English G 21

A6
für Gymnasien

English G 21 • Band A 6

Im Auftrag des Verlages herausgegeben von
Prof. Hellmut Schwarz, Mannheim
Jörg Rademacher, Mannheim

Erarbeitet von
Laurence Harger, Wellington, Neuseeland
Susan Abbey, Nenagh, Irland
Dr. James Pankhurst, Münster
Dr. Angelika Thiele, Münster
sowie Claire Lamsdale, Llangybi, Wales

unter Mitarbeit von
Wolfgang Biederstädt, Köln
Joachim Blombach, Herford
Roderick Cox, Freudenstadt
Helmut Dengler, Limbach
Dr. Annette Leithner-Brauns, Dresden
Jörg Rademacher, Mannheim
Jennifer Seidl, München
Sabine Tudan, Erfurt
sowie Miriam Lentzen, Hückelhoven; Heike Wirant, Jena

in Zusammenarbeit mit der Englischredaktion
Dr. Christiane Kallenbach (Projektleitung);
Dr. Christian v. Raumer, Gareth Evans (verantwortliche Redakteure); Susanne Bennetreu (Bildredaktion);
Britta Bensmann; Christiane Bonk; Dr. Philip Devlin;
Bonnie S. Glänzer; Stefan Höhne; Mara Leibowitz;
Uwe Tröger; Klaus G. Unger *sowie* Ulrike Berendt;
Sarah Silver

Beratende Mitwirkung
Peter Brünker, Bad Kreuznach; Helga Estor, Darmstadt;
Katja Fabel, Freiburg; Anette Fritsch, Dillenburg;
Patrick Handschuh, Köln; Ulrich Imig, Wildeshausen;
Bernd Koch, Marburg; Thomas Neidhardt, Bielefeld;
Wolfgang Neudecker, Mannheim; Birgit Ohmsieder, Berlin; Albert Rau, Brühl; Angela Ringel-Eichinger, Bietigheim-Bissingen; Dr. Jana Schubert, Genf/Leipzig;
Sieglinde Spranger, Chemnitz; Marcel Sprunkel, Köln;
Harald Weißling, Mannheim; Monika Wilkening, Wehretal

Illustrationen
Silke Bachmann, Hamburg; Roland Beier, Berlin;
Carlos Borrell, Berlin; Dylan Gibson, Pitlochry;
Christian Görke, Berlin; Graham-Cameron Illustration,
UK: Eoin Coveney; Alfred Schüssler, Frankfurt/Main

Layoutkonzept
Aksinia Raphael; Korinna Wilkes

Technische Umsetzung
Aksinia Raphael; Korinna Wilkes;
Stephan Hilleckenbach; Rainer Bachmaier

Umschlaggestaltung
Klein & Halm Grafikdesign, Berlin

www.cornelsen.de
www.EnglishG.de

Die Internetadressen und -dateien, die in diesem Lehrwerk angegeben sind, wurden vor Drucklegung geprüft. Der Verlag übernimmt keine Gewähr für die Aktualität und den Inhalt dieser Adressen und Dateien oder solcher, die mit ihnen verlinkt sind.

Dieses Werk berücksichtigt die Regeln der reformierten Rechtschreibung und Zeichensetzung.

1. Auflage, 1. Druck 2011

Alle Drucke dieser Auflage sind inhaltlich unverändert und können im Unterricht nebeneinander verwendet werden.

© 2011 Cornelsen Verlag, Berlin

Das Werk und seine Teile sind urheberrechtlich geschützt.

Jede Nutzung in anderen als den gesetzlich zugelassenen Fällen bedarf der vorherigen schriftlichen Einwilligung des Verlages.
Hinweis zu den §§ 46, 52a UrhG: Weder das Werk noch seine Teile dürfen ohne eine solche Einwilligung eingescannt und in ein Netzwerk eingestellt werden. Dies gilt auch für Intranets von Schulen und sonstigen Bildungseinrichtungen.

Druck: CS-Druck CornelsenStürtz, Berlin

ISBN 978-3-06-031309-9 – broschiert
ISBN 978-3-06-031359-4 – gebunden

 Inhalt gedruckt auf säurefreiem Papier aus nachhaltiger Forstwirtschaft.

Dein Englischbuch enthält folgende Teile:

Units **1** **2** **3** **4**	die vier Kapitel des Buches
Getting ready for a test	Hier kannst du dich gezielt auf einen Test vorbereiten.
EXTRA: Text File	viele interessante Texte zum Lesen (passend zu den Units)
Skills File (SF)	Beschreibung wichtiger Lern- und Arbeitstechniken
Grammar File (GF)	Zusammenfassung der Grammatik
Vocabulary	Wörterverzeichnis zum Lernen der neuen Wörter jeder Unit
Dictionary	alphabetisches englisch-deutsches Wörterverzeichnis zum Nachschlagen

Die Units bestehen aus diesen Teilen:

Lead-in	Einstieg in das neue Thema
Part A, B, C, D	neuer Lernstoff mit vielen Aktivitäten
Practice	Übungen

In den Units findest du diese Überschriften und Symbole:

Exploring language	Hier lernst du anhand von Beispielen, neue sprachliche Strukturen zu verstehen und richtig anzuwenden.
STUDY SKILLS	Einführung in Lern- und Arbeitstechniken
MEDIATION COURSE	In drei Kapiteln lernst du, zwischen zwei Sprachen zu vermitteln.
EVERYDAY ENGLISH	Übungen zum Bewältigen wichtiger Alltagssituationen
LISTENING	Aufgaben zu Hörtexten auf der CD
VIEWING	Aufgaben zu Filmausschnitten
REVISION	Übungen zur Wiederholung
WORDS	Übungen zu Wortfeldern und Wortverbindungen
Extra	zusätzliche Aktivitäten und Übungen
	Partnerarbeit / Gruppenarbeit
	nur auf CD / auf CD und im Schülerbuch
	Filmausschnitte auf DVD
	Schlage unbekannte Wörter in einem Wörterbuch nach.

Contents

Die folgenden Angebote sind nicht obligatorisch abzuarbeiten. Die Auswahl der Übungen und Übungsteile richtet sich nach den Schwerpunkten des schulinternen Curriculums.

 You and yours
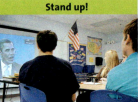 Stand up!
 Our one world
 Love reading

6 | Unit 1 — You and yours

Lead-in Going out
Part A Got friends?
Part B Addictions
Part C I hate my dad
Part D Boy meets girl around the world

Grammatical structures
- REVISION position of adverbs and adverbials
- REVISION modals and their substitutes

Word fields
- love and relationships
- friends and enemies
- family
- identity
- personal conflicts
- advertising
- addiction

STUDY SKILLS
Peer evaluation
Understanding adverts
Analysing films (1)
MEDIATION COURSE (1)
Oral mediation
EVERYDAY ENGLISH
Caring for others
VIEWING
Teens like you (scenes from an educational film)

26 | Unit 2 — Stand up!

Lead-in Human rights
Part A Speak out
Part B Get involved
Part C Make a change

Grammatical structures
- REVISION simple form and progressive form
- REVISION simple past vs. past progressive
- activity verbs and state verbs
- emphasis
- *used to* + infinitive

Word fields
- human/civil rights
- politics
- the media

STUDY SKILLS
Characterization in fiction
Analysing films (2)
Identifying style and register
Analysing newspaper articles
MEDIATION COURSE (2)
Written mediation
EVERYDAY ENGLISH
Staying cool in a conflict
VIEWING
- 'That's enough debate' (scene from a film)
- Vote! (promotional video)

44 | Extra — Revision – Getting ready for a test 1

52 Unit 3 Our one world

Lead-in Inventions and discoveries
Part A How our world works
Part B Our fragile world
Part C Our future world?

Grammatical structures
- REVISION passive
- REVISION conditional sentences 1 and 2
- passive: progressive tenses

Word fields
- science and technology
- inventions and discoveries
- environment
- climate change
- life sciences
- science fiction

STUDY SKILLS
Describing objects and processes
Writing a film review
Giving a group presentation
MEDIATION COURSE (3)
Translation
VIEWING
Who's the real Sam Bell? (scenes from a film)

68 Extra Revision – Getting ready for a test 2

74 Unit 4 Love reading

Lead-in Books and reading habits
Part A Can't put it down: fabulous fiction
Part B A quick fix: short stories
Part C Lifelines: saved by poetry
Part D All the world's a stage: thrilling theatre

Word fields
- literary terminology
- figurative language

STUDY SKILLS
Point of view
Giving a book report
Short stories
Rhyme and rhythm
Imagery
Sounds and language
Reading drama
VIEWING
Video book reviews (online videos)

106 Partner B and key to *Getting ready for a test 1 and 2*

107 Extra Text File
   108 TF 1: Amal's decision _____ (zu Unit 1)
   111 TF 2: Checks and balances _____ (zu Unit 2)
   112 TF 3: The monarchy and Parliament _____ (zu Unit 2)
   114 TF 4: **Bilingual module** Europe united _____ (zu Unit 2)
   118 TF 5: Into space _____ (zu Unit 3)
   120 TF 6: Electric wind _____ (zu Unit 3)
   123 TF 7: **Bilingual module** Global warming – how does it affect us? _____ (zu Unit 3)

125 Skills File
165 Grammar File
195 Grammatical terms
197 Vocabulary
231 Dictionary (English–German)
280 Irregular verbs
282 List of names
      Countries and continents
285 Acknowledgments

Unit 1 You and yours

1 What's going on?

a) Look at the photos and speculate about the teenagers (who, where, what, why, …).

b) Choose a photo and imagine what one of the teenagers in the photo is thinking. Make notes on their unspoken thoughts. Find other people in your class who have chosen the same photo and exchange ideas.

c) `Extra` Take similar photos of yourselves, print them out and write speech bubbles to go with them. Display them in class.

2 Going out

a) Listen and take notes. Compare what you discussed in 1a) and wrote in 1b) with what you've found out about the teenagers now.

b) Together, try to remember how many mini-scenes you listened to. Where did they each take place?

c) Listen again. Divide up the questions in your group and try to answer them.
1. Bella is interested in a new boy. Why?
2. Amber's mum is strict. What about?
3. Amber thinks her boyfriend's brother does something too much. What?
4. Amber is annoyed with her boyfriend. Why?
5. Sam criticizes Josh's girlfriend. How?
6. Paige tries to calm Amber down. How?
7. In the end they all go to the cinema. Why?
8. Amber wants to sit next to Paige. Why?
9. Bella and Sam are fine with that. Why?

Collect all your answers and decide together whether they are right.

d) *Line-up:* Read the statements below. Do you agree or disagree with them? For each statement do a line-up in class. Everyone shows their opinion from 'I totally agree' on the left to 'I totally disagree' on the right. Stand in the line at the position you think corresponds best with your opinion.
– Strict parents help me to grow up right.
– Boyfriends and girlfriends are too possessive.

GOT FRIENDS?

1 Forum on friends

a) In your opinion, what makes a 'real friend'?

heartdancer
15 Sep, 5:44 pm
Just looked at my Facebook page. Aaagghh! I haven't got a single friend. I argued with my mum the other evening and she de-friended me. I'm all alone.

dove999
15 Sep, 5:49 pm
Who cares about Facebook friends? People collect them like stamps. They think it shows how wonderful they are: 'Look at how many friends I've got. I'm amazing!'

caspianboy
15 Sep, 5:52 pm
Yeah, dove999, it really just shows how insecure they are. They wouldn't recognize a real friend if they saw one. You'd better find some real friends, heartbreaker.

heartdancer
15 Sep, 6:00 pm
So, caspianboy, you would recognize a real friend, right? How many of your 100 (150? 200?) social networking friends are real friends? Ten? If you're lucky!

dove999
15 Sep, 6:06 pm
What's a real friend anyway? Is it that old saying 'A friend in need is a friend indeed'?

heartdancer
15 Sep, 6:18 pm
Nah! The actor Peter Ustinov got it right: 'I do not believe that friends are necessarily the people you like best, they are merely the people who got there first.'

caspianboy
15 Sep, 6:20 pm
The writer C.S. Lewis has got a really good quotation on friends but I can't find it right now …

dove999
15 Sep, 6:30 pm
Who's C.S. Lewis anyway? I think, this has to be the best quotation. Oscar Wilde: 'True friends stab you in the front.' I love it!

b) Explain what dove999 and caspianboy think about 'friends' on social networking sites. What do you think a 'real friend' means to them?

c) Consider the following words and phrases (an English–English dictionary will help):
– in need
– necessarily, merely
– stab you in the front

Now discuss the meaning of the three quotations in the forum.

d) Imagine real-life situations which are good examples of the quotations. Write them down and read them to the class.

e) Which of the three quotations do you personally like best – and why?

f) **Extra** Write a comment to add to the forum. React to the other comments, say what made you think, what surprised/annoyed you, etc. Include your own idea of what a real friend is. You can put your comment in your DOSSIER.

▶ WB 1 (p. 2)

2 My best friend dumped me!

a) Look at the picture of the girl. What does it tell you about what she's like and how she's feeling? Consider clothes, body language, face, ...

My best friend dumped me

by Haylie, California

"We can't be friends anymore."

I was sitting at home, reading a magazine, when the text message popped up on my cell. It was from Samantha, my best friend, the person I cared about most in the world after my family. *What?* I thought. *Is this some kind of joke?* My fingers flew as I texted her right back: *Why???* *Seriously, what did I do?* I thought. I was so confused. I thought we were doing great. But then came her list of reasons. She was *really* unhappy with me – and she didn't hold back in telling me about it. I cared too much about what other people thought of me. I was really clingy, but I also insisted that we have a big circle of friends around us all the time. It could never be just her and me. "What, am I not enough?" she asked.

Samantha and I had been best friends for almost a year, ever since she'd come to my school as the new girl. I liked her right from the start. She was down-to-earth and friendly, and she didn't care too much about what others thought of her. We just kind of clicked. Samantha liked the same things I liked, and she'd never betray a trust or tell your secrets – she just wasn't like that. Because she was new at our school and made friends easily, she became popular in the good way – *everyone* really liked her. She was *really* special to me, and for some

reason I was always kind of scared I might lose her friendship.
I guess that's why I acted the way I did. All those things she said about me were actually true. At first I got really mad and said they weren't. But after I calmed down, I really thought about the way I'd been acting for the past few months. And the more I thought, the more I could see she was right. I had blown it big time.

Guilty as charged
First of all, I was *clingy*. I'd been so scared of losing Samantha's friendship that I'd stuck to her like glue. I'd go over to her house almost every day and call her a billion times on her cell phone just to talk. One time, she wasn't answering so I ended up calling her *brother's* cell phone to reach her! He wasn't too happy about that! I think I kind of burned her out with my neediness. You can have too much of a good thing!
Then there was the thing about always needing lots of friends around. Partly I just wanted to include everyone because I hate it when *I'm the one being excluded*. But mostly I did it because I was insecure. When I was surrounded by friends, I could prove to myself that I was "popular".
At the time, I didn't get how much that hurt Samantha. But when I thought about it later, I realized I wouldn't like to hang out with a friend if every single time, she also had to be with three or four of her other friends. It's great to be part of a group, and it's really nice to include everyone, but most people also want some one-on-one time with their best friend. If your best friend never wanted that, you'd end up feeling like you weren't very important to her.
The sad thing was, Samantha really was important to me. I just didn't do a very good job of showing her that. I spent so much time worrying that Samantha might not want to be my friend that I forgot how to be a sensitive friend to her.

It's really over
When I finally realized what I'd done, I felt terrible. I'd hurt my very best friend and ruined our friendship. I apologized over and over again, but Samantha just ignored me. She wouldn't talk to me at all. I got my other friends to apologize for me, but she ignored them too. That's when I realized that Samantha was more than just mad at me. She was done with our friendship. So, as much as it hurt, I had to accept that it was totally over. After a long time, we slowly started talking at school again. Now we've gotten back to being friends, but not best friends. We'll never be as close as we were because the way I acted pushed a wedge between us that won't go away. I wish we had the chance to start over again – I'd be a better friend this time.
I hope you learn from my mistakes too, because believe me … it's no fun being dumped by your best friend. ■

(abridged from Discovery Girls magazine, June/July 2009)

b) Summarize the reasons why Samantha no longer wanted to be friends with Haylie.

c) "It always takes two people for a problem to come up between them."
Do you think the end of the friendship was just Haylie's fault? Discuss your opinions in a group.

d) Suggest what Haylie could have done before the break-up to stay friends with Samantha. And what could she do now?

e) **Extra** In one of the paragraphs missing from Haylie's story, she explains what she has learned from her experience. Imagine you are Haylie and write that paragraph. Compare what you wrote with Haylie's actual words (which your teacher has).

▶ WB 2–6 (pp. 3–5)

Part A B C D   Practice   1   11

P1 STUDY SKILLS Peer evaluation

a) A writing task
Read the statement on the right. Discuss in writing why you agree or disagree with it.
👥 First, in a group, collect as many arguments for and against as you can.
On your own, write an outline:
1 Introduction
2 Arguments for
3 Arguments against
4 Conclusion, including your opinion
Then write a draft, proof-read it carefully (grammar, spelling, order, ideas, …) and write your final version.

b) Evaluate your partner's work
👥 Swap what you have written with a partner.
Step 1: Read your partner's work and make notes (you might like to use the evaluation sheet your teacher has):
– How well does it discuss the problem?
– Does it have the right structure?
– Are the ideas linked well?
Step 2: Underline or highlight in `green` parts of the text you think are good. Underline or highlight in `blue` parts of the text where you think there are mistakes or parts that don't sound right to you.

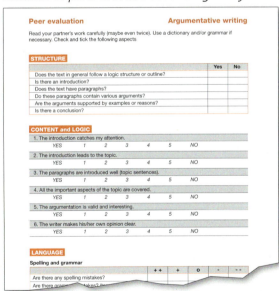

Think about grammar (tenses, word order, …), vocabulary (collocations, spelling, appropriate for the context) and logic.
Step 3: Think about how you could correct the parts that you think have mistakes. Make notes.

STUDY SKILLS Peer evaluation

Helping each other out
Reading and trying to correct each other's work can be very helpful in finding mistakes and improving your style. Discussing your ideas together makes it easier to find mistakes and think of ways of correcting them.

How to do it
– Read each other's work carefully.
– Make notes on how well it is written.
– Mark the good parts and what you think needs correcting.
– Note down corrections you would make.
– Discuss each other's ideas together and correct your own text as you now think necessary.

c) 👥 **Talk to your partner**
Discuss each other's work. Say what you think is very good. Make your suggestions for corrections and try to agree on a good version. Check in dictionaries or the Grammar File, or ask other students or your teacher for help if necessary.

▶ SF Outlining (p. 131) • SF Writing Course (pp. 150–151) • SF Peer evaluation (p. 136) • WB 7–8 (pp. 5–6)

P2 WORDS Emotions and relationships

a) Look at the following verbs connected with emotions and relationships. Most of them are used on pages 8–10. Find pairs (one from each box) that have a similar meaning and write them down.

be best friends • be caring • become good friends with sb. • be done with sb. • be really special to sb. • burn sb. out • calm down • feel guilty/sorry • get mad • get on sb.'s nerves • hurt sb. • leave sb. • stick to sb. • trick sb. • trust sb. • worry about sth./sb.

be clingy • be close • become less angry • be helpful • be insecure about sth./sb. • believe in sb. • betray sb. • be very important to sb. • click with sb. • decide a relationship is over • dump sb. • feel like apologizing • get angry • make sb. annoyed • make sb. feel bad • make sb. tired

be best friends – be close
become good friends with sb. – ...

b) On a large piece of paper, draw a line and label it as below. Then arrange the verbs from the box on the right along the line from most positive to most negative. There is not one correct solution. Discuss your line of verbs with a partner.

like • look down on • dislike • love • idolize • admire • fancy • respect • be attracted to • get along well with • look up to • take interest in • be pleased by • be excited about • hate • be in love with • care about • be annoyed by

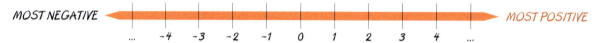

MOST NEGATIVE ... -4 -3 -2 -1 0 1 2 3 4 ... MOST POSITIVE

P3 Extra WORDS Perfect partners

a) Make eight 'personality cards'. On one side write down the name of a very popular or unpopular celebrity. On the other write 'male' or 'female', as appropriate.
Then make eight 'relationship cards'. Write a verb from task 2a) or 2b) above on them.

| Britney Spears | admire | like |
| hate | fancy | be annoyed by |

b) Put your personality and relationship cards face down in two piles.

Partner A: Pick one card from the personality pile and five cards from the relationship pile and lay them out in front of Partner B.

Partner B: You are a dating counsellor. Advise Partner A about their perfect partner by interpreting the cards.

Partner A: First listen and then react to the counsellor's advice.
Then both partners swap their roles.

Partner B: *Your perfect partner seems to be Britney Spears. You fancy her when she is on the stage and you admire her beautiful voice. You like her because – just like you – she hates drugs and is annoyed by wild parties.*
Partner A: *I completely agree with you. I'm so excited about this. We are perfectly suited to each other. She might be older than me, but she's such a friendly person and would never hurt anyone.*
Or:
Are you joking? I could never imagine being with Britney Spears because ...

Part **A** B C D Practice **1** 13

P4 REVISION Me and mine (Position of adverbs and adverbials)

a) *Go to page 167 in the Grammar File and read about the position of adverbs in English sentences.*

b) *Put the adverbs in brackets in the correct position in the sentences. There may be more than one correct answer.*

1 My friend Tony had an accident on his way to school because he was tired. (almost)
 My friend Tony almost had an accident ...
2 He goes to bed before midnight. (never)
3 My sister speaks French. (well)
4 She loves France and has travelled there. (often)
5 We have decided not to go to the party. (already)

6 I have enough time to finish my book. (at last)
7 I can't meet you at the cinema. (unfortunately)
8 I clean my room on Saturday mornings. (always)
9 Then the whole family has lunch together. (usually)
10 My sister goes to football. (in the afternoon)

c) *Check your answers on page 196. If you got any wrong, look at the Grammar File again and then discuss the correct answer with your partner.*
▶ *GF 1.2: Adverbs/Phrases of place and time (p. 167)*

P5 REVISION Friends and friendship (Modals and their substitutes)

Remember			
	Present	**Past**	**Future**
können:	I can	I could/I was able to	I will be able to
dürfen:	I may/I can	I was allowed to/I could	I will be allowed to
müssen:	I must/I have to	I had to	I will have to

musn̶t (handwritten beside *dürfen*)

▶ *GF 5: Modals and their substitutes (pp. 177–180)*

a) *Complete these statements.*

1 Good friends ... to know what the other thinks. (müssen nicht miteinander reden)
2 Often a real friend ... when you have a problem. (wird helfen können) *will be able to help*
3 With the internet, friends ... 24/7 – if their computers are on! (können kommunizieren) *can communicate*
4 In blogs, people ... about their friends. (sollten nicht lügen dürfen) *shouldn't be allowed to lie*

b) *Complete the dialogue with modals or their substitutes. There may be more than one correct answer.*

Father Don't stay out too late. I ... stay out so late at your age.
Son Yes, Dad, I know. You ... do anything unless Granny said so.
Father Don't be rude about my mum. I ... talk to her about anything, you know.
Son And I can talk to you about anything, I know. But I don't think I ... tell you everything. I'm 16, you know.
Father Well, I ... talk to my parents about everything either. But sometimes I did and I was glad I did. They ... give me some really good advice.

Son And I ... get really good advice from my friends now.
Father Oh, really? Did you get good advice from them the other week when you missed the last bus and I ... pick you up from town at one in the morning?
Son Dad, you know that was an accident. How ... we know they were going to cancel the last bus?
Father Well, your sister knew. Of course, she's had a good education, so she ... read the notice on the bus stop!

ADDICTIONS

1 Addicted to games

a) *Estimate the number of hours you spend a week on these activities:*

> video games • social networking sites • texting • e-mails • surfing the internet

Then, over the course of the next week, keep a log of how many hours it really is.

1 in 12 Teens Addicted to Video Games

A new nationwide survey of 1,178 American children, aged 8 to 18, suggests that about 1 in 12 teens are addicted to video games.

"It's not that the games are bad," said Douglas Gentile, the study's author. "It's not that the games are addictive. It's that some kids use them in a way that is out of balance and harms other areas of their lives."

On average, teens had few symptoms of addiction: boys typically had more than two, girls less than two. But 12% of boys and 8% of girls had at least six symptoms – enough to be considered addicted.

Symptoms included spending more and more time and money on video games; feeling annoyed or nervous when playing less; escaping problems through play; spending more time at the controller instead of on chores or homework; lying about how much they played; and stealing games or money to play more.

Those who researchers called "pathological gamers" received poorer grades in school and were more than twice as likely to have attention-deficit disorder and hand and wrist pain from playing for long hours. They were also more likely to have a video game system in their bedroom.

News not all bad

Fortunately, the news is not all bad for gamers. Video games are supposed to be good for hand-eye coordination and researchers have shown that is true. Another recent study compares gamers to bilingual people: they are said to think faster and are better at multitasking.

A little fix in the morning

Former games addict Carl Blunt describes his life as a gamer.

"I was addicted to a war game, the sort that has a series of levels. Gamers call these levels 'maps'. The main thing is: playing the game makes you feel good. Of course you want to feel good all the time, so you play as much as you can. As soon as you wake up you play a couple of maps. You need that little fix before you go to school.

"And then at school your mind is always on the game. You're in class but you're thinking about the map you're going to play when you get home. In fact, that's all you think about.

"It takes up all your free time. Wherever I was, I was always working out how I could play a map. Man, it was bad. I mean, the moment I got home from school I'd start playing video games. I'd play all evening. I'd only stop for dinner. Then play until I went to bed. And the next day I'd do exactly the same. I spent so much time on it."

b) Read the article. Then make a list of symptoms of addiction to video games and of the benefits of playing. Add your own ideas for other symptoms and benefits and then compare lists with a partner.

c) Which of the symptoms of addiction did Carl Blunt use to have? Explain what he sees as the main problem of video game addiction.

"No, it doesn't connect to an X-Box!"

2 Role play

a) Divide the class into four big groups. Each group works together on one role (Kerry Jones, Mrs Jones, school counsellor, Jaz). Study your role card carefully. Collect useful phrases you might need during the role play.

b) Now divide the class into groups of four so that there is one person for each role in every group. You are meeting in the student counsellor's room at school to discuss Kerry's computer use. Do the role play.

Kerry Jones

You spend several hours on video games and Facebook every day. You really enjoy the games and have made lots of interesting friends on Facebook. You think the games make you better at solving problems and that Facebook lets you keep in touch with lots of people.

School counsellor

You have arranged a meeting because Mrs Jones has phoned you. She is very worried about Kerry's computer use. You've spoken to Kerry's teachers and you think there is a problem. You want to help Kerry to reduce the time he/she spends on the computer.

Mrs Jones

You are worried that Kerry is currently spending too much time on the computer, not doing enough work for school and not meeting friends any more. You have tried talking to Kerry about this but he/she just gets angry and refuses to discuss or admit the problem.

Jaz

You're one of Kerry's friends. You also like video games but don't have much time to play as you're a keen footballer too and your parents are very strict about homework. You used to see Kerry more but only really talk to him/her on Facebook nowadays.

▶ WB 9 (p. 7)

3 Hard sell

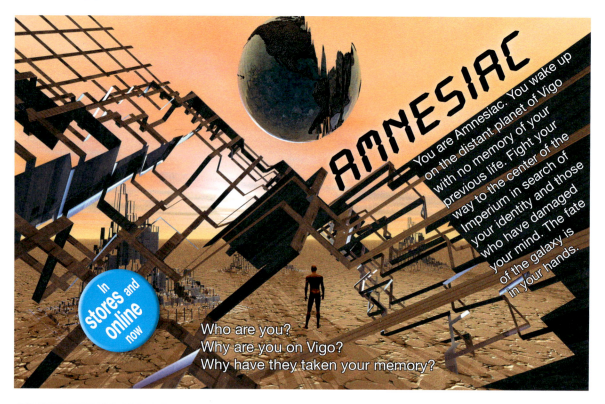

a) *Look at the two adverts on page 16. Write answers to the following questions about them.*

1 Which advert did you look at first? Why?
2 What are the two adverts for?
3 What are they trying to do and who is their target group?
4 Where would these adverts appear?

b) *Describe the graphics and the design (colours, layout, font, font size and colour, ...). Explain why the images suit the advert – or not.*

c) *Analyse the words.*
– *Make sure you know what all the words mean. Use a dictionary if necessary.*
– *How does the language grab your attention? Give examples.*

d) *Say which advert you think works best. Give reasons.*

e) **Extra** *Bring in one of your favourite print adverts and analyse it in the same way. Say why you like it.*

▶ *SF Understanding adverts (p. 144)*

4 **Extra** 👥 Designing your own advert

After looking at how print adverts work, use your imagination and produce your own advert.

Step 1

First brainstorm some ideas.

– What are you going to advertise?	An idea? A product? A real one or an imaginary one?
– Who is your target group?	Teenagers, children, women, men, ...?
– Where will your advert appear?	Billboard, magazine, internet, ...?

Step 2

Divide up the work.

– Who will work on the graphics? What will they be like?	What would suit the product and appeal to the target market: a drawing, photos, ...? What colours would work?
– Who will write the text?	How will the words grab people's attention? Can you use imagery or repetition? Can you write something funny? Will there be a story element?
– Who will think about the layout of text and graphics?	Where will you put the text on the graphics? What size, colour and font will you use?

Step 3

Produce the parts of your advert. Before you put them all together, look at everything again. How could you make the advert more effective? Proofread the text and make corrections.

Step 4

Display your adverts in class. Form groups with one person from each advert group. Walk round and look at the adverts. The experts present their advert to the group.

P1 WORDS The meanings of adverbs

Think about the meanings of the adverbs in blue and choose the correct one from each pair.

It is a sad fact that **luckily · unfortunately** some young people develop an addiction to illegal drugs. **However · Perhaps** this is because they don't feel accepted for who they are, but there are **usually · probably** many other reasons. This is **certainly · probably** a big problem in western societies. **Hopefully · Sadly** most of these young people do not admit that they have an addiction, which is **almost · exactly** why the families and other people caring for them **never · usually** have a hard time helping them. **At first · Of course**, there are bigger problems too. There are **definitely · maybe** even more young people who are addicted to the legal drugs – alcohol and cigarettes.

"Unfortunately, a few years back we had to start accepting advertising."

P2 Exploring language The English for German 'sollen'

Look at these sentences (the first two are from page 14). The words in blue can be translated by German 'sollen'. The meanings of the English words are explained more in brackets.
1 They **are supposed to be** good for hand-eye coordination. (what people say)
2 They **are said to** think faster. (what people say)
3 Children **shouldn't** spend too many hours on the computer every day. (the right thing to do or not to do)
4 They **ought to** do more sport. (the right thing to do)
5 Of course, adults **had better** set a good example or shut up. (the best thing to do in a situation)

Pia is writing an e-mail to her American friend, Nick. Look at what she is thinking. How can she say it in English? (There may be more than one correct answer.)

Ich weiß, ich sollte öfter schreiben.

Oder wir skypen einfach. Ja, das sollten wir tun. Dann können wir umsonst richtig miteinander reden.

Du solltest dich aber bei Facebook oder MySpace anmelden.

Twitter soll aber auch ganz gut sein. Bist du schon dabei? Ich nicht.

Ich habe gelesen, dass Facebook in den USA am populärsten sein soll.

Ich sollte jetzt besser aufhören, es ist schon sehr spät.

▶ GF 5.3: Modals – what do they express? (pp. 179–180) •
WB 10 (p. 8)

Part A **B** C D Practice **1** 19

P3 EVERYDAY ENGLISH Caring for others 🎧

a) Read the dialogue below. Then listen to the CD. Take notes and try to complete the dialogue.
A: I saw Jesse the other day.
B: Oh, yeah. How is he?
A: He didn't … too good.
B: No? I haven't seen him for ages.
A: That's because he's … playing video games.
B: Do you think he's …?
A: I don't know. He was always … video games.
B: I am too.
A: Yeah, but you don't play … You're not … to them.
B: Maybe not.
A: You have lots of other … Jesse is hooked. He doesn't do anything else.
B: Yeah, I remember when he said he needed his … every day.
A: Yes, I think he may …

b) 👥 *Work out the conversation in English together.*
A: Begrüße B.
B: Grüße auch. Sage, dass du keine Lust mehr hast, mit Alex und Jana auszugehen.
A: Frage, was los ist.
B: Sage, sie waren am Samstag wieder betrunken.
A: Frage, ob B meint, sie seien süchtig.
B: Bejahe dies. Sage, dass sie immer zu viel trinken, wenn sie ausgehen.
A: Sage, dass du denkst, dass sie Hilfe brauchen.
B: Sage, du hast es ihnen gesagt. Sie hätten aber gesagt, dass sie nicht süchtig seien.
A: Du meinst, dass man es oft nicht merkt, wenn man süchtig ist. Du denkst, ihr solltet euch um Hilfe kümmern.

P4 LISTENING Radio adverts 🎧

a) 👥 *Copy the table below. Then listen to four radio adverts and fill in the table. Check your answers in a group.*

	product or problem	for or against	speakers
ad 1			
ad 2			
…			

b) Listen again.
How does each ad get its message across? Think about
– the information given
– sound effects
– tone of voice
– humour
– surprises
– emotional elements
– …

c) 👥 *How effective are the adverts? Individually, rank them on a scale from 1 (very bad) to 10 (excellent). Then discuss your ranking in a group and choose the best ad.*

d) Extra *Write a description of your own favourite radio ad without mentioning what exactly it is advertising. Read out your description in class. Can anyone guess what the ad is for or against?*

▶ WB 11–12 (p. 8)

Radio – a medium that reaches people everywhere

I hate my dad (abridged from *Love Lessons* by Jacqueline Wilson) 🎧 ▶ 📄

👥 *Read the first sentence of the text and talk to your partner: What might the text be about? Make a list of common reasons for problems between teenagers and their parents.*

I hate my dad.

I know lots of teenage girls say that but they don't really mean it. Well, I don't *think* they do. I don't really know any other teenage girls. That's one of the reasons I hate Dad. He keeps me a virtual prisoner.

I'm interrogated[1] if I slip down the road to Krishna's Korner Shop. I'm not allowed to go into town by myself. I can't go to see any films. I can't eat in McDonald's.

Dad even fussed[2] about me making a simple bus ride by myself to go to Miss Roberts for maths tuition. He took my sister Grace and me out of school ages ago, when I'd just gone into the Juniors and she was still at the finger-painting stage. Dad said *he* was going to educate us.

We were left to get on with it for ages, but this summer we had a home visit from a Mr Miles, who was from some kind of education authority. He wanted to know what provision[3] Dad was making for my GCSE coursework. Dad said he didn't believe in examinations. Mr Miles smiled through Dad's tirade, obviously[4] having heard it all before.

'What do you want to do when you're older, Prudence and Grace?' he asked.

Grace mumbled something about working with animals. Dad won't let us have any proper[5] pets because he says he's allergic to them. Grace has a lot of secret, unsatisfactory pets, like the blackbird in the garden and the toads in the compost heap and for a while she kept a wormery hidden under her bed. Grace's pets are not exactly cuddly[6].

'You'll certainly need to pass lots of exams if you want to be a vet[7],' said Mr Miles.

Dad snorted. 'You'll find our Grace has got no more brains[8] than a donkey,' he said unkindly. 'She'll get a job in a shop somewhere and be happy enough.'

'In your bookshop?'

'She can help sell the books, but I doubt[9] she's up to the business side of things,' said Dad. 'But Prudence can do all the cataloguing and buying and book fairs.'

'Is that what you want to do, Prudence – run your father's business?' said Mr Miles.

I swallowed[10]. 'I – I'd like to go to art college.' Dad glared at me. 'For goodness' sake, I've told you to forget that nonsense. You don't need to go away to college to learn drawing and painting; you can do that already.'

'But I *want* to go, Dad.'

Dad was furious with me for arguing in front of Mr Miles, but decided not to pursue[11] it. 'All right, all right, go to art college, waste three years,' he said. He nodded triumphantly at Mr Miles. 'I guarantee she can pass her art GCSE standing on her head.'

'I dare say[12],' said Mr Miles. 'But I think you'll find art colleges require quite a few GCSEs, plus three good A-levels. You're going to have to make more provision for your daughter's education, Mr King. Otherwise we might have to pursue the matter[13] through the courts.'

'The courts!' said Mum, panicking.

'You've got no power to do any such thing,' said Dad, hands on his hips. 'You can't stop parents home-educating their children.'

'Not if they've been home-educated right from the start. But your girls have attended school in the past, so I think you'll find we have every power. However, let's hope we can avoid any unpleasant action. We all want what's best for Prudence and Grace.'

Dad seemed sure Mr Miles was bluffing, but nevertheless[14] he fixed up for me to go to this Miss Roberts for maths tuition on Wednesday afternoons. I only went once. It was unbearable[15].

Miss Roberts used to teach maths at a girls'

---

[1] (to) interrogate [ɪnˈterəgeɪt] *verhören* [2] (to) fuss [fʌs] *sich aufregen* [3] (to) make provision [prəˈvɪʒn] *Vorkehrungen treffen* [4] obviously ['ɒbvɪəsli] *offensichtlich* [5] proper ['prɒpə] *richtig* [6] cuddly ['kʌdli] *kuschelig* [7] vet *Tierarzt, -ärztin* [8] brains [breɪnz] *Intelligenz* [9] (to) doubt *bezweifeln* [10] (to) swallow ['swɒləʊ] *schlucken* [11] (to) pursue [pəˈsjuː] *(weiter)verfolgen* [12] I dare say. [deə] *hier: Das nehme ich an.* [13] matter *Angelegenheit, Sache* [14] nevertheless [ˌnevəðəˈles] *trotzdem* [15] unbearable [ʌnˈbeərəbl] *unerträglich*

school way back in the sixties. She seemed
preserved[1] in that time. She bent over me,
trying to explain some supposedly simple
point about algebra.

I couldn't understand any of it. I wrote down
random[2] letters of the alphabet but I couldn't
tease[3] any meaning from them. I expect letters
to arrange themselves into words. If I'm doing
sums I need numbers – though I'm actually
useless with numbers too. I can't always add
up accurately. The shop takings rarely[4] balance
on a Saturday when I help out.

Miss Roberts tried hard to be patient with
me. She explained it over and over again,
raising[5] her voice and speaking s-l-o-w-l-y.

I paid her the twenty pounds for the tuition
and she gave me a cup of tea.

'Don't look so woebegone[6], Prudence,' she
said. 'Your father says you're a very bright girl.
I'm sure you'll catch on[7] in no time.'

I thanked her politely.

I didn't go back. For the last three
Wednesdays I've walked into town and spent
my tuition fee. Sixty whole pounds.

I've never had so much money in my life
before. Dad gives Grace and me one pound
every Saturday. He behaves as if he's
bestowing[8] solid gold upon us, and even has
the nerve to lecture[9] us, telling us not to waste
it on rubbish. I've always saved mine up to buy
sketchpads and soft pencils and crayons[10].

I know I am very weird. I can't seem to
help[11] it. I don't know how to be a proper
teenager. I bought a couple of teenage
magazines out of my stolen tuition money.
They were astonishing[12], especially the
problem pages. I knew I didn't look anything
like girls my own age, but I didn't realize my
experiences were so different.

I've had *no* experiences; *they've* had plenty.
The girls writing to the problem pages spoke
a different language and behaved as if they
were from a totally different planet. They wore
astonishing clothes and got up to astonishing
things with their boyfriends. I read these

letters feeling hot, my heart beating.

The only letters I could identify with in any
way were the ones where the girls moaned[13]
about their mums and dads. They said they
couldn't stick[14] their parents. Their mums
wouldn't let them have a nose stud or platform
heels[15]; their dads nagged about bad marks at
school and got mad if they didn't come home
till midnight.

'They should try having my mum and dad,'
I muttered[16], as I flicked[17] through them by
torchlight[18] under the bedcovers.

Working with the text

1   Understanding the story
*Describe Prudence's situation. How do her
problems with her dad compare with your list
from page 20?*

2   Characters of the story
*a) Look at the following lines of the extract and
describe how you think the characters are feeling.*
ll. 38–41: Prudence and her father
ll. 49–50: Prudence
ll. 50–51: her father
l. 68: her mother
ll. 69–70: her father

*b) Which words helped you to understand how
they were feeling?*

3   Narrating the story
*Read the part about Miss Roberts again
(ll. 83–104). Write the scene from Miss Roberts's
perspective. What effect does changing the
narrator have on the story?*

▶ *SF Reading literature (pp. 141–143)* • *WB 13 (p. 9)*

---

[1] preserved *konserviert*   [2] random ['rændəm] *beliebige(r,s)*   [3] (to) tease [tiːz] *herauskitzeln*   [4] rarely *selten*   [5] (to) raise one's voice *die Stimme erheben*   [6] woebegone ['wəʊbɪɡɒn] *(fml) bekümmert*   [7] (to) catch on *kapieren*   [8] (to) bestow sth. upon sb. [bɪ'stəʊ] *(fml) jm. etwas schenken*   [9] (to) lecture sb. ['lektʃə] *jn. belehren*   [10] crayon ['kreɪən] *Buntstift*   [11] I can't help it. *Ich kann nicht anders.*   [12] astonishing [ə'stɒnɪʃɪŋ] *erstaunlich*   [13] (to) moan [məʊn] *jammern*   [14] (to) stick *ausstehen*   [15] platform heels [,plætfɔːm 'hiːlz] *Plateausohlen*   [16] (to) mutter *murmeln*   [17] (to) flick through sth. *etwas durchblättern*   [18] torch ['tɔːtʃ] *Taschenlampe*

P1 Antonyms, synonyms, word families

a) Match the expressions 1–10 to the words a–j.

1. a big test at the end of a term or a school year
2. a young person aged 13–19
3. a class
4. exercises and tasks you have to do outside school
5. what you call somebody who is very clever
6. all you can remember about what you have learned and experienced
7. the place you go to learn every day
8. what you get at a school or university
9. someone who attends a school
10. (to) catch on

a course
b education
c exam
d homework
e intelligent
f knowledge
g school
h student
i teenager
j (to) understand

b) Work with a partner. Try to find an antonym and/or a synonym for all the words (a–j above). Then add as many words from the same word families or collocations with the words as you can, e.g. course: training, class, do a course, take a course, ...
Use an English–English dictionary or a collocations dictionary for help.

P2 False friends

a) Look at this sentence from "I hate my dad" (p. 21, ll. 116–117):
I don't know how to be a **proper** teenager.

'Proper' is both an English and a German word. They are spelled the same but they don't mean the same:
proper = richtig, ordentlich   proper = neat, clean, tidy
'Proper' is a false friend, i.e. a word that looks or sounds similar in English and German but has a different meaning.

b) Write down the correct German translations of the English words in blue.
1. What's the **meaning** of this?
2. I **wonder** what's for dinner this evening.
3. Haylie has a big **circle** of friends.
4. Everything Samantha said was **actually** true.
5. Haylie called her a **billion** times.
6. Can you find your home town on this **map**?
7. How much time do you **spend** on the computer?
8. Jack's not **brave** enough to ask her out.
9. They **became** friends as soon as Samantha started at the school.

c) Write down the correct English translations of the German words in orange.
1. Hast du eine **Meinung** dazu?
2. Du wirst **dich** über das Abendessen **wundern**.
3. Kannst du mir deinen **Zirkel** leihen?
4. Wir stehen **aktuell** auf Platz vier.
5. Das Universum enthält viele **Billionen** Sterne.
6. Die Unterlagen sind in dieser **Mappe**.
7. Kannst du ein paar Euro für die Tsunami-Opfer **spenden**?
8. Lass mal die Sau raus. Sei nicht so **brav**!
9. Was **bekomme** ich dafür?

▶ WB 14–15 (p. 10)

Part A B **C** D   Practice   **1**   23

P3 VIEWING Teens like you? 🎥

a) 👥 *Look at the stills on the right. They are from a short film about US teenagers. Discuss when you think the film was made and give reasons.*

b) 👥 *Describe the setting and the people in the stills. Speculate about what is happening: who are the people? How are they related?*

c) **Extra** 👥 *Write a thought bubble (big enough for all to read) for one of the characters from the stills. Show the thought bubbles for each character in class. Vote for the best ones.*

d) Divide the class into two groups, A and B. Group A face the TV. Group B have their backs to it. Group A watch a scene from the film with their hands over their ears. Group B listen to the scene.

After that, Group A make notes on: the setting, the characters' actions and appearance, the events that take place in the scene

Group B make notes on: the number of speakers, their voices and feelings, what is said, the background noises or music.

👥 *Work in pairs (one from Group A, one from Group B). Use your notes and exchange information about the scene. Present your ideas to the class.*

e) Groups A and B now swap roles and do the same with a second scene from the film.

f) Now all watch four scenes from the film with the sound. What were you surprised by? What else did you find out? Who do you think this film was made for – teenagers or parents?

g) The teenagers in the film have a number of problems with their parents. Which of the problems do teenagers still have with their parents today?

Kay

Sally

Bill

STUDY SKILLS	Analysing films (1)

Feature films are **basically stories** told **using sound and moving pictures**. Documentary films also sometimes tell stories. So you can analyse a feature film and some documentaries with the same categories you use for **narrative literature: plot, setting/atmosphere and characters**. Films, however, also work via sound, music, lighting, camera work and special effects.

▶ *SF Analysing films (p.157)*

BOY MEETS GIRL AROUND THE WORLD

a) Boy meets girl: the oldest situation in the world. But how does it happen where you live? How do people get together, fall in love, start a relationship? And what happens after that? Quickly note down some ideas. Then read about getting together in some other places around the world.

Troy, 16, Cicero, Illinois, USA

I have a kind of ritual when I'm going on a date, especially a first date. I take a shower and make sure I smell good. I always wear my favorite clothes so that I feel good. Mostly we'll meet at a Starbucks or something and then go see a movie. Then after that we'll hang out in the mall and maybe get a pizza or a drink somewhere. If I'm lucky, she'll have a car and drive me home afterwards – and I'll get more than just a goodnight kiss.

Maya, 17, Chandigarh, India

Dating in Chandigarh is very different from what we see in American films and TV shows. Marriages here are arranged by parents in about 80% of the cases. So it's your parents who look for a suitable boy or girl for you. After they choose one, you meet the boy or girl, at your house or theirs, with your parents. If you happen to like each other (you are supposed to say 'Yes' or 'No' the same day or in the next few days), then you can start dating.

Yamila, 17, Irbid, Jordan

We go on dates, in a group, and sometimes just as a couple. Our parents mustn't know, of course – they wouldn't let us go on a date if they did. Irbid has hundreds of internet coffee houses. That's where my girlfriends and I go. There are boys there too, but we don't mix in the internet cafés – we go online and chat with boys, boys we know, about music and sports and what's going on. And even sex. Sometimes we arrange to meet.

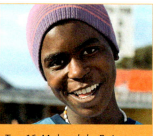
Tau, 16, Molepolole, Botswana

In our village we don't really go on dates. In Setswana culture, that's not really allowed. The idea is that boys and girls should not mix until they get married. But we're mixed at school and there is this place in the village where we meet after school and hang out together. That's where you can find a girlfriend. I want a girlfriend who is sexy, fun and a good dresser. And she should be faithful, of course, not a girl who looks at other boys.

b) 👥 Work in groups of four, with one student working on each teenager. Take notes on how 'getting together' happens for your teenager. Then report on your teenager to the others. Together, compare and contrast how 'getting together' happens for these teenagers and for teenagers where you live.

c) 👥 Think about what else you would like to know about dating, relationships, marriage, etc. for your teenager. With your ideas, write a letter to them, asking these questions and telling them how you feel about these things.
Read each other's letters and suggest corrections and improvements. ▶ **Text File 1** *(pp. 108–110)*

P1 MEDIATION Out in a boat (Oral mediation)

There are many situations where you might have to use your English and German knowledge to mediate between the two languages. For example, you're on holiday and a boy or girl says something in English that only you understand. You explain it to the others in your group. Or the same thing happens with an announcement at an airport. Or a visitor to your country needs help with the instructions on a ticket machine.
This first part of your mediation course deals with spoken mediation.

a) Only the gist 🎧
The most important thing to remember: don't try and translate word for word. You only need to get across the most important information.
1. Listen to the speaker and note down what you think is important.
2. 👥 Compare your results with a partner and agree on what is most important. Then each mediate what you heard into German.
3. 👥 Now read the text on the right and note down the important parts – or highlight them on a copy. Compare results and then mediate into English. Use a dictionary if you need to.
4. Listen to someone else mediating the text and compare.

b) 👥👥 Help! I didn't get that.
If you don't understand something in English, ask the speaker to slow down, say it again or explain what they mean. Collect and write down as many polite phrases as you can for asking someone to repeat something, speak more slowly or explain what they mean.

c) 👥 Help! How do I say that?
If you can't think of the right words when mediating into English, try paraphrasing.
Partner B: Go to page 106.
Partner A: You probably do not know the English words for the items in these pictures. Paraphrase them for your partner. Do they understand what you mean? Then listen to your partner.

Ihre Vorbereitung aufs Drachenbootfahren

Drachenbootfahren ist Wassersport. Das heißt, dass Sie ganz sicher nass werden, vor allem, wenn Sie mit anderen Anfängern in einem Boot sitzen. Bringen Sie also trockene Sachen mit, damit Sie sich nach dem Training umziehen können. Ihre Wertsachen wie Schlüssel, Handy, Papiere oder Geldbörse geben Sie bitte dem Team-Captain, der hat einen wasserdichten Sack dabei, den er am Boot befestigt, sodass auch bei einer sehr feuchten Fahrt oder gar einer Kenterung nichts verloren gehen kann. Jugendliche unter 18 Jahren müssen eine Rettungsweste tragen. Sie bekommen aber eine ganz dünne, die beim Paddeln nicht behindert.

d) 👥 Can you do it?
Listen to parts 1 and 2 and take notes.
Partner A: Mediate part 1 for your partner and ask them for feedback on how well you did.
Partner B: Give your partner feedback.
Partner B: Mediate part 2.
Partner A: Give feedback.

Remember
- Only get the gist across. Don't translate.
- Paraphrase words you don't know.
- Ask an English speaker to slow down, repeat or explain.

▶ SF Mediation Course (pp. 145–146) • WB 16 (p. 11) •
Skills check WB (pp. 12–21)

Unit 2 Stand up!

On 10 December 1948, the United Nations passed the Universal Declaration of Human Rights. Here are short versions of six of its 30 articles:

- Article 1: All humans are born free and equal. They should act towards each other in a spirit of brotherhood.
- Article 5: No one shall suffer torture or inhuman treatment. D
- Article 12: Everyone has the right to privacy. E
- Article 19: Everyone has the right to freedom of opinion and expression. B
- Article 21: Everyone has the right to take part in the government of his or her country. A
- Article 26: Everyone has the right to education. C

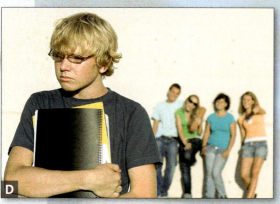

1 Human rights illustrated

a) Each of the illustrations on p. 26 comments on human rights. Match the illustrations to five of the UN articles listed above. Give reasons for your choice.

b) 👥 Make a list of violations of human rights that you have heard about or read about recently.

▶ SF Describing and analysing pictures (p. 128)

2 Human rights in poetry 🎧

a) Emmanuel Jal was a child soldier in the civil war in Sudan. He wrote a long poem about his experiences with the title "Forced to sin". Read the excerpts from Jal's poem printed below.

b) 👥 What are some of the topics of the poem? Which one is the most important for you? Say why. How is the poem connected with the Universal Declaration of Human Rights?

c) 👥 In groups of five, discuss how you would order the different parts below.

d) Listen to Jal reciting his poem and compare his order with your order of the parts.

e) 👥 Each member of the group learn one part of the poem, and then recite it, taking turns, in Jal's original order.

A Ah! The children of Darfur.
Your empty bellies on the telly and it's you that I'm fighting for.

B Sometimes you gotta lose to win.
Never give up. Never give in.
Left home at the age of seven.

C One year later, live with an AK-47 by my side.
Slept with one eye open wide.
Run, duck, play dead and hide.
I've seen my people die like flies.

D Left home. Don't even know the day I'll ever return.
My country is war-torn.
Music I used to hear was bombs and fire of guns.
So many people die that I don't even cry no more.

E Ask God a question what am I here for?
And why are my people poor?
And why, why when the rest of the children were learning how to read and write,
I was learning how to fight?

www.emmanueljal.com

3 Extra 👥 Human rights in your own life

In what way are human rights protected in your own life? Or perhaps you feel they are in danger? Exchange your ideas with a partner and agree on five examples.

▶ WB 1 (p. 22)

SPEAK OUT

1 First Amendment   (from the novel *Speak* by Laurie Halse Anderson)

Melinda, the narrator of the novel, is in the 8th grade at an American high school. In this extract she's in her History class.

Mr. Neck storms into class, a bull chasing thirty-three red flags. We slide into our seats. I think for sure he's going to explode. Which he does, but in an unpredictable, faintly
5 educational way.

IMMIGRATION. He writes it on the board. I'm pretty sure he spelled it right.

Mr. Neck: "My family has been in this country for over two hundred years. We built
10 this place, fought in every war from the first one to the last one, paid taxes, and voted."

A cartoon thought bubble forms over the heads of everyone in the class. ("WILL THIS BE ON THE TEST?")
15 Mr. Neck: "So tell me why my son can't get a job."

A few hands creep skyward. Mr. Neck ignores them. It is a pretend question, one he asked so he could give the answer. I relax. This
20 is like when my father complains about his boss. The best thing to do is to stay awake and blink sympathetically.

His son wanted to be a firefighter, but didn't get the job. Mr. Neck is convinced that this is
25 some kind of reverse discrimination. He says we should close our borders so that real Americans can get the jobs they deserve. The job test said that I would be a good firefighter. I wonder if I could take a job away from Mr.
30 Neck's son.

I tune out and focus on my doodle, a pine tree. [...]

Mr. Neck writes on the board again: "DEBATE: America should have closed her
35 borders in 1900." That strikes a nerve. Several nerves. I can see kids counting backward on their fingers, trying to figure when their grandparents or great-grandparents were born, when they came to America, if they would
40 have made the Neck Cut. When they figure out they would have been stuck in a country that hated them, or a place with no schools, or

a place with no future, their hands shoot up. They beg to differ with Mr. Neck's learned opinion.
45

I don't know where my family came from. Someplace cold, where they eat beans on Thursday and hang their wash on the line on Monday. I don't know how long we've been in America. We've been in this school district
50 since I was in first grade; that must count for something. I start an apple tree.

The arguments jump back and forth across the room. A few suck-ups quickly figure out which side Mr. Neck is squatting on, so they
55 fight to throw out the "foreigners". Anyone whose family immigrated in the last century has a story to tell about how hard their relatives have worked, the contributions they make to the country, the taxes they pay. A
60 member of the Archery Club tries to say that we are all foreigners and we should give the country back to the Native Americans, but she's buried under disagreement. Mr. Neck enjoys the noise, until one kid challenges him
65 directly.

Brave Kid: "Maybe your son didn't get that job because he's not good enough. Or he's lazy. Or the other guy was better than him, no matter what his skin color. I think the white
70 people who have been here for two hundred years are the ones pulling down the country. They don't know how to work – they've had it too easy."

The pro-immigration forces erupt in
75 applause and hooting.

Mr. Neck. "You watch your mouth, mister. You are talking about my son. I don't want to hear any more from you. That's enough debate – get your books out."
80

The Neck is back in control. Show time is over. I try to draw a branch coming out of a tree trunk for the 315th time. It looks so flat, a cheap, cruddy drawing. I have no idea how to

Part **A** B C 2 29

make it come alive. I am so focused I don't
notice at first that David Petrakis My Lab
Partner has stood up. The class stops talking.
I put my pencil down.

Mr. Neck: "Mr. Petrakis, take your seat."

David Petrakis is never, ever in trouble. He is
the kid who wins perfect attendance records,
who helps the staff chase down bugs in the
computer files of report cards. What is he
thinking? Has he flipped, finally cracked under
the pressure of being smarter than everyone?

David: "If the class is debating, then each
student has the right to say what's on his
mind."

Mr. Neck: "I decide who talks in here."

David: "You opened a debate. You can't close it
just because it is not going your way."

Mr. Neck: "Watch me. Take your seat, Mr.
Petrakis."

David: "The Constitution does not recognize
different classes of citizenship based on time
spent living in the country. I am a citizen, with
the same rights as your son, or you. As
a citizen, and as a student, I am protesting the
tone of this lesson as racist, intolerant, and
xenophobic."

Mr. Neck: "Sit your butt in that chair,
Petrakis, and watch your mouth! I try to get
a debate going in here and you people turn it
into a race thing. Sit down or you're going to
the principal."

David stares at Mr. Neck, looks at the flag for
a minute, then picks up his books and walks
out of the room. He says a million things
without saying a word. I make a note to study
David Petrakis. I have never heard a more
eloquent silence.

Fact File

The Constitution of the United States
(1789) set up the country's system of
government. Many other democracies such
as Germany have a basic law influenced by
the US Constitution.
Since 1789, 27 amendments have been
made to the Constitution. The first ten were
made together in 1791 and are known as
the Bill of Rights. The First Amendment
guarantees freedom of speech and the
press, freedom of religion, freedom of
assembly and the right to protest to the
government.

Working with the text

1 👥 **Understanding the story**
*After looking at the Fact File, give reasons why this
chapter of the novel is called 'First Amendment'.*

2 **The main characters**
a) *Write a character description of Mr Neck. Find
examples of implicit and explicit characterization
in the text and note the line numbers.*

b) *Contrast Mr Neck's views on immigration and
human rights with David's.*

3 **The topic: freedom of speech**
*Where do you see the limits to freedom of speech?
Are there things one should not be allowed to say?*

4 Extra 👥 **Game**
*Divide into five groups. Each group chooses a scene
from the story and does a freeze frame. The other
groups describe what they see and say where it
belongs in the text.*

STUDY SKILLS **Characterization in fiction**

The author of a story can describe or portray a character **directly or explicitly** by giving
information through the narrator or other characters. Characterization is **indirect or implicit**
when we learn about the character by what they say or do or through the setting they are put in.

▶ *SF Reading literature (pp. 141–143)* • **Text File 2** *(p. 111)* • *WB 2 (p. 23)*

2 VIEWING 'That's enough debate'

a) Watch the film extract. What is different from the novel? What is the same?

b) In the novel, Melinda is the narrator. How is this reflected in the film and why do you think it is done this way?

c) Look at the four stills from the film and describe the characters' facial expressions and posture. The words in the box below may help.

> The eyes/lips/forehead/eyebrows ...
> His/Her arms/fingers/shoulders ...
> The way ... stands/walks/moves his head/ arms ... suggest(s)/tell(s) us/express(es)/ show(s)/look(s)/mean(s)/makes us think ... angry/authoritarian/bored/excited/fed up/ determined/dominant/insecure/ worried/sarcastic/alarmed/ not paying attention/nervous ...

d) Watch the film extract again. Imitate the hand positions of Melinda and Mr Neck and imagine how they feel. How is their character reflected by their body language?

e) Which types of camera angle can you identify in pictures 1 and 3? Explain how these camera angles help to characterize the people in this scene.

f) Extra Watch the scene again, looking for implicit and explicit ways of characterizing Mr Neck.

STUDY SKILLS Analysing films (2)

Characterization in film
Explicit characterization in films can be achieved through voiceover comments.
Implicit characterization is achieved through what the character says and through their body language and facial expressions.

Camera angles
The camera can be used to present the characters in a certain way. Different **camera angles** have different effects.

Low-angle shot: The camera looks up at the character from below. This can make people appear important or scary.
Eye-level shot: The camera is level with the character's face. This is a rather neutral position.
High-angle shot: The camera looks down from above. This tends to make the characters seem less powerful.

▶ SF Analysing films (p. 157)

3 Free speech – hate speech

a) *Hate speech is spreading fast on modern electronic media. The snippets below all deal with the topic of hate speech. Read them and write down where you think each of them came from. The texts are (1) from the advice page of a magazine, (2) an internet chat room, (3) a student essay, (4) a scientific report, (5) a dictionary, (6) a blog.*

A I dont give a damn if you or anyone wants to dis me. That's what FREE SPEECH is. That's what i think. DONT interfere with my life and i'll leave u alone 2.

B Hate speech has led to much controversy in recent discussions. The problem is that if we try to prevent hate speech, we go against the basic right which allows us to express our opinions. In this paper, I will ask if the 'right' to freedom of expression can ever be challenged.

C It's my right to call someone an ugly bitch online, if that's what I want to do. And if they go and jump off a bridge, is it my fault? I can tell them they're stupid, and I wish they would get out of my life, but no one should blame me if they do what I tell them. They kill themselves for other reasons.

D Hate speech: Spoken or written communication which will probably be seen as offensive by minorities or anyone who sees themselves as a victim.

b) *Compare your results with those of your partner. With the help of the information in the study skills box, explain your decisions.*

c) *Choose the text you most agree with or disagree with. Give reasons.*

d) **Extra** *'Sticks and stones may break my bones, but names can never hurt me.' Explain this saying. Do you agree with it?*

E Although there is no significant difference in the percentage of foreign students and UK students who say that they have been victims of hate speech, 7% of all male foreign students experienced it as against 4% of UK males and 2% of all females.

F There's nothing you can do about hate talk. Don't try to – just try to get used to living with it. There are lots of people who are always talking crap online, so you'd better ignore it and forget it.

STUDY SKILLS | Identifying style and register

The way people speak changes depending on the topic and who they are addressing. The style may be formal, neutral, informal or very informal (slang).
- Formal language: less common words, complex sentences, no short forms
- Informal language: common words, short forms, use of questions, conversational style (e.g. frequent use of pronouns), unusual spelling
- The language used is also influenced by the topic: scientific reports will often contain numbers, formulas or statistics, letters of advice often use imperatives, legal texts are written in a very precise language, etc.

▶ SF Identifying style and register (p. 143) • WB 3 (p. 24)

P1 REVISION Free to decide (Simple form and progressive form)

Present or present perfect? Complete the sentences with the correct tense of the verbs in brackets. Decide if you need the simple form or the progressive form.

Mr Brown is successful, quite successful. He's a manager. He … (be) a manager for ten years now. He … (enjoy) being a manager very much. Mr Brown … (be) a keen hiker too. He … (often go) hiking with his friend Mr Green. Actually, right now they … (go) on a short hiking trip in the north of Scotland. They … (fly) back to England next Monday. Mr Brown's wife … (wait) for her husband. Impatiently! There are problems. Their only son Matthew, who … (celebrate) his 16th birthday this month, … (decide) to leave school and join the army. He says he … (think) about it for a long time and now he … (know) that it … (be) the right thing for him to do. He … (want) to experience real life and do something useful, like fighting for his country. Mrs Brown … (worry) because she … (find) the army jobs too dangerous. Matthew's decision will be a surprise for Mr Brown too. He is the manager of a humanitarian organization that … (give) help to child soldiers in Africa.

▶ GF 3: Aspect: the simple form and the progressive form (pp. 173–174)

P2 REVISION Censorship (Simple past vs. past progressive)

a) *Apart from the example in the first sentence, there are six more places in this text where the past progressive would be better than the simple past. Decide which form fits each gap best.*
Remember: The past progressive is used to describe an action or event that was in progress and not yet complete at a particular time in the past.

Jimmy Preston … (get) *was getting* more and more nervous. The 16-year-old schoolboy from Connecticut … (stand) backstage in a New York City theater, waiting for his call to go on stage. He … (read) his text once again. Jimmy … (have to) speak a powerful monologue, and he … (want) to get it right. He … (play) the role of an ex-soldier from the Iraq War. In the play the ex-soldier … (describe) the psychological problems he … (suffer) now he was back home from Iraq.
The lights in the theater dimmed. It was time for Jimmy to go on stage. He quickly … (move) forward, looking confused, like the soldier whose role he … (play).
Jimmy started his monologue: "My symptoms didn't appear straightaway. Then everything … (hit) me all at once. I had nightmares. I couldn't sleep …"
Two months ago Jimmy and the other actors, his mates from the school drama club, … (rehearse) because they wanted to put on the play *Voices in Conflict* for parents and friends at their school. When they … (get) ready for the first night, their head teacher suddenly … (ban) the drama project. Some parents didn't like the school putting on an anti-war play. The story … (reach) the newspapers in New York and shortly afterwards the drama club got an invitation to perform there.
Back on the New York stage Jimmy's nerves had gone and he … (do) his monologue confidently: "I can't seem to find happiness in anything …"

b) *Write the beginning of a story. Start by describing the setting and what the characters are doing, then let something happen. Here is an example:*

It was cold outside and the Smith family was sitting round the fire. Soft music was playing and … Suddenly somebody knocked on the window …

▶ WB 4 (p. 24)

Part A B C Practice 2 33

P3 Exploring language | Activity verbs and state verbs

a) *There are two groups of verbs: activity verbs and state verbs.*

Activity verbs describe activities (e.g. go, write) or events (e.g. rain). We can use activity verbs in the simple and progressive forms.

We always talk about the industrial revolution in History.
You are talking about my son.

State verbs (e.g. know) don't describe activities or events, but states. We generally use them only in the simple form.

I know where my family came from.
The Constitution does not recognize different classes of citizenship.

Which eight of the following verbs are state verbs (and not used in the progressive)? Use each one of the eight in a sentence.

believe – belong to – cost – discuss – explain – hate – mean – own – prefer – take – want – watch

---

b) *Now look at these sentences:*

I think for sure that Mr. Neck is going to explode.

(think = *meinen, glauben* – a state ▸ simple, not progressive)

What is Neck thinking?

(think = *überlegen, über etwas nachdenken* – an activity, in progress ▸ progressive)

Some verbs are used as activity verbs and *as state verbs – with different meanings. As activity verbs, they can be used either in the simple form or – if the activity is in progress – in the progressive form. As state verbs, they are always used in the simple form.*

Simple present or progressive? Complete the following pairs of sentences with the right form of the verb in brackets. Then translate the sentences into German.

1 Now I ... (see) why Ben isn't here. He ... (see) his teacher.
2 Just a minute, I ... (taste) the soup ... Hm, it ... (taste) good today.
3 I ... (look) at this job advert. It ... (look) interesting.

---

c) *Look at stills 1 and 4 on p. 30. Describe the pictures in detail, say who is doing what and speculate about the thoughts and feelings of Melinda, David and their classmates.*

You could use the following verbs:
appear, believe, dream, hate, have, imagine, know, look, seem, sit, stand, stare, think, understand, want, wish, wonder

---

d) *There are 14 mistakes in this text. Sometimes the writer has wrongly used the progressive for state verbs, and sometimes they have not used the progressive for activity verbs that describe an activity in progress. Correct the mistakes.*

I am not thinking that my friends want me to be with them any longer. Do they meet tonight without me? They have all said that they are busy with homework but I am having a feeling that they do something together. I heard someone say something about the cinema. I am not meaning that they are wanting to hurt me, but right now they act strangely towards me. Look, there they are, putting their heads together in deep conversation. Do they talk about me? I am betting that they make fun of my clothes because they keep turning their heads towards me. I guess they are hating me. Huh? What's that? Alex is waving! It's looking as if he's waving at me. Am I understanding this correctly? Yes, now he clearly calls me over ...

▸ *GF 3.2–3.3: Activity verbs and state verbs (p. 174)* ·
WB 5–6 (p. 25)

GET INVOLVED

1 Voting

Many young people in Britain want to be more involved in politics, but they are only allowed to vote when they are 18. Should this be changed? Read the following online article on the topic.

Home

Should the voting age be 16?

The government-backed Youth Citizenship Commission says 66 % of people want the voting age lowered to 16. Do you agree?

Open thread
guardian.co.uk, Friday 26 June 2009 10.30 BST
Article history

The Youth Citizenship Commission, set up in 2007 to look at young people's relationship with citizenship, says that 66 % of people it surveyed support the lowering of the voting age to 16.

The prime minister, Gordon Brown, meeting teenagers – but are they old enough to vote?

5 Opponents say that 16-year-olds are not mature enough to choose a government, and fear that they may be too easily influenced. Supporters of the commission's findings argue that reform in 1970, which lowered the voting age from 21 to 18 for all public elections in the UK, did not have
10 any catastrophic impact on the political landscape. They claim that if one can "leave school, work full-time and pay taxes, leave home, get married and join the armed forces", surely one can vote. The Labour party has officially adopted Votes at 16 as policy – joining the Liberal Democrats, the Scottish National party and the Green party. But what's your take? Are 16-year-olds too young to vote?

© Guardian News & Media Ltd 2009

---

a) List arguments for and against lowering the voting age given in the article.

b) The article says that lowering the voting age to 18 'did not have any catastrophic impact on the political landscape' (ll. 9–10). Explain.

c) Identify typical elements of print and online articles in the *Guardian* text above.

STUDY SKILLS Analysing newspaper articles

Elements of print and online articles
The **headline** in large type gives an idea of what the article is about and attracts the reader's attention. The **sub-heading** goes into greater detail than the headline. A **caption** describes a photo or another picture. A **byline** states who the article is by, or who took the photo.

Elements of online articles only
Online papers give their **web address**, the **date** and sometimes the **time** the article was published. The term **open thread** tells readers that they can write comments on the article. Words in blue or underlined are hyperlinks that can be clicked on for further information. The **article history** tells readers when the article was first published and when it was last modified.

▶ SF Analysing newspaper articles (p. 144) • Text File 3 (pp. 112–113) • Text File 4 (pp. 114–117)

d) These are some of the comments readers of the online article made:
- shud b able 2 vote by txt innit
- Given that half of 16-year olds leave school without 5 good GCSEs, the idea that they are informed enough to vote is laughable and the prospect of them voting is terrifying.
- NO, they aren't adults. And they shouldn't be able to join armed forces either
- yes it shud be coz people arent dum when they are 16. by the way i love michael jackson may he rest in peace god bless him
- They can already vote – it's called the X-factor, Big Brother, Britain's Got Talent.

Choose one of the comments above and explain the reader's intention.
Write your own comment on the Guardian article, making your own opinion on voting at 16 clear.

e) **Extra** What kind of newspaper do you prefer – online or print? Explain your preference. Do a class survey.

2 VIEWING Vote!

a) During the 2008 US presidential election campaign some Hollywood stars made a short film to encourage people to vote. Collect ideas on what you might see in this film. Then watch it.

b) List features of the film that you find unusual. Explain why they may have been used and discuss what effect they may have had on people watching the film.

c) Watch the film again. Write down as many reasons as you can which people give for wanting to vote. Compare your list with a partner's.

3 Responsibilities

a) On 20 September 2009, US President Barack Obama gave a speech to young students nationwide, which was broadcast live to all the schools in the country. Note down key words that you expect to hear.

b) Listen to the speech. While you listen, put these topics in the order they come up in the speech:
A Setting goals
B Getting up early
C Asking for help
D Not giving up
E Fulfilling responsibilities
F Working hard

d) Which of President Obama's topics speak to you most, and which ones leave you cold? Would it be a good idea if the German President or Chancellor gave a speech to students here during school time? If so, what topics should they address?

c) Listen again. Find examples for each topic. Take notes and compare with a partner.

▶ WB 7–8 (pp. 26–27)

P1 Exploring language — Emphasis

a) Find five different ways the writer uses emphasis in the following text. Try to do it without first looking at the box below.

Yes, it was President Obama who came to our school yesterday and gave a speech. So we were listening to the President himself. And he does smile a lot when he meets people. I think that he really enjoyed his visit. Never in my life have I seen such an enthusiastic crowd of kids at our school.

Now look at the box below and check.

b) Rewrite the following sentences, adding emphasis as shown in brackets.

Obama's mother helped him with his lessons early every morning. (It was …)
She never allowed him to sleep in from Monday to Friday. (Never …)
She made him work hard (… did …), but he was pleased about it (… really …).
The lessons were always interesting, he said. (-self pronoun)

c) **Extra** Read the following text, then make four statements to your partner about facts in the text that you could emphasize, e.g. 'It was X who/which …'.

The US Stars and Stripes is the most famous flag in the world, not the British Union Jack. George Washington asked Betsy Ross to make the very first flag in 1776. Betsy Ross did not design the flag, she only sewed it. In fact George Washington probably designed it. The Stars and Stripes has become the United States' most important national symbol. The flag is always at his side when a US president addresses his people.

Emphasis

When you talk or write, you might want to put special emphasis on certain words or expressions.

1. When speaking, any word can be emphasized by **stressing** it:
   None of it will matter unless all of you fulfill **your** responsibilities.
2. You can use **certain words** to add emphasis, like really, ever and completely here:
   I want you to really work at it.
   Don't ever give up on yourself.
   Not every homework assignment will seem completely relevant to your life.
3. You can use an **emphasizing -self pronoun** to stress a noun or pronoun.
   So my **mother** decided to teach me extra lessons **herself**.
4. You can change the **word order**, putting the part you want to emphasize at the front:
   It's you who can decide to stand up for kids who are being teased or bullied.
   That's the opportunity an education can provide. (*Not stressed:* An education can provide that opportunity.)
5. Some adverbials with negative meaning can go at the beginning of a sentence for special emphasis, but then an auxiliary verb must come before the subject. This we call inversion.
   Never should you give up.
   No way do you love all the books you have to read for school.
6. You can use do, does or did to stress the verb which follows it.
   No one's born being good at things, but you **do** become good at things through hard work.

▶ GF 12: Emphasis (pp. 193–194) • WB 9 (p. 27)

Part A B C Practice **2** 37

P2 Common verbs and their collocations

a) *Combinations of words that happen very often are called collocations. Which collocations do the verbs* **do** *and* **make** *form with nouns (left)? Which collocations do* **get** *and* **go** *form with adjectives (right)?*

do make	friends	the work
	nothing	a cake
	well	a call
	the dishes	a favour
	an exercise	a deal
	a speech	a drawing
	business	a project

get go	angry	dressed
	bad (*food*)	drunk
	blind	hard
	bored	involved
	crazy	ready
	deaf	red

b) 👥 *Partner A: Find a good German translation for each collocation.*
Partner B: Make up an English sentence with the collocation in it. Take turns.

P3 Common adjectives and their collocations ▸ ⊟⊟

a) *Use one of the adjectives* **hard, heavy** *and* **strong** *to fill the gaps. It will help you if you check the three adjectives in all their meanings in a dictionary.*

1 He won't be able to lift such a *heavy* bag. He's only nine years old.
2 She's got a really … timetable this term.
3 It's been a long … day today.
4 My teachers always made a … impression on me.
5 It was a … exam and the final question was just too difficult.
6 There is a … chance that he will get the job.
7 He's been a … smoker and drinker all his adult life.
8 Although I have … views on this, I can see your point too.
9 It was a very … meal – far too much meat and not enough vegetables.
10 There was a … and unpleasant smell coming from the kitchen.
11 They have had a … life in this country.
12 I'm not so good at maths but I am quite … in physics.
13 Her … breathing told me that she was deeply asleep.

b) 👥 *Compare your results with a partner.*

P4 Collocations in politics

a) *Work out which verb goes with which noun. Use a dictionary if necessary.*

achieve • break • cause • discriminate against • elect • lose • support • vote	an aim • Conservative • a mayor • minorities • a movement • a promise • support • trouble

b) *Use each collocation in a sentence beginning with* **If** *or* **When***:*
If you want to achieve an aim, you will have to work hard for it and be prepared for problems.

▸ WB 10 (p. 28)

THE WORDS PAGE

MAKE A CHANGE

1 Street scene

a) Look at the photo. Describe what you see in it. How does the scene make you feel?

b) Write a thought bubble for each person you see in the photo.

c) **Extra** A reporter comes to the scene and interviews one of the people. Write the interview with a partner and then act it out in front of the class.

2 We are all bystanders
(abridged and adapted from *Greater Good Magazine*, III Fall/Winter 2006–2007)

Peggy liked Stewart. They went to high school together, and Peggy always used to say hi when she passed Stewart in the hall. However every day when Stewart boarded their school bus, a couple of boys used to tease him mercilessly. And every day, Peggy just used to sit in her seat, silent.

"I was dying inside for him," she said. "There were enough of us on the bus who were feeling awful. We could have done something. But none of us said anything."

Peggy still can't explain why she didn't defend Stewart. She had known his tormentors since they were all little kids, and she didn't find them threatening. She thinks if she had said something, other kids might have joined in to make the teasing stop.

"I think I would say something now, but I don't know for sure," she said. "Maybe if I saw someone being beaten up and killed, I'd just stand there. That still worries me."

We've all found ourselves in similar situations: the times we've seen someone harassed on the street and didn't get involved; when we've driven past a car stranded by the side of the road, assuming another driver would stop to help; even when we've noticed litter on the sidewalk and left it for someone else to pick up. We witness a problem, think about some kind of positive action, then respond by doing … nothing. Something prevents us. We remain bystanders.

a) Read the article above and say in two sentences what it is about.

b) Why didn't Peggy speak up for Stewart when he was in trouble?

c) Make up a scene in which Peggy finally decides to speak up for Stewart. Work in groups of four and then act out the scene on the bus.

d) The text gives examples of bystander situations. Think of more examples.

e) 👥 *Read the text below and say why bystanders remain passive when others are in need.*

The bystander effect (abridged and adapted from an article in the *Toronto Star*, March 29, 2007)

Psychologists say that a person is less likely to help someone in need when other people are around. The more witnesses there are, the less likely it is one will get involved. That's because most people assume someone else will take responsibility. In an emergency, most people will wait to see what others do before offering to help. An individual bystander will be considerably influenced by the ways in which other bystanders are reacting. Everyone waits for someone else to take action yet no one is willing to step forward first.

f) Extra 👥 *Get into groups and make use of all the information on bystanders that you have. Discuss solutions to the problem of the bystander effect and prepare a one-minute talk.*

g) Extra 👥 *Albert Einstein is reported to have said: 'The world is a dangerous place, not because of those who do evil, but because of those who look on and do nothing.'*
From all you have learned, would you agree with this comment? Why or why not?

3 Filming injustice 🎧

a) World-famous musician Peter Gabriel is the co-founder of the human rights organization Witness. Their motto is 'See it, film it, change it'. Does this give you any idea of what they do?

b) Listen to Peter Gabriel's talk. He mentions four names and two years – note them down. Then answer these questions:
1 Who got Gabriel interested in human rights and when?
2 What human rights organization was supported on the tour that Gabriel went on?
3 When did Witness get started?
4 What is the name of the website that Gabriel mentions?

c) Listen to the talk again and find the following more detailed information:
1 How did Gabriel himself suffer inhuman treatment when he was a young boy and how did he feel about it?
2 Why couldn't he walk away from the topic of human rights after the tour?
3 How can cameras help with human rights?
4 What exactly does Witness do?
5 What would Gabriel like to do with all the film material from the cameras?

d) Cameras are often used 'for fun' to record violence. Contrast this with the use of cameras by Witness. Explain the difference.
▶ WB 11 (p. 28)

40 **2** Part A B C Practice

MEDIATION COURSE Part 2

P1 MEDIATION An e-mail to Britain (Written mediation)

a) *You have received an e-mail from a class in your exchange school in Britain. It says: 'Our citizenship class is doing a project on what other countries do to prevent crimes of violence. Can you give us some help?' Use the advice below for your reply.*

Find the main ideas

Read the whole text, then decide and write down for every section what the most important ideas are and what will be useful for the project in Britain. Compare your ideas with those of your partner and decide on a final list of points.

Check your vocabulary

Check with your classmates or in a dictionary for any words you need.

Mediate the text into English

Use your notes to put the main ideas of the German text into simple sentences that are easy to understand for young people in Britain. Don't stay too close to the German text. Explain what the text says instead of translating it.

Finish your reply

Check that you have covered all the important points on your list. Check for grammar and spelling. Finally, write a short e-mail to the class in Britain to tell them that the text is attached.

ZivilCOURAGE zeigen!

Was jeder im Alltag gegen Gewalt und Rassismus tun kann

Grundsätzlich gilt: Spielen Sie nicht den Helden. Es ist immer richtig, den Notruf der Polizei (Tel. 110) zu verständigen.

In der Bahn, im Bus: Es wird jemand angegriffen, erniedrigt, verletzt. Sie können den/die Fahrer/in auffordern, die Polizei zu rufen. Sie können andere Mitfahrende auffordern, mit Ihnen laut zu pfeifen und zu rufen: „Hört auf, hört auf!" Anfangs machen dabei wenige, dann in der Regel immer mehr mit. Jetzt wird die Situation für Gewalttäter/innen riskant, weil sie unüberschaubar und unberechenbar ist.

Bei Schlägereien: Wenn Kinder, Jugendliche oder Erwachsene sich schlagen, schlagen Sie Alarm, machen Sie Krach, stellen Sie Öffentlichkeit (aus sicherer Entfernung) her. Machen Sie andere auf die Schlägerei aufmerksam. Zeigen Sie, dass Sie bereit sind, gemäß Ihren Möglichkeiten einzugreifen. Eine Kleinigkeit zu tun ist besser, als über große Heldentaten nachzudenken. Ein einziger Schritt, ein kurzes Ansprechen, jede Aktion verändert die Situation und kann andere dazu anregen, ihrerseits einzugreifen.

Viele Kinder und Jugendliche behaupten, zur Rede gestellt, alles sei „nur ein Spaß" gewesen. Nennen Sie dann die vorausgegangene „Gewalt" beim Namen: „Dann lassen Sie mal den roten Fleck (die blutende Lippe, ...) sehen, nennen Sie das einen Spaß? Ich nenne das Körperverletzung."

---

b) *After you send your reply, you get another e-mail. Your British friends are going to take part in an anti-bullying conference and have invited you to take part too. Make a notice in German for your notice board with the relevant information about the trip and the conference.*

Many thanks for the information you sent us.

In connection with our project, some people in our class are going to attend this year's Actionwork anti-bullying conference – which is in our town. Our school is helping to organize it. It starts on Easter Tuesday and lasts three days. We would like to invite you and another five students from your school to join us. Families here have offered to be your hosts, so your only expense will be getting here.

These conferences attract hundreds of young people from around the country and abroad. This year the conference will focus on the good work that young people do to stop bullying and violence in their communities and schools. There will be lots of workshops. We are going to the one on 'Active Bystanders', which is what you would probably call people who show 'Zivilcourage'. If you are interested in coming, let us know and we can discuss the details.

▶ *SF Mediation Course (pp. 145–146) • WB 12 (pp. 29–30)*

Part A B **C** Practice **2** **41**

P2   WORDS The language of violence and non-violence ▸ ☰☰

a) *The words and expressions in the box on the left are taken from a newspaper article. Find synonyms from the box on the right.*

- achieve a compromise
- express one's anger
- accept differences
- be aggressive
- apologize
- provoke somebody
- reduce stress
- show sympathy
- show respect
- be kind

- be tolerant
- annoy somebody
- be polite
- calm somebody down
- be violent
- reach an agreement
- say sorry
- say what is upsetting you
- show you understand
- be nice

b) 👥 *Write the pairs on cards, one pair per card, and order them from non-violent to violent. Compare your order with your partner's.*

P3   👥 **EVERYDAY ENGLISH** SPEAKING Role play: staying cool in a conflict

Partner A: You are annoyed. Say one of the sentences 1–6 below.
Partner B: Try to stay calm, keeping in mind the tips in the box below right.
Swap roles after two turns. At the end, think about which sentence was most or least de-escalating.

1 Bus passenger sitting opposite you:
   'Why are you looking at me like that?'
2 Man bumping into you:
   'Can't you watch where you're going?'
3 Person waiting in a queue at a shop:
   'What do you think you're doing? I was here first.'

4 Woman in street to you about your dog:
   'Do you always let your dog do its business on the pavement?'
5 Train passenger annoyed about your mobile:
   'Do you have to talk at the top of your voice the whole time?'
6 Troublemaker in the street:
   'I just don't like the look of your face.'

> **Tip**
>
> When somebody speaks to you in such a way that you feel they are attacking you or not allowing you your rights, it's good to stay cool and polite, and to try to de-escalate.
>
> **How to behave in difficult situations**
> – It's better to begin a sentence with 'I' instead of 'You'.
> – Do not take unfriendliness personally.
> – Say sorry but don't beg.
> – Don't make things worse by saying things like 'Mind your own business' or 'Shut up'.
> – Keep your voice calm. It can make a lot of difference.
>
> **Some phrases to calm somebody down**
> – I'm sorry. I didn't realize that …
> – I think there is a misunderstanding …
> – My mistake, I'm sorry.
> – How stupid of me. I must be more careful…
> – Sorry but we disagree on this.
> – I see what you mean but it is not how I feel.

▸ WB 13–14 (p. 30)

P4 Remembering the past (used to + infinitive)

With *used to + infinitive*, you can talk about actions and states which took place regularly in the past but don't take place any longer.
Peggy always **used to say hi** when she passed Stewart in the hall.
She **used to be scared** to get involved.
It is also possible to use *would* instead of *used to* but mainly only for actions and not for states.
Peggy **would always say hi** when she passed Stewart in the hall.

a) *Peggy and Stewart meet as adults and talk about the time when they were teenagers. Make sentences with used to + infinitive.*

Peggy
1 Our fathers ... be very good friends.
2 I ... hate Math at school.
3 I ... feel bad when the others teased you.

Stewart
4 Your father ... visit our farm.
5 I ... hate history.
6 I ... wonder why nobody seemed to care.

b) *Tell your partner about some of the things you used to do when you were younger.*
I used to play in the garden all day long. / I would play in the garden all day long.

P5 WRITING Protesters and police

a) *Last Saturday afternoon some people were injured during a demonstration in the capital of a former British colony. Read the following statements by people who saw what happened.*

'There were about 250 of them, demonstrating for freedom of speech – as if they haven't got it already – marching to the parliament building, and haven't they got anything better to do? The police officers moved forward to stop them. Quite right in my opinion. They had to use their batons because the protesters were in the way. Then I saw some of them fighting with the police, so it was all their own fault. Four or five officers were injured and were taken to hospital. I hope the people who did it go to prison.'

'The marchers came from People's Park and they were going to the parliament building. It happened right in front of me. They wanted to turn into Victoria Street, but there was a group of police officers there and suddenly they ran forward and attacked the marchers with batons. I was shocked because there were 200 to 250 people protesting peacefully against this new law to limit freedom of speech. Some of them ran away and some were hit on the head as they tried to fight back. I counted 15 protesters taken away in ambulances.'

'I was standing at the corner of the street. I'd say there were at least 200 people marching, coming into Victoria Street, and the police were waiting for them. Suddenly the police ran towards the marchers and started hitting them with batons, hitting people on the head. It was awful. Some of the protesters ran away, but some of them fought with the police. Soon there were about 20 people lying on the ground, five of them officers. Then the ambulances came.'

b) *In groups, decide what are the facts and what are people's opinions. Then write your own reports, including the facts but not any opinions.*
▶ WB 15 (p. 31)

Part A B **C** Practice **2** 43

P6 LISTENING WTNX News Time 🎧

a) Listen to the news from Haybrook, Illinois. Put these stories into the correct order:

1 Court decision on use of language
2 Report on possible extremist activities
3 Dress shop doesn't accept the way assistant dresses
4 Latest statistics show big rise
5 Haybrook murder case still not solved

b) Listen again and correct the sentences.

– Speaking Spanish will be allowed at St Joseph's after the court's decision.
– The majority of prisoners are likely to get involved in terrorist activities again.
– A week after a manager gave a young Muslim woman a job, she was fired for wearing the hijab.
– Five cities in Illinois had a population increase of over 60 per cent in the last five years.
– A woman was shot in the stomach from the balcony of a third-floor apartment.

P7 👥 READING A campaigner for human rights ▶ 🗐

Bianca Jagger was born in Nicaragua in 1950. At the time, the country was suffering under a right-wing dictatorship. As a child she used to go on political protests with her mother. At 16 she was given the chance to study politics in Paris. In 1970, she married Mick Jagger of the Rolling Stones and spent a few years among the jet set, mixing with celebrities in the art and fashion world. It was at the beginning of the 80s that she started making headlines in a different way. She was deeply involved in drawing attention to human rights problems all over the world.

In South America Bianca Jagger campaigned for the protection of the tropical rain forests and for indigenous rights. In Bosnia she did everything she could to help stop the genocide and bring those responsible to an international court. She has been in the front line working to help the orphans of Africa, whose parents have died of AIDS. She made a significant speech at the start of Amnesty International's important "Stop Violence Against Women" campaign and has been a witness concerning violations of human rights at many international courts and committees. In addition, she writes articles for leading newspapers and regularly appears on television programmes in Britain and the US. She has spoken out worldwide against the death penalty and is now giving her attention to the international trade in young children for sex.

In 2004 she received the Right Livelihood Award, also known as the Alternative Nobel Prize for her work in the field of human rights, social justice and environmental protection. In her acceptance speech she said: "There is much each one of us can do to make a difference (...) We need to stand up for our principles and values, human rights, civil liberties and the rule of law. If we don't, our world will further descend into chaos."

Divide the class into four groups. Each member of a group first works individually on their task and then compares the result with other members of their section.

Group 1: *Choose ten key words from the text.*
Group 2: *Summarize the text in one sentence.*

Group 3: *Summarize the text in three sentences.*
Group 4: *Write down six phrases to express your own reaction to the text.*

Form new groups of four (one from each of the groups above), and share your results.
Discuss the best method of preparing for a talk.

▶ WB 16 (p. 31)

44 Extra Revision Getting ready for a test 1

1 WORDS Getting involved

Choose the correct words to complete the sentences.
1. The students are going to … (produce/protect/protest) against higher bus fares on Saturday. Let's all join their protest … (march/mark/match)!
2. What can we do to … (raise/rate/rise) money for our youth club holiday programme? – We could organize a charity match and ask people to … (deserve/donate/deliver) money.
3. Our local councillor took … (part/place/turns) in a radio discussion last week. She spoke … (down/up/through) for a lower voting age.
4. Would you like to … (sell/spend/support) our environmental project? We want to … (protect/share/revise) Cornwall's coasts.
5. How many people took part in the … (deal/debate/departure)? – All the teenagers who … (viewed/visited/volunteered) the European Parliament.

2 WORDS We need jobs!

Jenna and her friends are looking for summer jobs. Complete what she says with a future form of a verb from the box. Sometimes more than one form is possible.

apply • ask • find • give • help • look for • need • not be • not do • work

1. I … a job on the internet. I'm sure I … something suitable there.
2. Our teachers … us with the application. I hope it … too difficult.
3. … you … your father's boss for a job? I think he … you a chance.
4. Perhaps they … help at the new café in my street. My best friend and I … to the manager.
5. Have you heard about Sam? He … as a gardener. I certainly … that.

3 WORDS Paraphrasing

a) *If you can't think of the English word for something that you want to say, you have to paraphrase it. Here are some examples. Match the words in the box with the definitions.*

Fahrgeld • Klassensprecher/in • Untertitel • Ernte • Angestellte(r) • Schülerzeitung

1. It's a magazine that is written and sold by students.
2. It's somebody who represents the class.
3. They're words that translate what is said in a film into a different language and appear on the bottom of the screen.
4. It's the money that you pay to travel by bus, tram, tube, taxi, etc.
5. It is a person who gets money for working for a company.
6. It's the collecting, digging or picking of fruits and vegetable.

b) *Now look up the words in a German–English dictionary.*

Extra Revision Getting ready for a test 1   45

4 READING Working out the meaning of words

a) *Try to work out the meaning of the following words or phrases. The tips will help you.*

1   **Tip** You know a similar word in German.
   A *(to) charter* a plane
   B *(to) explode*
   C *(to) renovate* an old building

2   **Tip** You understand the word from its context.
   A It was a *blazing* summer day – 37 degrees in the shade.
   B The food was *inedible* – we sent it straight back to the kitchen.
   C The hotel offered great *facilities* such as a pool, a tennis court and a very nice restaurant.

3   **Tip** You know the main part of the word.
   A *Disconnect* the mouse from the computer.
   B Her statement is just *untrue*.
   C He's a real *worrier*.

4   **Tip** You know a similar English word.
   A an *adult* dog
   B a boy *aged* 13
   C a *debatable* question

b) *Read the text below. You probably don't know the underlined words. Try to guess their meaning and say which of the tips in a) can help you.*

If you are looking for a job, you should be aware that there are common <u>requirements</u> for all <u>employees</u>. This refers also to teenage workers. First of all, employers expect you to be hardworking. This might sound <u>self-evident</u> but <u>laziness</u> is one of the major reasons for being <u>fired</u>. In addition, your boss counts on your <u>dependability</u>. That is often <u>related to</u> being punctual. So, start using a <u>planner</u> and do not depend on your memory. It will soon get too difficult to remember all the appointments from school, work and private activities.

5 SPEAKING I've got a suggestion

There are different ways of suggesting things. Use the phrases in the box on the right to express the ideas below.

1 Du möchtest mit deinem Freund/deiner Freundin heute Abend tanzen gehen: *Let's ...*
2 Du hast eine Idee. Du möchtest mit deinen Freunden zu einer Live-Talkshow gehen.
3 Du schlägst vor, am nächsten Wochenende ein Picknick zu machen.
4 Du schlägst deinem Besuch vor, heute Abend ins Kino zu gehen.
5 Du sagst deiner Freundin, dass du an ihrer Stelle einfach zu Hause fernsehen würdest.
6 Du empfiehlst einigen Touristen, einen Spaziergang am Fluss zu machen.

Making suggestions:
– Let's ...
– I suggest that we ...
– If I were you, I'd ...
– What I'd recommend is ...
– What do you think about ...?
– Why don't we...?

1 READING Mosquito box

Read the text. Then answer the questions below, using keywords.

Beware of mosquitoes

The Mosquito Box is an electronic device invented in 2005 to stop teenagers from hanging around businesses and private property. It produces a very high sound about 16 kHz to 18 kHz, which is extremely irritating and which only disturbs people younger than 25 years, because people's hearing gets poorer the older one gets. Depending on the particular equipment, this high frequency noise can be heard at a distance of about 40 to 60 metres.

In 2006, the first Mosquito Boxes were put on sale, and since then they have been promoted as a safety device for preventing teenage gangs from annoying customers and residents alike. They are also said to lower vandalism and crime in public areas. Therefore the Mosquito Box is supported by business associations, such as the Association of Convenience Stores. More than 3,000 have been sold in Great Britain so far, but they are also used throughout Europe, Canada and the USA.

The Mosquito Box has caused a debate on human rights. On the one hand supporters point out the rights of shopkeepers, who are afraid of losing income due to badly-behaved teenagers. Critics, on the other hand, claim that the Mosquito Box discriminates against young people creating "a dangerous and widening divide between the young and the old," as Sir Al Aynsley-Green, the children's commissioner for England, warned. That's why he supports the 'Buzz off' campaign, initiated by the UK Youth Parliament, aiming to make Mosquito Boxes illegal because the devices are affecting all children and teenagers regardless of their behaviour. So, it was a huge success for the young people when Kent County Council decided to ban all Mosquito Boxes from council property in 2008.

1. What kind of sound does a Mosquito Box make?
2. How far does the sound reach? From … to …
3. When was the Mosquito Box first sold?
4. Why is this device supported by businesses? (Give two reasons.)
   a) …
   b) …
5. What does Sir Al Aynsley-Green criticize?
6. Who organized the 'Buzz off' campaign?
7. What is the campaign's aim?

2 READING Events

Five teenagers are looking for events they might be interested in. Read the teenagers' statements (1–4), then read the announcements (A–E) from a youth club notice board. Decide which event would suit each person. There is one more event than there are people.

1 Megan:
I love where I live, but it's ten miles from the nearest town and we're too young to drive cars yet. At least you can get back from town by public transport on a Saturday night now – thanks to our protests. But you still think twice about going out because it's so expensive.

2 Ethan:
I'm really interested in politics but I don't know any other young people here who are. I think that politicians in Britain should be more open to learn from other countries. There are lots of good ideas coming from the other side of the Channel, for example.

3 Jill:
I now have lots of different rights. But for some reason I'm still "too young" to select the person who will represent me in Parliament and make sure these rights are respected. Something needs to be done about this senseless situation.

4 Ben:
I love living where I do. I couldn't imagine living in the mountains or in a metropolitan area. Unfortunately a lot of people from big cities come to our town. And that often causes massive problems for the countryside.

A Political Friday
This week's debate will be all about lowering the voting age to 16. Frank Lloyd is a local councillor who thinks that young people learn so much in the two years from 16 to 18 that 16 is too early for voting. Diana Gee, from Radio Kent, says 16-year-olds know enough to vote. It promises to be an interesting discussion.

B Teen rules, OK?
Sunday 10 am. Local citizens' advice bureau officer Diane Fry explains what young people can and can't do. Find out about your rights and duties in many areas: voting, working, travelling at reduced fares, drinking, smoking, driving, passports, boyfriends, girlfriends, etc., etc.

C Coastal clean-up
Once again local clubs are being asked to come along to the beach (meet at North Bay) this Saturday morning to tidy it up after the summer season. Please take part. Wear gloves, bring plastic bags and give a couple of hours of your time for our most popular place.

D Protest march
Saturday, 2 pm. Young people over 14 have to pay full fare on our local buses, which is a problem if you need the bus to get out and about at the weekend. It's a £10 bus ride to and from the discos and clubs in Canterbury. Half-fare would be £5. Join our march to the town hall and demand "Teeny fares for teens"!

E Visit to the European Parliament for young people
Find out how Europe works. Come on our coach trip to the European Parliament in Brussels. There are 50 seats available and the trip only costs £15 because it is EU-sponsored. We leave Dover at 4 am (sorry!) and arrive home at midnight. Passport needed!

3 READING Sunderland votes in UKYP election

Read this text from a magazine.
Then decide if the statements below (1–11) are true, false or not given in the text.

Over 16,000 young people will be entitled to vote in the Sunderland constituency in this year's election to the UK Youth Parliament. Voting will take place at 55 schools over 7 days from 26th February and a week later, on the evening of 5th March, the names of the four young people elected will be announced.
UK Youth Parliament is an organization in which young people aged 11 to 18 come together to debate issues relevant to their age group and to plan campaigns to achieve their goals. About 600 members (MYPs) are elected nationally and can sit not just in the UK Youth Parliament, but also in their respective regional youth parliaments.
A record 22 candidates are standing in the Sunderland area this year. The youngest, eleven-year-old Will Mitchell from West Winton Primary School, is campaigning for a more efficient system of recycling at local schools. 'At the moment, schools have to pay for the collection of all rubbish. It would be better if the collection was free for anything that can be recycled. That would give schools a reason to reduce rubbish and recycle as much as possible.'
For Barbara McKenzie, 16, from St Ambrose School for Girls, cheaper public transport for students is a matter of urgency.

'We need to reduce the price of travelling by bus and train now. Young people need to be mobile, but they can't be expected to pay high fares while still at school. We should only have to pay half of what adults pay.' The manifesto of 17-year-old Nathan Wilde focuses on the lack of facilities for young people. 'There isn't a suitable venue for music concerts in the area. The places we have to use are too small, or they aren't available when we need them.'
Nathan, a student at Thornbrook Technology College, said: 'I think it's important that our voices are heard. There's so much negative stuff about young people in the media, but a lot of us really want to work to improve things for everyone.'
The UK Youth Parliament meets at different locations each year. This year's main sitting is scheduled to take place at the Jordanstown campus of the University of Ulster in Northern Ireland, where successful candidates will have three days to debate and to plan new campaigns. During the year, there is also likely to be an afternoon sitting in the chamber of the House of Commons. MYPs are the only group to have been granted this privilege in the history of parliament.

1 In the Sunderland constituency seven young people will be chosen for the UK Youth Parliament.
2 Students elected for the UK Parliament need to have excellent marks in English.
3 They discuss topics that are important for teenagers and organize activities.
4 Will Mitchell criticizes schools for producing too much waste.
5 Barbara McKenzie normally goes to school by bus.
6 She speaks out for cheaper tickets for public transport.
7 There should be more buses in the evenings.
8 Nathan Wilde is campaigning for better locations for youth events.
9 He wants to improve the image of teenagers in the media.
10 The UK Youth Parliament comes together in Jordanstown regularly.
11 The UK Youth Parliament is permitted to have a meeting in the Houses of Parliament.

Extra Practice test Getting ready for a test 1   49

4 MEDIATION A job advertisement

Portsmouth City Council Youth Service
is shortly going to employ a

Trainee Youth Club Leader

We're going to give you full training in all aspects of the job. We're going to want to interview you if you are really interested in young people. Good communicative skills will be necessary. Computer skills and some experience with working with young people will be an advantage. We will require the successful applicant to channel young people's energies into worthwhile projects.

Your responsibilities:
– you will organize activities for young people
– you will work with the local youth officer
– you will look after the youth club facilities

Please send your application and CV to:
Portsmouth City Council, Civic Offices, Guildhall Sq, Portsmouth, PO1 2AL

Write down in German what information the advertisement gives you about:
– *the trainee's tasks,*   – *the skills and the knowledge the trainee needs,*
– *the training itself,*   – *how and where to apply.*

5 MEDIATION Helping a visitor to Germany

In your local newspaper you have found two events which will take place this evening. Leave a message in English for your Scottish friend, who is interested in politics, describing briefly what will happen. Give the main information. Write down notes.

WAS?
Wir werden eine DVD zeigen, die in anschaulicher Form die politischen Ziele der größten Parteien in Deutschland erklärt. Wir zeigen den Film (45 Min.) mit englischen Untertiteln.

WANN UND WO?
Freitag, 19 Uhr, Jugendzentrum Schillerstraße

WIE?
Comicfiguren und lustige Zeichnungen werden die unterschiedlichen Intentionen in den großen Gebieten Außenpolitik, Innenpolitik, Gesundheit und Wirtschaft illustrieren.

WAS NOCH?
Anschließend werden wir diskutieren. Danach kann zu Live-Musik der Gruppe Poll Position getanzt werden.

WAS?
Live-Polit-Talk mit Studiogästen. Thema: „Wohin, Europa?" Moderation: Tom Meyer; Gäste: EU-Abgeordnete aus Deutschland, den Niederlanden, Belgien und Großbritannien. Dauer: 90 Minuten.

WANN UND WO?
Freitag, 18 Uhr, Fernsehzentrum Köln

WIE?
Meyer wird jungen Europa-Abgeordneten Fragen zur Zukunft Europas stellen. Insbesondere wird es um die Integration junger Wählerinnen und Wähler in politische Planungen gehen. Meyer wird in dieser Sendung in seinem Element sein, spricht er doch neben seiner Muttersprache noch Niederländisch, Französisch und natürlich Englisch.

Hi Lindsay,
I've found this in the newspaper and thought you might be interested. Call me on my mobile if you'd like to go to one of these events.
Event 1:
–

Extra Practice test Getting ready for a test 1

6 SPEAKING Summer jobs

You and your friend are looking for a job to earn some extra pocket money. Below are some possibilities, but you can also use your own ideas. Discuss the advantages and disadvantages of the different jobs (e.g. working hours, the money you get, skills/knowledge you need …). Try to agree on one job. Talk together for five minutes.

7 SPEAKING My school

Imagine some students from England have come on a visit. Give them a five-minute presentation on your school. You may have to do some research first. Prepare the presentation before you talk. Use notes in English. Include the following points:
– history of the school building
– facts and figures (number of students and teachers; head teacher; …)
– facilities (e.g. computer room; gym; science rooms …)
– clubs and extracurricular activities
– students' involvement in school matters (e.g. class spokesperson; school newspaper …)
– your personal attitude towards your school
– …

Extra Self-evaluation 51

How am I doing?

Reading
Tasks 1–3 in the test were reading tasks. Check your answers on page 106.
▶ SF Reading Course (pp. 139–140) • SF How to do well in a test (pp. 158–160)

Mediation
Tasks 4 and 5 were mediation tasks. The following questions will help you to assess how you did. Ask your teacher for a copy of the assessment sheet[1] and fill it in.

Assessment sheet	☹	😐	☺			
Name …	1	2	3	4	5	Comments
4 MEDIATION A job advertisement						
a) It was easy for me to take notes on the English text in German.						
b) In my notes, I concentrated on the most important information and didn't translate word for word.						
c) I found information on all the important points.						
5 MEDIATION Helping a visitor to Germany						
d) I found it easy to use German texts to write a message in English.						
e) In my message, I only gave the most important information about the events (when, where, what). I didn't translate word for word.						
f) I used short and simple sentences.						
g) If I didn't know an important word in English I tried to paraphrase it or to use a similar word or phrase.						

▶ SF Mediation Course (pp. 145–146)

👥 Speaking

1 Look at the checklist on the right and talk about how well you did in task 6, the dialogue about summer jobs.

2 Now copy and fill in the assessment sheet[1] below about your classmate's presentation in task 7 (My school).

– We listened to each other and tried to agree on one job.
– Our answers were long enough.
– We both showed interest in what our partner said.
– We were able to keep the conversation going.

Assessment sheet	☹	😐	☺			
Name …	1	2	3	4	5	Comments
Did your classmate …						
1 … speak clearly and loudly?						
2 … talk about all the important points?						
3 … have problems finding the right words?						
4 … make grammar or vocabulary mistakes?						
5 … look at the audience and not at his/her notes most of the time?						

▶ SF Giving a presentation (p. 132) • SF Speaking Course (pp. 148–149)

---

[1] assessment sheet *Beurteilungsbogen*

Unit 3 Our one world

Energy

1,500,000 years ago ▸

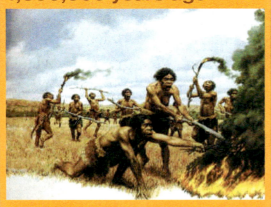

Humans (Homo erectus) learn to control fire. They grow in numbers because now they can eat cooked food and preserve it, be active at night and protect themselves from wild animals.

1769 ▸

James Watt invents his improved steam engine. Steam is the power behind the Industrial Revolution.

Life sciences

1543 ▸

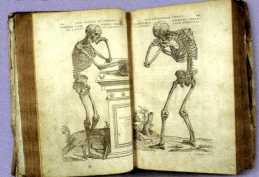

With his book *De humani corporis fabrica* (*On the fabric of the human body*), Flemish physician Andreas Vesalius revolutionizes medicine and founds modern human anatomy.

1859 ▸

Charles Darwin publishes *On the Origin of Species*, explaining how evolution works and showing that all species, including humans, have evolved over time from common ancestors.

1 Inventions and discoveries

a) Read about some milestones in the fields of **energy** and **life sciences**. Choose one and explain one of the following aspects to the class:
– why it was important for humanity in the past
– why it is still important for your life today
– how this field might develop in the future

b) Form a **double circle** in class. When your teacher names an invention or discovery, exchange ideas on its importance with your partner. After one minute your teacher will name a second invention or discovery and the inner circle will move one place clockwise. Exchange ideas on the second item with your new partner.
Then continue in the same way with a third, fourth, ... invention or discovery.

c) **Extra** What other milestone could you add to the fields **energy** or **life sciences**?

1879 ▶

One of Thomas Edison's many inventions is a practical electric light bulb.

The future? ▶

Will climate change destroy our civilization? Or will renewable energy like wind or solar power save us? And will we one day be able to use nuclear fusion, which powers the sun, and have endless energy?

1953 ▶

Using the results of work by Rosalind Franklin and Maurice Wilkins, Francis Crick and James Watson make the first correct model of the structure of DNA, discovering the secret of life on earth.

The future? ▶

Genetic engineering (GE) might let us cure diseases, clean up pollution and even design new life-forms – but how can we be sure what effects life-forms made by GE will have on our planet?

2 Unit task (1)
*While you are working on this unit, research one item from these two fields or from others, like **transport, communication, …**, in more detail.*
Prepare a presentation on the item.
Consider the inventor or discoverer's life, how the invention or discovery affected the world when it was made, why it is still important today and how the field might develop in the future.

▶ WB 1–3 (p. 32)

The future? ▶

Communication

Transport

…

HOW OUR WORLD WORKS

1 Science – what is it good for?

a) *Discuss in your group why you are or are not interested in science. Then agree on two good reasons why people should have an understanding of some areas of science and two ways of making science more popular. Collect all the ideas in class.*

b) *Read one of the two extracts **A** or **B**, which both come from books about science. Your partner reads the other.*

Think of a good title for your extract. Write four comprehension questions for your extract.

c) *Swap titles and questions, read the other extract and answer the questions. Then discuss the title suggestions and the answers to the questions together.*

d) *Exchange your ideas with another pair.*

A My own starting point was a school science book. The book was a standard 1950s schoolbook – battered, unloved – but near the front it had an illustration that just captivated me: a cutaway diagram showing the Earth's interior.

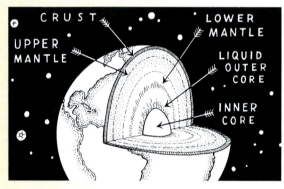

I suspect, in honesty, my initial interest was based on a private image of unsuspecting motorists plunging over the edge of a sudden four-thousand-mile cliff running between Central America and the North Pole, but gradually my attention did turn to the scientific importance of the drawing and the realization that the Earth consisted of layers, ending in the centre with a glowing sphere of iron and nickel, which was as hot as the Sun, according to the caption, and I remember thinking with real wonder: 'How do they know that?'

Then, much later, I was on a long flight across the Pacific, staring out the window at the moonlit ocean, when it occurred to me uncomfortably that I didn't know the first thing about the only planet I was ever going to live on. I had no idea, for example, why the oceans were salty but the Great Lakes weren't. I didn't know whether the oceans were growing more salty or less and whether I should be concerned about it or not. I didn't know what a proton was, or a protein, didn't know a quark from a quasar, didn't understand how geologists could look at a layer of rock on a canyon wall and tell you how old it was – didn't know anything, really. I became gripped by a quiet, unusual but insistent urge to know a little about these matters and to understand above all how people figured them out. That to me remained the greatest of all amazements – how scientists work things out. How does anybody know how much the Earth weighs or how old its rocks are or what really is way down there in the centre? How can they know how and when the universe started and what it was like when it did? How do they know what goes on inside an atom? And how, come to that – or perhaps above all – can scientists so often seem to know nearly everything but then still not be able to predict an earthquake or even tell us whether we should take an umbrella with us to the races next Wednesday?

Abridged from A Short History of Nearly Everything *by Bill Bryson, 2003*

Part A B C **3** **55**

B The most important thing that science has taught us about our place in the Universe is that we are not special. The process began with the work of Nicolaus Copernicus in the sixteenth century, which suggested that the Earth is not the centre of the Universe, and gained momentum after Galileo, early in the seventeenth century, used a telescope to obtain the crucial evidence that the Earth is indeed a planet orbiting the Sun. In the centuries that followed, astronomers found that just as the Earth is an ordinary planet, the Sun is an ordinary star (one of several hundred billion stars in our Milky Way galaxy) and the Milky Way itself is just an ordinary galaxy (one of several hundred billion in the visible Universe).

While all this was going on, biologists tried and failed to find any evidence for a special 'life force' that distinguishes living matter from non-living matter, concluding that life is just a rather complicated form of chemistry. For human life turned out to be no different from any other kind of life on Earth. As the work of Charles Darwin and Alfred Wallace

established in the nineteenth century, all you need to make human beings out of amoebas is the process of evolution by natural selection, and plenty of time.

In his *New Guide to Science*, Isaac Asimov said that the reason for trying to explain the story of science to non-scientists is that:

No one can really feel at home in the modern world and judge the nature of its problems – and the possible solutions to those problems – unless one has some intelligent notion of what science is up to.

I couldn't put it better myself. Science is one of the greatest achievements (arguably *the* greatest achievement) of the human mind, and the fact that progress has actually been made, in the most part, by ordinarily clever people building step by step from the work of their predecessors makes the story more remarkable, not less. Almost any of the readers of this book, had they been in the right place at the right time, could have made the great discoveries described here. And since the progress of science has by no means come to a halt, some of you may yet be involved in the next step in the story.

Abridged from Science: a History *by John Gribbin, 2003*

e) 👥 *Discuss the most important ideas in the two extracts. Which are the same or similar? Which are different? Compare and contrast what the extracts say with the ideas you had in 1a).*

f) **Extra** *Use everything you have found out and write a short comment on 'The importance of science in modern society'.*

2 WRITING Describing objects 🔼

a) Look at lines 14–16 of extract A on page 54. What is Bryson describing there?
Now listen to the person describing something. How quickly can you guess what it is?

b) **Extra** *Copy the table on the right. Listen to the description again and add words to the table.*
👥 *Compare your results with a partner's. Then add other words to the table that could be useful for describing objects.*

shape	square, …
made of	metal, …
size	a diameter of …, huge, …
colour	black, …
texture	rough, smooth, …
location	… km/cm/… from …, …
appearance	looks like, …
comparisons	…er than …, …

c) **Extra** 👥 *Think of an object you use in everyday life. Write a description of it. Read your description to a partner. How quickly can they guess what it is?*

▶ **Text File 5** *(pp. 118–119)* • *SF Describing objects and processes (p. 156)* • *WB 4 (p. 33)*

3 Changing the world

a) Look quickly at the headline of the article, the sub-headings and the pictures and say what you think the article is generally about.

The Washington Post

Self-Adjusting Lenses for the Poor

By Mary Jordan
Washington Post Foreign Service
Saturday, January 10, 2009

Oxford, England.
Joshua Silver remembers the first day he helped a man see. Henry Adjei-Mensah, a tailor in Ghana, could no longer see well enough to thread the needle of his sewing machine. He was too poor to afford glasses or an optometrist. Then Silver, an atomic physicist at Oxford University, handed him a pair of self-adjusting glasses he had designed, and suddenly the tailor's world came into crystal-clear focus. "He grinned and started operating his machine very fast," said Silver, 62, who aims to distribute his special glasses throughout the developing world. Silver said he wants to provide eyeglasses to more than a billion people with poor eyesight. [...]

Third world without glasses
In the United States, Britain and other wealthy nations, 60 to 70 per cent of people wear glasses, Silver said. But in many developing countries, only about 5 per cent have glasses because so many people, especially those in rural areas, have little or no access to optometrists. Even if they could visit an eye doctor, the cost of glasses can be more than a month's wages. This means that many school-children cannot see the blackboard, bus drivers can't see clearly and others can no longer fish, teach or do other jobs. [...]

One size fits all
The glasses, which are now being made in China, are not sleek. In fact, Silver acknowledged, people call them ugly. He said the design is being improved, but the current model [...] has thick dark frames with round lenses. The glasses work on the principle that the more liquid is pumped into a thin sac in the plastic lenses, the stronger the correction.
Silver has attached plastic syringes filled with silicone oil on each side of the glasses; the wearer adds or subtracts the clear liquid with a little dial on the pump until the focus is right. After that, the syringes are removed and the [...]

glasses are ready to go.
Currently, Silver said, a pair costs about $19, but his hope is to cut that to a few dollars. [...]
Silver said there has been some resistance from the eyewear industry. Years ago, one vision company offered a "substantial amount of money" to him if he sold them his technology, but Silver said no because he was not sure that it would be used to bring low-cost glasses to the poor. [...]

(Abridged and adapted)

b) Read the whole article and take notes on the most important information. Then talk to a partner to make sure you understand how Silver's invention works.

c) Prepare a one-minute speech to convince somebody to support Joshua Silver's work. Work in groups of three. Each group member makes notes from a different point of view for their speech: A as Joshua Silver; B as Henry Adjei-Mensah; C as a student in Germany.

Your speech could explain:
– why lots of people do not have glasses
– how Silver's invention can help those people
– who is already being helped
– why Silver will not sell his idea
– why your listeners should help
– how they could help

d) Each student gives his or her speech to the group. Who was most convincing? Why?

▶ **Text File 6** (pp. 120–122) • SF Speaking Course (pp. 148–149)
• SF Peer evaluation (p.136)

Part A B C Practice   **3** 57

P1 WORDS Compound nouns

> **Tip**
> Compound nouns consist of two or more words. They often come in the following types:
> **noun + noun** (e.g. schoolbook)   **gerund + noun** (e.g. chewing gum)
> **noun + gerund** (e.g. winemaking)   **adjective + noun** (e.g. secondary school)
> They are sometimes written as two words, sometimes as one, sometimes with a hyphen.

a) Look at the words in the two boxes and make up 20 meaningful compound nouns with them. Arrange them in the four types shown above, e.g.
noun + noun: *love affair*.
Check in a dictionary (a collocations dictionary if you can) to find out whether they really exist, what they mean and how they are pronounced.

b) Choose verbs from the right (or choose your own) and combine them with the compound nouns.

Nouns:	air • climate • computer • earth • eye • fire • life • light • school • steam • wind
Gerunds:	developing • driving • sewing • starting
Adjectives:	black • elementary • green • solar

Nouns:	board • bulb • change • country • engine • escape • force • form • game • house • licence • machine • point • power • quake • school • sight • system • wear
Gerunds:	conditioning • surfing

attend • break • cause • circulate • control • damage • design • destroy • discover • enjoy • evolve • get • grow • help • improve • invent • lose • make • need • operate • play • pump • run up/down • threaten • turn on/off • use • wipe • write on

P2 WRITING Describing processes

a) As well as describing objects and places, you might sometimes need to describe processes. Look at lines 40–49 of the article on page 56. Which process is described here? Find the verbs and the time expressions used in the description. Why are they well-chosen for describing a process? What tenses are the verbs in? Are there any passive forms?

b) Describe the process used to generate electricity with solar power, which is shown in the diagram. The words on the diagram and in the box will help you. Use passive forms where necessary.

sun's rays • reflect • heat (v.) • flow through • transfer • be used to • drive • generate

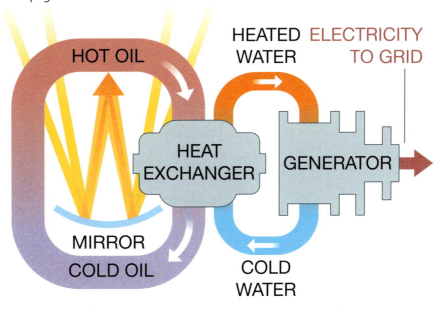

▶ SF Describing objects and processes (p. 156) • WB 5–6 (pp. 33–34)

P3 LISTENING Dial4Light 🎧

a) Listening for gist: Listen to the radio interview. Find out which country the report is about, what its topic is and who the presenter is talking to.

b) Listening for detail: Listen again. Take notes on how Dial4Light works, including these points:
– when the street lights in the town go off
– why the town turns them off
– how long the lights stay on under the Dial4Light system
– in how many streets
– how much the system saves the town

c) Extra Use your notes and write a short description of how the Dial4Light system works.

d) Extra Listen to the interview again. What word does Lena often use to fill gaps when she's explaining something? The word can also mean 'said'. What sort of language is this?

P4 REVISION Photosynthesis (Passive: mixed bag)

In Biology you have learned about photosynthesis. What can you remember? Fill in the gaps in the following text. Use passive constructions with these verbs:

> absorb • can store • capture • partly convert • emit • produce (2x) • understand

The process of photosynthesis *has been understood* since the 1800s: sugar … in plants using water, carbon dioxide and the sun's energy. Water … by the roots of the plant. Light energy … by chlorophyll in the plant's leaves. During this process oxygen … The sugar that … … into starch that … in the plant.

▶ GF 4: The passive (pp. 175–177)

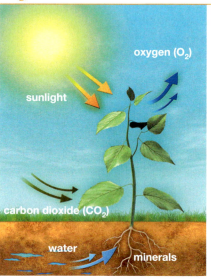

P5 Fighting climate change (Passive: progressive tenses)

Write sentences using passive progressive in the present and past tense.

1. In 1970/old rainforests/New Zealand/still cut down.
   In 1970, the old rainforests of New Zealand were still being cut down.
2. Then/global warming/not talk about/by anyone.
3. Nowadays/the same/do/to rainforests/around the world.
4. So even today/number of trees taking CO_2 out of the atmosphere/reduce considerably.
5. On the other hand/millions of tonnes of CO_2/produce/every day/by people driving to work/flying away on holiday.
6. Different solutions/discuss/to reduce carbon emissions.
7. Emission levels/of cars and factories/limit.
8. Further steps and laws/plan/to fight climate change.

▶ WB 7–9 (pp. 34–35)

Part **A** B C   Practice   **3**   59

P 6   MEDIATION COURSE What do I have to do? (Translation)

Translation is a special kind of mediation, something that only professional translators need to do. For most everyday use, ordinary mediation of the general meaning is more appropriate. But in certain cases, it might be important to do an exact translation of something, e.g. of the technical instructions that come with some new equipment like a digital camera or MP3 player, or of a recipe, or instructions on how to get somewhere. For this kind of thing, an exact translation will be useful.

a) Get the gist
Don't start translating straightaway. Read the whole text first to get a general idea of what it is about. Read the text on the right. What is it generally about?

b) 'Exact' is NOT 'word for word'
When translating from English into German, don't try to do it word for word. That won't work. Translate this sentence word for word. Is it good German?
After you've read through the whole text, translate it sentence by sentence. Now read that whole sentence again and try to translate it into good German. Do a rough translation first – leave gaps where you have problems. Go back to those parts afterwards Translate all the sentences you can understand easily. Leave the difficult ones and go back to them later when you use a dictionary.
Only write on every other line – you will need space for corrections. Using a pencil also makes corrections easier.

Using the R-09HR

Turning power on/off

Using the AC adaptor

NOTE
Be sure to use the AC adaptor when connecting to a PC.
If the batteries become exhausted while copying a song, the song may be corrupted.

1. **Check that power is turned off.**
   If the power is on, turn it off. Press and hold the [POWER switch] on the R-09HR to turn power on or off.

2. **Plug the DC plug of the AC adaptor into the [AC Adapter Jack] on the R-09HR.**
   Place the AC adaptor so that its lamp light is on the top side.
   (it lights up when connected to an AC outlet)

3. **Plug the AC adaptor into an electrical power outlet.**

4. **Turn power on.**
   Pressing and holding down the [POWER switch] turns on the power and shows an R-09HR image in the display. To turn off power, press and hold down the [POWER switch].

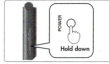

NOTE
• Be sure to use the AC adaptor supplied with this product.
• If the [HOLD Switch] is in the on position, no operations can be performed.
Be sure to slide it to the off position. (→ p. 12)

MEMO
• If the AC adaptor is connected while power is on, the power supply is drawn from the AC adaptor.
• You may still hear some sound when the power is switched on, but this is normal, and does not indicate a malfunction.

20

c) Using a dictionary
When you look up words in a dictionary, read the whole entry to make sure you find the right meaning for your context. What are the right German translations of these words (underlined in blue)?
exhaust • switch • jack • outlet • perform • slide • indicate

d) Finishing and correcting
When you have finished your translation, cover the English text and read your German translation carefully. Does it make sense? Is it good German or does some of it sound a little strange? Correct anything you think is not right yet. Check with the English version when you make corrections, so that you do not change the meaning.

▶ SF Mediation Course (p. 145–146) • WB 10 (p. 36)

OUR FRAGILE WORLD
1 Carbon footprints and global warming

According to scientists, emissions of carbon dioxide (CO_2) into the atmosphere are one of the causes of global warming, perhaps the biggest problem the world faces today.

5 And where do those CO_2 emissions come from? From people like you. All the modern technology you use allows you to have a comfortable lifestyle: it keeps you warm, it lets you communicate with your friends, it lets you travel. But almost every-
10 thing you do as an individual releases CO_2 into the atmosphere: like boiling water to make some tea, turning your heating on when you're cold, watching TV, getting the bus to school, texting your friends, buying a bottle of coke, or flying to
15 Majorca on holiday.

The amount of CO_2 you personally produce every year is known as your carbon footprint. So how big is YOUR footprint?

THE AVERAGE PERSON IN THE UK PRODUCES 9.8 TONNES OF CO_2 PER YEAR, SO THAT'S THEIR CARBON FOOTPRINT. THE PIE CHART BELOW SHOWS HOW THE AVERAGE PERSONAL FOOTPRINT IN THE UK IS MADE UP.

Other average carbon footprints in tonnes of CO_2 per person per year

- 20.4 USA
- 9.8 Germany
- 4 World average
- 3.8 China
- 0.1 Tanzania
- 2 Target for a world average to stop climate change

Source: www.carbonfootprint.com

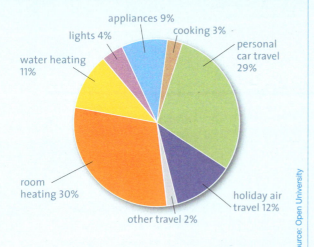

- appliances 9%
- cooking 3%
- lights 4%
- water heating 11%
- personal car travel 29%
- room heating 30%
- other travel 2%
- holiday air travel 12%

Source: Open University

a) Read "Carbon footprints and global warming". Then name one of the main causes of global warming.

b) 👥 Look at the seven examples of everyday activities in "Carbon footprints and global warming" (ll. 11–15). Discuss with a partner why and how you think they release carbon dioxide into the atmosphere.
A We boil water in an electric kettle at home. That uses electricity.
B Yeah, oil and gas are burned to produce electricity. That releases CO_2 into the atmosphere.
Collect the ideas in class.

c) Look at the carbon footprints and the pie chart for the UK. Explain what they tell you about carbon emissions worldwide and in the UK.

d) **Extra** Find out how these countries' carbon footprints have changed in the meantime.

e) **Extra** Use the carbon footprint calculator at www.EnglishG.de/footprint and calculate your own carbon footprint. Are you above or below average? Compare what makes up your individual footprint with that of the average person from the UK.

▶ SF Talking about statistics (p. 129)

2 Welcome to the future (abridged from *The Carbon Diaries 2015* by Saci Lloyd)

It's 2015. The UK wants to fight global warming. So the government is introducing carbon rationing on January 8th to reduce the country's carbon footprint. Now everyone will have a carbon allowance of 200 points a month. Nearly everything people do, like drive the car, listen to music and have a shower, will cost them carbon points. What will this mean for 16-year-old Laura Brown, her older sister Kim and their family?

Sat, Jan 3rd

Dad sat us all down tonight and took us thru a disgusting government online form to work out what our family CO allowance is. It's heavy. Basically we've got a carbon allowance of 200 Carbon Points per month to spend on travel, heat and food. All other stuff like clothes and technology and books have already got the Carbon Points built into the price, so say you wanna buy a PC but it's been shipped over from China and built using dirty fossil fuel then you're gonna pay a lot more for it in Euros – cos you're paying for all the energy that's gone into making it.

And the worst thing is, me and Kim have to give up loads of our points for the family energy allowance, which leaves us some pathetic amount for travel, college, going out … The car's gonna be cut way back, all of us get access to the PC, TV, HD, stereo for only two hours a day, heating is down to 16 °C in the living room and 1 hour a day for the rest of the house, showers max 5 minutes, baths only at weekend. We've got to choose – hairdryer, toaster, microwave, smartphone, kettle, lights, PDA, e-pod, fridge or freezer and on and on. Flights are a real no-no and shopping, travelling and going out not much better. It's all kind of a choice.

Mon, Jan 5th

Carbon cards came today … They've got these little blocks down one side going from green to red and as you use up your year's ration they fade away one by one till you're down to the last red and then you're all alone, sobbing in the dark. Kim won't unwrap her card, she says if she touches it then that's all her youth gone. I felt pretty shaky unwrapping mine, not that I really have a youth in my family. My sister's got it.

Thurs, Jan 8th
Rationing.

Back to college, and I got in late cos I had to take Mum to her bus stop. Her eyes filled up with tears as we walked past the Saab. She whispered, 'It's not for ever,' and stroked the bonnet. I pretended not to see.

We missed the first bus, so we had to wait 15 minutes in the drizzle till the next one. When it finally came I leapt on, swiped my card and was scooting upstairs, only to see Mum behind me going thru her purse, bag and pockets. She looked up at me.

'Laura, darling, I can't find my card. Can you lend me some …'

The driver shook his head. 'No carbon card, no ride, love.'

'But, please …'

A woman out in the rain shouted: 'Get off, yer stoopid cow! You're holding us up.'

And then Mum started to cry. I went back down and walked her off the bus. 'We'll have to go home and get your card, Mum.'

'Found it! In the lining! Bastards!' Mum shook the green plastic at the bus, now rumbling off into the traffic. 'Oh, I shouldn't get so upset. Sweetie, let's pop into Alfredo's for a cup of tea.'

'I'm so sorry, Laura.' Mum stirred her dodgy brown tea. 'I know I should be strong, but I feel so responsible for my generation – we're the ones who've messed it all up for you. I mean, what's going to become of you young things? Woodstock, freedom, women's rights, the Magic Bus ... that's what it was all about – but you'll never know ... Don't forget, I'm your mother and I'm always here if you need to talk.'

I kept quiet. I once worked out that if Mum had actually been to Woodstock, she'd be about 70 by now.

When I finally got to college there was a huge queue at the entrance cos everyone had to swipe their CO cards at the turnstile and the swipe machine kept breaking down. I don't know what we were swiping for anyway – the building was freezing cold.

'Welcome to the future,' muttered Adisa. 'They're ripping us off already.'

Adi's my best mate. He's so deep.

Tues, Jan 13th

My family has disappeared. Dad spends all night in his study on his laptop, Mum is always lost on a bus somewhere and Kim basically lives in her room – an evil ball of silent sulk. I actually feel sick being in the same atmosphere, she's radiating so much wicked energy. She's definitely got the TV going 24/7 in her room. I can hear it thru the wall.

Weds, Jan 14th

I woke up this morning and it was freezing, freezing cold. I'm only allowed heat on in my room between 7 and 8. I went and looked at the Smart Meter in the hall. It's this thing that tells you everything that's going on with energy in the house. Even for our one hour of heat Dad's locked the bedroom temp at 15 °C. What a joke – it's not even enough to melt the frost on the windows.

Thurs, Jan 15th

There's heavy snowstorms all over southern Europe.

Mon, Jan 19th

The blizzards in Europe are getting worse – and spreading north. Italy has just lost all its electricity. The news showed this footage of the Vatican going black, window after window.

Tues, Jan 20th

We had a powercut in the night. The house is so cold now, it feels like 200 years of evil chill creeping into my bones. Cuts give me the creeps – you know when you go to switch the light on and it's dead?

▶ **Text File 7** *(pp. 123–124)*

Working with the text

1 Carbon rationing
Explain how carbon rationing in the novel works. Then find parts of the text that show what Laura and other characters feel about it.

2 Utopia or dystopia?
A utopia paints an ideal picture of a future society, a dystopia creates a nightmare vision of it. Which sort is The Carbon Diaries 2015? *Could its vision become reality for you in the future? Give reasons.*

3 Give it up?
a) Look at ll. 19–28. Which of the things could you give up? Which not? Explain why.

b) **Extra** *How would you manage on 200 carbon points a month? In the week ahead, save some energy and reduce your carbon footprint. How? Take two-minute showers? Give up toast? Turn off your mobile? Stop watching TV? ...? Decide on one idea and do that for a week. Write about your experience and display what you write in class.*

▶ *WB 11–13 (pp. 37–38)*

Part A **B** C   Practice   **3**   63

P1   REVISION What will happen if …? (Conditional sentences 1)

a) *What will happen if we don't get a grip on global warming? Complete the conditional sentences.*
1 If we *don't do* (not do) something about global warming, more polar ice *will start* (start) to melt.
2 If a lot of polar ice … (melt), it … (cause) sea levels to rise.
3 Coastal areas and islands all over the world … (be affected) if sea levels … (rise).
4 If governments around the world … (not do) enough about it, climate change … (speed up).
5 … (there be) many more serious weather events if climate change … (speed up).
6 So let's do something, because if we … (not take) the first step, nobody else will.

b) *An old song starts like this: 'In the year 2525, if man is still alive, if woman can survive, they may find …'*
What do you think humans may find, if they are still alive in the year 2525? Use conditional sentences to talk about the possibilities for humans in the future.

P2   REVISION What would you do? (Conditional sentences 2)

What would you do if …? Write two conditional sentences (type 2) for each option below. Be careful with the verb forms. Don't forget that you can also use past auxiliaries other than 'would', like 'might', 'should' and 'could'. Write what you would do you if …
1 … you met the girl/boy of your dreams.
   If I met the boy/girl of my dreams, I …
2 … you were going to be a mother/father soon.
3 … you had to live on a desert island.
4 … you were seen dating an older person.
5 … you woke up tomorrow as a member of the opposite sex.
6 … you could talk to animals.
7 … you were able to understand what other people are thinking.
8 … you discovered how to travel through time.
▶ *GF 6: Conditional sentences (pp. 181–182)*

P3   WORDS Saying numbers 🎧

a) 👥 *Saying English numbers (very important in science and technology) is not as easy as you think! – Partner B: Go to page 106.*
Partner A: Read the numbers, dates, etc. below out loud. Your partner should write them down. Then listen together. Did you say them right? Did your partner get them right? Discuss any problems. Then listen to your partner and do the same.

1,500,000	55%	1990s
967	9.8	35 + 72 = 107
1879 AD	99,265	6 x 7 = 42
363 BC	1/3	49 ÷ 7 = 7
22/09/2015	1/2	$4^2 = 16$
Feb 27, 2018	32° C	$\sqrt{25} = 5$
23rd	30 km/h	

b) 👥 *Work out together how you would say the following numbers (**m** at the beginning = **miles**):*
900 mph • 19 mps • 1,000,000 mpd •
40,000 mph • 100,000,000,000 • 100,000 •
16,000 • 3,000 • 30,000 • 200,000,000 •
12,000,000 mpm

c) *The numbers above all come from a song. What do you think the song could be about?*

d) *Listen for the numbers in the song and try to hear what they refer to. Get as many as you can.*
👥 *Compare your results with a partner and make corrections.*
👥👥 *Then do the same with another pair.*

e) **Extra** *What is the message of the song?*
▶ *WB 14–17 (pp. 38–39)*

OUR FUTURE WORLD?

1 Tonight's films on TV

a) What was the last film you watched on TV? What sort of films do you like (comedy, science fiction, thrillers, …)? Who's your favourite actor/director?

b) Read the reviews below. Do you agree with the ratings (number of stars) given at the end? Which of the two films would you most like to see? Explain why.

Moon (2009)
★★★★★
(Friday 8.00 pm, Sky One)

This is the intelligent first film from David Bowie's son, Duncan Jones, with a great performance by Sam Rockwell as a lonely miner working for three years on the dark side of the moon, with just a robot, Gerty, for company (voice of Kevin Spacey).

When Sam starts to get painful headaches and hallucinations, he almost has a fatal accident in a lunar rover. Back at the base (with no memory of how he got there), Sam meets a younger, angrier clone of himself, who claims to be there on the same three-year job Sam started all those years ago. What is going on?

Although it has few digital effects, Jones's low-budget film is an exciting, sensitive investigation into what it is, and takes, to be human.

I, Robot (2004)
★★☆☆☆
(Friday 9.00 pm, Virgin 1)

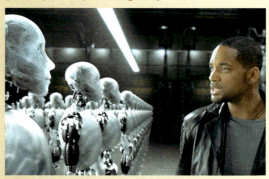

In the year 2035 robots are a part of everybody's everyday life. They are programmed to help humans and can never harm them. Or can they?

US Robotics (USR) plans to introduce its latest robot: the NS-5. When Detective Del Spooner (Will Smith) investigates the suicide of USR researcher Dr Alfred Lanning (James Cromwell), he becomes convinced it's a case of murder, not suicide, and that the NS-5 robots are responsible for it. He accepts the help of robot psychologist Dr Susan Calvin (Bridget Moynahan) and the hunt begins.

I, Robot looks great. Director Alex Proyas does a great job linking the fantastic digital effects with the action. But the story is illogical and never properly explains the relations between humans and robots in this new world. So when the robots go crazy, it makes no sense.

And Will Smith's talents as an actor don't help. In fact, he's no better than a robot himself.

2 Analysing a film review

a) On the right are some common features of film reviews. Examine the two reviews above and list which features they contain.

b) What else should a film review contain in your opinion? Give reasons. Add these to your list.

Plot summary

- **Credits:** when/where made, names of people involved • **Opinions on:** acting, casting, characters, effects, camera work, music, setting, story
- **Themes/message:** … • **Overall effect:** …
- **Recommendation:** strengths/weaknesses,

3 Writing a film review

a) Choose a film you know well or have seen recently. Your task will be to write a review of it.

b) Look back at the reviews on page 64 to find language that might be useful in a review, e.g. 'a great performance by', 'looks great', ...

c) 👥 Swap reviews with a partner. Read your partner's review considering the features of a film review that you have just learned about.
Give your partner feedback.
Explain why you found the review useful or not. Say especially what was missing from your point of view.

> **STUDY SKILLS** | **Writing a film review**
> – Decide which of the features of a film review you want to use (see page 64 and the list you made in 2b).
> – Order the features sensibly in an outline.
> – Make notes on your film for all these features.
> – Use your notes and outline to write your review.
> – Find a way of attracting your reader's attention at the beginning.
> – Don't spoil the film for others by giving away too much of the story or saying how it ends.

▶ SF Writing a film review (p. 156)

4 VIEWING Who's the real Sam Bell? 🎥

a) Imagine you wake up one morning and find a clone of yourself at home. How would you react? Write down how your first conversation with him/her might go.

b) When Sam Bell, a miner at a base on the moon, wakes up after an accident in a rover, he finds another man there too, another Sam Bell who looks just like him.

Watch an extract from the 2009 film *Moon* and answer the questions:
1 How are the two Sam Bells getting along? How do you know?
2 What does the injured Sam Bell think of the other Sam's character?
3 What does he want to know from Gerty, the base computer?
4 What does he find out and how does he react to it?

c) 👥 Check your answers with a partner. Then discuss how you think the injured Sam Bell is feeling.

d) Look at the film extract together again and discuss the following:
1 Describe what the injured Sam Bell's movements tell you about his state of mind at the beginning of the extract.
2 When do his movements change and what does this show?
3 How does the film show what Gerty thinks and feels about Sam's situation?
4 When does the music start? What sort of music is it and what effect does this have?

e) How did the film extract affect you? What do you think of Sam's situation? Do you feel sorry for him? Explain why or why not.

f) **Extra** 👥 The film *Moon* presents a negative example of how a technology – in this case cloning – could be used. In a group, collect other examples of technologies and list their pros and cons.
Use your lists in a class discussion on the topic.

66 **3** Part **A** **B** **C** Practice

THE WORDS PAGE

P1 Phrasal verbs ▸ 🗏🗏

a) *A **phrasal verb** is a combination of a verb and a short adverb, or 'adverb particle'. The main stress in a phrasal verb is on the adverb, e.g. find sth.* **out**, *use sth.* **up***. Here are a few examples from this unit:*

clean up pollution (p. 53); how people figured them out (p. 54); human life turned out to be no different (p. 55); the swipe machine kept breaking down (p. 62).

Using a different adverb with the same verb can change its meaning dramatically. Compare:

I broke down and cried when she broke up with me. On the way home the car broke down and a fire broke out.

*If a phrasal verb has an **object** and the object is a noun, it can come before or after the adverb:*

I used up all my **carbon points** last week.
I used all my **carbon points** up last week.

If the object is a pronoun, it must come before the adverb.

My carbon points? Oh, I used **them** up last week.

calm • come • cut • end • hang • hurry • look • slow • write

*Add **up** or **down** to the verbs in the box and complete the sentences. Think about the right tenses and whether the verbs should be used in the active or passive.*

1 Charles Darwin *wrote down* his ideas on evolution in his book *On the Origin of Species*.
2 Some great scientists … in prison.
3 Many scientists made their discoveries because solutions … accidentally.
4 Darwin was sometimes very annoyed by the attacks on his theory and people had to … him ….
5 I must … – I'm late for my science lesson.
6 In order to build a new laboratory, the company … a lot of trees …
7 You can … the laws of gravity in your science books.
8 Can we … a poster of Max Planck instead of Charles Darwin?
9 Thinking about too many things at once makes people …

b) *Phrasal verbs are mainly used in informal English. Formal written English often uses other verbs with a similar meaning.*

I soon caught on that stars are like our sun.
I soon understood that stars are like our sun.

Replace the underlined verbs with phrasal verbs made from the two boxes. Look up words you do not know in a dictionary if necessary.

chill • go • put • turn • work

down • off • on • out

1 They <u>relaxed</u> in the comfortable seats on the plane.
2 She'll <u>dress</u> in her prettiest clothes today.

3 The meeting <u>continued</u> longer than expected.
4 Did you hear the bomb <u>explode</u> last night?
5 Can you <u>reduce</u> the volume, please?
6 I wonder how scientists first <u>calculated</u> the speed of light.

c) **Extra** *Try to tell an interesting or exciting story using phrasal verbs made from the two boxes below. Always check they exist in a dictionary before you use them.*

drive • go • get • show • call • set • put • carry • work • turn • find

about • across • ahead • along • away • back • by • down • forward • in • off • on • out • over • through • up

▸ *WB 18–21 (pp. 40–41)*

P2 UNIT TASK (2) Milestones in science

Now that you have researched a milestone of science for your unit task as described on page 53, it is time to put your presentation together. You have already learned how to do this.
▶ SF Research (p. 130) • SF Outlining (p. 131) • SF Giving a presentation (p. 132)

But how can you give a successful group presentation? This page will help you.

a) *Look at the following phrases and match them to the different roles in a group presentation – team leader, co-leader, presenters.*
– Hello. We're going to give a presentation today about …
– I'd like to say a few words about our topic before <name> talks about … and <name> looks at …
– In this first part of our presentation, I want to look at …
– Just let me turn on the OHP.
– <name> is going to use presentation software for his/her part.
– Now the next part of the presentation is about … and I'm going to hand over to <name> for that.
– OK, now has anybody got any questions?
– So, let me end the presentation by summing up. …
– Thanks <name>. Now, as <name> told you, this next part of our presentation …
– We'll take questions from you at any time, but it would be easier if you asked questions at the end.
– You all know the members of our group.

b) *Listen to a group presentation. Take notes on the topic they are talking about. Use your notes to give a short oral summary of the main points of the presentation.*

c) *Carefully read the skills box on the right. Then listen again. Take notes on how well the students did. Discuss and evaluate the presentation in your group.*

d) *Give your presentation on a milestone of science. Listen to the other groups. Take notes and ask questions.*

STUDY SKILLS | Giving a group presentation

Each person in the group or team has one of the following roles:
The **team leader** is the person in charge. He/She welcomes the audience, introduces the topic, makes clear when questions will be accepted (during or after the presentation), and finishes the presentation, thanking the audience for listening and taking questions.
The **co-leader** keeps an eye on the time, makes sure all visual aids and media (computer, …) are in order.
Individual **presenters** each cover a different aspect of the topic and introduce the next speaker. Everybody must know what everybody else is going to do so that no one repeats information unnecessarily.
Rehearse your presentation together. Give each other feedback.

When giving a **computer-aided presentation**,
– do not use too many effects,
– make sure the images and text on your slides are big enough to be seen by everybody,
– only use key words on your slides,
– check that the classroom technology works,
– consider using video or sound to support your presentation.

▶ *SF Giving a group presentation (p. 132)*

68 Extra Revision Getting ready for a test 2

1 WORDS For a greener world

a) Which of the words doesn't belong in the group? Write it down.
1 wood • plastic • paper • glass
2 oil • coal • wind • gas
3 waste • recycle • reduce • save
4 pollute • destroy • burn • protect
5 dangerous • safe • poisonous • threatening

b) Now use each of the words you have written down in a sentence, e.g. wood: *Wood is a natural material.*

c) Match the beginning of the sentences (1–7) to the correct endings (a–g).
1 **Organic** food is good for you
2 Locally grown products
3 You can buy super clothes for little money
4 Having solar equipment on the roof
5 Give clothes that you don't need any more
6 Use recycled paper
7 Take empty bottles back to the shop

a reduces your electricity bill.
b are better for the environment.
c so they can be used again.
d to charity collections.
e at second-hand shops.
f as it hasn't been treated with **chemicals**.
g to save trees.

2 Our green holidays (Questions in the simple past/present perfect)

Lucy and her friend Sharon each went on a "green holiday" with their parents. After the holidays, Lucy is writing an e-mail to Sharon. Read Lucy's statements. Then complete her questions to Sharon. Use the simple past or present perfect.
1 Hi Sharon. I'm back from my "green holiday" in France. I went with my parents. *Who did you go with?*
2 We came back yesterday. *When …?*
3 I haven't washed all my dirty clothes yet. *Have you …?*
4 We stayed at a "green hotel" in the south. *Where …?*
5 We've stayed there before. *Have you …?*
6 We ate lots of wonderful fish in France. *What …?*
7 Most of the food we had came from the area. *Where …?*
8 We only had vegetables from the garden. *Did … too?*
9 I actually helped with the gardening. *… too?*
10 I even learned how to use kitchen herbs. *Have you ever …?*
11 But we also went down to the beach every day. *… too?*
12 So I was really pleased with our "green holiday". *Were … too?*
13 In fact, it was the best holiday I've ever had. *Was … too?*
14 I have already decided to go there again next year. *Have you already …?*

3 Better or worse? (Comparison)

a) Compare the following things. Use the adjectives from the box.
Example: Cars are more comfortable than bikes, but bikes are cleaner.

> cheap • clean • comfortable • effective • environmentally friendly • healthy • light • popular • safe • trendy

1 car – bike
2 plastic bottle – glass bottle
3 new clothes – second-hand clothes
4 food from your garden – fast food
5 nuclear energy – solar energy

b) Two things are almost the same, one is different. Make sentences with the adjective in brackets.
Example: Surfing is as dangerous as climbing. Dancing is less dangerous.

1 surfing/climbing/dancing (dangerous)
2 learning a new language / learning an instrument / learning a poem (difficult)
3 Mumbai/Singapore/Hamburg (crowded)
4 tigers/bears/deer (threatened)

c) Complete the sentences with the words in brackets. Give your opinion.

1 A camping holiday is … a holiday in a hotel. (exciting)
A camping holiday is as exciting as / more / less exciting than a holiday in a hotel.
2 A sports holiday is … a holiday on the beach. (cool)
3 Gardening is … going to a gym. (relaxing)
4 Cooking your own food is … going out for meals. (good)
5 Buying clothes made in Germany is … buying clothes from Asia. (environmentally friendly)

4 SPEAKING Expressing opinions

Use the phrases from the table and discuss the topics below (1–3) with a partner. Don't forget to give reasons and examples.

Giving an opinion	Asking for an opinion	Agreeing	Disagreeing
– I (don't) think/ believe/feel that … – In my opinion … – From my point of view … – I'm quite sure that …	– What do you think about …? – What is your opinion on …? – How do you feel about …? – Do you agree with me?	– That's right/true/ correct (but …) – I feel the same. – I think so too. – You are (absolutely) right.	– I'm afraid I can't agree with you. – I'm sorry but I don't think … – I can't believe that it is true that … – Actually, I see it differently …

1 Going on holiday with friends is better than going with your parents.
2 Online friends are not real and often lie about their identity.
3 Couples from different cultural backgrounds have more problems than couples from the same culture.

Revision Getting ready for a test 2

5 WORDS A teenage magazine

a) *Zink!* *is a US teenage magazine with eight sections:*

THEATRE – MUSIC – CINEMA & TV – BOOKS – COMPUTER – SPORTS – RELATIONS – RELIGION

Make lists of typical words for each section. First use the words from the box – some words can go into more than one section. Then add more words.

actor • athletics • audience • cable TV • Christianity • church • comic • divorced • ex-girlfriend • Hindu • husband • install • label • link • lovers • match • menu • Muslim • narrator • news network • novel • pitch • play • playlist • poem • prime-time TV • rehearsal • release • save • scene • sound file • stage • train

MUSIC   SPORTS   …
rehearsal   pitch
…

b) *You want to tell your friend about some of the things you have read in* Zink!. *Choose the right word for each sentence.*

1. A new play is starting soon at the theatre. *Zink!* went to the rehearsals/research/rituals.
2. The Huddersfield Half Pipes did pretty well, but you just can't collect/compare/impress them with a team like the South London Skaters.
3. Helsinki Motel have just installed/released/reviewed their new album. We thinks it's hot.
4. *Zink!* says this new software is cheap and easy to install/join/repair.
5. *Avatar* is going to be recycled/rehearsed/repeated. Don't miss it if you haven't seen it yet. *Zink!* loves it.
6. *Zink!* recommends a concert/playlist/tune of religious music at Bath Abbey tomorrow.

6 I'd never fall in love … (Prepositions)

Which of the two words in brackets fits the sentences? Complete the sentences with the correct prepositions.

1. I'd never fall in love … a boy my age! (in/with)
2. It won't work. We're just too different … each other. (from/of)
3. You can't judge a person … the clothes they wear. (after/by)
4. What do your parents feel … your new boyfriend? (about/of)
5. If I had known he'd be so upset … what I said, I would have been more careful. (about/across)
6. … my point of view, he's just jealous. (From/Out of)
7. The best thing … my parents is that they aren't prejudiced. (about/at)
8. His parents are so strict. He has to be home … 10 o'clock – always! (by/for)
9. … my opinion, he's very ugly. (After/In)
10. We're so fed up … our parents. They never understand! (of/with)

Extra   Practice test   Getting ready for a test 2   71

1 LISTENING What can we do this weekend? 🎧

Copy the table below. Now listen to two girls talking about their plans for the weekend. While listening, complete the table in key words.

– You will listen to the conversation **twice**.
– You have 20 seconds at the end of the recording to complete your notes.

Helen's ideas for Saturday evening	Tina's arguments against Helen's ideas – write down one for each idea
1 see *Romeo and Juliet* at the theatre	
2 play a new computer game at Helen's house	
3 listen to music, each girl at home	
4 listen to music and watch TV	
5 In the end, Helen decides to …	

2 LISTENING Living together 🎧

Listen to a radio phone-in. While listening, answer the questions below using one to seven words.
– You will hear the recording **twice**.
– You will have 15 seconds at the end of the recordings to complete your answers.
– You now have 30 seconds to look at the questions.

1 What is the topic of the radio show?
2 What attitude does Sharon's dad have towards Sharon's activities?
3 What does Sean's girlfriend find strange?
4 What did Afra's family think about her relationship?
5 How did Afra feel when they finally split up?
6 When did Bob get to know his girlfriend?
7 What makes their relationship easy? (Name two aspects.)

Extra Practice test Getting ready for a test 2

3 LISTENING Radio adverts 🎧

Listen to three radio adverts. While listening, note down the correct answer.
– *You will hear the recordings only **once**.*
– *You will have 10 seconds at the end of the recordings to complete your answers.*
– *You now have 30 seconds to look at the task.*

1 This advert is for
   A beautiful flowers.
   B expensive chocolate.
   C a health and fitness hotel.

   It addresses
   A women.
   B men.
   C women and men.

2 This advert is for a book that helps to
   A find a suitable partner.
   B divorce in a fair way.
   C stay happily married.

   It addresses
   A women.
   B men.
   C women and men.

3 This advert is for a
   A fitness class.
   B holiday on the beach.
   C men's health magazine.

   It addresses
   A women.
   B men.
   C women and men.

4 WRITING An environmentally-friendly school

Imagine your school wants to become more environmentally friendly. These ideas have come up:
– *The canteen should stop selling drinks in plastic bottles.*
– *Teachers should hand out fewer photocopies to save paper.*
– *Everyone should use recycled paper.*
Write a text of at least 200 words about whether you like or dislike these ideas. Give reasons for your opinion. You can also suggest alternatives.

Self-evaluation

Listening

The first three tasks in the test were listening tasks. Check your answers on p. 106. The following questions will help you to think about how you did.

1 What was difficult in the tasks?
a) I didn't understand the task.
b) People spoke quickly.
c) I found the accents difficult.
d) There was a lot of information. I couldn't find the exact answers.
e) I didn't have time to write the answers to the questions.
f) There were words and phrases that I just couldn't understand.
g) I didn't have time to finish all the tasks.

2 How did you do the tasks?
a) I looked quickly at the tasks first but only read them carefully while I was listening.
b) I read the tasks carefully first so I knew what I had to do and what I had to listen for.
c) I wrote as many answers as I could the first time I heard the text and checked them (or filled in gaps) the second time.
d) There were lots of things I couldn't understand and I panicked.

▶ *SF Listening (p. 137)* •
SF How to do well in a test (pp. 158–160)

Writing

The fourth task in your test was a writing task. Work with a partner. Exchange the texts you've written and read your partner's text. Copy and fill in the assessment sheet[1] below.

Assessment sheet	☹	😐	😊			
Name of partner:	1	2	3	4	5	Comments
Did your partner ...						
1 ... write about all three ideas?						
2 ... explain his/her opinion clearly?						
3 ... write enough?						
4 ... use interesting vocabulary and phrases?						
5 ... write longer sentences with linking words?						

▶ *SF Writing Course (pp. 150–151)*

---

[1] assessment sheet *Beurteilungsbogen*

Unit 4 Love reading

1 Pick up a book

a) Work in a group of four with a **placemat**. First look closely at the painting on the left for a few minutes. Then imagine you've just picked up a book that has this painting on the cover. Do the following tasks in your part of the placemat.
– Think of a title for the book.
– Write down what sort of book it is: a novel, a book of short stories, a drama, or a collection of poems.
– Write the first sentence of the novel or first short story. Or the first speech of the drama. Or the title and first line of the first poem in the collection.

Then discuss all your ideas in your group and agree which should go in the middle of the placemat. Read these out to the class.

b) Extra Think about your imagined book some more, then use your ideas to write the publisher's blurb for the book.

2 What I read last

a) Think about the last book you read (not one you had to read for school) and make notes about it (title, type of book, what language, why you read it, whether you enjoyed it, …)

b) Make **appointments** with two students and exchange information about the last book you read.

c) Extra Which book that you heard about would you most like to read? Note its title. Collect all these favourites in class. Which is the most popular book?

3 Extra Reading habits

a) What are the three sorts of things you read most? Write them down from 1 to 3. Here are some ideas: celebrity news in magazines • lyrics • video game info • popular series of novels (*Harry Potter, Alex Rider, Twilight,* …) • online newspapers • Facebook • blogs • chat rooms • text messages • …

b) Collect the class's results and make a class survey 'Our favourite reads'.

CAN'T PUT IT DOWN: FABULOUS FICTION

1 What are you going to read?

You want a really good novel to read while you're on holiday this summer, a real page-turner that you can't put down. Tell your group which of the following you would choose – or why you would choose none of these. The phrases on the right might help. Which book gets most votes?

- I've seen the film and …
- I like love stories/thrillers/historical novels/…
- It looks as if it's a … story.
- It sounds exciting/interesting/…
- I love the cover. / I don't like it at all because …
- I've already read one of …'s books.
- … recommends it so it must be good.
- I'm interested in …

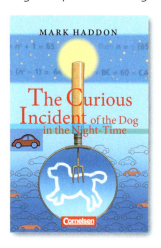

Late one night, Christopher finds his neighbour's dog dead in the neighbour's garden – killed with a garden fork. Christopher decides to find out who murdered the dog, which leads him on a journey of discovery. Through the eyes of the teenage narrator, readers will not only be given a look into the extraordinary mind of the protagonist, but will examine elements of life they take for granted while being led through an unusual detective story.

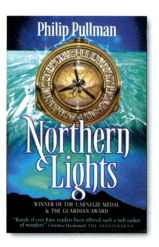

'Without this child, we shall all die.' The destiny that awaits Lyra and her animal dæmon will take them to the frozen lands of beautiful witches and armoured bears. Her journey will have consequences far beyond her own world.

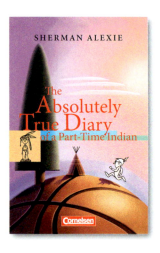

Junior is a member of the Spokane tribe living on a reservation in the north-west of the USA. At his Native American school he is always being beaten up by the other kids. When he realizes that the school cannot offer him any kind of future, he decides to go to a white school in the next town – where he stands out as the only Indian. Torn between both worlds, Junior has to find out where he belongs and who he is.

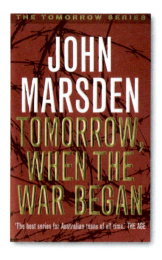

Ellie and her friends leave home one quiet morning, wave goodbye to their parents, and head up into the hills to camp out for a while. But the world is about to change forever. Their lives will never be the same again.

2 Reading a novel

Read through the tips for extensive reading below. Then, in 15 minutes at most, read the first 81 lines of the novel Looking for Alaska *by John Green.*

> **Tip**
>
> When you're reading a novel, or any longer text in a foreign language, try to read as if it was in your own language, without stopping at every difficult word or expression. After all, you want to enjoy what you're reading or inform yourself about something. This is called 'extensive reading' – and you probably do it like this in German too. The more you practise reading longer texts, the easier you will find it to enjoy real, authentic English writing. You have already learned how to understand new words without using a dictionary by considering
> – pictures, diagrams or symbols,
> – the context,
> – any similarity to words you know in German, French, Latin, …,
> – parts of the new word that you already know.
>
> ▶ SF Reading course (pp. 139–140)

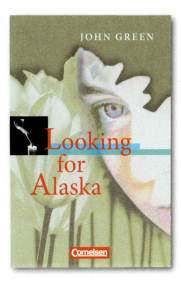

before

one hundred thirty-six days before

THE WEEK BEFORE I left my family and Florida and the rest of my minor life to go to boarding school in Alabama, my mother insisted
5   on throwing me a going-away party. To say that I had low expectations would be to underestimate the matter dramatically. Although I was more or less forced to invite all my "school friends," i.e., the ragtag bunch of drama people and English geeks I sat with by social necessity in the cavernous cafeteria of my public
10 school, I knew they wouldn't come. Still, my mother persevered, awash in the delusion that I had kept my popularity secret from her all these years. She cooked a small mountain of artichoke dip. She festooned our living room in green and yellow streamers, the colors of my new school. She bought two dozen champagne
15 poppers and placed them round the edge of our coffee table.

And when that final Friday came, when my packing was mostly done, she sat with my dad and me on the living-room couch at 4:56 P.M. and patiently awaited the arrival of the Good-bye to Miles Cavalry. Said cavalry consisted of exactly two people: Marie Lawson,
20 a tiny blonde with rectangular glasses, and her chunky (to put it charitably) boyfriend, Will.

"Hey, Miles," Marie said as she sat down.

"Hey," I said.

"How was your summer?" Will asked.
25   "Okay. Yours?"

"Good. We did *Jesus Christ Superstar*. I helped with the sets. Marie did lights," said Will.

---

4 minor ['maɪnə] *klein, unbedeutend*
4 boarding school ['bɔːdɪŋ ˌskuːl] *Internat*
6 expectation [ˌekspek'teɪʃn] *Erwartung*
6 dramatically [drə'mætɪkli] *hier: in höchstem Maße*
10 (to) persevere [ˌpɜːsɪ'vɪə] *beharrlich sein*
11 awash in [ə'wɒʃ] *erfüllt von*
19 said [sed] *besagte(r,s)*

"That's cool." I nodded knowingly, and that about exhausted our conversational topics. I might have asked a question about
Jesus Christ Superstar, except that 1. I didn't know what it was, and 2. I didn't care to learn, and 3. I never really excelled at small talk. My mom, however, can talk small for hours, and so she extended the awkwardness by asking them about their rehearsal schedule, and how the show had gone, and whether it was a success.

"I guess it was," Marie said. "A lot of people came, I guess." Marie was the sort of person to guess a lot.

Finally, Will said, "Well, we just dropped by to say good-bye. I've got to get Marie home by six. Have fun at boarding school, Miles."

"Thanks," I answered, relieved. The only thing worse than having a party that no one attends is having a party attended only by two vastly, deeply uninteresting people.

They left, and so I sat with my parents and stared at the blank TV and wanted to turn it on but knew I shouldn't. I could feel them both looking at me, waiting for me to burst into tears or something, as if I hadn't known all along that it would go precisely like this. But I *had* known. I could feel their pity as they scooped artichoke dip with chips intended for my imaginary friends, but they needed pity more than I did: I wasn't disappointed. My expectations had been met.

"Is this why you want to leave, Miles?" Mom asked.

I mulled it over for a moment, careful not to look at her. "Uh, no," I said.

"Well, why then?" she asked. This was not the first time she had posed the question. Mom was not particularly keen on letting me go to boarding school and had made no secret of it.

"Because of me?" my dad asked. He had attended Culver Creek, the same boarding school to which I was headed, as had both of his brothers and all of their kids. I think he liked the idea of me following in his footsteps. My uncles had told me stories about how famous my dad had been on campus for having simultaneously raised hell and aced all his classes. That sounded like a better life than the one I had in Florida. But no, it wasn't because of Dad. Not exactly.

"Hold on," I said. I went into Dad's study and found his biography of François Rabelais. I liked reading biographies of writers, even if (as was the case with Monsieur Rabelais) I'd never read any of their actual writing. I flipped to the back and found the highlighted quote ("NEVER USE A HIGHLIGHTER IN MY BOOKS," my dad had told me a thousand times. But how else are you supposed to find what you're looking for?)

"So this guy," I said, standing in the doorway of the living room. "François Rabelais. He was this poet. And his last words were 'I go to seek a Great Perhaps.' That's why I'm going. So I don't have to wait until I die to start seeking a Great Perhaps."

And that quieted them. I was after a Great Perhaps, and they knew as well as I did that I wasn't going to find it with the likes of Will and

---

33 awkwardness ['ɔːkwədnəs] *Peinlichkeit*
41 vastly [vɑːstli] *äußerst, völlig*
46 pity ['pɪti] *Mitleid*
47 intended for sb. [ɪn'tendɪd] *für jn. gedacht*
50 (to) mull sth. over [mʌl] *über etwas nachdenken*
53 (to) pose a question ['pəʊz] *eine Frage stellen*
60 (to) raise hell [ˌreɪz 'hel] *ein Höllenspektakel machen*
60 (to) ace classes [eɪs] *Bestnoten bekommen*
71 poet ['pəʊɪt] *Dichter/in*
75 the likes of [laɪks] *Leute wie*

Marie. I sat back down on the couch, between my mom and my dad, and my dad put his arm around me, and we stayed there like that, quiet on the couch together, for a long time, until it seemed okay to turn on the TV, and then we ate artichoke dip for dinner and watched the History Channel, and as going-away parties go, it certainly could have been worse.

Before you go on reading, check how well you have understood the story so far by answering these questions:
- Who is Miles and where is he from?
- What interesting facts do you find out about him?
- Where is he going soon?
- What happens at his going-away party?
- Why does he want to leave?

Compare and discuss your answers with a partner. What else can you add? Then read on to the end of the extract.

one hundred twenty-eight days before

FLORIDA WAS PLENTY HOT, certainly, and humid, too. Hot enough that your clothes stuck to you like Scotch tape, and sweat dripped like tears from your forehead into your eyes. But it was only hot outside, and generally I only went outside to walk from one air-conditioned location to another.

This did not prepare me for the unique sort of heat one encounters fifteen miles south of Birmingham, Alabama, at Culver Creek Preparatory School. My parents' SUV was parked in the grass just a few feet outside my dorm room, Room 43. But each time I took those few steps to and from the car to unload what now seemed like far too much stuff, the sun burned through my clothes and into my skin with a vicious ferocity that made me genuinely fear hellfire.

Between Mom and Dad and me, it only took a few minutes to unload the car, but my unair-conditioned dorm room, although blessedly out of the sunshine, was only modestly cooler. The room surprised me: I'd pictured plush carpet, wood-paneled walls, Victorian furniture. Aside from one luxury – a private bathroom – I got a box. With cinder-block walls coated with thick layers of white paint and a green-and-white-checkered linoleum floor, the place looked more like a hospital than the dorm room of my fantasies. A bunk bed of unfinished wood with vinyl mattresses was pushed against the room's back window. The desks and dressers and bookshelves were all attached to the walls in order to prevent creative floor planning. *And no air-conditioning.*

I sat on the lower bunk while Mom opened the trunk, grabbed a stack of the biographies my dad had agreed to part with, and placed them on the bookshelves.

"I can unpack, Mom," I said. My dad stood. He was ready to go.

"Let me at least make your bed," Mom said.

---

91 dorm room ['dɔːm ˌruːm] *Zimmer im Internat*
94 vicious ['vɪʃəs] *brutal, wütend*
94 ferocity [fə'rɒsəti] *Heftigkeit*
94 genuinely ['dʒenjuɪnli] *echt, wirklich*
101 cinder-block ['sɪndə blɒk] *Leichtbaustein*
106 dresser ['dresə] *(AE) Kommode*
108 trunk [trʌŋk] *Überseekoffer, Kiste*
109 (to) part with sth. *sich von etwas trennen*

"No, really. I can do it. It's okay." Because you simply cannot draw these things out forever. At some point, you just pull off the
115 Band-Aid and it hurts, but then it's over and you're relieved.

"God, we'll miss you," Mom said suddenly, stepping through the minefield of suitcases to get to the bed. I stood and hugged her. My dad walked over, too, and we formed a sort of huddle. It was too hot, and we were too sweaty, for the hug to last terribly long. I knew
120 I ought to cry, but I'd lived with my parents for sixteen years, and a trial separation seemed overdue.

"Don't worry," I smiled. "I's a-gonna learn how t'talk right Southern." Mom laughed.

"Don't do anything stupid," my dad said.
125 "Okay."

"No drugs. No drinking. No cigarettes." As an alumnus of Culver Creek, he had done the things I had only heard about: the secret parties, streaking through hay fields (he always whined about how it was all boys back then), drugs, drinking, and cigarettes. It had
130 taken him a while to kick smoking, but his badass days were now well behind him.

"I love you," they both blurted out simultaneously. It needed to be said, but the words made the whole thing horribly uncomfortable, like watching your grandparents kiss.
135 "I love you, too. I'll call every Sunday." Our rooms had no phone lines, but my parents had requested I be placed in a room near one of Culver Creek's five pay phones.

They hugged me again – Mom, then Dad – and it was over. Out the back window, I watched them drive the winding road off
140 campus. I should have felt a gooey, sentimental sadness, perhaps. But mostly I just wanted to cool off, so I grabbed one of the desk chairs and sat down outside my door in the shade of the overhanging eaves, waiting for a breeze that never arrived. The air outside sat as still and oppressive as the air inside. I stared out over
145 my new digs: Six one-story buildings, each with sixteen dorm rooms, were arranged in a hexagram around a large circle of grass. It looked like an oversize old motel. Everywhere, boys and girls hugged and smiled and walked together. I vaguely hoped that someone would come up and talk to me. I imagined the
150 conversation.

"Hey. Is this your first year?"

"Yeah. yeah. I'm from Florida."

"That's cool. So you're used to the heat."

"I wouldn't be used to this heat if I were from Hades," I'd joke.
155 I'd make a good first impression. *Oh, he's funny. That guy Miles is a riot.*

That didn't happen, of course. Things never happened like I imagined them.

Bored, I went back inside, took off my shirt, lay down on the
160 heat-soaked vinyl of the lowerbunk mattress, and closed my eyes.

---

115 Band-Aid ['bændeɪd] *Heftpflaster*
117 suitcase ['suːtkeɪs] *Koffer*
121 trial separation [ˌtraɪəl ˌsepəˈreɪʃn] *Trennung auf Probe*
121 overdue [ˌəʊvəˈdjuː] *überfällig*
128 (to) streak ['striːk] *(infml) blitzen (nackt laufen)*
130 (to) kick sth. *mit etwas aufhören*
136 (to) request [rɪˈkwest] *bitten*
145 digs [dɪgz] *(pl, infml) Bude, Bleibe*
145 one-story ['stɔːri] *(AE) einstöckig*
155 impression [ɪmˈpreʃn] *Eindruck*
156 (to) be a riot ['raɪət] *(infml) unglaublich lustig sein*

I'd never been born again with the baptism and weeping and all
that, but it couldn't feel much better than being born again as a guy
with no known past. I thought of the people I'd read about – John
F. Kennedy, James Joyce, Humphrey Bogart – who went to
165 boarding school, and their adventures – Kennedy, for example,
loved pranks. I thought of the Great Perhaps and the things that
might happen and the people I might meet and who my roommate
might be (I'd gotten a letter a few weeks before that gave me his
name, Chip Martin, but no other information). Whoever Chip
170 Martin was, I hoped to God he would bring an arsenal of high-
powered fans, because I hadn't packed even one, and I could
already feel my sweat pooling on the vinyl mattress, which
disgusted me so much that I stopped thinking and got off my ass to
find a towel to wipe up the sweat with. And then I thought, *Well,*
175 *before the adventure comes the unpacking.*

   I managed to tape a map of the world to the wall and get most of
my clothes into drawers before I noticed that the hot, moist air
made even the walls sweat, and I decided that now was not the
time for manual labor. Now was the time for a magnificently cold
180 shower.

   When I opened the bathroom door after my shower, a towel
wrapped around my waist, I saw a short, muscular guy with
a shock of brown hair. He was hauling a gigantic army-green duffel
bag through the door of my room. He stood five feet nothing, but
185 was well-built, like a scale model of Adonis, and with him arrived
the stink of stale cigarette smoke. *Great*, I thought. *I'm meeting my
roommate naked.* He heaved the duffel into the room, closed the
door, and walked over to me.

   "I'm Chip Martin," he announced in a deep voice, the voice of
190 a radio deejay. Before I could respond, he added, "I'd shake your
hand, but I think you should hold on damn tight to that towel till
you can get some clothes on."

   I laughed and nodded my head at him (that's cool, right? the
nod?) and said, "I'm Miles Halter. Nice to meet you."
195 "Miles, as in to go before I sleep?" he asked me.
   "Huh?"
   "It's a Robert Frost poem. You've never read him?"
   I shook my head no.
   "Consider yourself lucky." He smiled.
200 I grabbed some clean underwear, a pair of blue Adidas soccer
shorts, and a white T-shirt, mumbled that I'd be back in a second,
and ducked back into the bathroom. So much for a good first
impression.

   "So where are your parents?" I asked from the bathroom.
205 "My parents? The father's in California right now. Maybe sitting
in his La-Z-Boy. Maybe driving his truck. Either way, he's drinking.
My mother is probably just now turning off campus."

   "Oh," I said, dressed now, not sure how to respond to such

---

161 baptism ['bæptɪzəm] *Taufe*
166 prank [præŋk] *Streich*
177 drawer [drɔː] *Schublade*
182 waist [weɪst] *Taille*
183 (to) haul [hɔːl] *schleppen*
183–184 duffel bag ['dʌfl] *(AE)
Reisetasche*
206 La-Z-Boy ['leɪzibɔɪ]
(Markenname) Liegesessel

personal information. I shouldn't have asked, I guess, if I didn't
want to know.

Chip grabbed some sheets and tossed them onto the top bunk.
"I'm a top bunk man. Hope that doesn't bother you."

"Uh, no. Whatever is fine."

"I see you've decorated the place," he said, gesturing toward the
world map. "I like it."

And then he started naming countries. He spoke in a monotone,
as if he'd done it a thousand times before.

Afghanistan.

Albania.

Algeria.

American Samoa.

Andorra.

And so on. He got through the A's before looking up and
noticing my incredulous stare.

"I could do the rest, but it'd probably bore you. Something
I learned over the summer. God, you can't imagine how boring
New Hope, Alabama, is in the summertime. Like watching
soybeans grow. Where are you from, by the way?"

"Florida," I said.

"Never been."

"That's pretty amazing, the countries thing," I said.

"Yeah, everybody's got a talent. I can memorize things. And you
can ...?"

"Um, I know a lot of people's last words." It was an indulgence,
learning last words. Other people had chocolate: I had dying
declarations.

"Example?"

"I like Henrik Ibsen's. He was a playwright." I knew a lot about
Ibsen, but I'd never read any of his plays. I didn't like reading
plays. I liked reading biographies.

"Yeah, I know who he was," said Chip.

"Right, well, he'd been sick for a while and his nurse said to him,
'You seem to be feeling better this morning,' and Ibsen looked at
her and said, 'On the contrary,' and then he died."

Chip laughed. "That's morbid. But I like it."

I sat down next to him, and he looked over at me and suddenly
said, "Listen. I'm not going to be your entrée to Culver Creek social
life."

"Uh, okay," I said, but I could hear the words catch in my throat.
"Basically you've got two groups here," he explained, speaking with
increasing urgency. "You've got the regular boarders, like me, and
then you've got the Weekday Warriors; they board here, but they're
all rich kids who live in Birmingham and go home to their parents'
air-conditioned mansions every weekend. Those are the cool kids.
I don't like them, and they don't like me, and so if you came here
thinking that you were hot shit at public school so you'll be hot shit

---

212 (to) bother sb. ['bɒðə] *jm. etwas
ausmachen*
234 indulgence [ɪn'dʌldʒəns] *Luxus*
238 playwright ['pleɪraɪt]
Dramatiker/in
244 on the contrary ['kɒntrəri] *im
Gegenteil*
251 (to) increase [ɪn'kriːs] *zunehmen*
251 urgency ['ɜːgənsi] *Dringlichkeit*
251 regular ['regjələ] *(bes. AE) normal*
252 (to) board [bɔːd] *Internats-
schüler/in sein*

here, you'd best not be seen with me. You did go to public school, didn't you?"

"Uh ...," I said. Absentmindedly, I began picking at the cracks in
260 the couch's leather, digging my fingers into the foamy whiteness.

"Right, you did, probably, because if you had gone to a private
school your freakin' shorts would fit." He laughed.

I wore my shorts just below my hips, which I thought was cool.
Finally I said, "Yeah, I went to public school. But I wasn't hot shit
265 there, Chip. I was regular shit."

"Ha! That's good. And don't call me Chip. Call me the Colonel."
I stifled a laugh. "The *Colonel*?"

"Yeah. The Colonel. And we'll call you ... hmm. Pudge."
"Huh?"
270 "Pudge," the Colonel said. "Because you're skinny. It's called
irony, Pudge. Heard of it? Now, let's go get some cigarettes and
start this year off right."

We walked five doors down to Room 48. A dry-erase board was
taped to the door using duct tape. In blue marker, it read: *Alaska*
275 *has a single!*

The Colonel explained to me that *1.* this was Alaska's room, and
that *2.* she had a single room because the girl who was supposed to
be her roommate got kicked out at the end of last year, and that *3.*
Alaska had cigarettes, although the Colonel neglected to ask
280 whether *4.* I smoked, which *5.* I didn't.

He knocked once, loudly. Through the door, a voice screamed,
"Oh my God come in you short little man because I have the best
story."

We walked in. I turned to close the door behind me, and the
285 Colonel shook his head and said, "After seven, you have to leave the
door open if you're in a girl's room," but I barely heard him
because the hottest girl in all of human history was standing before
me in cutoff jeans and a peach tank top. And she was talking over
the Colonel, talking loud and fast.

(*Abridged from* Looking for Alaska *by John Green*)

---

270 Pudge [pʌdʒ] *etwa: Moppel*
270 skinny ['skɪni] *(infml) mager*
278 (to) kick sb. out *(infml) jn.*
rausschmeißen
279 (to) neglect [nɪ'glekt] *versäumen*

Working with the text

1   Your impression of the story
Say whether you like the story so far or not. Would you like to read on? Give reasons for your answers.

2   👥 Did you get it?
a) Read the following quotations from the story and explain their context. Share your ideas with a partner.

– l. 10: I knew they wouldn't come.
– ll. 37–38: "I've got to get Marie home by six. Have fun at boarding school, Miles."

– ll. 57–58: I think he liked the idea of me following in his footsteps.
– ll. 98–99: The room surprised me: ...

b) 👥 *Now pick out sentences from the story on your own and ask each other to explain the context in which they are used.*

c) `Extra` *Make notes for an oral summary of the beginning of* Looking for Alaska.
Then do a chain summary in class. Student A starts with the first sentence of the oral summary. Student B continues with the next, then Student C and so on. Each student contributes one sentence.

▶ *SF Speaking Course (pp. 148–149)*

3 The setting

a) 👥 *Partner A: Scan the text for descriptions of the appearance and atmosphere of Miles's home in Florida.*
Partner B: Scan the text for descriptions of the appearance and atmosphere of his boarding school in Alabama.
Discuss together what they are like and how they are different.

b) *Now explain Miles's decision to leave home and go to school somewhere else.*

4 The characters of Miles and Chip

a) *Describe the character of Miles. Remember to include direct as well as indirect clues to his appearance and personality.*

b) *Explain what impression Chip (the Colonel) makes on Miles. Find evidence for your ideas in the story.*

c) *What is your own impression of Chip? Say whether you'd like to make friends with him or not. Give reasons.*

5 How does the Colonel see it?

a) *Imagine you're Chip Martin (the Colonel) and you want to tell Alaska about your first meeting with Miles from your point of view. Make some notes and work out what you would say. Use the first person.*

b) 👥 *Present your monologues to each other in a small group.*
Listen closely so that you can evaluate each other's work. Which of the monologues best captures Chip's personality? Explain why.

▶ *SF Peer evaluation (p. 136)*

c) `Extra` 👥 *Discuss the possible reasons why John Green chose to tell his story from the perspective of Miles. What advantages might that have? What disadvantages? Thinking about the relationships between the characters might give you some ideas.*
Note down how the story would be different if it was told by an omniscient third-person narrator.

STUDY SKILLS **Point of view**

An author can choose to tell a story from different perspectives, using different kinds of narrator:

A limited point of view
A first-person narrator tells a story from his/her personal perspective. So he/she does not know everything that is going on. A third-person narrator is also sometimes limited to the experience of one or more characters and does not know every character's thoughts and feelings.

An unlimited point of view
Often, a third-person narrator is someone who knows everything about every character and can describe their actions and reveal their thoughts and feelings. We also call this sort of narrator an omniscient narrator.

▶ *SF Reading literature (pp. 141–143)*

3 LISTENING Listening to a novel 🎧

a) Think about when, where and why people listen to audiobooks.

b) Listen to an extract from the audiobook of *Looking for Alaska*. The words below might help.

- SAT = Scholastic Aptitude Test *Zulassungsprüfung für das Studium an einer amerikanischen Universität*
- honk [hɒŋk] *hupen, hier: drücken*
- boob [buːb] *(infml) Busen*

c) Explain what happened to Alaska in the summer and what Alaska does to Miles. How does he feel about this?

d) From what you have heard about Alaska, describe her character. Compare the two ways she is characterized: her actions and words (direct characterization), or what Miles says about her (indirect characterization)?

e) Extra Note down the advantages and disadvantages of listening to audiobooks as compared to reading a book. Does it make a difference if the audiobook is in English or your own language?
👥 Compare your ideas with a partner.
👥👥 Then compare your ideas in a group.

▶ SF Reading literature (pp. 141–143)

4 Extra Not just a writer

I happened to see a book by John Green the other day. Have you heard of him? He was born in Indianapolis and studied English and Religious Studies, a pretty unusual combination. And now he writes fiction for young adults. In fact, he's a good writer. How do I know? He's an award-winning novelist, so he can't be bad. His first novel, Looking for Alaska, won the Michael L. Printz Award for Excellence in Young Adult Literature in 2006, when he was just 29. Wow! Enough to make him a celebrity or pretty famous at least.
But John Green isn't just a writer. He's well-known in another pretty weird way too. It all started back in 2007. John and his brother Hank decided that, for a whole year, they would not communicate with each other in writing, but only by video blog. They called this project Brotherhood 2.0 and they put their video blogs on the Brotherhood 2.0 website – and on YouTube, where lots of people saw them, learned to love them and gave them a nickname. Which is why reviews of John Green's books often start something like this: 'This book is by John Green – you might know him better as one of the vlogbrothers.'

a) 👥 Read the short article about John Green. Imagine what reasons a writer could have for communicating only by video for a whole year. Discuss your ideas with a partner. Then collect them in class.

b) Find the 'vlogbrothers' on the internet and find out more about them.

c) 👥👥 Write down the names of six people you do not live with or see at school every day. How do you communicate with these people? Compare your answers in your group. What do you notice?

d) Find out something interesting about your favourite author, write it down on an index card. Collect all the cards for everyone to read.

86   **4**   Part **A** B C D   Practice

P1   VIEWING   Video book reviews

a) Have you ever watched book reviews on an online video site? Or filmed your own video book reviews and put them online?
Where else can you find written or video reviews of books?

b) If you were going to film a review of a book, how could you make it interesting visually?
Brainstorm ideas in a group. Pick the best three ideas and tell the class.
Collect all the ideas on the board.

c) On the right are stills from two reviews of the same book. Watch the first minute of each review without the sound. Say which you would now prefer to watch. Give reasons.
Take a vote in class and decide which review to watch first.

d) Watch your preferred video first.
Note down all the ways the reviewer tries to make their video more visually interesting. Did they use any of the ideas you collected on the board? Did they have better ideas? Which of the ideas on the board would have made the review more interesting?

e) Watch the second video and do the same. Then answer the following questions.
1 Which review used better visual ideas?
2 Which review gave you a better idea of what the book is about? How?
3 Which review most made you want or not want to read the book? Why?

f) Discuss your answers with a partner.

g) **Extra** Watch the two reviews again and do the following tasks:
1 Describe what you have learned about the main characters of the book. How does this change or underline what you already knew about them?
2 The boy talks a lot about the two parts of the novel, the 'before' and the 'after'. How are they different?
3 The girl is especially interested in famous last words. How many does she quote? Which did you find most interesting?
4 What emotional reaction to the book do both reviewers mention?

Part **A** B C D Practice **4** 87

P2 Preparing and presenting a book report

a) Give a book report on an interesting book you have read. You might find the Study Skills box on the right and the useful language given below helpful.

b) Match the sections of useful language (A–D) to the parts of a book report in the Study Skills box.

A

– … is a thriller / a fantasy / a collection of short stories / a book for young adults / a classic / … by …
– It deals with environmental problems / the historical events of … / the period …
  It's about this Australian girl who …
– The story is set in …
– It begins with …
– The main character is introduced at a moment when he/she …
– Later …
– I'm going to read a short extract from the book. I find it very moving/thrilling/…
  It starts when the protagonist …
  I chose the moment when the hero …
  It is the scene after …
– … creates a very unusual/frightening/romantic/… atmosphere in …
  The book is full of sudden developments.
  I love the way … uses language. It's so poetic/memorable/funny/striking/…

B

– This is one of the best books I have ever read.
– It's so thrilling/exciting/funny, I couldn't put it down.
– I highly recommend it.
– It's a great read for your holidays/boring weekends/…

C

– This is what Stephen King said about this book: "My all-time favorite … Astonishing."
– I'd like to start with this really funny/interesting/weird/shocking/… quotation from the book.
– Look at the cover of my book.

STUDY SKILLS | **Giving a book report**

Introduction
Grab your audience's attention right from the start.

About the book
– Give its title, author and genre.
– Give a short summary of the plot – don't give away the ending!
– Read an extract.
– Say something about specific features of the book (setting, language, atmosphere, developments, pace).

Background information
– Say when and where the book was published.
– Talk a little about the author.

Your opinion
Finish with a clear statement of your opinion.

D

– … was first published in … in …
– It is …'s first/second/… novel/…
– … comes from … and lives in … He/She's … years old and loves …
– This book won the …

c) **Extra** *Film a video version of your book report and show it to the class.
Or have a book slam in class. Each student presenting a book has three minutes to convince the class that their book is the best.
Vote for the best book at the end.*

▶ SF Giving a presentation (p. 132)

A QUICK FIX: SHORT STORIES ▶ ☰☰

How to do it   By Dave Eggers

The woman, named Puma, was forty-four, shaped like a gymnast, and had too many friends. She had lived in the same city, full of Mormons, for twenty-five years, and she was not impetuous or jealous or callous or cruel. Thus, the friends she had made twenty-
5 five years ago were still her friends now, and because her job – she was a veterinary surgeon, specializing in toucans – brought her in contact with new people all the time, she added friends with now-troubling regularity. Which was fine, it was nice to have new companions, but at this point Puma could no longer be a good
10 friend to all of them – to even half of them. She did the calculations one day: ten friends from her first few years in the city, and (at the very least) three more added every year thereafter. This brought her to a total, now, of about eighty-five good friends and close acquaintances, and this number, given birthdays and anniversaries
15 and sympathy calls and favors and lunches and various gift-giving showers, made her life untenable. Every day was something, every day was everyone. She couldn't enjoy her time with any one of them, knowing that she was neglecting the rest. And she certainly couldn't enjoy time alone, because at this point even an hour to
20 herself – when she hadn't, for example, seen William and Jeanette's new baby, now five months old! – was decadent, selfish, and utterly foreign. Her friends had made her unfriendly, her chums had sapped her charm. Something had to be done; she had to make a break. So she stopped answering her phone, and no
25 longer took walks. She ordered her groceries online, and pretended her email didn't work. And for a day, one glorious day, this worked. But they found her. Of course they did. They found her at work, at her home. They dropped cute notes in her mailbox, fastened them under her car's windshield wipers. They did so because her friends
30 were good friends, were persistent and not to be easily put off. They worried, they wished her well. But this only made Puma more perturbed, more desperate to be free, and more determined to bring them all together, for a grand dinner one night, where she would deal with the problem once and for all. It was extreme, yes,
35 but also necessary, and thankfully possible, for among her too-many friends (and the only ones she would spare) she had a caterer, an expert in untraceable and fast-acting poisons, and an excellent attorney.

---

3 impetuous [ɪmˈpetjʊəs] *impulsiv, ungestüm*
4 callous [ˈkæləs] *herzlos*
6 veterinary surgeon [ˈvetərɪnəri ˈsɜːdʒən] *Tierarzt/-ärztin*
6 toucan [ˈtuːkæn] *Tukan (südamerikanischer Vogel)*
8 regularity [ˌreɡjʊˈlærɪti] *Regelmäßigkeit*
9 companion [kəmˈpænjən] *Freund/in, Gefährte/Gefährtin*
12 thereafter [ˌθɜərˈɑːftə] *danach*
14 acquaintance [əˈkweɪntəns] *Bekannte/r*
16 untenable [ʌnˈtenəbl] *unhaltbar*
18 neglect [nɪˈɡlekt] *vernachlässigen*
21 selfish *egoistisch*
23 chum *(infml) Kumpel*
23 sap sth. *etwas schwächen*
28 fasten [ˈfɑːsn] *befestigen*
29 windshield wiper [ˈwɪndʃiːld ˈwaɪpə] *Scheibenwischer*
30 persistent [pəˈsɪstənt] *beharrlich*
30 put sb. off *jn. abschrecken*
32 perturbed [pəˈtɜːbd] *beunruhigt*
36 spare [speə] *verschonen*
37 untraceable [ʌnˈtreɪsəbl] *unauffindbar*
38 attorney [əˈtɜːni] *(AE) Rechtsanwalt/-anwältin*

Part A **B** C D   **4**   89

Working with the text

1   Did you get it?

a) *Sum up the plot of the story in one or two sentences.*

b) *Friendship – what makes a good friend, losing a friend, collecting friends, dating, etc.– was an important topic in Unit 1 of this book. Explain this story's view of the problem of collecting friends.*

2   Analysing the story

a) *Read the Study Skills box on the right. Then read "How to do it" again. Make notes on how it matches the features of a short story described in the box.*
– Is it short?
– Are the characters, plot and setting limited?
– How many characters are developed?
– Is there a beginning, climax and resolution?
– Or is there an abrupt start, a surprise or open ending?

b) *Compare and discuss your ideas in a group.*

3   A few details

Consider whether the following details are significant or not and discuss in class:
– the main character's name
– her level of fitness
– her job
– the large number of friends she has
– the jobs of some of the friends she is inviting to dinner

4   Extra   Another point of view

Imagine you are one of Puma's friends. Rewrite lines 24–34 of the story from your point of view. Explain how you feel about your invitation to a grand dinner.

5   The dinner

Continue the story, describing what happens at Puma's grand dinner.

STUDY SKILLS   **Short stories**

What makes a short story:
– Short stories are … **short**. How short? They can be less than a page or more than 50.
– Short stories usually focus on a **single plot and setting**. They usually have fewer characters and cover **shorter periods of time** than novels.
– Often there is just **one main character**: other characters are **not developed** or are just **stereotypes**.
– Short stories may have a clear **beginning** (introducing the setting, situation and main characters), **climax** (point of highest interest/drama/action) and a **resolution** (when the story comes to an end) – but modern short stories often **start abruptly**, in the middle of the action, and may have a **surprise ending** or **be open-ended**.

▶ *SF Reading literature (pp. 141–143)*

6   Extra   Short short stories

The American writer Ernest Hemingway once wrote a six-word short story:
For sale: baby shoes. Never worn.

Other writers later came up with these:

Computer, did we bring batteries? Computer?
Eileen Gunn

Longed for him. Got him. Shit.
Margaret Atwood

We crossed the border; they killed us.
Howard Waldrop

Do you think they can really be called stories? Write your own six-word story.

LIFELINES: SAVED BY POETRY

1 Unwanted literature

a) Discuss in your group what role poetry plays in your life. You could
– talk about whether or how often you read or listen to poetry and what you like or dislike about it,
– comment on songs you listen to (do you agree that songs are like poems?),
– mention poets you know/have heard of,
– recite your favourite poem (in English, German, or another language) and talk about why you like it and what it means for you.
– …

London Airport
Last night in London Airport
I saw a wooden bin
labelled UNWANTED LITERATURE
IS TO BE PLACED HEREIN.
So I wrote a poem
and popped it in.

Christopher Logue (born 1926)

b) Now read the poem "London Airport" and comment on its relevance for your discussion in a).

2 Tell me a story

a) Summarize the story told in the poem "Willow pattern".

b) What image does the poet choose to describe the Emperor's feelings in the sixth verse? Explain why it is a good image or not. Which words in the verse carry the emotion most?

c) Extra Which elements from the poem can you discover on the plate right?

Willow pattern
Look. On my plate
is a blue garden.
It happened in China
a long time ago.

There on a bridge
the soldiers are running
to capture the princess,
the Emperor's daughter.

She left with the young man
she wanted to marry.
They fled to an island
that lay on a lake.

The Emperor was angry.
He ordered his soldiers
to capture the princess
and kill the young man.

But the man and the princess
were turned into bluebirds.
They flew from the island
and never returned.

The Emperor, in sadness,
turned into a willow.
And always he droops
as he weeps in his sorrow.

He weeps on my plate
in a blue garden.
It happened in China
a long time ago.

Tony Mitton (born 1951)

Part A B C D **4** 91

d) 👥 *Make sure everyone in the group knows the fairy tale "Little Red Riding Hood".
Then read the poem below. What's different?*

Little Red Riding Hood and the Wolf

As soon as Wolf began to feel
That he would like a decent meal,
He went and knocked on Grandma's door.
When Grandma opened it, she saw
5 The sharp white teeth, the horrid grin,
And Wolfie said, 'May I come in?'
Poor Grandmamma was terrified,
'He's going to eat me up!' she cried.
And she was absolutely right.
10 He ate her up in one big bite.
But Grandmamma was small and tough,
And Wolfie wailed, 'That's not enough!
I haven't yet begun to feel
That I have had a decent meal!'
15 He ran around the kitchen yelping,
'I've *got* to have another helping!'
Then added with a frightful leer,
'I'm therefore going to wait right here
Till Little Miss Red Riding Hood
20 Comes home from walking in the wood.'
He quickly put on Grandma's clothes,
(Of course he hadn't eaten those.)
He dressed himself in coat and hat.
He put on shoes and after that
25 He even brushed and curled his hair,
Then sat himself in Grandma's chair.
In came the little girl in red.
She stopped. She stared. And then she said,
'*What great big ears you have, Grandma.*'
30 '*All the better to hear you with,*' the Wolf
replied.
'*What great big eyes you have, Grandma,*' said
Little Red Riding Hood.
'*All the better to see you with,*' the Wolf replied.

He sat there watching her and smiled.   35
He thought, I'm going to eat this child.
Compared with her old Grandmamma
She's going to taste like caviare.
Then Little Red Riding Hood said, '*But
Grandma, what a lovely great big furry coat you*   40
have on.'
'That's wrong!' cried Wolf, 'Have you forgot
To tell me what big teeth I've got?
Ah well, no matter what you say,
I'm going to eat you anyway.'   45
The small girl smiles. One eyelid flickers.
She whips a pistol from her knickers.
She aims it at the creature's head
And *bang bang bang*, she shoots him dead.
A few weeks later, in the wood,   50
I came across Miss Riding Hood,
But what a change! No cloak of red,
No silly hood upon her head.
She said, 'Hello, and do please note
My lovely furry WOLFSKIN COAT.'   55

Roald Dahl (1916–1990)

e) *Do you find the poem funny? What makes it
funny?*

f) *Examine the rhyme and rhythm of the poem.
What do you notice about them? What
advantages does this kind of rhyme and rhythm
have for moving the story along or learning the
poem by heart?*

▶ *SF Reading literature (pp. 141–143)*

STUDY SKILLS **Rhyme and rhythm**

Poems, like music, use **poetic devices** like
rhyme and **rhythm**.
Rhyme
– Matching sounds at the end of lines are
  called **end-rhymes**.
– Rhymes within a line give you an internal
  rhyme.
Both create a pattern you can hear. When
this pattern continues through a poem, it
gives the poem a **rhyme scheme**, which you
can write down like this: AABBCC; ABAB.
Rhythm
The sequence of stressed and unstressed
long and short syllables gives a poem its
rhythm.
If this rhythm is (more or less) regular, the
poem is written in a certain **metre**.

3 Paint me a picture

Castaway

The sea is a numberless army
Surrounding my desert isle.
The wind is its heartless general,
Howling mile after mile.
As wave after wave hits the beaches,
I catch sight of a hopeful white sail;
Then storm clouds hide the horizon
And all hope disappears in the gale.

Stephen Brock (born 1961)

The eagle

He clasps the crag with crooked hands;
Close to the sun in lonely lands,
Ring'd with the azure world, he stands.

The wrinkled sea beneath him crawls;
He watches from his mountain walls,
And like a thunderbolt he falls.

Alfred, Lord Tennyson (1809–1892)

Haiku

dawn is delicious
soup made from dew and birdsong
drink it with your ears

Sue Cowling (born 1946)

Amsterdam Avenue

Siren screams and car horns
Clog the air.
Still, the sparrow's song
Survives the blare.
And, though six-storied buildings
Crowd the sky,
The sun scissors through and shines –
And so will I.

Nikki Grimes (born 1950)

Stopping by woods on a snowy evening

Whose woods these are I think I know,
His house is in the village though;
He will not see me stopping here
To watch his woods fill up with snow.

My little horse must think it queer
To stop without a farmhouse near
Between the woods and frozen lake
The darkest evening of the year.

He gives his harness bells a shake
To ask if there is some mistake.
The only other sound's the sweep
Of easy wind and downy flake.

The woods are lovely, dark and deep,
But I have promises to keep,
And miles to go before I sleep,
And miles to go before I sleep.

Robert Frost (1874–1963)

a) *Choose one of the poems on this page and draw the most vivid picture it creates in your mind.*

STUDY SKILLS **Imagery**

To express emotions and to create such emotions in the reader's mind and senses, poets paint pictures with words. Some are immediately clear; others take time to make sense to you. This **imagery** often comes in the form of **metaphors** or **similes**, which show us a new way of seeing things.
In a **metaphor**, a poet talks about something as if it is something else, e. g. **The garden was a sea of flowers**, or as if it can do something that, in the real world, it cannot, e. g. **Time flies**.
In a **simile**, a poet creates an image by comparing one thing with another, e. g. **A face as white as snow** or **She fights like a tiger**.

▶ *SF Reading literature (pp. 141–143)*

---

azure ['æʒə] *azurblau*   castaway ['kɑːstəwei] *Schiffbrüchige(r)*   (to) catch sight of sth. *etwas erblicken*   (to) clasp [klɑːsp] *umklammern*
(to) clog (-gg-) [klɒg] *verstopfen*   crag [kræg] *Fels*   (to) crawl [krɔːl] *kriechen*   crooked ['krʊkɪd] *krumm, schief*   dew [djuː] *Morgentau*
downy ['daʊni] *flaumig, fedrig*   flake [fleɪk] *Flocke(n)*   gale [geɪl] *Sturm*   harness ['hɑːnɪs] *Pferdegeschirr*   paw [pɔː] *Tatze*   (to) scissor
['sɪzə] *schneiden*   sparrow ['spærəʊ] *Spatz*   sweep [swiːp] *wischende Bewegung*   wrinkled ['rɪŋkld] *faltig, zerknittert*

Part A B C D   4   93

STUDY SKILLS Sounds and language

Repetition of letters, sounds and words can help a poet create more effective images and underline the feeling, rhythm or the meaning of a poem.
In **alliteration**, the same letter/sound is repeated at the beginning of two or more neighbouring words, e.g. Godric Gryffindor, Helga Hufflepuff, Rowena Ravenclaw and Salazar Slytherin.
In **assonance**, the same vowel sound is repeated, e.g. The fat cat sat on the mat. Whole verses may be repeated, as in a chorus. Language that brings feelings, images or memories into the reader's mind also adds to the effect a poem creates.

▶ SF Reading literature (pp. 141–143)

b) Find a metaphor in "Castaway" and a simile in "The eagle". What do they describe? Talk or write about the picture they paint for you.

c) How are the meanings and the sounds of the words in the first line of "The eagle" used to create a picture in the reader's mind?

d) Choose one of the other poems on p. 92 and list the poetic devices used. Explain why they are effective, or not, in creating a picture.

e) Extra In several of the poems on p. 92, decisions are made. Find some of these decisions and explain what they are about.

4 Show me what you feel

She dwelt among the untrodden ways
She dwelt among the untrodden ways
Beside the springs of Dove,
A maid whom there were none to praise
And very few to love:

A violet by a mossy stone
Half-hidden from the eye!
– Fair as a star, when only one
Is shining in the sky.

She lived unknown, and few could know
When Lucy ceased to be;
But she is in her grave, and, oh,
The difference to me!

William Wordsworth
(1770–1850)

Sonnet number one
The moon doth shine as bright as in the
  day.
I sit upon the see-saw wondering why
She left me. Boys and girls come out to play.
But I'm bereft. I think I'm going to cry.
I gave her chocolate and I praised her skill
At skateboarding and at football not to
  mention
Arm wrestling. As we slowly climbed the
  hill
To fetch some water, did I sense a tension?
She seemed preoccupied. She hardly spoke.
And as we turned the handle to the well
I asked her, Jill, please tell me it's a joke.
She said, I've found another bloke. I fell,
I rolled, head over heels into the dark
Down to the bottom where I broke my heart.

Roger Stevens (born 1948)

---

bereft [bɪˈreft] (fml) beraubt · bloke [bləʊk] Kerl · (to) cease [siːs] (fml) aufhören · doth shine [dʌθ] (old) = does shine, shines · dwelt [dwelt] (fml, old) wohnte · grave [greɪv] Grab · handle [ˈhændl] Griff · hardly [ˈhɑːdli] kaum · head over heels [hiːlz] Hals über Kopf · maid [meɪd] (fml, old) Jungfer, Mädchen · (to) praise [preɪz] loben, preisen · preoccupied [priˈɒkjuːpaɪd] beschäftigt, abgelenkt · (to) roll [rəʊl] rollen · see-saw [ˈsiː sɔː] Wippe · tension [ˈtenʃn] Spannung · untrodden [ʌnˈtrɒdn] (fml) unbeschritten · well [wel] Brunnen

a) *Read the four poems on pp. 93–94 and identify which express which feelings from the word circle below:*

> passion
> love   boredom
> heartbreak   admiration
> pleasure   pain   thrill   despair
> excitement
>   anger   disappointment
>   wonder   sadness
>   joy   happiness
>   loss

Meeting Midnight

I met Midnight.
Her eyes were sparkling pavements after
   frost.
She wore a full-length, dark blue raincoat with
   a hood.
She winked. She smoked a small cheroot.

I followed her.
Her walk was more a shuffle, more a dance.
She took the path to the river, down she
   went.
On Midnight's scent,
I heard twelve cool syllables, her name,
chime from the town.
When those bells stopped,

Midnight paused by the water's edge.
She waited there.
I saw a girl in purple on the bridge.
It was One O'Clock.
Hurry, Midnight said, *it's late, it's late.*
I saw them run together.
Midnight wept.
They kissed full on the lips
and then I slept.

The next day I bumped into Half-Past Four.
He was a bore.

Carol Ann Duffy (born 1955)

Come. And be my baby

The highway is full of big cars
going nowhere fast
And folks is smoking anything that'll burn
Some people wrap their lives around a
   cocktail glass
And you sit wondering
where you're going to turn.
I got it.
Come. And be my baby.

Some prophets say the world is gonna end
   tomorrow
But others say we've got a week or two
The paper is full of every kind of blooming
   horror
And you sit wondering
what you're gonna do.
I got it.
Come. And be my baby.

Maya Angelou (born 1928)

b) *Now that you have recognized some of the feelings, say which poem you like best and why.*

c) *Examine your favourite poem's rhymes, rhyme scheme, rhythm and line lengths. Explain why they are suitable (or not) for the message and tone of the poem.*

d) *Practise reciting your favourite poem. Then recite it to the class. Or recite another poem, song or rap you know.*

e) **Extra** *Find your favourite word, image, rhyme, idea and line from the four poems. Use them to write your own poem. (It doesn't have to rhyme!)*

f) **Extra** *Imagine one of the four poems is a hit song. Which would it be? Give your reasons.*

---

blooming [ˈbluːmɪŋ] *(old, infml) verflixt*   (to) chime [tʃaɪm] *(Uhr) schlagen*   (to) pause [pɔːz] *eine Pause machen*   on the scent [sent] *auf der Spur*   shuffle [ˈʃʌfl] *Schlurfen*   sparkling [ˈspɑːklɪŋ] *glitzernd*   (to) wink [wɪŋk] *zwinkern*

5 Give me an insight

a) Look at the titles of the poems. Imagine what they could be about. Then read each poem and note down your impressions of them.

Absent

Dear Teacher,
my body's arrived
it sits at a table
a pen in its hand
as if it is able
to think and to act
perhaps write down the answer
to the question you've asked

but don't let that fool you

My mind is elsewhere
My thoughts are far away

So, apologies, teacher,
I'm not here today.

Bernard Young (born 1952)

The world is a beautiful place
       The world is a beautiful place
           to be born into
if you don't mind happiness
          not always being
              so very much fun
if you don't mind a touch of hell
         now and then
      just when everything is fine
            because even in heaven
     they don't sing
          all the time
     The world is a beautiful place
          to be born into
if you don't mind some people dying
         all the time
or maybe only starving
          some of the time
   which isn't half so bad
          if it isn't you.

Lawrence Ferlinghetti (born 1919)

Natural numbers
Example: Divide 5,000 buffaloes
by fifty hunters = almost nothing left.

1. Divide 200 elephants
by seventeen ivory poachers =

2. Divide two rainforests
by eight logging companies =

3. Divide one beautiful planet
by one greedy species =

Mike Johnson (born 1951)

Dreams
Here we are all, by day; by night we're
    hurled
By dreams, each one, into a several world.

Robert Herrick (1591–1674)

b) 👥 *Compare your impressions with a partner and add to your notes if necessary.*
👪 *Share your impressions in a group. Then, together, rank the poems from 1 (most insight) to 4 (least insight).*

c) Now read the poems again and consider the following:
– the text type of "Absent" and the layout of its verses
– what the text type of "Natural numbers" reminds you of
– the layout and the punchline of "The world is a beautiful place"
– the rhyme scheme in "Dreams" and the flow of the two lines

Considering what you have found out, change – if necessary – the rankings you gave the poems in b).

---

absent ['æbsənt] *abwesend*   (to) fool sb. [fuːl] *jm. etwas vormachen*   hell [hel] *Hölle*   (to) hurl [hɜːl] *schleudern*   ivory ['aɪvəri] *Elfenbein*
logging ['lɒgɪŋ] *Abholzung*   poacher ['pəʊtʃə] *Wilddieb/in*   several *(fml, old) separat*   (to) starve [stɑːv] *hungern*

P1 Create your own poems

One way of creating a poem is to follow a certain pattern, for example the pattern of a **cinquain**, which gets its name from the French cinq (five) because it always has five lines.

Line 1 – 2 syllables introducing the topic	Football.
Line 2 – 4 syllables saying something about the topic	Beautiful game.
Line 3 – 6 syllables saying how it feels	Great being in the team.
Line 4 – 8 syllables continuing the topic	It's a way of life: enjoy it
Line 5 – 2 syllables finishing the topic, often with a twist	and score.

Two other pattern poems are:
Haiku: a three-line Japanese poetry form. The first and last lines have 5 syllables, the second line 7. Haiku are often about the seasons of the year and the natural world and try to capture a moment of beauty.
Acrostic: the first letters of each line of an acrostic make up a word that is the topic of the poem.

Feet dribble the ball
Outside the left back.
One-two down
The touchline with
Ben, then send in
A magnificent cross for
Lynne to
Lift it over the goalie and score.

Think of a topic that is important to you and write your own cinquain.
and/or
What's your favourite season? Or your favourite place to go and enjoy the natural world? Make a few notes about it and create a haiku.
and/or
Create an acrostic about the same topic as your cinquain. Or use somebody's name or their job.

P2 Poems paint pictures

a) Now turn a picture (one of these, another one from somewhere else in this book, or one of your own) into a poem. Try to focus on the emotions and the atmosphere the picture conveys and find the right words and rhythm.

b) Use your poems to create a class collection which you could display, show to parents, …

▶ WB 1–3 (p. 42–43)

ALL THE WORLD'S A STAGE: THRILLING THEATRE

1 What's going on?

a) *Below are photos from different productions of a play for young people. Speculate about them on your own and note down some ideas on the following:*
- what the play is about
- when it takes place (past, present, future)
- where it is set
- what the relationship of the characters to each other is like
- …

b) *Present and discuss your ideas in your group.*

98 **4** Part A B C **D**

2 Kirsty and Gideon (abridged from *Fairytaleheart* by Philip Ridley) ▶ ▤▤

Characters
Kirsty
Gideon

The stage of an abandoned community centre in
the East End of London. Most of the windows are
broken and boarded over (concealing the snowy,
March evening outside), so what is about to be
5 described is, for the moment, barely discernible.
There's a couple of old chairs, several boxes,
a table and various scattered detritus. The table is
covered with painting materials: brushes, tubes of
paint, spray paint, whatever is needed to have
10 created –
The fairytale backdrop. This covers most of the
stage and has been created by adapting and
painting found objects: a pile of boxes has become
a mountain; an old mantelpiece, a cave; a sheet of
15 corrugated iron, a river; a large mirrorball, a sun
or moon. Also depicted are birds, flowers and
butterflies.
Some distance from the main backdrop – and
lying flat on the ground – is a large mirror.
20 Flowers have been painted around it, giving the
impression of a pond.
The general effect is of a magical landscape,
somewhere between a painting and a sculpture.
The magical quality will eventually intensify by
25 the shimmering light of –
Candles. These are everywhere on stage: across
the floor, on table. Candles of all shapes and sizes.
Most are in coloured-glass containers. They are, of
course, unlit at present.
30 Pause.
Then –
The entrance at the back of the auditorium noisily
unlocks and –
Kirsty enters. She is fifteen years old and
35 carrying a bag of hastily packed clothes in one
hand and a torch in the other. She is shivering
against the cold outside. Hardly surprising,
considering her clothing – obviously her 'party
best': a dress decorated with silver sequins and
40 rhinestones, silver stilettos and a short, white,

fake-fur coat. Her hair is neatly styled and
highlighted with silver glitter. She's tried hard to
make an impression and succeeded.
Kirsty closes the door behind her and switches on
the torch. The beam of light pokes through the   45
darkness like a luminous finger.
Kirsty   Hello?
Slight pause.
        Anyone there?

Kirsty walks through the auditorium and up onto   50
stage. She seems familiar with the community
hall as a whole, but not the paints and backdrop,
etc. She treads carefully round the candles, then
shines torch over backdrop.
Pause.   55
She puts bag down, then – a little awkwardly –
picks up a brush, dips it into some paint, and
adds some colour to one of the butterflies.
Pause.
Then –   60
The entrance at the back of the auditorium noisily
unlocks and –
Gideon enters. He is fifteen years old and
carrying a well-worn duffel bag in one hand and a
torch in the other. His hair is longish and aspires 65
to be dreadlocks. He is well insulated against the
cold: a thick and baggy (albeit worn) jumper, a
couple of coats, scarf, gloves and paint-spattered
boots. Nothing really goes together but – on him
– it works.   70
Kirsty turns torch off and puts brush down.
Gideon   Who ... who's there?
Closes door and fumbles to light torch.
        Who are you?
Kirsty   Don't panic.   75
Gideon   I don't mean you any harm.
Kirsty   Don't mean me any – What are you
        prattling on about?
Turns on her torch.
        I said, Don't panic.   80
Gideon turns on his torch and approaches stage.
Gideon   ... You're Kirsty.
Kirsty   How d'you know my bloody name?

---

1 (to) abandon [əˈbændən] *vernachlässigen*   **7** various [ˈveəriəs] *verschieden*   **8** brush [brʌʃ] *Pinsel*   **16** (to) depict [dɪˈpɪkt] *(fml) darstellen*
17 butterfly [ˈbʌtəflaɪ] *Schmetterling*   **24** eventually [ɪˈventʃuəly] *schließlich, irgendwann*   **32** entrance [ˈentrəns] *Eingang*   **36** torch [tɔːtʃ]
Taschenlampe   **48** slight [slaɪt] *klein*   **51** familiar with [fəˈmɪliə] *vertraut mit*   **64** well-worn [ˌwelˈwɔːn] *abgenutzt*   **64** duffel bag [ˈdʌfl
bæg] *(BE) Sporttasche*   **67** baggy [ˈbægi] *weit*   **67** albeit [ˌɔːlˈbiːɪt] *obwohl*   **67** jumper [ˈdʒʌmpə] *Pullover*   **81** (to) approach [əˈprəʊtʃ] *sich
nähern*   **83** bloody [ˈblʌdi] *(infml, rude) verdammt*

Gideon	Must have heard it around.

Gets on stage.

Slight pause.

	You live in the block of flats by the playground, don't you.
Kirsty	Yes, that's where I live. Heard that around too, did you?
Gideon	Must have.
Kirsty	You'll be telling me my flat number next.
Gideon	Thirteen.
Kirsty	You been spying on me?
Gideon	No.

Starts removing coats, gloves and scarf.

	How did you get in?
Kirsty	I unlocked the door.
Gideon	With what?
Kirsty	A pilchard with rigor mortis – What do you think I unlocked it with? A key!
Gideon	The only key belongs to me.
Kirsty	Correction. It belongs to your Dad. Who's the caretaker of the estate. And, as this is the community hall of said estate – or, it was – then the key is ... blah, blah, blah.

Slight pause.

Gideon	You been spying on me?
Kirsty	It's a small estate.

Pause.

Gideon	So where did you get your key from?
Kirsty	You get a degree in being nosy or something?
Gideon	Don't tell me if you don't want to.

Slight pause.

Kirsty	It's my Mum's, if you must know.
Gideon	Your Mum died, didn't she?
Kirsty	You asking me or telling me?

Slight pause.

	Yes, she died. Two years ago. Two years and seven months.

Slight pause.

Kirsty	Before she got sick she used to help out here. Help out – what am I saying? She ran it. When it was really a community centre. When the windows weren't boarded up. When people used to come to have tea and gossip. Or play bingo. Disco for kids. Mum knew everyone's name. This was her ... her ...
Gideon	Her kingdom.

Slight pause.

Kirsty	It was.
Gideon	I've heard people on the estate talk about her. She was real popular, your Mum. Beautiful too, they say.

Slight pause.

Kirsty	Bloody hell, it's like a fridge in here.
Gideon	There's no electric.
Kirsty	I know.
Gideon	Then you should have dressed properly.
Kirsty	I am dressed properly. I'm just not dressed ... suitably.
Gideon	You're welcome to one of my coats.
Kirsty	... They look a bit damp.
Gideon	My jumper then. It's warm with body heat.
Kirsty	... I'd rather not.
Gideon	But your lips are blue.
Kirsty	Must be the lipstick.
Gideon	Blue tights too, eh?
Kirsty	You leave my tights out of this.
Gideon	I'm wearing thermal pants.
Kirsty	Thank you for sharing that with me.
Gideon	It's snowing outside.
Kirsty	So that's what that white stuff's called.
Gideon	Ain't you got any thermal knickers?

Kirsty glares and gasps.

Slight pause.

Gideon takes flask from duffel bag.

Gideon	You want something warm to drink?
Kirsty	No, thank you.
Gideon	It's peppermint tea with a drop of lavender oil.
Kirsty	That's supposed to tempt me?
Gideon	Lavender helps you relax.
Kirsty	I am bloody relaxed!

Gideon pours himself a drink. He takes a few noisy slurps.

---

101 pilchard ['pɪltʃəd] *Sardine* **101** rigor mortis [ˌrɪgə 'mɔːtɪs] *Totenstarre* **106** estate [ɪ'steɪt] *Wohnsiedlung* **115** (to) get a degree in sth. [dɪ'griː] *etwas studieren* **115** nosy ['nəʊzi] *(infml) neugierig* **135** kingdom ['kɪŋdəm] *Königreich* **143** electric [ɪ'lektrɪk] *(infml) = electricity* **150** damp [dæmp] *feucht* **163** ain't [eɪnt] *(infml) = haven't, isn't* **166** flask [flɑːsk] *Thermosflasche* **171** (to) tempt [tempt] *in Versuchung führen* **174** (to) pour [pɔː] *eingießen*

Kirsty glances at him, irritated.
Slight pause.
Gideon takes a sandwich, wrapped in silver foil, from his duffel bag.

180	Gideon	Something to eat?
	Kirsty	I dread to ask. What is it?
	Gideon	Tofu and pine nut sandwich.
	Kirsty	Bloody hell! Ain't you got anything as basic as crisps and a Coke?
185	Gideon	Not on me, no.
	Kirsty	I'm not hungry.

Gideon takes a bite from the sandwich. He eats as noisily as he drinks.
Kirsty's irritation increases. Until –

190	Kirsty	Must you?
	Gideon	What?
	Kirsty	Eat ... like that!
	Gideon	Like what?

Slight pause.

195   I'll save the rest for later.
Puts sandwich and flask back in duffel bag.
Pause.

           Snow makes everything look beautiful.

200	Kirsty	Take more than snow to make this dump of an estate beautiful.
	Gideon	You're wrong ... Snow falling in the night sky. Like ... like twinkling bits of ... starlight. There! How's that?
205		And as it falls it changes colour. The street lights, you see – They turn the snow orange and yellow. Like burning feathers. Yes! It settles. The grey concrete – it's gone.
210		Piles of rubbish – gone. In their place? A twinkling wonderland. When you walk – crunch, crunch, crunch. Apart from that – silence.

Slight pause.

215   Your eyes look a bit bloodshot.

	Kirsty	... It's the cold. Makes my eyes water.
	Gideon	Wanna handkerchief?

Takes handkerchief from pocket.

	Kirsty	Ugh! No! I've got a clean one thank
220		you.

Rummages in her bag. Unable to find a handkerchief, she uses a T-shirt.

Slight pause.

	Gideon	You going to the launderette?
	Kirsty	Launder–? Oh, no.	225

Slight pause.

	Gideon	*indicating her coat* Hope that's not real fur.
	Kirsty	This? Baby seal. Culled it myself – Of course it's not real fur! What do you think of me?	230

Slight pause.

	Gideon	I'll light the candles. That'll warm things up. Mind over matter and all that.	235

Starts to light candles.

	Kirsty	I've never seen so many.
	Gideon	Every time I come I bring a few more. Some are amazing. Look at this one. Got gold bits in it.	240
	Kirsty	... Why?
	Gideon	Makes it look nice.
	Kirsty	Don't see the point. Candle's a candle. All that's important is the flame.	245

Slight pause.

           What's that smell?

	Gideon	Some of them are aromatic.
	Kirsty	Harry – what?
	Gideon	Smell of roses.	250

Holds candle out for Kirsty to smell.

	Kirsty	Gold! Roses! They'll be tap-dancing and cooking you pizza next.
	Gideon	You've got bits in your hair.
	Kirsty	... What?	255
	Gideon	Sparkling bits.
	Kirsty	Oh, that's hair gel. It's special. Got glitter in it. What did you think it was? Metallic dandruff?
	Gideon	No, I didn't think that.	260

Slight pause.

	Kirsty	Well, I dread to think what's in your hair. When was the last time you washed it?
	Gideon	Hair don't need washing. It cleans itself. The body's natural oils keep it healthy. Have a feel.	265
	Kirsty	You keep your natural oils to yourself.

---

176 irritated [ˈɪrɪteɪtɪd] *gereizt* **181** (to) dread [dred] *fürchten, nicht wagen* **201** dump [dʌmp] *(infml) Kaff, Dreckloch* **224** launderette [lɔːnˈdret] *Waschsalon* **227** (to) indicate [ˈɪndɪkeɪt] *deuten auf* **229** seal [siːl] *Robbe* **229** (to) cull [kʌl] *erlegen* **259** dandruff [ˈdændrʌf] *(Kopf-)Schuppen*

Part A B C **D** **4** **101**

270	*Gideon*	Don't you like the style?
	Kirsty	Oh, it's a *style*, is it?
	Gideon	Dreadlocks – well, almost, sort of.
	Kirsty	Dirty rat's tails – well, totally, definitely.
275	*Slight pause.*	
	Gideon	My name's Gideon.
	Kirsty	I know.
	Gideon	How?
	Kirsty	I ... Oh, don't start all that again. As
280		I said, small estate. New face, 'Who's that?' 'Oh, that's the new caretaker's son. His name's Gideon.' All there is to it.
	Pause.	
285	*Gideon*	The caretaker's not my Dad.
	Kirsty	What?
	Gideon	My real Dad left me and Mum years ago. I was a baby. Never seen him
290		since. Or heard from him. Can't remember what he looks like or anything. Mum had a photograph once – but she burnt it. Don't blame her. I'd have done the same if someone said, 'I love you', one day,
295		then packed their bags and cleared off the next, without so much as a 'take care of yourself'. So it was just me and Mum. Until she met this bloke. A few months ago. Love at first
300		sight or some such thing. Mum just looked at him and ... pow! She sort of ... changed. You know? Like before ... we agreed on everything, me and Mum. We'd giggle and stuff. Now
305		she giggles with him and ... Don't mind! Me! Not a bit. Anyway! Where was I ...? Yes! That's it! This bloke was just about to start a new job. Caretaker. Here. So ... well, blah,
310		blah, blah as you'd say.
	Pause.	
	Kirsty takes unlit candle from table and approaches Gideon.	
	Kirsty	Let me help.
315	*Gideon*	Sorry?
	Kirsty	The candles.

Gideon lights Kirsty's candle.
She starts lighting other candles.
Slight pause.

Kirsty	Where were you living before? When it was just you and your Mum?	320
Gideon	Oh, lots of places. Lived next to a warehouse once. Every Saturday night they'd have a rave. Ever been to one?	325
Kirsty	... No.	
Gideon	Music's so loud. Deafening. Used to make my bed shake. Real poltergeist stuff. Amazing.	
Kirsty	Didn't you complain?	330
Gideon	Why? Only people dancing.	
Kirsty	Must have kept you awake, though.	
Gideon	Sleep through anything, me. You like dancing?	

Takes small ghetto blaster from duffel bag. 335

	Got some amazing music here!	
Kirsty	I'm not into music.	
Gideon	How can you not be into music? It's like saying, 'I'm not into picking my nose.'	340
Kirsty	Well, I'm not into picking my nose either.	
Gideon	No, but you do it. Being into it or not's got nothing to do with it. You just do it. Same with music.	345
Kirsty	Music and snot. Why have I never seen the connection before?	

Slight pause.

Gideon	Last place we lived was under a flyover. Nothing but traffic all night. I slept through a car crash once. Police, sirens, ambulance, everything.	350
Kirsty	How come?	
Gideon	Told you, sleep through anything, me.	355
Kirsty	No – How come you were living under a flyover?	
Gideon	Oh, we were in a caravan. Staying with some friends of Mum's.	360
Kirsty	Gypsies?	
Gideon	Not really. Just ... well, just travellers, I guess. Gave me and Mum a caravan

---

273 tail [teɪl] *Schwanz*   **295** (to) clear off [ˌklɪərˈɒf] *(infml) abhauen*   **304** (to) giggle [ɡɪɡl] *kichern*   **323** warehouse [ˈweəhaʊs] *Lagerhaus*
346 snot [snɒt] *(infml) Rotz*   **350** flyover [ˈflaɪəʊvə] *Straßenüberführung*   **361** Gypsies *(pl)* [ˈdʒɪpsi] *Roma/Sinti*

365		to ourselves. They let me paint it. I put shooting stars and comets and rainbows all over. Looked amazing. At night we'd sit round a little campfire. Mum'd tell stories. She tells the most amazing things my
370		Mum. I loved that place. It was right by the canal too. I love the sound of running water, don't you?
	Kirsty	We've got a leaking toilet at the moment so the charm's lost on me.
375	Gideon	I remember one night. Lying in Mum's arms. By the campfire. Everything a flickering gold. And … oh, as I lay there, the sound of the
380		traffic seemed to change. Wasn't traffic anymore. It was tropical insects. Jungle sounds. And I imagined the concrete pillars of the flyover were gigantic tree trunks.
385		And the canal was a vast river. Like the Nile or something. Full of crocodiles and hippos. And I imagined all the exotic birds asleep
390		in the undergrowth. Flamingoes, cockatoos, parrots. And the insects. Beautiful, glittering things. Butterflies, with wings all colours of the rainbow. And then … then I actually felt something gently touch my fingertips. Guess what it was?
395	Kirsty	… A butterfly?
	Gideon	A rat!
	Kirsty	No!
	Gideon	The biggest, ugliest, slimiest rat
400		you'd ever seen. Big, pink tail. Yellow teeth. It'd crawled out of the canal and was nibbling at my thumbnail.
	Kirsty	Hope you killed it.
	Gideon	Why? Wasn't hurting anyone.
		Slight pause.
405	Kirsty	Bet your Mum was glad to get out of that caravan and come here.
	Gideon	She was in love. She'd have gone anywhere and been happy.
	Kirsty	But … how did you feel?

Gideon	Oh, live anywhere, me. Warehouse, council flat –	410
Kirsty	No – Your Mum being with this new bloke. Didn't it bother you at all?	
Gideon	I'm glad Mum's happy.	
Kirsty	That's not what I asked.	415
	Slight pause.	
Gideon	Turn your torch off.	
Kirsty	What? Oh, yes.	
	They both turn their torches off. All the candles are lit now.	420
Gideon	Magic or what?	
	Kirsty and Gideon look at the candlelit space.	
Kirsty	It does feel a bit warmer.	
Gideon	Sweltering, me.	
	He removes jumper to reveal a skimpy T-shirt underneath. Kirsty looks at him.	425
	Slight pause.	
	What's wrong?	
Kirsty	Oh – there's a hole in your shirt.	
Gideon	One in my jeans too.	430
	Bends over to reveal hole near his backside.	
	Good for ventilation. When I fart it –	
Kirsty	That's quite enough, thank you.	
	Gideon takes some painting materials over to mirror on floor and starts mixing paint.	435
Kirsty	You haven't spoken to many girls, have you?	
Gideon	What?	
Kirsty	Girls!	
Gideon	Girls! Oh … Sure! Zillions of times!	440
	Pause.	
Kirsty	What you doing?	
Gideon	Mixing paint.	
Kirsty	No! Here! All this!	
	Slight pause.	445
Gideon	A few weeks ago, when I first got here, I thought the whole estate was … well, amazing. Honestly. And Mum's boyfriend – he had the keys to everything! One key … one key let	450
	me into vast underground chambers. Where boilers vibrated and buzzed. Like … sleeping giants. Yes! That's it! Another key took me to the highest roof I'd ever been on. The view goes	455
	on for miles. At night the city lights	

---

373 leaking [liːkɪŋ] *undicht sein*   **382** pillar [ˈpɪlə] *Pfeiler*   **411** council flat [ˈkaʊnsl flæt] *Sozialwohnung*   **424** (to) swelter [ˈsweltə] *(vor Hitze) verschmachten*   **425** skimpy [ˈskɪmpi] *knapp*   **431** backside [ˈbæksaɪd] *Hintern*   **432** (to) fart [fɑːt] *furzen*   **451** chamber [ˈtʃeɪmbə] *Kammer, Raum*

up like a ... a billion flickering candles. All different colours. Another key –

460 *Kirsty* Let you in here.

Slight pause.

Gideon It felt so ... so safe and comfortable. You know! Warm with all the people who'd used this place. To drink tea
465 and gossip. Bingo.Disco.

Kirsty ... You felt that?

Slight pause.

Gideon So I asked Mum's boyfriend if I could have the only key – the only *other* key.

470 *Kirsty* And you started to come here?

Gideon Every evening.

Kirsty Eight o'clock.

Gideon On the dot. Not that you've been spying, of course.

475 *Slight pause.*

Kirsty And you're ... painting this – what?

Pause.

Gideon Just think of this: all this rubbish taken out. Windows mended. Walls
480 given a lick of paint. Something bright and cheerful. Floor, swept and polished. Perhaps a carpet. Above, lights – oh, yeah, the electric's back on. And up here, on the stage – we're
485 doing a play or something. And out there ...

Indicates audience.

The audience! I can imagine them. Their faces. See them almost. Can
490 you?

Kirsty ... No.

Gideon You're not trying hard enough.

Kirsty looks out into the audience with Gideon.

They're out there!

495 *Pause.*

Hear them?

Kirsty ... No.

Gideon Concentrate.

Kirsty I am. And I can't.

500 *Gideon* I'm sure if you try –

Kirsty Don't push it!

Slight pause.

Gideon What ... what was I saying? The audience. One day they'll ... they'll be out there for real. A theatre. That's it. 505 Amazing, eh?

Pause.

Kirsty You're bonkers.

Gideon I ... I believe if you ... if you show people something interesting then 510 they'll take an interest.

Kirsty Who said that? Your Mum?

Gideon What if she did?

Kirsty Listen. If you show people round here something interesting, they'll 515 steal it. That's if it was interesting in the first place. Which all this, believe me, ain't.

Gideon But ... but people ... people –

Kirsty You don't know the first thing about 520 people. You know what people want? What they *really* want? TV. Betting shop. Flash car. Pub. Video and takeaway curry on Saturday night –

Gideon But ... but I want to give them 525 something else too.

Kirsty What? A bunch of poncey actors.

Gideon No, no. We can do our own stuff. Write it, act it. Me, you, my Mum, your Dad – 530

Kirsty My Dad! Ha!

Gideon Please don't 'Ha!'. Please.

Slight pause.

Let me ... try to explain.

Slight pause. 535

Kirsty It's all yours.

Pause.

Well?

Gideon I'm trying to remember – Yes! Got it.

Slight pause. 540

Imagine this: you're a member of a tribe in the middle of a jungle –

Kirsty I'm what?

Gideon Give me a chance.

Slight pause. 545

You're a member of a tribe in the middle of a jungle. The date – it has no meaning for you. Why? Because things have remained the same for

---

473 on the dot [dɒt] *genau*   **479** (to) mend [mend] *reparieren*   **481** cheerful ['tʃɪəfl] *heiter, fröhlich*   **482** (to) polish ['pɒlɪʃ] *polieren*   **482** carpet ['kɑːpɪt] *Teppich*   **508** bonkers ['bɒŋkəz] *(infml) verrückt*   **523** flash [flæʃ] *protzig*   **527** poncey ['pɒnsi] *affektiert*

550 millenniums. Since the beginning of time. And for you – for you in particular – all your life has been the same. You live with your Dad. In that mud hut over there. See it? Since

555 your Mum died you look after your Dad. You fetch water from the nearby spring. You fish in the river. Your Dad's everything. See the hut yet?

Kirsty ... Yes.

560 **Gideon** And then ... a scream! Out in the jungle.

Kirsty What is it?

Gideon Someone's been killed.

Kirsty Who?

565 **Gideon** A member of the tribe.

Kirsty How?

Gideon There's a monster in the jungle. Some hideous thing. Claws. Teeth.

Kirsty Perhaps a Giant Rat, eh?

570 **Gideon** Very likely. And this Giant Rat is knocking off members of your tribe one by one. At night you tremble in fear as the Giant Rat howls and roars. What d'you think we should do?

575 **Kirsty** We've got to kill it.

Gideon You and the rest of your tribe get together. You arm yourself with sharpened lengths of bamboo –

Kirsty Is that all?

580 **Gideon** 'Fraid so. You scared?

Kirsty A little.

Gideon But you've got to go.

Kirsty Don't know if I can.

Gideon Aha! So that night the Witchdoctor

585 sits the tribe round a fire. The Witchdoctor gives everyone a ... a relaxing drink made from the pusy boils of giant frogs.

Hands her imaginary drink.

590 Have a sip.

Kirsty The pusy boils of giant frogs?

Gideon And a few worms.

Slowly, Kirsty drinks.

And as the pus 'n' worm mixture

595 takes effect, the Witchdoctor says, 'You're a member of a tribe in the

middle of a jungle. Your tribe is being threatened by the terrible Giant Rat. It must be killed. I know you are afraid. But you must face this fear ...'

600

Slight pause.

The next morning you sharpen your bamboo and go out into the jungle. In the distance you can hear the Giant Rat's massive pink tail slither

605 through the undergrowth. You say, 'In my dreams I have already faced the Giant Rat. I am not afraid.'

Pause.

Kirsty ... And?

610

Gideon There is no 'and'.

Kirsty You mean ... that's it?

Gideon Yes.

Kirsty And you think that explains something?

615

Gideon ... Doesn't it?

Kirsty You've been reading too many books.

Gideon It's supposed to explain ... supposed to ...

Kirsty Listen, I don't know what orbit you're

620 in, but tell me when the shuttle lands and we might actually have a conversation –

Gideon You listen! You live on an estate. An estate full of cracked concrete.

625 Graffiti. Ruined community centres. You know the date very well. It's one of millions of facts that fill your mind. You get these facts from computers. Television. Newspapers.

630 Faxes. Internet. You do not believe in Giant Rats. And yet – you're afraid. You don't know why. But something scares you. Oh, it doesn't have sharp teeth or claws or a gigantic, pink tail.

635 But still you're so, so afraid. The fear makes you feel so alone. Makes you cry. Makes you want to run away.

---

568 hideous ['hɪdɪəs] *grauenhaft*   **577** (to) arm [ɑːm] *bewaffnen*   **578** length [leŋθ] *Stück*   **587** pusy ['pʌsɪ] *eitrig*   **588** boil [bɔɪl] *Furunkel*
598 (to) threaten ['θretn] *bedrohen*   **605** massive ['mæsɪv] *riesig*   **634** (to) scare [skeə] *erschrecken*

Part A B C **D**   **4**   105

Working with the text

1   What's it all about?
a) 👥👥👥 *Compare the play and what happens in it with the ideas you talked about on page 97.*

b) *Write a short summary of the play for a flyer advertising a production of it. Try to make it sound interesting for the reader, but don't give too much of the story away.*

2   Reading the play
a) *Read all the stage directions on page 98 again. As you're reading, stop every now and again, close your eyes, and try to imagine how it would look on stage.*

b) 👥 *Read through lines 167–196 (pages 99–100) together. Then discuss how this should look on stage. Where are the two characters standing, sitting (close together, far apart, …)?*
What movements, actions do they make, when? How do they look at each other? What tone of voice do they use in their speeches?
Now read through the same lines again, as if you are on stage yourselves.

c) *Sum up in a sentence for each character what the stage directions tell you about Kirsty (lines 34–43) and Gideon (lines 63–70).*

d) *What do lines 75–95 reveal about Kirsty's character? Choose adjectives that describe her:*
aggressive • funny • hard • kind • lonely • panicky • suspicious • worried • …

e) *What do lines 198–213 reveal about Gideon's character? Choose an adjective to describe him:*
crazy • gentle • imaginative • kind • poetic • silly • unrealistic • weird

---

STUDY SKILLS   Reading drama

A play cannot be read in the same way as a novel or short story. Why is that?
– Plays are written mainly to be **performed**, not read.
– Most plays are written from the **points of view of various characters**. (Plays for one character are rather rare.)
– Plays consist of a series of speeches and stage directions. When reading a play you try to **imagine it on stage**, with the characters' expressions, gestures, movements, actions, tone of voice, etc.
– **Dramatic dialogue** may sound like real-life dialogue but is very different. It cuts out unnecessary talking and is used to reveal character or motives, give crucial information, build suspense, highlight important moments, create a dramatic climax and move the action forward.

▶ *SF Reading literature (pp. 141–143)*

---

f) Extra 👥 *Look for other pieces of dialogue that reveal aspects of the characters of Kirsty and Gideon's character. Explain to your partner what they reveal.*

3   👥 Performing
Choose an extract of between 50 and 100 lines from the play. Work out together how you would perform it. Experiment with intonation, gestures, movement and expressions. Learn your lines. Rehearse the extract. Then act it out for the class or film it.

4   Extra   What next?
Imagine how the play could continue.
How will Kirsty react to Gideon's last speech? Is she running away from anything? What problems does Gideon have? How could they play a role? Will any other characters appear?
Write the next part of the play.

▶ *WB 4 (p. 43)*

B Partner B

Unit 1 Part D

P1 MEDIATION Out in a boat (Oral mediation)

c) Help! How do I say that?
If you can't think of the right words when mediating into English, try paraphrasing.

Partner B: Listen to your partner paraphrasing some words. Do you know what they mean? You probably do not know the English words for the items in the pictures. Paraphrase them for your partner. Do they understand what you mean?

Unit 3 Part B

P3 WORDS Saying numbers

a) Partner B: Listen to your partner and write down the numbers. Did you get them right? Did your partner say them right? Discuss any problems. Then read the following numbers, dates, etc. to your partner and do the same.

3.8m	65%	1960s
1,498	44.75	$9 + 19 = 28$
1492 AD	155,711	$5 \times 5 = 25$
754 BC	1/4	$108 \div 12 = 9$
17/06/1954	3/4	$5^2 = 25$
Mar 06, 1888	68° F	$\sqrt{16} = 4$
32nd	100 mph	

Getting ready for a test 1   Key to the practice tests
▶ pp. 44–51

1 READING Mosquito box   ▶ p. 46
1 (very) high, (extremely) irritating, only heard by young people (16–18 kHz)
2 43–61 m
3 In 2006
4 a) improves safety around shops / stops teenagers from annoying customers
   b) lowers vandalism / reduces crime (in public areas)
5 It discriminates against young people / creates a (dangerous and widening) divide between generations (young and old people).
6 The UK Youth Parliament
7 make the Mosquito Box illegal / ban it

2 READING Events   ▶ p. 47
1 D; 2 E; 3 A; 4 C;

3 READING Sunderland   ▶ p. 48
1 false; 2 not given; 3 true; 4 false; 5 not given;
6 true; 7 not given; 8 true; 9 true; 10 false; 11 true

Getting ready for a test 2   Key to the practice tests
▶ pp. 68–73

1 LISTENING What can we do this weekend?
▶ p. 71

1 It's boring / read poems in school / been to ballet in Manchester (*Swan Lake*) / needs something more modern
2 not interested in computers
3 wants to do something together
4 doesn't like dancing / has often seen the film
5 do something on her own / stay at home (watch TV, read her new comic) alone / without Tina

2 LISTENING Living together   ▶ p. 71
1 mixed relationships / relationships (couples) with different religious background
2 tolerant/easy-going
3 going to church every week / telling the priest (Father O'Neill) what he's done wrong / confessing (to the priest)
4 not happy/not pleased/ … (Adjektive mit ähnlicher Bedeutung)
5 unhappy/terrible/sad/ … (Adjektive mit ähnlicher Bedeutung)
6 on holiday (in Ireland)
7 same language / both speak English / cheap flights / know something about their countries / neighbouring countries

3 LISTENING Radio adverts   ▶ p. 72
1 A / B (C); 2 C / C; 3 A / B

Text File

TF 1–7			Inhalt	Seite	
Unit 1	TF	1	Amal's decision	108–110	
Unit 2	TF	2	Checks and balances	111	
Unit 2	TF	3	The monarchy and Parliament	112–113	
Unit 2	TF	4	*Bilingual module – Social Studies* **Europe united**	114–117	
Unit 3	TF	5	Into space	118–119	
Unit 3	TF	6	Electric wind	120–122	
Unit 3	TF	7	*Bilingual module – Geography* **Global warming – how does it affect us?**	123–124	

TF 1 Amal's decision (abridged from *Does my head look big in this?* by Randa Abdel-Fattah)

What kinds of decisions have you made in your life? Were they easy or difficult?

Form groups of four to read the following text. Each member of the group will get a card from your teacher. Read the first part (ll. 1–35) and do the tasks on your card. Share your findings with the group. Then pass your card to another member of your group and work on the next part of the text (ll. 36–67). Share your findings again. Do the same for the final two parts (ll. 68–139 and l. 140 to end).

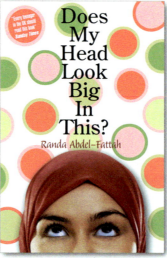

1 I'm lying in bed trying to figure out if I'm really ready to go ahead with my decision as I watch a guy on television try to persuade me that for forty-nine dollars and ninety-nine cents I can buy a can opener that will also slice a watermelon and probably pluck my eyebrows. I can't sleep from stressing about whether I've got the guts to do it. To wear the hijab, the head scarf, full-time.

I'm an Australian-Muslim-Palestinian. That means I was born an Aussie and whacked with some bloody confusing identity hyphens. I'm in Year Eleven and in four days' time I'll be entering my first day of term three at McCleans.

I'm terrified. But at the same time I feel like my passion and conviction in Islam are bursting inside me and I want to prove to myself that I'm strong enough to wear a badge of my faith. God says that men and women should act and dress modestly. The way I see it, I'd rather follow God's fashion dictates than some ugly solarium-tanned old fart in Milan who's getting by on a pretty self-serving theory of less is more when it comes to female dress.

What will Adam say?
Adam? Who gives a crap about Adam?
Not me. Uh-uh. Nope.
He'll probably laugh.
Hey, that's not fair. He's not like that.

2 I end up entering English with everybody already comfortably seated. I close the door behind me and am confronted by an instantly silent classroom, lines of faces staring up at me from their desks.

As I walk past the desks my eyes meet Adam's and he looks taken aback. He wriggles in his seat and is suddenly fascinated by the corner of his desk. I feel like somebody has got a stapler and started punching holes all over my guts. Then at approximately 11.45 a.m. on Friday, 24 May, we're in Chemistry and Adam's passing me a bunsen burner when I suddenly notice his sleeves are pulled up and I get a glimpse of his forearms. I'm telling you, I'm usually a 1) smile, 2) eyes, 3) skin, and 4) six-pack kind of girl. But the sight of Adam's forearms, with his veins bulging against his muscles and his shirt sleeves begging for oxygen just about made me dizzy. I started to notice his eyes – a deep navy-blue. OK there's a bit of dot-to-dot acne, but his imperfections are what kept me up all that Friday and Saturday night as I fantasized about cuddling up to his forearms, stroking his hair and listening to him tell me I'm the most beautiful girl in the world.

3 Simone, Eileen and I walk through the crowd. There are lots of people we don't recognize hanging around, huddled together, dancing, laughing, gossiping and drinking.

We end up sitting on the edge of the pergola studying the crowd and wondering why we bothered to come. Simone is on her fifth cigarette and is telling me how difficult it is to suck her stomach in as she inhales and

---

12 guts *(infml)* Mut   14 head scarf [skɑːf] *Kopftuch*   17 (to) whack [wæk] *(infml) hauen*   18 hyphen [ˈhaɪfn] *Bindestrich*   26 modestly [ˈmɒdɪstli] *sittsam*   28 old fart [fɑːt] *(infml, rude) „alter Sack"*   32 (to) not give a crap *(infml, rude) sich einen Dreck scheren*   44 taken aback [əˈbæk] *verblüfft*

Eileen's gone to the bathroom to fix her hair. I'm watching everybody, fascinated by the effect of alcohol on people. There's a girl who, when she arrived, had been looking at the floor as she walked, tugging her top down and avoiding eye contact. She's on a chair now doing a cheerleader routine. A guy who walked in with a scowl on his face is now clowning around in an attempted solo Zorba dance.

Simone suddenly motions at us to look towards the pool area. "Check it out!" She points to a circle of people cheering on Tia, as she stands on a table and slips her top off, throwing it into the crowd. She only has her bra on and is laughing and trying to keep her balance as she dances, winking at people in the crowd and blowing them kisses.

Adam appears before us. We smile sheepishly at him and I try to regain my composure, smoothing out my clothes and hijab.

"Can I speak to you alone?" he asks me and I stare back at him in surprise.

"Yeah, OK." I jump off the edge and walk with him through the crowd and inside, where the music is pumping loudly and people are dancing in a frenzy. I squash myself through a couple when a guy comes up to me and puts his arms around my shoulders, and I nearly choke on his breath.

"Scarf girl!" he shouts happily. "Helloooo scarf girl! Tell me, do you have hair? Take off your scarf and belly dance for us!" He laughs in my face and I want to gag, wondering why they don't make it compulsory to serve cool mints with alcohol. "Hey," he whispers in my ear, "the story goes that Adam's planning on getting you in the sack! Woo hoo! Who said you Middle Eastern girls don't have fun?"

My face crumbles into shock and I quickly walk away. I reach Adam and he grabs my hand, leading me away from the crowd and through the house to another courtyard.

I feel almost panicky, wondering whether I've just heard a drunken joke or if it's true.

I sit on a chair, not knowing if I should stay or go. Adam sits on a table, smiling at me.

"I've been looking all over for you."

"Have you?"

"Yep. So? Are you having fun?"

"Me? Yeah, yeah ... sure I am. Cool party." I crack my knuckles nervously.

"So ..." My head is going to burst through my scarf and explode into a shattered pulp on the floor. He doesn't say anything, just dangles his legs and stares at me with an intensity that makes me feel giddy. I look away, down at my hands, up again at his face, and then down again. I don't want things to change. I want things to stay as perfect as they are between us. I want to forget about what that guy just told me and for Adam to stop leaning towards me.

4   His face is inches from mine and as he moves in to kiss me I jolt back.

"I ... I ..."

"What's wrong? I thought you liked me – I thought –"

"Adam, I ... I don't do that stuff ..."

"What stuff?"

"Kissing – I mean dating – I mean, you know, physical –"

"Why not?"

"Because ..." I can feel my face blushing, "well, sex before marriage is uh-uh."

"Who said we were going to have sex, anyway?"

My face is now unbelievably cooked with embarrassment and I fidget uncomfortably in my seat.

"I did hear a rumour, though."

"You can't be serious."

"I heard ... you know, that you wanted to ..."

"What? Do it with you? Shit, Amal, how bloody naive are you?!" He runs his fingers through his hair and shakes his head. "If I was going to sleep with you, don't you think you'd have something to say about it? Look, Amal, just because I want to kiss you doesn't mean I'm running a Durex account at the local chemist."

---

83 routine *Nummer (bei einer Vorstellung)*   **84** scowl [skaʊl] *missmutiger Gesichtsausdruck*   **91** bra [brɑː] *BH*   **92** (to) wink *zwinkern*
103 in a frenzy ['frenzi] *wild, unbändig*   **110** (to) gag *(infml) an etwas würgen*   **111** compulsory [kəm'pʌlsəri] *verpflichtend*
133 giddy *schwindelig*   **141** (to) jolt back *zurückzucken*   **155** (to) fidget ['fɪdʒɪt] *zappeln*

"I should hope not," I say lightly, making an effort to smile at him.

"So you don't date then?"

"Er ... no."

"I don't get it ... that means you can never live for the moment. You'll always be repressing yourself."

I shake my head. "I don't see it like that."

"So if you meet a guy and you like him and he likes you ... what happens? You just ignore your feelings?"

"No. But I'm not ... look, I don't believe in the 'playing the field' and 'try before you buy' philosophies, OK? I don't want physical intimacy with a list of people in my life."

"Hey, whatever you believe in is up to you. I thought we had something more than *friendship*. But I guess we are different. *Too different*." He lets out a bitter laugh.

I feel like I'm about to suffocate on the tension and I run out of the courtyard and through the house. Tia bumps into me on my way out and stands in front of me, bursting into laughter as she looks me up and down.

"Piece of friendly advice: you should take that thing off before you do the dirty with him. It might get in his way."

I push her. She sprawls back on to the floor, her glass smashing next to her.

"You bitch!" she cries. "You could have cut me. How dare you! Why don't you just get out of our country and go back to some desert cave where you belong?"

I stand over her, my heart drumming in my chest. "This is *my* country and if you ever forget it again I'm going to rip your head off!" I turn away and plough through the crowd to find Eileen and Simone.

1 The characters

a) Make a list of all the characters, then think of adjectives to describe them. Rate them from 1 to 5, depending how much (5) or how little (1) they impress you. Justify your grading.

b) 👥 *Find out what Amal's feelings are on the following topics: fashion, boys, parties, alcohol, sex and head scarves. Illustrate how close or far away her feelings are from yours: draw a circle on paper to represent yourself and arrange the topics according to the distance between you and Amal. Compare illustrations with a partner.*

c) 👥 *Everyone prepares questions for Adam and Amal about what they said and did at the party. The class divides into two groups. In one group a boy plays Adam, and in the other a girl plays Amal. After Adam and Amal have answered questions in their groups, they change places and answer questions from the other group.*
With these answers in mind, write a letter of support to either Amal or Adam.

d) Explain Amal's reaction to the comments she gets from a boy and a girl at the party (ll. 103–117, 189–203).

2 Over to you

a) At one point Amal talks about "passion and conviction" (l. 22). Do you know of any examples of people acting out of passion and conviction?

b) Do your decisions about how you dress affect others? If so, in what way?

187 (to) suffocate [ˈsʌfəkeɪt] *ersticken*

Text File

TF 2 Checks and balances[1]

1 What do you know?
Say what you already know about politics in the USA. Can you name any US Presidents, past and present? What is the Constitution?

2 LISTENING
The US system of government

a) Look at the chart and listen.

b) Then try to complete a copy of the chart with the information you have heard. Listen again and add any missing information.

c) Compare your chart with that of a partner. Then ask each other questions to see if you have understood everything.

d) Do some research on the President and members of Congress. How are they elected and for how long? Add the information to your chart.

3 A government puzzle
Make five statements about the US system of government and write them down. For each statement you will need three of these pieces.

- are there for life
- The nine judges
- the basic law
- is to pass laws for the whole country
- that the President has
- The most important job
- that Congress has
- who sit on the Supreme Court
- The veto is
- The Supreme Court is
- that all other laws have to agree with
- the branch of government
- that interprets the laws
- a power
- The Constitution is

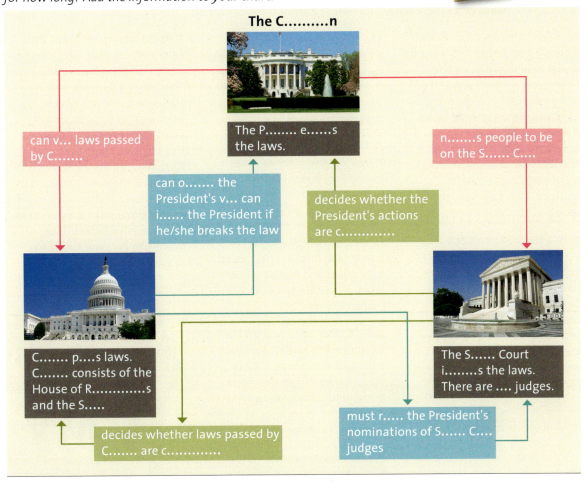

The C..........n

The P........ e......s the laws.

can v... laws passed by C.......

n.......s people to be on the S...... C....

can o....... the President's v... can i...... the President if he/she breaks the law

decides whether the President's actions are c.............

C....... p....s laws. C....... consists of the House of R.............s and the S.....

The S...... Court i........s the laws. There are .... judges.

decides whether laws passed by C....... are c............

must r..... the President's nominations of S...... C.... judges

---

[1] checks and balances [ˈbælənsɪz] gegenseitige Kontrolle (checks) und Machtgleichgewicht (balances) der Regierungsgewalten

2 Text File

TF 3 The monarchy and Parliament

1 The royal family

a) What do you know about the Queen and other members of the royal family? Why are people so interested in them?

b) Do you think the following statements are true or false? Check your answers when you have finished 3 on the next page.

The British monarch ...
... chooses the Prime Minister.
... writes a speech telling the government what to do.
... is head of the Church of England.
... is elected by Members of Parliament.

The Queen opening Parliament

2 From absolute monarchy to parliamentary democracy

a) Read the six texts A–F carefully and work out what the correct order is. Then you can complete the texts with these dates: 1215 • 1534 • 1649 • 1689 • 1832 • 1918 • 1969.

b) Match these six titles to the texts: More men get the vote • An early Parliament • A new kind of monarchy • Death of a king • Britain no longer Catholic • Votes for all

A William and Mary arrived with an army, and James fled[1]. In ▮, a year after this 'Glorious[2] Revolution', William and Mary signed the Bill[3] of Rights. This guaranteed Parliament's rights. Britain had become a constitutional monarchy. The Bill of Rights also said that a Catholic could never be monarch, and this is still the law today.

B Two hundred years ago only rich men (and no women) could vote. Several reform bills went through Parliament (the first, called the Reform Act[4], in ▮) and gave democratic rights to more and more people. But by the end of the 19th century women still did not have the vote.

C Up to the early 13th century, people had few rights. However, in ▮ a group of barons made King John sign the Magna Carta. The King agreed to consult[5] a council of barons before taking certain decisions. This council became a place for talking (French: parler) and discussing laws: a parliament.

D Three centuries later, King Henry VIII (the man who was married six times) wanted a divorce[6] from his first wife. The Pope[7] said no. So in ▮ King Henry broke with the Church of Rome and, with Parliament's agreement, founded the Church of England and made himself its head, a position still held by the monarch today.

E It was thanks to women like Emmeline Pankhurst and the suffragette[8] movement that women over 30 got the vote in ▮, and full voting equality followed ten years later. In ▮ the voting age was reduced to what it is today – 18.

F About a hundred years after Henry VIII, another king, Charles I, tried to rule without Parliament. This led to a civil war, which Parliament won. Charles was executed[9] in ▮, and for a few years England was a republic. But 40 years later the Catholic King James II again tried to rule without Parliament. So some of its members secretly invited James's daughter Mary and her Protestant husband William of Orange to become King and Queen.

Emmeline Pankhurst being arrested outside Buckingham Palace

[1] (to) flee – fled – fled *fliehen*   [2] glorious ['glɔːriəs] *ruhmreich*   [3] bill *Gesetzentwurf*   [4] act *Gesetz*   [5] (to) consult [kən'sʌlt] *zurate ziehen*
[6] divorce *Scheidung*   [7] Pope *Papst*   [8] suffragette [ˌsʌfrə'dʒet] *Kämpferin für das Frauenrecht*   [9] (to) execute *hinrichten*

3 Britain's political system today

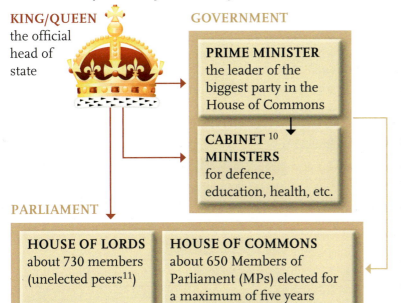

KING/QUEEN the official head of state

GOVERNMENT

PRIME MINISTER the leader of the biggest party in the House of Commons

CABINET[10] **MINISTERS** for defence, education, health, etc.

PARLIAMENT

HOUSE OF LORDS about 730 members (unelected peers[11])

HOUSE OF COMMONS about 650 Members of Parliament (MPs) elected for a maximum of five years

EUROPEAN PARLIAMENT Members of the European Parliament (MEPs) elected for five years

OTHER PARLIAMENTS OR ASSEMBLIES the Scottish Parliament, the Welsh Assembly and the Northern Ireland Assembly

VOTERS Every Briton over 18 may vote in a general election (for the House of Commons), in the European elections, for other Parliaments or assemblies (in certain areas) and in local elections.

→ elects   → chooses   → officially appoints[12]   → can usually control

a) Study the diagram and decide who or what statements 1–8 below refer to.
1 He/She is the most powerful British politician and has the same sort of job as the German *Bundeskanzler/in*.
2 He/She has no real power. The speech he/she gives at the opening of Parliament is written by the government.
3 Its role is to make the laws.
4 It can delay bills and suggest amendments, but it has little power.
5 It helps to make European laws.
6 They make important decisions. Each is head of a government department.
7 Almost all of them belong to a party such as Labour, the Conservatives or the Liberal Democrats.
8 They were created to give more independence to parts of the United Kingdom other than England.

b) Choose one of these three group tasks:
1 Compare the history of voting rights in Britain and Germany. Make a chart with two columns: one for Britain, one for Germany.
2 Prepare a presentation on Emmeline Pankhurst and the suffragettes. Use information from history books, the internet, etc.
3 How do you think the British system could be made more democratic? Exchange your ideas and then write one or two paragraphs for a political leaflet suggesting a programme of changes.

---
[10] cabinet [ˈkæbɪnət] *Kabinett*   [11] peer [pɪə] *Adlige(r)*   [12] (to) appoint [əˈpɔɪnt] *ernennen*

TF 4 Europe united

1 What does Europe mean to me?

a) *Describe the chart below. The skills box below right will help.*
Say
– what the chart is about,
– what form of chart it is,
– where the statistics come from,
– when they are from,
– what you have learned from the chart.

YOUNG PEOPLE AND EUROPE	
What the European Union means for Europeans aged 15–30	
Freedom to travel, study and work anywhere in the EU	90%
A way to protect the rights of citizens	72%
A means[1] of improving the economic situation in the EU	71%
A European government	56%
A lot of bureaucracy[2], a waste of time and money	40%
The risk of losing our cultural identity/diversity[3]	35%

Source: The European Commission (Flash Eurobarometer 202, February 2007)

b) 👥👥👥 *What does the European Union mean for you? Decide on six issues[4]. You can use the issues from the chart above, or replace some of them with your own ideas. Discuss possible ideas in your group first. Here are some possibilities:*
– democracy
– more crime
– other countries'
  economic problems
– the euro
– unemployment
– too much
  immigration
– ...

c) *When you have agreed on your issues, make a table like this and complete it for yourself.*

Issue	1 Peace	2 Ability to go where I want	3 ...
unimportant			
less important			
important			
very important			

d) *Produce a bar chart for your group's results like the one at the top of the page. Give each answer a score: unimportant = 0, less important = 25, important = 50, very important = 100. Divide the scores for each issue by the number of people in your group.*
Display the bar charts in class.
Discuss the other groups' results.

SOCIAL STUDIES SKILLS | Interpreting a chart

– Charts contain statistics on an issue[4] or question. This question/issue is normally shown at the top or bottom of a chart.
– The statistics in a chart can show the situation at a particular time (a source shows the date of the statistics), or it may show changes over time.
– Make sure you know what the numbers in a chart are: ordinary[5] numbers, percentages, rankings, ...
– Graphics illustrate the statistics. Common charts are bar charts, pie charts and line graphs[6].

▶ *SF Talking about statistics (p. 129)*

Activate your English
– This group's results are similar to ...
– The most important issue for them is ...
– Their results are completely different from ours.
– I find their results very interesting/strange/ hard to believe/...
– I'm very surprised by ...

---

[1] means [miːnz] *(pl.* means*) Mittel* [2] bureaucracy [bjʊəˈrɒkrəsi] *Bürokratie* [3] diversity [daɪˈvɜːsəti] *Vielfalt* [4] issue [ˈɪʃuː] *Streitfrage, Thema*
[5] ordinary [ˈɔːdnri] *gewöhnlich* [6] graph [ɡræf] *Diagramm*

Bilingual module – Social Studies

2 Young people in Europe

a) Read part of a speech by the President of the European Parliament, Jerzy Buzek from Poland. He made it in Brussels on 11 November, 2009, to 89 young Europeans born in November 1989.

My dear fellow[1] European Citizens, young people from across the 27 Member States of the European Union,

Let me begin by welcoming each and every one of you to the European Parliament today.

Most of you celebrated your 20th birthday this Monday 9 November. So I want to wish you all a very Happy Birthday!

You share your birthday with a most significant moment in the history of our shared European continent, the reunification[2] of not just Germany, but the reintegration of Europe.

You are from a different generation, one that has grown up entirely[3] in a free and democratic Europe. We would like to hear from you. Tell us, what does Europe mean to each of you?

You live in a European Union which is a community of shared values. Your dignity[4] and your freedom are protected and guaranteed. Whether you have come here today from Tallinn or Toledo, whether from Belfast or Budapest, you share in the same European rights. You can travel freely between these places, study or work wherever you choose throughout 27 Member States. You have the freedom to choose how to live your life, which religion to practise[5] or none, whom you want to associate with, what you want to say, think and believe. In a free and democratic society, that is your right. You have a right to hope for a better future and to work to realize[6] that future.

Perhaps you also have a vision of how our European Union will look 20 years from now? Will we have welcomed new Member States? In our reunited continent of democracy and human rights, how should we view our neighbours who are still striving for[7] these freedoms ?

We would all be delighted[8] to hear from you. Tell us what you think of this European Union of ours, what it means to you and how you would like to see it develop.

Ladies and Gentlemen, dear young citizens of Europe, thank you all once again for providing us in the European Parliament with this wonderful opportunity to hear from you.

The floor is yours[9].

b) Explain why these young people were chosen to go to Brussels for Buzek's speech and what he would like to find out from them.

c) Make a list of the important shared values of the European Union that the President of the European Parliament mentions. Compare this list to the issues on your charts from 1, p. 114.

d) Imagine you were one of the young people in Brussels. Use what you have discussed and learnt on these pages. Make notes and write a reply of about 150 words to Buzek's speech. Say what the EU means for you and how you think it should develop. Make this speech in class.

---

[1] fellow ['feləʊ] *Mit-*   [2] reunification [ˌriːjuːnɪfɪ'keɪʃn] *Wiedervereinigung*   [3] entirely [ɪn'taɪəli] *völlig*   [4] dignity ['dɪgnəti] *Würde*   [5] (to) practise ausüben   [6] (to) realize *verwirklichen*   [7] (to) strive for sth. [straɪv] *nach etwas streben*   [8] delighted [dɪ'laɪtɪd] *erfreut*   [9] The floor is yours. *Sie haben das Wort.*

3 Airbus – a European dream?

Over the last 40 years, Airbus, a truly[1] European company, has become one of the world's two largest aircraft[2] producers.

It all started with a group of European aircraft companies in 1969. These companies – from France, Germany, Spain and the United Kingdom – had enough good ideas, but still did not build many planes. On their own, they were too small to compete with a huge American producer like Boeing. So they came together and founded Airbus.

Would it be possible for companies from four different countries to work together successfully? Roger Béteille, one of Airbus's founding fathers, was worried that national interests would make it difficult. But in the end all the partners agreed, firstly, to produce different parts at sites[3] in each country and, secondly, to use just one assembly line[4] and test flight centre in Toulouse, France.

This meant that Airbus had to develop a transport system to move large aircraft parts from all over Europe to Toulouse, by road and sea and also with huge cargo planes[5] called Belugas. Today, 15 sites in France, Germany, Spain and the UK

The A380 can carry up to 525 passengers.

produce parts which are then transported to the Airbus assembly lines – there are three today – in Toulouse and Hamburg and in Tianjin in Northern China.

Starting with the A300 in the 1970s, Airbus has always produced aircraft that use little fuel and are quiet and cheap to run. Today the company produces a range[6] of eco-efficient planes with seats for between 107 and 525 passengers.

So is Airbus a perfect model of European co-operation? When things are going well, it seems so.

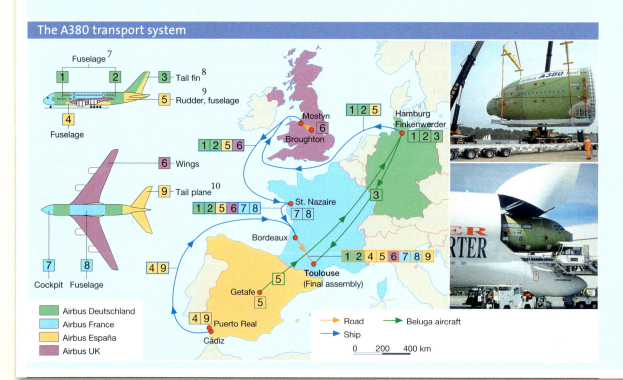

[1] truly ['truːli] *wahrhaft*   [2] aircraft ['eəkrɑːft] *Flugzeug*   [3] site *Standort*   [4] assembly line [ə'sembli laɪn] *Montagestraße*
[5] cargo plane ['kɑːgəʊ pleɪn] *Frachtflugzeug*   [6] range [reɪndʒ] *Sortiment, Reihe*   [7] fuselage ['fjuːzəlɑːʒ] *Flugzeugrumpf*
[8] tail fin ['teɪlfɪn] *Heckruder*   [9] rudder ['rʌdə] *Seitenruder*   [10] tail plane ['teɪlpleɪn] *Leitwerk*

But there are problems too. For example, the fact that production sites in different countries used different computer software was one reason behind big delays in delivering the A380 to the company's customers. These delays have caused a fall in profits[1], so that since 2007 production sites have been sold off and thousands of jobs lost. When Airbus has to decide where to cut jobs, it is then that national governments disagree, and national interests begin to play at least as big a role as the idea of European cooperation.

Sam – Apprentice[2]

'I joined Airbus as an apprentice after secondary school. I took part in an intercultural awareness[3] programme, working with British, French and German apprentices. It was a most enjoyable experience, from which I learned a lot and made a number of great friends from all three countries. I feel very lucky to have this apprenticeship. I would like to continue along the Airbus career path as far as I can, and later look for a chance to work in another country.'

a) Read about Airbus, then try to answer these questions:
1 What are the advantages for European countries of building airplanes together?
2 When does European cooperation become difficult for Airbus?
3 Why does Sam enjoy being an apprentice at Airbus?

b) Look at the map on p. 116 and with the help of the skills and language boxes say:
– what sort of map this is,
– which aircraft parts are produced in which countries and how they get to Toulouse.

c) Do you agree or disagree with the following? It would be a better idea if Airbus planes were all made in one place.
Make notes on your reasons and use them to discuss the question in class. You could think about

> European cooperation • transport problems • the environment • jobs in our country • competing with US companies • …

SOCIAL STUDIES SKILLS — Talking about maps

When you talk about maps,
– look at the title and the key[4] and make sure you understand what the map is about,
– start with a general statement about the map, then talk about the details.

Activate your English
– This is a physical[5]/political/thematic map.
– The map shows …
– Broughton/… is located/situated[6] in/near …
– … is about … km away from …
– … is between … and …
– The wings/… are produced/made/… in …
– They are carried/taken/transported/shipped/flown from … to …
– They are transported by road/ship/air/cargo plane …
– The aircraft parts are put together in …

4 Your opinion
Discuss one of the following with a partner:
– Should people fly less to protect our environment?
– Is this kind of European teamwork worth it for political and economic reasons or is it a waste of energy and time?

---

[1] fall in profits ['prɒfɪts] *Rückgang der Gewinne*   [2] apprentice [ə'prentɪs] *Auszubildende/r*   [3] intercultural awareness [ˌɪntəkʌltʃərəl_ə'weənəs] *interkulturelles Bewusstsein*   [4] key *Legende*   [5] physical ['fɪzɪkl] *physisch*   [6] (to) be situated ['sɪtʃueɪtɪd] *liegen, gelegen sein*

3 Text File

TF 5 Into space

1 On the way out

a) *Look at the pictures on this page and read the text below.*
Collect all the words belonging to the word field "universe" and use them to describe the pictures.

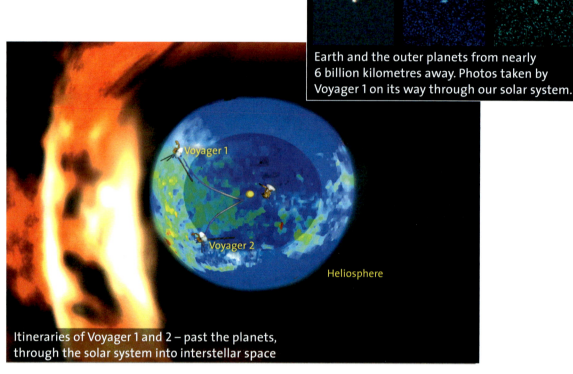

Earth and the outer planets from nearly 6 billion kilometres away. Photos taken by Voyager 1 on its way through our solar system.

Itineraries of Voyager 1 and 2 – past the planets, through the solar system into interstellar space

Voyagers 1 and 2 lifted off in August and September 1977 to explore the outer planets Jupiter (0.8 billion km from the sun), Saturn (1.4 billion km), Uranus (2.8 billion km) and Neptune (4.5 billion km). Both spacecraft sent such extraordinary pictures and scientific data back to NASA that more money was made available and their mission was extended. By the end of the 1980s, Voyager 1 and 2 had passed the outer planets and begun their trip out of the solar system at a speed of nearly one million miles a day. Right now the spacecraft are travelling through the heliosphere, the huge "bubble" that surrounds the solar system. No other human-made object has ever been further away from planet Earth and the journey is continuing every day. The information the two Voyagers are sending back has helped to solve some of the many mysteries of the universe, and data is still coming in. Although the spacecraft's nuclear batteries are slowly running low, they are expected to be a source of electrical power until sometime after 2025. By that time the spacecraft will probably have left the heliosphere and reached interstellar space. One of the last photos that Voyager 1 was able to make of Earth became known as the "pale[1] blue dot". It shows Earth from a distance of about 6 billion km away.

b) 👥 *With a partner, prepare five quiz questions based on this page. Make two of them easy, the other three more difficult. Then two pairs get together and do the quizzes.*

---

[1] pale *blass*

2 Exploring space – at what price?

"How do you put a price on a dream? I would go to space even if it was a one-way ticket, if it meant going and never returning, if it meant losing my life over it!" Anousheh Ansari had spent her childhood staring out into space and dreaming of travelling there. Her dream came true. She paid $ 20 million to fly to the International Space Station and so became the first female space tourist. She had to do seven months' training, and in 2010 a film called *Space Tourists* was released about her journey.

Ansari is one of a very exclusive group of tourists who have visited the ISS at enormous cost. But there are cheaper alternatives: you can experience weightlessness and view Earth from space in what is known as a suborbital flight with Virgin Galactic. There are already more than 340 would-be astronauts on their waiting list. You can book online or go to their official travel agent in Munich. Tickets cost $ 200,000 and a deposit of $ 20,000 is payable when you book.

The wish to explore space seems to be part of the human curiosity which has always driven us onwards to new horizons. Space travel has long been the subject of science fiction in books and in films. In 1969 NASA's Apollo programme set two men on the moon and this event captured the imagination of the whole world.

At that time NASA was using up almost five per cent of the US budget. Nowadays its finances have been severely cut back to about 0.5 per cent, although they are still substantial. Many argue that so much money should not be spent on space travel while people are suffering from disease and extreme poverty on Earth. At 0.5 per cent of the total budget, space expenditure may seem like a drop in the ocean, but to put it into perspective, the gross domestic product of Niger in Africa is around half of what the US spent on NASA in 2009.

Even in the US itself, many politicians believe that more money needs to be spent on health and education at home. The table below shows the US government spending in these areas for 2009.

NASA	$ 18.7 billion
Health and Human Services	$ 68.5 billion
Department of Education	$ 59.2 billion

On the other hand, space research has been extremely useful to us given its numerous medical and technological breakthroughs relevant to our daily life. In fact, the space programme may even be essential because our planet will soon be so hopelessly over-populated that we might have to move out into space. The famous astrophysicist Stephen Hawking believes that we will have to send people to live on other planets within the next 100 years to make sure that humans survive. For him the world is such a dangerous place that we cannot put our faith in this planet as our only home in the future. Getting to another planet and making it a suitable home for humanity will be a great challenge. But will moving out into space be a dream or a nightmare?

a) *List the reasons given in the text for and against space research and space tourism.*

b) 👥 *Find more arguments both for and against space research. Decide which side you are on, join three people who are of the same opinion and compare your arguments. Then have a class discussion.*

c) *Choose one of the following:*
– Free space flights are on offer. Write a letter to the company explaining why you should win such a flight.

– Your cousin in Australia has won a space flight. Explain to him/her why you think he/she should not accept it.

d) *Find examples of important discoveries and by-products resulting from space exploration.*

TF 6 Electric wind

(abridged from *The Boy Who Harnessed the Wind* by William Kamkwamba and Bryan Mealer)

From an early age William Kamkwamba wanted to become a scientist, but after primary school his father was unable to pay for him to go to secondary school. Before you read about William, talk about what it takes to become a scientist or an inventor.

Often while we fixed our radios, people would approach us and say, "Look at the little scientists! Keep it up, boys, and one day you'll have a good job."

I'd become very interested in how things worked, yet never thought of this as science. In addition to radios, I'd also become fascinated by how cars worked, especially how petrol operated an engine. I stopped the truckers in the trading center and asked them, "What makes this truck move? How does your engine work?" But no one could tell me. They'd just smile and shake their heads. Really, how can you drive a truck and not know how it works?

Even my father, who I assumed knew everything, said: "The fuel burns and releases fire and … well, I'm not really sure."

If solving such mysteries was the job of a scientist, then a scientist is exactly what I wanted to become.

Getting to know the library

Because my family still couldn't afford my school fees, I was forced to stay home doing nothing. I started wasting time in the trading center playing *bawo*. Someone also taught me a wonderful game called chess, which I started playing every day. But chess and *bawo* weren't enough to keep my mind occupied. I needed a better hobby, something to trick my brain into being happy. I missed school so terribly.

I remembered that the previous year a group called the Malawi Teacher Training Activity had opened a small library in Wimbe Primary School that was stocked with books donated by the American government. Perhaps reading could keep my brain from getting soft while being a dropout.

The library was in a small room near the main office. A woman was sitting behind a desk when I walked in. She smiled. "Come to borrow some books?" she said. This was Mrs. Edith Sikelo, a teacher at Wimbe who taught English and social studies and also operated the library. I nodded yes, then asked, "What are the rules of this place?" I'd never used such a facility.

Mrs. Sikelo took me behind a curtain to a smaller room, where three floor-to-ceiling shelves were filled with books. It smelled sweet and musty, like nothing I'd ever encountered. I took another deep breath. Mrs. Sikelo then explained the rules for borrowing books and showed me the collection.

After about a month, the school term finally ended and [my friend] Gilbert was free to hang out. One morning we went to the library to kill some time – we often stayed for hours, just sitting in chairs and reading – but today Mrs. Sikelo was in a rush.

"You boys spend hours in here taking my time," she said, "but today I have an appointment. Just find something quickly."

"Yes, madame."

Finding a book

I squatted down to grab one of the dictionaries, and when I did, I noticed a book I'd never seen, pushed into the shelf and slightly concealed. *What is this?* I thought. Pulling it out, I saw it was an American textbook called *Using Energy*, and this book has since changed my life.

The cover featured a long row of windmills – though at the time I had no idea what a *windmill* was. I opened the book and began to read.

(to) harness ['hɑːnɪs] *nutzen*   51 facility [fə'sɪləti] *Einrichtung*   56 (to) encounter sb./sth. [ɪn'kaʊntə] *jm./etwas begegnen*   73 (to) conceal [kən'siːl] *verstecken*   77 windmill *Windmühle, -rad*

"Energy is all around you every day," it said. "Sometimes energy needs to be converted to another form before it is useful to us. How can we convert forms of energy? Read on and you'll see."

I read on. It explained how Archimedes used his "Death Ray" – which was really a lot of mirrors – to reflect the sun onto the enemy ships until, one by one, they caught fire and sank. That was an example of how you can use the sun to produce energy.

Just like with the sun, windmills could also be used to generate power.

Suddenly it all snapped together. All I needed was a windmill, and then I could have lights. No more kerosene lamps that burned our eyes and sent us gasping for breath. With a windmill, I could stay awake at night reading instead of going to bed at seven with the rest of Malawi.

But most important, a windmill could also rotate a pump for water and irrigation. Having just come out of the hunger – and with famine still affecting many parts of the country – the idea of a water pump now seemed incredibly necessary. With a windmill, we'd finally release ourselves from the troubles of darkness and hunger. In Malawi, the wind was one of the few consistent things given to us by God, blowing in the treetops day and night. A windmill meant more than just power, it was freedom.

Standing there looking at this book, I decided I would build my own windmill. I'd never built anything like it before, but I knew if windmills existed on the cover of that book, it meant another person had built them. I felt confident I could build one, too.

Looking to a dark future

My father tried negotiating again with [my teacher] Mister Tembo, but [my head teacher] W. M. Phiri had already forbidden me to return. The Minister of Education was visiting various schools to ensure that all the students had paid their fees.

I was sitting on a chair in the yard when my father returned with the bad news. His eyes were pale and troubled, as if he'd wrestled with a ghost. I recognized the look on his face. It was one I knew well.

I couldn't blame my father for the famine or our troubles. But for the next week I couldn't look him in the eyes. Whenever I did, I saw the rest of my life.

My greatest fear was coming true: I would end up just like him, another poor Malawian farmer laboring in the soil, thin and dirty, with hands as rough as animal hides and feet that knew no shoes. I loved my father and respected him deeply, but I did not want to end up like him. If I did, my life would never be determined by me, but by rain and the price of fertilizer and seeds. I would do what every Malawian was supposed to do, what was written by God and the constitution: I would grow maize, and if I was lucky, maybe a little tobacco. And years when the crops were good and there was a little extra to sell, perhaps I could buy some medicine and a new pair of shoes. But most of the time, I knew, there would be hardly enough to simply survive. My future had been chosen, and thinking about it now scared me so much I wanted to be sick.

Busy building

When I wasn't in the scrapyard digging for treasure, I'd hang out at the library or sit in my hammock and read. Even if my father didn't fully understand my windmill, he felt so bad about my schooling that he no longer forced me to work in the field.

So with my father's blessing, the mornings and afternoons became my time to study. As I planned my windmill, I pored through chapters in *Explaining Physics* about electricity and how it moves and behaves and how it can be harnessed. Going to the library, I renewed the same three books over and over until one day Mrs. Sikelo raised her eyebrow.

"William, are you still preparing for exams? What are you up to?"

---

102 irrigation [ˌɪrɪˈɡeɪʃn] Bewässerung   **103** famine [ˈfæmɪn] *Hungersnot*   **120** (to) negotiate [nɪˈɡəʊʃɪeɪt] *verhandeln*   **143** fertilizer [ˈfɜːtəlaɪzə] *Dünger*   **143** seeds *(pl)* Saatgut   **155** scrapyard *Schrottplatz*   **157** hammock [ˈhæmək] *Hängematte*

"Nothing," I said. "Just building something. You'll see."

Enjoying success

Once the windmill was fastened we looked at each other and smiled. It felt sturdy and very strong. Sweat poured down my face and cooled with the breeze. I could hardly wait to watch the blades spin. While Geoffrey made his way down the tower, I remained atop my perch taking in the scenery. Then something strange began to happen. A line of people began trickling through the alleys from the shops and heading in my direction. They'd seen the tower from the market and were walking toward my house. Within a few minutes, a dozen people were gathered at the base. One of them was named Kalino.

"What is this thing?" he asked.

Since there's no word in Chichewa for windmill, I used the phrase *magetsi a mphepo*. "Electric wind," I answered.

"What does it do?"

"Generates electricity from the wind. I'll show you."

"That's impossible," Kalino said, smiling.

Aside from my family, about thirty adults

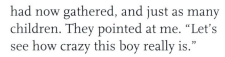

had now gathered, and just as many children. They pointed at me. "Let's see how crazy this boy really is."

"Quiet down! This is going to be a good show." Just then a gust of wind slammed against my body, and the blades kicked up like mad. The tower rocked once, knocking me off balance. I held the bulb before me, waiting for my miracle. It flickered once. Just a flash at first, then a surge of bright, magnificent light. My heart nearly burst.

"Look," someone said. "He's made light!" "It's true what he said!"

A gang of school kids pushed through the crowd so they could see better.

"Electric wind!" I shouted. "I told you I wasn't mad!" One by one, the crowd began to cheer. They raised their hands in the air clapping and shouting, "*Wachitabwina!* Well done!" "You did it, William!"

For the next month, about thirty people showed up each day to stare at the light.

"We doubted you, but look at you now!"

"How did you manage such a thing?" they asked.

"Hard work and lots of research," I'd say, trying not to sound too smug.

---

1 William's story

a) Talk about your first reactions to William's story.

b) With a partner, say what happened. Partner A begins with one sentence on the first part (ll. 1–23), Partner B adds one sentence, Partner A finalizes the summary for that part. Partner B starts on the second part (ll. 24–68), and so on.

c) Mrs Sikelo, the librarian, was very impressed with William. Imagine she had wanted to tell her boss about him, explaining what he had done and suggesting he should be getting some support. Write the letter.

2   A profile of William

Get into five groups. Each group collects information from the text on one of these topics: William's personality, his interests, his attitude towards his country, his feelings for his father, his motivation for building a windmill. Then form new groups with one expert for each topic. Share your findings. Prepare a complete profile on William.

3 The media

Listen to the interview with William and compare it with what you have read. What additional information does it give you?

---

179 blade *(Windmühlen-)Flügel* 181 perch *(hoher) Sitz* 103 smug *selbstzufrieden*

TF 7 Global warming – how does it affect us?

1 What's happening?

a) Describe the photos and say what the diagram below shows.

Glaciers in Austria's Zillertal: 1905 (left) and 2003 (right)

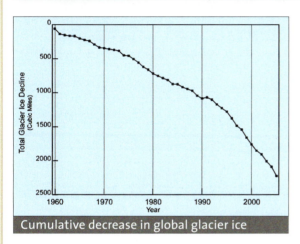

Cumulative decrease in global glacier ice

Activate your English
- The photo/graph ... shows/gives information about ...
- It says that ... / It shows ...
- This is a photo of ...
- In 2003, glaciers ... compared with 1905.

▶ *SF Talking about statistics (p. 129)*

b) 👥 Give reasons for the differences between the two photos. Make notes. Present your ideas to the class.

c) Analyse the diagrams below. How do they support your ideas from b)?

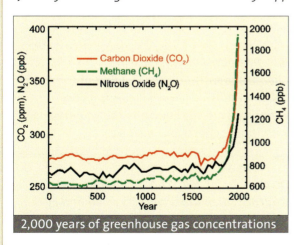

2,000 years of greenhouse gas concentrations

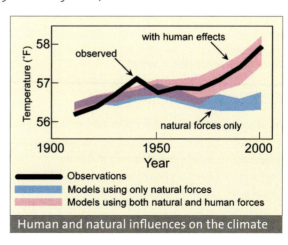

Human and natural influences on the climate

2 Causes and effects

a) *Explain how the atmosphere regulates the earth's climate. Use the information given in the picture below.*

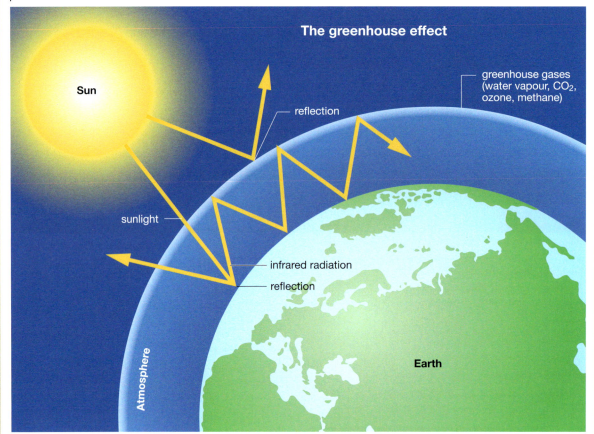

b) *What effect does an increase of the concentration of greenhouse gases in the atmosphere have on the earth's climate? Draw a flow chart by putting the steps in the box on the right in the correct order.*

- temperatures in the atmosphere rise
- fewer infrared rays can leave the earth
- more greenhouse gases are produced
- the layer of greenhouse gases around the earth gets thicker

3 Who should do what?

a) *What can you yourself do to stop global warming?*

b) *Should people decide for themselves whether and how they want to produce fewer greenhouse gases or should the government put more pressure on them and tell them what to do? Discuss.*

4 Project

Choose a country (e.g. the Maldives or Bangladesh). Find out what effects global warming is already having on this country and what future effects it could have.

OR

Do a survey for your school magazine, asking students, parents and teachers whether they think they are doing enough to prevent global warming.

Skills File

Skills File – Inhalt

Seite

STUDY AND LANGUAGE SKILLS

REVISION	Using a bilingual dictionary	126
REVISION	Using an English–English dictionary	127
REVISION	Using a grammar	127
REVISION	Learning words	128
REVISION	Describing and analysing pictures	128
REVISION	Talking about statistics	129
REVISION	Research	130
REVISION	Outlining	131
REVISION	Giving a presentation	132
	Giving a group presentation	132
REVISION	Handouts	133
REVISION	Visual aids in presentations	133
REVISION	Project skills	134–135
	Peer evaluation	136

LISTENING AND READING SKILLS

REVISION	Listening	137
REVISION	Taking notes	138
REVISION	Marking up a text	138
REVISION	READING COURSE	139–140
	Working out the meaning of words	139
	Skimming and scanning	139
	Finding the main ideas of a text	139
	Careful reading	140
	Text types: fiction and non-fiction	140
REVISION	Reading literature	141–143
	Identifying style and register	143
	Analysing newspaper articles	144
	Understanding adverts	144

MEDIATION SKILLS

MEDIATION COURSE – Zusammenfassung	145–146

SPEAKING AND WRITING SKILLS

REVISION	Paraphrasing	147
REVISION	Brainstorming	147
REVISION	SPEAKING COURSE	148–149
	Having a conversation	148
	Asking for, confirming, giving information	148
	Giving an oral summary	149
	Having a discussion	149
REVISION	WRITING COURSE	150–151
	Writing better sentences	150
	Using paragraphs	150
	Linking ideas	151
	Correcting your text	151

Writing different types of text		152–156
REVISION	Writing a report	152
REVISION	Writing a letter to a magazine	152
REVISION	Writing formal letters	152
REVISION	Argumentative writing	153
REVISION	Writing a CV	154
REVISION	Summary writing	155
	Writing a film review	156
	Describing objects and processes	156

VIEWING SKILLS

Analysing films	157

EXAM SKILLS

REVISION	How to do well in a test	158

GLOSSARY 161

Im **Skills File** findest du Hinweise zu Arbeits- und Lerntechniken. Was du in den Skills-Kästen der Units gelernt hast, wird hier näher erläutert.

Was du bereits aus Band 5 von English G 21 kennst, ist mit **REVISION** gekennzeichnet, z. B.
– **REVISION** Research, Seite 130
– **REVISION** Paraphrasing, Seite 147.

Viele neue Hinweise helfen dir bei der Arbeit mit Hör- und Lesetexten, beim Sprechen, beim Schreiben von eigenen Texten und beim Lernen von Methoden.

STUDY AND LANGUAGE SKILLS

SF REVISION   Using a bilingual dictionary

Wann brauche ich ein zweisprachiges Wörterbuch?

Du verstehst einen Text nicht, weil er zu viele Wörter enthält, die dir unbekannt sind, und die Worterschließungstechniken (▶ *Working out the meaning of words, p. 136*) helfen dir nicht weiter?
Du sollst einen Text auf Englisch schreiben, und dir fehlt das eine oder andere Wort, um deine Ideen auszudrücken? Du willst z. B. über die Ankunft eines Einwanderers in einem neuen Land schreiben und kennst das Wort für „Grenze" nicht? Dann hilft dir ein zweisprachiges Wörterbuch.

Wie benutze ich ein zweisprachiges Wörterbuch?

- Die **Leitwörter** *(running heads)* oben auf der Seite helfen dir, schneller zu finden, was du suchst. Auf der linken Seite steht das erste Stichwort, auf der rechten Seite das letzte Stichwort der Doppelseite.
- **drehen** ist das **Stichwort** *(headword)*. Stichwörter sind alphabetisch geordnet: **d** vor **e**, **da** vor **de** und **dre** vor **dri** usw.
- Die *kursiv* gedruckten Hinweise helfen dir, die für deinen Text passende Bedeutung zu finden.
- Die **Ziffern** 1, 2 usw. zeigen, dass ein Stichwort mehrere ganz verschiedene Bedeutungen hat.
- **Beispielsätze** und **Redewendungen** sind dem Stichwort zugeordnet. In den Beispielsätzen und Redewendungen ersetzt eine **Tilde** (~) das Stichwort.
- Im englisch-deutschen Teil der meisten Wörterbücher findest du außerdem Hinweise auf **unregelmäßige Verbformen**, auf die **Steigerungsformen der Adjektive** und Ähnliches.
- Die **Lautschrift** gibt Auskunft darüber, wie das Wort ausgesprochen und betont wird.
- Bei kniffligen Wörtern gibt es in vielen Wörterbüchern **Info-Boxes**, in denen dir mehr Hilfen und Hinweise gegeben werden.

Also: Lies immer erst den **gesamten Wörterbucheintrag**, bevor du dich für eine bestimmte Übersetzung entscheidest. Nimm nicht einfach die erste Übersetzung, die dir angeboten wird.
Wenn du unsicher bist, ob du die richtige Übersetzung gefunden hast, schau dir den Eintrag zu dieser Übersetzung an. Wenn du z. B. überprüfen willst, ob „spin" im zweiten Satz unten die richtige Übersetzung für „drehen" ist, such einen Eintrag unter „spin" und lies ihn dir durch.

> **Dr.**
> **Dr.** (*Abk. für* **Doktor**) Dr., Doctor
> **Drache** dragon
> **Drachen** *Papierdrachen* kite; *Fluggerät* hang glider
> **Drehbuch** screenplay, script
> **drehen 1** *Verb mit Obj* turn; *Film* shoot*; *Zigarette* roll **2**: **sich ~** turn; *schnell* spin*; **sich ~ um** *übertragen* be* about
> **Drehkreuz** turnstile; **Drehorgel** barrel organ ['ɔːgən]; **Drehort** location; **Drehstuhl** swivel chair; **Drehtür** revolving door
> **Drehung** turn; *um eine Achse* rotation
> **Drehzahl** (number of) revolutions *Pl od.* revs *Pl*
> **Drehzahlmesser** rev counter
> **drei** three
> **Drei** three; *Note etwa* C; **ich habe eine ~ geschrieben** I got a C
> **dreidimensional 1** *Adj* three-dimensional **2** *Adv:* **etwas ~ darstellen** depict sth. three-dimensionally; **Dreieck** triangle ['traɪæŋgl]; **dreieckig** triangular [traɪ-'æŋgjʊlə]

> **bringen**
> **bring** (*herbringen; mitbringen*) wird nur verwendet, wenn jemand oder etwas zum Ort des Sprechers oder Hörers gebracht wird:
>
> **Schön, dass du zu meiner Party** | I'm glad you can come to my party. Can
>
> **take** (*weg-, hinbringen; mitnehmen*) wird verwendet, wenn jemand oder etwas woanders hingebracht oder mitgenommen wird:
>
> **Kannst du morgen deinen Bruder zur Schule bringen?** | Can you take your brother to school tomorrow?

„drehen"=?

She's a good dancer, she loves to … round and round as fast as she can.

Lots of Hollywood stars come to Berlin to … their films here.

Skills File

SF REVISION   Using an English–English dictionary

Wenn du englische Texte liest oder selbst einen englischen Text schreibst, kannst du ein einsprachiges englisches Wörterbuch zur Hilfe nehmen. Hier findest du mehr über ein englisches Wort heraus als in einem zweisprachigen Wörterbuch:

– Das einsprachige Wörterbuch erklärt die **Bedeutung** eines englischen Wortes **auf Englisch**. Manche Wörter haben mehrere Bedeutungen. Lies alle Einträge und Beispielsätze genau und vergleiche sie mit deinem englischen Text, um die richtige Bedeutung herauszufinden.

– Das Wörterbuch hilft dir auch, die passende **Verbindung mit anderen Wörtern** zu finden, z.B. zu Verben, Präpositionen oder in bestimmten Wendungen. Das ist besonders nützlich, wenn du selbst einen englischen Text schreiben willst und nach den richtigen Wörtern suchst.

---

deadly ['dedli] *adj*

1 *able or likely to kill people* {= lethal}: This is no longer a deadly disease. ***deadly to*** The HSN virus is deadly to chickens. ***a deadly weapon*** The new generation of biological weapons is more deadly than ever.

2 *(only before noun)* {= complete}: ***deadly silence*** There was deadly silence after his speech. ***a deadly secret*** Don't tell anyone – this is a deadly secret. ***in deadly earnest*** completely serious: Don't you laugh – I am in deadly earnest!

3 *(informal) very boring*: Many TV programmes are pretty deadly!

4 *always able to achieve something*: The new Chelsea striker is said to be a deadly goal scorer.

SF REVISION   Using a grammar

Vielleicht hast du beim Schreiben oder Korrigieren deiner Klassenarbeiten schon einmal bemerkt, dass du immer die gleichen Fehler machst. Um diese Fehler zu vermeiden, kannst du ein Grammatikbuch zu Hilfe nehmen, das dir bei der Verwendung bestimmter grammatischer Strukturen helfen kann. In einem zweiten Schritt kannst du mit einer Grammatik auch an der Verbesserung deines Stils arbeiten, wenn es z.B. um die Verwendung von Partizipien in formalen Texten geht.

Schritt 1: Lege eine individuelle Fehlerstatistik an, d.h. notiere dir aus den Korrekturen deiner Klassenarbeiten die Fehlersorten *Wortschatz, Grammatik, Satzbau, Stil, …*

Schritt 2: Suche dir aus dem Bereich, in dem am häufigsten Fehler auftreten, einen Schwerpunkt heraus, z.B. *Grammatik ▸ tenses*.

Schritt 3: Suche im Inhaltsverzeichnis deiner Grammatik die betreffenden Kapitel heraus und lies sie dir nochmals gründlich durch. Vergleiche sie mit den Fehlern, die du in deinen Klassenarbeiten machst.

Schritt 4: Schreib dir einige wenige Mustersätze und Merkregeln zu diesen grammatischen Strukturen auf einen Merkzettel. Vor der nächsten Klassenarbeit solltest du ihn dir nochmals anschauen.

Clause elements	**20**	17-20
The verb		
Summary	**23**	21
Modal auxiliaries	**23**	22-48
Be, have and do	**36**	49-57
The short forms of the auxiliaries	**40**	58-60
Full verbs	**42**	61-71
Summary: the tenses of the full verbs	**50**	72-73
The tenses of the full verbs	**54**	74-94
Simple present	**54**	74-75
Present progressive	**56**	76-77
Simple present and present progressive in contrast	**57**	78
Present perfect (simple form)	**58**	79-80
Present perfect progressive	**60**	81-82

He goes to school every day.
he, she it, ein –s muss mit!!!

SF REVISION   Learning words

- Lerne neue und wiederhole alte Vokabeln regelmäßig – am besten jeden Tag ca. 15 Minuten.
- Schreib die neuen Wörter auch auf und überprüfe die Schreibweise mithilfe des Dictionary oder Vocabulary.
- Sammle **Gegensatzpaare**, z. B. **alive – dead**, **majority – minority**, **find – lose**.
- Sammle Wörter mit **gleicher Bedeutung**, z. B. **(to) train – (to) practise**.
- Sammle Wörter in **Wortfamilien**, z. B. **(to) dance, dance, dancer, dancing lessons, shop, shopper, shopping, shopping list, shop assistant**, ...
- Sammle und ordne Wörter in **Wortnetzen** (networks) – ein Beispiel siehst du rechts.
- Lerne Wörter in **Kollokationen** und in sinnvollen **Zusammenhängen**.
- Besonders gut prägen sie sich ein, wenn Du Beispielsätze bildest oder kurze Texte schreibst, in denen Du die neuen Wörter verwendest.

Wortnetz *(network)*
Topic: Youth
People: teenagers, young people, adolescents, ...
Education: school, college, university, professional training, ...
Lifestyle: fashion, music, sports, dancing, hanging out, dating, ...
Aims: good job, family, having fun, travelling, adventure, volunteering, ...

SF REVISION   Describing and analysing pictures

Wenn du ein Bild **beschreiben** sollst, lies zuerst die Bildunterschrift, falls es eine gibt. Sieh dir dann das Bild genau an um zu sehen, worum es vor allem geht.
This picture/photo/poster/cartoon is about .../shows ...
Beschreibe das Bild nun systematisch – vom Vordergrund zum Hintergrund, von oben nach unten, von links nach rechts.
In the centre/foreground/background of the photo you can see ...
The poster shows three almost identical pictures next to each other. The picture on the left/right/behind .../between ... and .../ in front of ...
In the cartoon there are two ..., one on the left, one ...
Um zu beschreiben, was die Personen auf dem Bild tun, verwende das present progressive.
The young woman is holding the book upside down.

Wenn du aufgefordert wirst, ein Bild zu **analysieren**, sollst du herausfinden, was das Bild bewirken will, ob es sein Ziel erreicht und wenn ja, wie es dies tut. Stelle dir bei einem Bild oder Foto folgende Fragen: Was will der Zeichner oder Fotograf sagen und wie sagt er/sie es (Technik, Farbgebung, ...)? Welche Wirkung hat das Bild auf den Betrachter bzw. auf mich selbst?
The picture/photo clearly shows that .../wants us to .../provides proof of .../ makes the point that ... /...
It's a good example of ... / ... is very attractive because ...

Frage bei einem Plakat oder einer Karikatur, ggf. aber auch bei einem Foto: Wer war der Auftraggeber (Zeitung/Zeitschrift, Wohltätigkeitsorganisation, politische Kampagne, Werbekampagne, ...)? Wann entstand das Plakat/die Karikatur? Was will die Abbildung sagen bzw. kritisieren, wozu ruft sie auf?
The poster/cartoon was meant to show voters / readers of the paper / ...
It's very eye-catching through its use of ...
It speaks to the reader directly by ...
The layout/use of colour ...
... is criticizing/making fun of ...
... makes the point that ...

SF REVISION Talking about statistics

Welche Arten von Diagrammen gibt es?

Diagramme bilden statistische Vergleiche zwischen mindestens zwei Sachverhalten grafisch ab. Die **Überschrift** des Diagramms ist sehr wichtig, denn sie gibt bereits genaue Informationen darüber, worum es bei der betreffenden Abbildung geht. Die **Darstellungsform** richtet sich häufig danach, ob man Zahlen oder Prozentsätze miteinander vergleichen will:
- *Bar chart* (**Säulendiagramm**): Anzahl oder Größe von zwei oder mehr Dingen
- *Pie chart* (**Kreis-/Tortendiagramm**): prozentuale Verteilung
- *Table* (**Tabelle**): Vergleich unterschiedlicher Daten anhand von Zahlen und Prozentsätzen
- *Line graph* (**Kurvendiagramm**): Entwicklung im Verhältnis unterschiedlicher Größen

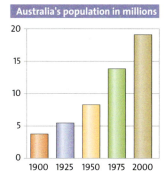

Wie beschreibe ich ein Diagramm?

Um ein Diagramm zu beschreiben, solltest du folgende Fragen beantworten:
- What is the graph/chart about?
  The bar/pie chart is about … / It deals with … / It is taken from …
- What does the graph/chart/table refer to/compare?
  The pie chart compares the size/number of … / It shows the different … in … / It is divided into … slices which show … / The graph/chart/table shows the relation between … and … / The table compares the population in terms of / with regard to …
- What does the chart tell you? What information does it give you?
  … has the largest/second largest/… / … is twice/three times /… as big as … / A huge majority/small minority is … / … per cent are … / There are more than/ nearly twice as many … as there are …

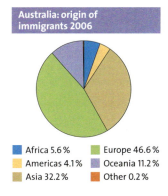

Manchmal kann es hilfreich sein, wenn du auch noch Aussagen über den Zeitraum der Statistik und/oder die Form der Darstellung machst:
It covers a period of … months/years. / It shows a development of three months/ years from 2002 to 2005. / The vertical/horizontal line shows/represents … / The figures are expressed as a percentage of the total population / total number of …

Achte bei der Beschreibung von Diagrammen auf die **Zeitformen** des Englischen:
- Benutze das *simple past*, wenn du dich auf einen Zeitpunkt in der Vergangenheit beziehst: The rainfall was 2207 mm in Cairns in 2008.
- Das *simple present* verwendest du bei allgemeingültigen Aussagen (The average rainfall in Cairns is 1992 mm per year) oder wenn du deine Schlussfolgerungen wiedergibst.
- Benutze das *present perfect*, wenn du dich auf einen Zeitraum beziehst, der von der Vergangenheit bis heute reicht: Three millions Asians have come to Australia since 2000.

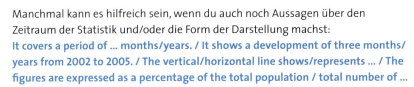

Wenn du dich auf die Zahlen bzw. Größen eines Diagramms beziehst, dann verwende **amount** für nicht zählbare Nomen: A large amount of meat/rain/ food/… Für zählbare Nomen benutzt du das englische Wort **number**: The number of immigrants/Asians/people/…

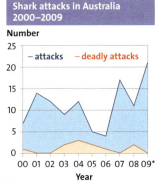

SF REVISION Research

Material sammeln (recherchieren)

Wenn du über ein Thema etwas schreiben oder einen Vortrag halten sollst, suchst du zuerst Informationen in Büchern oder in Zeitschriften, im Internet und in anderen Quellen. Verwende möglichst englischsprachige Quellen.

Damit du die Übersicht behältst, solltest du das Gefundene in einem Ordner sammeln und von vornherein sortieren. Orientiere dich dafür an der Gliederung bzw. *outline*, die du für deinen Text oder deine Präsentation vorbereitet hast (▶ *Outlining, p. 131*). Du kannst deine Materialien auch danach ordnen, ob es sich um sachliche Informationen, also Tatsachen, oder um persönliche Meinungen handelt.

Wichtiges herausschreiben (exzerpieren)

Sichte das Material und entscheide, welche Informationen du tatsächlich verwenden möchtest. Du kannst die betreffenden Passagen markieren (▶ *Marking up a text, p. 138*), herausschreiben oder auch ausschneiden und in fortlaufender Reihenfolge auf DIN-A4-Blätter kleben. Vergiss die Quellenangabe nicht. Deine eigenen Gedanken fügst du in Stichpunkten an den entsprechenden Stellen hinzu. Wenn du eine Präsentation vorbereitest, kannst du am Rand notieren, welche Medien du jeweils einsetzen möchtest.

Aus Materialien, die du im Internet gefunden und in elektronischen Ordnern gesammelt hast, überträgst du die wichtigen Informationen mit „Kopieren" und „Einfügen" in ein neues Dokument, wo du sie dann bearbeiten (also kürzen, ergänzen, umschreiben usw.) kannst.

Zitieren, umschreiben, Quellen angeben

Formuliere deinen Text oder deine Präsentation mit deinen eigenen Worten – schreibe nicht einfach aus deinen Quellen ab. Wenn du deine Argumentation einmal mit einer Expertenaussage unterstützen oder deinen Text mit einem Auszug aus einem Buch, einem Interview o. Ä. interessanter und abwechslungsreicher gestalten möchtest, markiere solche Zitate durch Anführungszeichen und gib Autor und Quelle einschließlich Seitenzahl an (bei Internetquellen die Webadresse und das Datum des Aufrufs). Das gilt auch dann, wenn du eine fremde Aussage mit eigenen Worten umschreibst. Gib auch bei einer Abbildung den Fundort an.

Kündige in deiner mündlichen Präsentation deine Zitate an und erkläre schwierige Wörter. Schaffe logische Übergänge zu deinen eigenen Argumenten.

Aber denk daran: Lange Zitate können deine Leser oder Zuhörer auch ermüden und erwecken leicht den Eindruck, dass du selbst nur wenig zu sagen hast. In der Kürze liegt die Würze!

http://www.shootingjozi.net/assets/images/gallery/142.jpg (17 April, 2010)

SF REVISION Outlining

Wenn du zu einem komplexen Thema einen Text schreiben oder eine Präsentation vorbereiten sollst, sammelst du zunächst Informationen und Unterlagen (▶ *Research, p. 130*). Eine zuvor erstellte Gliederung (*outline*) hilft dir dabei, denn so weißt du von vornherein genau, was du suchst. Und auch beim Ordnen deines Materials solltest du dich gleich an einer *outline* orientieren.

Outlines werden in Stichpunkten oder kurzen Sätzen verfasst. Schreibe dir zunächst deine Hauptpunkte auf. Bestimme dann Unterthemen und überlege dir, mit welchen Beispielen und Erläuterungen du deine Gedanken dazu unterstützen möchtest. Wenn du eine Mindmap erstellt hast, kannst du sie für deine Gliederung verwenden.

Achte auf eine logische Reihenfolge deiner Gedanken. Sie sollen sich in deiner *outline* widerspiegeln. Beim Gliedern kannst du verschiedene Möglichkeiten der Aufzählung (Zahlen, Groß- und Kleinbuchstaben, ...) nutzen. Mach dir einen Vermerk, z. B. am Rand des Blattes, welche Zitate, Statistiken, Bilder, Medienbeiträge usw. du an welcher Stelle einsetzen möchtest.

Die *outline* dient dir als Vorlage für deinen Text bzw. als Ausgangspunkt für deine Präsentation. Darüber hinaus kannst du sie dazu verwenden, deinen Lesern oder Zuhörern einen Überblick über dein Thema zu geben, indem du sie deinem Text oder deiner Präsentation voranstellst, z. B. bei einem mündlichen Vortrag auf einer Folie.

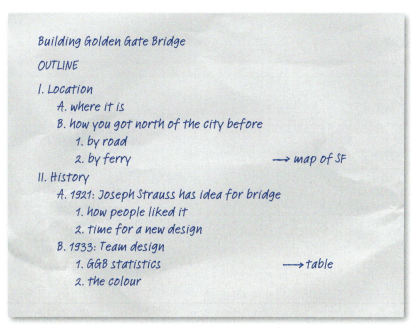

Merke dir also:
- Eine Gliederung (*outline*) hilft dir beim Recherchieren und beim Ordnen deines Materials.
- Bestimme zuerst die Hauptpunkte, dann die Unterthemen.

SF REVISION Giving a presentation

Vorbereitung

– Ordne deine Gedanken und notiere sie, z.B. auf nummerierten Karteikarten oder als Mindmap.
– Bereite ein Poster, eine Folie oder ein Handout. (▶ *Handouts, p. 133*) vor. Schreib groß und für alle gut lesbar.
– Überlege dir einen guten Einstieg: eine überraschende Tatsache, etwas Lustiges, ein Zitat aus dem Buch, das du vorstellen möchtest, ...
– Übe deine Präsentation zu Hause vor einem Spiegel. Sprich laut, deutlich und langsam, mach Pausen.
– Reicht die Zeit?

Durchführung

– Bevor du beginnst, bereite deine Medien vor und sortiere deine Vortragskarten.
– Warte, bis es ruhig ist. Schau die Zuhörer an.
– Erkläre zu Anfang, worüber du sprechen wirst: ein Land, ein kontroverses Thema, ein spannendes Buch, ...
– Lies nicht von deinen Karten ab, sondern sprich frei.
– Schreibe die Gliederung sowie unbekannten Wortschatz und Eigennamen an die Tafel.

> I'm going to talk about Saci Lloyd's novel *The Carbon Diaries 2015*.

Schluss

– Sag, dass du fertig bist, und frag die Zuhörer, ob sie Fragen haben.
– Bedanke dich fürs Zuhören.

> If you want to know the surprising end of the story, you'll have to read the novel yourself. It's worth it!

SF Giving a group presentation ▶ *Unit 3 (p. 67)*

Wird ein Projekt von mehreren Teilnehmern bearbeitet, wird das Produkt meist von allen Teammitgliedern gemeinsam präsentiert. Dabei hat jede Person eine bestimmte Rolle:

– Der oder die **Leiter/in der Gruppe (*team leader*)** hat die Gesamtverantwortung für die Präsentation. Er/Sie begrüßt die Zuhörer, stellt das Thema vor, erläutert den Ablauf der Präsentation, steuert die Diskussion, fasst die Ergebnisse zusammen und bedankt sich im Namen der Gruppe bei den Zuhörern.
– Der oder die **Stellvertreter/in (*co-leader*)** kontrolliert die Vollständigkeit und Einsatzbereitschaft des Präsentationsmaterials und der Medien.
– Die einzelnen **Referenten (*presenters*)** stellen die unterschiedlichen Aspekte des Projektes dar und leiten zum nachfolgenden Sprecher über.

> Here's an overview of our presentation. Just let me turn on the OHP.

> My part of the presentation deals with ...

Alle Beteiligten des Projektes müssen die Beiträge jedes einzelnen Teammitgliedes kennen, um keine Informationen zu wiederholen, keine Lücken entstehen zu lassen und in der Diskussion aufeinander Bezug nehmen zu können.

Das Team sollte den Ablauf der Präsentation – einschließlich des Medieneinsatzes – mehrmals wiederholen. Dabei können sich die Teammitglieder gegenseitig konstruktives Feedback geben.

SF REVISION Handouts

Ein Handout enthält die wichtigsten Informationen einer Präsentation. Man kann es vor, während oder nach der Präsentation austeilen:
- vor oder während der Präsentation, damit die Zuhörer die Gliederung des Vortrags verstehen und ihm besser folgen können;
- nach der Präsentation, damit die Zuhörer später noch einmal nachlesen und sich besser an die Präsentation erinnern können.

Ein Handout sollte übersichtlich strukturiert sein, z. B. durch eine Überschrift, deinen Namen, das Datum, durch Teilüberschriften, Beispiele, tabellarische oder grafische Übersichten. Du kannst in ganzen Sätzen schreiben, z. B. bei einer Zusammenfassung, oder in Stichpunkten.

Abbildungen sollten mit einer Bildunterschrift einer Quellenangabe versehen sein. Mit Symbolen kann man ein Handout übersichtlicher gestalten und die wesentlichen Informationen hervorheben.

Lass ausreichend Platz für die Notizen der Zuhörer, z. B. durch einen breiten Rand an der Seite oder im unteren Teil des Blattes.

SF REVISION Visual aids in presentations

Präsentationsmedien wie Poster, Overhead-Folien, Tafelzeichnungen und Computerpräsentationen geben einem Vortrag Struktur und erleichtern den Zuhörern das Verständnis.

1. Verwende eine **Schriftgröße**, die von überall im Klassenraum gelesen werden kann. Überprüfe vor deiner Präsentation die Lesbarkeit von verschiedenen Stellen im Klassenzimmer aus.
2. Deine Folien, Poster usw. sollten eine **klare Struktur** haben. Benutze Fettdruck, Großbuchstaben und Symbole, um besonders wichtige Dinge hervorzuheben.
3. **Vermeide zu viele Informationen auf einmal.** Eine Idee pro Folie reicht bei einer elektronischen Präsentation vollkommen aus. Vermeide längere Texte. Lies deine Folien nicht vor – sie geben nur den Extrakt deiner Aussagen wieder oder stellen zusätzliches Material zur Verfügung.
4. **Bilder, Illustrationen und Grafiken** unterstützen das Gesagte und die Anschaulichkeit deines Vortrags. Auch hier gilt: auf die Größe achten!
5. Die einzelnen Visualisierungen brauchen einen **klaren Ablaufplan**. Verwende sie nacheinander und gib deinen Zuhörern die Möglichkeit, sie parallel zu deinem Vortrag lange genug wahrzunehmen.
6. Vermeide es, während der Präsentation selbst auf deine visuellen Hilfsmittel zu schauen. Halte zu jeder Zeit den **Blickkontakt** mit deinen Zuhörern aufrecht und achte auf deine **Körpersprache**. Verstecke dich nicht hinter einem Skript. Auch ein Lächeln kann sehr überzeugend sein!

SF REVISION   Project skills

Organisation ist (fast) alles

Bei einer Projektarbeit, die du mit anderen gemeinsam durchführst, kommt es darauf an, dass du dich und deine Arbeit sehr gut organisierst und die einzelnen Phasen eines Projektes berücksichtigst. Meistens findet die Bearbeitung eines Projektauftrags innerhalb einer gewissen Zeitspanne statt, während parallel dazu der Unterricht weitergeht. Oft findet also ein Großteil der Arbeit außerhalb des Unterrichts statt – ein guter Grund, um nochmals auf die einzelnen Schritte einer Projektarbeit zu schauen, die dir helfen sollen, zur verabredeten *deadline* dein fertiges Produkt abgeben zu können.

Projektarbeit Schritt für Schritt

Schritt 1: Entscheide dich für dein Thema
Zuerst musst du dir darüber klar werden, welches Thema dich interessieren könnte. Zu welchem Thema weißt du vielleicht schon etwas, sodass du auf diesem Wissen aufbauen kannst?

Schritt 2: Finde deine Projektpartner
Nun musst du Mitschülerinnen und Mitschüler finden, die dein Thema ebenfalls interessant finden. Bei einer Projektarbeit kommt es auch darauf an, dass sich Menschen mit unterschiedlichen Talenten in einer Gruppe finden: Wer kennt sich gut mit dem Internet aus, wer kann zeichnen, wer schreiben, …?

Schritt 3: Tauscht eure Ideen aus
Was weiß eure Gruppe schon über das gewählte Thema? Wie soll eure Arbeit aussehen? Sammelt alle Ideen und Anregungen – vielleicht in Form einer *placemat* oder Mindmap? Vergesst nicht, euch auch auf die Form eures Handlungsproduktes, dem Ergebnis eurer Projektarbeit, zu einigen. Das kann zum Beispiel ein Poster, ein Text, ein Booklet oder eine Präsentation sein.

Schritt 4: Plant eure Arbeit
Wer übernimmt welche Aufgabe? Setzt euch einen realistischen Zeitrahmen und überprüft regelmäßig euren Arbeitsstand.

Schritt 5: Recherchiert Material
Für euer Produkt braucht ihr Informationen, Material, Bilder und vieles mehr. Stellt sicher, dass jeder etwas beiträgt.
▶ *Research, p. 130*

Schritt 6: Seid effizient
Haltet euch nicht zu lange an Materialien und Ideen auf, die euch nicht zum Ziel führen. Bei der Auswahl helfen euch unter anderem die Lesetechniken *skimming* und *scanning*.
▶ *Skimming and scanning, p. 139*

Schritt 7: Schreibt eine Outline
Wenn ihr ausreichend Material zusammengetragen habt, dann ordnet es anhand einer Outline an.
▶ *Outlining, p. 131*

Schritt 8: Beginnt mit der Herstellung eures Produktes
Beginnt recht zügig, die einzelnen Teile eures Produktes zusammenzufügen. Text, Bilder, aber auch Poster oder elektronische Präsentationen brauchen viel Zeit. Zeigt euch regelmäßig den Stand eurer Arbeiten, um mögliche Fehler frühzeitig zu bemerken.

Schritt 9: Kontrolliert gemeinsam das Produkt
Bevor ihr fertig seid, müsst ihr einen letzten Durchgang der Fehlersuche und -korrektur durchführen. Auch an Stil und Layout kann man jetzt noch Verbesserungen vornehmen.

Schritt 10: Präsentiert eure Ergebnisse
Wenn ihr eure Ergebnisse in einer Präsentation vorstellen wollt, müsst ihr diese gut vorbereiten. Denkt an eine aussagekräftige Visualisierung und ein Handout.

- ▶ *Giving a presentation, p. 132*
- ▶ *Giving a group presentation, p. 132*
- ▶ *Handouts, p. 133*
- ▶ *Visual aids in presentations, p. 133*

Schritt 11 (fakultativ): Beurteile deine eigene Arbeit
Denke zum Schluss an dein nächstes Projekt und beurteile daraufhin nochmals das gerade durchgeführte. Was ist euch gut gelungen? Worauf müsst ihr das nächste Mal stärker achten?
- ▶ *Peer evaluation, p. 136*

Schritt 12: Genießt die Ergebnisse
Ihr habt ganz selbstständig eine Aufgabe gemeistert und seid sicherlich zu tollen Ergebnissen gekommen. Genießt die Produkte der anderen Gruppen, lasst euch Zeit beim Anschauen und lobt eure Mitschülerinnen und Mitschüler für die Dinge, die ihnen besonders gut gelungen sind!

SF Peer evaluation ▸ Unit 1 (p. 11)

In allen Klassenstufen ist die Zusammenarbeit im Unterricht wichtig. Dabei geht es aber nicht nur um das gemeinsame Erstellen von Arbeitsprodukten, sondern zunehmend auch darum, die erbrachten Leistungen einzuschätzen und gegenseitig zu beurteilen. Damit die Rückmeldungen (*evaluations*) zielgerichtet und hilfreich sein können, muss man systematisch vorgehen und sich an bestimmte Regeln halten.

Schriftliches Englisch beurteilen *(evaluation of written English)*

Hier nimmt der Partner die Rolle eines Korrektors ein. Im gemeinsamen Gespräch soll ermittelt werden, wie sich der Stil, die Sprache, aber auch der Inhalt des betreffenden Textes verbessern lassen. In folgenden Schritten geht man vor:

Schritt 1: Der Text des Partners muss in Ruhe und genau gelesen werden.

Schritt 2: Positive Aspekte des Gesamtausdrucks werden notiert.

Schritt 3: Besonders gelungene Passagen werden im Text unterstrichen, damit sie als Beispiele herangezogen werden können.

Schritt 4: Verbesserungsvorschläge werden notiert. Das können einfache Rechtschreibkorrekturen sein, aber auch strukturelle oder inhaltliche Verbesserungen; in diesen Bereichen führt die individuelle Rückmeldung am schnellsten zum Erfolg.

Schritt 5: Man sollte auch immer über Verbesserungsmöglichkeiten sprechen – erst im Austausch der Ideen werden die Aspekte klar formuliert und helfen dem Verfasser weiter.

Mündliches Englisch beurteilen *(evaluation of spoken English)*

Gleichgültig, welche Art von mündlicher Leistung – ob nun ein Dialog oder ein Vortrag – evaluiert wird, kann man immer nach den gleichen Kriterien vorgehen:

1. Inhalt: Die Informationen sind sinnvoll ausgewählt und strukturiert und belegen ein sicheres Verständnis des Themas.

2. Strategie: Die Sprache wurde klar und gut formuliert eingesetzt, Lücken in Lexik und Grammatik konnten kompensiert werden, das Interesse der Zuhörer wurde geweckt.

3. Stil/Ausdruck: Die Sprache wurde präzise eingesetzt, der Wortschatz war differenziert, besondere Redemittel (z. B. zur Strukturierung oder zur Betonung) wurden eingesetzt.

Am effektivsten ist es, wenn man einen vorgefertigten Feedback-Bogen (*evaluation sheet*) verwendet, der es erlaubt, Kategorien des Sprechens schnell und zielgerichtet wahrzunehmen und zu beurteilen.

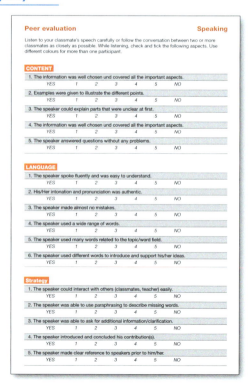

LISTENING AND READING SKILLS

SF REVISION   Listening

Vor dem Hören

- Frag dich, was du schon über das Thema weißt.
- Nutze Überschriften oder Bilder um zu erahnen, was dich z. B. bei einer Geschichte erwarten könnte.
- Lies dir die Aufgaben auf deinem Aufgabenblatt genau durch und überlege, auf welche Informationen du dich konzentrieren musst.
- Bereite dich darauf vor, Notizen zu machen. Leg z. B. eine Tabelle oder Liste an.

Während des Hörens

Listening for gist:
Konzentriere dich beim ersten Hören auf allgemeine Informationen, z. B. die Personen (unterschiedliche Stimmen), das Thema, die Umgebung (Geräusche), die Atmosphäre (die Sprechweise der Leute).

Listening for detail:
- Mach dir noch einmal bewusst, worauf du genau achten willst (Hörauftrag), besonders bei Durchsagen (*announcements*), die du vielleicht nur einmal hören kannst.
- Gerate nicht in Panik, wenn du meinst, du hättest gerade etwas Wichtiges verpasst. Konzentriere dich auf die nächste wichtige Information.
- Lass dich nicht von anderen Einzelheiten oder Geräuschen ablenken.
- Mach nur kurze Notizen, z. B. Anfangsbuchstaben, Symbole oder Stichworte.
- Manche Signalwörter machen es dir leichter, den Hörtext zu verstehen.
  Aufzählung: **and**, **another**, **too**
  Gegensatz: **although**, **but**
  Grund, Folge: **because**, **so**, **so that**
  Vergleich: **larger/older/... than**, **as ... as**, **more**, **most**
  Reihenfolge: **before**, **after**, **then**, **next**, **later**, **when**, **at last**, **at the same time**
- Auch andere Details wie z. B. die Stimme, der Akzent oder der Tonfall des Sprechers oder der Sprecherin können dir helfen, Informationen über seine oder ihre Gefühle, Herkunft usw. zu bekommen.
- Unterteile Telefonnummern beim Aufschreiben: 0171 572 4258.

Nach dem Hören

- Vervollständige deine Notizen sofort.
- Wenn du den Text ein zweites Mal hören kannst, konzentriere dich auf das, was du beim ersten Mal nicht genau verstanden hast.
- Schau dir noch einmal die Aufgabenstellung an. Sollst du die gehörten Informationen nutzen, um einen neuen Text zu schreiben? Dann achte auf die richtige Textform: Bericht, Beschreibung, ...

SF REVISION Taking notes

Worum geht es beim Notizen machen?

Wenn du beim Lesen oder Zuhören Notizen machst, kannst du dich später besser daran erinnern, wenn du etwas vortragen, nacherzählen oder einen Bericht schreiben sollst.

Wie mache ich Notizen?

In Texten oder Gesprächen gibt es immer wichtige und unwichtige Wörter. Die wichtigen Wörter werden **Schlüsselwörter** *(key words)* genannt und nur die solltest du notieren. Meist sind das Substantive und Verben, manchmal auch Adjektive oder Zahlen.

Deine Notizen sollten knapp sein:
- Verwende Ziffern (z. B. „7" statt „seven").
- Verwende Symbole und Abkürzungen, z. B. ✔ (für Ja) und + (für und) oder GB für Great Britain, K für Katrina.
  Du kannst auch eigene Symbole erfinden.
- Verwende not oder ╳ statt „doesn't" oder „don't".

Hmm, da hab ich wohl ein paar Symbole zu viel benutzt …

SF REVISION Marking up a text

Wann sollte ich einen Text markieren?

Du hast einen Text mit vielen Fakten vor dir liegen und sollst später über bestimmte Dinge berichten. Dann wird es dir helfen, die für dich wichtigen Informationen im Text zu markieren.

Wie gehe ich am besten vor?

Lies den Text und markiere nur die für dein Thema wichtigen Informationen. Nicht jeder Satz enthält Informationen, die für deine Aufgabe wichtig sind, und oft reicht es aus, nur ein oder zwei Wörter in einem Satz zu markieren.
- Du kannst wichtige Wörter einkreisen.
- Du kannst sie unterstreichen.
- Du kannst sie mit einem Textmarker hervorheben.

ABER:
Markiere nur auf Fotokopien von Texten oder in deinen eigenen Büchern.

Sydney Opera House
The Sydney Opera House is (one of the most famous buildings in the world.) It houses the large Concert Hall (2,678 seats), the Opera Theatre (1,507 seats), other smaller theatres and a place for open-air events.

Sydney Opera House
The Sydney Opera House is one of the most famous buildings in the world. It houses the large Concert Hall (2,678 seats), the Opera Theatre (1,507 seats), other smaller theatres and a place for open-air events.

Sydney Opera House
The Sydney Opera House is one of the most famous buildings in the world. It houses the large Concert Hall (2,678 seats), the Opera Theatre (1,507 seats), other smaller theatres and a place for open-air events.

Skills File

REVISION Reading course – Zusammenfassung

Working out the meaning of words

Das Nachschlagen unbekannter Wörter im Wörterbuch kostet Zeit und nimmt auf Dauer den Spaß am Lesen. Oft geht es auch ohne Wörterbuch:

1. Bilder und Zeichen erklären und ergänzen oft Dinge aus dem Text. Schau sie dir deshalb vor und nach dem Lesen genau an.
2. Manche Wörter erklären sich aus dem Textzusammenhang, z. B. *When we reached the station, Judy bought our tickets.*
3. Zu manchen englischen Wörtern fallen dir vielleicht deutsche, französische oder lateinische Wörter ein, die ähnlich geschrieben oder ausgesprochen werden, z. B. **excellent**, **millionaire**, **nation**, **reality**.
4. Es gibt neue Wörter, in denen du bekannte Teile entdeckst, z. B. **friendliness**, **helpless**, **understandable**, **gardener**, **tea bag**, **waiting room**.

Skimming and scanning

Beim **Skimming** überfliegst du einen Text schnell, um dir einen **Überblick** zu verschaffen. Du willst dabei herausfinden, worum es in dem Text geht. Achte dabei auf
– die **Überschrift**,
– die **Zwischenüberschriften** und hervorgehobene Wörter oder Sätze,
– die **Bilder** und **Bildunterschriften**,
– den **ersten Satz** und den **letzten Satz** jedes Absatzes,
– **Grafiken**, **Statistiken** und die **Quelle** des Textes.

Beim **Scanning** suchst du nach **bestimmten Informationen**. Dazu suchst du den Text nach Schlüsselwörtern (*key words*) ab und liest nur dort genauer, wo du sie findest. Geh dabei so vor:

Schritt 1: Denk an die Schlüsselwörter und geh mit deinen Augen oder dem Finger schnell durch den Text, in breiten Schlingen wie bei einem „S" oder „Z" oder von oben nach unten wie bei einem „U". Die gesuchten Wörter werden dir sofort „ins Auge springen".

Schritt 2: Wenn das gesuchte Wort nicht im Text vorkommt, überlege dir andere, themenverwandte Wörter (z. B. **lesson** → **school**, **subject**) und suche nach diesen.

Finding the main ideas of a text

Zeitungsartikel, Berichte oder Kommentare verstehst du besser, wenn du ihre wesentlichen Aussagen erkennst und dir klar machst, wie sie zusammenhängen. Die wichtigsten Aussagen findest du so:

1. Jeder Text hat ein Thema mit mindestens einer Hauptaussage, z. B.: *Drinking soda is one of the worst things you can do to your health.* Diese Hauptaussage findest du oft im **ersten Absatz**.

2. Die Hauptaussage wird in der Regel durch weitere Aussagen bzw. Gedanken unterstützt, z. B.: *Experts agree that sugary soft drinks and fast food are the main reasons why so many American teenagers are fat.*

3. Diese weiteren Aussagen bzw. Gedanken werden oft durch Beispiele und Begründungen ergänzt, z. B.: *About 7 % of the calories that they take in come from soft drinks alone.*

Careful reading

Schwierige Texte musst du besonders sorgfältig und konzentriert lesen, damit du alle darin enthaltenen Informationen und Gedanken verstehst.

1. Lies den Text genau. Welches sind seine wesentlichen Aussagen? (▶ *Finding the main ideas of a text, pp. 136–137*)

2. Manchmal musst du dir die Antwort auf eine Frage aus einzelnen Informationen erschließen, die du an verschiedenen Stellen im Text findest. Nimm zum Beispiel den Text auf S. 38: Warum heißt es in der Überschrift, wir seien alle *bystanders*? Für die Antwort musst du mehrere Aussagen aus dem Text zusammentragen:

<u>FACTS:</u> Concrete example: Peggy, who did not act when Stewart was bullied by other boys. Everybody has experienced similar situations where we witness a problem, realize we should do something and still don't do anything.

<u>CONCLUSION:</u> We are all bystanders or at least we are all at risk of remaining bystanders.

Text types: fiction and non-fiction

Wenn du einen Text liest, ist es sinnvoll sich klar zu machen, ob er von einer vom Autor erdachten Welt handelt (*fictional text,* deutsch: Dichtung) oder sich mit der Wirklichkeit auseinandersetzt (*non-fictional text,* deutsch: Sachtext).

Fiktionale Texte sind z. B. Kurzgeschichten und Romane. Der Autor wählt Figuren (*characters*) aus und erzählt von ihren Gefühlen und Handlungen, von deren Motiven und Hintergründen. Die Handlungen finden in einem oder mehreren Handlungsrahmen statt, z. B. an einem Ort, zu einer bestimmten Zeit und unter bestimmten Umständen (*setting*). Die Ereignisse können aus verschiedenen Perspektiven erzählt werden (*point of view*). Oft verwendet der Autor für seine Geschichte eine anschauliche Sprache, z. B. ausschmückende Adjektive, Metaphern, Vergleiche, direkte Rede oder er lässt den Leser an den Gedanken seiner Figuren oder des Erzählers teilhaben.

Nicht-fiktionale Texte sind z. B. Berichte in Zeitungen, wissenschaftliche Artikel, Aufsätze oder Kommentare. Hier informiert der Autor über ein Thema der realen Welt oder nimmt Stellung dazu.

Es gibt auch Texte, die ein **Mischform** aus beiden Textarten sind.

SF REVISION   Reading literature

Sachtexte und literarische Texte

Wie bei allen Texten handelt es sich auch bei englischen Texten entweder um Sachtexte oder um literarische Texte. **Sachtexte** – z.B. Zeitungsberichte oder Reden – wollen vorwiegend informieren oder zu etwas auffordern. **Literarische Texte**, die oft in einer besonderen Form oder Sprache verfasst sind, zeigen eine Welt oder Umgebung, die der Autor oder die Autorin erdacht hat. Im Englischen nennt man diese Texte auch *fiction*, weil sie von einer erdachten oder erfundenen (englisch: *fictional*) Welt handeln, im Gegensatz zu *non-fiction*, die sich mit der wirklichen Welt auseinandersetzt. Manche Texte liegen in einem Grenzbereich dazwischen.

Alles, was für das Lesen von Texten im Allgemeinen gilt (▶ *Reading Course, pp. 139–140*), trifft auch für das Lesen von Literatur zu. Deshalb ist es ratsam, auch in literarischen Texten Dinge zu markieren, die auffallen oder wichtig erscheinen.

Literarische Gattungen und ihre Merkmale

Grundsätzlich unterscheidet man drei Arten von literarischen Texten bzw. **literarischen Gattungen** (*genre*): Gedichte (Lyrik = *poetry*), Erzähltexte (Epik = *prose literature* oder *fiction*; damit wird der Begriff *fiction* im Englischen auch in einem etwas anderen, engeren Sinne gebraucht) und Dramen (Dramatik = *drama*).

Die Gattungen unterscheiden sich meist bereits in ihrer äußeren Form. In der Regel
- bestehen Gedichte aus gebundener Sprache, d.h. aus Verszeilen und Strophen *(lines/verses and stanzas)*,
- haben Erzähltexte fortlaufenden Text *(prose)*,
- ist ein Drama in Monologen und Dialogen *(monologues/dialogues)* als direkte Rede gesetzt.

Man kann Literatur einfach zum Vergnügen lesen, zum Beispiel, weil die Geschichte, ein bestimmtes Thema oder die dargestellten Personen interessant, spannend oder unterhaltend erscheinen. Zum besseren Verständnis kann es aber beitragen, wenn man etwas über formale, stilistische oder technische Besonderheiten des Textes weiß. Dann kann man sich beim Lesen überlegen, warum der Autor oder die Autorin wohl ausgerechnet diese Mittel einsetzt und welcher Eindruck oder welches Gefühl dadurch während des Lesens entsteht. Solche Besonderheiten sind beispielsweise

in Erzähltexten *(prose literature/fiction)*
- die Entwicklung der Handlung *(plot)*, die sich in verschiedene Handlungsstränge *(subplots)* unterteilen kann,
- die Figur des Erzählers *(narrator)*, dessen Beziehung zur Handlung oder Verhältnis zu anderen handelnden Personen die Erzählperspektive *(point of view)* prägt; im Englischen unterscheidet man zwischen einem *limited* und einem *unlimited point of view*, was gleichzeitig beschreibt, wie viel der Erzähler über die Geschehnisse und deren Vorgeschichte und Auswirkungen weiß,
- die Beschreibung der Figuren *(characters)*, die direkt oder indirekt erfolgen kann *(direct or indirect characterization)*,
- die Atmosphäre *(atmosphere)*,

It was one January morning, very early – a pinching, frosty morning – the cove all grey with hoar-frost, the ripple lapping softly on the stones, the sun still low and only touching the hilltops and shining far to seaward. The captain had risen earlier than usual and set out down the beach [...] I remember his breath hanging like smoke in his wake as he strode off.
From Treasure Island *by Robert Louis Stevenson*

In Erzähltexten wird der Schauplatz (*setting*) häufig durch bildhafte Adjektive, Vergleiche und Metaphern beschrieben.

– der Aufbau von Spannung (*suspense*),
– die vom Autor gewählte Form oder Strukturierung des Erzähltextes als Roman (*novel*), Kurzgeschichte (*short story*) o. Ä., die durch ihre charakteristischen Elemente die Aussage des Textes mitformen.

in Gedichten (*poetry*)
– die äußere Aufteilung in Strophen (*stanzas*),
– die Verwendung von Reim am Ende, aber auch innerhalb der Zeile (*end rhyme and internal rhyme*), wobei ein Muster (*rhyme scheme*) entstehen kann, das z.T. auf etablierte Formen zurückgreift (z.B. beim Sonett) oder auch ein ganz individuell neues Schema begründet,
– ein Rhythmus (*rhythm*), dessen Folge von betonten und unbetonten Silen ein mehr oder minder regelmäßiges Metrum (*metre*) ergeben kann,
– eine auffällige bildhafte Sprache (*imagery: metaphors, similes and symbols*),
– weitere strukturelle Elemente wie das Verwenden eines Refrains (*refrain*), inhaltliche oder formale Wiederholungen (*repetitions*) oder lautliche Besonderheiten (*alliteration, assonance*),

in Dramen (*drama*)
– die Art und Weise, wie Handlung in Dialogen (*dialogues*) und Monologen (*monologues*) sichtbar gemacht wird,
– Textmerkmale, die daher rühren, dass der Text für die Aufführung auf einer Bühne (*stage performance*) geschrieben wurde,
– die Aufteilung der Handlung in Akte und Szenen (*acts and scenes*), durch deren Anordnung Spannung entwickelt werden kann,
– die Konstellation von Charakteren, die Held bzw. Heldin (*protagonist*), Gegner (*antagonist*) oder Partner sein können; sie ist der Auslöser für einen oder mehrere Grundkonflikte (*conflicts*), die das Drama prägen,
– die dramatische Sprache, die alltäglich klingen kann, aber verschiedene Funktionen hat: Information über Motive und Hintergründe oder Pläne, Beschreibung der Charaktere, Vorantreiben der Handlung, Spannungsaufbau,
– die Bedeutung von Bühnenanweisungen (*stage directions*).

Es kommt auch vor, dass man – vor allem literarische – Texte nicht nur verstehen, sondern umsetzen muss, indem man sie darstellt oder einfach nur ausdrucksvoll spricht, indem man eigene Formen von Literatur verfasst, sie um- oder weiterschreibt. Gerade dann ist es wichtig, dass man die Besonderheiten des zugrundeliegenden Textes klar analysiert.

Castaway

The sea is a numberless army
Surrounding my desert isle.
The wind is its heartless general,
Howling mile after mile.
As wave after wave hits the beaches,
I catch sight of a hopeful white sail;
Then storm clouds hide the horizon
And all hope disappears in the gale.

Stephen Brock

Gedichte können Reime und Metaphern enthalten.

Enter Jack.
Gwendolen — (*Catching sight of him.*) Ernest! My own Ernest!
Jack — Gwendolen! Darling! (*Offers to kiss her.*)
Gwendolen — (*Draws back.*) A moment! May I ask if you are engaged to be married to this young lady? (*Points to Cecily.*)
Jack — (*Laughing.*) To dear little Cecily! Of course not! What could have put such an idea into your pretty little head?
Gwendolen — Thank you. You may! (*Offers her cheek.*)
Cecily — (*Very sweetly.*) I knew there must be some misunderstanding, Miss Fairfax. The gentleman *whose arm is at present round your waist* is my guardian, Mr. John Worthing.

From The Importance of Being Earnest *by Oscar Wilde*

In einem Drama ergeben sich sowohl aus den Dialogen als auch als den Bühnenanweisungen (*stage directions*) Handlungsanweisungen für die Darsteller.

Über literarische Texte sprechen

Wenn man über literarische Texte schreiben oder sprechen will, sind folgende Formulierungen hilfreich:

The story/novel/play/poem/song is about ...
The story is set in ...
The text tells the story of ...
The author uses a ...

XY is the narrator of the story; he/she only has a limited point of view.
The main character/hero/is …
He/She comes across as a strong/weak/aggressive/brave/… person.
He/She is characterized indirectly by his/her way of …

I liked it/didn't like it when …
I found the ending/story/characters interesting/funny/confusing …
The words and expressions in the text create an exciting/thrilling/… atmosphere.
It makes me feel compassionate for … / frustrated / … like/unlike the main character.
The text conveys a happy/sad/angry/… feeling.

The poem consists of … verses/stanzas, each with … lines.
The lines of the poem (don't) rhyme.
Every other line rhymes.
The speaker of the poem describes/utters/is in doubt about …
I think … is a metaphor for/symbol of …
In lines … and … you can find an alliteration/parallelism/rhetorical question.
This focuses our attention on the fact that …
With it the author wants to express …

In the play the dramatist is concerned with the issue/topic …
In the dialogue between … and … there is a lot of emotion/tension/anger/humour/arrogance …
The action takes place during … / in …
The stage directions are (not) very detailed.
In the play a conflict develops between … and … which refers to …
At the end there is a lot of suspense whether there will be a catastrophe or a happy ending.

SF Identifying style and register   ▶ Unit 2 (p. 31)

Je nach Situation, Themenbereich und beabsichtigter Wirkung können sich Menschen spezifischer Sprachstile *(style, register)* bedienen, die sich hinsichtlich der Wortwahl und der Satzstrukturen voneinander unterscheiden. Man spricht allgemein von den folgenden Stilebenen:

- **Förmliche Sprache *(formal language)*:** Gebrauch von weniger geläufigen Wörtern (oft Fachbegriffe, Latinismen oder Gräzismen), sehr schwierige Satzstrukturen (viele Nebensätze, Partizipien), keine Verkürzungen (wie z. B. *he's*).
- **Neutrale Sprache *(neutral language)*:** Allgemein leichter verständlich. Die Wortwahl weist auf keine Wertung hin. Keine umgangssprachlichen Wörter oder Wendungen, leicht nachvollziehbarer Satzaufbau.
- **Umgangssprache *(informal language)*:** Viele einfachere Wörter, oftmals Abbildung gesprochener Sprache – häufiger Gebrauch von Verkürzungen, hohe Frequenz an Fragen („You know what I mean?"), dabei auch oft fehlerhafte Verwendung der Grammatik.
- **Saloppe Umgangssprache *(slang)*:** Einfachstes sprachliches Niveau, oft mit fehlerhafter Verwendung von Grammatik und Lexik, bildhafte Ausdrücke und Redewendungen, verstärkter Gebrauch verknappter Satz- und Wortstrukturen.

SF Understanding adverts ▶ Unit 1 (pp. 16–17)

Werbung folgt fast immer dem so genannten AIDA-Prinzip:

- **Attention:** Zuerst muss die Aufmerksamkeit des Kunden gewonnen werden. Das erreicht man meist durch Bildbotschaften, oft in Kombination oder im Kontrast mit einer Überschrift oder einem Slogan.
- **Interest:** Nun wird das Interesse der potenzieller Kunden geweckt, die wissen möchten, was hinter den auffälligen Botschaften der Werbeanzeige steht.
- **Desire:** Die dargebotene Produktinformation muss so gestaltet sein, dass der Kunde ein spontanes Verlangen verspürt, das Produkt besitzen zu wollen.
- **Action:** Um ihm oder ihr nun noch die (Kauf-)Entscheidung zu erleichtern, muss man ihm klar machen, wie leicht es ist aktiv zu werden und das Produkt zu kaufen.

Nach dem gleichen Prinzip funktionieren auch Werbeanzeigen, die dem Betrachter weniger einen Kauf als vielmehr ein Verhalten nahe legen wollen.

SF Analysing newspaper articles ▶ Unit 2 (p. 34)

Zeitungsartikel setzen sich größtenteils mit aktuellen Vorgängen auseinander, je nach gewählter Textsorte (z.B. Nachricht, Reportage, Kommentar oder Leserbrief/ *letter to the editor*) mit der Absicht der Informations- oder Meinungsvermittlung geschieht dies mehr oder minder objektiv. Folgende Aspekte spielen bei ihrer Analyse eine Rolle:

- **Inhalt *(contents)*:** Aus dem Text, aber auch den möglicherweise beigefügten Illustrationen muss der Informationsgehalt erschlossen werden (*wh-questions*).
- **Aufbau *(structure)*:** Die innere Struktur eines Artikels wird oft durch das Layout unterstützt, z.B. durch die Überschrift (*headline*), die Unter- oder Zwischenüberschrift (*subheading*) oder Bildunterschriften (*captions*). In der so genannten *byline* wird die Verfasserin bzw. der Verfasser des Artikels genannt.
- **Stil *(style and register)*:** Besonders in seriösen Zeitungen wird ein förmlicher Stil bevorzugt.
- **Argumentation *(argumentation)*:** Die Verfasserin bzw. der Verfasser stellt bestimmte Thesen auf, die mit Argumenten unterstützt werden. Als Leser sollte man diese Argumentation nachvollziehen und stets kritisch hinterfragen.
- **Grafische Gestaltung *(layout)*:** Zeitungen können sich voneinander durch ihre Gestaltung unterscheiden, z.B. durch die Art, Größe und evtl. Farbe der Schrift, die Art der Seitenaufteilung oder die spezifische Verwendung von Illustrationen und Fotos.

Für die Beiträge in Online-Zeitungen gilt all dies entsprechend. Hyperlinks und Foren (*open threads*) ermöglichen den Lesern weitere Recherche und Kommentierung.

MEDIATION COURSE – Zusammenfassung

Sprachmittlung (*mediation*) ist die Überführung eines Inhalts von einer Ausgangssprache in eine Zielsprache wie es zum Beispiel geschieht, wenn sich zwei Menschen miteinander verständigen wollen, die nicht dieselbe Sprache sprechen, und ein Dritter die Mittlerrolle übernimmt.

Unter Sprachmittlung versteht man sowohl freie Formen der Übertragung in die jeweils andere Sprache, bei denen der Inhalt gekürzt und zusammengefasst wird (das ist Mediation im engeren Sinne des Wortes), als auch strenge Formen, bei denen ein Text ungekürzt und wortgetreu in eine andere Sprache übersetzt wird.

Sprachmittlung kann sowohl mündlich als auch schriftlich und in beide Sprachrichtungen (zum Beispiel vom Englischen ins Deutsche und umgekehrt) erfolgen, wobei die wörtliche Übersetzung in der Schule in der Regel nur schriftlich erfolgt.

Oral and written mediation ▶ *Unit 1 (p. 25), Unit 2 (p. 40)*

Bei der Mediation im engeren Sinne wird immer auch gekürzt, d.h. nur die wichtigsten Informationen werden ausgewählt und in die andere Sprache übertragen. Insofern kann man die Mediation auch als eine Art mündliche oder schriftliche *summary* in der jeweils anderen Sprache bezeichnen. Alle Tipps und Hilfsmittel, die zu einer erfolgreichen *summary* beitragen (im Schriftlichen z.B. die Wegstreich- oder Zettelmethode), können also auch bei der Mediation angewendet werden. (▶ *Summary writing, p. 147*)

Folgende Tipps sind für schriftliche wie mündliche Formen der Mediation hilfreich:

– Die gegebene Situation sowie die Wünsche und Bedürfnisse des Adressaten sollten berücksichtigt werden. Es macht einen Unterschied, ob man für die eigene Großmutter, für einen Freund oder für die zukünftige Chefin sprachmittelt.
– Der Text sollte nur die wichtigen und zentralen Informationen wiedergeben, die zum Gesamtverständnis notwendig sind. Unwichtige Informationen sollte man weglassen.
– Die Struktur und die Logik des Originaltextes dürfen geändert werden, wenn die Botschaft auf diese Weise klarer und verständlicher beim Adressaten ankommt.
– Begriffe, z.B. Fachtermini, deren Übersetzung man nicht kennt oder für die es in der anderen Sprache vielleicht gar keine Entsprechung gibt, muss man umschreiben. Dies kann z.B. mit Relativsätzen geschehen:
  It's somebody/a person who … / It's something that you use … / It's an animal that … / It's a place that/where …
   (▶ *Paraphrasing, p. 147*)

Bei der Mediation kann es also notwendig sein, Informationen *hinzuzufügen*, nämlich dann, wenn ein bestimmter Name, ein Begriff oder eine Tätigkeit dem Adressaten aufgrund kultureller Unterschiede vermutlich nichts sagt. In diesem Fall sollte man eine zusätzliche Erläuterung geben, also ausführlicher sein, als es der Ausgangstext ist:

In Hindelang erlebten wir den Almabtrieb. → In Hindelang we saw the 'Almabtrieb', the ceremonial driving down of cattle from the mountain pastures into the valley in the autumn.

Speziell bei der mündlichen Sprachmittlung ist es wichtig, genau auf die Reaktionen des Gegenübers zu achten und auf diese ggf. mit weiteren Erläuterungen einzugehen. Auch Rückfragen sind möglich. In der mündlichen Sprachmittlung können unterstützend auch Gestik und Mimik eingesetzt werden.

Translation ▶ *Unit 3 (p. 59)*

Für Übersetzungen gilt als Faustregel: „So nah am Originaltext wie möglich, so frei wie nötig". Einerseits soll die Übersetzung die allgemeine Tendenz und Aussage des Originals, aber auch seine Formulierungen bis ins Detail so genau wie möglich wiedergeben. Andererseits soll man dem so entstandenen Text möglichst gar nicht ansehen, dass er eine Übersetzung aus einer anderen Sprache ist; er soll sich also so natürlich lesen, als sei er selbst das Original.

So dürfen Ausdrücke und Redensarten (*idioms and sayings*) nicht Wort für Wort übersetzt werden, sondern man muss ihre Entsprechung in der Zielsprache finden – wenn es denn überhaupt eine gibt:

He acted like a bull in a China shop. → Er verhielt sich wie ein Elefant im Porzellanladen.
It's Greek to me. → Ich verstehe nur Bahnhof.
The early bird catches the worm. → Morgenstund hat Gold im Mund.

Auch sollten bestimmte grammatische Strukturen wie z. B. englische Partizipialkonstruktionen aufgelöst und so formuliert werden, wie es in der Zielsprache üblich ist:

Standing at the window he saw his friend. → Er stand am Fenster, als er seinen Freund sah.

Für eine gelungene Übersetzung sollte man Folgendes beachten:

- Am besten beginnt man nicht sofort mit dem Übersetzen, sondern versucht zunächst, den Text in seiner Gesamtheit zu erfassen, indem man ihn mehrmals vollständig durchliest. Wenn man mit einer Kopie arbeitet, kann man dabei unklare oder schwierige Passagen markieren; unbekannte Wörter lassen sich im Wörterbuch nachschlagen und ihre Übersetzung notieren.
- Eine Rohübersetzung lässt sich schrittweise korrigieren, wenn man von vornherein Platz für Verbesserungen (Leerzeilen) lässt. Am Schluss wird der Text ins Reine geschrieben.
- Nach der Fertigstellung sollte die Übersetzung nochmals geprüft werden: auf Zusammenhang und Verständlichkeit („Ergibt dieser Abschnitt überhaupt einen Sinn?"), auf Vollständigkeit (übersehen werden oft so genannte „kleine" Wörter, z. B. *however, yet, also* die Überschrift, manchmal auch ein Nebensatz) und auf die Idiomatik („Klingt der Text stilistisch gut und richtig?").

SPEAKING AND WRITING SKILLS

SF REVISION   Paraphrasing

Worum geht es beim Paraphrasing?

„Paraphrasing" bedeutet, etwas mit anderen Worten zu erklären. Das ist hilfreich, wenn dir ein bestimmtes Wort nicht einfällt oder wenn dein Gegenüber dich nicht verstanden hat. Paraphrasing ist auch besonders nützlich für **mediation** (▶ *Mediation, p. 140*).

Wie gehe ich beim Paraphrasing vor?

– Man kann mit einem Ausdruck umschreiben, der dieselbe Bedeutung hat:
  'To wonder' is the same as 'to ask yourself'.
  Oder man sagt das Gegenteil:
  'Alive' is the opposite of 'dead'.
– Manchmal braucht man mehrere Wörter, z. B. wenn man etwas beschreibt oder erklären will, wie man etwas verwendet. Dabei verwendet man ein allgemeines Wort (**general word**) und nennt weitere Eigenschaften:
  A skyscraper is a very tall building.
– Oder du umschreibst das Wort mit **... is/are like ...**
  A lodge is like a small house or cabin. You find it in the country.
– Du kannst auch einen Relativsatz (**relative clause**) verwenden:
  She is somebody who looks after small children. – Ah, she's a nanny!
  A ticket office is a shop where you can buy tickets for shows and concerts.

SF REVISION Brainstorming

Was ist Brainstorming und wofür ist es gut?

Bei vielen Aufgaben ist es nützlich, wenn du im ersten Schritt möglichst viele Ideen zum Thema sammelst. Beim Sammeln und beim Auswerten der Ideen helfen dir die folgenden Techniken.

Drei verschiedene Brainstorming-Techniken

Technik 1: Making a list
Schreib die Ideen so auf, wie sie dir einfallen, und zwar für jede Idee eine neue Zeile. Lies im zweiten Schritt alle deine Ideen durch. Überlege, welche Ideen davon für dein Thema sinnvoll sind und nummeriere sie nach Nützlichkeit.

Technik 2: Making a mind map
Leg eine Mindmap an. Überlege dafür, welche Oberbegriffe zu deinem Thema passen. Verwende unterschiedliche Farben für jeden Oberbegriff. Ergänze jede Idee, die zu einem Oberbegriff passt, auf einem Nebenast. Nimm dafür nur wichtige Schlüsselwörter. Du kannst statt Wörtern auch Symbole verwenden und Bilder ergänzen.

Technik 3: The 5 Ws
Schreib die Fragewörter **Who? What? When? Where? Why?** in eine Tabelle. Die Ideen, die dir zu der jeweiligen Frage kommen, werden darunter geschrieben.

6. watch DVDs
3. swimming pool
   no jobs for parents
   parents not at home
1. sleep late – every morning
   hang out
2. no homework
5. disco/party with friends
   watch TV
4. see friends cinema

REVISION Speaking course – Zusammenfassung

Having a conversation

Ein Gespräch beginnen

Ein Gespräch auf Englisch zu beginnen ist einfacher, als du vielleicht denkst. Es gibt immer mehrere Möglichkeiten:
- **Wenn du etwas erfragen willst** (z. B. den Weg oder die Uhrzeit) **oder um Hilfe bitten möchtest:**
  Excuse me, do you know … • Excuse me, can you tell me … • Excuse me, do you know where… • Could you help me, please?
- **Wenn du jemanden begrüßen möchtest oder kennenlernst:**
  Hi! • Hello! • Good morning. • (bei Erwachsenen) Good afternoon.
  Oft kann man das Gespräch dann mit einer allgemeinen Bemerkung weiterführen: Great day today! • Nice concert, isn't it? • …
  Oft hört man zur Begrüßung auch How are you? oder How do you do? Das sind einfache Begrüßungsformeln, auf die keine ausführliche Antwort erwartet wird. Am besten sagst du einfach Fine, thanks. How about you?
- **Wenn du jemanden wiedertriffst:**
  Hi, …, how are things? • Hi, how is it going? • How are you? • Hi, good to see/meet you.

Fantastic concert, isn't it?

Ein Gespräch führen

Für den weiteren Verlauf des Gesprächs sind diese Wendungen nützlich:
- **Sich vorstellen:** By the way, my name's … • I'm …
- **Sich kennen lernen:** Have you … before? • Have you ever …? • What about you?
- **Sich bedanken/auf Dank reagieren:** Thanks! • Thanks for your help. • You're welcome.
- **Sich verabschieden:** See you tomorrow/next week. • Bye!

Und wenn du einmal etwas nicht verstanden hast, kannst du nachfragen:
Sorry, I didn't get that. • Sorry, can you say that again, please?

Asking for, confirming, giving information

Ein Gespräch ist mehr als nur der Austausch von Informationen; es kommt auch auf einen höflichen und angenehmen Ton an. Das gilt natürlich auch für Gespräche auf Englisch. Diese Wendungen können hilfreich sein:
- **Asking for information:** Oft beginnt man eine Anfrage oder Auskunft mit
  Excuse me… • Excuse me, could you tell me, … • Would you mind telling me … • Sorry, I'd just like to know … • I'm not quite sure about … • Is it/Are they …? • Is it right that …? • Can I just ask … • Excuse me, I've just got a question. • Excuse me, do you think you could …?
- **Confirming information:** Wenn du nachfragen oder sicher gehen möchtest, dass du etwas richtig verstanden hast, kannst du das z. B. so tun: Can I just confirm …? • Is it right that …? • Have I got that right …? • …, (is that) right? • Could you just say that again, please? Auch question tags drücken den Wunsch nach Bestätigung aus: This is the library, isn't it?

Denke auch daran, dich für die erhaltenen Informationen freundlich zu bedanken.

– **Giving information:** Auch wenn du selbst eine Auskunft erteilst, versuche freundlich und höflich zu sein, z. B. mit einer kurzen Einleitung:
Sure. • Of course, no problem. • Well, just a second. • Give me a minute to think about it.
Wenn du nicht weiter helfen kannst, drückst du dein Bedauern aus:
Oh, I'm sorry, I don't know. • Sorry, I'm afraid I can't help you.

Giving an oral summary

Wenn du etwas, was du gehört, gesehen oder gelesen hast, für jemanden anderen zusammenfassen willst, tust du dies oft spontan. Du hast also nicht lange Zeit zum Überlegen und solltest auch nicht zu lange reden.
– Gib **nur das Wesentliche** des Inhalts wieder. Du brauchst dich nicht unbedingt an die chronologische Reihenfolge der Handlung zu halten:
I watched that film … last night. • Yesterday I read that web article about … • I've recently come across that ad/article about … • I've just read that story about …
– Verwende das **Präsens** zum Nacherzählen:
There's this kid … In this one scene he's running away from … then it starts raining … and he's trying … so she has to get out of the car …
– **Halte deine Meinung** zu dem betreffenden Film, Buch usw. **zurück**. Natürlich kannst du durch die Art und Weise, wie du erzählst, indirekt deinen Eindruck wiedergeben, z. B. durch den Ton deiner Stimme, deine Körpersprache und deine Wortwahl.

Having a discussion

Seine Meinung sagen und erklären

– **Expressing an opinion:** In einer Diskussion ist es gut, wenn du möglichst klar und deutlich sagst, was du zu einer bestimmten Frage denkst:
I think … • I feel … • In my opinion …
– **Giving reasons and examples**: Es ist aber noch wichtiger, dass du Beispiele und Argumente nennst, die deine Meinung unterstützen – schließlich willst du deine Gesprächspartner ja überzeugen: because … • First … / Second … • For example … • Let me explain … • That's why …

Auf andere reagieren

– **Asking for clarification:** Manchmal ist es notwendig nachzuhaken:
Could you say that again? • Sorry, but I don't understand what you mean.
– **Agreeing with someone:** Die Meinung eines anderen unterstützt du mit
I agree (with you/…). • That's a good point. • You're right.
– **Disagreeing with someone:** Oft widerspricht man nicht direkt, sondern leitet seine Reaktion z. B. mit Sorry, … ein. Zeig immer Respekt für die Meinung anderer.
I don't think you can say … • I see what you mean but … • No, that's not right. • Sorry, I don't agree with you. • Yes, but …, • Well, I don't think you can say that … • Ah, come on, …

REVISION Writing course – Zusammenfassung

The steps of writing

1. Brainstorming – Ideen sammeln und ordnen (▶ *Brainstorming, p. 147*)

2. Schreiben. Dabei achte darauf,
   - deine Sätze zu verbinden und auszubauen (*Writing better sentences*),
   - deinen Text gut zu strukturieren (*Using paragraphs*),
   - bei einem Bericht die 5 Ws abzudecken (▶ *Writing a report, p. 152*),
   - bei einem Leserbrief an eine Zeitschrift eine höfliche Anrede und Schlussformel zu verwenden (▶ *Writing a letter to a magazine, p. 152*).

3. Deinen Text inhaltlich und sprachlich überprüfen (*Correcting your text*)

Writing better sentences

Linking words verbinden Sätze und machen sie interessanter. Verwende z.B.
- **Time phrases** wie *at 7 o'clock, every morning, in the afternoons, a few minutes later, suddenly, then, next …,*
- **Konjunktionen** wie *although, and, because, but, so … that, that, when, while,*
- **Relativpronomen** wie *who, which* und *that.*

Auch mit **Adjektiven** und **Adverbien** kannst du deine Sätze verbessern.
- **Adjektive** bestimmen Personen, Orte, Gegenstände oder Erlebnisse genauer und machen sie ebenfalls interessanter:
  The man looked into the room. → *The young man looked into the empty room.*
- Mit **Adverbien** kannst du beschreiben, wie jemand etwas macht:
  The young man looked nervously into the empty room.

Using paragraphs

Structuring a text

Einen Text versteht man viel besser, wenn er in Absätze gegliedert ist:
- eine Einleitung (**beginning**) – hier schreibst du, worum es geht;
- einen Hauptteil (**middle**) – hier schreibst du mehr über dein Thema,
- einen Schluss (**end**) – hier bringst du den Text zu einem interessanten Ende.

Am Anfang eines Absatzes sind kurze, einleitende Sätze (**topic sentences**) gut, die den Lesern sofort sagen, worum es geht, z.B.
- Orte: *My trip to … was fantastic. / … is famous for … / … is a great place.*
- Personen: *… is great/funny/interesting/clever/…*
- Aktivitäten: *… is great fun. / Lots of people … every day.*

Wie kann ich meine Absätze interessant gestalten?

- Beginne mit einem interessanten Einstiegssatz:
  Guess what happened to me today! / Did I tell you that …?
- Fang für jeden neuen Aspekt einen neuen Absatz an.
- Beende deinen Text mit einer Zusammenfassung oder etwas Persönlichem.

Linking ideas

Damit sich dein Text flüssig liest und beim Leser Interesse weckt, solltest du auf gute Übergange von einem Absatz zum nächsten achten. Die folgenden Formulierungen kannst du verwenden
- um zu zeigen, wie dein Text aufgebaut ist:
  In the article, the writer describes how ... **Firstly, he states that** ... **Secondly,** ...
  Then he goes on to say that ... **Another point he makes is that** ... **Finally,** ...
- um etwas zu begründen:
  Because of / As a result of the growing population, ...
  ... had been in trouble with the police, so ...
- um zwei oder mehr Gedanken einander gegenüberzustellen:
  Although one could say that ..., I believe ...
  While most people would ..., the Prime Minister has said ...
  Serious scientists all say that ... **However/But some politicians** ...
- um Beispiele zu geben:
  This is true in a number of cases, for example / for instance / e.g. ...
- um Ergebnisse und Folgen zu erklären:
  As a consequence, / All in all, one can say that ...
  To sum up, I would like to say ...

Correcting your text

Lies jeden Text, den du geschrieben hast, mehrmals durch
- um zu sehen, ob er vollständig und gut verständlich ist,
- um ihn auf Fehler zu überprüfen, z. B. **Rechtschreibfehler** *(spelling mistakes)* und **Grammatikfehler** *(grammar mistakes)*.

Spelling mistakes

Beachte folgende Regeln:
- Manche Wörter haben Buchstaben, die man nicht spricht, aber schreibt, z. B. **talk**, **climb**.
- Manchmal ändert sich die Schreibweise, wenn ein Wort eine Endung erhält, z. B. **take** → **taking**, **terrible** → **terribly**, **lucky** → **luckily**, **try** → **tries** (aber **stay** → **stays**), **run** → **running**, **drop** → **dropped**.
- Beim Plural tritt manchmal noch ein *-e* zum *-s*, z. B. **church** → **churches**.

Grammar mistakes

Diese Tipps helfen dir, typische Fehler zu vermeiden:
- Im **simple present** wird in der 3. Person Singular *-s* angehängt: **she knows**
- **Unregelmäßige Verben**: Manche Verben bilden die Formen des *simple past* und des Partizip Perfekt *(past participle)* unregelmäßig. Die unregelmäßigen Formen musst du lernen. Die Liste steht auf S. 280–281.
  go – went – gone; **buy – bought – bought**
- **Verneinung**: Im *simple present* werden Vollverben mit **don't/doesn't** verneint, im *simple past* mit **didn't**.
- **Satzstellung**: Im Englischen gilt immer (auch im Nebensatz):
a) subject – verb – object (SVO):   ... when **I saw my brother**.
                                    ... als **ich meinen Bruder sah**.
b) Orts- vor Zeitangabe: **I bought a nice book in the city yesterday**.

Writing different types of text

SF REVISION Writing a report – organizing ideas

Hierauf kommt es bei einem Bericht an:
– Gib dem Leser eine **schnelle Orientierung**, was passiert ist.
– Beginne mit **wichtigen Informationen** und gib erst dann Detailinformationen.
– Gib Antwort auf die **5 Ws**: **Who? What? When? Where? Why?** und manchmal auch auf **How?**.
– Verwende das *simple past*.

SF REVISION Writing a letter to a magazine

Wenn du auf einen Zeitschriftenartikel reagieren und einen Leserbrief schreiben möchtest,
– beginne deinen Brief mit **Dear + (Name der Zeitschrift/des Autors des Artikels)**,
– lege deine Meinung dar und begründe sie (**I would like to comment on …, I agree/disagree with …, I think …, That is why …, For example, …**),
– beende deinen Brief mit **Yours sincerely** oder **Yours**.

SF REVISION Writing formal letters

Bei Briefen unterscheidet man zwischen privaten Briefen (*informal letters*) und Geschäftsbriefen (*formal letters*). Da du mit Geschäftsbriefen ein Anliegen bei einer Behörde, einer Firma oder einer Organisation verfolgst, sollten sie knapp, präzise, objektiv, aber trotzdem höflich formuliert sein (*KISS rule: Keep it short and simple*).

① Schreibe deine Adresse (ohne Namen) und das Datum in die rechte obere Ecke. Verwende keine typisch deutschen Buchstaben wie z. B. ß, ä, ö oder ü.
② Die Anschrift steht links.
③ Die Anrede lautet *Dear Sir or Madam*. Wenn du den Namen des Adressaten kennst, beginne deinen Brief mit *Dear Mr/Mrs/Ms …*
④ Verwende Langformen (*I am, I would like* statt *I'm, I'd like* usw.), vermeide unnötige Abkürzungen.
⑤ Nenne zu Beginn den Grund deines Briefes.
⑥ Bedanke dich bei Bitten und Anfragen im Voraus (*I look forward to hearing from you. Thank you.*).
⑦ Beende den Brief mit *Yours faithfully*, wenn du den Adressaten nicht kennst. Hast du den Adressaten am Anfang des Briefes mit Namen angeredet, dann schreibe *Yours sincerely*. (Im amerikanischen Englisch heißt es dagegen in beiden Fällen *Sincerely*.)
⑧ Unterschreibe den Brief und tippe zusätzlich deinen Namen.

① Schillerstr. 17
   37067 Goettingen
   Germany

② Jane Hall   4 May 2010
   Meadows Home Farm Shop
   Harston
   Cambridge CB22 4BE
   Great Britain

③ Dear Ms Hall
   ④
⑤ I am writing to you about the advertisement from April 21st in the Cambridge Weekly News. I would love to work for you at Meadows Home Farm this summer. ④

I am 16 years old and I have a good level of English but would like to improve my speaking skills. I am hard-working, friendly and a fast learner. At home I look after two horses so farm work is not new to me. I have also worked in a sports shop so I have experience in serving people and working in a team. My hobbies are horse riding, playing volley ball and hiking. Please find my CV with this letter.

Thank you for your time. I look forward to hearing from ⑥ you.

⑦ Yours sincerely
   Tamara Wille
⑧ Tamara Wille

SF REVISION Argumentative writing

„Schriftliche Diskussion"

Argumentative writing ist ähnlich der deutschen Erörterung die **schriftliche Diskussion eines Gedankens oder eines Themas**. Dabei müssen Argumente, Beispiele und Belege zu einer logisch aufgebauten Struktur zusammengefügt werden.

Oft verlangt die Aufgabenstellung von dir, dass du **Argumente für und gegen etwas** findest (z. B. *"Students should wear school uniforms." Discuss.*). Manchmal musst du auch eine Problemstellung oder eine Frage mit Argumenten belegen (häufig als W-Frage formuliert, z. B. *What should young people do in their free time?*). In beiden Fällen sollst du – in der Regel am Ende deines Textes – auch deine **eigene Meinung** äußern. Bemühe dich aber dennoch um einen **objektiven Stil**. Formulierungen wie *That's total nonsense* oder *I think it's very stupid* sind völlig fehl am Platz!

Wie gehe ich vor?

Vorbereitung:
- Lies die Aufgabenstellung sorgfältig, achte besonders auf die Arbeitsanweisungen oder „Operatoren" (▶ *How to do well in a test: Aufgabenstellungen verstehen, p. 159*) und entscheide, um welche Art von *argumentative writing* es sich handelt.
- Werde dir über deine eigene Meinung zum Thema klar.
- Sammle Ideen, Argumente, Belege und Beispiele (▶ *Brainstorming, p. 147*) und ordne sie, z. B. in einer Mindmap.
- Fertige eine Gliederung (▶ *Outlining, p. 131*).

Verfassen des Textes:
- Wie fast jeder Text ist auch das Ergebnis deines *argumentative writing* grundsätzlich in drei Hauptabschnitte gegliedert: Mit der Einleitung führst du zum Thema hin und weckst das Interesse deiner Leser, im Hauptteil entwickelst du deine Argumente (dies kann auch in mehreren Absätzen geschehen), mit dem Schluss fasst du zusammen und präsentierst deine Meinung oder auch einen Kompromiss.
- Verbinde die einzelnen Teile gut miteinander (z. B. mit **on the one hand, on the other hand, first/second/third, however, additionally, moreover, contrary to that**) und belege und begründe die jeweiligen Argumente (**that's why, because, a reason for it is**).
- Im Schlussteil (**all in all, to come to a conclusion, I would like to finish by saying**) solltest du keine neuen Argumente mehr anführen.

Überprüfen des Geschriebenen:
- Wie immer beim schriftlichen Arbeiten solltest du deinen Text am Ende überprüfen und korrigieren (▶ *Correcting your text, p. 151*). In Zweifelsfällen hilft dir ein Wörterbuch (▶ *Using a bilingual dictionary, p. 126, Using an English–English dictionary, p. 127*).

Introduction	Most students have mobiles. Should they be allowed in school?
Main body	Pros: student might miss bus parents might need to call … Cons: student might cheat in test …
Conclusion	More disadvantages than advantages → Should not be allowed

SF REVISION Writing a CV

Das Leben auf einen Blick

Dein Lebenslauf ist eine **klar gegliederte Zusammenfassung** deiner persönlichen Daten, Fähigkeiten und Erfahrungen und gibt Auskunft über die wichtigen Stationen deines Lebens. Da der Adressat sich schnell informieren will, ist es wichtig, dass der Lebenslauf fehlerfrei und übersichtlich, d.h. in der Regel in tabellarischer Form, erstellt worden ist.

Wie sollte ein Lebenslauf aussehen?

Weil Lebensläufe ganz persönliche, individuelle Dokumente sind, unterscheiden sie sich inhaltlich natürlich stark voneinander. Dennoch gelten bestimmte **inhaltliche und formale Regeln** – für englische Lebensläufe manchmal andere als für deutsche:

– Der Lebenslauf muss Namen, Kontaktdaten (Adresse, Telefonnummer, ggf. E-Mail-Adresse) und Nationalität enthalten. Das Geburtsdatum oder Auskünfte zur Familie sind nicht unbedingt notwendig.

– Die Lebensstationen sollten zeitlich lückenlos dargestellt werden. Sie können chronologisch (also beginnend mit den frühesten Daten) oder umgekehrt chronologisch (beginnend mit der Gegenwart) angeordnet sein.

– Die Daten und Informationen werden nach unterschiedlichen Aspekten gegliedert, z.B. *Education* (welche Schulen hast du wann besucht?), *Qualification/Skills* (welche besonderen Fähigkeiten hast du?), *Work experience* (wo hast du schon gearbeitet?), *Achievements* (hast du vielleicht eine Auszeichnung erhalten, einen Preis gewonnen oder etwas Besonderes erreicht?), *Hobbies and interests, References* (schriftliche Beurteilungen, Empfehlungsschreiben).

– Empfehlungsschreiben musst du, außer wenn es ausdrücklich verlangt wird, nicht sofort zur Verfügung stellen, sondern kannst sie auf Nachfrage zusenden.

– Im Englischen kann der Lebenslauf z.B. zusätzlich zu den nüchternen Daten und Fakten auch einige persönliche Ausführungen enthalten. In einem solchen *personal statement* kannst du einige deiner persönlichen Vorzüge hervorheben und erläutern, warum du die betreffende Position oder diesen bestimmten Arbeitsplatz anstrebst. Übertreibe es aber nicht – also nicht: *I am a very clever and intelligent person*, sondern etwas bescheidener (und leichter zu belegen): *I have always been quite successful at school*.

– In der Regel musst du einem englischen Lebenslauf kein Bild beifügen. Auch unterschreiben musst du ihn nicht.

Skills File

SF REVISION   Summary writing

Wenn du einen Lese- oder Hörtext oder einen Filmausschnitt zusammenfassen möchtest, schreibst du eine *summary*. Dabei gehst du folgendermaßen vor:

1. Lies dir den Text noch mindestens einmal genau durch (bzw. hör ihn dir ein weiteres Mal an oder sieh dir den Filmausschnitt noch einmal an). Bei einem Lesetext markierst du wichtige Passagen oder machst am Rand des Textes kurze Anmerkungen. Auch bei Hörtexten und Filmausschnitten machst du dir Notizen (▶ *Listening, p. 137*).

2. Wenn es sich um einen geschriebenen Text handelt, lies ihn jetzt ein weiteres Mal, Satz für Satz. Wenn du mit einer Kopie arbeitest, unterstreiche die Passagen im Text, die dir Antwort auf die **5 Ws** geben:

   Who?   Who does … / Who is the … about?
   What?   What happens? / What does he/she do?
   When?   When does it take place?
   Where? Where does it happen?
   Why?   Why does he/she act in this way?

   Zusätzlich zum Unterstreichen kannst du alle Sätze, Satzteile und Wortgruppen einklammern, die *nicht* zu den wesentlichen Gedanken des Autors gehören. Dazu gehören auch Beispiele, Vergleiche, symbolhafte Ausdrücke, Zitate, direkte Rede, ausschmückende Adjektive und andere Textteile, die der Beschreibung dienen.

3. Notiere dir alles, was du nicht eingeklammert hast, in Stichpunkten auf einem separaten Blatt Papier. Überprüfe noch einmal, ob du wirklich alle unnötigen Textstellen weggelassen hast.

4. Alternativ kannst du deine Notizen auch so anfertigen: Teile ein Blatt Papier in zwei Spalten ein. Notiere die Hauptaussagen des Textes auf der linken Seite. Suche dann zu diesen Aussagen Beispiele, Erläuterungen, Zitate, Zahlen und Fakten. Entscheide, welche du für besonders wichtig hälst, und notiere sie auf der rechten Seite deines Arbeitsblatts, neben den Hauptaussagen.

5. Nun schreibe mit deinen eigenen Worten einen neuen Text im *simple present* (auch wenn du eine Geschichte zusammenfasst, die in der Vergangenheit spielt). Bringe die Informationen in eine logische Reihenfolge. So kannst du anfangen:

   The story is about … • The text describes … • The article shows … • In the story we get to know …

   Im Hauptteil solltest du die wichtigsten Ereignisse einer Geschichte oder die Hauptpunkte eines Artikels wiedergeben. Verwende dafür deine Notizen zu den 5 Ws. Schreib den Text nicht ab, sondern verwende deine eigenen Worte.

6. Überprüfe deinen Entwurf noch einmal. Enthält dein Text wirklich die wichtigsten Gedanken, Ereignisse, Ideen aus dem Original? Achte auch auf sprachliche Fehler, besonders auf
   – die Rechtschreibung,
   – die Verwendung des *simple present*,
   – die Wortstellung,
   – logische Übergänge zwischen den Sätzen durch *linking words* (*and, therefore, that's why, but, because …*).

7. Bringe den korrigierten Entwurf in eine Reinschrift.

SF Writing a film review ▶ Unit 3 (p. 65)

In einer Filmbesprechung (*film review*) gibst du einen Überblick über die Eckdaten und den Inhalt eines Films und gibst eine persönliche Einschätzung.

Schritt 1: Mach dir Notizen zu den Rahmendaten des Films. Wann und wo wurde er gedreht? Wer führte Regie (*director*), wer waren die Hauptdarsteller (*starring actors*) und der Nebendarsteller (*supporting actors*)? Um welche Art von Film (*genre*) handelt es sich? Was ist die Handlung (*plot*) des Films? Was gibt es über die schauspielerische Leistung (*acting*) der Haupt- und Nebendarsteller zu sagen, was über die Kameraführung (*camera work*), die Musik (*soundtrack*), den Drehort (*setting*), die Kostüme (*costumes*), eventuell auch Requisiten (*props*) und Spezialeffekte (*special effects*)? Entscheide, auf welche dieser Aspekte du dich in deiner Besprechung beziehen möchtest.

Schritt 2: Überlege und notiere dir, was die **Aussage** des Films (*message*) ist.

Schritt 3: Überlege dir, wie dir der Film **gefallen** hat und ob du den Lesern **empfehlen** würdest, sich den Film ebenfalls anzusehen (*recommendation*). Notiere dir ein bis zwei wichtige Gründe dafür.

Schritt 4: Schreibe deine Filmbesprechung. Beginnen kannst du mit dem Filmtitel, einem interessanten oder lustigen Zitat oder einer Szene aus dem Film. Erzähle aber nicht zu viele Details – und verrate nicht das spannende Ende!

SF Describing objects and processes ▶ Unit 3 (p. 55, p. 57)

Im Alltag begegnen uns recht häufig Beschreibungen von Gegenständen und Vorgängen, sei es auf Deutsch oder in einer Fremdsprache. Dabei kann es sich z. B. um Bedienungsanleitungen (*manuals*), Wegbeschreibungen (*giving directions*) oder um Personen- und Bildbeschreibungen handeln.

Damit eine Beschreibung ein objektives und nachvollziehbares sprachliches „Abbild" des betreffenden Gegenstands oder Vorgangs darstellt, muss man bezüglich der Wortwahl, des Stils und der Struktur folgende Aspekte beachten:

– Äußerst wichtig ist die Reihenfolge in der Beschreibung. Bei einem Vorgang ist dies der zeitliche Ablauf, bei einem Gegenstand oder einem Bild kann es die Richtung von oben nach unten, von links nach rechts, vom Hintergrund zum Vordergrund o. Ä. sein. Die einmal gewählte Reihenfolge sollte konsequent eingehalten werden, um dem Leser oder Zuhörer das Verständnis zu erleichtern.
– Die zu verwendende Zeitform ist das Präsens (*present tense*).
– Größen, Farben, Formen, Zeiten und andere objektiv messbare Größen sind – wenn nötig – möglichst genau anzugeben.
– Hilfreich bei der Beschreibung sind treffende Adjektive, auch Relativsätze und Vergleiche, Passivkonstruktionen sowie notwendige Fachbegriffe. Besonders bei der Vorgangsbeschreibung ist es wichtig, die einzelnen Teilvorgänge geschickt miteinander zu verbinden (*linking words*) und auch bezüglich ihrer Funktion oder Wirkung kurz zu erläutern.

VIEWING SKILLS

SF Analysing films ▶ Unit 1 (p. 23), Unit 2 (p. 30)

Da es manchmal schwer ist, einem fremdsprachlichen Film zu folgen, sollte man vorher möglichst viel über den betreffenden Film in Erfahrung zu bringen:
Welchem Genre gehört er an – handelt es sich um einen Dokumentarfilm (*documentary*), einen Spielfilm (*feature film*) wie z. B. ein *western*, einen *thriller*, ein *science-fiction/sci-fi movie* oder ein *melodrama*? Oder ist es ein Videoclip oder ein Werbefilm? In welchem Land und wann wurde er gedreht?
Wo und wann spielt er? Werden Untertitel angeboten oder ist es eine synchronisierte Fassung (*dubbed version*)?

Bei vielen filmischen Elementen spielen ähnliche Gesichtspunkte eine Rolle wie bei der Rezeption von Literatur; deshalb werden Filme manchmal auch als eine Form von Literatur bezeichnet. Solche vergleichbaren Aspekte sind die Besetzung und Charakterisierung der Rollen (*cast*), der Schauplatz (*setting*) und die Handlung (*plot*). Andere Mittel dagegen sind filmspezifisch und müssen besonders beachtet werden: Ton und Beleuchtung (*sound and light effects, music, voice-over comments*), technische Effekte (*special effects*) und Kameraführung (*camera work*).

Durch die Kameraführung werden besondere Akzente gesetzt, zum Beispiel hinsichtlich der Beziehung, in der die Charaktere zueinander stehen. Auch die Stimmung oder Spannung in einer Szene wird von der Kameraführung beeinflusst. Ebenso lenkt die Kamera die Aufmerksamkeit der Zuschauer und macht klar, worauf sie sich konzentrieren sollen. Folgende Möglichkeiten stehen der Regie und den Kameraleuten zur Verfügung:

Mittels der Kameraperspektive (*camera angle*) können Besonderheiten in den Macht- oder Abhängigkeitsbeziehungen der Figuren ausgedrückt werden. Man unterscheidet zwischen *low-angle*, *eye-level* und *high-angle shots*. Ein weiteres Gestaltungsmittel ist die Bewegung der Kamera (*camera movement*), zum Beispiel beim Heranfahren an eine Szene oder ein Objekt im Zoom oder bei einzelnen Aufnahmen, die als Nahaufnahme (*close shot*) oder aus der Distanz (Totale – *long shot*) gefilmt werden können.

Wenn man eine Szene oder einen ganzen Film sehr intensiv analysieren möchte, hilft es, ein Filmtagebuch (*viewing log*) anzulegen, in dem man die Handlung oder einzelne wichtige Szenen nach den W-Fragen und filmischen Besonderheiten aufschlüsselt.

Die Erkenntnisse über einen Film, aber auch Fragen der Identifikation und des persönlichen Urteils über einen Film können schließlich in einer Filmkritik (*film review*) mündlich oder schriftlich zusammengefasst werden.
▶ SF Writing a film review, p. 156

EXAM SKILLS

SF REVISION   How to do well in a test

▶ *Getting ready for a test (pp. 44–51, 68–73)*

Countdown zum Testerfolg

Ein Test ist angekündigt? Kein Grund zur Panik. Wichtig ist, dass du weißt, worauf du dich vorbereiten musst. Im Zweifelsfall frag deine Lehrerin oder deinen Lehrer. Der Countdown kann beginnen!

Eine Woche vor dem Test

1. Lies noch einmal die **Texte** der zuletzt durchgenommenen Unit. Fasse mündlich oder schriftlich zusammen, worum es ging.

2. Wiederhole den **Wortschatz** der Unit mit Hilfe des *Vocabulary* oder des *Wordmaster*. Schreibe dir die Wörter und Wortverbindungen, die du immer wieder vergisst, auf ein Blatt Papier. Eine Mindmap oder ein Wortfeld helfen beim Behalten.

3. Geh auch noch mal die neue **Grammatik** durch. Aufgaben zur Selbstüberprüfung und zum Üben findest du im *Practice*-Teil, im *Grammar File* (S. 165–196), in deinem *Workbook* und im *e-Workbook*.

Zwei Tage vor dem Test

1. Wiederhole den **Wortschatz**. Manche Wörter sitzen noch nicht? Schreibe einen kurzen Text, in dem du sie verwendest.

2. Lies die **Texte** ein weiteres Mal.

3. Erkläre einem Freund oder einer Freundin die neue **Grammatik**. Das klappt nicht richtig? Dann lies nochmal im *Grammar File* nach.

Am Abend vor dem Test

1. Entspanne dich. Du kannst lesen, dich in die Badewanne legen, Musik hören, fernsehen, …

2. Geh zur gewohnten Zeit ins Bett.

Am Morgen des Tests

1. Steh rechtzeitig auf, damit du nicht hetzen musst.

2. Lies irgendetwas „zum Aufwärmen", aber schau nicht mehr in dein Schülerbuch.

Während des Tests

1. Denk daran: Du hast dich gut vorbereitet. Es gibt keinen Grund, nervös zu sein.

2. Konzentriere dich auf den Test, lass dich nicht ablenken.

3. Lies dir die Aufgaben genau durch. Dann löse zuerst die Aufgaben, die dir einfach scheinen. Wende dich erst danach den schwereren Aufgaben zu.

4. Aufgaben, die du bearbeitet hast, hakst du ab. So siehst du, wie du vorankommst, und behältst den Überblick.

5. Schau ab und zu auf die Uhr. Du solltest dir für den Schluss noch etwas Zeit einplanen, um deine Antworten noch einmal durchzulesen und wenn nötig zu korrigieren.

Aufgabenstellungen verstehen

Bevor du anfängst, die Aufgaben zu bearbeiten, vergewissere dich, dass du genau weißt, was du tun sollst. Lies die Aufgabe Wort für Wort langsam und gründlich und von Anfang bis Ende durch. Du kannst besonders wichtige Teile der Aufgabenstellung unterstreichen und die Aufgabe, wenn nötig, für dich in einzelne Schritte unterteilen.

Den folgenden Arbeitsanweisungen begegnest du häufig:

Add Verbinde eine Information oder einen Sachverhalt mit einer/einem anderen auf die geforderte Art und Weise.

Choose Wähle zwischen verschiedenen Möglichkeiten die passende Information aus.

Comment Kommentiere einen Sachverhalt durch die Darstellung deiner eigenen Meinung dazu. Begründe und erläutere sie möglichst genau.

Compare Vergleiche Dinge, Wörter oder Sachverhalte, indem du prüfst, ob und auf welche Weise sie gleiche oder verschiedene Eigenschaften, Aussehen, Bedeutungen oder Funktionen haben.

Complete Ergänze eine Information, indem du sie an dem dafür vorgesehenen Platz einträgst und damit z. B. einen Satz sinnvoll beendest.

Describe Beschreibe ein Objekt oder eine Person, d. h. stelle dar, wie sie aussehen, wie das Objekt funktioniert oder die Personen handeln. Vermeide eigene Wertungen wie z. B. „beautiful", „useful" oder „great".

Discuss Diskutiere ein Thema, eine Behauptung oder eine Aussage. Untersuche möglichst viele Seiten davon, z. B. Vor- und Nachteile, und stelle diese geordnet dar.

Explain Erkläre einen Sachverhalt, d. h. gib wesentliche Fakten über ihn und erläutere, wie sie logisch zusammenhängen.

Fill in Trage die geforderten Informationen in den dafür vorgesehenen Platz ein, z. B. in eine Lücke oder eine Tabelle.

List Schreibe einzelne oder mehrere Informationen übersichtlich und geordnet auf, z. B. in einer Reihe, Tabelle oder einem anderen Verzeichnis.

Listen Höre dir einen Text, einzelne Informationen oder Sachverhalte an.

Match Ordne die angegebenen Informationen einander zu, wie es die Aufgabe erfordert. Finde z. B. Satzanfänge und passende Satzenden und füge sie zusammen.

Use Verwende eine Tatsache, ein Wort usw. so, wie es in der Aufgabe gefordert wird.

Write a ... Schreibe etwas in einem geforderten Textformat auf, z. B. deinen Kommentar zu etwas oder eine Geschichte.

Ein besonderer Aufgabentyp sind **Multiple-choice-Fragen**. Tipps für den Umgang mit solchen Aufgaben findest du im folgenden Abschnitt. ▶▶

Multiple-choice-Aufgaben

Bei Multiple-choice-Aufgaben ist auf Folgendes zu achten:
– Die betreffende Frage oder der Satz sollten sehr genau gelesen werden.
– Bevor man sich die Lösungsangebote anschaut, deckt man sie mit Papier ab und überlegt, was die richtige Antwort sein könnte. Wenn diese dann auch als Lösungsmöglichkeit angeboten wird, ist sie wahrscheinlich richtig.
– Man sollte erst alle vorgegebenen Lösungen lesen, bevor man sich für eine entscheidet.
– Nur **eine** der Antworten sollte angekreuzt werden – es sei denn, es heißt in der Aufgabenstellung ausdrücklich, dass mehrere Antworten richtig sein können.
– Man sollte im ersten Durchgang alle Aufgaben so gut bearbeiten, wie man kann, also keine auslassen. Zum Schluss geht man dann zu denjenigen Fragen zurück, bei denen man unsicher ist.
– Wenn das alles nichts hilft, sollte man nicht mehr nach der *richtigen* Antwort suchen, sondern nach den *falschen*. Wenn man von vier Antwortmöglichkeiten drei als falsch identifiziert hat, kann man daraus schließen, dass die vierte Antwort die richtige ist.

Mündliche Prüfungen (*oral exams*)

Neben schriftliche Klassenarbeiten, Tests und Klausuren treten im Lauf der Zeit ergänzend mündliche Prüfungen der kommunikativen Fähigkeiten in den Bereichen „Vortragen (monologisches Sprechen)" und „Sprechen miteinander (dialogisches Sprechen)".

In diesen Prüfungen geht es um ein klar umrissenes Thema und einen Arbeitsauftrag, der auch aus einem Bildimpuls bestehen kann. Vor Beginn bekommt man ausreichend Zeit, sich mit dem Thema zu beschäftigen, sich Stichworte zu notieren und auch eine kleine Strukturskizze der Argumente anzufertigen. Für Vortragsprüfungen (so genannte Präsentationsprüfungen) sind manchmal mehrere Tage Vorbereitungszeit vorgesehen. Gesprächsprüfungen hingegen werden meist spontan und mit geringer Vorbereitungszeit (ca. 20 Minuten) angesetzt.

Für die Vorbereitung einer **Vortragsprüfung** können die SF-Abschnitte *Giving a presentation* (p. 132) und *Visual aids in presentations* (p. 133) hilfreich sein. Wichtig ist es, sowohl den Wortschatz für den Themenbereich (z. B. das Wortfeld „Environment") sicher zu beherrschen, als auch die Redemittel für die Moderation („I'm going to talk about ...") noch einmal zu üben. Nichts ist schlimmer, als in einer Präsentation lange nach den richtigen Wörtern suchen zu müssen. Notfalls muss man das gesuchte Wort umschreiben (▶ *SF Paraphrasing*, p. 147).

In einer **Gesprächsprüfung** kommt es nicht nur auf Inhalte an, sondern auch darauf, dass man sich auf die Redebeiträge der Vorredner bezieht (▶ *Having a discussion, p. 149*). Trotz der verkürzten Vorbereitungszeit ist es auch hier ratsam, sich einige Stichpunkte zu notieren, auf die man während des Gesprächs zurückgreifen kann. Themen- und Moderationswortschatz werden natürlich ebenso benötigt wie in der Vortragsprüfung.

Skills File

x-wichtig

GLOSSARY

abridged [ə'brɪdʒd]	gekürzt	An **abridged** version of a text is a shortened version.
act	Akt	Traditionally, plays are divided into **acts**.
action	Handlung	everything that happens in a story or play **External** ~ describes actual events that happen. **Internal** ~ is what goes on in a character's mind.
acrostic [ə'krɒstɪk]	Akrostichon	a poem in which the first letters of the lines form a word or phrase
adapted	bearbeitet, adaptiert	An **adapted** text has been changed to be suitable for its readers.
alliteration [ə,lɪtə'reɪʃn]	Alliteration	repetition of the same consonant sound in words close together in a poem, e.g. 'Along came a crowd of crazy cats.'
antonym ['æntənɪm]	Antonym, Gegenwort	*Slow* is an **antonym** of *fast*.
article	Artikel	a story or report in a newspaper or magazine **print** ~ *(gedruckter Artikel)* • **online** ~ *(Artikel im Internet)*
assonance ['æsənəns]	Assonanz	repetition of the same vowel sound in words close together, e.g. 'Oh no, my mobile's broken.'
atmosphere	Atmosphäre, Stimmung	the feeling or mood created in a piece of literature
audiobook	Hörbuch	a sound recording of a book
author ['ɔ:θə]	Schriftsteller/in, Autor/in	the writer of a piece of literature
biography [baɪ'ɒgrəfi]	Biografie	the story of a person's life • **autobiography** [,ɔ:təʊbaɪ'ɒgrəfi] – the story of a person's life written by the person
character	Figur, Charakter	a person in a story; the qualities of a person • **main** ~ *(Hauptfigur)*
characterization [,kærəktəraɪ'zeɪʃn]	Figurencharakterisierung	the way an author presents characters to readers **Implicit** or **indirect** ~ is when the reader finds out about a character through his/her words, actions. **Explicit** or **direct** ~ is when the author describes a person's character.
chorus ['kɔ:rəs]	Refrain	Everyone joined in with the **chorus** of the song.
chronological [,krɒnə'lɒdʒɪkl]	chronologisch	(events) arranged as they happened in time
cinquain [sɪŋ'keɪn]	Cinquain	a type of five-line poem
climax ['klaɪmæks]	Höhepunkt	the most exciting or important point in the action of a story or play
collection	Sammlung, Anthologie	a number of short stories or poems in one book
comedy ['kɒmədi]	Komödie, Lustspiel	a play, often meant to be funny or amusing, with a happy ending
conflict ['kɒnflɪkt]	Konflikt, Widerstreit	the key struggle between different characters in a piece of literature
context ['kɒntekst]	Zusammenhang, Kontext	the situation in which events happen and which helps you understand them
dialogue	Dialog	conversation in a story or play between two or more people
drama	Drama, Theater, Schauspiel, Stück	If you like acting, join the school **drama** club. adj: **dramatic** [drə'mætɪk] *(dramatisch)*
dystopia [dɪs'təʊpɪə]	Dystopie	an imaginary place or society in which life is terrible or a piece of literature describing such a place

ending	Schluss, Ende	Most comedies have happy **endings**.
essay ['eseɪ]	Aufsatz, Essay	a short piece of writing on a particular subject, often written at school or university
event	Ereignis	The events of a story make up the **plot**.
exaggeration [ɪɡˌzædʒə'reɪʃn]	Übertreibung	**Exaggeration** makes characters or events larger than life and memorable.
extract ['ekstrækt]	Auszug	a part taken from a longer piece of literature
fairy tale	Märchen	a traditional fantasy story
fantasy ['fæntəsi]	Fantasie	a story set in an imagined world where unreal or unlikely things happen
fiction	Erzählliteratur, Belletristik	*Robinson Crusoe* is a famous work of **fiction**.
flashback ['flæʃbæk]	Rückblende	Events that happened before the story takes place are sometimes told in **flashbacks**.
foreshadowing [fɔː'ʃædəʊɪŋ]	Vorahnung, Andeutung	What she saw in her dream was a **foreshadowing** of what would happen the next day.
genre	Genre, Gattung	a type or style of literature, e.g. science fiction
haiku ['haɪkuː]	Haiku	three-line poem with lines of 5, 7 and 5 syllables, originally from Japan
heading	Überschrift	a title printed at the beginning of a text
headline	Schlagzeile, Überschrift	the heading of a newspaper or magazine article, especially on the front page
hero, heroine ['hɪərəʊ, 'herəʊɪn]	Held/in	the main character in a piece of literature
humour ['hjuːmə]	Humor; humoristischer Text	what makes something funny; a piece of funny writing
image ['ɪmɪdʒ]	Bild, Vorstellung	The **images** the writer uses help you to create pictures in your mind.
imagery ['ɪmɪdʒəri]	bildhafte Sprache, Metaphorik	Metaphors and similes are both types of **imagery**.
irony ['aɪrəni]	Ironie	humorous use of words saying the opposite of what you really mean • adj: **ironic** [aɪ'rɒnɪk] *(ironisch)*
line	Zeile	A sonnet always has 14 **lines**.
lyrics ['lɪrɪks]	Text eines Lieds	I don't like the music but the **lyrics** are great.
message	Botschaft, Aussage	The **message** of the story is: love is wonderful but it can also hurt.
metaphor ['metəfɔːr]	Metapher	'He looked at us with *eyes of stone*' – that's a very strong **metaphor**. adj: **metaphorical** [metə'fɒrɪkl] *(metaphorisch)*
metre	Metrum	a regular rhythm pattern in a poem
monologue ['mɒnəlɒɡ]	Monolog	a long speech in a play by one person, especially when alone
moral ['mɒrəl]	Moral	the message of a piece of literature or something that you can learn from it
motif [məʊ'tiːf]	Motiv, Leitgedanke	a subject, idea or phrase that is developed in the course of a piece of literature

Skills File

narrator [nə'reɪtə]	Erzähler	the character or 'voice' in a piece of literature who is telling the story, not the same as the author, e.g. Miles is the **narrator** of *Looking for Alaska*, John Green is the author. • **first-person ~** *(Ich-Erzähler)* • **third-person ~** *(personaler Erzähler)* • **omniscient ~** [ɒm'nɪsɪənt] *(allwissender, auktorialer Erzähler)*
non-fiction	nichtfiktionale Texte, Sachtexte	I never read novels. I prefer **non-fiction**.
novel ['nɒvl]	Roman	*Looking for Alaska* was John Green's first **novel**.
novelist ['nɒvəlɪst]	Romanautor/in	My favourite **novelist** is James Joyce.
open-ended; open ending	offen, nicht entschieden	In an **open-ended** story, the reader is left to think about what really happens.
parody ['pærədi]	Parodie	a piece of writing that copies the style of something or somebody to be amusing
(to) perform [pə'fɔːm]	auftreten; aufführen	The actor Jon Wyatt **performed** as Hamlet last night. Our drama club is **performing** *Woyzeck* next month.
performance [pə'fɔːməns]	Vorstellung, Auftritt	Wyatt's **performance** was described as 'fantastic'.
personification [pə,sɒnɪfɪ'keɪʃn]	Verkörperung, Personifizierung	representing something (an object, an animal, an idea) as a person, like Midnight in Carol-Ann Duffy's poem "Meeting Midnight" (p. 94).
perspective [pə'spektɪv]	Blickwinkel, Perspektive	the point of view from which a character sees things
play	Stück, Schauspiel	*Hamlet* is probably the most famous **play** in English literature.
playwright ['pleɪraɪt]	Dramatiker/in	someone who writes plays
plot	Handlung, Plot	the sequence of events of a story or play
poem	Gedicht	I prefer **poems** to novels because of their rhythm and imagery.
poet	Dichter/in	someone who writes poems
poetry	Lyrik	I love literature but almost never read **poetry**.
point of view	Standpunkt, Erzählperspektive	the situation from which a character sees, writes or evaluates something **unlimited/limited ~ ~ ~** *(unbegrenzte/begrenzte Perspektive)*
production	Inszenierung, Aufführung	There is a great new **production** of *The Mousetrap* at our local theatre.
prose	Prosa	writing that is not poetry or drama
protagonist [prə'tægənɪst]	Protagonist/in	a main character in a piece of literature
punchline ['pʌntʃlaɪn]	Pointe	the last (often surprising) sentence or few words of a joke or story that make it funny
quotation	Zitat	a short extract from a piece of literature that shows something interesting or useful
realistic	realistisch	A **realistic** story shows things as they really are.
recite [rɪ'saɪt]	vortragen, rezitieren	Learn the poem so you can **recite** it to the class.
register ['redʒɪstə]	Register, Stilebene	the level and style of a text
repetition [,repə'tɪʃn]	Wiederholung	Songs and poetry often create effects by use of **repetition**.
resolution [,rezə'luːʃn]	Auflösung, Lösung	the moment at the end of a drama, novel, etc., where all the conflicts are solved
review [rɪ'vjuː]	Besprechung, Rezension	a report discussing a piece of literature or a film and giving an opinion on it

rhyme [raɪm]	Reim; sich reimen	a word that has or ends in the same sound as another word, e.g. *cat* **rhymes** with *hat* • **end-~** *(Endreim)* • **internal ~** *(Reim inmitten der Zeile)* • **~ scheme** *(Reimschema)*
rhythm ['rɪðəm]	Rhythmus	the pattern of stress in a poem
satire ['sætaɪər]	Satire	a piece of writing criticizing someone or something by making fun of them so that people will clearly see their faults
scene	Szene	A play or the acts of a play are divided into **scenes**.
science fiction (SF)	Science-Fiction	a genre that deals with imagined results of scientific discoveries, usually in the future
setting	Schauplatz, Handlungsrahmen	the time and place and sometimes the atmosphere of a piece of literature
(to) be set in	spielen in	*Looking for Alaska* **is set in** Alabama.
simile ['sɪməliː]	Vergleich	a poetic device comparing one thing to another, e.g. 'Her skin was white as snow'
sonnet ['sɒnɪt]	Sonnett	poem with 14 lines of 10 or 11 syllables each
speech	Rede, Sprechbeitrag	I only had a small part in the play, just three **speeches**.
stage directions [steɪdʒ dəˈrekʃnz]	Bühnen-, Regieanweisungen	notes in a play describing the scene and telling actors when to enter and exit and what to do
stanza ['stænzə]	Strophe	Poems are often divided into **stanzas** or verses.
stereotype ['sterɪətaɪp]	Klischeevorstellung, Stereotyp	I can't identify with this character. She's just the **stereotype** of a romantic schoolgirl.
story	Geschichte, Erzählung	*Treasure Island* is an exciting **story**.
short story	Kurzgeschichte	"The Garden Party" is a famous **short story** by Katherine Mansfield.
stress	Betonung; betonen	Each line of a sonnet has five **stressed** syllables.
style	Stil	the way a piece of literature is written, e.g. a thriller might have an exciting **style**
stylistic device [staɪˈlɪstɪk dɪˈvaɪs]	stilistisches Mittel	Poets create effects with **stylistic devices** like metaphors, rhymes or repetition.
suspense [səˈspens]	Spannung	It's a great thriller, full of **suspense**.
symbol ['sɪmbl]	Symbol	A heart is a **symbol** of love.
synonym ['sɪnənɪm]	Synonym	a word that means the same as another word, like *big* = *large*
tension ['tenʃn]	Spannung	The atmosphere of **tension** in the book makes it so exciting.
text	Text	any form of written material, e.g. **argumentative ~** *(Erörterung)* • **descriptive ~** *(Beschreibung)* • **expository ~** *(Darlegung)* • **fictional ~** *(Erzähltext)* • **instructive ~** *(Lehrtext)* • **non-fictional ~** *(Sachtext)*
text type	Textsorte	An argumentative text is a common **text type** in exams.
title	Titel	the name of a piece of literature
tone [təʊn]	Ton	Roald Dahl's poems always have a humorous **tone**.
tragedy ['trædʒədi]	Tragödie	a serious play with an unhappy ending, in which the main character(s) often die(s)
utopia [juːˈtəʊpɪə]	Utopie	a story about an imagined place where everything is perfect
verse [vɜːs]	Vers, Dichtung; Strophe	A narrative poem is a story told in **verse**.
free verse	freier Vers, reimlose Dichtung	poetry with no regular rhythm or rhyme scheme
writer	Autor/in, Schriftsteller/in	someone who writes

Grammar File – Inhalt

Seite

GF 1 **REVISION Word order** Wortstellung **166**
  1.1 S – V – O **166**
  1.2 Adverbs / Phrases of place and time Adverbien / Orts- und Zeitangaben **167**

GF 2 **The tenses** Die Zeitformen **168**
  2.1 Tense and time Grammatische Zeitform und wirkliche Zeit **168**
  2.2 Talking about the present Über die Gegenwart sprechen **168**
  2.3 Talking about the past Über die Vergangenheit sprechen **169**
  2.4 Talking about the past and the present Über die Vergangenheit und die Gegenwart sprechen __ **170**
  2.5 Talking about the future Über die Zukunft sprechen **171**

GF 3 **Aspect: the simple form and the progressive form** Aspekt: die einfache Form und die Verlaufsform __ **173**
  3.1 Simple and progressive form in contrast Einfache Form und Verlaufsform im Vergleich **173**
  3.2 Activity verbs Tätigkeitsverben **174**
  3.3 State verbs Zustandsverben **174**

GF 4 **REVISION The passive** Das Passiv **175**
  4.1 Active and passive Aktiv und Passiv **175**
  4.2 Use Gebrauch **175**
  4.3 Form Form **176**
  4.4 Passive sentences with by ... Passivsätze mit by **176**
  4.5 The passive of verbs with two objects Das Passiv von Verben mit zwei Objekten **176**

GF 5 **REVISION Modals and their substitutes** Modale Hilfsverben und ihre Ersatzverben **177**
  5.1 Modal auxiliaries Modale Hilfsverben **177**
  5.2 Substitutes Ersatzverben **178**
  5.3 Modals – what do they express? Modalverben – was drücken sie aus? **179**

GF 6 **REVISION Conditional sentences** Bedingungssätze **181**

GF 7 **REVISION Relative clauses** Relativsätze **182**
  7.1 Defining relative clauses Bestimmende Relativsätze **182**
  7.2 Contact clauses Relativsätze ohne Relativpronomen **182**
  7.3 Relative clauses with which to refer to a whole clause Satzbezogene Relativsätze mit which ___ **183**
  7.4 Non-defining relative clauses Nicht bestimmende Relativsätze **183**

GF 8 **REVISION Indirect speech** Indirekte Rede **184**
  8.1 Statements Aussagesätze **184**
  8.2 Questions Fragen **184**
  8.3 Advice, requests, commands Ratschläge, Bitten, Aufforderungen **185**

GF 9 **REVISION The to-infinitive** Der Infinitiv mit to **186**
  9.1 Verb + object + to-infinitive Verb + Objekt + to-Infinitiv **186**
  9.2 Question word + to-infinitive Fragewort + to-Infinitiv **186**
  9.3 The to-infinitive instead of a relative clause Der to-Infinitiv anstelle eines Relativsatzes **186**

GF 10 **REVISION The gerund** Das Gerundium **188**
  10.1 The gerund as subject and object Das Gerundium als Subjekt und als Objekt **188**
  10.2 The gerund after prepositions Das Gerundium nach Präpositionen **189**
  10.3 The gerund with 'its own subject' Das Gerundium mit „eigenem Subjekt" **189**

166 Grammar File

GF 11	**REVISION Participles** Partizipien		**190**
	11.1 **Participle forms** Formen des Partizips		**190**
	11.2 **Participle clauses instead of relative clauses** Partizipialsätze anstelle von Relativsätzen		**190**
	11.3 **The present participle after certain verbs** Das Partizip Präsens nach bestimmten Verben		**190**
	11.4 **Participle clauses instead of adverbial clauses**		**191**
	Partizipialsätze anstelle von adverbialen Nebensätzen		
	11.5 **Participle clauses giving additional information**		**192**
	Partizipialsätze zur Angabe von Zusatzinformationen		
GF 12	**Emphasis** Hervorhebung		**193**
Grammatical terms Grammatische Fachbegriffe			**195**

Additional information

We **stood** watching the street artists.
Wir standen da und sahen den Straßenkünstlern zu.

Abschnitte mit der Überschrift **Additional information** enthalten Grammatik, die du verstehen solltest, aber nicht selbst anwenden musst.

GF 1 REVISION Word order   Wortstellung

1.1 S – V – O   S – V – O

Subject – Verb – Object

		Subject	Verb	Object	
1		Rob	likes	ice cream.	
		The Clarks	have bought	a house	in Bath.
2		Ella	didn't like	the film.	
		Ava	can't speak	German	very well.
3	Can	Jamie	speak	German?	
	Did	you	like	the film?	

Die wichtigste Wortstellungsregel ist
Subject – **V**erb – **O**bject
(Subjekt – Prädikat – Objekt).
Sie gilt in bejahten und verneinten Aussagesätzen (1, 2) und in Fragen (3).

---

1 We're going to have **a big party**.
   Wir werden **eine große Party** veranstalten.

2 We often have fish on Fridays.
   Wir essen freitags oft Fisch.

3 Yesterday **we** celebrated Grandpa's birthday.
   Gestern feierten **wir** Opas Geburtstag.
   When I arrived, **the film** had already begun.
   Als ich ankam, hatte **der Film** schon begonnen.

4 He'll go out with you if you ask **him**.
                                ..., wenn du **ihn** fragst.
   Elisabeth told me   that she loves **Jeremy**.
   ..., dass sie **Jeremy** liebt.

! Beachte die Unterschiede zum Deutschen:

1 Die Teile des Prädikats (*are going to have*) dürfen nicht durch das Objekt (*a big party*) getrennt werden.

2 Prädikat und Objekt (*have fish*) dürfen nicht durch Adverbien (*often*) oder Zeitangaben (*on Fridays*) getrennt werden.

3 Die Wortstellung ist auch dann S – V – ..., wenn der Satz mit einer Zeitangabe (*yesterday*) oder einem Nebensatz (*When I arrived*) beginnt.

4 Die Wortstellung S – V – O gilt auch in Nebensätzen (*if you ask him; that she loves Jeremy*).

Grammar File

1.2 Adverbs / Phrases of place and time

1 Unfortunately it started to rain.
Luckily they had their anoraks with them.
At first I couldn't see anything.
Maybe we should start without him.

2 We don't often get up before 10 on Sundays.
I usually make breakfast for everybody.
We had never been to Spain before.

3 Try to speak clearly, then you'll do well.
The guide answered the questions politely.
They went outside and played in the garden.
We're flying to France tomorrow.

We were in Italy last summer.

Wir waren letzten Sommer in Italien.

4 That camera looks very/quite/too expensive.
She really believes she'll be famous one day.
I almost fell off my bike when I saw the dog.

Every Friday evening we do the shopping.
Sometimes you can see foxes from my window.
In Britain, school usually starts at 8.45 or 9.00.

Adverbien / Orts- und Zeitangaben

1 **Satzadverbien** wie *luckily, unfortunately, maybe, suddenly, finally, at last, at first, of course* beziehen sich auf den ganzen Satz. Sie stehen in der Regel am Satzanfang.

2 **Adverbien der unbestimmten Zeit oder Häufigkeit** wie *already, always, ever, just, never, often, sometimes, usually* stehen gewöhnlich vor dem Vollverb.

3 Nach dem Vollverb (+ Objekt) stehen gewöhnlich
– **Adverbien der Art und Weise** (*clearly, politely, well*)
– **Ortsangaben** (*outside, in Bristol, on the roof*)
– **Zeitangaben** (*tomorrow, a year ago, in 2008*).

! Wenn ein Satz mit einer Orts- <u>und</u> einer Zeitangabe endet, dann gilt die Regel **Ort vor Zeit** – wie im Alphabet: **O vor Z**.

4 **Gradadverbien** wie *very, quite, too, really, almost* stehen meist direkt vor dem Wort, auf das sie sich beziehen.

◄ Manchmal stehen Adverbien, Ortsangaben und Zeitangaben auch an anderen Stellen im Satz.

In English: Word order

1 The most important word order rule is **S – V – O**.

2 In contrast to German,
– the parts of the verb are not separated by the object	Jake **is going to have** a birthday party.
– verb and object are not separated by adverbs or time phrases	I **always go shopping** on Friday evening.
– the word order S – V in the main clause does not change when there is an adverb or a subordinate clause at the beginning of the sentence	Perhaps **you can help** me with the dishes. If you like, **we can go** to the cinema.
– the word order in the subordinate clause is the same as in the main clause	Dad will help you **if you ask him**.

3
– **Sentence adverbs** like *luckily, maybe, finally* go in front-position	**Luckily** she was able to stop the car.
– **Adverbs of indefinite time** or **frequency** usually come before the main verb	I **often help** Dad in the garden.
– **Adverbs of manner, place** and **definite time** usually come after the main verb (and its object, if there is one)	He **answered the questions politely**. We**'ll leave home early** and **arrive in Italy in the evening**.
– **Adverbs of degree** usually come before the word they relate to	That wasn't **too difficult**, was it?

GF 2 The tenses — Die Zeitformen

2.1 Tense and time

1a Emily **is visiting** her aunt in Bath right now.
1b Next week she **'s visiting** her uncle in Bristol.

2a I **bought** a new computer last week.
2b If Dad **bought** a new computer, he would give my sister his old one.

I**'ve been** in the team since 2007.	**Present perfect**
Ich **bin** seit 2007 in der Mannschaft.	**Präsens**
I**'ll take** the fish, please.	***will*-future**
Ich **nehme** den Fisch, bitte.	**Präsens**

▶ *The simple form and the progressive form: GF 3 (pp. 173–174)*

Grammatische Zeitform und wirkliche Zeit

◀ Die **grammatischen Zeitformen** können sich auf verschiedene **Zeiten in der Wirklichkeit** beziehen:
In Satz **1a** bezieht sich das *present progressive* auf die Gegenwart, in Satz **1b** auf die Zukunft.
In Satz **2a** bezieht sich das *simple past* auf die Vergangenheit, in Satz **2b** auf die Zukunft.

◀ Außerdem werden im Englischen und im Deutschen in vergleichbaren Situationen oft unterschiedliche Zeitformen verwendet.

2.2 Talking about the present

The simple present

Dave Wilson **usually gets** the bus to school.
On Mondays his mother **takes** him in the car.
He **never cycles** to school because it's too far.

Dave and his family **live** in Manchester.
He **plays** hockey and **collects** models of old cars.
His dad **works** for a computer company.

The present progressive

What**'s** Dave **doing**? –
Just now he**'s cleaning** his bike.

Dave (on the phone) I'm busy, Jack. I**'m cleaning** my bike.

This week Dave's grandma **is staying** at the Wilsons' because Dave's mum is ill.

Additional information

I**'m** always **forgetting** my keys.
He**'s** always **making** the same mistake.

Über die Gegenwart sprechen

Das *simple present* wird verwendet,

◀ um über Handlungen und Ereignisse zu sprechen, die **wiederholt, regelmäßig, immer** oder **nie** geschehen (oft mit Zeitangaben wie *always, usually, sometimes, often, every week, on Mondays, never* usw.).

◀ um über **Dauerzustände** sowie über **Hobbys** und **Berufe** zu sprechen.

Das *present progressive* wird verwendet,

◀ um über Handlungen und Ereignisse zu sprechen, die **jetzt gerade** im Gange sind (oft mit Angaben wie *at the moment, now, just*).

❗ Die Handlung, um die es geht, kann für einen Augenblick unterbrochen sein, z. B. durch ein Telefonat. Wichtig ist, dass sie noch nicht abgeschlossen ist.

◀ um über **vorübergehende Zustände** zu sprechen (begrenzter Zeitraum: *this week*).

◀ Das *present progressive* kann mit *always* verwendet werden, um Verärgerung oder Überraschung auszudrücken.

In English: Talking about the present

Simple present:	when something happens regularly, often, always or never
	when we talk about something permanent, for example hobbies, jobs, abilities
Present progressive:	when an action or event is in progress and not yet complete

Grammar File

169

2.3 Talking about the past

The simple past

Last Friday Katie's family flew to Spain.
Two years ago they went to Italy.
Letzten Freitag ist Katies Familie nach Spanien ge-
flogen / flog Katies Familie nach Spanien. ...

Yesterday Katie went to town with a friend.
First they looked round the shops and Katie
bought a CD. **Then** they tried on shoes in four
shops, but they didn't buy any. **After that** they
had an ice cream.

„Früher ...": *used to* + infinitive / *would* + infinitive

We used to live in Manchester.
Wir wohnten früher in Manchester.
Manchester United used to be my favourite team.
Früher war Manchester United meine Lieblingsmannschaft.
I used to spend lots of money on sports magazines.
Ich habe früher immer viel Geld für Sportzeitschriften ausgegeben.

Grandpa would visit us every Sunday after church.
Opa besuchte uns jeden Sonntag nach der Kirche. /
Opa pflegte uns jeden Sonntag nach der Kirche zu besuchen.
We would often go for long walks in the woods.
Wir haben oft lange Spaziergänge im Wald gemacht. /
Wir pflegten lange Spaziergänge im Wald zu machen.

The past progressive

Yesterday at 3.30 Angela was walking home
from school. It was raining, so lots of people
were hurrying to the bus stop.

Angela was just crossing the road when she
saw her boyfriend.

The past perfect (simple)

When Emma arrived home, her parents had
already eaten.
Als Emma zu Hause eintraf, hatten ihre Eltern bereits
gegessen.

I couldn't buy a bus ticket because I had
forgotten my money.
Ich konnte keine Busfahrkarte kaufen, weil ich mein
Geld vergessen hatte.

Über die Vergangenheit sprechen

Das *simple past* wird verwendet,

◄ um über <u>abgeschlossene</u> Handlungen und Ereignisse zu
sprechen, die **zu einem bestimmten Zeitpunkt in der
Vergangenheit** stattfanden (oft mit genauen Zeitangaben wie *last Friday, two years ago, yesterday, in 2006, ...*).

◄ wenn man über vergangene Ereignisse berichtet oder
eine Geschichte erzählt (oft mit *first ..., then ..., after
that ...*).

! Im Deutschen steht oft das Perfekt, wo im Englischen
das *simple past* stehen muss.

Wenn man beschreiben will, was **früher
der Fall war**, aber heute nicht mehr,
dann kann man die Konstruktion
used to + **Infinitiv** verwenden.

Zum Ausdruck von **früher gewohnheits-
mäßig wiederholten** <u>Handlungen</u> wird
auch *would* + **Infinitiv** verwendet.

Das *past progressive* wird verwendet,

◄ um über Handlungen und Ereignisse zu sprechen, die **zu
einem bestimmten Zeitpunkt in der Vergangenheit**
<u>noch im Gange, also noch nicht abgeschlossen</u> waren.

◄ wenn man beschreiben will, was gerade vor sich ging
(she was just crossing the road), als etwas anderes
passierte *(she saw her boyfriend)*.

Das *past perfect* (Plusquamperfekt, Vorvergangenheit)
wird verwendet, um auszudrücken, dass etwas **vor
etwas anderem in der Vergangenheit** stattgefunden
hatte.

► ► ►

The past perfect progressive

Emma was very tired when she arrived home because she had been studying for a test all day.
... denn sie hatte den ganzen Tag für einen Test gelernt.

We had been playing tennis for half an hour when it started to rain.
Wir hatten eine halbe Stunde Tennis gespielt, ...

Das *past perfect progressive* wird verwendet, um auszudrücken, dass eine Handlung **vor einem Zeitpunkt in der Vergangenheit** begonnen hatte und bis (oder fast bis) zu jenem Zeitpunkt andauerte.

In English: Talking about the past

Simple past:	when we want to say or ask <u>when</u> something happened
	when we talk about things in the past or tell a story
Past progressive:	when an action or event was in progress at a particular time in the past
Past perfect:	when an action or event had already happened before a time in the past
Past perfect progressive:	when an action or event had already begun before a time in the past and had continued up to (or almost up to) that time

2.4 Talking about the past <u>and</u> the present

Über die Vergangenheit <u>und</u> die Gegenwart sprechen

Present perfect und *present perfect progressive* haben mit der **Vergangenheit <u>und</u>** mit der **Gegenwart** zu tun.

Das *present perfect* wird verwendet,

The present perfect (simple)

1 Will Smith is great. I've seen all his films.
2 My sister loves books about horses. She's read hundreds of them.
3 Mel has lost her mobile. Now she can't phone her friends and her mum is angry.
4 I've bought some new jeans, look. They'll look good with my red top.
5 Luke has **already** done his Maths homework, but he has**n't** started his French **yet**.
6 I've **never** been to Paris. Have you **ever** been there?
   – No, I haven't. But I've **always** wanted to go.

◄ um über Handlungen und Ereignisse zu sprechen, die **irgendwann in der Vergangenheit** geschehen sind. Oft hat das Geschehen **Auswirkungen auf die Gegenwart oder die Zukunft (3, 4)**.
Ein genauer Zeitpunkt wird nicht genannt. Häufig werden jedoch Adverbien der unbestimmten Zeit wie *already, always, just, not ... yet, often, never* in *present perfect*-Sätzen verwendet **(5, 6)**.

We've had our new car **since April**.
Wir haben unser neues Auto <u>seit April</u>.

since + Zeitpunkt

We've had our new car **for three months**.
Wir haben unser neues Auto <u>seit drei Monaten</u>.

for + Zeitraum

◄ um über **Zustände** zu sprechen, die in der Vergangenheit begonnen haben und jetzt noch andauern (oft mit *since* bzw. *for* = deutsch „seit").
Zustandsverben, die oft mit der einfachen Form des *present perfect* verwendet werden, sind z.B. *be, have, know, like, hate.*
▶ *Zustandsverben: 3.3 (p.174)*

How long have you lived in Bristol?
Wie lange wohnt ihr in Bristol?
– **Since last August**.
– <u>Seit letztem August</u>.
– **For two years**.
– <u>Seit zwei Jahren</u>.

Mit *How long ...?* + *present perfect* kann man fragen, seit wann oder wie lange ein Zustand schon andauert.

! Im **Deutschen** benutzt man meist das **Präsens**, aber im **Englischen** <u>muss</u> das *present perfect* stehen:
Ich kenne ihn seit ...   I've known him since/for ...

Grammar File

The present perfect progressive

1 I've been writing e-mails all day.
Ich schreibe (schon) den ganzen Tag E-Mails.

2 Anna has been playing in the hockey team since May.
Anna spielt seit Mai in der Hockeymannschaft.

3 We've been learning French for four years.
Wir lernen seit vier Jahren Französisch.

Das **present perfect progressive** wird verwendet, um auszudrücken, dass eine Handlung **in der Vergangenheit** begonnen hat und jetzt noch andauert (auch wenn die Handlung nicht ununterbrochen im Gange war wie etwa in den Sätzen 2 und 3).

! Auch in diesen Fällen benutzt man im **Deutschen** meist das **Präsens**. Im **Englischen** steht das **present perfect progressive**:

Wir spielen seit ...   We've been playing since/for ...

In English: Talking about the past _and_ the present

Present perfect: when we want to say <u>that</u> something has happened (not when it happened)
when we want to say since when or how long a state has already lasted

Present perfect progressive: when an action or event began in the past and has continued up to (or almost up to) the present

2.5 Talking about the future

Über die Zukunft sprechen

The _will_-future

I'll be 15 next October.
It will be cold and windy, and we will get some rain in the afternoon.

I suppose Ella will be late again as usual.
Ich nehme an, Ella kommt wie üblich wieder zu spät.

Just a moment. I'll open the door for you.
Moment. Ich mache Ihnen die Tür auf.
I won't tell anyone what's happened. I promise.
Ich sage niemandem, was passiert ist. ...

Das **Futur mit _will_** wird verwendet,

◄ um **Vorhersagen** über die Zukunft zu äußern. Oft geht es dabei um Dinge, die man nicht beeinflussen kann, z.B. das Alter oder das Wetter.

◄ um eine **Vermutung** auszudrücken (oft eingeleitet mit _I suppose, I think, I'm sure, I expect, maybe_).

◄ wenn man sich **spontan** – also ohne es im Voraus geplant zu haben – zu etwas **entschließt**. Oft geht es dabei um **Hilfsangebote** oder **Versprechen**.

The _going to_-future

After school I'm going to study IT – I hope.
Nach der Schule werde ich IT studieren /
                    habe ich vor, IT zu studieren ...
My boyfriend says he's going to be an engineer.
Mein Freund sagt, er will Ingenieur werden.

Look at those clouds. There's going to be a storm.
... Es wird ein Gewitter geben.

Das **Futur mit _going to_** wird verwendet,

◄ um über **Vorhaben** und **Pläne** für die Zukunft zu sprechen.

◄ um auszudrücken, dass etwas **wahrscheinlich gleich geschehen wird** – es gibt bereits deutliche **Anzeichen** dafür.

The present progressive (future meaning)

We're driving to Scotland next weekend to visit my grandparents.
I'm meeting a friend in town tomorrow at 12.
All my friends are coming to my birthday party on Friday.

Auch das **present progressive** kann futurische Bedeutung haben. Es wird verwendet, wenn etwas **für die Zukunft fest geplant** oder **fest verabredet** ist (manchmal spricht man vom _diary future_). Durch eine Zeitangabe _(next weekend; tomorrow)_ oder aus dem Zusammenhang muss klar sein, dass es um etwas Zukünftiges geht.

►►►

Grammar File

The simple present (future meaning)

The next train to Bath **goes** in ten minutes.
Our cookery classes **start** on 2 September.

Auch das *simple present* kann futurische Bedeutung haben. Es wird verwendet, wenn ein **zukünftiges Geschehen** durch einen **Fahrplan**, ein **Programm** oder Ähnliches festgelegt ist (manchmal spricht man vom *timetable future*). Verben wie *arrive, leave, go, open, close, start, stop* werden häufig so verwendet.

The future progressive

This time next week my sister **will be flying** to Spain – and I**'ll be doing** my Maths exam.
Nächste Woche um diese Zeit wird meine Schwester (gerade) nach Spanien fliegen – und ich werde dabei sein, meine Mathe-Prüfung zu machen.

Das *future progressive* wird verwendet, um über Handlungen und Ereignisse zu sprechen, die **zu einem zukünftigen Zeitpunkt im Gange** sein werden (noch nicht abgeschlossen sein werden).
Typische Zeitangaben sind *a week today* („heute in einer Woche"), *this time next week* oder Ähnliches.

The future perfect

On Friday we **will have finished** all our exams.
Am Freitag werden wir alle unsere Prüfungen geschafft haben.

And **by the end of next week** we**'ll have received** our results.
Und bis Ende nächster Woche werden wir unsere Ergebnisse erhalten haben.

Das *future perfect* wird verwendet um auszudrücken, dass etwas **zu einem bestimmten Zeitpunkt in der Zukunft geschehen oder getan sein wird**. (Meist wird dieser Zeitpunkt auch genannt – hier: *on Friday; by the end of next week*.)

In English: Talking about the future

***will*-future:**	for predictions or assumptions about the future
	for spontaneous decisions (e.g. offers and promises)
***going to*-future:**	for intentions and plans for the future
	when something will very probably happen (there are already signs of it happening)
Present progressive:	when something is definitely planned or arranged for the future
Simple present:	for future events that are a fixed part of a timetable, programme, schedule, etc.
Future progressive:	when an action or event will be in progress at a point of time in the future
Future perfect:	when an action or event will be complete at a point of time in the future

Hold on, Dad, I'll run and borrow our neighbour's ladder.

Grammar File

173

GF 3 Aspect: the simple form and the progressive form
Aspekt: die einfache Form und die Verlaufsform

3.1 Simple and progressive form in contrast
Einfache Form und Verlaufsform im Vergleich

Tense	Simple form	Progressive form
present tense	sing(s)	am/are/is singing
present perfect	have/has sung	have/has been singing
past tense	sang	was/were singing
past perfect	had sung	had been singing
will-future	will sing	will be singing

Anders als im Deutschen gibt es im Englischen eine **einfache Form** *(simple form)* und eine **Verlaufsform** *(progressive form)* des Verbs. Mit diesen Formen bringt man im Englischen zum Ausdruck,
– ob eine Handlung regelmäßig oder wiederholt stattfindet <u>oder</u> ob sie sich gerade im Verlauf befindet,
– ob eine Handlung abgeschlossen ist <u>oder</u> ob sie noch andauert.
Vergleiche die folgenden Beispiele.

The simple form

1a Tom works at a garage on Saturdays.
(regelmäßig, jeden Samstag)
2a Mr Jones goes to work by bike.
(immer, jeden Tag)
3a Olivia has written two letters this morning.
(sie ist fertig und kann die Briefe jetzt abschicken)

◀ Die *simple form* wird verwendet
 – für regelmäßig oder wiederholt stattfindende Handlungen (**1a**)
 – für Dauerzustände (wenn etwas immer so ist) (**2a**)
 – für abgeschlossene Handlungen (**3a**).

The progressive form

1b Tom is working at the garage right now.
(er ist gerade dabei, die Arbeit ist im Gange)
2b This week Mr Jones is going to work by bus.
(nur diese Woche, denn sein Rad ist kaputt)
3b Olivia has been writing letters all morning. *(sie ist noch dabei)*

◀ Die *progressive form* wird verwendet
 – für Handlungen, die gerade im Verlauf sind (**1b**)
 – für vorübergehende Zustände (wenn etwas nur vorübergehend der Fall ist) (**2b**)
 – für Handlungen, die noch nicht abgeschlossen sind (**3b**).

! Im Deutschen gibt es keine Verlaufsform. Aber manchmal sagt und hört man Sätze wie „Ich bin gerade dabei, meine Hausaufgaben zu machen" oder „Er war (gerade) beim Abwaschen", um zum Ausdruck zu bringen, dass etwas im Gange und noch nicht abgeschlossen ist bzw. war.

He was doing the dishes when he heard a funny noise.
Er war gerade beim Abwaschen, ...

! **Beachte:** Nur **Tätigkeitsverben** *(activity verbs)* wie *do, drink, go, sit, write* können in der *progressive form* verwendet werden.

▶ Tätigkeits- und Zustandsverben: 3.2–3.3 (p. 174)

▶▶▶

3.2	**Activity verbs**	Tätigkeitsverben

(in a shop window) This shop repairs bikes!
(on the phone) Jack is repairing his bike.
Can he call you back?

It gets dark very early here in winter.
At 6 o'clock it was already getting dark.

Tätigkeitsverben bezeichnen **Tätigkeiten** *(do, go, read, repair, ...)* oder **Vorgänge** *(become, get, rain, ...)*.
Sie können sowohl in der *simple form* als auch in der *progressive form* verwendet werden.

3.3	**State verbs**	Zustandsverben

Zustandsverben *(state verbs)* bezeichnen keine Tätigkeiten oder Vorgänge, sondern **Zustände**. Sie werden in der Regel **nur in der *simple form*** verwendet.

Zu den **Zustandsverben** gehören

The price doesn't include breakfast.
Emily seems really happy at her new school.
Jake's uncle owns a nice house in the country.

– Verben, die **Eigenschaften**, **Besitz** oder **Zugehörigkeit** ausdrücken: *be, include, seem, sound, mean* („bedeuten"), *need, own, belong, ...*

Do you believe their story?
I don't know the answer to question 5.
Anna didn't understand what Julie meant.

– Verben des **Meinens** und des **Wissens**: *believe, know, mean* („meinen"), *remember, suppose, understand, ...*

Lucy doesn't like people who talk a lot.
I don't mind waiting for you here.
We prefer brown bread to white. It's healthier.

– Verben des **Mögens** und **Wollens**: *like, love, hate, mind, prefer, want, ...*

States and activities

Julie has dark hair.	**state:**	*haben*
Julie is having a shower.	**activity:**	*duschen*
We were having fun/a great time.	**activity:**	*Spaß/eine tolle Zeit haben, erleben*
Do I look silly with my hair like this?	**state:**	*aussehen*
I didn't see the man. I wasn't looking.	**activity:**	*(hin)schauen, gucken*
The flowers smell wonderful.	**state:**	*riechen*
Sophie is smelling the roses.	**activity:**	*riechen (an etwas)*
The pasta tastes good.	**state:**	*schmecken*
I'm tasting the soup.	**activity:**	*kosten, probieren*
I think that's a great idea.	**state:**	*denken, meinen*
He was thinking of moving to Paris.	**activity:**	*überlegen, nachdenken*

Einige wenige englische Verben können als **Tätigkeits- oder als Zustandsverb** verwendet werden (mit jeweils unterschiedlichen deutschen Entsprechungen).

Als **Zustandsverb** stehen diese Verben immer in der *simple form*.

Als **Tätigkeitsverb** kommen sie in beiden Formen vor.

Vergleiche die Beispiele links.

In English: Activity verbs and state verbs

1 **Activity verbs** *(do, read, watch, work, ...)* can be used in the simple form and in the progressive form:
 *Tom **does** his homework every evening. Look, Tom **is doing** his homework now.*
2 **State verbs** *(seem, belong, believe, know, like, need, ...)* are not used in the progressive form:
 *I **believe** you. (not: I'm believing you.)*
3 A few verbs are used as state verbs and as activity verbs – with different meanings:
 *The soup **tastes** good. Look, Grandpa **is tasting** the soup now.*

Grammar File

175

GF 4 REVISION The passive — Das Passiv

4.1 Active and passive — Aktiv und Passiv

Active: Alexander Fleming discovered penicillin in 1928.
Alexander Fleming entdeckte 1928 das Penicillin.

Passive: Penicillin was discovered in 1928.
Penicillin wurde 1928 entdeckt.

◀ Beide Sätze beschreiben denselben Sachverhalt, betrachten ihn aber aus unterschiedlichen Blickwinkeln:

Der **Aktivsatz** handelt von Fleming und informiert uns über eine Entdeckung, die er 1928 machte.

Der **Passivsatz** handelt von Penicillin und informiert uns über den Zeitpunkt seiner Entdeckung.

Active: The manager asked Mel to help out.
Passive: Mel was asked to help out.
Mel wurde gebeten auszuhelfen.

Active: The manager paid her £6 an hour.
Passive: She was paid £6 an hour.
Ihr wurden £6 die Stunde bezahlt. /
Sie erhielt £6 die Stunde.

◀ Das Passiv lässt sich im Englischen von allen Verben bilden, die im Aktivsatz ein Objekt haben.

4.2 Use — Gebrauch

1 A new sports centre has been opened in Paddington.   ... ist eröffnet worden ...

2 The first goal was scored in the seventh minute.   ... wurde erzielt ...

3 Breakfast is served from 7 to 10.30 am.
... wird serviert ...

4 The two bank robbers have been sentenced to ten years.   ... sind verurteilt worden ...

Mit einem **Passivsatz** kann man Handlungen beschreiben, ohne zu sagen, wer die Handlung ausführt.

Oft ist nicht bekannt oder dem Sprecher nicht wichtig, wer die Handlung ausführt (Sätze 1 und 2), manchmal ist es auch offensichtlich und daher nicht erwähnenswert (Sätze 3 und 4).

Das Passiv findet man oft in Nachrichten, in Zeitungsartikeln (z. B. über Unfälle, Sportereignisse, Verbrechen), in offiziellen Texten, in technischen Beschreibungen und auf Schildern.

> Library books must be returned before July 15.

... müssen vor dem 15. Juli zurückgegeben werden.

The woman was taken to hospital.
Man brachte die Frau ins Krankenhaus.

Their CDs can be ordered online now.
Man kann ihre CDs jetzt online bestellen.

Das Passiv wird im Englischen häufiger verwendet als im Deutschen. Einem englischen Passivsatz entspricht oft ein deutscher Aktivsatz mit „man".

Lunch will be served in a minute.

▶▶▶

4.3 Form / Form

The passive

Simple present	I am often invited to parties.
Present progressive	Some new shops are being built in Carlton Street.
Simple past	The bridge was completed in 1952.
Past progressive	I couldn't mail you. My computer was being repaired.
Present perfect (simple)	All the sandwiches have been eaten.
Past perfect (simple)	Ed didn't go to the party because he hadn't been invited.
will-future and modal auxiliaries	The last match of the season will be played next Friday. Mobile phones must be turned off during lessons. Concert tickets can be bought online.
going to-future	Look, the lions are going to be fed soon.
Future perfect	I hope my bike will have been repaired by Saturday.

Das Passiv bildet man mit einer **Form von be** und der 3. Form des Verbs (Partizip Perfekt, *past participle*).

Bei den *progressive forms* wird das Passiv mit *being* gebildet: *are being built; was being repaired.*

4.4 Passive sentences with *by* ... / Passivsätze mit *by* ...

The *Times* **is read** by 2 million people every day.
... wird jeden Tag von 2 Millionen Menschen gelesen.

This picture **was painted** by a 12-year-old girl.
... wurde von einem 12-jährigen Mädchen gemalt.

Part of this building **was destroyed** by fire.
... wurde durch ein Feuer zerstört.

Wenn man in einem Passivsatz den „Täter" oder „Verursacher" der Handlung nennen möchte, verwendet man die Präposition **by** („von", „durch").

4.5 The passive of verbs with two objects / Das Passiv von Verben mit zwei Objekten

<u>Active</u>	Indirect object	Direct object
The manager offered	her	a part-time job.

Der Geschäftsführer bot ihr eine Teilzeitstelle an.

<u>Passive (English)</u>

Subject		
She	was offered	a part-time job.

<u>Passive (German)</u>

Dativobjekt		Subjekt	
Ihr	wurde	eine Teilzeitstelle	angeboten.

* Manchmal wird auch im Englischen das Sachobjekt zum Subjekt des Passivsatzes. In diesem Fall wird das Personenobjekt mit *to* angehängt: A part-time job was offered <u>to</u> her.

Manche Verben haben zwei Objekte nach sich:
– ein **indirektes Objekt** (meist eine Person, daher auch: **Personenobjekt**)
– ein **direktes Objekt** (meist eine Sache, daher auch: **Sachobjekt**).

◄ Im Englischen wird meist das **indirekte Objekt** (das **Personenobjekt**) zum **Subjekt des Passivsatzes**. * Diese Art des Passivs nennt man *personal passive* (deutsch: „persönliches Passiv").

◄ Im Deutschen kann nur das **direkte Objekt** (das **Sachobjekt**) zum **Subjekt des Passivsatzes** werden. Die Dativform des Personenobjekts bleibt im deutschen Passivsatz erhalten: *Ihr wurde ... angeboten.*

Weitere Beispiele für das *personal passive* findest du auf der nächsten Seite.

Grammar File

177

We were given the necessary information.
Man hat uns die nötigen Informationen gegeben.

I've been promised a new computer if I pass my exams.
Mir ist ein neuer Computer versprochen worden, wenn ich meine Prüfungen bestehe.

The students were shown the film of the book.
Den Studenten wurde die Verfilmung des Buches gezeigt.

We were told the true story about the first Thanksgiving.
Uns wurde die wahre Geschichte über ... erzählt. / Man erzählte uns die wahre Geschichte über ...

◀ Häufig vorkommende Verben mit zwei Objekten sind *give, offer, pay, promise, send, show, tell*.

Vergleiche die englischen Passivsätze mit ihren deutschen Übersetzungen – im Deutschen verwendet man oft einen Aktivsatz.

I was given a violin for my birthday. It's my best present ever – Dad gives me two pounds every time I don't play it.

In English: The passive

1. The **passive** is used more in English than in German. In German an active sentence with 'man' is often preferred.
2. We find the passive mainly in news reports, official texts, signs, etc. when the 'doer' of the action is not named (because the 'doer' is not known or not important or because it's clear who does the action): *The thief was arrested.*
   (it's clear who did it: the police)
3. If you want to name the 'doer', you use **by** (German 'von', 'durch'):
   Penicillin was discovered in 1928 by A. Fleming.
   Our car was damaged by falling stones.
4. In English, the indirect object of an active sentence (the 'person object') can be the subject of a passive sentence ('personal passive'):
   Active: *They've offered him a job in London.*
   Passive: *He has been offered a job in London.*

GF 5 REVISION Modals and their substitutes
Modalverben und ihre Ersatzverben

5.1 Modal auxiliaries

1. Can you play the piano?
2. – Yes, I can. / No, I can't.
3. Sue is good at drawing. She should study art.
4. Could you do the exercise? I couldn't.
5. Can we help you in the kitchen, Mum?
6. We can play tennis on Saturday if you like.

Modale Hilfsverben

Modale Hilfsverben wie **can, may, must, should** drücken aus, was jemand tun **kann, darf, muss, soll** usw.

– Sie werden zusammen mit dem **Infinitiv eines Vollverbs** verwendet (1). Nur in Kurzantworten können sie allein stehen (2).
– Sie haben nur eine Form, es gibt also keine Endungen auf *-s, -ing* oder *-ed* (3).
– Frage und Verneinung werden ohne *do/does/did* gebildet (4).
– Sie beziehen sich in der Regel auf die Gegenwart oder die Zukunft (5, 6).

5.2 Substitutes

1 I'd love to be able to speak Spanish.
2 Being able to speak Spanish must be great.
3 We weren't allowed to use a dictionary.

„können": can – (to) be able to

My little brother can / is able to swim.

Tim could / was able to read when he was four.
I could smell fire, but I couldn't see any smoke.

Jacob hasn't been able to finish his essay.

I'm taking driving lessons, so next year I'll be able to drive.

„dürfen": can, may – (to) be allowed to

Can / May I have a sleepover on Friday, Mum?
We aren't allowed to stay up late in the week.

Under-12s couldn't / weren't allowed to see the film without an adult.

I've always been allowed to have pets.

Will you be allowed to go to the party on Friday?

Jeans must not be worn at this school.
At my school we're not allowed to wear jeans.

„müssen": must – (to) have to

Teacher You must work harder, Noah.
His teacher says Noah has to work harder.
I needn't get up at 6 tomorrow. / I don't have to get up at 6 tomorrow.

I had to rewrite my essay.
We didn't have to wait long.

Lauren has had to go to the dentist's.

You will have to go to the dentist's too if you eat so many sweets.

Everyone needs to take a break now and again.
You don't need to wait for me.
I didn't need to tell her. She knew it already.
Do we need to book a table?

Ersatzverben

Modale Hilfsverben können **nicht alle Zeitformen** bilden. Daher gibt es zu bestimmten modalen Hilfsverben **Ersatzverben** mit ähnlicher Bedeutung, von denen man den Infinitiv (1), die *-ing*-Form (2) und alle Zeitformen (3, *simple past*) bilden kann.

present:	*can* und *am/is/are able to*
past:	*could* und *was/were able to*
	could steht vor allem in verneinten Sätzen und Fragen sowie mit Verben der Wahrnehmung *(smell, see, hear, …)*.
present perfect:	*have/has been able to*
will-future:	*will/won't be able to*

present:	*can, may* und *am/is/are allowed to*
past:	*could* und *was/were allowed to*
present perfect:	*have/has been allowed to*
will-future:	*will/won't be allowed to*

! Für ausdrückliche **Verbote** wird *must not (mustn't)* oder *be not allowed to* verwendet.

present:	*must* und *have/has to* (*have/has to* ist häufiger als *must*)
	! **Verneinung:** *needn't* oder *don't/doesn't have to*
past:	*had to*
	! **Verneinung:** *didn't have to*
present perfect:	*have/has had to*
will-future:	*will/won't have to*

◄ Auch das Vollverb *need to* wird verwendet, um zu sagen, dass jemand etwas tun muss oder nicht zu tun braucht.

5.3 Modals – what do they express?

Modalverben – was drücken sie aus?

Ability (Fähigkeit)

I can speak French and a little German.	Ich **kann** Französisch und ein bisschen Deutsch.
My sister could read when she was only four.	Meine Schwester **konnte** lesen, als sie erst vier war.

Request (Bitte / Aufforderung)

Can I borrow this CD?	**Kann** ich diese CD ausleihen?
Can/Could you be quiet, please?	**Kannst/Könntest** du bitte leise sein?
Would you help me to wash the dishes?	**Würdest** du mir helfen abzuwaschen?

Permission / Prohibition (Erlaubnis / Verbot)

Can/May I use your phone, please?	**Kann/Darf** ich mal dein Telefon benutzen, bitte?
You can't take photos in the museum.	Du **darfst** im Museum **nicht** fotografieren.
In 1968, children could leave school at 15.	... **konnten/durften** Kinder mit 15 die Schule verlassen.
But they couldn't vote till they were 21.	Aber sie **konnten/durften** erst mit 21 wählen.
You mustn't tell Mel about the concert. It's a surprise.	Du **darfst** Mel **nichts** von dem Konzert erzählen. ...

Suggestion (Vorschlag)

Can/Can't we go on a bike trip?	**Können** wir **(nicht)** eine Radtour machen?
Shall we eat first and go shopping later?	**Sollen/Wollen** wir erst essen ...?
Couldn't you ask your grandma?	**Könntest** du **nicht** deine Oma fragen?
You could talk to your teacher.	Du **könntest (doch)** mit deiner Lehrerin sprechen.

Offer (Angebot)

Can/Could I get you a drink?	**Kann** ich Ihnen (vielleicht) etwas zu trinken holen?
Would you like to stay for dinner?	**Möchten** Sie **(nicht)** zum Essen bleiben?
Shall I help you with the dishes?	**Soll** ich dir beim Abwasch helfen?

Refusal, rejection (Weigerung, Ablehnung)

My parents won't let me stay out after ten.	Meine Eltern **wollen nicht**, dass ich nach zehn noch draußen bin.
I can't get in. The gate won't open.	... Das Tor **will nicht** aufgehen / geht nicht auf.
He knew the answer, but he wouldn't tell me.	..., aber er **wollte** sie mir nicht sagen /
	..., aber er **weigerte sich**, sie mir zu sagen.

Necessity, strong obligation (Notwendigkeit, Zwang)

You needn't tell Mel about the concert. She already knows.	Du **brauchst** Mel **nicht** von dem Konzert zu erzählen. ...
You've got a temperature. You must stay in bed.	Du hast Fieber. Du **musst** im Bett bleiben.

▶▶▶

Obligation, advice (Verpflichtung, Ratschlag)

Dogs should be left outside.	Hunde sollten draußen gelassen werden / draußen bleiben.
You should tell her the truth. / You ought to tell her the truth.	Du solltest ihr die Wahrheit sagen.

I'd better go now. It's late.
Ich sollte jetzt besser gehen. …
It's cold. You'd better (= had better) not go out.

We're not supposed to use our mobiles at school.
Wir sollen … unsere Handys nicht benutzen.
I was supposed to be home by ten but I missed the bus, and now I'm in trouble.

The Carpenters are supposed to be very rich. They're said to have six houses.
Die Carpenters sollen sehr reich sein. Sie sollen sechs Häuser haben. / Man sagt, sie hätten sechs Häuser.
Carrots are supposed to be good for your eyes.

◀ Auch *had better* und *be supposed to* können für das deutsche „**sollen**" verwendet werden:
 – *had better* ist stärker als *should* und *ought to*; es bringt zum Ausdruck, was jemand in einer bestimmten Situation am besten tun sollte
 – *be supposed to* drückt aus, dass etwas von jemandem erwartet wird bzw. wurde, z. B. weil etwas vereinbart wurde.

◀ *be supposed to* (oder *be said to*) wird verwendet, wenn etwas (angeblich) der Fall sein soll („die Leute sagen", „man sagt").

Possibility, probability (Möglichkeit, Wahrscheinlichkeit)

That must be Luke.	Das muss Luke sein.
– No, it can't be Luke. Luke is in Spain.	– Nein, das kann nicht Luke sein. Luke ist in Spanien.
Where's Dad? – He could be at Grandma's.	… – Er könnte bei Oma sein.
Sarah may still be at her friend's.	Sarah ist vielleicht noch bei ihrer Freundin.
John might come today if he's in town.	John kommt vielleicht heute vorbei, …
Kathy should be here by now. / Kathy ought to be here by now.	Kathy sollte jetzt (eigentlich) hier sein.
There's somebody at the door. It will be Janet.	Es ist jemand an der Tür. Das wird Janet sein.

In English: Modals and their substitutes

1 Modal auxiliaries (or **modals**) like *can, could, may, might, must,* etc.

– have only one form:	*Tom may come tomorrow.*
– form negatives and questions without *do/does/did*:	*They can't hear you. Can you hear them?*
– are followed by an infinitive without *to*:	*You should relax more.*
– usually refer to the present or future:	*Could I have a glass of water, please?*
	Can you call me back tomorrow?
– can express more than one speech function:	**can** *I can play tennis.* (ability)
	Can I borrow your ruler? (request)
	You can borrow my pen. (permission)
	That can't be Joe. Joe's in Italy. (possibility)
– cannot form all tenses.	

2 Substitutes are used to form other tenses:

– *can* („können") – *(to) be able to*:	*I'll be able to drive next year.*
– *can, may* („dürfen") – *(to) be allowed to*:	*Were you allowed to use a dictionary in the test?*
– *must* („müssen") – *(to) have to*:	*I had to do extra homework yesterday.*

GF 6 REVISION Conditional sentences Bedingungssätze

Subordinate clause	Main clause
If you give me your number,	I'll call you.
Wenn du mir deine Nummer gibst, rufe ich dich an.	

Main clause	Subordinate clause
I'll call you	if you give me your number.
Ich rufe dich an,	wenn du mir deine Nummer gibst.

Bedingungssätze („Wenn …, dann …"-Sätze) bestehen aus einem **Hauptsatz** *(main clause)* und einem **Nebensatz** *(subordinate clause)*.
Der Nebensatz wird in der Regel durch die Konjunktion ***if*** („wenn/falls") eingeleitet und nennt eine Bedingung. Der *if*-Satz kann vor dem Hauptsatz stehen (er wird dann mit einem Komma abgetrennt) oder auf den Hauptsatz folgen (ohne Komma).

Es gibt **drei Grundtypen** von Bedingungssätzen:

if + present	*will*-future

If I miss the bus,   I'll take a taxi.
Wenn ich den Bus verpasse, nehme ich ein Taxi.

If Dan misses the bus, he can/should/must
                            take a taxi.
If you miss the bus, take a taxi.

◄ **Typ 1 („Was ist, wenn …"-Sätze)**
Diese Bedingungssätze beziehen sich auf die **Gegenwart** oder die **Zukunft**. Sie drücken aus, was unter bestimmten Bedingungen **geschieht/geschehen wird** oder **nicht geschieht/nicht geschehen wird**.
Statt des Futurs mit *will* können im Hauptsatz auch die modalen Hilfsverben *can, should, must* usw. oder ein Imperativ stehen.

if + past	*would* + infinitive

If I missed the bus,   I would take a taxi.
Wenn ich den Bus verpasste/verpassen würde, würde ich ein Taxi nehmen.

If Dan missed the bus, he could/might take
                            a taxi.

◄ **Typ 2 („Was wäre, wenn …"-Sätze)**
Diese Bedingungssätze beziehen sich auch auf die **Gegenwart** oder die **Zukunft**. Sie drücken aus, was unter bestimmten Bedingungen **geschehen** oder **nicht geschehen würde**.
Statt *would* können im Hauptsatz auch *could* oder *might* stehen.

if + past perfect	*would have* + past participle

If I had missed the bus, I would have taken
                            a taxi.
Wenn ich den Bus verpasst hätte, hätte ich ein Taxi genommen.

If Dan had missed the bus, he could/might
                            have taken a taxi.

◄ **Typ 3 („Was wäre gewesen, wenn …"-Sätze)**
Diese Bedingungssätze beziehen sich auf die **Vergangenheit**. Sie drücken aus, was unter bestimmten Bedingungen **geschehen** oder **nicht geschehen wäre**.
Der *if*-Satz nennt eine Bedingung, die <u>nicht</u> eingetreten ist *(Ich habe **nicht** den Bus verpasst)*. Der Sprecher stellt sich nur vor, was geschehen wäre, aber in Wirklichkeit nicht geschehen ist *(Ich hätte ein Taxi genommen)*.
Statt *would have* können im Hauptsatz auch *could have* oder *might have* stehen.

Additional information

If I **knew** the answer, I **would have told** you.
If I **had had** his chances in life, I**'d be** rich now.
If she **could have told** you the reason,
  she **would have done**.

◄ Wie im Deutschen sind **je nach Situation auch Mischformen** möglich, besonders bei Typ 2 und Typ 3.
Es kommen also auch andere Kombinationen von Zeitformen vor als die oben beschriebenen.

▶ ▶ ▶

In English: Conditional sentences

Type 1:

present	**will**-future or **modal auxiliary + infinitive**	**!** No present tense
If you *give* me your number,	I *will/can call* you.	in the main clause.

Type 2:

past	**would/could/might + infinitive**	**!** No *would*
If you *gave* me your number,	I *would/could/might call* you.	in the *if*-clause.

Type 3:

past perfect	**would have/could have/might have + past participle**
If you *had given* me your number,	I *would have/could have/might have called* you.

GF 7 REVISION Relative clauses Relativsätze

7.1 Defining relative clauses

1 Do you know **the girl** who/that works at the Oxfam shop?
... das Mädchen, das im Oxfam-Shop arbeitet?

2 That's **the shop** which/that sells cheap books and CDs.
... der Laden, der billige Bücher und CDs verkauft.

Bestimmende Relativsätze

Bestimmende Relativsätze werden mit den Relativpronomen **who** oder **that** für **Personen (1)** und **which** oder **that** für **Dinge (2)** eingeleitet.

Ein bestimmender Relativsatz gibt Informationen über ein Nomen, die **zum Verständnis des Satzes notwendig** sind. Ohne die <u>Relativsätze</u>
– ... *the girl <u>who/that works at the Oxfam shop</u>* bzw.
– ... *the shop <u>which/that sells cheap books and CDs</u>*
wüsste man nicht, welches Mädchen bzw. welcher Laden gemeint ist.

! Beachte, dass ein bestimmender Relativsatz nicht durch Kommas abgetrennt wird.

7.2 Contact clauses

1 Lilly is **the girl** who I met at the library.
or Lilly is **the girl** I met at the library.
... das Mädchen, das ich ... kennengelernt habe.

2 These are **the photos** that Dad took.
or These are **the photos** Dad took.
... die Fotos, die Dad gemacht hat.

3 Jake is **the boy** who invited us to the party.
... der Junge, der uns auf die Party eingeladen hat.

Relativsätze ohne Relativpronomen

Wenn das Relativpronomen **Objekt des Relativsatzes** ist, wird es oft **weggelassen (1, 2)**.
Relativsätze ohne Relativpronomen werden *contact clauses* genannt.

! Wenn das **Relativpronomen direkt vor dem Verb** steht, ist es **Subjekt** und darf **<u>nicht</u>** weggelassen werden **(3)**.
Vergleiche:
– ... *the boy <u>who invited</u> us to the party*
   („... der Junge, der uns ... eingeladen hat")
– ... *the boy <u>who</u> we <u>invited</u> to the party* oder
   ... *the boy we <u>invited</u> to the party*
   („... der Junge, den wir ... eingeladen haben")

Grammar File

183

7.3 Relative clauses with *which* to refer to a whole clause

We're moving to Leeds in the summer, which means I'll have to change school.
..., was bedeutet, dass ich die Schule wechseln muss.

My sister thinks I should do a language course in France in the holidays, which is a good idea.
..., was ich für eine gute Idee halte.

Satzbezogene Relativsätze mit *which*

Relativsätze mit *which* können sich auch auf einen ganzen Satz beziehen. Sie kommentieren die Aussage im vorausgehenden Hauptsatz.

Im Deutschen werden solche Relativsätze mit „was" eingeleitet.

! Beachte das Komma vor satzbezogenen Relativsätzen.

Additional information

7.4 Non-defining relative clauses

Agatha Christie, **who died in 1976**, wrote about 70 detective novels and 17 plays.

At 11.35 we landed at Atlanta International, **which is one of the world's busiest airports**.

Nicht bestimmende Relativsätze

Nicht bestimmende Relativsätze kommen hauptsächlich in geschriebenem Englisch vor. Sie geben **zusätzliche Informationen**, die zum Verständnis des Satzes nicht notwendig sind.

! – In nicht bestimmenden Relativsätzen können *who*, *which* und *whose* verwendet werden, aber nicht *that*!
– Nicht bestimmende Relativsätze werden durch Kommas abgetrennt.

In English: Relative clauses

1 A **defining relative clause** gives **necessary** information about the noun that it refers to:
   *That's the boy **who sold Jack the cheap DVDs***.
   We can only leave out the relative pronoun when it is the **object** of the relative clause:
   *That's the boy **who Jack asked about cheap DVDs***. or
   *That's the boy **Jack asked about cheap DVDs***. (contact clause)
2 Relative clauses with **which** can **refer to the whole main clause**:
   *I got an 'A' in my Maths test**, which was a big surprise***.
3 A **non-defining relative clause** gives **extra** information about the noun that it refers to:
   *My friend Michael**, whose parents are German**, is bilingual*.

Excuse me.
We're looking for our car.
We parked it in a street that is called 'Einbahnstraße'.

GF 8   REVISION   Indirect speech   Die indirekte Rede

8.1   Statements

Kate	I **love** basketball. I'**m training** hard for our next match.	

Direct speech	Kate says, 'I **love** basketball. I'**m training** hard for our next match.'	◄ In der **direkten Rede** wird **wörtlich** wiedergegeben, was jemand sagt, schreibt oder denkt.
Indirect speech (reporting verb: simple present)	Kate says that she loves basketball. She says she's training hard for their next match.	◄ In der **indirekten Rede** (*indirect* oder *reported speech*) wird berichtet, was jemand sagt, schreibt oder denkt. Einleitende Verben sind *say, tell sb., answer, add, explain, think.*
Indirect speech (reporting verb: simple past)	Kate said that she loved basketball. She told me she was training hard for their next match.	◄ Steht das **einleitende Verb im *simple past*** (*said, told sb., answered* usw.), werden die Zeitformen der direkten Rede meist um eine Zeitstufe in die Vergangenheit „zurückverschoben" *(backshift of tenses).*

! Im Englischen steht vor der indirekten Rede **kein Komma** und das Wort *that* wird oft weggelassen.

Backshift of tenses after a reporting verb in the past

present	►	past	*will*-future	►	*would* + infinitive
past	►	past perfect	*going to*-future	►	*was/were going to* + infinitive
present perfect	►	past perfect	*can, may*	►	*could, might*

! Verben im *past perfect* bleiben unverändert, da man sie nicht weiter „zurückverschieben" kann.
In der Umgangssprache bleiben *past*-Formen der direkten Rede oft unverändert,
werden also nicht ins *past perfect* „zurückverschoben":
Gina   I didn't go out last Friday.   ►   Gina said she didn't go out last Friday.

8.2   Questions

Fragen

Wenn das einleitende Verb im *simple past* steht *(asked, wanted to know),* erfolgt auch bei **Fragen** in der indirekten Rede die Rückverschiebung der Zeiten.

Direct question (yes/no question)	'Do you train every day, Kate?'	◄ Handelt es sich bei der direkten **Frage** um eine **Frage ohne Fragewort** *(yes/no question),* dann wird die indirekte Frage mit *if* oder ***whether*** („ob") eingeleitet.
Indirect question	Alex asked Kate if/whether she trained every day.	
Direct question (with question word)	'When did you join the team?'	◄ Wenn die direkte **Frage mit einem Fragewort** beginnt (*why, how, what, when, where* usw.), dann wird das Fragewort in der indirekten Frage beibehalten.
Indirect question	Alex wanted to know when Kate had joined the team. ..., wann Kate sich der Mannschaft angeschlossen hat.	! Die Wortstellung in indirekten Fragen ist wie in Aussagesätzen: **S – V – ...** Es gibt keine Umschreibung mit *do/does/did.*

Grammar File

185

8.3 Advice, requests, commands

Ratschläge, Bitten, Aufforderungen

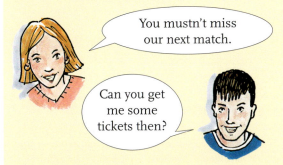

Kate **advised Alex not to miss** their next match.
Kate riet Alex, ihr nächstes Spiel nicht zu verpassen.

Alex **asked Kate to get** him some tickets.
Alex bat Kate, ihm Eintrittskarten zu besorgen.

◀ **Ratschläge** können mit **advise sb. to do sth.** (bzw. **advise sb. not to do sth.**) wiedergegeben werden.

◀ **Bitten** werden meist mit **ask sb. to do sth.** (bzw. **ask sb. not to do sth.**) wiedergegeben.

◀ **Aufforderungen** und **Anordnungen** werden meist mit **tell sb. to do sth.** (bzw. **tell sb. not to do sth.**) wiedergegeben.

In English: Indirect speech

1. If the reporting verb is in the past *(said, told sb., asked, ...)*, there is usually a 'backshift' of tenses (present ▶ past, present perfect ▶ past perfect etc.).
   Kate: 'I've hurt my knee.' ▶ Kate **said** that she **had hurt** her knee.
2. In indirect questions the word order is the same as in statements: **subject – verb** – ...
   Alex wanted to know when **Kate had joined the team**.
3. Indirect advice can be given with *advise sb.* + *to*-infinitive.
   Kate **advised Alex not to miss** the next match.
4. In indirect requests and commands the *to*-infinitive is used after *ask sb.* and *tell sb.*
   Alex **asked Kate to get** him some tickets.   The doctor **told me not to do** any sport.

GF 9 REVISION The *to*-infinitive — Der Infinitiv mit *to*

9.1 Verb + object + *to*-infinitive

Kim **helped** me to write my French essay.
Kim half mir, meinen französischen Aufsatz zu schreiben.

Sharon **asked** me not to use her photo.
Sharon bat mich, ihr Foto nicht zu verwenden.

Grandma **expects** us to save our pocket money.
Oma erwartet, dass wir unser Taschengeld sparen.

Ed **would like** me to go to town with him.
Ed möchte, dass ich mit ihm in die Stadt fahre.

We **want** you to help us to clean up the beach.
Wir wollen, dass du uns hilfst, den Strand zu säubern.

Verb + Objekt + *to*-Infinitiv

Nach bestimmten Verben kann ein **Objekt + *to*-Infinitiv** stehen, z. B. *ask/help/invite/teach sb. (not) to do sth*.

Nach den entsprechenden deutschen Verben steht meist ein Infinitiv mit „zu“:
jn. bitten/jm. helfen/…, etwas (nicht) zu tun.

◄ Auch nach den Verben *cause, expect, tell, want, would like, would love* kann ein **Objekt + *to*-Infinitiv** stehen.

! Nach den entsprechenden deutschen Verben steht ein Nebensatz mit „dass". Auf die englischen Verben darf jedoch <u>kein</u> *that*-Satz folgen:
*Wir **wollen**, dass du uns hilfst. We **want** you to help us.*
Nicht: *We want ~~that you help~~ us.*

9.2 Question word + *to*-infinitive

We **don't know** what to do.
(… what we should/could do)
Wir wissen nicht, was wir tun sollen/könnten.

Let's **ask** someone how to get to the bus station.
…, wie wir zum Busbahnhof kommen (können).

Can you **tell** us which direction to take?
…, welche Richtung wir nehmen müssen?

They **wondered** whether to go or to stay.
…, ob sie gehen oder bleiben sollten.

Fragewort + *to*-Infinitiv

Der *to*-Infinitiv steht oft nach einem **Fragewort** (*what, who, when, where, how* usw.) sowie nach *whether* („ob"). Er entspricht meist einem Nebensatz mit modalem Hilfsverb *(can, could, might, must, should)*.

Die Kombination aus Fragewort und *to*-Infinitiv steht oft nach den Verben *ask, explain, find out, know, show, tell, wonder*.

9.3 The *to*-infinitive instead of a relative clause

1 I expect **the last (person)** to arrive will be Jo.
  (… the last person who arrives …)
Tim was **the first (one)** to tell me the news.
  (… the first one who told me …)
We're **the only shop** to offer this service.
  (… the only shop that offers this service)
Sophie was **the only person/the only one** to say what she thought.
  (… the only person/one who said …)

2 Who was **the youngest (girl or boy)** to take part in the competition?
  (… the youngest girl or boy who took part …)

Der *to*-Infinitiv anstelle eines Relativsatzes

Der *to*-Infinitiv kann **anstelle eines Relativsatzes** stehen:

1 nach *the first, the last, the next, the only*

! Nach *the only* muss ein Nomen oder *one/ones* stehen.

2 nach einem Superlativ.

Grammar File

1 There are **clothes** to wash and **meals** to cook.
    (... clothes that I/we must wash ...)
James is **the person** to ask about computers.
    (... the person who you should ask)
Luigi's is the **place** to go for a good pizza.
    (... the place that you must/should go to)
Look, this is **the way** to do it.
    (... the way that you should do it)

2 I'm looking for **someone** to share a flat with.
    (... someone who I can share a flat with)
Lucy doesn't know **anybody** to play with.
    (... anybody who she can/could play with)
There's **nothing** to do and **nowhere** to go.
    (... nothing that I can do and nowhere that I can go)

Der *to*-Infinitiv kann **anstelle eines Relativsatzes <u>mit modalem Hilfsverb</u>** stehen:

1 nach einem **Nomen** (häufig nach *person, place, way*)

2 nach den Zusammensetzungen mit **some-, any-** und **no-** (*someone, something, somewhere, anything, nowhere* usw.).

In English: The *to*-infinitive

The *to*-infinitive is used
– after *ask, cause, expect, help, tell, want, would like, ...* + object   Dad **would like you to help** him.
– after a question word, instead of a subordinate clause   I don't know **who to ask**.
– after *the first (person), the last (one)*, etc., instead of a relative clause   Sue is always **the first to arrive**.
     Tom was **the oldest to join** us.
– after nouns and *someone, anything, nowhere*, etc., instead of a relative clause   I've got **some letters to write**.
     Is there **anybody to ask**?

*(to) disturb [dɪˈstɜːb] *stören*

GF 10 REVISION The gerund Das Gerundium

10.1 The gerund as subject and object

Subject	Object
Cycling is fun.	I love cycling.
Radfahren macht Spaß.	Ich liebe das Radfahren. / Ich fahre sehr gern Rad.

I like riding **motorbikes**.
Ich fahre gern Motorrad.
Cycling **in the rain** can be fun too.
Radfahren im Regen kann auch Spaß machen. /
Im Regen Rad zu fahren kann auch Spaß machen.

1 Nobody **enjoys** going to the dentist's.
Niemand geht gern zum Zahnarzt.
Imagine living in California!
Stell dir vor, in Kalifornien zu leben!
Tom **suggested** going for an ice cream.
Tom schlug vor, ein Eis essen zu gehen.

2 When it **started** raining / to rain we all went home.
Als es anfing zu regnen, gingen wir alle nach Haus.
Will **loves** doing / to do crazy things.
Will liebt es, verrückte Sachen zu machen.

3 I'll never **forget** talking to Robbie Williams.
Ich werde nie vergessen, wie ich mit Robbie Williams gesprochen habe.
I **forgot** to phone Grandpa. I'm sorry.
Ich habe vergessen, Opa anzurufen. Es tut mir leid.

I **remember** posting the letter last Friday.
Ich erinnere mich daran, letzten Freitag den Brief eingeworfen zu haben.
I must **remember** to post this card tomorrow.
Ich muss daran denken (= ich darf nicht vergessen), morgen diese Karte einzuwerfen.

I've **stopped** talking to Rob. We had a fight.
Ich habe aufgehört, mit Rob zu reden. / Ich rede nicht mehr mit Rob. ...
I **stopped** to talk to Jo. We chatted for a while.
Ich hielt an, um mit Jo zu reden.

I can't open the door. – **Try** kicking it.
... Probier mal, dagegen zu treten.
I **tried** to kick the door open and hurt myself.
Ich versuchte/bemühte mich, die Tür aufzutreten ...

Das Gerundium als Subjekt und als Objekt

Wenn die -ing-Form eines Verbs die Funktion eines **Nomens** hat, wird sie **Gerundium** (gerund) genannt. Das Gerundium kann **Subjekt** oder **Objekt** eines Satzes sein.

Wie ein Verb kann das Gerundium erweitert werden, z.B. durch ein Objekt (hier: *motorbikes*) oder eine Orts- oder Zeitangabe (hier: *in the rain*).

! Beachte:

◄ **1** Nach einigen Verben – z.B. *dislike, enjoy, finish, imagine, miss, practise, suggest* – muss ein weiteres Verb als Gerundium stehen:
I *enjoy* going ...; He *suggested* going ...
Anders als im Deutschen darf nach diesen Verben **kein Infinitiv** stehen!
Also nicht: I ~~enjoy to go~~ ...; He ~~suggested to go~~ ...

◄ **2** Nach *begin/start, continue, hate, like, love, prefer* kann jedoch – bei gleicher Bedeutung – entweder ein Gerundium oder ein *to*-Infinitiv stehen.

◄ **3** Nach *forget*, *remember*, *stop*, *try* kann entweder ein Gerundium oder ein *to*-Infinitiv stehen, aber mit unterschiedlicher Bedeutung:

– *forget doing* sth.	vergessen, dass/wie man etwas (in der Vergangen- heit) getan hat
forget to do sth.	vergessen, etwas zu tun
– *remember doing* sth.	sich daran erinnern, dass man etwas (in der Vergan- genheit) getan hat
remember to do sth.	daran denken, etwas zu tun
– *stop doing* sth.	aufhören, etwas zu tun
stop to do sth.	anhalten, um etwas (anderes) zu tun
– *try doing* sth.	etwas (aus)probieren
try to do sth.	versuchen/sich bemühen, etwas zu tun

Grammar File

10.2 The gerund after prepositions

Boots are made for walking. So let's go!
... zum Wandern ...
In future, don't use my mobile without asking.
... ohne zu fragen
You can save petrol by driving more slowly.
... indem man langsamer fährt

My little brother is **afraid** of sleeping in the dark.
... hat Angst davor, im Dunkeln zu schlafen.

I'm very **keen** on playing rugby.
Ich spiele leidenschaftlich gern Rugby.

Is there any **hope** of winning the final match?
Besteht Hoffnung, das Endspiel zu gewinnen?
What are his **reasons** for leaving school?
Was sind die Gründe dafür, dass er die Schule verlässt?

Sue **is talking** about moving to London.
Sue redet davon, nach London zu ziehen.
I don't **feel** like going out tonight. Do you?
Ich habe keine Lust, heute Abend auszugehen. Und du?

Das Gerundium nach Präpositionen

Nach einer Präposition *(by, for, of, without, ...)* muss ein Verb als Gerundium stehen.

Adjektiv/Nomen/Verb + Präposition + Gerundium:

–	*(to) be*	***afraid of*** ***good/bad at*** ***interested in*** ***keen on*** ***sick/tired of***	***doing*** *sth.*	**Adjektiv +** **Präposition**
–	*the*	***advantage of*** ***chance of*** ***hope of*** ***reason for***	***doing*** *sth.*	**Nomen +** **Präposition**
–	*(to)*	***dream of*** ***feel like*** ***talk about*** ***think of***	***doing*** *sth.*	**Verb +** **Präposition**

Additional information

10.3 The gerund with 'its own subject'

1a **Ella** can't **imagine moving** to Africa.
　Ella kann sich nicht vorstellen, nach Afrika zu ziehen.
1b **Ella** can't **imagine** <u>her family</u> **moving** to Africa.
　Ella kann sich nicht vorstellen, dass ihre Familie
　nach Afrika zieht.

2a His parents talked **about** <u>him</u> **going** to Paris.
2b His parents talked **about** <u>his</u> **going** to Paris.
　Seine Eltern redeten davon, dass er nach Paris fährt.

Das Gerundium mit „eigenem Subjekt"

◀ In Satz **1b** hat das Gerundium ein „eigenes Subjekt":
moving bezieht sich auf *her family* (und nicht auf *Ella*,
das Subjekt des ganzen Satzes).

◀ Wenn wie in Satz **2a** das Subjekt des Gerundiums ein Personal-
pronomen ist, dann steht es in der Objektform: ***him*** (nicht: *he*).
In sehr formellem Englisch wird wie in Satz **2b** oft ein Possessiv-
pronomen bevorzugt: ***his*** *going* ...

In English: The gerund

1 A **gerund** is an *-ing* form used as a noun.
　It can be the subject or the object of a sentence.　　　　　*Singing is fun. I like singing.*
2 After some verbs *(enjoy, imagine, suggest, ...)* we use a gerund,
　<u>not</u> an infinitive.　　　　　*Lucy <u>suggested</u> asking the head teacher.*
3 Verbs which follow a <u>preposition</u> take the form of a gerund.　　*Don't cross the road <u>without</u> looking.*
4 Gerunds can have <u>their own subject</u>.　　　　　*Is there any chance of <u>Pete/him</u> winning?*

GF 11 REVISION Participles Partizipien

11.1 Participle forms

Formen des Partizips

Present participle *(-ing):*

work	→	**working**	try	→	**trying**
danc**e**	→	**dancing**	plan	→	**plan**n**ing**

◄ Das **Partizip Präsens** *(present participle)* bildet man durch Anhängen von **-ing** an den Infinitiv. Beachte die Besonderheiten bei der Schreibung.

Past participle, regular verbs *(-ed):*

work	→	**worked**	try	→	**tri**ed
danc**e**	→	**danced**	plan	→	**plann**ed

◄ Das **Partizip Perfekt** *(past participle)* eines <u>regelmäßigen</u> Verbs wird durch Anhängen von **-ed** an den Infinitiv gebildet. Beachte auch hier die Besonderheiten bei der Schreibung.

<u>Unregelmäßige</u> Verben haben eigene *past participle*-Formen, die man einzeln lernen muss.

▶ *Unregelmäßige Verben (pp. 280–281)*

Past participle, irregular verbs:

build	→	**built**	grow	→	**grown**
make	→	**made**	see	→	**seen**
teach	→	**taught**	write	→	**written**

11.2 Participle clauses instead of relative clauses

Partizipialsätze anstelle von Relativsätzen

Partizipialsätze können Relativsätze verkürzen und werden daher oft anstelle von Relativsätzen verwendet.

The girl talking **to Leo** is my sister.
   (The girl <u>who is talking</u> to Leo ...)
The man driving **the red car** didn't stop.
   (The man <u>who was driving</u> the red car ...)

◄ Das *present participle* entspricht einem Relativpronomen + Verb im **Aktiv**: *is talking; was driving.*

We often buy strawberries grown **in California**.
   (... strawberries <u>which were grown</u> ...)
The girls chosen **for the team** were only 15.
   (The girls <u>who were chosen</u> for the team ...)

◄ Das *past participle* entspricht einem Relativpronomen + Verb im **Passiv**: *were grown; were chosen.*

11.3 The present participle after certain verbs

Das Partizip Präsens nach bestimmten Verben

Verb of perception + object + present participle			
	Verb	Object	Present participle
1 I	heard	people	shouting.
2 Rob	saw	two men	running out of the bank.
3 Sue	noticed	some men	getting into a blue car.
4 We	watched	the car	driving down the street.

Mit einem **Verb der Wahrnehmung + Objekt + Partizip Präsens** sagt man, dass man etwas wahrnimmt, das gerade im Verlauf ist.

Verben der Wahrnehmung sind *feel, hear, listen to, notice, see, smell, watch.*

1 Ich hörte Leute schreien.
2 Rob sah zwei Männer aus der Bank laufen.
3 Sue bemerkte, wie/dass einige Männer in ein blaues Auto stiegen.
4 Wir beobachteten, wie das Auto die Straße hinunterfuhr.

Im Deutschen verwendet man einen Infinitiv (1, 2) oder einen Nebensatz mit „wie" oder „dass" (3, 4).

Grammar File

Additional information

1 Rob **watched the car <u>stop</u>** at the corner.
2 He **saw a man <u>get out</u>**.
3 Rob **heard him <u>shout</u>** something to the others.
4 Then he **watched the car <u>disappear</u>** round the corner.

1 Rob beobachtete, wie das Auto an der Ecke anhielt.
2 Er sah einen Mann aussteigen.
3 Rob hörte, wie er den anderen etwas zurief.
4 Dann beobachtete er, wie/dass das Auto um die Ecke verschwand.

Nach **Verben der Wahrnehmung + Objekt** kann auch ein **Infinitiv** stehen (ohne *to*). Damit drückt man aus, dass das Geschehen **vollständig – von Anfang bis Ende –** wahrgenommen wird. Oft handelt es sich um kurze Handlungen. Vergleiche:

– *I saw a man **cross** the street.*
  (Er überquerte die Straße.)
– *I saw a man **crossing** the street when a car hit him.*
  (Er war dabei, die Straße zu überqueren, wurde aber angefahren, bevor er die andere Straßenseite erreichte.)

Additional information

We **stood <u>watching</u>** the street artists.
Wir standen da und sahen den Straßenkünstlern zu.

We **sat <u>chatting</u>** in a café.
Wir saßen in einem Café und unterhielten uns.

The dog **came <u>running</u>** towards me.
Der Hund kam auf mich zugerannt.

Das Partizip Präsens kann nach **Verben der Ruhe** *(stand, sit, stay, lie)* und nach **Verben der Bewegung** *(come, go)* stehen.

11.4 Participle clauses instead of adverbial clauses

Partizipialsätze anstelle von adverbialen Nebensätzen

Time

Seeing **Ellis Island for the first time**, Ava was very excited.
(When Ava saw Ellis Island for the first time, …)
Als Ava zum ersten Mal Ellis Island sah, …

Arriving **at the station**, we went straight to the platform.
Als wir am Bahnhof ankamen, …

Asked **to turn down his MP3 player**, the boy started to shout at the bus driver.   (When he was asked to turn down …)
Als er gebeten wurde, seinen MP3-Spieler leiser zu stellen, …

Partizipialsätze können **Nebensätze der Zeit** oder **des Grundes** verkürzen.

Solche Partizipialsätze gehen oft dem Hauptsatz voran. Sie sind **typisch für das geschriebene Englisch**.

In gesprochenem Englisch werden meist adverbiale Nebensätze bevorzugt.

Reason

Feeling **tired**, Emily took the bus home.
(Because/Since she felt tired, …)
Weil/Da sie sich müde fühlte, …

Being **a doctor**, Marie knew exactly what to do.
Weil/Da sie Ärztin ist, …

Warned **by his wife**, the man was able to escape.
(Because he was warned by his wife, …)
Von seiner Frau gewarnt, … / Weil er … gewarnt wurde, …

►►►

Having + past participle

1 **Having passed** his exams, Mike applied for a job.
(After he had passed his exams, ...)
Nachdem Mike seine Prüfungen bestanden hatte, ...

2 **Having been** to Italy twice, we decided to go to Spain.
(Because/Since we had been to Italy twice, ...)
Da wir schon zweimal in Italien gewesen waren, ...

Not having seen the film, I bought the DVD.
(Because/Since I hadn't seen the film, ...)
Da ich den Film nicht gesehen hatte, ...

Partizipialsätze mit **having** + **Partizip Perfekt** drücken immer **Vorzeitigkeit** aus.

Partizipialsätze mit **having** + **Partizip Perfekt** entsprechen

1 einem adverbialen Nebensatz der **Zeit**, meist mit *after* eingeleitet

2 einem adverbialen Nebensatz des **Grundes**.

Additional information

1a **Reading** a really boring book, I fell asleep.
Als/Weil ich ein wirklich langweiliges Buch las, ...

1b **When/While reading** a really boring book,
I fell asleep. *or* I fell asleep **when/while reading** a really boring book.

◄ Nicht immer ist eindeutig zu erkennen, ob ein Partizipialsatz einem Nebensatz der Zeit oder einem Nebensatz des Grundes entspricht (Satz **1a**).

Durch Voranstellen der **Konjunktion** *when* oder *while* macht man deutlich, dass der Satz **zeitlich** zu verstehen ist (Satz **1b**).

2a I saw a huge black dog **when/while walking** down the street.
(= I was walking down the street)
Ich habe einen riesigen schwarzen Hund gesehen, als/während ich die Straße hinunterging.

2b I saw a huge black dog **walking** down the street.
(= the dog was walking down the street)
Ich habe gesehen, wie ein riesiger schwarzer Hund die Straße hinunterging.

◄ Wenn der Hauptsatz ein Objekt enthält (hier: *a huge black dog*), gibt es oft große Bedeutungsunterschiede, je nachdem, ob der Partizipialsatz mit Konjunktion (Satz **2a**) oder ohne Konjunktion (Satz **2b**) verwendet wird.

3 **Although asked** to stop by the police, the man drove on.
He will have to wait outside **until asked** to enter.
If posted before 12 o'clock, the letter should arrive tomorrow.

◄ Partizipialsätze können auch durch andere Konjunktionen eingeleitet werden, z. B. *although, until, if, after, before* (Sätze **3**).

11.5 Participle clauses giving additional information

'I'll be back at 6,' he shouted, banging **the door** behind him.
... rief er und knallte die Tür hinter sich zu.

Using **a knife**, he was able to open the door.
Indem er ein Messer benutzte, ...

Lynn ran down the stairs, losing **a shoe**.
..., wobei sie einen Schuh verlor.

Partizipialsätze zur Angabe von Zusatzinformationen

Partizipialsätze werden oft verwendet, um Zusatzinformationen zu geben oder die Begleitumstände einer Handlung zu beschreiben. (Meist handelt es sich um zeitgleich oder fast zeitgleich stattfindende Handlungen oder Vorgänge.)

Im Deutschen steht meist ein Hauptsatz mit „und" oder ein Nebensatz mit „indem" oder „wobei".

Grammar File

193

In English: Participles

Participle clauses can be used
- instead of relative clauses — *The girl **talking to Jack** ... / Wine **produced in Australia** ...*
- after verbs of perception + object — *I can **see somebody running** down the street.*
  (when the action is not yet completed)
- instead of adverbial clauses of time or reason — ***Travelling** by train, you meet some interesting people.*
  ***Not having** much money, we stayed at a small B&B.*
- to give additional information — *Maggie ran down the road, **singing** her favourite song.*

GF 12 **Emphasis**   Hervorhebung

Word stress

nicht betont	He says he**'ll** do his Maths homework now.
zur Hervor-hebung betont	He says he will do his Maths homework now.

◄ Man kann **beim Sprechen** einzelne Wörter oder Satzteile stark **betonen**, um sie hervorzuheben.
Bei Hilfsverben (z. B. *is, have, will, would*) wird dann die Langform benutzt.

Es gibt auch eine Reihe **besonderer Wörter und Strukturen zur Hervorhebung**:

Certain adverbs

I couldn't answer some of the interviewer's questions. I felt really/so/completely stupid.
I'll never go to an interview unprepared again.
Don't ever make the same mistake!

◄ Bestimmte **Adverbien** werden benutzt, um einzelne Wörter oder Satzteile hervorzuheben.
Beispiele: *really, completely, so, such, never, ever.*

Emphasizing pronouns

The work itself isn't difficult. You just need the right tools. (Die Arbeit selbst ...)
So I'm going to repair the motorbike myself.

◄ **Verstärkende Pronomen** auf *-self/-selves* werden benutzt, um Nomen oder Pronomen hervorzuheben.

It's ... / It was ... + relative clause

It's **French** that I don't like. German is OK.
It was **me** who/that told him about the party.
It was **in the shopping mall** that I first met my boyfriend.

It was **my grandparents** who/that paid for the flat, not my parents.

It's **the tenses** that I don't always get right.
The rest of the grammar is OK.

◄ Man kann einen Satz mit ***It's ... that/who ...*** oder ***It was ... that/who ...***beginnen, um ein Nomen, ein Pronomen oder eine adverbiale Bestimmung hervorzuheben. Beachte, dass Pronomen nach *It's/It was* in der Objektform stehen (*It was **me** ...*).

◄ Oft wird mit dieser Konstruktion ein Gegensatz ausgedrückt.

! Auch bei Pluralnomen steht das Verb im Singular:
*It **was** my **grandparents** ... / It**'s** the **tenses** ...*

►►►

'Negative' adverbials + inversion

Never have I seen so many people.
Noch nie habe ich so viele Leute gesehen.

Under no circumstances did he want to see her again.
Unter keinen Umständen wollte er sie wiedersehen.

◄ In eher förmlichem Englisch können einige **Adverbien** und **adverbiale Bestimmungen** mit **einschränkender oder verneinender Bedeutung** besonders betont werden, indem man sie an den Satzanfang stellt.
Beispiele: *never, rarely (*„selten"*), hardly (*„kaum"*), no way, under no circumstances (*„unter keinen Umständen"*).*
Beachte, dass sich in diesem Fall die Wortstellung ändert (Inversion):

	Hilfsverb	Subjekt	Vollverb
Never	*have*	*I*	*seen ...*
Under no circumstances	*did*	*he*	*want to ...*

Emphatic *do/does/did*

ohne Hervorhebung	I **think** you should talk to your teacher.
mit Hervorhebung	I **do think** you should talk to your teacher.
	Ich bin wirklich der Meinung ...
ohne Hervorhebung	Well, you needn't help me, but you **promised**.
mit Hervorhebung	Well, you needn't help me, but you **did promise**.
	... aber eigentlich hast du es versprochen.

Do have another biscuit.
Nehmen Sie doch noch einen Keks.

Oh **do be** quiet!
Oh sei jetzt endlich still!

◄ Im *simple present* oder *simple past* kann man der Aussage eines Satzes Nachdruck verleihen, indem man betontes **do**, **does** oder **did** vor das Vollverb stellt.
Das Vollverb selbst steht dann im Infinitiv.
Im Deutschen benutzt man in solchen Fällen meist verstärkende Adverbien wie „wirklich" oder „doch".

◄ Oft werden auf diese Weise Aufforderungen und Anweisungen verstärkt.

In English: Emphasis

To **emphasize** a word or sentence part you can ...

1 stress it in speech — *Lucy is doing volunteer work in **South Africa**, not South America.*

2 use adverbs such as *really, completely, ever, never* — *That's a **completely** crazy idea. Don't **ever** suggest such a thing again.*

3 use *myself, yourself, ourselves* etc. to emphasize a noun or pronoun — *Liz can repair her computer **herself**. Can't **we** design the website **ourselves**?*

4 use *It's/It was ... that/who ...* to put the stressed word at the beginning of the sentence — *It's tomorrow **that** we're doing the Maths test. **It was** the French **who** signed the agreement, not the Chinese.*

5 use inversion after negative adverbials such as *never, rarely, under no circumstances* — ***Never** had they seen such a fantastic sight.*

6 use *do/does/did* in the *simple present* and *simple past* to stress the full verb — *I **do** like her new boyfriend. He **does** seem to be right for her. We **did** enjoy our meal. It was delicious.*

Grammar File

Grammatical terms (Grammatische Fachbegriffe)

English	German	Example
active ['æktɪv]	Aktiv	*Beckham **scored** the final goal.*
activity verb [æk'tɪvəti vɜːb]	Tätigkeitsverb	*do, go, make, read, repair*
adjective ['ædʒɪktɪv]	Adjektiv	*good, red, new, boring*
adverb ['ædvɜːb]	Adverb	*always, badly, here, really, today*
adverb of frequency ['friːkwənsi]	Häufigkeitsadverb	*always, often, never*
adverb of indefinite time [ɪn,defɪnət 'taɪm]	Adverb der unbestimmten Zeit	*already, ever, just, never*
adverb of manner ['mænə]	Adverb der Art und Weise	*badly, happily, quietly, well*
adverbial [æd'vɜːbiəl]	Adverbialbestimmung	*I play football **on Sunday mornings**.*
adverbial clause [æd,vɜːbiəl 'klɔːz]	adverbialer Nebensatz	*I went to bed **because I was tired**.*
article ['ɑːtɪkl]	Artikel	*the, a/an*
aspect ['æspekt]	Aspekt	
auxiliary [ɔːg'zɪliəri]	Hilfsverb	*be, have, do; will, can, must*
backshift of tenses ['bækʃɪft]	Verschiebung der Zeitformen	*'**I'm** glad.' ▶ He said he **was** glad.*
command [kə'mɑːnd]	Befehl, Aufforderungssatz	*Open your books. Don't talk.*
comparison [kəm'pærɪsn]	Steigerung	*old – older – oldest*
complex sentence [,kɒmpleks 'sentəns]	Satzgefüge (Verbindung aus Haupt- und Nebensatz)	*I can't go to school because I'm ill.*
conditional sentence [kən,dɪʃənl 'sentəns]	Bedingungssatz	*I'd call him if I knew his number.*
conjunction [kən'dʒʌŋkʃn]	Konjunktion	*and, or, but; because, before*
contact clause ['kɒntækt klɔːz]	Relativsatz ohne Relativpronomen	*She's the girl **I love**.*
countable noun ['kaʊntəbl]	zählbares Nomen	*girl – girls, pound – pounds*
defining relative clause [dɪ'faɪnɪŋ]	bestimmender Relativsatz	*There's the girl **who helped me**.*
definite article ['defɪnət]	bestimmter Artikel	*the*
direct speech [,daɪrekt 'spiːtʃ]	direkte Rede, wörtliche Rede	*'**I'm sorry**.'*
emphasis ['emfəsɪs]	Hervorhebung, Betonung	
future perfect [,fjuːtʃə 'pɜːfɪkt]	vollendete Zukunft, Futur II	*On Friday we will have finished our exams.*
future progressive [,fjuːtʃə prə'gresɪv]	Verlaufsform des *will-future*	*A week today I will be lying on the beach.*
gerund ['dʒerənd]	Gerundium	*I like **dancing**. **Dancing** is fun.*
going to-**future**	Futur mit *going to*	*I**'m going to watch** TV tonight.*
if-**clause** ['ɪf klɔːz]	*if*-Satz, Nebensatz mit *if*	***If I see Jack**, I'll tell him.*
imperative [ɪm'perətɪv]	Imperativ (Befehlsform)	*Open your books. Don't talk.*
indirect speech [,ɪndərekt 'spiːtʃ]	indirekte Rede	*Sam said **(that) he was sorry**.*
infinitive [ɪn'fɪnətɪv]	Infinitiv (Grundform des Verbs)	*(to) open, (to) see, (to) read*
inversion [ɪn'vɜːʃn]	Inversion, Umkehrung	*Never before **had she** lied to me.*
irregular verb [ɪ,regjələ 'vɜːb]	unregelmäßiges Verb	*(to) go – went – gone*
main clause	Hauptsatz	***I like Scruffy** because I like dogs.*
modal, modal auxiliary [,məʊdl_ɔːg'zɪliəri]	Modalverb, modales Hilfsverb	*can, could, may, must*
negative statement [,negətɪv 'steɪtmənt]	verneinter Aussagesatz	*I don't like bananas.*
non-defining relative clause [dɪ'faɪnɪŋ]	nicht bestimmender Relativsatz	*Madison**, who lives in Atlanta,** goes to M. L. King High School.*
noun [naʊn]	Nomen, Substantiv	*Sophie, girl, brother, time*
object ['ɒbdʒɪkt]	Objekt	*My sister is writing **a letter**.*
object form ['ɒbdʒɪkt fɔːm]	Objektform (der Personalpronomen)	*me, you, him, her, it, us, them*
participle ['pɑːtɪsɪpl]	Partizip	*planning, taking; planned, taken*
participle clause [,pɑːtɪsɪpl 'klɔːz]	Partizipialsatz	*I saw a boy **playing in the street**.*
passive ['pæsɪv]	Passiv	*The goal **was scored** by Beckham.*
past participle [,pɑːst 'pɑːtɪsɪpl]	Partizip Perfekt	*cleaned, planned, gone, taken*
past perfect [,pɑːst 'pɜːfɪkt]	Plusquamperfekt, Vorvergangenheit	*He cried – he **had hurt** his knee.*

past perfect progressive [ˌpɑːst ˌpɜːfɪkt prəˈɡresɪv]	Verlaufsform des *past perfect*	She **had been working** in the garden since 12 o'clock.
past progressive [ˌpɑːst prəˈɡresɪv]	Verlaufsform der Vergangenheit	At 7.30 I **was having** dinner.
personal passive [ˌpɜːsənl ˈpæsɪv]	persönliches Passiv	I was offered a job.
personal pronoun [ˌpɜːsənl ˈprəʊnaʊn]	Personalpronomen (persönliches Fürwort)	I, you, he, she, it, we, they; me, you, him, her, it, us, them
plural [ˈplʊərəl]	Plural, Mehrzahl	
positive statement [ˌpɒzətɪv ˈsteɪtmənt]	bejahter Aussagesatz	I like oranges.
possessive determiner [pəˌzesɪv dɪˈtɜːmɪnə]	Possessivbegleiter (besitzanzeigender Begleiter)	my, your, his, her, its, our, their
possessive form [pəˌzesɪv fɔːm]	s-Genitiv	Jo's brother; my sister's room
possessive pronoun [pəˌzesɪv ˈprəʊnaʊn]	Possessivpronomen	mine, yours, his, hers, ours, theirs
preposition [ˌprepəˈzɪʃn]	Präposition	after, at, in, next to, under
present participle [ˌpreznt ˈpɑːtɪsɪpl]	Partizip Präsens	cleaning, planning, going, taking
present perfect [ˌpreznt ˈpɜːfɪkt]	*present perfect*	We**'ve made** a cake for you.
present perfect progressive	Verlaufsform des *present perfect*	We**'ve been waiting** for an hour.
present progressive [ˌpreznt prəˈɡresɪv]	Verlaufsform der Gegenwart	The Hansons **are having** lunch.
pronoun [ˈprəʊnaʊn]	Pronomen, Fürwort	
quantifier [ˈkwɒntɪfaɪə]	Mengenangabe	some, a lot of, many, much
question tag [ˈkwestʃən tæɡ]	Frageanhängsel	This place is great, **isn't it?**
question word [ˈkwestʃən wɜːd]	Fragewort	what?, when?, where?, how?
reflexive pronoun [rɪˌfleksɪv ˈprəʊnaʊn]	Reflexivpronomen	myself, yourself, themselves
regular verb [ˌreɡjələ ˈvɜːb]	regelmäßiges Verb	(to) help – helped – helped
relative clause [ˌrelətɪv ˈklɔːz]	Relativsatz	There's the girl **who helped me**.
relative pronoun [ˌrelətɪv ˈprəʊnaʊn]	Relativpronomen	who, that, which, whose
reported speech [rɪˌpɔːtɪd ˈspiːtʃ]	indirekte Rede	Sam said **(that) he was sorry**.
request [rɪˈkwest]	Bitte	Can you help me with this?
short answer [ˌʃɔːt ˈɑːnsə]	Kurzantwort	Yes, I am. / No, I don't.
simple past [ˌsɪmpl ˈpɑːst]	einfache Form der Vergangenheit	Jo **wrote** two letters yesterday.
simple present [ˌsɪmpl ˈpreznt]	einfache Form der Gegenwart	I always **go** to school by bike.
singular [ˈsɪŋɡjələ]	Singular, Einzahl	
state verb [ˈsteɪt vɜːb]	Zustandsverb	be, know, like, own, sound, want
statement [ˈsteɪtmənt]	Aussagesatz	
subject [ˈsʌbdʒɪkt]	Subjekt	**My sister** is writing a letter.
subject form [ˈsʌbdʒɪkt fɔːm]	Subjektform (der Personalpronomen)	I, you, he, she, it, we, they
subordinate clause [səˌbɔːdɪnət ˈklɔːz]	Nebensatz	I like Scruffy **because I like dogs**.
substitute [ˈsʌbstɪtjuːt]	Ersatzverb (eines modalen Hilfverbs)	be able to, be allowed to, have to
tense [tens]	Zeitform	
uncountable noun [ʌnˈkaʊntəbl]	nicht zählbares Nomen	bread, milk, money, news, work
verb [vɜːb]	Verb	hear, open, help, go
verb of perception [pəˈsepʃn]	Verb der Wahrnehmung	feel, hear, listen to, see, smell
will-future	Futur mit *will*	I think it **will be** cold tonight.
word order [ˈwɜːd ˌɔːdə]	Wortstellung	
yes/no question	Entscheidungsfrage	Are you 13? Do you like comics?

Unit 1, Part A, P4 (p. 13): Lösung

1 My friend Tony almost had an accident on his way to school.
2 He never goes to bed before midnight.
3 My sister speaks French well.
4 She loves France and has travelled there often. / ... and has often travelled there.
5 We have already decided not to go to the party.
6 At last I have enough time to finish my book.
7 Unfortunately, I can't meet you at the cinema. / ... at the cinema unfortunately.
8 I always clean my room on Saturday mornings.
9 Then the whole family usually has lunch together.
10 In the afternoon my sister goes to football. / ... to football in the afternoon.

Vocabulary

Diese Wörterverzeichnisse findest du in deinem Englischbuch:

- Das **Vocabulary** (S. 197–230) enthält alle Wörter und Wendungen aus Band 6, die du lernen musst. Sie stehen in der Reihenfolge, in der sie in den Units vorkommen.
- Das **Dictionary** (S. 231–279) enthält den Wortschatz der Bände 1 bis 6 in alphabetischer Reihenfolge. Dort kannst du nachschlagen, was ein Wort bedeutet, wie man es ausspricht oder wie es genau geschrieben wird.

So ist das Vocabulary aufgebaut:

- Hier siehst du, wo die Wörter vorkommen.
  p. 17   = Seite 17
  p. 18/P 1 = Seite 18, Übung 1
- Die Lautschrift zeigt dir, wie ein Wort ausgesprochen und betont wird.
  (→ Englische Laute: S. 284)
- Eingerückte Wörter lernst du am besten zusammen mit dem vorausgehenden Wort, weil die beiden zusammengehören.
- Die blauen Kästen solltest du dir besonders gut ansehen.
- Auf den Seiten 204, 212 und 223 findest du Zusammenstellungen von Wörtern und Wendungen zu Themenfeldern der Units 1–3. Neue Wörter oder Wendungen sind durch ⁺ gekennzeichnet.

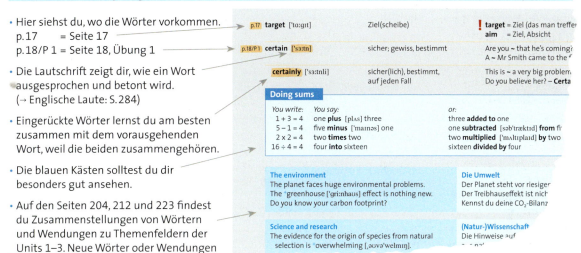

Abkürzungen:

n	= noun	v	= verb	
adj	= adjective	adv	= adverb	
prep	= preposition	conj	= conjunction	
pl	= plural	no pl	= no plural	
p.	= page	pp.	= pages	
jd.	= somebody	etw.	= something	
jn.	= jemanden	jm.	= jemandem	
AE	= American English	infml	= informal	
BE	= British English	fml	= formal	

Symbole:

! Hier stehen Hinweise auf Besonderheiten, bei denen man leicht Fehler machen kann.

◄► ist das „Gegenteil"-Zeichen: **alive** ◄► **dead**
(**alive** ist das Gegenteil von **dead**)

~ Die **Tilde** in den Beispielsätzen steht für das neue Wort.

Ⓕ verwandtes Wort im Französischen
Ⓛ verwandtes Wort im Lateinischen

Unit 1: You and yours

p. 7 (to) **go on**	los sein, abgehen, laufen	Is anything **going ~** tonight? – Yes, Jack's having a party. Dan and Sue are together?! How long has this been **going ~**?
(to) **criticize (for)** ['krɪtɪsaɪz]	kritisieren (wegen)	He **~d** me **for** not listening to him. Ⓕ critiquer
in the end	schließlich, am Ende, zum Schluss	At first no one clapped, but **in the end** everybody joined in. **!** **in the end** = schließlich **at the end (of)** = am Ende (von) **At the end of** the concert everybody clapped.
possessive [pə'zesɪv]	besitzergreifend, vereinnahmend	Nina's boyfriend is so **~** that she can't even go out with her girlfriends. Ⓕ possessif, -ve

Irregular verbs → S. 280–281 · List of names, places and countries → S. 282–284

Vocabulary

PART A   Got friends?

p.8	**single** ['sɪŋgl]	einzige(r, s), nur ein(e/n)	There was a ~ cake left and I bought it. He's 34 and hasn't had a ~ girlfriend yet. **!** **single** = **1.** ledig; 　　　　　**2.** Einzel- 　　　　　**3.** einzige(r, s) *(nur ein/e)* 　　　　　　　　　Ⓛ singuli, -ae, -a
	insecure [ˌɪnsɪˈkjʊə]	unsicher	I felt ~ when I started to wear glasses.
	secure [sɪˈkjʊə]	sicher; selbstsicher	She has a very ~ job: she's a teacher. He seems very ~ but actually he's quite shy. 　　　　　　　　　Ⓛ securus, -a, -um
	You**'d better** ... (= You **had** better ...)	Du solltest lieber ...	It's cold: we**'d better** (= we **had better**) take our pullovers. ► Grammar File 5.3: Modals (p.179)
p.9	(to) **dump** sb. [dʌmp]	jn. sitzen lassen, mit jm. Schluss machen	= to chuck sb., to end a relationship with sb.
	clingy ['klɪŋi] *(infml)*	anhänglich, klammernd	
	(to) **insist (on** sth.) [ɪnˈsɪst]	bestehen (auf etwas)	I didn't want to go to Granny's but Mum ~**ed**. Dad always ~**s on** me helping him clean the car. 　　　　　　　　　Ⓕ insister
	down-to-earth [ˌ--ˈ-]	praktisch, nüchtern	He's not a dreamer but a very ~**-to-**~ sort of person. (= *steht mit beiden Füßen auf dem Boden.*)
	kind of ['kaɪnd_əv] *(infml)*	irgendwie (schon)	He isn't really stupid, he's ~ **of** not intelligent. You like her? – **Kind** ~, but she annoys me too.
	(to) **click** [klɪk] *(infml)*	sich auf Anhieb gut verstehen	They met at a party and ~**ed** straightaway.
	(to) **betray** sb./sth. [bɪˈtreɪ] *(fml)*	jn./etwas verraten	The spy was ~**ed** by a friend and caught.
	trust [trʌst]	Vertrauen; vertrauliche Mitteilung	(to) **betray a** ~ = etwas Vertrauliches ausplaudern
	(to) **be special (to** sb.) ['speʃl]	(jm.) besonders, außergewöhnlich sein; (jm.) viel bedeuten	This ring is ~ **to** me as it was my grandma's. The dodo was a ~ bird because it couldn't fly. 　　　　　　　　　Ⓕ spécial,e
p.10	**friendship** ['frendʃɪp]	Freundschaft	
	(to) **act** [ækt]	handeln, sich verhalten	Simon is ~**ing** strangely. I wonder what's wrong. 　　　　　　　　　Ⓛ agere **!** (to) **act** = **1.** handeln, sich verhalten; 　　　　　　**2.** spielen, schauspielern
	mad (at sb.) [mæd] *(bes. AE, infml)*	wütend (auf jn.)	**!** **mad** = **1.** *(especially BE)* wahnsinnig, verrückt; 　　　　**2.** wütend
	the more ... the more ...	je mehr ... desto mehr ...	**The more** I do now, **the more** I can relax later. Is it true that **the prettier** a girl is, **the more** boyfriends she has?
	guilty ['gɪlti]	schuldbewusst; schuldig	I felt so ~ because I forgot my mum's birthday. He would never steal anything. He can't be ~.
	I'd go (= I *would* go)	ich pflegte zu gehen; ich ging oft	► Grammar File 2.3: „Früher" (p.169)

Tips on learning words→ S.128 · Glossary of literary terms → S.161–164 · Dictionary (English – German) → S.231–279

Vocabulary

(to) **end up doing** sth.	schließlich etwas tun	My uncle started his career doing the dishes in a hotel. He ~**ed up owning** the hotel.
partly ['pɑːtli]	zum Teil, teilweise	Tomorrow's weather: ~ sunny, ~ cloudy. Ⓛ partim
(to) **exclude** sb./sth. **(from** sth.) [ɪk'skluːd]	jn./etwas ausschließen (von etwas)	There are gentlemen's clubs in London which still ~ women. Ⓕ exclure Ⓛ excludere
mostly ['məʊstli]	hauptsächlich, meistens	The milk we drink is ~ from cows.
(to) **prove** sth. **(to** sb.) [pruːv]	(jm.) etwas beweisen, nachweisen	**!** noun: **proof** – verb: (to) **prove** Ⓕ prouver Ⓛ probare
sensitive ['sensətɪv]	einfühlsam, empfindsam; empfindlich, sensibel	She's a good listener and ~ to my feelings. Don't say anything about his big nose: he's very ~ about it.
very best/most/... ['veri]	allerbeste(r, s), allermeiste(r, s), ...	**!** very + superlative = German *aller*- The ~ best book I have ever read is *Oliver Twist*. The ~ first film I saw was *Peter Pan*.
(to) **ignore** [ɪg'nɔː]	nicht beachten, ignorieren	She completely ~**d** me. It was as if I just wasn't there. Ⓕ ignorer Ⓛ ignorare
(to) **get** sb. **to do** sth.	jn. dazu bringen, etwas zu tun; jn. zwingen, etwas zu tun	If you don't want to clean your room, **get** your sister **to do** it for you. She always says yes. = (to) **make** sb. **do** sth.
total ['təʊtl]	Gesamt-, gesamt, völlig, total	The ~ costs, with drinks, were over £300. Smoking is ~**ly** banned in all UK pubs.
evaluation [ɪˌvæljuˈeɪʃn]	Beurteilung, Einschätzung	What is your ~ of the problem? Can we solve it? Ⓕ l'évaluation (f)
task [tɑːsk]	Aufgabe	= a job that has to be done
(to) **break up (with** sb.) [ˌbreɪkˈʌp]	Schluss machen (mit jm.), sich trennen (von jm.)	My parents have **broken** ~ and are getting divorced soon.
(to) **evaluate** [ɪˈvæljueɪt]	beurteilen, einschätzen; auswerten	From 1 to 10, how would you ~ his talent? The new design is still being ~**d**. Ⓕ évaluer
(to) **note** sth. **down** [ˌnəʊtˈdaʊn]	(sich) etwas notieren	= (to) write sth. down quickly Ⓕ noter Ⓛ notare
emotion [ɪˈməʊʃn]	Gefühl, Emotion	**!** stress: em**o**tion [-'--] Ⓕ l'émotion (f)
nerve [nɜːv]	Nerv	If you didn't have ~**s**, your body wouldn't feel pain. She **had the** ~ to ask if I could do the job for her! (= besaß die Frechheit)
(to) **get on** sb.'s **nerves**	jm. auf die Nerven gehen	My little brother often ~**s on** my **nerves**.
(to) **feel like doing** sth. [fiːl]	Lust haben, etwas zu tun	Do you ~ **like coming** to a concert with me?

p.11/P 1 · p.12/P 2

Irregular verbs → S. 280–281 · List of names, places and countries → S. 282–284

(to) **look down on** sb.	auf jn. herabsehen	

Why do some drivers ~ ~ **on** other people's cars?
(to) look down on sb. ◄► (to) look up to sb.

(to) **dislike** [dɪsˈlaɪk]	nicht mögen, nicht leiden können	**!** No infinitive after **dislike**: I **dislike** gett**ing** up early. *not:* I dislike ~~to get up~~ early.
(to) **idolize** [ˈaɪdəlaɪz]	vergöttern, abgöttisch lieben	

PART B   Addictions

p.14 **addiction (to** sth.) [əˈdɪkʃn]	Sucht (nach etwas)	The official name for an ~ **to** shopping is *oniomania*. (F) l'addiction (f)
(to) **be addicted (to** sth.) [əˈdɪktɪd]	süchtig sein (nach etwas), abhängig sein (von etwas)	He didn't know he **was ~ to** games until his computer crashed and he started sweating.
(to) **be addictive** [əˈdɪktɪv]	süchtig/abhängig machen	Smoking **is** very **~**: if you start, it's very difficult to stop.
addict [ˈædɪkt]	Süchtige(r), Abhängige(r)	**!** stress: **addict** [ˈ--]
nationwide [ˌneɪʃnˈwaɪd]	landesweit, im ganzen Land	U2's ~ tour of the USA starts tomorrow. The new disease was first noticed in the south and then spread ~.
(to) **suggest** sth. [səˈdʒest]	auf etwas hindeuten	He fell asleep, which ~ed the lesson was boring.
study [ˈstʌdi]	Studie	**!** verb: (to) **study** – noun: **study**
(to) **harm** sb./sth. [hɑːm]	jn. verletzen; einer Sache schaden	No animals were ~ed while making the film. His last film didn't help his career; it ~ed it.
harm [hɑːm]	Schaden	Doctors say this drug causes more ~ than good. There was an accident, but no one came to ~. My dog **means no ~**: he just wants to play. *(= er meint es nicht böse)*
symptom [ˈsɪmptəm]	Symptom, Anzeichen	**!** stress: **symptom** [ˈ--] A headache and a sore throat are among the ~s of a cold.
(to) **consider** sb. **(to be)** sth. [kənˈsɪdə]	jn. als etwas betrachten, jn. für etwas halten	The Beatles are ~ed **(to be)** one of the greatest bands ever. (F) considérer (L) considerare
chore [tʃɔː]	(Haus-)Arbeit; *(lästige)* Pflicht	What ~s do you do at home? – I have to do the dishes and walk the dog.
fortunately [ˈfɔːtʃənətli]	glücklicherweise	Jane got to the bus stop ten minutes late but ~ the bus was late too.
unfortunately [ʌnˈfɔːtʃənətli]	leider, unglücklicherweise	**Unfortunately** there is nothing we can do.
(to) **be supposed to do/be** sth. [səˈpəʊzd]	tun sollen; angeblich sein sollen	We**'re** not **~** to use our mobiles at school, but some of us do. He must be rich. He**'s ~ to** own three houses. ► Grammar File 5.3: Modals (p.179)

Tips on learning words→ S.128 · Glossary of literary terms → S.161–164 · Dictionary (English – German) → S.231–279

Vocabulary

coordination [kəʊˌɔːdɪˈneɪʃn]	Koordinierung, Koordination	Mr Jones is responsible for the ~ of the teams. You need good ~ if you want to catch a ball.
p.15 **in fact** [ɪn ˈfækt]	um genau zu sein	Yes, I know her. **In ~**, we were in the same class. *(F)* en fait
(to) **take** sth. **up** [ˌteɪk ˈʌp]	etwas in Anspruch nehmen, etwas einnehmen *(Zeit, Raum)*	I don't want to ~ **up** too much of your time. These old comics ~ **up** a lot of space in my room.
counsellor [ˈkaʊnsələ]	Berater/in	John's parents are having problems. They're going to see a ~. *(F)* conseiller, -ère
(to) **arrange** [əˈreɪndʒ]	vereinbaren; planen; anordnen	The meeting was ~**d** for Tuesday at 9 am. I'm **arranging** a party for next weekend. Please ~ the chairs around the table. *(F)* arranger
current [ˈkʌrənt]	aktuelle(r, s), gegenwärtige(r, s); gebräuchlich	This song is the ~ number 1 in the UK. The word 'thou' [ðaʊ] means 'du' but it's not ~ any more. Now people say 'you'. *(F)* courant,e
(to) **refuse (to do** sth.**)** [rɪˈfjuːz]	sich weigern (etwas zu tun); verweigern, ablehnen	He ~**d to** help her although she had problems. She asked him to help, but he ~**d**. *(F)* refuser
(to) **admit (-tt-)** [ədˈmɪt]	zugeben, eingestehen	After a long discussion I ~**ted** I was wrong. Do you ~ stealing the watch? *(F)* admettre *(L)* admittere
keen [kiːn]	begeistert, leidenschaftlich	Tiger is a ~ golfer: he plays every week.
p.16 **memory** [ˈmeməri]	Gedächtnis; Erinnerung; Speicher *(Computer)*	Grandpa is very old but still has a good ~. My first ~ is of my third birthday. How much ~ does your computer have? *(F)* la mémoire *(L)* memoria
distant [ˈdɪstənt]	(weit) entfernt, fern	a ~ country, a ~ relative, the ~ past, the ~ future *(F)* distant,e *(L)* distans
previous [ˈpriːvɪəs]	frühere(r, s), vorherige(r, s)	The ~ owner of our car was from Manchester. Last night I watched football on TV and on the ~ evening I watched rugby. *(L)* praevius, -a, -um

Today's photos
Previous photo ◀ 3 of 10 ▶ Next photo

search [sɜːtʃ]	Suche	verb: (to) **search** – noun: **search**
(to) **damage** [ˈdæmɪdʒ]	beschädigen, schädigen	The house was ~**d** in the storm. Alcohol can seriously ~ your health.
fate [feɪt]	Schicksal, Bestimmung	'This is how ~ knocks at the door!' – Ludwig van Beethoven *(L)* fatum
galaxy [ˈgæləksi]	Sternsystem, Galaxie	Earth's ~ is called the **Milky Way**.
nightmare [ˈnaɪtmeə]	Albtraum	= a frightening dream

Irregular verbs → S. 280–281 · List of names, places and countries → S. 282–284

202　1　Vocabulary

p.17	**target** ['tɑ:gɪt]	Ziel(scheibe)	❗ **target** = Ziel (das man treffen/erreichen will) **aim** = Ziel, Absicht
p.18/P1	(to) **accept** [ək'sept]	annehmen, akzeptieren	I've asked 20 people to my party and 13 have already **~ed** the invitation. Ⓕ accepter　Ⓛ accipere
	certain ['sɜ:tn]	sicher; gewiss, bestimmt	Are you **~** that he's coming? – Yes, he promised. A **~** Mr Smith came to the flat today. Ⓕ certain,e　Ⓛ certus, -a, -um
	certainly ['sɜ:tnli]	sicher(lich), bestimmt, auf jeden Fall	This is **~** a very big problem, but we'll manage it. Do you believe her? – **Certainly**! She never lies.
	society [sə'saɪəti]	(die) Gesellschaft	❗ *No article:* **modern ~** and its problems = die moderne Gesellschaft und ihre Probleme Ⓕ la société　Ⓛ societas
	hopefully ['həʊpfəli]	hoffentlich	**Hopefully**, my dad will get a new job. =I hope my dad will get a new job.
	at first [ət 'fɜ:st]	zuerst, anfangs, am Anfang	**At ~** John seems rude, but soon I realized he was just shy.
	even more/taller/... ['i:vn]	(sogar) noch mehr/größer/...	The Eiffel Tower is tall, the CN Tower is taller, but the Burj Khalifa is **~ taller**: it's the tallest building in the world.
	cigarette [ˌsɪgə'ret]	Zigarette	My dad used to smoke 20 **~s** a day. Ⓕ la cigarette
p.18/P2	they **ought to** do more sport [ɔ:t]	sie sollten mehr Sport treiben	= they **should** do more sport ▶ Grammar File 5.3: Modals (p.179)

PART C　I hate my dad

p.20	**obviously** ['ɒbviəsli]	offensichtlich	The dog was wet. It had **~** been raining outside.
	proper ['prɒpə]	richtige(r, s), ordentliche(r, s)	When we said good night, she gave me a **~** kiss. Adverb: **properly** – Please do your homework **~**.
	brain [breɪn]	Gehirn	Your **~** is inside your head. You think with it.
	brains *(pl)* [breɪnz]	Verstand, Intelligenz	He hasn't got enough **~** to be a doctor.
	(to) **doubt** [daʊt]	bezweifeln	❗ silent letter **b**: **doub̲t** [daʊt] We've waited two hours. I **~** she's coming. Ⓕ douter　Ⓛ dubitare
	doubt [daʊt]	Zweifel, Bedenken	I can't say yes because I still have too many **~s**.
	(to) **guarantee** [ˌgærən'ti:]	garantieren, versprechen	The Basic Law **~s** many freedoms. I **~** that I will help you tomorrow. ❗ spelling: **g̲uarantee**
	matter ['mætə]	Angelegenheit, Sache	If our neighbours are loud again, we'll ask the police to deal with the **~**.

Tips on learning words→ S.128 · Glossary of literary terms → S.161–164 · Dictionary (English – German) → S.231–279

Vocabulary 1 203

(to) **stop** sb. **doing** sth. [stɒp]	jn. daran hindern, etwas zu tun	I wanted to visit the Queen but a guard **~ped** me **getting** into the palace.
unpleasant [ʌnˈpleznt]	unangenehm	**unpleasant ◄► pleasant** [ˈpleznt] angenehm
nevertheless [ˌnevəðəˈles]	trotzdem	Generally, I don't like TV soaps. **Nevertheless**, I sometimes watch *Marienhof*.
p.21 (to) **preserve** [prɪˈzɜːv]	konservieren; erhalten, bewahren	(to) save and keep
(to) **bend** [bend], **bent, bent**	sich beugen	Yoga helps you to **~**.
sum [sʌm]	Summe	(to) **do sums** = rechnen
(to) **add up** [ˌædˈʌp]	addieren, zusammenzählen	Ⓛ addere

Doing sums

You write:	You say:	or:	
1 + 3 = 4	one **plus** [plʌs] three	three **added to** one	
5 − 1 = 4	five **minus** [ˈmaɪnəs] one	one **subtracted** [səbˈtræktɪd] **from** five	
2 x 2 = 4	two **times** two	two **multiplied** [ˈmʌltɪplaɪd] **by** two	equals/is four.
16 ÷ 4 = 4	four **into** sixteen	sixteen **divided by** four	
2^2 = 4	two **squared** [skweəd]	**the square of** two	
√16 = 4	the **square root** [ˌskweə ˈruːt] of sixteen		

---

rare [reə]	selten	**rare ◄► common** adv: **rarely** – I've **~** seen such a lovely face. Ⓕ rare Ⓛ rarus, -a, -um
(to) **raise** sth. [reɪz]	etwas (er)heben	After the accident he couldn't **~** his arm above his shoulder.
(to) **lower** sth. [ˈləʊə]	etwas hinunterlassen; senken	They **~ed** the boat into the water. She **~ed** her voice and told me her secret. (to) **raise ◄► (to) lower**
(to) **catch on (to** sth.**)** [ˌkætʃ ˈɒn]	(etwas) kapieren, begreifen	Our dog **~es on** very fast. She learns a new trick every week.
I can't help it.	Ich kann nicht anders.; Ich kann es nicht ändern.	Sorry, I **can't help laughing** – it's so funny. (= *ich kann nicht anders, als zu lachen*)
(to) **identify (with)** [aɪˈdentɪfaɪ]	identifizieren; sich identifizieren (mit)	The bank robber was **identified** by an old lady. I really **~ with** you: I understand how you feel.
p.22/P 1 **knowledge** *(no pl)* [ˈnɒlɪdʒ]	Wissen; Kenntnis(se)	**!** verb: (to) **know** [nəʊ] – noun: **knowledge** [ˈnɒlɪdʒ]
p.22/P 2 **false** [fɔːls]	falsch	'Bekommen' and '(to) become' are examples of '**~** friends'. **true ◄► false** Ⓛ falsus, -a, -um
p.23/P 3 (to) **view** [vjuː] *(fml)*	betrachten, sehen; fernsehen	How do you **~** the problem? Can we solve it? A study of **~ing** trends shows teenagers watch more TV now than 20 years ago. Ⓛ videre

Irregular verbs → S. 280–281 · List of names, places and countries → S. 282–284

204 | 1 — Word field: **Me and others**

Family
My ancestors came from Poland.
We've lived here for five generations.
Many of my relatives are very artistic.
My older brother is a role model for me.

Childhood days
I was born in ... on 3rd May, 1992.
My sister grew up in the 90s.
I spent my childhood in ...
At the age of seven I moved to ...
I made friends with lots of kids my age.

As a young teenager I was/liked (to) ...
I'll move out as soon as I'm 18.

Adult life
I share a room/flat with ...
I'm planning to move in with my girlfriend.
I feel very much at home in/with ...
Most people I know are single.
My best friend has got married to a teacher.
They want to have a baby.
My cousin ⁺gave birth to healthy twins.
Not only married couples argue – partners do too.
It's always hard to end a relationship.
My uncle and his wife have broken up.
My aunt got divorced from her husband.
Being a single parent is hard work.

Old age
I'd like to retire at the age of 63.
Some old people's homes are very nice.
My grandmother ⁺lived to be 98 years old.
I inherited a magnificent desk from her.

Likes and dislikes
I love/like/hate going to the zoo.
I can't stand people who show off.
I enjoy being with my friends.
My favourite dish is pizza.
I'm into folk music.
I much prefer Belgium to France.

Friendship and conflicts
I know that I can always depend on you.
Sometimes I'm jealous of you.
Let's not argue.
Stop calling me names.
Mind your own business.
I'm very disappointed in you.
I didn't mean to hurt you.
I'd like to apologize to you.
Please forgive me for being rude.

Familie
Meine Vorfahren kamen aus Polen.
Wir leben hier seit fünf Generationen.
Viele meiner Verwandten sind künstlerisch sehr begabt.
Mein älterer Bruder ist ein Vorbild für mich.

Kinder- und Jugendzeit
Ich wurde am 3. Mai 1992 in ... geboren.
Meine Schwester ist in den 90er-Jahren aufgewachsen.
Ich verbrachte meine Kindheit in ...
Mit sieben / Im Alter von sieben Jahren zog ich nach ...
Ich habe mich mit vielen Kindern in meinem Alter angefreundet.
Als junge(r) Teenager/in war/mochte ich ...
Sobald ich 18 werde, ziehe ich aus.

Erwachsenenleben
Ich teile mir ein Zimmer/eine Wohnung mit ...
Ich habe vor, bei meiner Freundin einzuziehen.
Ich fühle mich in/bei ... sehr zu Hause.
Die meisten Leute, die ich kenne, sind ledig.
Mein bester Freund hat eine Lehrerin geheiratet.
Sie wünschen sich ein Baby.
Meine Cousine brachte gesunde Zwillinge zur Welt.
Nicht nur Ehepaare, sondern auch Partner streiten sich.
Es ist immer schwer, eine Beziehung zu beenden.
Mein Onkel und seine Frau haben sich getrennt.
Meine Tante wurde von ihrem Ehemann geschieden.
Alleinerziehend zu sein ist harte Arbeit.

Alter
Ich würde gern mit 63 in den Ruhestand gehen.
Manche Altenheime sind sehr schön.
Meine Großmutter wurde 98 Jahre alt.
Ich habe einen herrlichen Schreibtisch von ihr geerbt.

Was man mag, was man nicht mag
Ich liebe/mag es/mag es gar nicht, in den Zoo zu gehen.
Ich kann Leute nicht ausstehen, die angeben.
Ich bin gern mit meinen Freunden zusammen.
Mein Lieblingsessen ist Pizza.
Ich stehe auf Folkmusik.
Belgien gefällt mir viel besser als Frankreich.

Freundschaft und Konflikte
Ich weiß, dass ich mich immer auf dich verlassen kann.
Manchmal bin ich neidisch auf dich.
Lass uns nicht streiten.
Hör auf, mich zu hänseln.
Das geht dich nichts an.
Ich bin sehr von dir enttäuscht.
Ich wollte dich nicht verletzen.
Ich möchte mich bei dir entschuldigen.
Entschuldige bitte, dass ich unhöflich war.

Tips on learning words→ S.128 · Glossary of literary terms → S.161–164 · Dictionary (English – German) → S.231–279

Vocabulary · 1–2

PART D Boy meets girl around the world

p.24	**ritual** ['rɪtʃuəl]	Ritual	**!** stress: **ri̱tual** ['---]
	especially [ɪ'speʃəli]	besonders, vor allem, insbesondere	I love chocolate, ~ if it's from Belgium. *(F)* spécialement
	afterwards ['ɑːftəwədz]	nachher, danach	We met him in 2008 and saw him again soon ~.
	marriage ['mærɪdʒ]	Ehe	verb: (to) **marry** – noun: **marriage** *(F)* le mariage
	(to) happen to do sth. ['hæpn]	etwas zufällig(erweise) tun	Do you ~ **to** know the way to the post office? He ~**ed to** be in London at the same time as me.
	faithful (to sb./sth.**)** ['feɪθfəl]	(jm./einer Sache) treu	When you marry, you promise to be ~ **to** your wife or husband.
p.25/P1	**oral** ['ɔːrəl]	mündlich	We have two exams next week: a written exam and an ~ exam. = spoken *(F)* oral,e
	(to) slow down [ˌsləʊ 'daʊn]	langsamer werden	
	(to) speed up [ˌspiːd_'ʌp]	schneller werden	(to) **slow down** ◄► (to) **speed up**

Unit 2: Stand up!

p.26	**(to) stand up (for** sth./sb.**)**	eintreten/sich einsetzen (für etwas/jn.)	A good way to avoid bullies is to have a big brother who ~**s up for** you.
	declaration [ˌdeklə'reɪʃn]	Erklärung, Mitteilung	**!** *German* **Erklärung** = **1. explanation** *(Erläuterung)* **2. declaration** *(Mitteilung)* *(F)* la déclaration *(L)* declaratio
	human ['hjuːmən]	menschlich, Menschen-	**!** **human** ◄► **inhuman** [ɪn'hjuːmən] *(F)* humain,e *(L)* humanus, -a, -um
	spirit ['spɪrɪt]	Geist; Seele	team ~, community ~, fighting ~, the human ~ **!** *German* **Geist** = **1. ghost** *(Gespenst)* **2. spirit** *(Seele)* *(F)* l'esprit *(m)* *(L)* spiritus
	brotherhood ['brʌðəhʊd]	Brüderlichkeit	
	torture ['tɔːtʃə]	Folter	*(F)* la torture
	treatment ['triːtmənt]	Behandlung *(auch medizinisch)*	He needed ~ on his leg after the accident. She suffered terrible ~ in prison. *(F)* le traitement
	privacy ['prɪvəsi]	Privatsphäre	**!** adj: **pri̱vate** ['praɪvət] – n: **pri̱vacy** ['prɪvəsi]
p.27	**belly** ['beli] *(infml)*	Bauch	= stomach

Irregular verbs → S. 280–281 · List of names, places and countries → S. 282–284

(to) **give in** [ˌɡɪv‿ˈɪn]	sich ergeben, nachgeben	The soldiers couldn't escape and **gave ~**. My dad doesn't really smoke any more but sometimes he **~s in** and has just one cigarette.
(to) **return** [rɪˈtɜːn]	zurückkehren	I left London on 23rd May and **~ed** on 4th June. ⒡ retourner

PART A Speak out

p.28 (to) **speak out** [ˌspiːk‿ˈaʊt]	seine Meinung (offen) sagen	If you think something in the world is wrong, you should publicly **~ out** against it.
amendment (to sth.) [əˈmendmənt]	(Ab-)Änderung (einer Sache); (oft A~) Verfassungszusatz (zur Verfassung der USA)	If we make a small **~ to** this document, it will be perfect. ⒡ l'amendement (m) The 18th **Amendment** made alcohol illegal.
(to) **explode** [ɪkˈspləʊd]	explodieren, ausrasten	A bomb has **~d**, killing 33 people. When my mum saw my bedroom, she **~d**.
faint [ˈfeɪnt]	schwach, leicht (ein wenig)	As I went past the house, I heard a **~** cry. Her face looks **~ly** like the Queen's.
tax [tæks]	Steuer	The **~ on** petrol is about 70 % of the price. ⒡ la taxe
bubble [ˈbʌbl]	(Luft-)Blase	a **speech ~** a **thought ~** There'll be a test tomorrow. Oh no.
(to) **complain (to** sb. **about** sth./sb.) [kəmˈpleɪn]	sich beklagen/beschweren (bei jm. über etwas/jn.)	My mum had to **~ to** the waiter **about** the quality of the food. ⒡ se plaindre
(to) **be awake** [əˈweɪk]	wach sein	**awake ◄► asleep**
sympathetic [ˌsɪmpəˈθetɪk]	mitfühlend, verständnisvoll, wohlwollend	❗ ~~German **sympathisch** = English **sympathetic**~~ German **sympathisch** = English nice, friendly
sympathy (for sb.) [ˈsɪmpəθi]	Mitgefühl, Verständnis, Anteilnahme (für jn., jm. gegenüber)	Lots of people expressed their **~** after my grandfather died.
(to) **convince** sb. **(of** sth.) [kənˈvɪns]	jn. (von etwas) überzeugen	After a long argument, he **~d** me **of** the disadvantage of my plan. ⒡ convaincre ⒧ convincere
backwards [ˈbækwədz], **backward** [ˈbækwəd] (bes. AE)	rückwärts	My dream is to travel **~** through time and see my grandfather as a little boy.
forwards [ˈfɔːwədz], **forward** [ˈfɔːwəd] (bes. AE)	vorwärts	It's easier to count **forwards** from 1 to 100 than to count **backwards** from 100 to 1.
(to) **figure** sth. **(out)** [ˈfɪɡə]	etwas ausrechnen; etwas herausfinden (oft mit Zahlen)	I can't **~ out** how this machine works.
district [ˈdɪstrɪkt]	Gegend, Bezirk	Sophie lives in the Cotham **~** of Bristol.

Tips on learning words→ S.128 · Glossary of literary terms → S.161–164 · Dictionary (English – German) → S.231–279

Vocabulary

argument [ˈɑːgjumənt]	Argument	He listed five ~s against my idea. **!** stress: **argument** [ˈ---] **argument** = **1.** Streit, Auseinandersetzung **2.** Argument
contribution [ˌkɒntrɪˈbjuːʃn]	Beitrag	Please could you **make a ~** to our local soup kitchen? (= einen Beitrag leisten) Ⓕ la contribution Ⓛ tributum
(to) **contribute** (sth.) (**to/towards** sth.) [kənˈtrɪbjuːt]	(etwas) beitragen; einen Beitrag leisten (für etwas)	I'm shy and don't ~ much **to** class discussions. Ⓕ contribuer Ⓛ contribuere
disagreement [ˌdɪsəˈgriːmənt]	Uneinigkeit; Meinungsverschiedenheit	We all knew he was rich. But there was ~ about exactly how much money he had. My parents had a little ~ last Monday and haven't talked to each other since then.
agreement [əˈgriːmənt]	Einigung; Vereinbarung	We **reached** ~ after a long discussion. (= Wir haben uns geeinigt ...)
(to) **challenge** sb. (**to** sth.) [ˈtʃælɪndʒ]	jn. herausfordern (zu etwas)	He ~d me **to** a game of chess after school. Maths doesn't really ~ me at the moment.
lazy [ˈleɪzi]	faul	**lazy ◄► hard-working**
no matter what [ˈmætə]	ganz gleich, was	I don't want to see him ... **no ~** who he is, **no ~** where he has come from, **no ~** why he is here, and **no ~** how often he says he loves me.
forces (pl) [ˈfɔːsɪz]	Kräfte	the armed ~ (= die Streitkräfte, das Militär), security ~, the ~ of nature (= Naturgewalten), market ~ Ⓕ les forces (f, pl)
pressure [ˈpreʃə]	Druck, Belastung	We're always under a lot of ~ just before a test. Ⓕ la pression Ⓛ pressus
(to) **debate** (sth.) [dɪˈbeɪt]	debattieren (über etwas); hin und her überlegen	We ~d the topic of bringing mobiles to school. Our visitors ~d whether to go or stay.
constitution [ˌkɒnstɪˈtjuːʃn]	Verfassung	Ⓕ la constitution Ⓛ constitutio
citizenship [ˈsɪtɪzənʃɪp]	Staatsangehörigkeit, Staatsbürgerschaft	My uncle moved to the UK 20 years ago and has now applied for British ~.
citizen [ˈsɪtɪzən]	(Staats-)Bürger/in	If they say yes, my uncle will become a British ~. Ⓕ le/la citoyen, -ne
intolerant (**of** sth./sb.) [ɪnˈtɒlərənt]	intolerant (etwas/jm. gegenüber)	**intolerant ◄► tolerant** [ˈtɒlərənt]
xenophobic [ˌzenəˈfəʊbɪk]	fremdenfeindlich, xenophob	Ⓕ xénophobe
(to) **turn** sb./sth. **into** sth.	jn./etwas in etwas verwandeln	He ~ed the rabbit **into** a bird. It was magic!
silence [ˈsaɪləns]	Stille, Schweigen	The orchestra finished playing, there was ~ for five seconds, then everybody cheered. Ⓕ le silence Ⓛ silentium
silent [ˈsaɪlənt]	still, schweigend	Being quiet is not enough: be absolutely ~. Ⓕ silencieux, -se Ⓛ silens
(to) **influence** [ˈɪnfluəns]	beeinflussen	The Beatles still ~ musicians today. Ⓕ influencer
the press [pres]	die Presse, Zeitungen	His death was a big story on TV and in **the ~**.
assembly [əˈsembli]	Versammlung	Has Obama made his speech to the UN General **Assembly**? Ⓕ l'assemblée (f)

p.29 *(intolerant row)*

Irregular verbs → S. 280–281 · List of names, places and countries → S. 282–284

Vocabulary

p.30	**eyebrow** [ˈaɪbraʊ]	Augenbraue	**eyebrows** 

authoritarian [ɔːˌθɒrɪˈteərɪən]	autoritär	an ~ leader, system, state, government, parent, teacher
(to) **be fed up (with** sth.**)** [ˌfed_ˈʌp]	die Nase voll haben (von etwas)	I'm ~ ~ **with** you. You're boring and I can't stand being with you any more.
dominant [ˈdɒmɪnənt]	dominant, vorherrschend	❗ stress: d**o**minant [ˈ---]
sarcastic [sɑːˈkæstɪk]	sarkastisch	When she said my essay was 'the best story in the world', I think she meant it **~ally**.
(to) **alarm** sb. [əˈlɑːm]	jn. beunruhigen, erschrecken	I don't want to ~ you, but there's a problem. You look **~ed**. Is there something wrong?
attention [əˈtenʃn]	Aufmerksamkeit	Listen to me, please. Can I have everybody's ~? ⓕ l'attention *(f)* ⓛ attentio

attention

(to) **attract/grab/catch** sb.'s ~	It was her smile that first **attracted** my ~. I shouted to **grab** her ~.	..., das mir ins Auge fiel. ..., um sie auf mich aufmerksam zu machen.
(to) **pay/give** ~ **to** sb.	Don't **pay** any ~ **to** him: he's nobody. Please **give** me your full ~.	Achte/Höre nicht auf ihn ... Schenken Sie mir bitte Ihre volle Aufmerksamkeit.
(to) **draw** sb.'s ~ **to** sth.	May I **draw** your ~ **to** a few mistakes?	Kann ich dich auf ein paar Fehler aufmerksam machen?
(to) **come to** sb.'s ~	Sorry, sir, but it has **come to** our ~ that you have not paid for your food.	... wir haben bemerkt, dass ...

(to) **analyse** [ˈænəlaɪz]	analysieren	❗ stress: (to) an**a**lyse: [-ˈ---]
facial [ˈfeɪʃl]	Gesichts-	Some religions say that men must have ~ hair.
angle [ˈæŋgl]	Winkel; Blickwinkel	This is a 40° **angle**. He drew the bridge from an unusual ~: he was lying under it! ⓕ l'angle *(m)* ⓛ angulus
low [ləʊ]	niedrig	Mali has a **~er** standard of living than Germany. **low** ◀▶ **high**
shot [ʃɒt]	(Film-)Aufnahme, Dreh	❗ verb: (to) **shoot** = 1. schießen; 2. drehen – noun: **shot** = 1. Schuss; 2. Dreh
p.31	**controversy** [ˈkɒntrəvɜːsi]	Auseinandersetzung, Kontroverse	There was a lot of ~ about that building at first, but now people like it. ⓛ controversia
communication [kəˌmjuːnɪˈkeɪʃn]	Kommunikation	❗ stress: communic**a**tion [-,--ˈ--] ⓕ la communication ⓛ communicatio
(to) **communicate (with** sb.**)** [kəˈmjuːnɪkeɪt]	(mit jm.) kommunizieren, sich (mit jm.) verständigen	If you want to ~ **with** foreigners, the best thing to do is learn their language. ⓕ communiquer ⓛ communicare

Tips on learning words → S.128 · Glossary of literary terms → S.161–164 · Dictionary (English – German) → S.231–279

Vocabulary 2

	offensive [ə'fensɪv]	beleidigend, Anstoß erregend	I consider your behaviour not just rude but ~.
	significant [sɪg'nɪfɪkənt]	bedeutend, wichtig	You made a ~ contribution to the team's victory.
	male *(adj; n)* [meɪl]	männlich; männliche Person	Most of the workers here are ~. The police are looking for a 40-year-old white ~.
	female *(adj; n)* ['fi:meɪl]	weiblich; weibliche Person	'Hostess' is the ~ form of 'host'. **Females** often earn less money than males.
	depending (on) [dɪ'pendɪŋ]	je nachdem (wie)	Dad takes between 20 and 40 minutes to get to work, ~ **on** how much traffic there is.
	(to) address sb. [ə'dres]	jn. ansprechen, anreden	You ~ the Queen as 'Your Majesty' or 'Ma'am'.
	neutral ['nju:trəl]	neutral	Switzerland was ~ in World War II. ⓕ neutre Ⓛ neuter, -utra, -utrum
	frequent ['fri:kwənt]	häufig	People who fly often are called '~ flyers'. ⓕ fréquent,e Ⓛ frequens
	(to) contain [kən'teɪn]	enthalten	ⓕ contenir Ⓛ continere
	precise [prɪ'saɪs]	präzise, genau	You say you saw him 'about' ten days ago, but can you be more ~? ⓕ précis,e
p.32/P 1	**decision (on** sth.**)** [dɪ'sɪʒn]	Entscheidung (über etwas)	The court will **make** its ~ tomorrow. (= ... seine Entscheidung treffen/fällen) ⓕ la décision
	humanitarian [hju:ˌmænɪ'teəriən]	humanitär	Oxfam is a ~ charity that helps people all over the world.
p.32/P 2	**censorship** ['sensəʃɪp]	Zensur	Press ~ is common in dictatorships. ⓕ la censure Ⓛ censura
	psychological [ˌsaɪkə'lɒdʒɪkl]	psychisch, psychologisch	❗ silent **p**: **psychological** [ˌsaɪkə'lɒdʒɪkl]
	psychology [saɪ'kɒlədʒi]	Psychologie	❗ silent **p** and different stress: **psychology** [ˌ-'---]
	psychologist [saɪ'kɒlədʒɪst]	Psychologe, Psychologin	❗ silent **p** and different stress: **psychologist** [ˌ-'---]
	conflict ['kɒnflɪkt]	Konflikt, Auseinandersetzung	The ~ in Palestine has been going on for years.
p.33/P 3	**state** [steɪt]	Zustand	

❗ **state** = **1.** Staat; **2.** Zustand   Ⓛ status

Irregular verbs → S. 280–281 · List of names, places and countries → S. 282–284

PART B   Get involved

p.34	(to) **back** sth./sb. [bæk]	etwas/jn. unterstützen	The UN is **~ing** the USA's plan to end the war. = (to) support sth./sb.
	(to) **want** sth. **done**	wollen, dass etwas geschieht; wollen, dass etwas getan wird	She **wanted** her hair **cut** so she went to the hairdresser's.
	mature [mə'tʃʊə]	reif, vernünftig	She's younger than him, but much more **~**. Ⓕ mature Ⓛ maturus, -a, -um
	(to) **fear** sth./sb. [fɪə]	vor etwas/jm. Angst haben; etwas/jn. (be)fürchten	'The only thing we have to **~** is fear itself.' – President Franklin D. Roosevelt, 1882–1945 **!** **verb:** (to) **fear** – noun: **fear**
	findings *(pl)* ['faɪndɪŋz]	Ergebnisse *(einer Untersuchung u.Ä.)*	The committee's **~s** show that cats are now more popular than dogs.
	(to) **argue** ['ɑːgjuː]	argumentieren, behaupten	He tried to **~** that Shakespeare was German! **!** (to) **argue** = **1.** sich streiten, sich zanken **2.** argumentieren
	impact ['ɪmpækt]	Auswirkung	Laptops have had a huge **~** on the way we relax. Ⓕ l'impact *(m)*
	political [pə'lɪtɪkl]	politisch	**!** nouns: **p̲olitics**, **politi̲cian** – adj: **poli̲tical**
	(to) **claim** [kleɪm]	behaupten	The stranger **~ed** to be the mayor of London.

certainly – surely

You use **certainly** when you have **no doubts** so **certainly** means *sicher(lich)* in the sense *zweifellos, bestimmt, ganz sicher, auf jeden Fall.*

It's **certainly** very warm today.
Do you agree? – I **certainly** do.
I'd **certainly** like to see that film again.

You use **surely** when you have doubts or can't really believe that something is true.
Sentences with **surely** are really questions (= Is it really true that ...?) and often have a question mark.

Surely that's not snow, in the middle of July.	Das ist doch nicht (wirklich) Schnee, mitten im Juli?
You don't believe that, **surely**?	Das glaubst du doch wohl nicht wirklich, oder?
We'll be home by ten, **surely**?	Wir sind doch bestimmt vor 22 Uhr zu Hause, oder?

party ['pɑːti]	Partei	**!** **party** = **1.** Party, Feier; **2.** Partei

Political parties in Britain

These are the biggest parties in Britain:*

National parties:	Seats (2010)	Political views
the **Conservative** Party [kən'sɜːvətɪv]	307	centre-right, supports the free market economy
the **Liberal Democrats** [ˌlɪbrəl 'deməkræts]	57	centre, supports the rights of the individual
the **Labour** Party ['leɪbə]	258	centre-left, supports working people
the **Green** Party	1	centre-left, protects the environment
Non-English parties:		
the **Scottish National** Party	6	centre-left, wants Scotland to be a separate country
Plaid Cymru [ˌplaɪd 'kʌmrɪ] *(Welsh: the Party of Wales)*	3	centre-left, wants Wales to be a separate country

*There are different parties in Northern Ireland.

Tips on learning words→ S.128 · Glossary of literary terms → S.161–164 · Dictionary (English – German) → S.231–279

Vocabulary

(to) **adopt** [əˈdɒpt]	adoptieren; beschließen, sich entscheiden (für) *(Maßnahme, Politik)*	Our neighbours can't have their own children, so they've **~ed** a boy from a children's home. The new government has **~ed** very green plans.
policy (on) [ˈpɒləsi]	Politik *(politische Maßnahme, Linie, Verfahrensweise)*	❗ *German* **Politik** = **1. politics** *(no pl)* *(politisches Leben/Geschehen)*: Are you interested in **politics**? **2. policy** *(politische Maßnahmen, Linie)*: economic **policies** *(Wirtschaftspolitik)*, **policy on** education *(Bildungspolitik)*
element [ˈelɪmənt]	Element	❗ stress: **element** [ˈ---]
further [ˈfɜːðə]	weitere(r, s), zusätzliche(r, s)	If you're interested, write to us for **~** details.
p.35 **given** his intelligence *(fml)*	angesichts/bei seiner Intelligenz	**Given** her beauty, it's no surprise that Granny attracted lots of boys when she was young. **Given that** he is rich, he dresses like a beggar. *(= Angesichts der Tatsache, dass er reich ist, ...)*
laughable [ˈlɑːfəbl]	lächerlich	The idea that the world is round used to be **~**.
prospect [ˈprɒspekt]	Aussicht, Vorstellung	50 years ago there was no **~** of a black US president. ⓛ prospectus
terrifying [ˈterɪfaɪɪŋ]	schrecklich, unheimlich	= very frightening
(to) **rest** [rest]	ruhen, sich ausruhen	Some believe that God **~ed** on the seventh day. We **~ed** for an hour then continued our walk.
peace [piːs]	Frieden	ⒻF la paix ⓛ pax
peaceful [ˈpiːsfl]	friedlich; ruhig	The march began **~ly** but got violent later. Babies look so **~** when they're asleep.
(to) **fulfil (-ll-)**, *(AE:* **fulfill)** [fʊlˈfɪl]	erfüllen; ausführen	Will the new president **~** what he promised? He **~led** his dream at 57 and got a sports car.
p.36/P 1 **emphasis** [ˈemfəsɪs]	Betonung, Hervorhebung	❗ *German* **Betonung** = **1. stress** *(less formal)* **2. emphasis** *(more formal)*
(to) **emphasize** sth. [ˈemfəsaɪz]	etwas betonen, etwas hervorheben	Germans sometimes **~** 'Hyde Park' on the word 'Hyde', but that's wrong. Why did you highlight the word? – I wanted to **~** it.
(to) **sleep in** [ˌsliːp ˈɪn]	ausschlafen	On Sundays I **~ in** till about 11 am. ❗ (to) **sleep in** = ausschlafen (to) **fall asleep** = einschlafen
assignment [əˈsaɪnmənt]	Arbeit, Aufgabe, Auftrag	The journalist's next **~** was in Iran. ❗ *Often used in AE for* **homework**: I can't come with you because I have a Math **~** to finish.
relevant (to sth.**)** [ˈreləvənt]	relevant (für etwas)	❗ stress: **relevant** [ˈ---]

Word field: Human rights and politics

Human rights
In many countries people's basic rights are +at risk.

Many suffer from +extreme [ɪkˈstriːm] poverty.
Not all countries allow freedom of speech.

Censorship is a big problem.
The US civil rights movement fought +racial [ˈreɪʃl] discrimination.
But +racism [ˈreɪsɪzəm] has not entirely disappeared.
Freedom of religion is in danger.
Everybody has the right to an education.
The freedom of assembly must not be +restricted [rɪˈstrɪktɪd].

Menschenrechte
In vielen Ländern sind die Grundrechte der Menschen gefährdet.
Viele leiden unter extremer Armut.
Nicht in allen Länder herrscht das Recht auf freie Meinungsäußerung.
Zensur ist ein großes Problem.
Die US-Bürgerrechtsbewegung kämpfte gegen Rassendiskriminierung.
Aber der Rassismus ist nicht völlig verschwunden.
Die Religionsfreiheit ist in Gefahr.
Jeder hat das Recht auf Erziehung.
Die Versammlungsfreiheit darf nicht eingeschränkt werden.

Democracy in action
The 'Basic Law' is the German constitution.
The +chancellor [ˈtʃɑːnsələ] is the head of government.
In a general election, voters elect a new parliament.

I love watching debates from parliament.
When the president has signed a law, it +comes into force.
Should the voting age be lowered to 16?

The British Prime Minister is the leader of the largest party in parliament.
Parties sometimes form coalition governments.
Parties that are not in government form the opposition.
What's our mayor's policy on transport?

I think the state should pay for education.
Isn't that what people pay taxes for?
Three candidates are standing.

Demokratie in Aktion
Das 'Grundgesetz' ist die deutsche Verfassung.
Der/Die Kanzler/in ist der/die Regierungschef/in.
In den Parlamentswahlen wählen die Wähler/innen ein neues Parlament.
Ich sehe mir sehr gern Parlamentsdebatten an.
Wenn der/die Präsident/in ein Gesetz unterzeichnet hat, tritt es in Kraft.
Sollte das Mindestwahlalter auf 16 Jahre gesenkt werden?
Der/Die britische Premierminister/in ist der/die Partei-vorsitzende der größten Partei im Parlament.
Parteien bilden manchmal Koalitionsregierungen.
Parteien, die nicht in der Regierung sind, bilden die Opposition.
Welche Linie vertritt unser Bürgermeister in Verkehrsfragen?
Ich finde, die öffentliche Hand sollte für Bildung zahlen.
Zahlen die Leute nicht dafür Steuern?
Drei Kandidaten/-innen bewerben sich.

Justice and the law
The legal system should be independent from politics.
Taking +bribes [braɪb] is illegal.
The +Supreme [suːˈpriːm] Court decides in +constitutional [ˌkɒnstɪˈtjuːʃənl] questions.
Judges have a very responsible job.

The crime rate has been quite +stable [ˈsteɪbl].
She was +accused [əˈkjuːzd] of +robbery [ˈrɒbəri].
The +defendant [dɪˈfendənt] was found guilty and sentenced to 15 months in prison.
The defence considered this punishment too +harsh [hɑːʃ].
The court +sits again next Monday.

Recht und Gesetz
Das Rechtssystem sollte von der Politik unabhängig sein.
Es ist illegal, Bestechungsgelder anzunehmen.
Der Oberste Gerichtshof / das Verfassungsgericht entscheidet in Fragen der Verfassung.
Richter/innen haben einen sehr verantwortungsvollen Beruf.
Die Kriminalitätsrate ist ziemlich stabil gewesen.
Sie wurde des Raubes beschuldigt.
Der/Die Angeklagte wurde für schuldig befunden und zu 15 Monaten Gefängnis verurteilt.
Die Verteidigung hielt diese Strafe für zu hart.

Das Gericht tagt am kommenden Montag wieder.

Tips on learning words→ S.128 · Glossary of literary terms → S.161–164 · Dictionary (English – German) → S.231–279

Vocabulary

PART C   Make a change

p.38	**bystander** ['baɪstændə]	Zuschauer/in, „Dabeistehende(r)"	Lots of ~s saw Grandma fall, but no one helped.
	(to) pass sb./sth. [pɑːs]	an etwas/jm. vorbeigehen/-fahren	If you ~ a shop on the way home, please buy me a newspaper. Ⓕ passer
	(to) board (sth.) [bɔːd]	(in etwas) einsteigen, an Bord (von etwas) gehen	The gate had actually closed, but luckily we were still allowed to ~ the plane.
	merciless ['mɜːsɪləs]	gnadenlos	Vlad III was a ~ king who killed all his enemies.
	(to) defend sb./sth. **(against** sb./sth.) [dɪ'fend]	jn./etwas verteidigen (gegen jn./etwas)	Leningrad was ~ed **against** the German army from September 1941 to January 1944. Ⓕ défendre Ⓛ defendere
	threatening ['θretnɪŋ]	drohend, bedrohlich	Those clouds look ~: I think it's going to rain.
	(to) threaten sb. ['θretn]	jn. bedrohen, jm. drohen	He ~ed me with a knife and I ran away.
	similar (to sth./sb.) ['sɪmələ]	(etwas/jm.) ähnlich	'Silent' and 'quiet' aren't the same, but very ~. Ⓕ similaire Ⓛ similis, -e
	(to) assume [ə'sjuːm]	annehmen, ausgehen von	She ~d he was African because of his skin colour, but he was actually German. Ⓛ assumere
	(to) witness sth. ['wɪtnəs]	bei/von etwas Zeuge sein	Did anyone ~ the accident? **!** noun: **witness to** sth. – verb: **(to) witness** sth.
	(to) respond (to sth.**)** [rɪ'spɒnd] *(fml)*	reagieren (auf etwas); antworten (auf etwas)	If I need help, he **responds** fast. (= **reacts**) I said hi, but he didn't **respond**. (= **answer**) Ⓕ répondre Ⓛ respondere
	(to) remain [rɪ'meɪn] *(fml)*	bleiben	My parents are divorced but they have ~ed quite good friends. = (to) **stay** Ⓛ remanere
p.39	**(to) be likely to do/be** sth. ['laɪkli]	etwas wahrscheinlich tun/sein	How ~ **are** we **to go** to Spain this year? It**'s** ~ **to be** sunny in the afternoon.
	sb. **in need** [niːd]	ein/e Notleidende(r)	I gave £1 to a man **in** ~ who was begging outside a shop.
	(to) be around [ə'raʊnd]	da sein, anwesend sein, in der Nähe sein	Friends **are** always ~ when you need them.
	individual [ˌɪndɪ'vɪdʒuəl]	einzelne(r, s)	The ~ members of the team were very good, but as a group, they played terribly. Ⓕ individuel, le Ⓛ individuus, -a, -umi
	considerable [kən'sɪdərəbl] *(fml)*	erheblich, beträchtlich	**Considerable** progress was made at the UN peace conference last week. Ⓕ considérable
	(to) be willing to do sth. ['wɪlɪŋ]	bereit/gewillt sein, etwas zu tun	Are you really ~ **to** help me? I don't want to make you do something you don't want to do.
	(to) step forward (-pp-) ['fɔːwəd]	vortreten, sich melden	The teacher asked who would like to help and ten students immediately ~ped **forward**.
	injustice [ɪn'dʒʌstɪs]	Ungerechtigkeit, Unrecht	He suffered great ~ when he went to prison because he hadn't committed the crime. Ⓕ l'injustice (f) Ⓛ iniustitia
	justice ['dʒʌstɪs]	Gerechtigkeit; Recht, Justiz	Peace without ~ isn't really peace at all. The ~ systems in the UK and USA are similar. Ⓕ la justice Ⓛ iustitia
p.40/P1	**(to) attend** sth. [ə'tend]	etwas besuchen, an etwas teilnehmen	Emily ~ed the same school as her mother. I was unable to ~ the meeting because I was ill. Ⓛ attendere

Irregular verbs → S. 280–281 · List of names, places and countries → S. 282–284

(to) **last** [lɑːst]	(an-, fort)dauern	❗ *German* **dauern** = **1.** *(Zeit benötigen)* (to) **take**: It normally **takes** 30 minutes to get home, but last night it **took us** an hour. **2.** *(andauern, im Gange sein)* (to) **last**: A football match **lasts** 90 minutes.
expense [ɪk'spens]	Kosten	Before buying a dog, think of the ~ of keeping it. I had it repaired at my ~. (= *auf meine Kosten*)
p.41/P 2 **non-violence** [ˌnɒn'vaɪələns]	Gewaltlosigkeit, Gewaltfreiheit	Gandhi used ~ to make the British leave India.
p.41/P 3 **misunderstanding** [ˌmɪsʌndə'stændɪŋ]	Missverständnis	There was a ~ about my meal. I had ordered chicken but the waiter brought me fish.
p.42/P 5 (to) **demonstrate (for/ against** sth.**)** ['demənstreɪt]	(für/gegen etwas) demonstrieren	In London yesterday, 20,000 people **~d against** the war.
(to) **march** [mɑːtʃ]	marschieren, demonstrieren	

They're **~ing**.   Ⓕ marcher

police officer [pə'liːs ˌɒfɪsə]	Polizist/in	
(to) **injure** sb. ['ɪndʒə]	jn. verletzen	❗ *German* **verletzen** = **1.** (to) **hurt** *(cause pain)* **2.** (to) **injure** *(break, cut, etc. a part of the body)*
(to) **limit** sth. **(to)** ['lɪmɪt]	etwas einschränken; etwas beschränken/begrenzen (auf)	This new law **~s** our right to go on strike. The audience was **~ed to** 500 people. Ⓕ limiter

Unit 3: Our one world

p.52 **discovery** [dɪ'skʌvəri]	Entdeckung	❗ verb: (to) **discover** – noun: **discovery** Ⓕ la découverte
steam engine ['stiːm ˌendʒɪn]	Dampfmaschine	
life sciences *(pl)* ['laɪf ˌsaɪənsɪz]	Biowissenschaften	= the study of humans, animals and plants
anatomy [ə'nætəmi]	Anatomie	❗ stress: an<u>a</u>tomy [-'---]
evolution [ˌiːvə'luːʃn]	Evolution	= the way life-forms change over generations
(to) **evolve** [ɪ'vɒlv]	sich entwickeln	Over time, Berlin **~d** from a village into a city.
common ['kɒmən]	gemeinsam	Germany and Austria have a ~ language. ❗ **common** = **1.** weit verbreitet Ⓕ commun/e **2.** gemeinsam Ⓛ communis, -e
p.53 **invention** [ɪn'venʃn]	Erfindung	❗ verb: (to) **invent** – nouns: **inventor, invention** Ⓕ l'invention *(f)* Ⓛ inventio
light bulb ['laɪt bʌlb]	Glühlampe	**light bulbs**

Tips on learning words→ S.128 · Glossary of literary terms → S.161–164 · Dictionary (English – German) → S.231–279

Vocabulary

renewable [rɪ'njuːəbl]	erneuerbar	We need to depend on ~ sources of energy.
solar ['səʊlə]	Solar-, Sonnen-	❗ stress: **solar** ['--]
power ['paʊə]	Kraft, Energie, Strom	
nuclear ['njuːklɪə]	Kern-, Atom-	Hiroshima was destroyed by a ~ bomb in 1945. Ⓕ nucléaire
(to) **power** sth. ['paʊə]	etwas antreiben, etwas mit Energie versorgen	Cars that are ~ed by electricity are better for the environment.
genetic engineering [dʒə,netɪk ˌendʒɪ'nɪərɪŋ]	Gentechnik	
(to) **cure** sth./sb. [kjʊə]	etwas/jn. heilen	Will doctors soon be able to ~ AIDS?
form [fɔːm]	Gestalt	❗ **form** = **1.** *(class)* Klasse **2.** *(shape)* Gestalt

PART A   How our world works

p.54 (to) **captivate** ['kæptɪveɪt] *(fml)*	fesseln, faszinieren	Her beauty ~s me. I can think of nothing else.
interior [ɪn'tɪərɪə]	Innere	The car looks small from outside but its ~ is surprisingly big. Ⓕ l'intérieur *(m)*
core [kɔː]	Kern	The ~ of all his problems is his poverty.
(to) **suspect** [sə'spekt]	vermuten	Look at those dark clouds. I ~ it's going to rain. ❗ *You usually* **suspect** sth. **bad**. Ⓛ suspicari
honesty ['ɒnəsti]	Ehrlichkeit	❗ silent letter **h**: **honesty** ['ɒnəsti]
initial [ɪ'nɪʃl]	anfängliche(r, s)	My ~ reaction was to say no, but then I thought about it a bit more. Ⓕ initial,e
(to) **be based on** sth. [beɪst]	auf etwas basieren	The new film **is ~ on** a novel by Dickens.
motorist ['məʊtərɪst]	Autofahrer/in	**Motorists** are warned to avoid the city centre.
edge [edʒ]	Rand, Kante	We live on the ~ of the town, not in the centre. I hurt my leg on the ~ of the table.
gradual ['grædʒʊəl]	allmählich, langsam	He ~**ly** started to realize he might be wrong. **gradual ◄► sudden** Ⓕ graduel,e
scientific [ˌsaɪən'tɪfɪk]	(natur)wissenschaftlich	❗ nouns: **science, scientist** – adj: **scientific** Ⓕ scientifique
importance [ɪm'pɔːtəns]	Wichtigkeit, Bedeutung	The book is of great ~ to me. Ⓕ l'importance *(f)*
realization [ˌriːəlaɪ'zeɪʃn]	Erkenntnis	❗ verb: (to) **realize** – noun: **realization**
(to) **consist of** sth. [kən'sɪst]	aus etwas bestehen	My family ~**s of** my parents, my two sisters and me. Ⓕ consister (en/dans) Ⓛ consistere
sphere [sfɪə]	Kugel	The earth, like all planets, is a ~ in shape.
iron ['aɪən]	Eisen	❗ silent letter **r**: **iron** ['aɪən]
according to [ə'kɔːdɪŋ]	laut, zufolge	It's true ~ **to** the papers, but can we trust them?
(to) **occur to** sb. (-rr-) [ə'kɜː]	jm. einfallen	The idea ~**red to** me in a dream.

Irregular verbs → S. 280–281 · List of names, places and countries → S. 282–284

concerned (about sth./sb.**)** [kən'sɜːnd]	besorgt (um etwas/jn.)	If you're **~ about** the environment, get involved. I'm very **~ about** Bill. He never looks happy.
(to) **grip** (-pp-) [grɪp]	*(von Film, Buch)* fesseln, faszinieren	This film doesn't really **~** me. In fact, it's boring.
urge [ɜːdʒ]	Bedürfnis, Verlangen	The music was so beautiful that he suddenly had the **~** to cry.
amazement [ə'meɪzmənt]	Erstaunen, Verwunderung	When he told me the news, I reacted with **~**.
universe ['juːnɪvɜːs]	Universum	**!** stress: <u>u</u>niverse ['---]
(to) **predict** [prɪ'dɪkt]	voraussagen, vorhersagen	I can't **~** the result accurately; I can only guess. Ⓕ prédire Ⓛ praedicere
umbrella [ʌm'brelə]	Regenschirm	an **umbrella**

p.55 (to) **obtain** [əb'teɪn] *(fml)*	erhalten, erwerben	= (to) get Ⓕ obtenir Ⓛ obtinere
crucial ['kruːʃl]	äußerst wichtig, entscheidend	This is not just important, it's **~**. Ⓕ crucial,e
evidence *(no pl)* ['evɪdəns]	Beweis(e), Hinweis(e)	There was just one **piece of ~** to suggest that Mr Wainwright was the murderer. **!** German **Beweis** = **1.** proof (sth. that *shows you* that sth. is true) **2.** evidence (sth. that *suggests* that sth. is true)
(to) **orbit** sth. ['ɔːbɪt]	etwas umkreisen	Before Copernicus, people used to believe that the sun **~ed** the earth.
(to) **fail (to do** sth.**)** [feɪl]	versagen (beim Versuch, etwas zu tun)	I **~ed** to lift the rock: it was just too heavy.
(to) **distinguish** A **from** B [dɪ'stɪŋgwɪʃ]	A von B unterscheiden	Bill and Ben are twins, but you can **~** Bill **from** Ben because his hair is longer. Ⓕ distinguer
rather ['rɑːðə] *(bes. BE)*	ziemlich	Olivia is a **~** nice girl: yes, I **~** like her. = quite a nice girl
complicated ['kɒmplɪkeɪtɪd]	kompliziert	This is too **~** for me: I just don't understand it.
for [fɔː] *(fml, old-fashioned)*	denn	'Yes!' she cried. 'I will marry you! **For** I love you!' **!** **for** = **1.** *(preposition)* für; **2.** *(conjunction)* denn
(to) **turn out (to be** sth.**)** [ˌtɜːn_'aʊt]	sich (als etwas) herausstellen	She looked poor but it **~ed out** that she's rich. The murderer **~ed out to be** the police officer.
(to) **establish** [ɪ'stæblɪʃ]	feststellen	Scientists have **~ed** a link between climate change and earthquakes.
solution (to) [sə'luːʃn]	(Auf-)Lösung (für)	The **~s to** *Getting ready for a test* are on p.106. Ⓕ la solution Ⓛ solutio
notion ['nəʊʃn] *(fml)*	Vorstellung, Idee	Democracy is based on the **~** of freedom. Ⓕ la notion Ⓛ notio
predecessor ['priːdɪsesə]	Vorgänger/in, Vorläufer/in	Barack Obama's **~** was George Bush. The **~** of the CD was the cassette. Ⓕ le prédécesseur
remarkable [rɪ'mɑːkəbl]	beachtlich, außergewöhnlich	My grandmother died at the **~** age of 105.

Tips on learning words→ S.128 · Glossary of literary terms → S.161–164 · Dictionary (English – German) → S.231–279

Vocabulary

	since [sɪns]	weil, da	I won't eat ~ we're going to a restaurant later. ! **since** = **1.** seit; **2.** weil
	by no means [miːnz]	keineswegs	He's **by no** ~ a millionaire, but he's still very rich.
	object [ˈɒbdʒɪkt]	Gegenstand	(F) l'objet (m)
p.56	(to) **adjust (to)** [əˈdʒʌst]	(sich) einstellen (auf); (sich) anpassen (an)	**Adjust** the car mirror to see what's behind you. It took a long time to ~ **to** the speed of city life. (F) ajuster
	lens [lenz]	Linse *(in der Optik)*; (Brillen-)Glas	I can't see the board very well – I think I need new **~es** for my glasses.

the rich, the poor, etc.

We can use **the + adjective** to talk about whole groups of people, e.g. the rich, the poor, etc.

The old are less active than **the young**.
Here, 'The old' means 'all old people', so we could also say: **Old people** are less active than **young people**.

Compare:
The rich have more power than **the poor**. = **Rich people** have more power than **poor people**.
We should help **the homeless** more. = We should help **homeless people** more.

But when we talk about one person or about a few people, we use *woman*, *man*, *people*, etc.
I bought a magazine from **a poor woman**.   ! not: ... from a poor
The rich man spent the night in a beautiful hotel.   not: The rich spent ...
The homeless people got on the bus in front of the hostel.   not: The homeless got on ...

tailor [ˈteɪlə]	Schneider/in	

needle

tailor

needle [ˈniːdl]	Nadel	
(to) **be able to afford** sth. [əˈfɔːd]	sich etwas leisten können	Now that Mum has a new job, we'll **be able to** ~ a holiday abroad.
(to) **come into focus** [ˈfəʊkəs]	scharf werden	If someone in a photo is **in focus**, you can see them clearly. If they are **out of focus**, you can't. ! **focus** = **1.** Schwer-, Mittel-, Hauptpunkt **2.** Brennpunkt
(to) **grin (-nn-)** [grɪn]	grinsen	He was so happy he was **~ning** from ear to ear.
(to) **aim (at)** [eɪm]	beabsichtigen; zielen (auf)	He **~s** to have his own business when he's 25. She **~ed** her gun **at** the bird but missed.
(to) **provide** sb. **with** sth. [prəˈvaɪd]	jm. etwas zur Verfügung stellen, jn. mit etwas ausstatten	My dad travels a lot for his company, so they have **~d** him **with** a nice big car. (L) providere
access (to) [ˈækses]	Zugang (zu)	(F) l'accès (m) (L) accessus No **access**

Irregular verbs → S. 280–281 · List of names, places and countries → S. 282–284

wages *(pl)* [ˈweɪdʒɪz]	Lohn	His ~s are about £300 a week.	
(to) **acknowledge** [əkˈnɒlɪdʒ] *(fml)*	zugeben	He ~d that he was wrong and apologized. = (to) admit	
thick [θɪk]	dick	**!** *German* **dick** = 1. **fat** *(person, animal)* 2. **thick** *(book, cloud, pullover, sauce, skin, wall)*	
frame [freɪm]	Gestell, Rahmen	the **frame** of his glasses the picture **frame**	
thin [θɪn]	dünn	Philip used to be fatter but now he's quite ~. **thin ◄► thick/fat**	
syringe [sɪˈrɪndʒ]	Injektionsspritze	a **syringe** (F) la seringue	
oil [ɔɪl]	Öl		
(to) **remove** [rɪˈmuːv] *(fml)*	entfernen, beseitigen	(L) removere *Bikes left here will be removed!*	
resistance *(no pl)* [rɪˈzɪstəns]	Widerstand	Sophie Scholl was a famous member of the German ~ to Hitler. (F) la résistance	
vision [ˈvɪʒn]	Sehvermögen	When old people's ~ becomes bad, they need glasses.	
substantial [səbˈstænʃl] *(fml)*	erheblich, beträchtlich	= considerable (F) substantiel, -le	
amount (of) [əˈmaʊnt]	Menge, Betrag	You can add a small ~ of salt to the soup. £300! I wouldn't pay that ~ for a pair of jeans.	
p.57/P 2 (to) **reflect** [rɪˈflekt]	zurückwerfen, reflektieren, spiegeln	A mirror ~s images. (F) refléter (L) reflectere	
(to) **transfer (-rr-)** [trænsˈfɜː]	übertragen	Can the disease be ~red through kissing? (F) transférer (L) transferre	
(to) **drive** [draɪv]	(an)treiben	This machine is ~n by water power.	
(to) **generate** [ˈdʒenəreɪt]	erzeugen	Steam is ~d by the boiling of water. (F) générer (L) generare	
p.58/P 4 **photosynthesis** [ˌfəʊtəʊˈsɪnθəsɪs]	Photosynthese	**!** stress: **photosynthesis** [ˌ--ˈ---]	

Tips on learning words→ S.128 · Glossary of literary terms → S.161–164 · Dictionary (English – German) → S.231–279

Vocabulary 3 219

(to) **absorb** [əb'sɔːb, əb'zɔːb]	absorbieren, aufnehmen	Over time, immigrants are usually ~ed into the culture of their new country.
(to) **store** [stɔː]	speichern	Squirrels often ~ food for the winter.
(to) **capture** ['kæptʃə]	(ein)fangen	The lion was ~d 30 km from the zoo. Ⓕ capter Ⓛ capere, captare
(to) **convert** [kən'vɜːt]	umwandeln	The old castle has been ~ed into a hospital. Ⓕ convertir Ⓛ convertere
(to) **emit (-tt-)** [ɪ'mɪt] *(fml)*	ausstoßen, freisetzen, abgeben	Poisonous gases were ~ted from the factory. Ⓛ emittere
emission [ɪ'mɪʃn]	Emission, (Schadstoff-)Ausstoß	❗ stress: em**i**ssion [-'--] Ⓕ l'émission (f)
carbon dioxide (CO₂) [ˌkɑːbən daɪ'ɒksaɪd]	Kohlendioxid (CO₂)	❗ stress: di**o**xide [-'--] Sometimes **carbon** is used alone to mean CO₂, especially in compound nouns, e.g. ~ **emissions**, ~ **footprint** ['fʊtprɪnt] (CO₂-Fußabdruck)
root [ruːt]	Wurzel	leaves roots
leaf [liːf], *pl* **leaves** [liːvz]	Blatt	
p.58/P 5 **tonne** [tʌn]	Tonne *(Gewichtseinheit)*	❗ pronunciation: [tʌn]
(to) **discuss** sth. [dɪ'skʌs]	über etwas diskutieren, etwas besprechen	We need to ~ the problem before we can find a solution. ❗ noun: **discussion** – verb: (to) **discuss** sth.
p.59/P 6 **appropriate** [ə'prəʊpriət]	passend, angemessen	We're going to a posh party at the weekend and need to wear ~ clothes. Ⓕ approprié/e
recipe ['resəpi]	Kochrezept	This cake is so delicious! Can I have the recipe? ❗ pronunciation: **recipe** ['---]

PART B   Our fragile world

p.60 **fragile** ['frædʒaɪl]	zerbrechlich; gebrechlich	Ⓕ fragile Ⓛ fragilis, -e
(to) **release** [rɪ'liːs]	freilassen *(Gefangene)*; freisetzen, ablassen *(Gas)*	After 25 years the murderer was ~d from prison. How much CO₂ do cars ~?

Irregular verbs → S. 280–281 · List of names, places and countries → S. 282–284

heating [ˈhiːtɪŋ]	Heizung	It was really cold in our classroom today. The ~ wasn't working.
appliance [əˈplaɪəns]	(Haushalts-)Gerät	Most homes have ~s like dishwashers and washing machines.
kettle [ˈketl]	(Wasser-)Kessel, Wasserkocher	Let's have a cup of tea. Turn the ~ on, please.
p.61 (to) **ration** [ˈræʃən]	rationieren	During the war, the government ~ed food so that everybody would have enough.
disgusting [dɪsˈgʌstɪŋ]	ekelhaft, widerlich	Your feet smell ~. I feel sick.
(to) **disgust** [dɪsˈgʌst]	anwidern, anekeln	They were behaving like animals. It ~ed me.
form [fɔːm]	Formular	**!** **form** = 1. Klasse; 2. Gestalt; 3. Formular
basically [ˈbeɪsɪkli]	im Grunde, im Prinzip	*Appliance* and *machine* ~ mean the same thing, but *appliances* are usually found in the home.
fossil fuel [ˌfɒsl ˈfjuːəl]	fossiler Brennstoff	Oil, petrol, gas and **coal** [kəʊl] *(Kohle)* are all **fossil ~s**.
loads of [ləʊdz] *(BE, infml)*	viel, viele	= lots of
pathetic [pəˈθetɪk]	jämmerlich; lächerlich	We found a ~ little dog in the park. Dad says his wages are ~**ally** low.
freezer [ˈfriːzə]	Tiefkühltruhe, -schrank	Please get some ice cream from the ~.
(to) **freeze** [friːz], **froze** [frəʊz], **frozen** [ˈfrəʊzn]	(ge)frieren; zufrieren; einfrieren	Rivers and lakes sometimes ~ in winter. Don't throw that food away, you can ~ it. **!** It's **freezing** outside. (= It's very cold outside.)
(to) **fade away** [ˌfeɪd_əˈweɪ]	schwächer werden	The sound of the car ~d away into the distance.
(to) **sob (-bb-)** [sɒb]	schluchzen	She was ~bing so much she couldn't breathe.
(to) **unwrap (-pp-)** [ʌnˈræp]	auspacken, auswickeln	He ~ped his presents excitedly. **!** silent letter **w**: un**w**rap [ʌnˈræp]
(to) **wrap (-pp-)** [ræp]	einwickeln	I need to ~ this present and take it to the post office. **!** silent letter **w**: **w**rap [ˈræp]
(to) **swipe** a card [swaɪp]	eine Karte durchziehen	We had to ~ a card at the door to get into our hotel room.
(to) **hold** sb./sth. **up** [ˌhəʊld_ˈʌp]	jn./etwas aufhalten	Sorry for ~ing you **up**; I needed the toilet. = (to) delay sb./sth.
(to) **pop** somewhere **(-pp-)** [pɒp] *(BE, infml)*	(schnell) irgendwo hingehen	Dad's not at home. He's ~ped over to the shop to get a newspaper.
p.62 (to) **rip** sb. **off (-pp-)** [ˌrɪp_ˈɒf] *(infml)*	jn. übers Ohr hauen, jn. abzocken	I wouldn't shop there. It's much too expensive and they'll ~ you **off** if they can.
study [ˈstʌdi]	Arbeitszimmer	**!** **study** *(n)* = 1. Studie; 2. Arbeitszimmer
evil [ˈiːvl]	übel, schlimm; böse *(bösartig, feindselig)*	There was an ~ smell in the room, as if an ~ monster had died there.
(to) **radiate** [ˈreɪdieɪt] ⓛ radiare	ausstrahlen, abstrahlen	Her smile ~s confidence and happiness.

Tips on learning words→ S.128 · Glossary of literary terms → S.161–164 · Dictionary (English – German) → S.231–279

Vocabulary 3

wicked ['wɪkɪd]	böse, schlecht	**!** pronunciation: **wicked** ['--]
24/7 [ˌtwentifɔː'sevn]	rund um die Uhr, sieben Tage die Woche	= twenty-four hours, seven days a week
meter ['miːtə]	(Gas-, Strom-)Zähler	a **gas meter**
(to) **melt** [melt]	schmelzen	The sun came out, and the snow began to ~. The sun ~ed the ice on the windows.
blizzard ['blɪzəd]	Schneesturm	
footage (no pl) ['fʊtɪdʒ]	Film(material)	The documentary used some old ~ from 1942.
chill [tʃɪl]	Kühle, Kälte	The heating is on but there's still a ~ in the room.
(to) **creep** [kriːp], **crept, crept** [krept]	kriechen	Hoping she wouldn't see me, I tried to ~ slowly past her.
(to) **give** sb. **the creeps** [kriːps] (infml)	jm. unheimlich sein; jm. nicht geheuer sein	Let's get out of this place. It **gives** me **the** ~. That man **gives** me **the** ~. He looks so scary.
(to) **switch** sth. **on** [ˌswɪtʃ_'ɒn]	etwas anschalten	= (to) turn sth. on (to) **switch on** ◄► (to) **switch off**
p.63/P1 (to) **affect** sth./sb. [ə'fekt]	etwas/jn. betreffen; sich auf etwas/jn. auswirken	The rain didn't ~ us because we were inside. I was badly ~ed by the accident. (to) **affect** sth./sb. = (to) have an **effect** on sth./sb. Ⓛ afficere
p.63/P2 **sex** [seks]	Geschlecht	What ~ is your dog, male or female? Teens are sometimes shy of the opposite ~. Ⓕ le sexe Ⓛ sexus **!** **sex** = **1.** Sex, Geschlechtsverkehr **2.** Geschlecht

PART C   Our future world

p.64 **miner** ['maɪnə]	Bergarbeiter/in	
robot ['rəʊbɒt]	Roboter	**!** stress: **robot** ['--]
investigation (into sth.**)** [ɪn'vestɪɡeɪt]	Untersuchung (von etwas)	The ~ **into** the accident took six months. **!** **investigation into** sth.
(to) **investigate** [ɪn'vestɪɡeɪt]	ermitteln	Police are **investigating** a murder that happened last night. Ⓛ investigare
suicide ['suːɪsaɪd]	Selbstmord	After being unhappy for years, he committed ~. Ⓕ le suicide
sense [sens]	Sinn	The five ~s are the ~s of **sight**, **hearing**, **smell**, **taste** and **touch**. I don't get this. It **makes no** ~ at all. (= Es ergibt gar keinen Sinn.)
review [rɪ'vjuː]	Rezension, Kritik	Before I buy a book, I try to read a few ~s of it.
message ['mesɪdʒ]	Botschaft, Aussage	The film's ~ is that we must all love each other.
overall [ˌəʊvə'rɔːl]	Gesamt-, allgemeine(r, s)	To get an ~ view of the subject, you need to learn more about it.

Irregular verbs → S.280–281 · List of names, places and countries → S.282–284

recommendation [ˌrekəmen'deɪʃn]	Empfehlung	*F* la recommandation
(to) **recommend** sth. (**to** sb.) [ˌrekə'mend]	(jm.) etwas empfehlen	May I ~ the fish to you, sir? *F* recommander ❗ No infinitive after **recommend**: I'd ~ hav<u>ing</u> the fish. *or* I'd ~ that you have the fish. *(Ich würde empfehlen, den Fisch zu nehmen.)*
p.65 **feature** ['fiːtʃə]	*(physisches)* Merkmal, Kennzeichen	The prettiest ~ of this town is its park. ❗ *German* **Merkmal** = **1. characteristic** *(describing sb.'s character)* **2. feature** *(describing a place or thing)*
sensible ['sensəbl]	vernünftig	I wouldn't cycle in the rain. It would be more ~ to take a bus. ❗ *false friends:* **sensible** ['sensəbl] = vernünftig **sensitive** ['sensətɪv] = sensibel
(to) **spoil** sth. (**for** sb.) [spɔɪl]	(jm.) etwas verderben	Don't tell me how the book ends, because that would ~ the story **for** me.
(to) **give** sth. **away** [ˌgɪv_ə'weɪ]	etwas verraten	He was shot because he had **given** secrets ~ to the enemy.
p.66/P1 **volume** ['vɒljuːm]	Lautstärke	
(to) **calculate** ['kælkjuleɪt]	berechnen, ausrechnen	I've ~d we'll need £40 for the shopping. *F* calculer
p.67/P2 (to) **hand over** (**to** sb.) [ˌhænd_'əʊvə]	(die Führung / das Wort) übergeben (an jn.)	After five years, the junta **~ed over to** a new president. That's all from me. Now I'll **~ ~ to** my colleague John Smith.
(to) **cover** ['kʌvə]	behandeln, abdecken	In History last term, we **~ed** the 18th century. Any more questions? – No, you've **~ed** them all. ❗ (to) **cover** = **1.** bedecken, zudecken **2.** behandeln, abdecken
(to) **aid** sb. [eɪd] *(fml)*	jm. helfen	A good dictionary should ~ you with your English. *F* aider

Tips on learning words→ S.128 · Glossary of literary terms → S.161–164 · Dictionary (English – German) → S.231–279

Word field: Environment, science, technology

The environment

The planet faces huge environmental problems.
The ⁺greenhouse ['griːnhaʊs] effect is nothing new.
High carbon dioxide (CO_2) emissions lead to global warming and climate change.
Do you know your carbon footprint?
⁺Methane ['miːθeɪn] is a greenhouse gas.
Plants absorb CO_2 and release oxygen.
⁺Environmentalists [ɪnˌvaɪrən'mentəlɪst] are worried about ⁺glacier ['glæsiə] ⁺retreat [rɪ'triːt].
Cars have a big environmental impact.
Oil, coal, gas and wood are fossil fuels.
Germany's energy resources are limited.
We should use more renewable energy.
Public transport is environmentally friendly.
⁺Non-deposit [dɪ'pɒzɪt] bottles produce waste.
The recycling of waste helps to save energy.
Deserts are areas of very low rainfall.

Earthquakes cannot be reliably predicted.

Pollution is a serious global problem, not just for the Third World.
⁺Drinking water is ⁺scarce [skeəs] in this area.
⁺Overfishing is bad for the ⁺ecosystem ['iːkəʊsɪstəm].
The tiger is an ⁺endangered [ɪn'deɪndʒəd] species.
Its survival is at risk.

Die Umwelt

Der Planet steht vor riesigen Umweltproblemen.
Der Treibhauseffekt ist nichts Neues.
Ein hoher Ausstoß an Kohlendioxid führt zu Erderwärmung und Klimawandel.
Kennst du deine CO_2-Bilanz?
Methan ist ein Treibhausgas.
Pflanzen nehmen CO_2 auf und setzen Sauerstoff frei.
Umweltschützer machen sich Sorgen über den Rückgang der Gletscher.
Autos haben einen großen Einfluss auf die Umwelt.
Öl, Kohle, Gas und Holz sind fossile Brennstoffe.
Deutschlands Energiequellen sind begrenzt.
Wir sollten mehr erneuerbare Energie verwenden.
Öffentliche Verkehrsmittel sind umweltfreundlich.
Einwegflaschen erzeugen Müll.
Müll wiederaufzubereiten hilft Energie zu sparen.
Wüsten sind Gegenden mit sehr wenig Niederschlag/ Regen.
Erdbeben können nicht verlässlich vorausgesagt werden.
Umweltverschmutzung ist ein ernstes weltweites Problem, nicht nur für die Dritte Welt.
Trinkwasser ist in dieser Region knapp.
Überfischung ist schlecht für das Ökosystem.

Der Tiger ist eine bedrohte Tierart.
Sein Überleben ist in Gefahr.

Science and research

Scientists are usually curious.
The life sciences deal with living ⁺organisms ['ɔːgənɪzəm].
The discovery of ⁺penicillin [ˌpenə'sɪlən] made it possible to treat and cure many diseases.
The evidence for the origin of species from natural selection is ⁺overwhelming [ˌəʊvə'welmɪŋ].
A lot of research is done in physics, chemistry and medicine.
⁺Astronomers [ə'strɒnəmə] study objects in space, like planets, stars and galaxies.
All findings are carefully recorded.

(Natur-)Wissenschaft und Forschung

Wissenschaftler sind normalerweise neugierig.
Biowissenschaften beschäftigen sich mit lebenden Organismen.
Die Entdeckung des Penicillins ermöglichte die Behandlung und Heilung vieler Krankheiten.
Die Hinweise auf / Beweise für den Ursprung der Arten aus natürlicher Auslese sind überwältigend.
In Physik, Chemie und Medizin wird viel Forschung betrieben.
Astronomen/-innen erforschen Gegenstände im Weltall wie Planeten, Sterne und Galaxien.
Alle Ergebnisse werden sorgfältig aufgezeichnet.

Technology

A steam engine is used to power a generator.

With nuclear energy, the problem of waste ⁺disposal [dɪ'spəʊzl] has not been solved yet.
Nuclear ⁺radiation [ˌreɪdi'eɪʃn] is very dangerous.
The use of solar and wind energy is getting more and more ⁺efficient [ɪ'fɪʃnt].
Nuclear fusion would provide lots of energy.
A generator is a machine that generates electricity.
⁺Civil engineers build roads and bridges.
Some inventors and discoverers are poor.
The world of computers is also called 'IT' (information technology).

Technologie

Mit einer Dampfmaschine lässt sich ein Generator antreiben.
Im Fall der Kernenergie ist das Problem der Müllbeseitigung noch nicht gelöst.
Kernstrahlung ist sehr gefährlich.
Die Nutzung von Solar- und Windenergie wird immer effizienter.
Die Kernfusion würde eine Menge Energie bereitstellen.
Ein Generator ist eine Maschine, die Strom erzeugt.
Bauingenieure/-innen bauen Straßen und Brücken.
Manche Erfinder/innen und Entdecker/innen sind arm.
Die Welt der Computer wird auch als „IT" (Informationstechnologie) bezeichnet.

Irregular verbs → S. 280–281 · List of names, places and countries → S. 282–284

Unit 4: Love reading

PART A   Can't put it down: fabulous fiction

p.76	**fabulous** ['fæbjələs] *(infml)*	fabelhaft, fantastisch	You'll love this book: it's really ~. Ⓕ fabuleux, se Ⓛ fabulosus, -a, -um
	historical [hɪ'stɒrɪkl]	historisch, geschichtlich	This old book is of great ~ importance. Ⓕ historique
	curious ['kjʊəriəs]	seltsam; wissbegierig	He wears ~ clothes, as if he wants to look old. She's a ~ girl and always loves to find out new things. Ⓕ curieux, se Ⓛ curiosus, -a, -um
	incident ['ɪnsɪdənt]	Vorfall, Zwischenfall	The march finished without ~. Ⓕ l'incident *(m)*
	(to) **examine** [ɪg'zæmɪn]	prüfen, untersuchen	Let's ~ all the ideas before we decide. I had a stomach ache, so the doctor ~**d** me. Ⓕ examiner Ⓛ examinare
	(to) **take** sth. **for granted** ['grɑːntɪd]	etwas für (allzu) selbst-verständlich halten	In Europe we ~ fresh water **for granted**.
	(to) **stand out** [ˌstænd_'aʊt]	hervorstechen, auffallen	Charles ~**s** out because of his very large ears. My dad says the summer of 1976 ~**s** ~ as the hottest of his life so far.
	destiny ['destɪni]	Schicksal	My parents say that ~ brought them together. = **fate** *(but more positive)* Ⓕ le destin
	(to) **await** [ə'weɪt] *(fml)*	bevorstehen, erwarten	What ~**s** us on our journey through life? ❗ *German* **erwarten** = **1.** Wir erwarten etwas. = We **expect** sth. **2.** Etwas erwartet uns. = Sth. **awaits** us.

a **witch**

	witch [wɪtʃ]	Hexe	

an **armoured** car

	armoured ['ɑːməd]	gepanzert	Ⓕ armé/e Ⓛ armatus, -a, -um
	beyond [bɪ'jɒnd]	jenseits (von), über ... hinaus/hinweg	The road leads ~ the village and into the fields. If you look ~ his big nose, he's quite handsome.
	(to) **be about to do** sth. ['ə'baʊt]	im Begriff sein, etwas zu tun	

I **was** ~ **to** go to bed when the doorbell rang.

Tips on learning words→ S.128 · Glossary of literary terms → S.161–164 · Dictionary (English – German) → S.231–279

Vocabulary

p.77	**after all** [ˌɑːftər_ˈɔːl]	schließlich	Why isn't Jo here? **After ~,** it was her who told us to come. Tim said he wouldn't be at the party, but then he came ~ ~.
	symbol (of sth.) [ˈsɪmbl]	Symbol (für etwas)	The heart is the ~ **of** love. ❗ stress: **symbol** [ˈ--] Ⓕ le symbole
	similarity (to, between) [ˌsɪməˈlærəti]	Ähnlichkeit (mit, zwischen)	The twins look very different: there's no ~ **between** them at all. ❗ adjective: **similar** – noun: **similarity**
	minor [ˈmaɪnə]	klein, unbedeutend	Bach was considered a ~ musician ... Ⓕ mineur/e
	major [ˈmeɪdʒə]	groß, bedeutend	... until he was rediscovered as a ~ composer in the 19th century. Ⓕ majeur/e
	boarding school [ˈbɔːdɪŋ ˌskuːl]	Internat	My grandmother's family lived in Jamaica and she went to ~ **school** in England.
	expectation [ˌekspekˈteɪʃn]	Erwartung	I'm not sure who will win, but my ~ is that it will be the Conservatives. Ⓛ expectatio ❗ verb: (to) **expect** – noun: **expectation**
p.78	**awkwardness** [ˈɔːkwədnəs]	Peinlichkeit, Unbehaglichkeit; Unbeholfenheit	The ~ of the silence was made even worse when somebody started to laugh. He tries to hide his ~ by talking very loudly.
	awkward [ˈɔːkwəd]	peinlich, unbehaglich; unbeholfen; ungünstig	This is a bit ~, but I don't want you at my party. Although she's pretty, she's very ~ with boys. This is an ~ time: we're just having dinner.
	vast [vɑːst]	riesig	The country has ~ gold resources, worth billions. Ⓛ vastus, -a, -um
	vastly [ˈvɑːstli]	äußerst, völlig	Without his beard, he looked ~ different.
	pity for sb. [ˈpɪti]	Mitleid mit jm.	I feel real ~ **for** people who can't find a job.
	(to) intend [ɪnˈtend]	beabsichtigen	Mr Smith ~**s** to get married next month. That meat wasn't ~**ed** for you, but for the dog.
p.79	**genuine** [ˈdʒenjuɪn]	echt, wirklich	
	carpet [ˈkɑːpɪt]	Teppich	

Genuine flying carpet $99

p.80	**suitcase** [ˈsuːtkeɪs]	Koffer	a heavy **suitcase**
	trial [ˈtraɪəl]	Test, Probe, Versuch	**Trials** of the new drug will take place next year.
	separation [ˌsepəˈreɪʃn]	Trennung	The friends met again after a ~ of ten years. ❗ verb: (to) **separate** – noun: **separation** Ⓕ la séparation Ⓛ separatio

Irregular verbs → S.280–281 · List of names, places and countries → S.282–284

	(to) **request** sth. **(from** sb.) [rɪ'kwest] *(fml)*	(jn.) um etwas bitten	We ~ an answer **from** you by tomorrow. ❗ noun: **request** – verb: (to) **request**
	impression [ɪm'preʃn]	Eindruck	He made the ~ of being very confident. What ~ does this song make? Is it sad, happy? Ⓕ l'impression *(f)* Ⓛ impressio
p.81	**drawer** [drɔː]	Schublade	a **drawer**
	waist [weɪst]	Taille	❗ **waist** [weɪst] = Taille **waste** [weɪst] = Verschwendung
p.82	(to) **bother** sb. ['bɒðə]	jn. stören; jn. belästigen	Would it ~ you if we stayed home this summer? I don't want to ~ you, sir, but a man has been waiting to see you for over an hour.
	on the contrary ['kɒntrəri]	im Gegenteil	You hate me! – **On the ~**, I love you! Ⓕ au contraire Ⓛ e contrario
	(to) **increase (by)** [ɪn'kriːs]	ansteigen, zunehmen (um); erhöhen (um)	The number of road accidents has ~d again. They've ~d the price **by** 10 %. Last week it was lower.
	(to) **decrease (by)** [dɪ'kriːs]	abnehmen, nachlassen, zurück-gehen (um); reduzieren, ver-ringern (um)	The storm was over and the wind ~d again. The ship ~d speed as it entered the harbour. (to) decrease ◄► (to) **increase**
p.83	(to) **neglect** [nɪ'glekt]	vernachlässigen; versäumen *(zu tun)*	The children were cruelly ~ed by their parents. I ~ed to inform you of my new address. Ⓕ négliger Ⓛ neglegere
p.84	(to) **reveal** [rɪ'viːl]	offenbaren, preisgeben, verraten	The murderer isn't usually ~ed until the end of the film. Ⓕ révéler
p.86/P1	**visual** ['vɪʒuəl]	optisch, visuell	❗ stress: **visual** ['---] Ⓕ visuel, le
p.87/P2	**development** [dɪ'veləpmənt]	Entwicklung	The situation has changed. There have been some interesting new ~s. ❗ verb: (to) **develop** – noun: **development** Ⓕ le développement
	pace [peɪs]	Tempo	Is this ~ OK for you, or shall we run a bit slower?
	classic ['klæsɪk]	Klassiker	I think the song 'Thriller' is a ~ of the 1980s.
	period ['pɪəriəd]	Zeit(-raum, -spanne)	The second half of the 20th century was a ~ of peace in western Europe. Ⓕ la période
	extract (from) ['ekstrækt]	Auszug (aus)	At the cinema, they always show ~s **from** other films before the one you've come to see. ❗ stress: **extract** ['--] Ⓕ l'extrait *(m)*
	moving ['muːvɪŋ]	bewegend	My mum usually finds love films ~.
	thrilling ['θrɪlɪŋ]	aufregend, spannend	I love to get excited by a really ~ book.
	memorable ['memərəbl]	unvergesslich	I'll never forget my first time in London: it was a really ~ experience. Ⓕ mémorable Ⓛ memorabilis, -e
	striking ['straɪkɪŋ]	auffallend	His most ~ feature is his friendliness.

Tips on learning words→ S.128 · Glossary of literary terms → S.161–164 · Dictionary (English – German) → S.231–279

Vocabulary

PART B A quick fix: short stories

p.88	**thus** [ðʌs] *(fml)*	daher, folglich	He is only 16. **Thus** he is unable to drive. *or:* He is **thus** unable to drive. = … so he can't drive.
	acquaintance [əˈkweɪntəns]	Bekannte(r)	I wouldn't say he's a real friend: he's just an ~.
	selfish [ˈselfɪʃ]	egoistisch	You never think of other people! You're so ~!
	chum [tʃʌm] *(infml)*	Kumpel	= friend, mate
	groceries *(pl)* [ˈgrəʊsəriz]	Lebensmittel	I need to go to the corner shop for some cheese and eggs and other ~.
	(to) **be desperate to be/do** sth. [ˈdespərət]	unbedingt etwas sein/tun wollen	I was so ~ **to** escape that I didn't think of the danger. (F) désespéré,e (L) desperatus, -a, -um
	attorney [əˈtɜːni] *(bes AE)*	(Rechts-)Anwalt, Anwältin	
p.89	**abrupt** [əˈbrʌpt]	abrupt, plötzlich	There was an ~ change in the weather, which was a surprise for us all.

PART C Lifelines: saved by poetry

p.90	**lifeline** [ˈlaɪflaɪn]	Rettungsleine	
	(to) **comment (on** sth.**)** [ˈkɒment]	sich (zu etwas) äußern, einen Kommentar (zu etwas) abgeben	He refused to ~ **on** the news until he had looked at the facts more closely. (F) commenter
	(to) **mention** [ˈmenʃn]	erwähnen; nennen	Did I ~ that I was going on holiday next week? He ~**ed** the names of several famous poets. (F) mentionner
	(to) **recite** [rɪˈsaɪt]	vortragen, rezitieren, aufsagen	Learn the poem so that you can ~ it to the class.
	pattern [ˈpætn]	Muster	I like the ~ of your pullover, but not the colour.
p.91	**sharp** [ʃɑːp]	scharf	Careful, that knife is very ~.
	coat [kəʊt]	Mantel	It's cold today. You'll need a pullover and a ~.

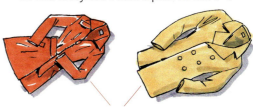

coats

	(to) **brush** [brʌʃ]	bürsten; putzen	Please ~ your hair and your teeth.
	creature [ˈkriːtʃə]	Lebewesen	Last night I watched a scary film about ~s from another planet. (F) la créature (L) creatura
	(to) **match** [mætʃ]	zusammenpassen	Some people say blue and brown don't ~.
	sequence [ˈsiːkwəns]	Abfolge, Reihenfolge	What's the next number in this ~? 2, 4, 16, … (F) la séquence
p.92	**beneath** [bɪˈniːθ] *(fml)*	unter	= under

	promise [ˈprɒmɪs]	Versprechen	He **made** a ~ to her. She thought he would **keep** his ~, but in the end he **broke** his ~. ❗ verb: (to) **promise** – noun: **promise** Ⓕla promesse Ⓛpromissum
p.93	(to) **praise** [preɪz]	loben, preisen	He ~**d** me by saying I was the best student he had ever known.
	(to) **cease** [siːs] *(fml)*	aufhören	Suddenly the noise ~**d** and all was silent. = (to) stop Ⓕcesser Ⓛcessare
	grave [greɪv]	Grab	Grandpa was buried in Africa and I have never visited his ~.
	tension [ˈtenʃn]	Spannung	There was ~ when I came in, as if everyone was afraid of what I would say. Ⓕla tension
	hardly [ˈhɑːdli]	kaum	He has ~ any friends, just Tom and Jon. ▶ Grammar File 12: Emphasis (p.193)
	handle [ˈhændl]	Griff, Klinke	

handles

	bloke [bləʊk] *(infml, BE)*	Kerl	That Dave seems a posh kind of ~, doesn't he? = guy
	(to) **roll** [rəʊl]	rollen	Tears ~**ed** down his face as he heard the news.
p.94	**admiration (for)** [ˌædməˈreɪʃn]	Bewunderung (für)	I have great ~ **for** Rooney as a footballer. ❗ verb: (to) **admire** – noun: **admiration** Ⓕl'admiration *(f)* Ⓛadmiratio
	(for) pleasure [ˈpleʒə]	(zum) Vergnügen	I didn't stay up till midnight **for** ~! I was studying for my English test. Ⓕle plaisir
	excitement [ɪkˈsaɪtmənt]	Aufregung, Erregung	The ~ about the next day made it hard to sleep.
	disappointment [ˌdɪsəˈpɔɪntmənt]	Enttäuschung	Don't go to that restaurant. The meal we had there was a big ~. ❗ verb: (to) **disappoint** – noun: **disappointment**
	anger [ˈæŋgə]	Wut, Ärger	❗ adj: **angry** – noun: **anger**
	joy [dʒɔɪ]	Freude	= great happiness Ⓕla joie
	loss [lɒs]	Verlust	The motorist had suffered so much ~ of blood that the doctors were unable to save him.
	(to) **pause** [pɔːz]	eine Pause machen	After an hour on the road, we ~**d** to have lunch.
	pause [pɔːz]	Pause	There was a short ~ before he started playing.
p.95	**insight** [ˈɪnsaɪt]	Verständnis; Einsicht, Einblick	Her work shows a deep ~ into the human mind.
	absent [ˈæbsənt]	abwesend	Why were you ~? – I was ill, sir. Ⓕabsent Ⓛabsens
	hell [hel]	Hölle	Some religions believe in heaven and ~.
	flow [fləʊ]	Fluss, Strom	❗ verb: (to) **flow** – noun: **flow**
p.96	**twist** [twɪst]	(überraschende) Wendung	Roald Dahl is famous for writing stories with a ~ at the end.

Tips on learning words→ S.128 · Glossary of literary terms → S.161–164 · Dictionary (English – German) → S.231–279

Vocabulary

magnificent [mæg'nɪfɪsənt]	großartig, herrlich	This beautiful bridge is a ~ example of modern architecture. *(F)* magnifique *(L)* magnificus, -a, -um

PART D   All the world's a stage: thrilling theatre

p.98 (to) **abandon** [ə'bændən]	verlassen, im Stich lassen	He went to live with another woman, **~ing** his wife and children. *(F)* abandonner
various ['veərɪəs]	verschieden	There are ~ ways to solve this problem. *(F)* varié,e *(L)* varius, -a, -um
brush [brʌʃ]	Pinsel	❗ verb: (to) **brush** – noun: **brush**
(to) **depict** [dɪ'pɪkt] *(fml)*	darstellen, abbilden	The novel **~s** the life of a man on a desert island.
butterfly ['bʌtəflaɪ]	Schmetterling	a **butterfly**
eventually [ɪ'ventʃuəli]	schließlich, irgendwann	I waited for him at school, and he ~ came after two hours. ❗ *false friends:* **eventually** = schließlich **perhaps** = eventuell
entrance ['entrəns]	Eingang	I entered the building through the main ~. *(F)* l'entrée *(f)*
torch [tɔ:tʃ]	Taschenlampe	a **torch**
slight [slaɪt]	klein, leicht, unwichtig	I have a ~ headache, but it will go away.
familiar with [fə'mɪlɪə]	vertraut mit	Are you ~ **with** Elgar's music? – Yes, I know a few pieces. *(L)* familiaris, -e
(to) **approach** [ə'prəʊtʃ]	sich nähern	As we **~ed** our house, we saw that the front door was open. *(F)* s'approcher
p.99 **estate** [ɪ'steɪt]	Wohnsiedlung	He lives in the middle of a huge ~ of new flats.
kingdom ['kɪŋdəm]	Königreich	The United **Kingdom** is a constitutional monarchy.
damp [dæmp]	feucht	Those clothes aren't dry yet: they're still ~.
(to) **tempt** [tempt]	in Versuchung führen	I was **~ed** to have some more chocolate, but knew that I shouldn't. *(L)* temptare
(to) **pour** [pɔ:]	eingießen	He **~ed** the wine into six glasses.
p.100 **irritated** ['ɪrɪteɪtɪd]	gereizt	I felt ~ because she was behaving so rudely. ❗ *false friends:* **irritated** = gereizt **confused** = irritiert
launderette [lɔ:n'dret]	Waschsalon	Our washing machine is broken, so we will have to go to the ~ until it has been repaired.
(to) **indicate** sth. ['ɪndɪkeɪt]	deuten auf etwas	Unable to speak, the injured man just **~d** the parts of his body that hurt. *(F)* indiquer *(L)* indicare

---

Irregular verbs → S. 280–281 · List of names, places and countries → S. 282–284

230 4 Vocabulary

p.101	**tail** [teɪl]	Schwanz	
p.103	(to) **mend** [mend]	reparieren	My watch is broken. I need to have it **~ed**. = (to) repair
	cheerful ['tʃɪəfl]	heiter, fröhlich	He was poor but always **~**.
	(to) **polish** ['pɒlɪʃ]	polieren	He **~ed** his shoes till they shone.
	(to) **concentrate (on** sth.) ['kɒnsntreɪt]	sich konzentrieren (auf etwas)	Be quiet, I can't **~ on** my homework. Ⓕ se concentrer
p.104	(to) **arm** [ɑːm]	bewaffnen	The enemy was **~ed** with only bows and arrows. Ⓕ armer Ⓛ armare
	length [leŋθ]	Länge; Dauer; Stück	The unit of **~** is the metre. The **~** of the play is two hours and 20 minutes. He hit me with a **~** of rope.
	massive ['mæsɪv]	riesig, massig	❗ stress: m**a**ssive ['--] Ⓕ massif, -ve
	(to) **scare** sb. [skeə]	jn. erschrecken, jm. Angst machen	Being alone in that big dark forest really **~d** me. = (to) frighten
p.105	**aggressive** [ə'gresɪv]	aggressiv	Some people get **~** after drinking alcohol. ❗ stress: aggr**e**ssive [-'--] Ⓕ aggressif, -ve
	panicky ['pænɪki] *(infml)*	in Panik, panisch	I tried to calm him down, but he was still **~**.
	suspicious (of/about) [sə'spɪʃəs]	misstrauisch (gegenüber); verdächtig	I'm still **~ about** his version of the story. I don't think I believe him. There was a **~** man waiting in the shadows.
	gentle ['dʒentl]	sanft(mütig)	The dog looks aggressive, but he's really very **~**.
	imaginative [ɪ'mædʒɪnətɪv]	fantasievoll, einfallsreich	My aunt always has really exciting and **~** ideas about what to do at the weekend.
	gesture ['dʒestʃə]	Geste, Handbewegung	This **~** means 'peace' or 'victory'. Ⓕ le geste Ⓛ gestus

Tips on learning words → S.128 · Glossary of literary terms → S.161–164 · Dictionary (English – German) → S.231–279

Dictionary (English – German)

231

Das **Dictionary** (S. 231–279) enthält den Wortschatz der Bände 1 bis 6 von *English G 21*.
Wenn du wissen möchtest, was ein Wort bedeutet, wie man es ausspricht oder wie es genau geschrieben wird, kannst du hier nachschlagen.

Im **Dictionary** werden folgende **Abkürzungen und Symbole** verwendet:

jm. = jemandem	sb. = somebody	*pl* = *plural*	*AE* = *American English*
jn. = jemanden	sth. = something	*no pl* = *no plural*	*infml* = *informal*

° Mit diesem Kringel sind Wörter markiert, die nicht zum Lernwortschatz gehören.
▶ Der Pfeil verweist auf Kästchen im **Vocabulary** (S. 197–230), in denen du weitere Informationen zu diesem Wort findest.

Die **Fundstellenangaben** zeigen, wo ein Wort zum ersten Mal vorkommt.
Die Ziffern in Klammern bezeichnen Seitenzahlen:

I = Band A1 • II = Band A2 • III = Band A3 •
IV = Band A4 • V = Band A5 • VI = Band A6

VI 1 (15)	= Band 6, Unit 1, Seite 15
VI 1 (34/210)	= Band 6, Unit 1, Seite 210 (im Vocabulary, zu Seite 34)
VI 1 (10/G)	= Band 6, Unit 1, Seite 10; wird im *Glossary* (S. 161– 164) behandelt

---

Tipp

Auf der **Audio-CD im Workbook** findest du sowohl dieses englisch-deutsche Wörterverzeichnis als auch ein deutsch-englisches Wörterverzeichnis mit dem Lernwortschatz der Bände 1–6.

1

1800s [ˌeɪtiːn 'hʌndrədz]: **in the mid-1800s** Mitte des 19. Jahrhunderts V

1950s [ˌnaɪntiːn'fɪftiz] die Fünfzigerjahre (des 20. Jahrhunderts) III

24/7 [ˌtwentifɔːˈsevn] rund um die Uhr, sieben Tage die Woche; fortlaufend, ununterbrochen VI 3 (62)

9/11 [ˌnaɪn_ɪ'levn] Nine Eleven *(der Terroranschlag am 11. September 2001)* IV

A

a [ə]
1. ein, eine I
2. once/twice a week einmal/zweimal pro Woche III • **a bit** ein bisschen, etwas II • **a few** ein paar, einige II • **a lot (of)** eine Menge, viel, viele II • **He likes her a lot.** Er mag sie sehr. I

abandon [ə'bændən] verlassen, im Stich lassen VI 4 (98)

abbey ['æbi] Abtei II

abbreviation [əˌbriːvi'eɪʃn] Abkürzung IV

able ['eɪbl]: **be able to do sth.** etwas tun können; fähig sein/in der Lage sein, etwas zu tun II

Aboriginal [ˌæbə'rɪdʒənəl] Aborigine- *(die Ureinwohner/innen Australiens betreffend)* V • **the Aboriginal people** die Ureinwohner/innen Australiens V

Aborigine [ˌæbə'rɪdʒəni] *Ureinwohner/in Australiens* V

about [ə'baʊt]
1. über I
2. ungefähr II
ask about sth. nach etwas fragen I • **be about to do sth.** im Begriff sein, etwas zu tun VI 4 (76) • **know about sth.** von etwas wissen; über etwas Bescheid wissen II • **learn about sth.** etwas über etwas erfahren, etwas über etwas herausfinden II • **This is about Mr Green.** Es geht um Mr Green. I • **What about ...? 1.** Was ist mit ...? / Und ...? I; **2.** Wie wär's mit ...? I • **What are you talking about?** Wovon redest du? I • **What was the best thing about ...?** Was war das Beste an ...? II

above [ə'bʌv] über, oberhalb (von) III • **above all** vor allem VI 3 (54)

abridged [ə'brɪdʒd] gekürzt VI 1 (10/G)

abroad [ə'brɔːd] im Ausland II
go abroad ins Ausland gehen/fahren II

abrupt [ə'brʌpt] abrupt, plötzlich VI 4 (89)

absent ['æbsənt] abwesend VI 4 (93)

absolute ['æbsəluːt] absolut V

absolutely [ˌæbsə'luːtli] absolut, völlig IV

absorb [əb'sɔːb, əb'zɔːb] absorbieren, aufnehmen VI 3 (58)

accent ['æksənt] Akzent II

accept [ək'sept] annehmen, akzeptieren VI 1 (18)

access (to) ['ækses] Zugang (zu) VI 3 (56)

accident ['æksɪdənt] Unfall II; Zufall VI 1 (13)

accommodation [əˌkɒmə'deɪʃn] Unterkunft IV

according to [ə'kɔːdɪŋ] laut, zufolge VI 3 (54)

accurate ['ækjərət] genau, akkurat III

AC [ˌeɪ'siː] *siehe* **air conditioning**

achieve [ə'tʃiːv] erreichen, erzielen, zustande bringen IV • **achieve an end** ein Ziel erreichen IV

achievement [ə'tʃiːvmənt] Leistung, Errungenschaft V

acid ['æsɪd] Säure IV

acknowledge [ək'nɒlɪdʒ] zugeben VI 3 (56)

acquaintance [ə'kweɪntəns] Bekannte(r) VI 4 (88)

acrobat ['ækrəbæt] Akrobat/in III

across [ə'krɒs]
1. (quer) über II
2. hinüber, herüber III

acrostic [ə'krɒstɪk] Akrostichon VI 4 (96/G)

act [ækt]
1. aufführen, spielen I
°**act sth. out** etwas vorspielen
2. handeln, sich verhalten VI 1 (10)

action ['ækʃn] Action; Handlung, Tat III

active ['æktɪv] aktiv III

activist ['æktəvɪst] Aktivist/in IV

activity [æk'tɪvəti] Aktivität, Tätigkeit I

actor ['æktə] Schauspieler/in II

actual ['æktʃʊəl] eigentlich VI 4 (78)

actually ['æktʃʊəli] eigentlich, tatsächlich, übrigens, zwar IV

ad [æd] Anzeige, Inserat; *(im Fernsehen)* Werbespot IV

AD [,eɪ 'diː] *(from Latin: Anno Domini)* nach Christus III

adapt [ə'dæpt] adaptieren VI 2 (38/G)

add (to) [æd] hinzufügen, ergänzen, addieren (zu) I

add up [,æd_'ʌp] addieren, zusammenzählen VI 1 (21)

addict ['ædɪkt] Süchtige(r), Abhängige(r) VI 1 (14)

addicted [ə'dɪktɪd]: **be addicted (to sth.)** süchtig (nach etwas) sein, abhängig (von etwas) sein VI 1 (14)

addiction (to sth.) [ə'dɪkʃn] Sucht (nach etwas) VI 1 (14)

addictive [ə'dɪktɪv]: **be addictive** süchtig/abhängig machen VI 1 (14)

address [ə'dres] Anschrift, Adresse II

address sb. [ə'dres] jn. ansprechen, anreden VI 2 (31) • °**address sth.** sich mit etwas befassen

adjust (to sth.) [ə'dʒʌst] sich (an etwas) gewöhnen, sich (auf etwas) einstellen IV • **adjust sth. (to sth.)** (sich) einstellen (auf); (sich) anpassen (an) VI 3 (56) • °**self-adjusting** sich selbst regulierend VI 3 (56)

admiration (for) [,ædmə'reɪʃn] Bewunderung (für) VI 4 (93)

admire [əd'maɪə] bewundern IV

admit (-tt-) [əd'mɪt] zugeben, eingestehen VI 1 (15)

adopt [a'dɒpt] adoptieren; beschließen, sich entscheiden (für) *(Maßnahme, Politik)* VI 2 (34)

adult ['ædʌlt] Erwachsene(r) III
adult life das Leben als Erwachsene(r) III

advanced [əd'vɑːnst] fortgeschritten; für Fortgeschrittene V

advantage (over sb./sth.) [əd'vɑːntɪdʒ] Vorteil (gegenüber jm./etwas) IV

adventure [əd'ventʃə] Abenteuer II

advert ['ædvɜːt] Anzeige, Inserat; *(im Fernsehen)* Werbespot II

advertise ['ædvətaɪz] Werbung machen (für); inserieren V

advertisement [əd'vɜːtɪsmənt] Anzeige; Inserat; *(im Fernsehen)* Werbespot V

advertiser ['ædvətaɪzə] Inserent/in; Werbekunde/-kundin V

advertising ['ædvətaɪzə] Werbung V

advice (no pl) [əd'vaɪs] Rat, Ratschlag, Ratschläge V • **Take my advice.** Hör auf meinen Rat. V

advise sb. [əd'vaɪz] jn. beraten V

adviser [əd'vaɪzə] Berater/in V

°**affairs (pl)** [ə'feəz] Angelegenheiten

affect sth./sb. [ə'fekt] etwas/jn. betreffen VI 3 (63)

afford [ə'fɔːd]: **be able to afford sth.** sich etwas leisten können VI 3 (56)

afraid [ə'freɪd]
1. be afraid (of) Angst haben (vor) I
2. I'm afraid leider II

after ['ɑːftə] nach *(zeitlich)* I
after all schließlich VI 4 (77)
after that danach I • **after-school** nach dem Unterricht stattfindende(r, s) V

after ['ɑːftə] nachdem II

afternoon [,ɑːftə'nuːn] Nachmittag I • **in the afternoon** nachmittags, am Nachmittag I • **on Friday afternoon** freitagnachmittags, am Freitagnachmittag I

afterwards ['ɑːftəwədz] nachher, danach VI 1 (24)

again [ə'gen] wieder; noch einmal I
now and again ab und zu, von Zeit zu Zeit III

against [ə'genst] gegen I

age [eɪdʒ] Alter III • **at (the age of) 16** mit 16; im Alter von 16 III **she's my age** sie ist in meinem Alter V • **under age** minderjährig V

agency ['eɪdʒənsi]: **news agency** Nachrichtenagentur IV

aggressive [ə'gresɪv] aggressiv VI 4 (105)

ago [ə'gəʊ]: **a minute ago** vor einer Minute I

agree [ə'griː]: **agree (on)** sich einigen (auf) I • **agree (to sth.)** sich (zu etwas) bereit erklären V • **agree (with sb.)** (jm.) zustimmen I

agreement [ə'griːmənt] Abkommen, Vertrag V; Einigung; Vereinbarung VI 2 (28) • **reach (an) agreement** sich einigen VI 2 (28)

agriculture ['ægrɪkʌltʃə] Landwirtschaft IV

ahead (of sb./sth.) [ə'hed] (jm./etwas) voraus V • **the road ahead** die Straße vor uns V

aid [eɪd] *(fml)* helfen VI 3 (67)
computer-aided computergestützt VI 3 (67)

AIDS [eɪdz] AIDS V

aim [eɪm] Ziel III

aim (to do sth.) [eɪm] beabsichtigen (etwas zu tun), zielen (auf) VI 3 (56)

air [eə] Luft II

air conditioning (no pl) ['eə kən,dɪʃənɪŋ] Klimatisierung, Klimaanlage V

airport ['eəpɔːt] Flughafen III

°**AK-47** Kalaschnikow, sowjetisch-russisches Sturmgewehr

alarm sb. [ə'lɑːm] jn. beunruhigen, erschrecken VI 2 (30)

alarm clock [ə'lɑːm klɒk] Wecker I

album ['ælbəm] Album II

alcohol ['ælkəhɒl] Alkohol III

A-level exams, A-levels (pl) ['eɪ ,levl] *die höchsten Abschlussprüfungen des Schulsystems in England, Wales und Nordirland* V

alive [ə'laɪv]: **be alive** leben, am Leben sein IV • **keep sth. alive** etwas am Leben halten IV

all [ɔːl] alle; alles I • **2 all** 2 beide (2:2 unentschieden) III • **all day** den ganzen Tag (lang) I • **all over the world** auf der ganzen Welt III **all right** [ɔːl 'raɪt] gut, in Ordnung II • **All the best** Viele Grüße IV **all the time** die ganze Zeit I • **all we have to do now ...** alles, was wir jetzt (noch) tun müssen, ... II **from all over the world** aus der ganzen Welt II • **This is all wrong.** Das ist ganz falsch. I • **all year round** das ganze Jahr hindurch IV

allergic (to sth.) [ə'lɜːdʒɪk] allergisch (gegen etwas) III

alliteration [ə,lɪtə'reɪʃn] Alliteration VI 4 (93/G)

allow [ə'laʊ] erlauben, zulassen II
be allowed to do sth. [ə'laʊd] etwas tun dürfen II

°**allowance** [ə'laʊəns] erlaubte Menge

all-time [,ɔːl'taɪm]: **my all-time favourite** mein Liebling aller Zeiten VI 4 (87)

almost ['ɔːlməʊst] fast, beinahe II

alone [ə'ləʊn] allein I

along [ə'lɒŋ]: **along the road** entlang der Straße / die Straße entlang II • **get along** zurechtkommen IV

along with sb./sth. [ə'lɒŋ] neben jm./etwas, (zusammen) mit jm./etwas V

alphabet ['ælfəbet] Alphabet I

already [ɔːl'redi] schon, bereits II

also ['ɔːlsəʊ] auch IV • **not only ... but also ...** nicht nur ... sondern auch ... IV

although [ɔːl'ðəʊ] obwohl III

altogether [,ɔːltə'geðə] insgesamt V

always ['ɔːlweɪz] immer I

am [,eɪ_'em]: **7 am** 7 Uhr morgens/vormittags I

Dictionary

amazement [əˈmeɪzmənt] Erstaunen, Verwunderung VI 3 (54)

amazing [əˈmeɪzɪŋ] erstaunlich, unglaublich II

ambition [æmˈbɪʃn] Ehrgeiz V

ambitious [æmˈbɪʃəs] ehrgeizig V

ambulance [ˈæmbjələns] Krankenwagen III

amendment (to sth.) [əˈmendmənt] (Ab-)Änderung (einer Sache); *(oft* **Amendment***)* Verfassungszusatz *(zur Verfassung der USA)* VI 2 (28)

American football [əˌmerɪkən ˈfʊtbɔːl] Football I

°**amnesiac** [æmˈniːziæk] ein(e) unter Gedächtnisschwund Leidende(r)

among [əˈmʌŋ] unter, zwischen *(mehreren Personen oder Dingen)* IV

amount (of) [əˈmaʊnt] Menge, Betrag VI 3 (56)

an [ən] ein, eine I

analyse [ˈænəlaɪz] analysieren VI 2 (30)

anarchy [ˈænəki] Anarchie V

anatomy [əˈnætəmi] Anatomie VI 3 (52)

ancestor [ˈænsestə] Vorfahr/in IV

ancient [ˈeɪnʃənt] antik; alt V **ancient cities** antike Städte V • **in ancient Rome** im antiken/alten Rom V • **the ancient world** die Antike V

and [ənd, ænd] und I • **and now for** und jetzt … *(kündigt ein neues Thema an)* III • **nice and cool/ clean/…** schön kühl/sauber/… I

angel [ˈeɪndʒl] Engel II

anger [ˈæŋgə] Wut, Ärger, Zorn VI 4 (93)

angle [ˈæŋgl] Winkel; Blickwinkel VI 2 (30)

angry (about sth./with sb.) [ˈæŋgri] wütend, böse (über etwas/auf jn.) II

animal [ˈænɪml] Tier I

anniversary [ˌænɪˈvɜːsəri] Jahrestag IV • **anniversary of sb.'s death** Todestag IV

announce [əˈnaʊns] bekanntgeben III

announcement [əˈnaʊnsmənt] Bekanntgabe, Ankündigung; Durchsage; Ansage III

annoy [əˈnɔɪ] ärgern, verärgern V **be/get annoyed (with sb., about sth.)** sich (über jn./etwas) ärgern V

annoying [əˈnɔɪɪŋ] ärgerlich, lästig V

anorak [ˈænəræk] Anorak, Windjacke III

another [əˈnʌðə] ein(e) andere(r, s); noch ein(e) I • **another 70 metres** weitere 70 Meter, noch 70 Meter II

answer [ˈɑːnsə] (be)antworten I **answer (the phone)** rangehen *(ans Telefon)* IV

answer (to) [ˈɑːnsə] Antwort (auf) I

anti- [ˈænti] anti-, gegen- V **anti-social** asozial, antisozial V

antonym [ˈæntənɪm] Antonym IV

any [ˈeni]: **any …?** (irgend)welche …? I • **not (…) any** kein(e) I **not (…) any more** nicht mehr II **any** irgendeine(r) V

anybody [ˈenibɒdi]: **anybody?** (irgend)jemand? II • **not (…) anybody** niemand II • **anybody** jede(r) (beliebige) V

anymore *(AE)* [ˌeniˈmɔː]: **not (…) anymore** nicht mehr VI 1 (9)

anyone [ˈeniwʌn]: **anyone?** (irgend)jemand? III • **not (…) anyone** niemand III • **anyone** jede(r) (beliebige) V

anything [ˈeniθɪŋ]: **anything?** (irgend)etwas? II • **Did you do anything special?** Habt ihr irgendetwas Besonderes gemacht? I **not (…) anything** nichts II • **anything** alles, egal was V

anyway [ˈeniweɪ] **1.** sowieso I **2. trotzdem** II

Anyway, … [ˈeniweɪ] Aber egal, … / Wie dem auch sei, … V

anywhere [ˈeniweə]: **anywhere?** irgendwo(hin)? II • **not (…) anywhere** nirgendwo(hin) II **anywhere** überall hin V

apart [əˈpɑːt] voneinander getrennt, auseinander IV

apart from [əˈpɑːt] außer V

apartment [əˈpɑːtmənt] Wohnung IV

apologize (to sb. for sth.) [əˈpɒlədʒaɪz] sich (bei jm. für etwas) entschuldigen V

°**appeal to sb./sth.** [əˈpiːl] *(den Verstand, das Gefühl usw.)* ansprechen

appear [əˈpɪə] erscheinen, auftauchen III

°**appearance** [əˈpɪərəns] Aussehen, äußere Erscheinung

appetite [ˈæpɪtaɪt] Appetit III

°**applause** [əˈplɔːz] Beifall

apple [ˈæpl] Apfel I

appliance [əˈplaɪəns] (Haushalts-) Gerät VI 3 (60)

applicant [ˈæplɪkənt] Bewerber/in V

application [ˌæplɪˈkeɪʃn] Bewerbung V • **letter of application** Bewerbungsschreiben V

apply for [əˈplaɪ] sich bewerben (um/für etwas); etwas beantragen IV

appointment [əˈpɔɪntmənt] Termin, Verabredung I

approach [əˈprəʊtʃ] sich nähern VI 4 (99)

appropriate [əˈprəʊpriət] passend, angemessen VI 3 (59) • **as appropriate** wie zutreffend

April [ˈeɪprəl] April I

°**archery** [ˈɑːtʃəri] Bogenschießen

architect [ˈɑːkɪtekt] Architekt/in III

archive [ˈɑːkaɪv] Archiv IV

are [ɑː] bist; sind; seid I • **How are you?** Wie geht es dir/Ihnen/euch? II • **The pencils are 35 p.** Die Bleistifte kosten 35 Pence. I

area [ˈeəriə] Gebiet, Gegend; Bereich III

argue [ˈɑːgjuː] **1.** sich streiten, sich zanken I **1.** argumentieren, behaupten VI 2 (34)

argument [ˈɑːgjumənt] **1.** Streit, Auseinandersetzung II • **have an argument** eine Auseinandersetzung haben, sich streiten II **2.** Argument, Begründung VI 2 (28)

argumentative writing [ˌɑːgjuˈmentətɪv] Erörterung V

arm [ɑːm] Arm I

arm [ɑːm] bewaffnen VI 4 (104) **the armed forces** *(pl)* die Streitkräfte VI 2 (28/207)

armchair [ˈɑːmtʃeə] Sessel I

armoured [ˈɑːməd] gepanzert VI 4 (76)

army [ˈɑːmi] Armee, Heer IV • **join the army** zum Militär gehen VI 2 (32)

around [əˈraʊnd] in … umher, durch, um … (herum) III • **around six** um sechs Uhr herum, gegen sechs III **around the lake** um den See (herum) III • **around the town** in der Stadt umher, durch die Stadt III • **be around** da sein, anwesend sein, in der Nähe sein VI 2 (39) **look around** sich umsehen III **turn around** sich umdrehen IV **walk/run/jump around** herumgehen/-rennen/-springen, umhergehen/-rennen/-springen III

arrange [əˈreɪndʒ] vereinbaren; planen; (an)ordnen VI 1 (15)

arrival [əˈraɪvl] Ankunft III

arrive [əˈraɪv] ankommen, eintreffen II

arrow [ˈærəʊ] Pfeil IV • **bow and arrow** Pfeil und Bogen IV

art [ɑːt] Kunst I • **rock art** *(no pl)* Felsmalerei(en) V

article ['ɑːtɪkl] (Zeitungs-)Artikel I

artificial [ˌɑːtɪ'fɪʃl] künstlich, Kunst- III

artistic [ɑː'tɪstɪk] künstlerisch; künstlerisch begabt V

as [əz, æz]
1. als, während II
2. wie II • **as you know** wie du weißt II
3. as nice/big/exciting as so schön/groß/aufregend wie II **just as … as** ebenso … wie IV **as soon as** sobald, sowie II
4. weil V

as if [əz ˈɪf] als ob IV

ask [ɑːsk] fragen I • **ask about sth.** nach etwas fragen I • **ask questions** Fragen stellen I • **ask sb. for sth.** jn. um etwas bitten II **ask someone out (on a date)** sich mit jm. verabreden; jn. einladen, mit ihr/ihm auszugehen V • **ask sb. the way** jn. nach dem Weg fragen II

asleep [ə'sliːp]: **be asleep** schlafen II • **fall asleep** einschlafen V

assembly [ə'sembli] Versammlung VI 2 (29)

assess [ə'ses] einschätzen, beurteilen V

assessment [ə'sesmənt] Einschätzung, Beurteilung V

assignment [ə'saɪnmənt] Arbeit, Aufgabe, Auftrag VI 2 (36); *(AE)* Hausaufgabe IV

assistant [ə'sɪstənt] Verkäufer/in I

assonance ['æsənəns] Assonanz VI 4 (93/G)

assume [ə'sjuːm] annehmen, ausgehen von VI 2 (38)

at [ət, æt]: **at 7 Hamilton Street** in der Hamiltonstraße 7 I • **at 8.45** um 8.45 I • **at (the age of) 16** mit 16; im Alter von 16 III • **at break** in der Pause *(zwischen Schulstunden)* II • **at home** zu Hause, daheim I • **at first** zuerst, anfangs, am Anfang VI 1 (18) • **at last** endlich, schließlich I • **at least** zumindest, wenigstens I • **at night** nachts, in der Nacht I • **at school** in der Schule I • **at sea** auf See II **at that table** an dem Tisch (dort) / an den Tisch (dort) I • **at the back (of the room)** hinten, im hinteren Teil (des Zimmers) II • **at the bottom (of)** unten, am unteren Ende (von) II • **at the chemist's/ doctor's/hairdresser's** beim Apotheker/Arzt/Friseur III • **at the**

end (of) am Ende (von) I • **at the moment** im Moment, gerade, zurzeit I • **at the Shaws' house** im Haus der Shaws, bei den Shaws zu Hause I • **at the station** am Bahnhof I • **at the top (of)** oben, am oberen Ende, an der Spitze (von) I • **at the weekend** am Wochenende I • **at work** bei der Arbeit / am Arbeitsplatz I

ate [et, eɪt] *siehe* **eat**

atheism ['eɪθiɪzəm] Atheismus V

atheist ['eɪθiɪst] Atheist(in) V

atheistic [ˌeɪθi'ɪstɪk] atheistisch V

athletics [æθ'letɪks] Leichtathletik III

atmosphere ['ætməsfɪə] Atmosphäre; Stimmung V

°**atom** ['ætəm] Atom

attach to [ə'tætʃ] anhängen, anheften (an) *(an Brief, Mail)* V; befestigen VI 3 (56)

attack [ə'tæk] Angriff III • **heart attack** Herzinfarkt IV

attack [ə'tæk] angreifen III

attend sth. [ə'tend] etwas besuchen, an etwas teilnehmen VI 2 (40)

°**attendance record** [ə'tendəns ˌrekɔːd] Anwesenheitsliste

attention [ə'tenʃn] Aufmerksamkeit VI 2 (30) • **attract/catch/grab sb.'s attention** jm. ins Auge fallen; sich (bei jm.) aufmerksam machen VI 2 (30/208) • **come to sb.'s attention** auf etwas aufmerksam werden VI 2 (30/208) • **draw sb.'s attention to sth.** jn. auf etwas aufmerksam machen VI 2 (30/208) • **give attention (to sth./sb.)** jm. zuhören, auf jn. hören/aufpassen VI 2 (30/208) • **pay attention (to sth./sb.)** jm. zuhören, auf jn. hören/aufpassen VI 2 (30/208)

°**attention-deficit disorder** [ə'tenʃn ˌdefɪsɪt dɪsˌɔːdə] Aufmerksamkeitsdefizitsstörung

attitude to/towards ['ætɪtjuːd] Haltung gegenüber, Einstellung zu IV

attorney [ə'tɜːni] (Rechts-)Anwalt, Anwältin VI 4 (88)

attract [ə'trækt] anziehen, anlocken V • **attract sb.'s attention** jm. ins Auge fallen; sich (bei jm.) aufmerksam machen VI 2 (30/208)

attractive [ə'træktɪv] attraktiv, verlockend V

audience ['ɔːdɪəns] Zuschauer/ innen, Zuhörer/innen, Publikum V

°**audiobook** ['ɔːdiəʊbʊk] Hörbuch

August ['ɔːɡəst] August I

aunt [ɑːnt] Tante I • **auntie** ['ɑːnti] Tante II

author ['ɔːθə] Autor/in V

authoritarian [ɔːˌθɒrɪ'teəriən] autoritär VI 2 (30)

auto ['ɔːtəʊ] *(AE)* Auto, PKW IV

autobiography [ˌɔːtəʊbaɪ'ɒɡrəfi] Autobiografie IV

autumn ['ɔːtəm] Herbst I

available [ə'veɪləbl] erhältlich; vorrätig IV

avenue ['ævənjuː] Allee, Boulevard IV

average ['ævərɪdʒ] Durchschnitt; durchschnittlich IV

avoid [ə'vɔɪd] vermeiden V

await [ə'weɪt] *(fml)* erwarten, bevorstehen VI 4 (76)

awake [ə'weɪk]: **be awake** wach sein VI 2 (28)

award [ə'wɔːd] Auszeichnung, Preis V

away [ə'weɪ] weg, fort I • **get away from sth./sb.** von etwas/jm. weggehen, sich entfernen III **put sth. away** wegräumen IV

awesome ['ɔːsəm] *(AE, infml)* klasse, großartig IV

awful ['ɔːfl] furchtbar, schrecklich II

awkward ['ɔːkwəd] peinlich, unbehaglich; unbeholfen; ungünstig VI 4 (78)

awkwardness ['ɔːkwədnəs] Peinlichkeit, Unbehaglichkeit; Unbeholfenheit VI 4 (78)

B

baby ['beɪbi] Baby I • **have a baby** ein Baby/Kind bekommen II

back [bæk]: **at the back (of the room)** hinten, im hinteren Teil (des Zimmers) II • **back home** zurück zu Hause IV • °**back and forth** hin und her

back sth./sb. [bæk] etwas/jn. unterstützen VI 2 (34)

back door [ˌbæk 'dɔː] Hintertür II

background ['bækɡraʊnd] Hintergrund II • **background file** *etwa:* Hintergrundinformation II

°**backstage** [ˌbæk'steɪdʒ] hinter der Bühne

backwards, backward *(bes. AE)* ['bækwədz, 'bækwəd] rückwärts VI 2 (28)

bacon ['beɪkən] Schinkenspeck II

bacteria *(pl)* [bæk'tɪəriə] Bakterien IV

Dictionary

bad [bæd] schlecht, schlimm I
bad timing schlechtes Timing, schlechte Wahl des Zeitpunkts III
badge [bædʒ] Abzeichen, Button V
badminton ['bædmɪntən] Badminton, Federball I • **badminton racket** Federballschläger III
bag [bæg] Tasche, Beutel, Tüte I; Handtasche III
bagel ['beɪgl] Bagel *(ringförmiges Brötchen)* IV
°**baggy** ['bægi] weit
balcony ['bælkəni] Balkon V
ball [bɔːl]
  1. Ball *(zum Sport)* I
  2. Ball *(Tanz)* II
  °**3.** Klumpen
balloon [bə'luːn] Heißluftballon; Luftballon II
ban (-nn-) [bæn] sperren; ein (Aufenthalts-)Verbot erteilen V
banana [bə'nɑːnə] Banane I
band [bænd] Band, (Musik-)Gruppe I
banjo ['bændʒəʊ] Banjo III
bank [bæŋk] Bank, Sparkasse I
  bank robber ['bæŋk ˌrɒbə] Bankräuber/in I
bar [bɑː] Bar II
bar chart ['bɑː tʃɑːt] Balkendiagramm V
barbecue ['bɑːbɪkjuː] Grillfest, Grillparty V
bark [bɑːk] bellen II
°**base** [beɪs] Station, Basis
baseball ['beɪsbɔːl] Baseball I
  baseball cap Baseballmütze II
based [beɪst]: **be based on sth.** auf etwas basieren VI 3 (54)
basic ['beɪsɪk] grundlegend, Grund-; einfach, elementar V
  Basic Law Grundgesetz *(der Bundesrepublik)* V
basically ['beɪsɪkli] im Grunde, im Prinzip VI 3 (61)
basket ['bɑːskɪt] Korb I • **a basket of apples** ein Korb Äpfel I
basketball ['bɑːskɪtbɔːl] Basketball I
bass [beɪs] Kontrabass; Bassgitarre III • **bass guitar** Bassgitarre III **double bass** Kontrabass III
bat [bæt]: **table tennis bat** Tischtennisschläger III
bath [bɑːθ] Bad, Badewanne II
  have a bath baden, ein Bad nehmen II
bathe [beɪð] *(AE)* baden *(sich waschen)* V
bathroom ['bɑːθruːm; 'bɑːθrʊm] Badezimmer I
°**baton** ['bætɒn] Schlagstock

°**battery** ['bætri] Batterie, Akku
°**bay** [beɪ] Bucht III
BC [ˌbiː 'siː] v. Chr. IV
be [biː], **was/were, been** sein I
  be into sth. *(infml)* etwas mögen III • **be a farmer, a teacher, ...** Bauer/Bäuerin, Lehrer/in, ... werden IV
beach [biːtʃ] Strand II • **on the beach** [biːtʃ] am Strand II
bean [biːn] Bohne IV
bear [beə] Bär II • **teddy bear** Teddybär III
beat [biːt], **beat, beaten** schlagen; besiegen III • **beat sb. up** jn. zusammenschlagen VI 2 (38)
beaten ['biːtn] *siehe* **beat**
beautiful ['bjuːtɪfl] schön I
beauty ['bjuːti] Schönheit III
became [bɪ'keɪm] *siehe* **become**
because [bɪ'kɒz] weil I
because of [bɪ'kɒz ˌəv] wegen IV
become [bɪ'kʌm], **became, become** werden II
bed [bed] Bett I • **Bed and Breakfast (B&B)** [ˌbed ˌən 'brekfəst] Frühstückspension I • **double bed** Doppelbett V • **go to bed** ins Bett gehen I • **put sb. to bed** jn. ins Bett bringen III • **single bed** Einzelbett V
bedroom ['bedruːm; 'bedrʊm] Schlafzimmer I
beef [biːf] Rindfleisch V
been [biːn] *siehe* **be**
before [bɪ'fɔː] vor *(zeitlich)* I • **the day before yesterday** vorgestern II
before [bɪ'fɔː] bevor II
before [bɪ'fɔː] (vorher) schon mal II
beg [beg] betteln V
began [bɪ'gæn] *siehe* **begin**
beggar ['begə] Bettler/in V
begin (-nn-) [bɪ'gɪn], **began, begun** beginnen, anfangen (mit) I
beginner [bɪ'gɪnə] Anfänger/in V
beginning [bɪ'gɪnɪŋ] Anfang, Beginn III
begun [bɪ'gʌn] *siehe* **begin**
behave [bɪ'heɪv] sich verhalten, sich benehmen V
behaviour [bɪ'heɪvjə] Verhalten, Benehmen V
behind [bɪ'haɪnd] hinter I • **leave behind** zurücklassen IV
believe [bɪ'liːv] glauben III
  believe in sth./sb. an etwas/jn. glauben IV/VI 1 (12) • **She couldn't believe her eyes.** Sie traute ihren Augen kaum. III
bell [bel] Klingel, Glocke I
belly ['beli] Bauch VI 2 (27)

belong (to) [bɪ'lɒŋ] gehören (zu) II
below [bɪ'ləʊ] unter, unterhalb (von) III
bend [bend], **bent, bent** sich beugen VI 1 (21)
beneath [bɪ'niːθ] *(fml)* unter VI 4 (92)
°**benefit** ['benɪfɪt] Vorteil, Nutzen
bent [bent] *siehe* **bend**
beside [bɪ'saɪd] neben V
besides [bɪ'saɪdz] außerdem IV
besides [bɪ'saɪdz] außer V
best [best] am besten II • **All the best** Viele Grüße IV • **Best wishes** Viele Grüße IV • **the best** ... der/die/das beste ...; die besten ... I **What was the best thing about ...?** Was war das Beste an ...? II
bet (-tt-) [bet], **bet, bet** wetten III **You bet!** *(infml)* Aber klar! / Und ob! IV
betray sb./sth. [bɪ'treɪ] jn./etwas verraten VI 1 (9) • **betray a trust** etwas Vertrauliches ausplaudern VI 1 (9/198)
better ['betə] besser I • **like sth. better** etwas lieber mögen II **You'd better ... (= You had better ...)** Du solltest lieber ... VI 1 (8)
between [bɪ'twiːn] zwischen II
beyond [bɪ'jɒnd] jenseits (von), über ... hinaus/hinweg VI 4 (76)
Bible ['baɪbl] Bibel IV
big [bɪg] groß I • **big wheel** Riesenrad III
bike [baɪk] Fahrrad I • **bike tour** Radtour II • **ride a bike** Rad fahren I
bilingual [ˌbaɪ'lɪŋgwəl] zweisprachig IV
bill [bɪl] *(AE)* (Geld-)Schein, Banknote V
°**Bill of Rights** [bɪl] Zusatzartikel 1-10 zu den Grundrechten der USA
°**billboard** *(especially AE)* ['bɪlbɔːd] Reklametafel
billion ['bɪliən] Milliarde V
bin [bɪn] Mülltonne II
binoculars *(pl)* [bɪ'nɒkjuləz] Fernglas IV
biography [baɪ'ɒgrəfi] Biografie III
biological [ˌbaɪə'lɒdʒɪkl] biologisch IV
biology [baɪ'ɒlədʒi] Biologie I
bird [bɜːd] Vogel I
birth [bɜːθ] Geburt IV • **birth rate** Geburtsrate V • **date of birth** Geburtsdatum IV
birthday ['bɜːθdeɪ] Geburtstag I **Happy birthday.** Herzlichen Glückwunsch zum Geburtstag. I • **My birthday is in May.** Ich habe im

Mai Geburtstag. I • **My birthday is on 13th June.** Ich habe am 13. Juni Geburtstag. I • **When's your birthday?** Wann hast du Geburtstag? I • **for his birthday** zu seinem Geburtstag III

biscuit ['bɪskɪt] Keks, Plätzchen I

bit [bɪt]: **a bit** ein bisschen, etwas II

°**bitch** (infml, rude) [bɪtʃ] Schlampe

black [blæk] schwarz I

blame sb. (for) [bleɪm] jm. die Schuld geben (an); jm. Vorwürfe machen (wegen) III

blanket ['blæŋkɪt] Decke (zum Zudecken) V

bled [bled] siehe **bleed**

bleed [bli:d], **bled, bled** bluten IV

bleep [bli:p] piepsen II

bleep [bli:p] Piepton II

°**bless** [bles] segnen

blessing ['blesɪŋ] Segen IV

blew [blu:] siehe **blow**

blind [blaɪnd] blind III

°**blink** [blɪŋk] blinzeln

blizzard ['blɪzəd] Schneesturm VI 3 (62)

block [blɒk] blockieren, (ver)sperren IV

block [blɒk] (Häuser-, Wohn-)Block IV

blog [blɒg] Blog (Weblog, digitales Tagebuch) IV

bloke [bləʊk] (infml, BE) Kerl, Typ VI 4 (94)

blond (bei Frauen oft: **blonde**) [blɒnd] blond IV

blood [blʌd] Blut III

blouse [blaʊz] Bluse II

blow [bləʊ], **blew, blown** pusten, blasen; wehen III

blown [bləʊn] siehe **blow**

blue [blu:] blau I

blues [blu:z] Blues III

°**blurb** [blɜ:b] Klappentext, kurzer Werbetext

board [bɔ:d] (Wand-)Tafel I • **on the board** an der/die Tafel I

board (sth.) [bɔ:d] (in etwas) einsteigen, an Bord (von etwas) gehen VI 2 (38)

boarding school ['bɔ:dɪŋ ˌsku:l] Internat VI 4 (77)

boat [bəʊt] Boot, Schiff I

body ['bɒdi] Körper I

bodyguard ['bɒdigɑ:d] Bodyguard, Leibwächter/in, Leibwache IV

boil [bɔɪl] kochen (Flüssigkeit, Speise) IV

bold (type) [ˌbəʊld 'taɪp] Fettdruck V

bomb [bɒm] Bombe IV

bone [bəʊn] Knochen IV

book [bʊk] Buch I • °**book slam** etwa: Bücher-Wettstreit

booklet ['bʊklət] Broschüre II

boot [bu:t] Stiefel I

boot camp ['bu:t kæmp] Erziehungslager (für junge Straftäter/innen) V

border ['bɔ:də] Grenze IV

bored [bɔ:d]: **get bored** sich langweilen; gelangweilt sein IV

boring ['bɔ:rɪŋ] langweilig I

born [bɔ:n]: **be born** geboren sein/werden II

borough ['bʌrə, AE: 'bɜ:rəʊ] (Stadt-)Bezirk III

borrow sth. ['bɒrəʊ] sich etwas (aus)leihen, etwas entleihen II

boss [bɒs] Boss, Chef/in I

both [bəʊθ] beide I

bother sb. ['bɒðə] jn. stören; jn. belästigen VI 4 (82)

bottle ['bɒtl] Flasche I • **a bottle of milk** eine Flasche Milch I **bottle cap** (Flaschen-)Deckel V

bottom ['bɒtəm] unteres Ende II **at the bottom (of)** unten, am unteren Ende (von) II

bought [bɔ:t] siehe **buy**

bow [bəʊ] Bogen (Waffe und zum Musizieren) IV • **bow and arrow** Pfeil und Bogen IV

bowl [bəʊl] Schüssel I • **a bowl of cornflakes** eine Schale Cornflakes I

box [bɒks] Kasten, Kästchen, Kiste I

box office ['bɒks ˌɒfɪs] (Theater-, Kino-)Kasse III

boy [bɔɪ] Junge I • **boy!** (AE, infml) Mann! Mensch! III

boycott ['bɔɪkɒt] Boykott IV

boyfriend ['bɔɪfrend] (fester) Freund VI 1 (7)

bracket ['brækɪt] Klammer (in Texten) IV • **round brackets** runde Klammern IV • **square brackets** eckige Klammern IV

brain [breɪn] Gehirn VI 1 (20)

brains (pl) [breɪnz] Verstand, Intelligenz VI 1 (20)

brainstorm ['breɪnstɔ:m] brainstormen (so viele Ideen wie möglich sammeln) III

°**branch** [brɑ:ntʃ] Ast, Zweig

brave [breɪv] tapfer, mutig IV

bread (no pl) [bred] Brot I

break [breɪk], **broke, broken** (zer)brechen; kaputt machen; kaputt gehen II • **break a rule/order** gegen eine Regel/Anordnung verstoßen IV • **break out** ausbrechen VI 3 (66) • **break sth.**

open etwas aufbrechen IV **break up (with sb.)** Schluss machen (mit jm.), sich trennen (von jm.) VI 1 (11)

break [breɪk] Pause I • **at break** in der Pause (zwischen Schulstunden) II • **take a break** eine Pause machen IV

break down [ˌbreɪk 'daʊn] **1.** eine Panne haben V **2.** zusammenbrechen V

breakfast ['brekfəst] Frühstück I **have breakfast** frühstücken I

°**break-up** ['breɪkʌp] Auflösung, Trennung

breathe [bri:ð] atmen IV

bridge [brɪdʒ] Brücke I

bridle path ['braɪdl ˌpɑ:θ] Reitweg III

brief [bri:f] kurz (gefasst), knapp, von kurzer Dauer V • **be brief** sich kurz fassen V

bright [braɪt] hell, leuchtend II; klug, intelligent, „hell" VI 1 (21)

bring [brɪŋ], **brought, brought** (mit-, her)bringen I

British ['brɪtɪʃ] britisch II

broadcast ['brɔ:dkɑ:st], **broadcast broadcast** senden; (eine Sendung) ausstrahlen IV

broke [brəʊk] siehe **break**

broken ['brəʊkən] siehe **break**

broken ['brəʊkən] gebrochen; zerbrochen, kaputt II

brother ['brʌðə] Bruder I

brotherhood ['brʌðəhʊd] Brüderlichkeit VI 2 (26)

brought [brɔ:t] siehe **bring**

brown [braʊn] braun I

brush [brʌʃ] bürsten; fegen; putzen VI 4 (91)

brush [brʌʃ] Pinsel VI 4 (98)

°**BST** = British Summer Time (Britische oder Westeuropäische Sommerzeit)

bubble ['bʌbl] (Luft-)Blase VI 2 (28) **speech bubble** Sprechblase VI 2 (28/206) • **thought bubble** Denkblase VI 2 (28/206)

bucket ['bʌkɪt] Eimer V

Buddhism ['bʊdɪzm] Buddhismus V

Buddhist ['bʊdɪst] Buddhist/in, buddhistisch V

budgie ['bʌdʒi] Wellensittich I

°**bug** [bʌg] (Programm)fehler

build [bɪld], **built, built** bauen II **the ship was built in Bristol** das Schiff wurde in Bristol gebaut II

builder ['bɪldə] Bauarbeiter/in V

building ['bɪldɪŋ] Gebäude II

built [bɪlt] siehe **build**

bulb [bʌlb]: **light bulb** Glühlampe VI 3 (53)

bulletin board ['bʊlətɪn bɔːd] schwarzes Brett, Anschlagtafel IV

bully ['bʊli] einschüchtern, tyrannisieren II

bully ['bʊli] (Schul-)Tyrann III

bummer ['bʌmə]: **What a bummer!** (infml) So ein Mist! Wie schade! III

bump into sb./sth. [bʌmp] sich an etwas stoßen; gegen jn. stoßen V

bunk (bed) [bʌŋk] Etagenbett, Koje II

burn [bɜːn] brennen; verbrennen IV

bury ['beri] begraben, vergraben; beerdigen IV

bus [bʌs] Bus I

bush [bʊʃ] Busch, Strauch V • **the bush** der Busch (unkultiviertes, „wildes" Land in Australien, Afrika) V

bus pass ['bʌs pɑːs] Bus-Monatskarte III

bus stop ['bʌs stɒp] Bushaltestelle III

business ['bɪznəs] Unternehmen; Geschäfte V • **business people** (pl) Geschäftsleute V • **do business (with)** Geschäfte machen (mit); Handel treiben (mit) V • **do one's business** (dog or baby) sein Geschäft machen/verrichten VI 2 (41) **Mind your own business.** Das geht dich nichts an! / Kümmere dich um deine eigenen Angelegenheiten! II **start a business** ein Unternehmen gründen V

busy ['bɪzi]
1. beschäftigt I
2. belebt, verkehrsreich; hektisch III

but [bət, bʌt]
1. aber I
2. sondern IV • **not only ... but also ...** nicht nur ... sondern auch ... IV

°**butt** [bʌt] (infml) Hinterteil V

butter ['bʌtə] Butter IV

butterfly ['bʌtəflaɪ] Schmetterling VI 4 (98)

button ['bʌtn] Knopf III

buy [baɪ], **bought, bought** kaufen I

by [baɪ]
1. von I
2. an; (nahe) bei II
3. by two degrees/ten per cent um zwei Grad/zehn Prozent V **by asking** indem du fragst V • **by car/bike/...** mit dem Auto/Rad/... II • **by day and by night** bei Tag und bei Nacht V • **by far** bei weitem; mit Abstand V • **by no means**

keineswegs VI 3 (55) • **by the end of the song** (spätestens) bis zum Ende des Lieds III • **by the way** übrigens; nebenbei (bemerkt) III

Bye. [baɪ] Tschüs! I

°**byline** ['baɪlaɪn] Zeile mit Angabe des Verfassers eines Zeitungsartikels

bystander ['baɪstændə] (gleichgültige(r)) Zuschauer/in, „Dabeistehende(r)" VI 2 (38)

C

cabin ['kæbɪn] Hütte III

café ['kæfeɪ] (kleines) Restaurant, Imbissstube, Café I

cafeteria [ˌkæfəˈtɪəriə] Cafeteria, Selbstbedienungsrestaurant II

cage [keɪdʒ] Käfig III

cake [keɪk] Kuchen, Torte I

calculate ['kælkjuleɪt] berechnen, ausrechnen VI 3 (66)

°**calculator** ['kælkjuleɪtə] Taschenrechner

calendar ['kælɪndə] Kalender I

call [kɔːl] rufen; anrufen; nennen I **be called** heißen, genannt werden II • **call for help** um Hilfe rufen V **call sb. names** jn. mit Schimpfwörtern hänseln, jm. Schimpfwörter nachrufen III

call [kɔːl]
1. Ruf, Schrei; Anruf II
give sb. a call jn. anrufen V
make a call ein Telefongespräch führen, telefonieren II
°**2.** Aufruf

calm [kɑːm] ruhig, still V • **keep calm** ruhig/still bleiben; Ruhe bewahren V

calm down [ˌkɑːm ˈdaʊn] sich beruhigen II • **calm sb. down** jn. beruhigen II

came [keɪm] siehe **come**

camel ['kæml] Kamel II

camera ['kæmərə] Kamera, Fotoapparat I

camp [kæmp] zelten III

camp [kæmp] Camp, Lager IV

campaign [kæm'peɪn] Kampagne V

campground ['kæmpˌɡraʊnd] (AE) Zeltplatz III

camping gear ['kæmpɪŋ ˌɡɪə] Campingausrüstung IV

campsite ['kæmpsaɪt] Zeltplatz III

can [kæn] Dose V

can [kən, kæn]
1. können I
2. dürfen I
Can I help you? Kann ich Ihnen

helfen? / Was kann ich für Sie tun? (im Geschäft) I

canal [kə'næl] Kanal III

cancel ['kænsəl] absagen V; streichen VI 1 (13)

cancer ['kænsə] Krebs (Krankheit) V

candidate ['kændɪdət] Kandidat/in; Bewerber/in V

candle ['kændl] Kerze IV

cannot [kæ'nɒt] kann nicht IV

canoe [kə'nuː] Kanu III

canoe [kə'nuː] paddeln, Kanu fahren III

canyon ['kænjən] Cañon IV

cap [kæp] Mütze, Kappe II

capital ['kæpɪtl] Hauptstadt III

capital letter [ˌkæpɪtl 'letə] Großbuchstabe III

captain ['kæptɪn] Kapitän/in III

caption ['kæpʃn] Bildunterschrift IV

captivate ['kæptɪveɪt] (fml) fesseln, faszinieren VI 3 (54)

capture ['kæptʃə] (ein)fangen VI 3 (58)

car [kɑː] Auto I

caravan ['kærəvæn] Wohnwagen II

carbon ['kɑːbən] Kohlenstoff; (oft auch kurz für:) Kohlendioxid VI 3 (58/219) • **carbon dioxide (CO$_2$)** Kohlendioxid (CO$_2$) VI 3 (58) **carbon footprint** „CO$_2$-Fußabdruck", CO$_2$-Bilanz VI 3 (58/219)

card [kɑːd] (Spiel-, Post-)Karte I **swipe a card** eine Karte durchziehen VI 3 (61)

care (about) [keə] sich interessieren (für); sich kümmern (um); wichtig nehmen III • **I care about the environment.** Die Umwelt liegt mir am Herzen. III • **I don't care about money.** Geld ist mir egal. III • **Who cares?** Ist doch egal! / Na und? III

care [keə]: **take care of sth.** sich um etwas kümmern III

career [kə'rɪə] Karriere III

careful ['keəfl] vorsichtig I

caretaker ['keəteɪkə] Hausmeister/in II

carpet ['kɑːpɪt] Teppich VI 4 (79)

car park ['kɑː pɑːk] Parkplatz III

carrot ['kærət] Möhre, Karotte I

carry ['kæri] tragen V

cart [kɑːt] Wagen, Karren IV

cartoon [kɑː'tuːn] Cartoon (Zeichentrickfilm; Bilderwitz) II

case [keɪs] Fall II

casino [kə'siːnəʊ] (Spiel)kasino IV

°**casting** ['kɑːstɪŋ] Auswahlverfahren in der Vorproduktion von Inszenierungen

castle [ˈkɑːsl] Burg, Schloss II
cat [kæt] Katze I
°**catastrophic** [ˌkætəˈstrɒfɪk] katastrophal, verhängnisvoll
catch [kætʃ], **caught, caught** fangen; erwischen II • **be catching** ansteckend sein V • **catch sb.'s attention** jm. ins Auge fallen; sich (bei jm.) aufmerksam machen VI 2 (30/208)
catch on (to sth.) [ˌkætʃˈɒn] (etwas) kapieren, begreifen VI 1 (21)
cathedral [kəˈθiːdrəl] Kathedrale, Dom III
cattle (pl) [ˈkætl] Vieh, Rinder IV
caught [kɔːt] siehe **catch**
cause [kɔːz] verursachen IV
cause [kɔːz] Ursache IV
cave [keɪv] Höhle V
CD [ˌsiːˈdiː] CD I • **CD player** CD-Spieler I
cease [siːs] (fml) aufhören VI 4 (94)
ceilidh [ˈkeɪli] Musik- und Tanzveranstaltung, vor allem in Schottland und Irland III
ceiling [ˈsiːlɪŋ] (Zimmer-) Decke V
celebrate [ˈselɪbreɪt] feiern IV
celebration [ˌseləˈbreɪʃn] Feier IV
celebrity [səˈlebrəti] berühmte Persönlichkeit, Prominente(r) III
cell [sel] Zelle V
cello [ˈtʃeləʊ] Cello III
cellphone [ˈselfəʊn] (kurz auch: **cell**) (AE) Mobiltelefon, Handy III
censorship [ˈsensəʃɪp] Zensur VI 2 (32)
cent (c) [sent] Cent I
cent: per cent [pəˈsent] Prozent III
centimetre (cm) [ˈsentɪmiːtə] Zentimeter III
central [ˈsentrəl] Zentral-, Mittel- III
centre [ˈsentə] Zentrum, Mitte I
century [ˈsentʃəri] Jahrhundert II
certain [ˈsɜːtn] sicher; gewiss, bestimmt VI 1 (18) • **certainly** sicher(lich), bestimmt, auf jeden Fall VI 1 (18)
   ▶ S.210 certainly – surely
certificate [səˈtɪfɪkət] Urkunde, Zeugnis, Bescheinigung V
°**chain** [tʃeɪn] Kette
chair [tʃeə] Stuhl I
challenge sb./sth. [ˈtʃælɪndʒ] jn. herausfordern (zu etwas) VI 2 (28)
champion [ˈtʃæmpiən] Meister/in, Champion I
championship [ˈtʃæmpiənʃɪp] Meisterschaft III
chance [tʃɑːns] Chance II
change [tʃeɪndʒ]
   1. Wechselgeld I

2. (Ver-)Änderung, Wechsel IV
   climate change Klimaveränderung, -wandel VI 3 (53)
change [tʃeɪndʒ]
   1. umsteigen III
   2. (sich) (ver-)ändern IV
   3. wechseln IV
   4. umtauschen IV
   5. umwandeln IV
   6. change stations (Radio) umschalten IV
   7. sich umziehen IV
chapel [ˈtʃæpl] Kapelle, Kirche (für manche protestantische Gemeinden) V
°**chapter** [ˈtʃæptə] Kapitel
character [ˈkærəktə] Charakter, Persönlichkeit IV
characteristic [ˌkærəktəˈrɪstɪk] (charakteristisches) Merkmal IV
characterization [ˌkærəktəraɪˈzeɪʃn] Charakterisierung VI 2 (29/G)
charge (at sb.) [tʃɑːdʒ] stürmen; (jn.) angreifen IV
charge [tʃɑːdʒ]: **be in charge of sth./ sb.** für etwas/jn. verantwortlich sein; etwas leiten V
charged [tʃɑːdʒd]: **guilty as charged** schuldbewusst; schuldig VI 1 (10)
charity [ˈtʃærəti] Wohlfahrtsorganisation II
chart [tʃɑːt] Diagramm I
chase sb. [tʃeɪs] jn. jagen; jm. hinterherjagen IV
chat (-tt-) [tʃæt] chatten, plaudern II
chat [tʃæt] Chat, Unterhaltung II
chat room [ˈtʃæt ruːm] Chatroom III
chat show Talkshow II
cheap [tʃiːp] billig, preiswert II
cheat [tʃiːt]: **cheat sb.** jn. betrügen V • **cheat on sb.** jn. betrügen, jm. untreu sein V
check [tʃek] (über)prüfen, kontrollieren I
checklist [ˈtʃeklɪst] Checkliste III
check out (of a hotel) [ˌtʃekˈaʊt] (aus einem Hotel) auschecken, abreisen V
checkpoint [ˈtʃekpɔɪnt] Kontrollpunkt (zur Selbstüberprüfung) I
cheer [tʃɪə] jubeln II
cheerful [ˈtʃɪəfl] heiter, fröhlich VI 4 (103)
cheerleader [ˈtʃɪəliːdə] Cheerleader (Stimmungsanheizer/in bei Sportereignissen) IV
cheese [tʃiːz] Käse I
chemist [ˈkemɪst] Drogerie, Apotheke II • **at the chemist's** beim Apotheker III
chew [tʃuː] kauen V • **chew gum** Kaugummi kauen V

chewing gum [gʌm] Kaugummi V
°**Chichewa** [tʃɪˈtʃeɪwə] eine der Amtssprachen in Malawi
chicken [ˈtʃɪkɪn] Huhn; (Brat-)Hähnchen I
chief [tʃiːf] Häuptling IV
child [tʃaɪld], pl **children** [ˈtʃɪldrən] Kind I • **children's home** Kinderheim V • °**child soldier** Kindersoldat/in
childhood [ˈtʃaɪldhʊd] Kindheit V
childproof [ˈtʃaɪldpruːf] kindersicher V
chill [tʃɪl] Kühle, Kälte VI 3 (62)
chill out [ˌtʃɪlˈaʊt] (infml) sich entspannen, relaxen III
Chinese [tʃaɪˈniːz] chinesisch IV
chips (pl) [tʃɪps]
   1. (BE) Pommes frites I
   2. (AE) Chips IV
chocolate [ˈtʃɒklət] Schokolade I
°**choice** [tʃɔɪs] Wahl, Auswahl
choir [ˈkwaɪə] Chor I
choose [tʃuːz], **chose, chosen** (sich) aussuchen, (aus)wählen I
chore [tʃɔː] (Haus-)Arbeit; (lästige) Pflicht VI 1 (14)
chorus [ˈkɔːrəs] Refrain VI 4 (93/G)
chose [tʃəʊz] siehe **choose**
chosen [ˈtʃəʊzn] siehe **choose**
Christ [kraɪst] Christus IV
Christian [ˈkrɪstʃən] Christ/in, christlich V
Christianity [ˌkrɪstiˈænəti] Christentum V
Christmas [ˈkrɪsməs] Weihnachten V • **at Christmas** an/zu Weihnachten V • **Christmas tree** Christ-, Weihnachtsbaum V • **for Christmas** zu Weihnachten V
chuck sb. [tʃʌk] (infml) mit jm. Schluss machen V
chum (infml) [tʃʌm] Kumpel VI 4 (88)
church [tʃɜːtʃ] Kirche I • **go to church** in die Kirche gehen III
cigarette [ˌsɪgəˈret] Zigarette VI 1 (18)
cinema [ˈsɪnəmə] Kino II • **go to the cinema** ins Kino gehen II
°**cinquain** [sɪŋˈkeɪn] Cinquain (fünfzeiliges Gedicht)
circle [ˈsɜːkl] Kreis III
circumstances (pl) [ˈsɜːkəmstənsɪz]: **under no circumstances** unter keinen Umständen (194/Grammar File)
circus [ˈsɜːkəs] (runder) Platz III
citizen [ˈsɪtɪzən] (Staats)Bürger/in VI 2 (28)
citizenship [ˈsɪtɪzənʃɪp] Staatsangehörigkeit, Staatsbürgerschaft (auch als Schulfach Sozialkunde/Politik) VI 2 (28)

Dictionary

city ['sɪti] Stadt, Großstadt I
city centre [ˌsɪti 'sentə] Stadtzentrum, Innenstadt I
civilization [ˌsɪvəlaɪ'zeɪʃn] Zivilisation V
civil rights *(pl)* [ˌsɪvl 'raɪts] Bürgerrechte IV
civil war [ˌsɪvl 'wɔː] Bürgerkrieg IV
claim [kleɪm] behaupten VI 2 (34)
clap (-pp-) [klæp] (Beifall) klatschen IV
clarification [ˌklærəfɪ'keɪʃn] Klarstellung, Klärung V
clarinet [ˌklærɪ'net] Klarinette III
class [klɑːs]
1. (Schul-)Klasse I • **class teacher** Klassenlehrer/in I
2. Unterricht; Kurs IV
classic [klæsɪk] klassisch III
classic ['klæsɪk] Klassiker VI 4 (87)
classical ['klæsɪkl] klassisch III
classmate ['klɑːsmeɪt] Klassenkamerad/in, Mitschüler/in I
classroom ['klɑːsruːm; 'klɑːsrʊm] Klassenzimmer I
clause [klɔːz] (Teil-, Glied-)Satz III
clean [kliːn] sauber II
clean [kliːn] sauber machen, putzen I • **clean one's teeth** sich die Zähne putzen III • °**clean sth. up** etwas sauber machen, etwas säubern
cleaner ['kliːnə] Putzfrau, -mann II
clear [klɪə] klar, deutlich I
clever ['klevə] klug, schlau I
cleverness ['klevənəs] Klugheit, Schlauheit IV
click *(infml)* [klɪk] sich auf Anhieb gut verstehen VI 1 (9)
click on sth. [klɪk] etwas anklicken II
cliff [klɪf] Klippe III
climate ['klaɪmət] Klima V
climate change Klimaveränderung, -wandel VI 3 (53)
climax ['klaɪmæks] Höhepunkt V
climb [klaɪm] klettern; hinaufklettern (auf) I • **Climb a tree.** Klettere auf einen Baum. I
clingy *(infml)* ['klɪŋi] anhänglich, klammernd VI 1 (9)
clinic ['klɪnɪk] Klinik II
clock [klɒk] (Wand-, Stand-, Turm-) Uhr I
°**clockwise** ['klɒkwaɪz] im Uhrzeigersinn
°**clone** [kləʊn] Klon, Kopie
close (to) [kləʊs]
1. nahe (bei, an) III
2. eng V
That was close. Das war knapp. II

close [kləʊz] schließen, zumachen I
closed [kləʊzd] geschlossen II
closely ['kləʊsli] **look closely at sth.** etw. genau anschauen III
°**close-up** ['kləʊs_ʌp] Closeup (Großaufnahme als Einstellungsgröße bei Filmaufnahmen)
clothes *(pl)* [kləʊðz, kləʊz] Kleider, Kleidungsstücke I
clothing ['kləʊðɪŋ] Kleidung IV
piece of clothing Kleidungsstück IV
cloud [klaʊd] Wolke II
cloudy ['klaʊdi] bewölkt II
clown [klaʊn] Clown/in I
club [klʌb] Klub; Verein I
°**co-** [kəʊ] Mit-, Ko-
°**CO** [ˌsiː_'əʊ] *(falsche) Abkürzung für Kohlendioxid*
CO_2 [ˌsiː_əʊ'tuː] CO_2 VI 3 (58)
coach [kəʊtʃ] Trainer/in III • **life coach** Lebensberater/in V
coal [kəʊl] Kohle VI 3 (61/220)
coast [kəʊst] Küste II
°**coastal** ['kəʊstl] Küsten-
coat [kəʊt] Mantel VI 4 (91)
coconut ['kəʊkənʌt] Kokosnuss V
coffee ['kɒfi] Kaffee IV • **coffee to go** Kaffee zum Mitnehmen IV
°**coffee house** Café, Kaffeehaus
coin [kɔɪn] Münze V
cola ['kəʊlə] Cola I
cold [kəʊld] kalt I • **be cold** frieren I • **freezing cold** eisig; eiskalt VI 3 (61/220) • °**leave sb. cold** jn. kaltlassen
cold [kəʊld] Erkältung II • **have a cold** erkältet sein, eine Erkältung haben II
collapse [kə'læps] zusammenbrechen; einstürzen IV
collect [kə'lekt] sammeln I
collection [kə'lekʃn] Sammlung IV
collector [kə'lektə] Sammler/in II
college ['kɒlɪdʒ] Hochschule, Fachschule III
collocation [ˌkɒlə'keɪʃn] Kollokation (Wörter, die oft zusammen vorkommen) IV
colonist ['kɒlənɪst] Kolonist/in; Siedler/in IV
colony ['kɒləni] Kolonie IV
colour ['kʌlə] Farbe I • **What colour is ...?** Welche Farbe hat ...? I
colourful ['kʌləfl] bunt IV
column ['kɒləm]
1. Säule III
2. Spalte V
°**combination** [ˌkɒmbɪ'neɪʃn] Kombination

come [kʌm], **came, come** kommen I • °**come alive** lebendig werden
come from stammen von/aus IV
come home nach Hause kommen I • **come in** hereinkommen I
Come on. 1. Na los, komm. II; **2.** Ach komm! / Na hör mal! II
come together zusammenkommen IV • **come true** wahr werden II • °**come up** auftauchen
come up with sth. sich etwas ausdenken, sich etwas einfallen lassen IV
comedy ['kɒmədi] Comedyshow, Komödie II
comfort ['kʌmfət] trösten IV
comfortable ['kʌmftəbl] bequem I
comic ['kɒmɪk] Comic-Heft I
comment ['kɒment] Kommentar IV
comment (on sth.) ['kɒment] sich äußern (über/zu etwas); einen Kommentar abgeben (zu etwas) VI 4 (90)
°**commission** [kə'mɪʃn] Kommission
commit (-tt-) [kə'mɪt]: **commit a crime** ein Verbrechen begehen IV
committee [kə'mɪti] Ausschuss, Komitee V
common ['kɒmn]
1. weit verbreitet, häufig V
2. gemeinsam VI 3 (52)
Commonwealth ['kɒmənwelθ]: **the Commonwealth** *Gemeinschaft der Länder des ehemaligen Britischen Weltreichs* III
communicate (with sb.) [kə'mjuːnɪ'keɪt] (mit jm.) kommunizieren, sich (mit jm.) verständigen VI 2 (31)
communication [kəˌmjuːnɪ'keɪʃn] Kommunikation VI 2 (31)
community [kə'mjuːnəti] Gemeinschaft, Gemeinde V • **community hall** Gemeinschaftshalle, -saal / Gemeindehalle, -saal III
community service gemeinnützige Arbeit V
commuter [kə'mjuːtə] Pendler/in V
company ['kʌmpəni] Firma, Gesellschaft III
compare [kəm'peə] vergleichen II
comparison [kəm'pærɪsn] Steigerung; Vergleich II
competition [ˌkɒmpə'tɪʃn] Wettbewerb III
complain (to sb. about sb./sth.) [kəm'pleɪn] sich beklagen/beschweren (bei jm. über etwas/jn.) VI 2 (28)
complete [kəm'pliːt]
1. komplett, vollständig V
°**2.** abgeschlossen

complete [kəmˈpliːt] vervollständigen; abschließen, beenden v

complicated [ˈkɒmplɪkeɪtɪd] kompliziert VI 3 (55)

°**comprehension** [ˌkɒmprɪˈhenʃn] Verständnis

computer [kəmˈpjuːtə] Computer I **computer-aided** computergestützt VI 3 (67) • **computer science** Computerwissenschaft, Informatik III

°**con** [kɒn]: **pros and cons** *(pl)* Vor- und Nachteile

concentrate (on sth.) [ˈkɒnsntreɪt] sich konzentrieren (auf etwas) VI 4 (103)

concern [kənˈsɜːn]: **To whom it may concern** *(bes. AE)* Sehr geehrte Damen und Herren IV

concerned (about sth./sb.) [kənˈsɜːnd] besorgt (um etwas/jn.) VI 3 (54)

concert [ˈkɒnsət] Konzert II

conclude (sth. from sth.) [kənˈkluːd] (etwas aus etwas) schließen v

conclusion [kənˈkluːʒn] Schluss(folgerung) v • **draw a conclusion** einen Schluss ziehen v

concrete [ˈkɒŋkriːt] Beton, Beton- v

confident [ˈkɒnfɪdənt] selbstbewusst, (selbst)sicher v

confirm [kənˈfɜːm] bestätigen v

conflict [ˈkɒnflɪkt] Konflikt, Auseinandersetzung VI 2 (32)

confuse [kənˈfjuːz] verwirren IV

confusion [kənˈfjuːʒn] Verwirrung IV

Congratulations! [kənˌgrætʃuˈleɪʃnz] Herzlichen Glückwunsch! III

connect A with/to B [kəˈnekt] A mit B verbinden v

connection [kəˈnekʃn] Verbindung v

conscious [ˈkɒnʃəs] bei Bewusstsein v • **conscious of sth.** sich einer Sache bewusst v

consequence [ˈkɒnsɪkwəns] Folge, Konsequenz IV

consider [kənˈsɪdə]
°**1.** nachdenken über, berücksichtigen, in Betracht ziehen
2. consider sb./sth. (to be) sth. jn./etwas als etwas betrachten, jn./etwas für etwas halten VI 1 (14)

considerable [kənˈsɪdərəbl] *(fml)* erheblich, beträchtlich VI 2 (39)

consist of sth. [kənˈsɪst] aus etwas bestehen VI 3 (54)

console [ˈkɒnsəʊl]: **game console** Spielkonsole v

Constitution [ˌkɒnstɪˈtjuːʃn] Verfassung VI 2 (28)

constitutional monarchy [ˌkɒnstɪˈtjuːʃənl] konstitutionelle Monarchie v

°**construction** [kənˈstrʌkʃn] Konstruktion

contact sb. [ˈkɒntækt] sich mit jm. in Verbindung setzen; mit jm. Kontakt aufnehmen III

contact [ˈkɒntækt] Kontakt IV **contact details** Kontaktdaten v

contain [kənˈteɪn] enthalten VI 2 (31)

context [ˈkɒntekst] Zusammenhang, Kontext IV

continent [ˈkɒntɪnənt] Kontinent IV

continue [kənˈtɪnjuː] weitermachen (mit); weiterreden; weitergehen II

contrary [ˈkɒntrəri]: **on the contrary** im Gegenteil VI 4 (82)

contrast (to/with sth., between two things) [ˈkɒntrɑːst] Gegensatz (zu) v

contrast sth. and/with sth. [kənˈtrɑːst] A mit B kontrastieren *(die Unterschiede aufzeigen)* v

contribute [kənˈtrɪbjuːt] (etwas) beitragen; einen Beitrag leisten (für etwas) VI 2 (28)

contribution [ˌkɒntrɪˈbjuːʃn] Beitrag VI 2 (28) • **make a contribution** einen Beitrag leisten VI 2 (28/207)

control (over) [kənˈtrəʊl] Kontrolle (über) v • **under control** unter Kontrolle IV

controller [kənˈtrəʊlə] Steuergerät, Regler VI 1 (14)

controversy [ˈkɒntrəvɜːsi] Auseinandersetzung, Kontroverse VI 2 (31)

conversation [ˌkɒnvəˈseɪʃn] Gespräch, Unterhaltung II

°**conversational** [ˌkɒnvəˈseɪʃənl] Unterhaltungs-, Gesprächs-

convert [kənˈvɜːt] umwandeln, verwandeln VI 3 (58)

°**convey** [kənˈveɪ] vermitteln

convict [ˈkɒnvɪkt] Sträfling, Strafgefangene(r) v

convince sb. (of sth.) [kənˈvɪns] jn. (von etwas) überzeugen VI 2 (28)

convinced [kənˈvɪnst]: **be convinced** überzeugt sein VI 2 (28)

cook [kʊk] kochen, zubereiten II

cook [kʊk] Koch, Köchin II

cooker [ˈkʊkə] Herd I

cookie [ˈkʊki] *(AE)* Keks IV

cool [kuːl]
1. kühl I
2. cool I

coordination [kəʊˌɔːdɪˈneɪʃn] Koordinierung, Koordination VI 1 (14)

copy [ˈkɒpi] kopieren II

copy [ˈkɒpi] Kopie, Abschrift IV

core [kɔː] Kern VI 3 (54)

corn [kɔːn] *(AE, no pl)* Mais IV

corner [ˈkɔːnə] Ecke I • **on the corner of Sand Street and London Road** Sand Street, Ecke London Road II

cornflakes [ˈkɔːnfleɪks] Cornflakes I

correct [kəˈrekt] korrigieren, verbessern II

correct [kəˈrekt] richtig, korrekt II

correction [kəˈrekʃn]
1. Korrektur, Berichtigung IV
2. (Sehstärken-)Korrektur VI 3 (56)

°**correspond (with sth.)** [ˌkɒrəˈspɒnd] (mit etwas) übereinstimmen

cost [kɒst], **cost, cost** kosten III

cost [kɒst] Preis, Kosten IV

costume [ˈkɒstjuːm] Kostüm, Verkleidung I

cotton [ˈkɒtn] Baumwolle IV

could [kəd, kʊd]: **he could ...** er konnte ... II

could [kəd, kʊd]: **we could ...** wir könnten ... II

°**could** [kəd, kʊd]: **I could have done** ich hätte machen können

counsellor [ˈkaʊnsələ] Berater/in VI 1 (15)

count [kaʊnt] zählen II

countdown [ˈkaʊntdaʊn] Countdown III

counter [ˈkaʊntə]
1. Spielstein II
2. Theke, Ladentisch IV

country [ˈkʌntri] Land *(auch als Gegensatz zur Stadt)* II • **in the country** auf dem Land II

couple [ˈkʌpl]: **a couple of** ein paar/ Paar III

course [kɔːs] Kurs, Lehrgang III

course: of course [əv ˈkɔːs] natürlich, selbstverständlich I

°**course** [ˈkɔːs]: **over the course of** im Laufe von

court [kɔːt]
1. Platz, Court III
2. Gericht(shof) IV

cousin [ˈkʌzn] Cousin, Cousine I

cover [ˈkʌvə]
1. zudecken, bedecken IV
2. abdecken, behandeln VI 3 (67)

cover [ˈkʌvə]
1. (CD-)Hülle I
°**2.** (Buch-)Umschlag

cow [kaʊ] Kuh II

°**crack** [kræk] zusammenbrechen, verrückt werden

°**crap** [kræp] *(infml)* Mist

crash [kræʃ] abstürzen III • **crash in(to) sth.** gegen etwas fahren/ laufen v

Dictionary

crazy ['kreɪzi] verrückt III

cream [kriːm] Sahne; Creme IV

cream cheese [ˌkriːm 'tʃiːz] Frischkäse IV

create [kri'eɪt] (er)schaffen, kreieren V

creative [kri'eɪtɪv] kreativ, einfallsreich IV

creature ['kriːtʃə] Lebewesen VI 4 (91)

creep [kriːp], **crept, crept**
1. sich langsam bewegen VI 3 (62)
°**2.** kriechen

creeps [kriːps]: **give sb. the creeps** jm. unheimlich sein; jm. nicht geheuer sein VI 3 (62)

crept [krept] *siehe* **creep**

crew [kruː] Crew, (Schiffs-)Mannschaft III

cricket ['krɪkɪt] Kricket III

crime [kraɪm] Verbrechen; Kriminalität IV • **commit a crime** ein Verbrechen begehen IV • **crime film** Krimi IV • **crime rate** Kriminalität(srate) V • **crime story** Krimi IV

crisis ['kraɪsɪs] Krise IV

crisps (pl) [krɪsps] Kartoffelchips I

critic ['krɪtɪk] Kritiker/in IV

criticize (for) ['krɪtɪsaɪz] kritisieren (wegen) VI 1 (7)

crocodile ['krɒkədaɪl] Krokodil II

cross [krɒs] überqueren; (sich) kreuzen II

°**cross** [krɒs] Flanke, Querpass

crosswalk ['krɒswɔːk] *(AE)* Fußgängerüberweg IV

crowd [kraʊd] (Menschen-)Menge III

crowded ['kraʊdɪd] voller Menschen, überfüllt III

crucial ['kruːʃl] äußerst wichtig, entscheidend VI 3 (55)

°**cruddy** *(infml)* ['krʌdi] schlecht

cruel ['kruːəl] grausam IV

cry [kraɪ]
1. schreien I • **cry in pain** vor Schmerzen schreien I
2. weinen III

culture ['kʌltʃə] Kultur V

cup [kʌp]
1. Tasse II • **a cup of tea** eine Tasse Tee II
2. Pokal III

cupboard ['kʌbəd] Schrank I

cure [kjʊə] heilen VI 3 (53)

curious ['kjʊəriəs] seltsam; neugierig VI 4 (76)

current ['kʌrənt] aktuelle(r, s), gegenwärtige(r, s); gebräuchlich VI 1 (15)

curriculum vitae [kəˌrɪkjələm 'viːtaɪ] *(BE)* Lebenslauf V

cut (-tt-) [kʌt], **cut, cut** schneiden II; reduzieren VI 3 (56) • °**cut sth. down** etwas zurückschneiden; *(Baum)* fällen, *(Wald)* abholzen
cut sth. off etwas abschneiden, abtrennen III • **cut sth. out** ausschneiden III • **cut the grass** Rasen mähen IV

cut [kʌt] Schnitt IV

°**cutaway** ['kʌtəweɪ] Querschnitts-

CV [ˌsiː 'viː] *(BE)* Lebenslauf V

cycle ['saɪkl] (mit dem) Rad fahren II

cycle path ['saɪkl pɑːθ] Radweg II

D

dad [dæd] Papa, Vati; Vater I

°**dæmon** ['diːmən] Dämon

daily ['deɪli] täglich IV

damage ['dæmɪdʒ] beschädigen, schädigen VI 1 (16)

damn [dæm] verdammt IV
°**I don't give a damn.** Es ist mir egal.

damp [dæmp] feucht VI 4 (99)

dance [dɑːns] tanzen I

dance [dɑːns] Tanz I • **dance floor** Tanzfläche III

dancer ['dɑːnsə] Tänzer/in II

dancing ['dɑːnsɪŋ] Tanzen I
dancing lessons Tanzstunden, Tanzunterricht I

danger (to) ['deɪndʒə] Gefahr (für) I

dangerous ['deɪndʒərəs] gefährlich II

dark [dɑːk]
1. dunkel I
2. dunkelhaarig V

dark [dɑːk]: **after dark** nach Einbruch der Dunkelheit IV

darling ['dɑːlɪŋ] Liebling, Schatz V

date [deɪt]
1. Datum I • **date of birth** Geburtsdatum IV • **to date** bis heute, bis dato V
2. Verabredung, Date V • **go on a date with sb.** mit jm. ausgehen V

date [deɪt] *(bes. AE)* mit jm. (aus)gehen; sich (regelmäßig) mit jm. treffen III

daughter ['dɔːtə] Tochter I

day [deɪ] Tag I • **by day and by night** bei Tag und bei Nacht V
one day eines Tages I • **days of the week** Wochentage I • **the day before yesterday** vorgestern II • **that day** an jenem Tag III

daylight ['deɪlaɪt] Tageslicht VI 1 (16)

dead [ded] tot I • °**play dead** sich totstellen

deaf [def] taub, gehörlos III

deal with sb./sth. [diːl], **dealt, dealt** sich mit jm./etwas beschäftigen; handeln von etwas IV

deal [diːl] Angebot IV • **make a deal** ein Abkommen / eine Abmachung treffen III • **It's a deal!** Abgemacht! III

dealt [delt] *siehe* **deal**

dear [dɪə] Schatz, Liebling I • **Oh dear!** Oje! II

dear [dɪə]: **Dear Jay ...** Lieber Jay, ... I
Dear Sir or Madam ... Sehr geehrte Damen und Herren IV

death [deθ] Tod IV • **death rate** Sterberate V • **death sentence** Todesstrafe IV • **fall to one's death** zu Tode stürzen IV

debate [dɪ'beɪt] Debatte V

debate (sth.) [dɪ'beɪt] debattieren (über etwas); hin und her überlegen VI 2 (28)

debts (pl) [dets] Schulden IV

December [dɪ'sembə] Dezember I

decide (on sth.) [dɪ'saɪd] sich entscheiden (für etwas), (etwas) beschließen II

decision (on sth.) [dɪ'sɪʒn] Entscheidung (über etwas) VI 2 (32) • **make a decision** eine Entscheidung treffen/fällen VI 2 (32/209)

declaration [ˌdeklə'reɪʃn] Erklärung, Mitteilung VI 2 (26)

decrease [dɪ'kriːs] abnehmen, nachlassen, zurückgehen (um); reduzieren, verringern (um) VI 4 (82)

deep [diːp] tief IV

deer, *pl* **deer** [dɪə] Reh, Hirsch II

°**de-escalate** [ˌdiː'eskəleɪt] deeskalieren

defence [dɪ'fens] Verteidigung III

defend sb./sth. (against sb./sth.) [dɪ'fend] jn./etwas verteidigen (gegen jn./etwas) VI 2 (38)

definite ['defɪnət] fest, bestimmt; endgültig, eindeutig V

°**de-friend sb.** *(infml)* [ˌdiː'frend] jm. die Freundschaft kündigen

degree [dɪ'griː] Grad II

delay [dɪ'leɪ] aufhalten IV

delay [dɪ'leɪ] Verspätung IV

deli ['deli] Deli *(Lebensmittelgeschäft mit Fastfoodrestaurant)* IV

delicious [dɪ'lɪʃəs] köstlich, lecker II

deliver [dɪ'lɪvə] (aus)liefern, austragen IV

democracy [dɪ'mɒkrəsi] Demokratie; demokratischer Staat V

democrat ['deməkræt] Demokrat/in V

democratic [ˌdeməˈkrætɪk] demokratisch V

demonstrate (for/against sth.) [ˈdemənstreɪt] (für/gegen etwas) demonstrieren VI 2 (42)

dentist [ˈdentɪst] Zahnarzt, -ärztin IV

department store [dɪˈpɑːtmənt stɔː] Kaufhaus II

departure [dɪˈpɑːtʃə] Abfahrt; Abflug IV

depend on sth./sb. [dɪˈpend] sich auf etwas/jn verlassen IV

depending (on) [dɪˈpendɪŋ] je nachdem (wie) VI 2 (31)

dependable [dɪˈpendəbl] zuverlässig IV

depict [dɪˈpɪkt] (fml) darstellen VI 4 (98)

describe sth. (to sb.) [dɪˈskraɪb] (jm.) etwas beschreiben II

description [dɪˈskrɪpʃn] Beschreibung II

desert [ˈdezət] Wüste IV • **desert island** Wüsteninsel VI 3 (63)

deserve [dɪˈzɜːv] verdienen (zu Recht bekommen) V

design [dɪˈzaɪn] Muster, Entwurf; Design, Gestaltung V • **design school** Kunsthochschule V

design [dɪˈzaɪn] entwickeln, entwerfen I

desk [desk] Schreibtisch I

desperate [ˈdespərət]: **be desperate to be/do sth.** unbedingt etwas sein/tun wollen VI 4 (88)

despite [dɪˈspaɪt] trotz V

destination [ˌdestɪˈneɪʃn] (Reise-)Ziel V

destiny [ˈdestɪni] Schicksal VI 4 (76)

destroy [dɪˈstrɔɪ] zerstören III

detail [ˈdiːteɪl] Detail, Einzelheit III **contact details** Kontaktdaten V

detailed [ˈdiːteɪld] ausführlich, detailliert V

detective [dɪˈtektɪv] Detektiv/in I **detective story** Krimi VI 4 (76)

determination [dɪˌtɜːmɪˈneɪʃn] Entschlossenheit V

determined [dɪˈtɜːmɪnd] (fest) entschlossen V

develop (from ... into ...) [dɪˈveləp] entwickeln; sich (aus ... zu ...) entwickeln V • **developing country** Entwicklungsland V • **developing world** Entwicklungsländer VI 3 (56)

development [dɪˈveləpmənt] Entwicklung VI 4 (87)

device [dɪˈvaɪs]: **poetic device** poetisches (Stil-)Mittel VI 4 (91/G)

diagonal [daɪˈægənəl] diagonal, schräg IV

dial (-ll-) [ˈdaɪəl] wählen (Telefonnummer) II

°**dial** [ˈdaɪəl] Anzeige (eines Geräts)

dialect [ˈdaɪəlekt] Dialekt, Mundart V

dialogue [ˈdaɪəlɒg] Dialog VI 4 (105/G)

°**diameter** [daɪˈæmɪtə] Durchmesser V

diamond [ˈdaɪəmənd] Diamant V

diary [ˈdaɪəri] Tagebuch; Terminkalender I

dice, pl **dice** [daɪs] Würfel II **throw the dice** würfeln II

dictator [dɪkˈteɪtə] Diktator/in V

dictatorship [ˌdɪkˈteɪtəʃɪp] Diktatur V

dictionary [ˈdɪkʃənri] Wörterbuch, (alphabetisches) Wörterverzeichnis I

did [dɪd] siehe do • **Did you go?** Bist du gegangen? / Gingst du? I **we didn't go** [ˈdɪdnt] wir sind nicht gegangen/wir gingen nicht I

die (of) (-ing form: **dying**) [daɪ] sterben (an) II

difference [ˈdɪfrəns] Unterschied III

different (from) [ˈdɪfrənt] verschieden, unterschiedlich; anders (als) I

difficult [ˈdɪfɪkəlt] schwierig, schwer I

°**digital effects** [ˌdɪdʒɪtəl_ɪˈfekts] Digitaleffekte (in Filmen)

°**dim (-mm-)** [dɪm] schwächer werden

dining room [ˈdaɪnɪŋ ruːm; ˈdaɪnɪŋ rʊm] Esszimmer I

dinner [ˈdɪnə] Abendessen, Abendbrot I • **have dinner** Abendbrot essen I

dinosaur [ˈdaɪnəsɔː] Dinosaurier IV

dioxide [daɪˈɒksaɪd]: **carbon dioxide (CO₂)** Kohlendioxid (CO₂) VI 3 (58)

direct [dəˈrekt] direkt V

direct [dəˈrekt] Regie führen III

direct speech [dəˈrekt] direkte Rede III

directions (pl) [dəˈrekʃnz] Wegbeschreibung(en) II • **stage directions** Regieanweisungen VI 4 (105/G)

director [dəˈrektə] Regisseur/in III

dirt [dɜːt] Schmutz, Dreck V

dirt bike [ˈdɜːt baɪk] Geländemotorrad V

dirt road [ˈdɜːt rəʊd] unbefestigte Straße V

dirty [ˈdɜːti] schmutzig II

°**dis sb.** (infml for **disrespect**) [dɪs] jn. beleidigen, jn. „dissen", jn. respektlos behandeln

disabled [dɪsˈeɪbld] (körper)behindert III

disadvantage [ˌdɪsədˈvɑːntɪdʒ] Nachteil IV

disagree (with sb. on sth.) [ˌdɪsəˈgriː] (zu etwas) anderer Meinung sein (als jemand), (zu etwas) nicht übereinstimmen (mit jm.) II

disagreement [ˌdɪsəˈgriːmənt] Uneinigkeit; Meinungsverschiedenheit VI 2 (28)

disappear [ˌdɪsəˈpɪə] verschwinden II

disappoint sb. [ˌdɪsəˈpɔɪnt] jn. enttäuschen IV

disappointed (with/in sb., with/about sth.) [ˌdɪsəˈpɔɪntɪd] enttäuscht (von jm./etwas) IV

disappointment [ˌdɪsəˈpɔɪntmənt] Enttäuschung VI 4 (93)

discipline [ˈdɪsəplɪn] Disziplin V

disc jockey [ˈdɪsk dʒɒki] Diskjockey III

disco [ˈdɪskəʊ] Disko I

discover [dɪˈskʌvə] entdecken; herausfinden II

°**discoverer** [dɪsˈkʌvərə] Entdecker/in

discovery [dɪˈskʌvəri] Entdeckung VI 3 (52)

discriminate against sb. [ˌdɪˈskrɪmɪneɪt] jn. diskriminieren, jn. benachteiligen IV

discrimination (against) [dɪˌskrɪmɪˈneɪʃn] Diskriminierung (von), Benachteiligung (von) IV

discuss sth. [dɪˈskʌs] über etwas diskutieren, etwas besprechen VI 3 (58)

discussion [dɪˈskʌʃn] Diskussion II

disease [dɪˈziːz] (ansteckende) Krankheit IV

disgust [dɪsˈgʌst] anwidern, anekeln VI 3 (61)

disgusting [dɪsˈgʌstɪŋ] ekelhaft, widerlich VI 3 (61)

dish [dɪʃ] Gericht (Speise) III

dishes (pl) [ˈdɪʃɪz] Geschirr I • **do the dishes** das Geschirr abwaschen I

dishwasher [ˈdɪʃwɒʃə] Geschirrspülmaschine I

dislike [dɪsˈlaɪk] nicht mögen, nicht leiden können VI 1 (12)

dislikes (pl) [ˈdɪslaɪks]: **likes and dislikes** (pl) Vorlieben und Abneigungen V

display [dɪsˈpleɪ] Display IV • **be on display** ausgestellt sein IV

°**display** [dɪsˈpleɪ] zeigen, ausstellen

distance [ˈdɪstəns] Entfernung IV

distant [ˈdɪstənt] (weit) entfernt, fern VI 1 (16)

distinguish A from B [dɪˈstɪŋgwɪʃ] A von B unterscheiden VI 3 (55)

Dictionary

district ['dɪstrɪkt] Gegend, Bezirk VI 2 (28)

diver ['daɪvə] Taucher/in v

divide (into) [dɪ'vaɪd] (sich) teilen (in), (sich) aufteilen (in) II

divorced [dɪ'vɔːst] geschieden I

DJ ['diːdʒeɪ] Diskjockey III

DJ ['diːdʒeɪ] (Musik/CDs/Platten) auflegen (in der Disko) III

do [duː], **did, done** tun, machen I • **do a gig** einen Auftritt haben, ein Konzert geben III • **do a good job** gute Arbeit leisten II • **do an exercise** eine Übung machen II **do a project** ein Projekt machen, durchführen II • **do sb. a favour** jm. einen Gefallen tun IV • **do sport** Sport treiben I • °**do sth. about sth.** etwas an etwas ändern • **do the dishes** das Geschirr abwaschen I • **How am I doing?** Wie komme ich voran? (Wie sind meine Fortschritte?) III • **learning by doing** Lernen durch Handeln/ Tun v

doctor ['dɒktə] Arzt/Ärztin, Doktor I • **at/to the doctor's** beim/zum Arzt III

documentary [ˌdɒkju'mentri] Dokumentarfilm II

dog [dɒg] Hund I • **walk the dog** den Hund ausführen v

doll [dɒl] Puppe IV

dollar ($) ['dɒlə] Dollar IV

dolphin ['dɒlfɪn] Delfin v

dominant ['dɒmɪnənt] dominant, vorherrschend VI 2 (30)

donate [dəʊ'neɪt] spenden, schenken v

done [dʌn] siehe **do**

don't [dəʊnt]: **Don't listen to Dan.** Hör/Hört nicht auf Dan. I • **I don't like ...** Ich mag ... nicht. / Ich mag kein(e) ... I

°**doodle** ['duːdl] Kritzelei

door [dɔː] Tür I

doorbell ['dɔːbel] Türklingel I

dossier ['dɒsieɪ] Mappe, Dossier (des Sprachenportfolios) I

double ['dʌbl] zweimal, doppelt, Doppel- I • **double bed** Doppelbett v

double bass [ˌdʌbl 'beɪs] Kontrabass III

doubt [daʊt] bezweifeln VI 1 (20)

doubt [daʊt] Zweifel, Bedenken VI 1 (20)

dough [dəʊ] Teig IV

down [daʊn] hinunter, herunter, nach unten I • **down there** (nach) dort unten II • **down-to-earth** praktisch, nüchtern VI 1 (9)

download [ˌdaʊn'ləʊd] runterladen, downloaden II

downstairs [ˌdaʊn'steəz] unten; nach unten I

downtown ['daʊntaʊn] Stadtzentrum IV • **downtown bus** (AE) Bus in Richtung Stadtzentrum IV

Dr., Dr ['dɒktə] Dr. IV

draft [drɑːft] Entwurf IV

dragon ['drægən] Drache III

drama ['drɑːmə]
  1. Schauspiel, darstellende Kunst I
  2. Fernsehspiel; Drama IV

dramatic [drə'mætɪkli] dramatisch
  dramatically [drə'mætɪkli] dramatisch, in höchstem Maße VI 4 (77/G)

drank [dræŋk] siehe **drink**

draw [drɔː], **drew, drawn** zeichnen III

draw a conclusion [drɔː] einen Schluss ziehen v

draw sb.'s attention to sth. [drɔː] jn. auf etwas aufmerksam machen VI 2 (30/208)

draw [drɔː] Unentschieden III

drawer [drɔː] Schublade VI 4 (81)

drawing ['drɔːɪŋ] Zeichnung III

drawn [drɔːn] siehe **draw**

dream [driːm] Traum I • **dream house** Traumhaus I

dream (of, about) [driːm] träumen (von) III • **dream on** weiterträumen III

dress [dres] sich kleiden, sich anziehen IV

dress [dres] Kleid I

dressed [drest]: **get dressed** sich anziehen I

°**dresser** ['dresə]: **She's a good dresser.** Sie ist immer gut gekleidet.

drew [druː] siehe **draw**

°**dribble** ['drɪbl] dribbeln (mit)

drink [drɪŋk] Getränk I

drink [drɪŋk], **drank, drunk** trinken I

drinker ['drɪŋkə] Trinker/in VI 2 (37)

drive [draɪv], **drove, driven**
  1. (also **drive a/the car**) (ein Auto / mit dem Auto) fahren II • **driving instructor** Fahrlehrer/in v
  2. (an)treiben VI 3 (57)

drive [draɪv] (Auto)fahrt IV

driven ['drɪvn] siehe **drive**

driver ['draɪvə] Fahrer/in II

driving licence ['draɪvɪŋ ˌlaɪsəns] Führerschein, Fahrerlaubnis v

drop (-pp-) [drɒp]
  1. fallen lassen I
  2. fallen I
  drop sb. off jn. absetzen (aussteigen lassen) IV

drove [drəʊv] siehe **drive**

drown [draʊn] ertrinken IV

drug [drʌg] Droge; Medikament v **drug dealer** Dealer/in v

drum [drʌm] Trommel; Schlagzeug III • **drumstick** Trommelstock III **play the drums** Schlagzeug spielen III

drunk [drʌŋk]
  1. siehe **drink**
  2. betrunken IV • **get drunk** sich betrinken v

dry [draɪ] trocken III

°**duck** [dʌk] sich ducken

dump sb. [dʌmp] sitzen lassen, mit jm. Schluss machen VI 1 (9)

during (prep) ['djʊərɪŋ] während III

dust [dʌst] Staub IV

dustbin ['dʌstbɪn] Mülltonne II

dusty ['dʌsti] staubig v

duvet ['duːveɪ] Bettdecke, Federbett v

DVD [ˌdiː viː 'diː] DVD I

°**dystopia** [dɪs'təʊpiə] Dystopie

E

each [iːtʃ] jeder, jede, jedes (einzelne) I • **each other** einander, sich (gegenseitig) III

eagle ['iːgl] Adler v

ear [ɪə] Ohr I

earache ['ɪəreɪk] Ohrenschmerzen II

early ['ɜːli] früh I

earn money [ɜːn] Geld verdienen v

earring ['ɪərɪŋ] Ohrring I

earth [ɜːθ] (also **Earth**) Erde v **down-to-earth** praktisch, nüchtern VI 1 (9)

earthquake ['ɜːθkweɪk] Erdbeben IV

earthworm ['ɜːθwɜːm] Regenwurm IV

east [iːst] Osten; nach Osten; östlich II • **eastbound** ['iːstbaʊnd] Richtung Osten III • **eastern** ['iːstən] östlich, Ost- III

easy ['iːzi] leicht, einfach I • **easy-to-read** leicht zu lesende(r, s) v

easy-going [ˌiːzi 'gəʊɪŋ] gelassen, unbeschwert v

eat [iːt], **ate, eaten** essen I

eaten ['iːtn] siehe **eat**

economic [ˌiːkə'nɒmɪk] wirtschaftliche(r, s); Wirtschafts- v

economy [ɪ'kɒnəmi] (Volks-)Wirtschaft v

edge [edʒ] Rand, Kante VI 3 (54)

edit ['edɪt] redigieren III

editor ['edɪtə] Redakteur/in III

educate ['edʒukeɪt] unterrichten; erziehen; aufklären v

education [ˌedʒuˈkeɪʃn] (Schul-, Aus-)Bildung; Erziehung IV

°**educational** [ˌedʒuˈkeɪʃənl] pädagogisch

effect (on) [ɪˈfekt] Wirkung, Auswirkung (auf) IV • °**digital effects** Digitaleffekte (in Filmen)

effective [ɪˈfektɪv] effektiv, wirksam, wirkungsvoll V

e-friend [ˈiːfrend] Brieffreund/in (im Internet) I

°**e.g.** [ˌiː ˈdʒiː] z.B.

egg [eg] Ei I

eightish [ˈeɪtɪʃ] ungefähr acht (Jahre/Uhr) IV

either [ˈaɪðə, ˈiːðə]: **either … or …** entweder … oder … V • **not (…) either** auch nicht II

elect sb. sth. [ɪˈlekt] jn. zu etwas wählen IV

election [ɪˈlekʃn] Wahl (von Kandidaten bei einer Abstimmung) IV

electric [ɪˈlektrɪk] elektrisch, Elektro- III

electrical engineer [ɪˌlektrɪkəl ˌendʒɪˈnɪə] Elektrotechniker/in V

electricity [ɪˌlekˈtrɪsəti] Strom, Elektrizität III • **static electricity** elektrische Aufladung IV

electronic [ɪˌlekˈtrɒnɪk] elektronisch III

element [ˈelɪmənt] Element VI 2 (34)

elementary school [ˌelɪˈmentri skuːl] (USA) Grundschule (für 6- bis 11-Jährige) IV

elephant [ˈelɪfənt] Elefant I

elevator [ˈelɪveɪtə] (AE) Fahrstuhl, Aufzug II

°**eloquent** [ˈeləkwənt] eloquent, gewandt

else [els]: **anybody/anything else** sonst (noch) jemand/etwas • **anywhere else** sonst (noch) irgendwo(hin) • **somebody else** jemand anders • **something else** etwas anderes • **somewhere else** woanders(hin) • **who/what/ where/why/… else?** wer/was/ wo/warum/… (sonst) noch? III

e-mail [ˈiːmeɪl] (also **email**) E-Mail I

embarrassed [ɪmˈbærəst] verlegen IV

embarrassing [ɪmˈbærəsɪŋ] peinlich IV

emergency [ɪˈmɜːdʒənsi] Notfall, Not- IV

emission [iˈmɪʃn] Emission, (Schadstoff-)Ausstoß VI 3 (58)

emit (-tt-) [iˈmɪt] ausstoßen, freisetzen, abgeben VI 3 (58)

emotion [ɪˈməʊʃn] Gefühl, Emotion VI 1 (12)

°**emotional** [ɪˈməʊʃənl] emotionell

emphasis [ˈemfəsɪs] Betonung, Hervorhebung VI 2 (36)

emphasize [ˈemfəsaɪz] betonen, hervorheben VI 2 (36)

employer [ɪmˈplɔɪə] Arbeitgeber/in V

empty [ˈempti] leer I

emu [ˈiːmjuː] Emu V

enclose [ɪnˈkləʊz] etwas (einem Brief) beilegen V

encourage [ɪnˈkʌrɪdʒ] (jn.) ermutigen, ermuntern; (etwas) fördern V

encyclopedia [ɪnˌsaɪkləˈpiːdiə] Enzyklopädie, Lexikon II

end [end] Ende; Schluss I • **at the end (of)** am Ende (von) I **achieve an end** ein Ziel erreichen IV **end-rhyme** Endreim VI 4 (91/G) **in the end** schließlich, am Ende, zum Schluss VI 1 (7)

end [end]
1. zu Ende gehen IV
2. (etwas) beenden V • **end a relationship** mit jm. Schluss machen V • **end up doing sth.** schließlich etwas tun VI 1 (10)

ending [ˈendɪŋ] Ende, (Ab-)Schluss (einer Geschichte, eines Films usw.) III • **happy ending** Happyend II **have an open ending** offen sein, nicht entschieden sein VI 4 (89/G)

endless [ˈendləs] endlos V

enemy [ˈenəmi] Feind/in II

energetic [ˌenəˈdʒetɪk] dynamisch, tatkräftig, energisch V

energy [ˈenədʒi] Energie, Kraft V
°**light energy** Lichtmenge

engine [ˈendʒɪn]: **steam engine** Dampfmaschine VI 3 (52)

engineer [ˌendʒɪˈnɪə] Ingenieur/in II

engineering [ˌendʒɪˈnɪərɪŋ] Technik VI 3 (53) • **genetic engineering** Gentechnik VI 3 (53)

English [ˈɪŋglɪʃ] Englisch; englisch I

enjoy [ɪnˈdʒɔɪ] genießen I

enough [ɪˈnʌf] genug I

enroll for/in/on sth. [ɪnˈrəʊl] sich (für etwas) anmelden IV

enter [ˈentə]
1. betreten IV • **enter a country** in ein Land einreisen IV
2. eingeben, eintragen II

entertain sb. [ˌentəˈteɪn] jn. unterhalten IV

entertainment [ˌentəˈteɪnmənt] Unterhaltung (Vergnügen) IV

entrance [ˈentrəns] Eingang VI 4 (98)

entry [ˈentri]
1. Eintrag, Eintragung (im Wörterbuch/Tagebuch) III

2. Einsendung, Beitrag (zu einem Wettbewerb) III

environment [ɪnˈvaɪrənmənt] Umwelt IV

environmental [ɪnˌvaɪrənˈmentl] Umwelt- IV

epidemic [ˌepɪˈdemɪk] Epidemie V

equal [ˈiːkwəl] gleich IV

equal (-ll-) [ˈiːkwəl] gleich sein VI 1 (21/203) • **2 plus 3 equals 5** 2 plus 3 ist (gleich) 5 VI 1 (21/203)

equalize [ˈiːkwəlaɪz] ausgleichen; das Ausgleichstor erzielen III

equator [ɪˈkweɪtə] Äquator V

equipment [ɪˈkwɪpmənt] Ausrüstung III

eraser [ɪˈreɪzə(r), ɪˈreɪsə(r)] (AE) Radiergummi IV

°**erupt** [ɪˈrʌpt] ausbrechen

escape from sb./sth. [ɪˈskeɪp] vor jm./aus etwas fliehen; entkommen IV

especially [ɪˈspeʃəli] besonders, vor allem, insbesondere VI 1 (24)

essay (about, on) [ˈeseɪ] Aufsatz (über) I

establish [ɪˈstæblɪʃ] feststellen VI 3 (55)

estate [ɪˈsteɪt] Wohnsiedlung VI 4 (99)

°**estimate** [ˈestimeɪt] schätzen

etc. (et cetera) [etˈsetərə] usw. (und so weiter) IV

ethnic [ˈeθnɪk] ethnisch, Volks- IV

euro (€) [ˈjʊərəʊ] (also **Euro**) Euro I

evaluate [ɪˈvæljueɪt] beurteilen, einschätzen; auswerten VI 1 (11)

evaluation [ɪˌvæljuˈeɪʃn] Beurteilung, Einschätzung VI 1 (11) • **peer evaluation** Partnerbeurteilung

even [ˈiːvn]
1. sogar II
even more/taller (sogar) noch mehr/größer/… VI 1 (18)
2. (sogar) schon III

evening [ˈiːvnɪŋ] Abend I • **in the evening** abends, am Abend I • **on Friday evening** freitagabends, am Freitagabend I

event [ɪˈvent] Ereignis II

eventually [ɪˈventʃuəli] schließlich, irgendwann VI 4 (98)

ever [ˈevə] je, jemals III • **ever?** je? / jemals? / schon mal? II **more than ever** mehr als je (zuvor), mehr denn je V • **ever since** (ununterbrochen) seit VI 1 (9) **for ever** für immer VI 3 (61)

every [ˈevri] jeder, jede, jedes I

everybody [ˈevribɒdi] jeder, alle II

everyday (adj) [ˈevrideɪ] Alltags-; alltäglich III

Dictionary 245

everyone ['evriwʌn] jeder; alle III
everything ['evriθɪŋ] alles I
everywhere ['evriweə] überall I
evidence *(no pl)* ['evɪdəns] Beweis(e), Hinweis(e) VI 3 (55) • **piece of evidence** Beweis, Hinweis VI 3 (55)
evil ['i:vl] übel, schlimm; böse *(bösartig, feindselig)* VI 3 (62)
evolution [,i:və'lu:ʃn] Evolution VI 3 (52)
evolve [ɪ'vɒlv] sich entwickeln VI 3 (52)
exact [ɪg'zækt] genau III
exam [ɪg'zæm] Prüfung V
examine [ɪg'zæmɪn] prüfen, untersuchen VI 4 (76)
example (of) [ɪg'zɑ:mpl] Beispiel (für) I • **for example** zum Beispiel I
excellent ['eksələnt] ausgezeichnet, hervorragend IV
except [ɪk'sept] außer, bis auf IV
°**excerpt (from sth.)** ['eksɜ:pt] Auszug (aus etwas)
exchange [ɪks'tʃeɪndʒ] (Schüler-) Austausch III
exchange [ɪks'tʃeɪndʒ] aus-, umtauschen III; *(Geld)* wechseln III
°**exchanger** [ɪks'tʃeɪndʒə]: **heat exchanger** Wärmetauscher
excited [ɪk'saɪtɪd] *(positiv)* aufgeregt, begeistert II
excitement [ɪk'saɪtmənt] Aufregung, Erregung VI 4 (93)
exciting [ɪk'saɪtɪŋ] aufregend, spannend II
exclude sb./sth. (from sth.) [ɪk'sklu:d] jn./etwas (von etwas) ausschließen VI 1 (10)
Excuse me, ... [ɪk'skju:z mi:] Entschuldigung, ... / Entschuldigen Sie, ... I
execution [,eksɪ'kju:ʃn] Hinrichtung IV
exercise ['eksəsaɪz] Übung, Aufgabe I • **do an exercise** eine Übung machen II • **exercise book** Schulheft, Übungsheft I • **prewriting exercise** Übung vor dem Schreiben III
exhibition (on) [,eksɪ'bɪʃn] Ausstellung (über) IV
exist [ɪg'zɪst] existieren V
expect [ɪk'spekt] erwarten, annehmen, vermuten V
expectancy [ɪk'spektənsi]: **life expectancy** Lebenserwartung V
expectation [,ekspek'teɪʃn] Erwartung VI 4 (77)
expense [ɪk'spens] Kosten VI 2 (40) **at my expense** auf meine Kosten VI 2 (40/214)

expensive [ɪk'spensɪv] teuer I
experience [ɪk'spɪəriəns] Erfahrung; Erlebnis IV • **work experience** *(no pl)* Arbeits-, Praxiserfahrung(en) V
experience [ɪk'spɪəriəns] erfahren, erleben V
experienced [ɪk'spɪəriənst] erfahren IV
°**expert** ['ekspɜ:t] Experte, Expertin, Fachmann, Fachfrau
explain sth. to sb. [ɪk'spleɪn] jm. etwas erklären, erläutern II
explanation [,eksplə'neɪʃn] Erklärung II
explicit [ɪk'splɪsɪt] explizit, klar, ausdrücklich VI 2 (29/G)
explode [ɪk'spləʊd] explodieren, ausrasten VI 2 (28)
explore [ɪk'splɔ:] erkunden, erforschen I
explorer [ɪk'splɔ:rə] Entdecker/in, Forscher/in II
explosion [ɪk'spləʊʒn] Explosion IV
express [ɪk'spres] äußern, zum Ausdruck bringen, ausdrücken V
expression [ɪk'spreʃn] Ausdruck III **freedom of expression** Redefreiheit VI 2 (26)
°**extensive** [ɪk'stensɪv] ausgedehnt, ausführlich • **extensive reading** extensives Lesen
extra ['ekstrə] zusätzlich I
extract (from) ['ekstrækt] Auszug (aus) VI 4 (87)
extracurricular activities *(kurz: **extracurriculars**)* [,ekstrəkə'rɪkjələz] *schulische Angebote außerhalb des regulären Unterrichts, oft als Arbeitsgemeinschaften* IV
extraordinary [ɪk'strɔ:dnri] außergewöhnlich IV
°**extremist** [ɪk'stri:mɪst] Extremist/in
eye [aɪ] Auge I • **eye-level** auf gleicher Höhe mit den Augen VI 2 (30) • **keep an eye on sth./ sb.** nach jm./etwas Ausschau halten IV • **She couldn't believe her eyes.** Sie traute ihren Augen kaum. III
eyebrow ['aɪbraʊ] Augenbraue VI 2 (30)
eyeglasses *(pl)* ['aɪ,glɑ:sɪz] Brille VI 3 (56)

F

°**fabric** ['fæbrɪk] Bau, Struktur
fabulous ['fæbjələs] *(infml)* fabelhaft, fantastisch VI 4 (76)
face [feɪs] Gesicht I • **face down** mit der Schrift nach unten

°**face sth.** [feɪs] mit dem Gesicht zu etwas sitzen/stehen
facial ['feɪʃl] Gesichts- VI 2 (30)
fact [fækt] Tatsache, Fakt III • **in fact** um genau zu sein VI 1 (15)
factory ['fæktri] Fabrik II
factual text ['fæktʃu:l] Sachtext IV
fade away [,feɪd ə'weɪ] schwächer werden VI 3 (61)
fail to do sth. [feɪl] versagen (beim Versuch, etwas zu tun) VI 3 (55)
failure ['feɪljə] ungenügend IV
faintly ['feɪntli] schwach, leicht *(ein wenig)* VI 2 (28)
fair [feə]
1. fair, gerecht II
2. hell *(Haut; Haare)* V
faith (in sb./sth.) [feɪθ] Vertrauen (in jn./etwas); Glaube V
faithful (to sb./sth.) ['feɪθfəl] (jm./ einer Sache) treu VI 1 (24)
faithfully ['feɪθfəli]: **Yours faithfully** *(BE)* mit freundlichen Grüßen IV
fall [fɔ:l], **fell, fallen** fallen, stürzen; hinfallen II • **fall asleep** einschlafen V • **fall down** runterfallen; hinfallen II • **fall in love (with sb.)** sich verlieben (in jn.) IV • **fall off** herunterfallen (von) II • **fall to one's death** zu Tode stürzen IV
°**fall** [fɔ:l] *(AE)* Herbst
fallen ['fɔ:lən] *siehe* **fall**
false [fɔ:ls] falsch VI 1 (22) • **false friend** *ein Wort, das wie ein Wort in einer anderen Sprache ähnlich aussieht aber eine andere Bedeutung hat* VI 1 (22/202)
familiar with [fə'mɪliə] vertraut mit VI 4 (98)
family ['fæməli] Familie I • **family man** Familienmensch IV • **family tree** (Familien-)Stammbaum I
famous (for) ['feɪməs] berühmt (für, wegen) II
fan [fæn] Fan, Anhänger/in III
fan [fæn] Ventilator V
fancy sth. ['fænsi] *(infml)* Lust auf/zu etwas haben V • **fancy sb.** auf jn. stehen VI 1 (12)
fancy ['fænsi] schick, ausgefallen *(etwas abwertend)* V
fantastic [fæn'tæstɪk] fantastisch, toll V
fantasy ['fæntəsi] Fantasy *(Genre)* V
far [fɑ:] weit (entfernt) I • **by far** bei weitem; mit Abstand V • **far and wide** weit und breit IV • **so far** bis jetzt, bis hierher III
faraway ['fɑ:rəweɪ] abgelegen III
farm [fɑ:m] Bauernhof, Farm II
farmer ['fɑ:mə] Bauer/Bäuerin, Landwirt/in; (Fisch-)Züchter/in III

farmhouse ['fɑːmhaʊs] Bauernhaus III

fascinate ['fæsəneɪt] faszinieren V

fashion ['fæʃn] Mode II • **military-style fashion** Mode im Militärstil V

fast [fɑːst] schnell II

fat [fæt] dick IV

fate [feɪt] Schicksal, Bestimmung VI 1 (16)

father ['fɑːðə] Vater I

fault [fɔːlt] Schuld, Fehler IV • **it's your fault** du hast Schuld IV

favour ['feɪvə]: **do sb. a favour** jm. einen Gefallen tun IV

favourite ['feɪvərɪt] Lieblings- I **my favourite colour** meine Lieblingsfarbe I

favourite ['feɪvərɪt] Favorit/in; Liebling III • **my all-time favourite** mein Liebling aller Zeiten VI 4 (87)

fear (of) ['fɪə] Furcht, Angst (vor) III

fear sth./sb. [fɪə] vor etwas/jm. Angst haben; etwas/jn. (be)fürchten VI 2 (34)

fearless ['fɪələs] furchtlos V • **the fearless** die Furchtlosen V

feature ['fiːtʃə] (physisches) Merkmal, Kennzeichen VI 3 (65)

February ['februəri] Februar I

fed [fed]
1. siehe **feed**
2. be fed up (with sth.) die Nase voll haben (von etwas) VI 2 (30)

feed [fiːd], **fed, fed** füttern I

°**feedback** ['fiːdbæk] Reaktion, Feedback

feel [fiːl], **felt, felt** fühlen; sich fühlen II; sich anfühlen II • **feel like doing sth.** Lust haben, etwas zu tun VI 1 (12) • **I feel sick.** Mir ist schlecht. IV

feeling ['fiːlɪŋ] Gefühl III

feet [fiːt] Plural von „foot" I

fell [fel] siehe **fall**

felt [felt] siehe **feel**

felt tip ['felt tɪp] Filzstift I

female ['fiːmeɪl] weiblich VI 2 (31)

female ['fiːmeɪl]
1. weibliche Person VI 2 (31)
2. Weibchen II

fence [fens] Zaun IV

ferry ['feri] Fähre III

festival ['festɪvl] Fest, Festival II

fetch [fetʃ] holen, abholen IV

few [fjuː] wenige IV • **a few** ein paar, einige II

fewer ['fjuːə] weniger IV

fiction ['fɪkʃn] Belletristik; Prosaliteratur IV

fiddle ['fɪdl] (infml) Fiedel, Geige III **play the fiddle** Geige spielen III

field [fiːld]
1. Feld, Acker, Weide II • **in the field** auf dem Feld II
°**2.** (Sach-)Gebiet

fight sth. [faɪt], **fought, fought** etwas bekämpfen VI 3 (61) • **fight (for)** kämpfen (für, um) III

fight [faɪt] Kampf IV

figure ['fɪgə] Zahl, Ziffer, Betrag V

figure sth. (out) ['fɪgə] etwas ausrechnen; etwas herausfinden (oft mit Zahlen) VI 2 (28)

°**file** [faɪl] **1.** Datei; **2.** Ordner

file [faɪl]: **background file** etwa: Hintergrundinformation II **grammar file** Grammatikanhang I • **skills file** Anhang mit Lern- und Arbeitstechniken I

fill sth. (with sth.) [fɪl] etwas (mit etwas) (aus)füllen IV

filling ['fɪlɪŋ] (Brot-)Belag IV

film [fɪlm] Film I • **crime film** Krimi IV • **film star** Filmstar I

film [fɪlm] filmen III

final ['faɪnl] Finale, Endspiel III

final ['faɪnl] letzte(r, s); End- III

finally ['faɪnəli] endlich, schließlich IV

finance ['faɪnæns] Finanzwesen V

financial [faɪ'nænʃl] finanziell, Finanz- V

find [faɪnd], **found, found** finden I **find out (about)** herausfinden (über) I • **find sb. guilty (of a crime)** jn. (eines Verbrechens) schuldig befinden VI 1 (10)

findings (pl) ['faɪndɪŋz] Ergebnisse (einer Untersuchung u.Ä.) VI 2 (34)

fine [faɪn]
1. gut, ausgezeichnet; in Ordnung II
2. (gesundheitlich) gut II **I'm/He's fine.** Es geht mir/ihm gut. II • °**be fine with sth.** mit etwas kein Problem haben

fine [faɪn] Geldstrafe IV

finger ['fɪŋgə] Finger I

finish ['fɪnɪʃ] beenden, zu Ende machen; enden I

fire ['faɪə]
1. Feuer, Brand II • **There's no smoke without fire.** Wo Rauch ist, ist auch Feuer. IV
2. (von Waffen) Feuer, Schüsse VI 2 (27)

°**fire sb.** [faɪə] jn. entlassen, feuern

firefighter ['faɪəfaɪtə] Feuerwehrmann, -frau IV

fireman ['faɪəmən] Feuerwehrmann II

fireproof ['faɪəpruːf] feuerbeständig, -fest V

fire station ['faɪə ˌsteɪʃn] Feuerwache IV

firewoman ['faɪəˌwʊmən], pl **firewomen** Feuerwehrfrau II

first [fɜːst]
1. erste(r, s) I
2. zuerst, als Erstes I
at first zuerst, anfangs, am Anfang VI 1 (18) • **be first** der/die Erste sein I • **for the first time** zum ersten Mal II • **First Nations** die Ersten Nationen (indianische Ureinwohner/innen Kanadas) III

first floor [ˌfɜːst flɔː] erster Stock (BE) / Erdgeschoss (AE) IV

fish, pl **fish/fishes** [fɪʃ] Fisch I

fish [fɪʃ] fischen, angeln III

fisherman ['fɪʃəmən], pl **fishermen** ['fɪʃəmən] Angler, Fischer III

fist [fɪst] Faust IV

fit (-tt-) [fɪt] passen I

fitness ['fɪtnəs] Fitness VI 4 (89)

°**fix (infml)** [fɪks] Dosis, Schuss

°**fix** [fɪks] anbringen, befestigen

flag [flæg] Fahne, Flagge V

flash [flæʃ] aufblitzen; leuchten IV

flash [flæʃ] Lichtblitz III

flashback ['flæʃbæk] Rückblende V

flat [flæt] Wohnung I

flat [flæt] flach, eben II

flattered ['flætəd]: **be/feel flattered** sich geschmeichelt fühlen V

flavour ['fleɪvə] Geschmack, Geschmacksrichtung II

flea market ['fliː ˌmɑːkɪt] Flohmarkt III

flew [fluː] siehe **fly**

flexible ['fleksəbl] flexibel, anpassungsfähig V

flight [flaɪt] Flug II

floor [flɔː]
1. Fußboden I • **dance floor** Tanzfläche III
2. Stock(werk) IV • **first floor** erster Stock (BE) / Erdgeschoss (AE) IV • **ground floor** (BE) Erdgeschoss IV • **on the second floor** im zweiten Stock (BE) / im ersten Stock (AE) IV

flow [fləʊ] fließen IV

flow [fləʊ] Fluss, Strom VI 4 (93) **flow chart** Flussdiagramm I

flower ['flaʊə] Blume; Blüte II

flown [fləʊn] siehe **fly**

flu [fluː] Grippe II

flute [fluːt] Querflöte III

fly [flaɪ], **flew, flown** fliegen II **flying instructor** Fluglehrer/in V

fly [flaɪ] Fliege V

flyer ['flaɪə] Flugblatt, Flyer IV

Dictionary

focus ['fəʊkəs]
1. Schwerpunkt, Mittelpunkt, Hauptpunkt v
2. Brennpunkt VI 3 (56/217) • **be in focus** scharf sein VI 3 (56/217) • **be out of focus** unscharf sein VI 3 (56/217) • **come into focus** scharf werden VI 3 (56)
focus (on) ['fəʊkəs] sich konzentrieren (auf) v
fog [fɒg] Nebel II
foggy ['fɒgi] neblig II
folk (music) ['fəʊk ˌmjuːzɪk] Folk (meist englischsprachige, volkstümliche Musik mit Elementen der Rockmusik) III
folks [fəʊks] (infml, bes. AE) Leute III
follow ['fɒləʊ] folgen; verfolgen I
the following ... die folgenden ... III
font [fɒnt] Schrift(art) v
food [fuːd] Essen; Lebensmittel; Futter I
foot [fʊt], pl **feet** [fiːt]
1. Fuß I • **on foot** zu Fuß III
2. Fuß (Längenmaß; ca. 30 cm) IV
footage (no pl) ['fʊtɪdʒ] Film(material) VI 3 (62)
football ['fʊtbɔːl] Fußball I
football boots Fußballschuhe, -stiefel I • **football pitch** Fußballplatz, -feld II
footballer ['fʊtbɔːlə] Fußballspieler/in III
footnote ['fʊtnəʊt] Fußnote, Anmerkung IV
footprint ['fʊtprɪnt] Fußabdruck VI 3 (60) • **carbon footprint** „CO_2-Fußabdruck", CO_2-Bilanz VI 3 (60/219)
for [fə, fɔː]
1. für I • **for a moment** einen Moment lang II • **for a while** eine Weile, einige Zeit IV • **for break-fast/lunch/dinner** zum Frühstück/Mittagessen/Abendbrot I • **for ever** für immer VI 3 (61) • **for example** zum Beispiel I • **for his birthday** zu seinem Geburtstag III **for lots of reasons** aus vielen Gründen I • **for miles** meilenweit II • **(in prison) for murder** (im Gefängnis) wegen Mordes IV • **for sale** (auf Schild) zu verkaufen IV **for the first time** zum ersten Mal II • **for three days** drei Tage (lang) I • **for years** seit Jahren III • **just for fun** nur zum Spaß I • **What for?** [ˌwɒt 'fɔː] Wofür? II • **What's for homework?** Was haben wir als Hausaufgabe auf? I
2. (fml, old-fashioned) denn VI 3 (55)

force sb. to do sth. [fɔːs] jn. dazu bringen/jn. zwingen, etwas zu tun IV
force [fɔːs] Gewalt v • **use force** Gewalt anwenden v
forces (pl) ['fɔːsɪz] Kräfte VI 2 (28)
the armed forces die Streitkräfte VI 2 (28/207) • **market forces** Marktkräfte VI 2 (28/207) • **natural forces** Naturgewalten VI 2 (28/207) **security forces** Sicherheitskräfte VI 2 (28/207)
foreground ['fɔːgraʊnd] Vordergrund II
forehead ['fɒhed, 'fɒrɪd] Stirn IV
foreign ['fɒrɪn]
1. ausländisch v • **foreign language** Fremdsprache v
°**2.** fremd v
foreigner ['fɒrɪnə] Ausländer/in v
forest ['fɒrɪst] Wald II
forever [fər'evə]
1. endlos; ewig v
°**2.** für immer v
forgave [fə'geɪv] siehe **forgive**
forget (-tt-) [fə'get], **forgot, forgotten** vergessen III
forgive sb. for sth. [fə'gɪv], **forgave, forgiven** jm. etwas vergeben, verzeihen IV
forgiven [fə'gɪvn] siehe **forgive**
forgot [fə'gɒt] siehe **forget**
forgotten [fə'gɒtn] siehe **forget**
fork [fɔːk] Gabel III
form [fɔːm] bilden IV
form [fɔːm]
1. (Schul-)Klasse I • **form teacher** Klassenlehrer/in I
2. Gestalt VI 3 (53)
3. Formular VI 3 (61)
formal ['fɔːml] formell, förmlich v
format ['fɔːmæt] Format v
former ['fɔːmə] ehemalige(r, s), frühere(r, s) v
formula ['fɔːmjələ] Formel v
fort [fɔːt] Fort III
°**forth** [fɔːθ]: **back and forth** hin und her
fortunately ['fɔːtʃənətli] glücklicherweise VI 1 (14)
fortune ['fɔːtʃuːn] Vermögen; Glück v
forum ['fɔːrəm] Forum IV
forwards ['fɔːwədz] (bes. AE: **forward**) vorwärts VI 2 (28) • **look forward to sb./sth.** sich auf jn./etwas freuen IV
fossil fuel [ˌfɒsl 'fjuːəl] fossiler Brennstoff VI 3 (61)
fought [fɔːt] siehe **fight**
foul [faʊl] foulen III
found [faʊnd] siehe **find**

found [faʊnd] gründen IV
fox [fɒks] Fuchs II
fragile ['frædʒaɪl] zerbrechlich; gebrechlich VI 3 (60)
frame [freɪm] Gestell, Rahmen VI 3 (56)
freak out [ˌfriːk_'aʊt] ausflippen v
free [friː]
1. frei I • **free time** Freizeit, freie Zeit I • **free-time activities** Freizeitaktivitäten II
2. kostenlos I
free [friː] freilassen v
freedom ['friːdəm] Freiheit v
freeway ['friːweɪ] (USA, Australien) Autobahn IV
freeze [friːz], **froze, frozen** (ge)frieren; zufrieren; einfrieren VI 3 (61)
°**freeze frame** ['friːz ˌfreɪm] Standbild
freezer ['friːzə] Tiefkühltruhe, -schrank VI 3 (61)
French [frentʃ] Französisch I
French fries [ˌfrentʃ 'fraɪz] (bes. AE) Pommes frites IV
frequent ['friːkwənt] häufig VI 2 (31)
Friday ['fraɪdeɪ, 'fraɪdi] Freitag I
fridge [frɪdʒ] Kühlschrank I
friend [frend] Freund/in I • **make friends (with)** Freunde finden; sich anfreunden (mit) II
friendliness ['frendlinəs] Freundlichkeit IV
friendly ['frendli] freundlich II; sympathisch VI 2 (28/206)
friendship ['frendʃɪp] Freundschaft VI 1 (10)
fries ['fraɪz]: **(French) fries** (bes. AE) Pommes frites IV
frighten ['fraɪtn] verängstigen, erschrecken v
frightening ['fraɪtnɪŋ] schrecklich, erschreckend v
frisbee ['frɪzbi] Frisbee IV
frog [frɒg] Frosch II
from [frəm, frɒm]
1. aus I
2. von I
dresses from the 60s Kleider aus den 60ern / aus den 60er Jahren II
from all over the UK / England aus dem gesamten Vereinigten Königreich / aus ganz England III
from all over the world aus der ganzen Welt II • **from Monday to Friday** von Montag bis Freitag III • **from my point of view** aus meiner Sicht; von meinem Standpunkt aus gesehen II • **I'm from ...** Ich komme/bin aus ... I • **Where are you from?** Wo kommst du her? I

front [frʌnt]**: at the front** vorne, im vorderen Teil III • **in front of** vor (*räumlich*) I • **to the front** nach vorn I • **front door** [ˌfrʌnt ˈdɔː] Wohnungstür, Haustür I • **front page** Titelseite III

frost [frɒst] Frost VI 3 (62)

froze [frəʊz] *siehe* **freeze**

frozen [ˈfrəʊzn] *siehe* **freeze**

fruit [fruːt] Obst, Früchte; Frucht I **fruit salad** Obstsalat I • **pick fruit** Obst pflücken IV

fry [fraɪ] braten III

fuel [ˈfjuːəl] Brenn-, Treib-, Kraftstoff VI 3 (61)

fulfil (-ll-), *(AE:* **fulfill)** [fʊlˈfɪl] erfüllen; ausführen VI 2 (35)

full [fʊl] voll I

°**full-time** [ˌfʊlˈtaɪm] ganztags

fun [fʌn]
1. Spaß I • **have fun** Spaß haben, sich amüsieren I • **Have fun!** Viel Spaß! I • **just for fun** nur zum Spaß I • **Riding is fun.** Reiten macht Spaß. I
2. lustige(r, s) V

funeral [ˈfjuːnərəl] Trauerfeier IV

funny [ˈfʌni] witzig, komisch I

furniture *(no pl)* [ˈfɜːnɪtʃə] Möbel III

further [ˈfɜːðə] weiter VI 2 (34)

fusion [ˈfjuːʒn]**: nuclear fusion** Kernfusion VI 3 (53)

future [ˈfjuːtʃə] Zukunft I

°**future** [ˈfjuːtʃə] zukünftig, künftig

G

°**gain momentum** [ɡeɪn] in Schwung/Fahrt kommen

galaxy [ˈɡæləksi] Sternsystem, Galaxie VI 1 (16)

gallery [ˈɡæləri] Galerie III

game [ɡeɪm] Spiel I • **a game of football** ein Fußballspiel II **game console** Spielkonsole V

gamer [ˈɡeɪmə] Gamer VI 1 (14)

gang [ɡæŋ] Bande, Gang V

°**gap** [ɡæp] Pause; Lücke

garage [ˈɡærɑːʒ] Garage II

garbage [ˈɡɑːbɪdʒ] *(AE)* Müll, Abfall IV

garden [ˈɡɑːdn] Garten I

gas [ɡæs]
1. Gas IV
2. *(AE)* Benzin IV • **gas station** *(AE)* Tankstelle IV

gate [ɡeɪt] Flugsteig III

gave [ɡeɪv] *siehe* **give**

GCSE exams [ˌdʒiː siːˈes ˈiː] *(also* **GCSEs)** *(GB)* der mittleren Reife oder Fachoberschulreife vergleich-

bare Schulabschlussprüfung(en) VI 1 (20)

gear *(no pl)* [ɡɪə] Ausrüstung IV **camping gear** Campingausrüstung IV • **sports gear** Sportausrüstung, Sportsachen II

general [ˈdʒenrəli] allgemeine(r, s) III

generally [ˈdʒenrəl] im Allgemeinen III

generate [ˈdʒenəreɪt] erzeugen VI 3 (57)

generation [ˌdʒenəˈreɪʃn] Generation V

generator [ˈdʒenəreɪtə] Generator VI 3 (57)

genetic [dʒəˈnetɪk] genetisch VI 3 (53) • **genetic engineering** Gentechnik VI 3 (53)

genre [ˈʒɒnrə] *(fml)* Genre VI 4 (87)

gentle [ˈdʒentl] sanft(mütig) VI 4 (105)

gentleman [ˈdʒentlmən]**,** *pl* **gentlemen** [ˈdʒentlmən] Herr V **Ladies and gentlemen** Meine Damen und Herren V

genuine [ˈdʒenjuɪn] echt, wirklich VI 4 (79)

geography [dʒiˈɒɡrəfi] Geografie, Erdkunde I

German [ˈdʒɜːmən] Deutsch; deutsch; Deutsche(r) I

Germany [ˈdʒɜːməni] Deutschland I

gesture [ˈdʒestʃə] Geste, Handbewegung VI 4 (105)

get (-tt-) [ɡet]**, got, got**
1. bekommen, kriegen II
2. holen, besorgen II
3. gelangen, (hin)kommen I
4. get angry/hot/... wütend/heiß/... werden II
5. get off (the train/bus) (aus dem Zug/Bus) aussteigen I • **get on (the train/bus)** (in den Zug/Bus) einsteigen I
6. get up aufstehen I
I don't get it. Das versteh ich nicht. / Das kapier ich nicht. II
get sth. across (to sb.) (jm.) etwas klarmachen/rüberbringen V
get along zurechtkommen IV
get away from sth./sb. von etwas/jm. weggehen, sich entfernen III
get bored sich langweilen, gelangweilt sein IV • **get drunk** sich betrinken V • **get involved (in)** sich engagieren (für, bei); sich beteiligen (an) IV • **get lost** sich verlaufen III • **get married** heiraten V
get on sb.'s nerves jm. auf die Nerven gehen VI 1 (12/199) • **get out (of a car)** (aus einem Auto) aussteiー

gen V • **Get out of my sight.** Geh mir aus den Augen. IV • °**get out of sb.'s life** aus dem Leben von jm. verschwinden • **get ready (for)** sich fertig machen (für), sich vorbereiten (auf) I • **get sb. to do sth.** jn. zwingen, etwas zu tun; jn. dazu bringen, etwas zu tun VI 1 (10) **get sth. right** etwas richtig machen III • **get sth. wrong** etwas falsch machen III • **get things ready** Dinge fertig machen, vorbereiten I • **get together** sich treffen VI 1 (24) • **get used to sth./sb.** sich gewöhnen an jn./etwas IV **What can I get you?** Was kann/darf ich euch/Ihnen bringen? II

getting by in English [ˌɡetɪŋ ˈbaɪ] *etwa:* auf Englisch zurechtkommen I

ghost [ɡəʊst] Gespenst, Geist V

giant [ˈdʒaɪənt] riesige(r, s), Riesen- IV

gig [ɡɪɡ] *(infml)* Gig, Auftritt III **do a gig** einen Auftritt haben, ein Konzert geben III

giraffe [dʒəˈrɑːf] Giraffe II

girl [ɡɜːl] Mädchen I

girlfriend [ˈɡɜːlfrend] Freundin III

gist [dʒɪst] das Wesentliche III

give [ɡɪv]**, gave, given** geben I **give sth. back** etwas zurückgeben I • **give sb. a call** jn. anrufen V **give sb. a hug** jn. umarmen IV **give information** Information(en) angeben V • **give attention (to sth./sb.)** jm. zuhören, auf jn. hören/aufpassen VI 2 (30/208) **give an impression** einen Eindruck vermitteln VI 4 (80/226) • **give a smile** lächeln IV • **give sb. a smile** jn. anlächeln IV • **give a source** eine Quelle angeben IV • **give a speech** eine Rede halten IV • **give sth. away** etwas verraten VI 3 (65) **give in** sich ergeben, nachgeben VI 2 (27) • **give sb. the creeps** jm. unheimlich sein; jm. nicht geheuer sein VI 3 (62) • **give (sth./sb.) up** (etwas/jn.) aufgeben V • **give up on sb./oneself** jn./sich aufgeben VI 2 (36)

given [ˈɡɪvn]
1. *siehe* **give**
2. given his intelligence *(fml)* angesichts/bei seiner Intelligenz VI 2 (35) • **given that he is rich** *(fml)* angesichts der Tatsache, dass er reich ist VI 2 (35)

glad [ɡlæd] froh, dankbar IV

glass [ɡlɑːs] Glas I • **a glass of water** ein Glas Wasser I

Dictionary

glasses (pl) ['glɑːsɪz] (eine) Brille I
global ['gləʊbl] weltweit, Welt- V
global warming Erwärmung der Erdatmosphäre V
gloves (pl) [glʌvz] Handschuhe II
glue [gluː] (auf-, ein)kleben II
glue [gluː] Klebstoff I • **glue stick** ['gluː stɪk] Klebestift I
go [gəʊ], **went, gone**
1. gehen I; fahren II
2. go hard/bad/deaf/blind/crazy/... hart/schlecht/taub/blind/verrückt/... werden III • **go red in the face** rot werden V • °**go abroad** ins Ausland gehen/fahren II • °**go against sth.** einer Sache widersprechen • **go ahead** in Führung gehen III • **go by** vergehen, vorübergehen (Zeit) V • **go by car/ bike/...** mit dem Auto/Rad/... fahren II • **go for a run** laufen gehen IV • **go for a walk** spazieren gehen, einen Spaziergang machen II • **go home** nach Hause gehen I °**go into doing sth.** für etwas aufgewendet werden • **go off 1.** losfahren, -gehen IV; **2.** (Waffe) losgehen; (Bombe) explodieren IV °**go off** (Licht) ausgehen • **go on 1.** weitergehen; weiterreden III; **2.** angehen (Licht) III **3.** los sein, abgehen, laufen VI 1 (7) • **go on a date with sb.** mit jm. ausgehen V **go on a hike** eine Wanderung machen IV • **go on a trip** einen Ausflug machen II • **go on a walk** eine Wanderung / einen Spaziergang machen IV • **go on doing sth.** etwas weiter tun IV • **go on holiday** in Urlaub fahren II • **go on to do sth.** dann etwas tun IV **go on tour** auf Tournee gehen VI 2 (39) • **go out** weg-, raus-, ausgehen I • **go out with sb.** mit jm. (aus)gehen V • **go riding/shopping/swimming** reiten/einkaufen/schwimmen gehen I • **go skiing** Ski laufen/fahren III • **go surfing** wellenreiten gehen, surfen gehen II • **go to** führen nach (Straße, Weg) II • **go to bed** ins Bett gehen I **go to mass** die Messe besuchen IV • **go to the cinema** ins Kino gehen II • **go to university** mit dem Studium anfangen V • **go well** gut (ver)laufen, gutgehen II • **go with** gehören zu, passen zu III **Let's go.** Auf geht's! (wörtlich: Lass uns gehen.) I • **coffee to go** Kaffee zum Mitnehmen IV • **What are you going to do?** Was wirst du tun? / Was hast du vor zu tun? I

goal [gəʊl]
1. Tor (im Sport) III • **score a goal** ein Tor schießen, einen Treffer erzielen III
2. Ziel V • **set a goal** ein Ziel setzen VI 2 (35)
°**goalie** ['gəʊli] (infml) siehe **goalkeeper**
goalkeeper ['gəʊlkiːpə] Torwart, Torfrau III
goat [gəʊt] Ziege IV
God [gɒd] Gott IV
gold [gəʊld] Gold III
gone [gɒn]
1. siehe **go**
2. be gone weg sein, nicht da sein II
good [gʊd]
1. gut I • **Good afternoon.** Guten Tag. (nachmittags) I • **Good luck (with ...)!** Viel Glück (bei/mit ...)! I **Good morning.** Guten Morgen. I **Good night, Goodnight.** Gute Nacht. VI 1 (24)
2. brav II
Goodbye. [ˌgʊd'baɪ] Auf Wiedersehen. I • **say goodbye** sich verabschieden I
good-looking [ˌgʊd'lʊkɪŋ] gut aussehend V
goods (pl) [gʊdz] Waren, Güter V
goose bumps (pl) ['guːs ˌbʌmps] Gänsehaut (AE) IV
goose pimples (pl) ['guːs 'pɪmpəlz] (BE) Gänsehaut IV
gorge [gɔːdʒ] Schlucht IV
gorgeous ['gɔːdʒəs] (infml) äußerst schön und attraktiv V
gorilla [gə'rɪlə] Gorilla IV
gossip ['gɒsɪp] schwatzen, klatschen, tratschen III
got [gɒt] siehe **get**
got [gɒt]: **I've got ...** Ich habe ... I **I haven't got a chair.** Ich habe keinen Stuhl. I
°**gotta** ['gɒtə] (infml) = **have got to**
gotten (AE) ['gɒtn] siehe **get**
govern ['gʌvən] regieren V
government ['gʌvənmənt] Regierung (als Schulfach etwa: Staatskunde) IV
governor ['gʌvənə] Gouverneur/in IV
grab (-bb-) [græb] schnappen, packen III • **grab sb.'s attention** jm. ins Auge fallen; sich (bei jm.) aufmerksam machen VI 2 (30/208)
grade [greɪd]
1. (AE) Jahrgangsstufe, Klasse IV
2. (Schul-)Note, Zensur IV
gradual ['grædʒʊəl] allmählich, langsam VI 3 (54)

graduate ['grædʒʊeɪt] (AE) den Schulabschluss machen IV (BE) den Hochschulabschluss machen IV
graffiti [grə'fiːti] Graffiti V
grammar ['græmə] Grammatik I **grammar file** Grammatikanhang I **grammar school** Gymnasium III
grand [grænd] eindrucksvoll, beeindruckend IV
grandchild ['græntʃaɪld], pl **grandchildren** ['-tʃɪldrən] Enkel/in I
granddaughter ['grændɔːtə] Enkelin II
grandfather ['grænfɑːðə] Großvater I
grandma ['grænmɑː] Oma I
grandmother ['grænmʌðə] Großmutter I
grandpa ['grænpɑː] Opa I
grandparents ['grænpeərənts] Großeltern I
grandson ['grænsʌn] Enkel II
granny ['græni] Oma II
granted ['grɑːntɪd]: **take sth. for granted** etwas für (allzu) selbstverständlich halten VI 4 (76)
grape [greɪp] Weintraube IV
°**graphics** (pl) ['græfɪks] Grafik(en), grafische Darstellung V
grass [grɑːs] Gras, Rasen IV • **cut the grass** Rasen mähen IV
grateful ['greɪtfl] dankbar V
grave [greɪv] Grab VI 4 (94)
great [greɪt] großartig, toll I
great-grandmother/-father [ˌgreɪt 'grænmʌðə], [ˌgreɪt 'grænfɑːðə] Urgroßmutter/-vater III
greedy ['griːdi] gierig; habgierig V
green [griːn] grün I
greet [griːt] begrüßen IV
grew [gruː] siehe **grow**
grey [greɪ] grau II
grid [grɪd] Gitter; Rechteckschema IV
grin (-nn-) [grɪn] grinsen VI 3 (56)
grip (-pp-) [grɪp] (von Film, Buch) fesseln, faszinieren VI 3 (54)
°**grip** [grɪp]: **get a grip on sth./sb.** etwas in den Griff bekommen V
groceries (pl) ['grəʊsəriz] Lebensmittel VI 4 (88)
ground [graʊnd] (Erd-)Boden III
ground floor [ˌgraʊnd 'flɔː] (BE) Erdgeschoss IV
Ground Zero [ˌgraʊnd 'zɪərəʊ] Bodennullpunkt (Bezeichnung für das zerstörte World Trade Center in New York) IV
group [gruːp] Gruppe I • **group word** Oberbegriff II • **target group** Zielgruppe VI 1 (17)

grow [grəʊ], **grew, grown**
1. wachsen II • **grow up** erwachsen werden; aufwachsen III
2. *(Getreide usw.)* anbauen, anpflanzen IV
grown [grəʊn] *siehe* **grow**
growth [grəʊθ] Wachstum, Zunahme V
grumble [ˈgrʌmbl] murren, nörgeln II
guarantee [ˌgærənˈtiː] garantieren, versprechen VI 1 (20)
guard [gɑːd] Wachposten IV
guess [ges] raten, erraten, schätzen II; annehmen VI 1 (10) • **Guess what!** [ˌges ˈwɒt] Stell dir vor! / Stellt euch vor! II
guest [gest] Gast I
guide [gaɪd] Fremdenführer/in, Reiseleiter/in IV • **(travel) guide** Reiseführer *(Buch)* V
guided tour [ˌgaɪdɪd ˈtʊə] Führung IV
guilty [ˈgɪlti]: **find sb. guilty (of a crime)** jn. (eines Verbrechens) schuldig befinden VI 1 (10) • **guilty as charged** schuldbewusst; schuldig VI 1 (10)
guinea pig [ˈgɪni pɪg] Meerschweinchen I
guitar [gɪˈtɑː] Gitarre I • **play the guitar** Gitarre spielen I
gum [gʌm]: **chewing gum** Kaugummi V • **chew gum** Kaugummi kauen V
gun [gʌn] Schusswaffe IV
guy [gaɪ] Typ, Kerl II • **guys** *(pl)* Leute II
gym [dʒɪm] Sporthalle, Turnhalle; Fitnessstudio IV

H

°**habit** [ˈhæbɪt] Gewohnheit
had [hæd] *siehe* **have**
°**haiku** [ˈhaɪkuː] Haiku
hair *(no pl)* [heə] Haar, Haare I
hairdresser [ˈheədresə] Friseur/in III
at the hairdresser's beim Friseur III
half [hɑːf], *pl* **halves** [hɑːvz]
1. Hälfte III
2. Halbzeit III
half [hɑːf] halbe(r, s) II • **half an hour** eine halbe Stunde II • **half past 11** halb zwölf (11.30 / 23.30) I
half-time Halbzeit(pause) III
three and a half days/weeks dreieinhalb Tage/Wochen IV
half-pipe [ˈhɑːfpaɪp] Halfpipe *(halbierte Röhre für Inlineskater)* III

hall [hɔːl]
1. Flur, Diele I
2. Halle, Saal III • **community hall** Gemeinschaftshalle, -saal III **sports hall** Sporthalle III
hallway [ˈhɔːlweɪ] *(AE)* Korridor, Gang IV
hamburger [ˈhæmbɜːgə] Hamburger I
hamster [ˈhæmstə] Hamster I
hand sb. sth. [hænd] jm. etwas reichen IV • **hand over (to sb.)** die Führung (an jn.) übergeben VI 3 (67)
hand [hænd] Hand I • **second-hand** gebraucht; aus zweiter Hand III
handkerchief [ˈhæŋkətʃiːf] Taschentuch IV
handle [ˈhændl] Griff VI 4 (94)
handout [ˈhændaʊt] Arbeitsblatt, Informationsblatt, Handout IV
handsome [ˈhænsəm] attraktiv, gut aussehend V
hang sb. [hæŋ] jn. hängen IV
hang sth. (up) [hæŋ], **hung, hung** etwas aufhängen IV
hang out [ˌhæŋ ˈaʊt], **hung, hung** *(infml)* hängen, rumhängen, abhängen III
happen (to) [ˈhæpən] geschehen, passieren (mit) I • **happen to do sth.** etwas zufällig(erweise) tun VI 1 (24)
happiness [ˈhæpinəs] Glück IV
happy [ˈhæpi] glücklich, froh I
Happy birthday. Herzlichen Glückwunsch zum Geburtstag. I
happy ending Happyend II
harass [ˈhærəs, həˈræs] belästigen V
harbour [ˈhɑːbə] Hafen III
hard [hɑːd] hart; schwer, schwierig II • **work hard** hart arbeiten II
hardly [ˈhɑːdli] kaum VI 4 (94)
°**hard sell** [ˌhɑːd ˈsel] aggressive Verkaufstechnik
hard-working [ˌhɑːdˈwɜːkɪŋ] fleißig V
harm [hɑːm] Schaden VI 1 (14)
mean no harm es nicht böse meinen VI 1 (14/200)
harm sth. [hɑːm] jn. verletzen; einer Sache schaden VI 1 (14)
harvest [ˈhɑːvɪst] Ernte IV
hat [hæt] Hut I
hate [heɪt] hassen, gar nicht mögen I
°**hate speech** [ˈheɪt ˌspiːtʃ] Hetzrede
have [həv, hæv], **had, had** haben, besitzen II • **have an argument** eine Auseinandersetzung haben, sich streiten II • **have a baby** ein Baby/Kind bekommen II • **have**

a bath baden, ein Bad nehmen II • **have a cold** erkältet sein, eine Erkältung haben II • **have a massage** sich massieren lassen II • **have a sauna** in die Sauna gehen II • **have a shower** (sich) duschen I • **have a sore throat** Halsschmerzen haben II • **have a temperature** Fieber haben II **have breakfast** frühstücken I **have dinner** Abendbrot essen I **have ... for breakfast** ... zum Frühstück essen/trinken I • **have fun** Spaß haben, sich amüsieren I **Have fun!** Viel Spaß! I • **have a good/great time** sich gut amüsieren III • **have sex** miteinander schlafen, sich lieben V • **have sth. done** etwas machen lassen V **have to do** tun müssen I
have got: I've got ... [aɪv ˈgɒt] Ich habe ... I • **I haven't got a chair.** Ich habe keinen Stuhl. I
he [hiː] er I
head [hed] Kopf I • **nod (one's head)** (mit dem Kopf) nicken III **shake one's head** den Kopf schütteln III
head for/to/towards sth. [hed] auf etwas zugehen, -fahren, -steuern V
headache [ˈhedeɪk] Kopfschmerzen II
heading [ˈhediŋ] Überschrift IV
headline [ˈhedˌlaɪn] Schlagzeile III
headphones *(pl)* [ˈhedfəʊnz] Kopfhörer III
head teacher [ˌhed ˈtiːtʃə] Schulleiter/in III
health [helθ] Gesundheit; Gesundheitslehre IV
healthy [ˈhelθi] gesund II
hear [hɪə], **heard, heard** hören I
heard [hɜːd] *siehe* **hear**
hearing [ˈhɪərɪŋ] Hören, auditive Wahrnehmung VI 3 (64/221)
heart [hɑːt] Herz I • **heart attack** Herzinfarkt IV
heat [hiːt] Hitze V • **heat exchanger** Wärmetauscher IV
heating [ˈhiːtɪŋ] Heizung VI 3 (60)
heaven [ˈhevn] Himmel *(im religiösen Sinn)* IV
heavy metal [ˌhevi ˈmetl] Heavymetal III
hedgehog [ˈhedʒhɒg] Igel II
held [held] *siehe* **hold**
helicopter [ˈhelɪkɒptə] Hubschrauber, Helikopter II
hell [hel] Hölle VI 4 (93)
Hello. [həˈləʊ] Hallo. / Guten Tag. I
helmet [ˈhelmɪt] Helm III

Dictionary

help [help] helfen I • **Can I help you?** Kann ich Ihnen helfen? / Was kann ich für Sie tun? *(im Geschäft)* I • **help (sb.) out** (jm.) aushelfen V • **I can't help it.** Ich kann nicht anders; Ich kann es nicht ändern. VI 1 (21) • **I can't help laughing.** Ich kann nicht anders, als zu lachen. VI 1 (21/203)

help [help] Hilfe I

helpful ['helpfl] hilfreich, nützlich IV

helpless ['helpləs] hilflos IV

her [hə, hɜː]
  1. ihr, ihre I
  2. sie; ihr I

herb [hɜːb] (Gewürz-)Kraut III

here [hɪə]
  1. hier I • **round here** hier (in der Gegend) IV
  2. hierher I
  Here you are. Bitte sehr. / Hier bitte. I

heritage ['herɪtɪdʒ] Erbe IV

hero ['hɪərəʊ], *pl* **heroes** ['hɪərəʊz] Held/in II

hers [hɜːz] ihrer, ihre, ihrs II

herself [hɜː'self]
  1. sich III
  2. selbst IV

Hey! [heɪ] Hallo! III

Hi! [haɪ] Hallo! I • **Say hi to your parents for me.** Grüß deine Eltern von mir. I

hid [hɪd] *siehe* **hide**

hidden ['hɪdn] *siehe* **hide**

hide [haɪd], **hid, hidden** sich verstecken; (etwas) verstecken I

high [haɪ] hoch III

highlight ['haɪˌlaɪt] Höhepunkt III

°**highlight** ['haɪlaɪt] *(einen Textabschnitt farbig)* hervorheben, markieren

°**highly** ['haɪli] sehr, höchst, wärmstens

high school ['haɪ skuːl] *(USA)* Schule für 14- bis 18-Jährige IV

highway ['haɪweɪ] *(USA)* Fernstraße *(oft mit vier oder mehr Spuren)* IV

°**hijab** [hɪ'dʒɑːb] Hidschab

hijacker ['haɪdʒækə] (Flugzeug-)-Entführer/in IV

hike [haɪk] wandern IV

hike [haɪk] Wanderung, Marsch IV

hiker ['haɪkə] Wanderer, Wanderin VI 2 (32)

hill [hɪl] Hügel II

hilly ['hɪli] hügelig III

him [hɪm] ihn; ihm I

himself [hɪm'self]
  1. sich III
  2. selbst IV

Hindu ['hɪnduː] Hindu V

Hinduism ['hɪnduːɪzm] Hinduismus V

hip hop ['hɪp ˌhɒp] Hiphop IV

hippo ['hɪpəʊ] Flusspferd II

his [hɪz]
  1. sein, seine I
  2. seiner, seine, seins II

historical [hɪ'stɒrɪkl] historisch, geschichtlich VI 4 (76)

history ['hɪstri] Geschichte I

hit (-tt-) [hɪt], **hit, hit**
  1. schlagen III
  2. treffen IV

°**hit song** [ˌhɪt 'sɒŋ] Hit

hobby ['hɒbi] Hobby I

hockey ['hɒki] Hockey I • **hockey pitch** Hockeyplatz, -feld II **hockey shoes** Hockeyschuhe I

hold [həʊld], **held, held** halten II **hold a competition** einen Wettbewerb veranstalten III • **hold sb./ sth. up** jn./etwas aufhalten VI 3 (61)

hole [həʊl] Loch I

holiday(s) ['hɒlədeɪ] Ferien I • **be on holiday** in Urlaub sein II • **go on holiday** in Urlaub fahren II **holiday home** Ferienhaus, -wohnung III

home [həʊm] Heim, Zuhause I **at home** daheim, zu Hause I **children's home** Kinderheim V **come home** nach Hause kommen I • **get home** nach Hause kommen I • **go home** nach Hause gehen I • **old people's home** Altenheim, Seniorenresidenz V

homeland ['həʊmlænd] Heimat(land) IV

homeless ['həʊmləs] obdachlos IV
  ▶ S.217 the rich, the poor, etc.

homeowner ['həʊmˌəʊnə] Eigenheimbesitzer/in IV

hometown ['həʊmˌtaʊn] Heimat(stadt) IV

homework *(no pl)* ['həʊmwɜːk] Hausaufgabe(n) I • **do homework** die Hausaufgabe(n) machen I **What's for homework?** Was haben wir als Hausaufgabe auf? I

honest ['ɒnɪst] ehrlich II

honesty ['ɒnəsti] Ehrlichkeit VI 3 (54)

°**hooked** [hʊkt] abhängig, süchtig

Hooray! [hu'reɪ] Hurra! II

hope [həʊp] hoffen I • **I hope so.** Ich hoffe es. II

hope (of) [həʊp] Hoffnung (auf) III

°**hopeful** ['həʊpfʊl] hoffnungsvoll IV

hopefully ['həʊpfəli] hoffentlich VI 1 (18)

hopeless ['həʊpləs] hoffnungslos IV • **You're hopeless.** Dir ist nicht zu helfen. IV

horizon [hə'raɪzn] Horizont V

horrible ['hɒrəbl] scheußlich, grauenhaft II

horror ['hɒrə] Entsetzen, Grauen, Horror III

horse [hɔːs] Pferd I • **(horse) racing** Pferderennsport V

hose [həʊz] Schlauch IV

hospital ['hɒspɪtl] Krankenhaus II **He's gone to hospital.** Er ist ins Krankenhaus gegangen. III • **He's in hospital.** Er ist im Krankenhaus. III

host [həʊst] Gastgeber IV

hostel ['hɒstl] Herberge, Wohnheim III • **youth hostel** Jugendherberge III

hostess ['həʊstes] Gastgeberin *(in USA auch: Frau, die in einem Restaurant die Gäste in Empfang nimmt)* IV

hot [hɒt] heiß I • **hot chocolate** heiße Schokolade I • **hot-water bottle** Wärmflasche II

hotel [həʊ'tel] Hotel II

hotline ['hɒtlaɪn] Hotline II

hour ['aʊə] Stunde I • **half an hour** eine halbe Stunde II • **a 24-hour supermarket** ein Supermarkt, der 24 Stunden geöffnet ist III • **a two-hour operation** eine zweistündige Operation III

house [haʊs] Haus I • **at the Shaws' house** im Haus der Shaws / bei den Shaws zu Hause I

how [haʊ] wie I • **How about you grabbing that table?** Wie wär's, wenn ihr den Tisch dort schnappt? IV • **How are you?** Wie geht es dir/Ihnen/euch? II • **How do you know …?** Woher weißt/kennst du …? I • **how many?** wie viele? I • **how much?** wie viel? I • **How much is/are …?** Was kostet/kosten …? / Wie viel kostet/kosten …? I • **How old are you?** Wie alt bist du? I • **How was …?** Wie war …? I • **How shall I put it?** Wie soll ich es formulieren/ausdrücken? IV **how to do sth.** wie man etwas tut / tun kann / tun soll IV

however [haʊ'evə] trotzdem IV

hug (-gg-) [hʌg] umarmen IV

hug [hʌg] Umarmung IV • **give sb. a hug** jn. umarmen IV

huge [hjuːdʒ] riesig, sehr groß III

human ['hjuːmən] *(also **human being**)* Mensch, menschliches Wesen IV

human ['hjuːmən] menschlich, Menschen- VI 2 (26)

Dictionary

humanitarian [hjuːˌmænɪˈteəriən] humanitär VI 2 (32)

°**humanity** [hjuːˈmænɪti] Menschheit

hundred [ˈhʌndrəd] hundert, Hundert I

hung [hʌŋ] *siehe* **hang**

hunger [ˈhʌŋgə] Hunger V

hungry [ˈhʌŋgri] hungrig I • **be hungry** Hunger haben, hungrig sein I

hunt [hʌnt] Jagd III

hunt [hʌnt] jagen III

hurry [ˈhʌri] eilen; sich beeilen II **hurry up** sich beeilen I

hurry [ˈhʌri]: **be in a hurry** in Eile sein, es eilig haben I

hurt [hɜːt], **hurt, hurt** wehtun; verletzen I

hurt [hɜːt] verletzt II

husband [ˈhʌzbənd] Ehemann II

hut [hʌt] Hütte IV

hutch [hʌtʃ] (Kaninchen-)Stall I

°**hyperlink** [ˈhaɪpəlɪŋk] Hyperlink

I

I [aɪ] ich I • **I'm** [aɪm] ich bin I **I'm from …** Ich komme aus … / Ich bin aus … I • **I'm … years old.** Ich bin … Jahre alt. I • **I'm sorry.** Entschuldigung. / Tut mir leid. I

ice [aɪs] Eis II

ice cream [ˌaɪs ˈkriːm] (Speise-)Eis I

ice hockey [ˈaɪs hɒki] Eishockey III

ice rink [ˈaɪs rɪŋk] Schlittschuhbahn II

ID [ˌaɪ ˈdiː] Ausweis IV

idea [aɪˈdɪə]
  1. Idee, Einfall I
  °**2.** Vorstellung

ideal [aɪˈdiːəl] Ideal, Idealvorstellung V

°**ideal** [aɪˈdiːəl] ideal

identification [aɪˌdentɪfɪˈkeɪʃn] Ausweis IV

identify (with) [aɪˈdentɪfaɪ] identifizieren; sich identifizieren (mit) VI 1 (21)

identity [aɪˈdentɪti] Identität IV

idolize [ˈaɪdəlaɪz] vergöttern, abgöttisch lieben VI 1 (12)

if [ɪf]
  1. wenn, falls II
  2. ob II

ignore [ɪgˈnɔː] nicht beachten, ignorieren VI 1 (10)

ill [ɪl] krank II

illegal [ɪˈliːgl] illegal, ungesetzlich IV

illness [ˈɪlnəs] Krankheit IV

illogical [ɪˈlɒdʒɪkl] unlogisch VI 3 (64)

illustrate [ˈɪləstreɪt] veranschaulichen, illustrieren IV

image [ˈɪmɪdʒ] Bild V

imagery [ˈɪmɪdʒəri] Metaphorik V

imaginable [ɪˈmædʒɪnəbl] vorstellbar, erdenklich V

°**imaginary** [ɪˈmædʒɪnəri] imaginär *(nur in der Vorstellung vorhanden, nicht wirklich)*

imagination [ɪˌmædʒɪˈneɪʃn] Fantasie, Vorstellung(skraft) IV

imaginative [ɪˈmædʒɪnətɪv] fantasievoll, einfallsreich VI 4 (105)

imagine sth. [ɪˈmædʒɪn] sich etwas vorstellen III • **imagine doing sth.** sich vorstellen, etwas zu tun V

imitate [ˈɪmɪteɪt] nachmachen III

immediately [ɪˈmiːdɪətli] sofort IV

immigrant [ˈɪmɪgrənt] Einwanderer/Einwanderin IV

immigrate [ˈɪmɪgreɪt] einwandern IV

immigration [ˌɪmɪˈgreɪʃn] Einwanderung IV

impact [ˈɪmpækt] Auswirkung VI 2 (34)

impatient [ɪmˈpeɪʃnt] ungeduldig V

imperfect [ɪmˈpɜːfɪkt] unvollkommen, mangelhaft V

impersonal [ɪmˈpɜːsənl] unpersönlich V

implicit [ɪmˈplɪsɪt] implizit, unausgesprochen VI 2 (29/G)

impolite [ˌɪmpəˈlaɪt] unhöflich V

importance [ɪmˈpɔːtəns] Wichtigkeit, Bedeutung VI 3 (54)

important [ɪmˈpɔːtnt] wichtig II

impossible [ɪmˈpɒsəbl] unmöglich II

impress [ɪmˈpres] beeindrucken V

impression [ɪmˈpreʃn] Eindruck VI 4 (80)

impressive [ɪmˈpresɪv] beeindruckend, eindrucksvoll III

improve [ɪmˈpruːv] (sich) verbessern III

°**improvement** [ɪmˈpruːvmənt] Verbesserung

in [ɪn] in I • **the best view in the world** die beste Aussicht der Welt IV • **in 2050** im Jahr 2050 II • **in … Street** in der …straße I • **in English** auf Englisch I • **in front of** vor *(räumlich)* I • **in here** hier drinnen I • **in next to no time** im Nu III **in other places** an anderen Orten, anderswo III • **in school** *(AE)* in der Schule IV • **in the afternoon** nachmittags, am Nachmittag I **in the country** auf dem Land II **in the evening** abends, am Abend I • **in the field** auf dem Feld II

in the morning am Morgen, morgens I • **in the photo/picture** auf dem Foto/Bild I • **in there** dort drinnen I • **in the sky** am Himmel II • **in the world** auf der Welt II • **in the yard** auf dem Hof II **in time** [ɪn ˈtaɪm] rechtzeitig II

inaccurate [ɪnˈækjərət] ungenau V

inactive [ɪnˈæktɪv] inaktiv, untätig V

incident [ˈɪnsɪdənt] Vorfall, Zwischenfall VI 4 (76)

include [ɪnˈkluːd] einschließen IV

incorrect [ˌɪnkəˈrekt] inkorrekt, falsch V

increase [ɪnˈkriːs] ansteigen, zunehmen (um); erhöhen (um) VI 4 (82)

incredible [ɪnˈkredɪbl] unglaublich IV

independent [ˌɪndɪˈpendənt] unabhängig V

index [ˈɪndeks] Index, Register V

Indian [ˈɪndiən]
  1. Inder/in I
  2. Indianer/in IV

indicate sth. [ˈɪndɪkeɪt] deuten auf etwas VI 4 (100)

°**indigenous** [ɪnˈdɪdʒənəs] eingeboren, einheimisch

indirect [ˌɪndəˈrekt] indirekt V **indirect speech** indirekte Rede III

individual [ˌɪndɪˈvɪdʒuəl] einzelne(r, s) VI 2 (39)

industrial [ɪnˈdʌstriəl] industriell III

industry [ˈɪndəstri] Industrie III

inexact [ˌɪnɪgˈzækt] ungenau V

inexpensive [ˌɪnɪkˈspensɪv] preiswert V

infinitive [ɪnˈfɪnətɪv] Infinitiv *(Grundform des Verbs)* I

influence [ˈɪnfluəns] beeinflussen VI 2 (29)

inform sb. (about/of sth.) [ɪnˈfɔːm] jn. (über etwas) informieren IV

informal [ɪnˈfɔːml] informell; umgangssprachlich V

information (about/on) *(no pl)* [ˌɪnfəˈmeɪʃn] Information(en) (über) I • **give information** Information(en) angeben V

informed [ɪnˈfɔːmd] (wohl/gut) informiert VI 2 (35)

inhabit [ɪnˈhæbɪt] bewohnen, leben in V

inhabitant [ɪnˈhæbɪtənt] Einwohner/in, Bewohner/in V

inherit sth. (from sb.) [ɪnˈherɪt] etwas (von jm.) erben V

inhuman [ɪnˈhjuːmən] unmenschlich VI 2 (26/205)

initial [ɪˈnɪʃl] anfängliche(r, s) VI 3 (54)

injure sb. [ˈɪndʒə] jn. verletzen VI 2 (42)

Dictionary

injury ['ɪndʒəri] Verletzung II
injustice [ɪn'dʒʌstɪs] Ungerechtigkeit, Unrecht VI 2 (39)
°**inner** ['ɪnə] inner, Innen-
°**innit?** ['ɪnɪt] *(infml; = isn't it?)* nicht wahr?
innovation [ˌɪnə'veɪʃn] Innovation, Neuerung IV
insect ['ɪnsekt] Insekt IV
insecure [ˌɪnsɪ'kjʊə] unsicher VI 1 (8)
inside [ˌɪn'saɪd]
  1. innen (drin), drinnen I; Innen- IV
  2. nach drinnen II
  3. inside the car ins Auto (hinein), ins Innere des Autos II
insight ['ɪnsaɪt] Verständnis; Einsicht, Einblick VI 4 (93)
insist (on sth.) [ɪn'sɪst] bestehen (auf etwas) VI 1 (9)
install [ɪn'stɔːl] installieren, einrichten II
installation [ˌɪnstə'leɪʃn] Installation, Einrichtung II
instant message [ˌɪnstənt 'mesɪdʒ] *Nachricht, die man im Internet austauscht (in Echtzeit)* III
instead of [ɪn'sted_əv] anstelle von, statt IV
instructions (on) *(pl)* [ɪn'strʌkʃnz] (Gebrauchs-)Anweisung(en) (zu, hinsichtlich, für), Anleitung(en) II
instructor [ɪn'strʌktə] Lehrer/in, Ausbilder/in V
instrument ['ɪnstrəmənt] Instrument III
intend [ɪn'tend] beabsichtigen VI 4 (78)
interest ['ɪntrəst] Interesse V • **take interest in sb./sth.** sich für jn./etwas interessieren VI 1 (12)
interest sb. ['ɪntrəst] jn. interessieren IV
interested [ɪntrəstɪd]: **be interested (in)** interessiert sein (an), sich interessieren (für) III
interesting ['ɪntrəstɪŋ] interessant I
interior [ɪn'tɪəriə] Innere VI 3 (54)
intermediate [ˌɪntə'miːdɪət] Mittel-, für fortgeschrittene Anfänger/innen V
internal [ɪn'tɜːnəl]: **internal rhyme** Binnenreim VI 4 (91/G)
international [ˌɪntə'næʃnəl] international II
internet ['ɪntənet] Internet I • **surf the internet** im Internet surfen II
°**interpret** [ɪn'tɜːprɪt] deuten, interpretieren
interrupt [ˌɪntə'rʌpt] unterbrechen IV
interview ['ɪntəvjuː] befragen, interviewen IV

interview ['ɪntəvjuː]
  1. Interview *(Zeitung, TV, usw.)* V
  2. Vorstellungsgespräch V
into ['ɪntə, 'ɪntʊ]
  1. in ... (hinein) I
  2. be into sth. *(infml)* etwas mögen III
intolerant (of sth./sb.) [ɪn'tɒlərənt] intolerant (etwas/jm. gegenüber) VI 2 (29)
°**intonation** [ˌɪntə'neɪʃn] Intonation
introduce sb. (to sb.) [ˌɪntrə'djuːs] jn. (jm.) vorstellen IV
introduce sb. to sth. [ˌɪntrə'djuːs] jn. in etwas einführen IV
introduction (to) [ˌɪntrə'dʌkʃn] Einführung (in) III
invent [ɪn'vent] erfinden III
invention [ɪn'venʃn] Erfindung VI 3 (53)
inventor [ɪn'ventə] Erfinder/in III
°**inversion** [ɪn'vɜːʃn] Inversion, Umstellen von Wörtern im Satz
investigate [ɪn'vestɪgeɪt] ermitteln VI 3 (64)
investigation (into sth.) [ɪnˌvestɪ'geɪʃn] Untersuchung (von etwas) VI 3 (64)
invitation (to) [ˌɪnvɪ'teɪʃn] Einladung (zu) I
invite (to) [ɪn'vaɪt] einladen (zu) I
involved [ɪn'vɒlvd]: **get involved (in)** sich engagieren (für, bei); sich beteiligen (an) IV
iron ['aɪən] Eisen VI 3 (54)
irregular [ɪ'regjələ] unregelmäßig III
irritated [ɪrɪteɪtɪd] gereizt VI 4 (99)
is [ɪz] ist I
Islam ['ɪzlɑːm] Islam V
island ['aɪlənd] Insel II • **desert island** Wüsteninsel VI 3 (63)
it [ɪt] er/sie/es I • **It's £1.** Er/Sie/Es kostet 1 Pfund. I
IT [ˌaɪ 'tiː], **information technology** IT (Informationstechnologie) II
°**itch** [ɪtʃ] jucken
°**item** ['aɪtəm] Gegenstand
its [ɪts] sein/seine; ihr/ihre I
itself [ɪt'self]
  1. sich III
  2. selbst IV

J

jacket ['dʒækɪt] Jacke, Jackett II
January ['dʒænjuəri] Januar I
jazz [dʒæz] Jazz III
jealous (of) ['dʒeləs] neidisch (auf); eifersüchtig (auf) V
jeans *(pl)* [dʒiːnz] Jeans I

jet lag ['dʒet ˌlæg] Jetlag IV
Jew [dʒuː] Jude/Jüdin V
Jewish ['dʒuːɪʃ] jüdisch IV
job [dʒɒb] Aufgabe, Job I • **do a good job** gute Arbeit leisten II
join sb./sth. [dʒɔɪn] sich jm. anschließen; bei jm./etwas mitmachen II • **join the army** zum Militär gehen VI 2 (32)
join in [ˌdʒɔɪn_'ɪn] mitmachen III
joke [dʒəʊk] Witz I
joke [dʒəʊk] scherzen, Witze machen II
journalist ['dʒɜːnəlɪst] Journalist/in IV
journey ['dʒɜːni] Reise, Fahrt III
joy [dʒɔɪ] Freude VI 4 (93)
Judaism ['dʒuːdeɪɪzm] Judaismus V
judge [dʒʌdʒ] Richter/in V
judge sb. (by) [dʒʌdʒ] jn. beurteilen, einschätzen (nach) IV
judo ['dʒuːdəʊ] Judo I • **do judo** Judo machen I
jug [dʒʌg] Krug I • **a jug of milk** ein Krug Milch I
juice [dʒuːs] Saft I
July [dʒu'laɪ] Juli I
jumble sale ['dʒʌmbl seɪl] Wohltätigkeitsbasar I
jump [dʒʌmp] springen II
June [dʒuːn] Juni I
jungle ['dʒʌŋgl] Dschungel IV
junior ['dʒuːniə]
  1. Junioren-, Jugend- I
  2. junior (to sb.) jm. untergeordnet IV
junta ['dʒʌntə, 'hʊntə] Junta V
just [dʒʌst]
  1. (einfach) nur, bloß I
  2. gerade (eben), soeben II
  just then genau in dem Moment; gerade dann II
  3. just like you genau wie du II
  just as ... as ebenso ... wie IV
  4. einfach III
justice ['dʒʌstɪs] Gerechtigkeit; Recht, Justiz VI 2 (39)

K

kangaroo [ˌkæŋgə'ruː] Känguru II
keen [kiːn] begeistert, leidenschaftlich VI 1 (15) • **keen to do sth. / on doing sth.** wild darauf sein, etwas zu tun V
keep [kiːp], **kept, kept** (be)halten; aufbewahren III • °**keep a log** Buch führen • **keep an eye on sth./sb.** nach jm./etwas Ausschau halten IV • **keep calm** ruhig/still bleiben; Ruhe bewahren V • **keep**

(on) doing sth. etwas weiter tun; etwas ständig tun IV • **keep in touch** in Verbindung bleiben, Kontakt halten III • **keep quiet** still sein, leise sein IV • **keep sth. alive** etwas am Leben halten IV • **keep sb./sth. out of sth.** jn./etwas (aus etwas) heraushalten V • **keep sth. warm/cool/open/...** etwas warm/kühl/offen/... halten II

keeper ['ki:pə] Torwart, Torfrau III

kept [kept] *siehe* **keep**

ketchup ['ketʃəp] Ketchup IV

kettle ['ketl] (Wasser-)Kessel, Wasserkocher VI 3 (60)

key [ki:] Schlüssel I • **key word** Stichwort, Schlüsselwort I • **key ring** Schlüsselring IV

key [ki:] Haupt-, entscheidende(r, s) V

keyboard ['ki:bɔ:d] Keyboard *(elektronisches Tasteninstrument)* III

kick [kɪk] *(mit dem Fuß)* treten (gegen) IV

kid [kɪd] Kind, Jugendliche(r) I

kill [kɪl] töten I

kilogram (kg) ['kɪləgræm]**, kilo** ['ki:ləʊ] Kilogramm, Kilo III • **a kilogram of oranges** ein Kilogramm Orangen III • **a 150-kilogram bear** ein 150 Kilogramm schwerer Bär III

kilometre (km) ['kɪləmi:tə] Kilometer III • **a ten-kilometre walk** eine Zehn-Kilometer-Wanderung III • **square kilometre** Quadratkilometer III

kind (of) [kaɪnd] Art (von) III

kind of scary *(infml)* irgendwie unheimlich III • **We kind of clicked.** *(infml)* Wir haben uns auf Anhieb irgendwie (schon) gut verstanden. VI 1 (9)

kind [kaɪnd] freundlich V

kindergarten ['kɪndəgɑ:tn] Kindergarten; *(USA)* Vorschule *(für 5-bis 6-Jährige)* IV

king [kɪŋ] König I

kingdom ['kɪŋdəm] Königreich VI 4 (99)

kiss [kɪs] (sich) küssen IV

kiss [kɪs] Kuss IV

kitchen ['kɪtʃɪn] Küche I

kite [kaɪt] Drachen I

knee [ni:] Knie I

kneel (down) [ni:l]**, knelt, knelt** sich hinknien V

knelt [nelt] *siehe* **kneel**

knew [nju:] *siehe* **know**

knife [naɪf]**, pl knives** [naɪvz] Messer III

knock (on) [nɒk] (an)klopfen (an) I

know [nəʊ]**, knew, known**
1. wissen I
2. kennen I
How do you know ...? Woher weißt du ...?/Woher kennst du ...? I • **know about sth.** von etwas wissen; über etwas Bescheid wissen II • **..., you know.** ..., wissen Sie. / ..., weißt du. I • **You know what, Sophie?** Weißt du was, Sophie? I

knowledge *(no pl)* ['nɒlɪdʒ] Wissen; Kenntnis(se) VI 1 (22)

known [nəʊn]
1. *siehe* **know**
2. bekannt IV

koala [kəʊˈɑ:lə] Koala V

L

°**label** ['leɪbl] beschriften, etikettieren

°**labelled** ['leɪbəld] mit der Aufschrift

labour ['leɪbə] Arbeit VI 3 (34/210)

ladder ['lædə] *(die)* Leiter IV

lady ['leɪdi] Dame V • **Ladies and gentlemen** Meine Damen und Herren V

laid [leɪd] *siehe* **lay**

lain [leɪn] *siehe* **lie**

lake [leɪk] (Binnen-)See II

lamp [læmp] Lampe I

land [lænd] landen II

land [lænd] Land III • **on land** auf dem Land III

landlady ['lændleɪdi] Vermieterin V

landline ['lændlaɪn] Festnetzleitung V

landlord ['lændlɔ:d] Vermieter V

landscape ['lændskeɪp] Landschaft V

lane [leɪn] Gasse, Weg III

language ['læŋgwɪdʒ] Sprache I • **foreign language** Fremdsprache V

laptop ['læptɒp] Laptop V

large [lɑ:dʒ] groß III

lasagne [ləˈzænjə] Lasagne I

last [lɑ:st]
1. letzte(r, s) I; • **the last day** der letzte Tag I • **at last** endlich, schließlich I
°2. als Letzte(r, s)

last [nn] (adv)

last [lɑ:st] (an-, fort)dauern VI 2 (40)

last-minute [ˌlɑ:st ˈmɪnɪt]**: a last-minute shot** ein Schuss in der letzten Minute III

late [leɪt] spät; zu spät I • **be late** zu spät sein/kommen I • **late at night** spät abends V • **Sorry, I'm late.** Entschuldigung, dass ich zu spät bin/komme. I

later ['leɪtə] später I

latest ['leɪtɪst] neueste(r, s) III

laugh [lɑ:f] lachen I • **laugh at sb.** jn. anlachen V • **laugh out loud** laut lachen II

laughable ['lɑ:fəbl] lächerlich VI 2 (35)

laughter ['lɑ:ftə] Gelächter II

launderette [lɔ:n'dret] Waschsalon VI 4 (100)

law [lɔ:]
1. Gesetz IV • **Basic Law** Grundgesetz *(der Bundesrepublik)* V • **pass a law** ein Gesetz verabschieden V
2. Jura V

lay [leɪ] *siehe* **lie**

lay the table [leɪ]**, laid, laid** den Tisch decken I

°**lay sth. out** [leɪ] etwas ausbreiten

layer ['leɪə] Schicht IV

°**layout** ['leɪaʊt] Layout, Gestaltung

lazy ['leɪzi] faul VI 2 (28)

lead (to sth.) [li:d]**, led, led** (zu etwas) führen IV

leader ['li:də] (An-)Führer/in, Leiter/in IV

leaf [li:f]**, pl leaves** [li:vz] Blatt VI 3 (58)

learn [lɜ:n] lernen I • **learn about sth.** etwas über etwas erfahren, etwas über etwas herausfinden II • **learning by doing** Lernen durch Handeln/Tun V

°**learned** ['lɜ:nɪd] *(fml)* gelehrt

least [li:st] am wenigsten IV • **at least** zumindest, wenigstens I

leather ['leðə] Leder III

leave [li:v]**, left, left**
1. (weg)gehen; abfahren II
2. verlassen II
3. **leave (behind)** zurücklassen IV
4. **leave sth. out** etwas auslassen V
°5. **leave sb. cold** jn. kaltlassen

led [led] *siehe* **lead**

left [left] *siehe* **leave** • **be left** übrig sein II

left [left] linke(r, s) I • **look left** nach links schauen I • **on the left** links, auf der linken Seite I • **take a left** *(AE)* nach links/rechts abbiegen IV • **to the left** nach links III **turn left** (nach) links abbiegen II

°**left back** [ˌleft ˈbæk] Linksverteidiger/in

leg [leg] Bein I

legal ['li:gl] legal IV

leisure centre ['leʒə sentə] Freizeitzentrum, -park II

lemonade [ˌleməˈneɪd] Limonade I

lend sb. sth. [lend], **lent, lent** jm. etwas leihen II

length [leŋθ] Länge; Dauer; Stück VI 4 (104)

lens [lenz] Linse (in der Optik) VI 3 (56)

lent [lent] siehe **lend**

lentil ['lentəl] Linse (Hülsenfrucht) III

leotard ['liːətɑːd] Gymnastikanzug; Turnanzug III

less [les] weniger IV • **more or less** mehr oder weniger IV

lesson ['lesn] (Unterrichts-)Stunde I • **lessons** (pl) Unterricht I

let [let], **let, let** lassen II • **Let's ...** Lass uns ... / Lasst uns ... I • **Let's go.** Auf geht's! (wörtlich: Lass uns gehen.) I • **Let's look at the list.** Sehen wir uns die Liste an. / Lasst uns die Liste ansehen. I • **let sb. do sth.** jm. erlauben, etwas zu tun; zulassen, dass jd. etwas tut III

letter ['letə]
1. Buchstabe I • **capital letter** Großbuchstabe III • **small letter** Kleinbuchstabe III
2. letter (to) ['letə] Brief (an) II **letter of application** Bewerbungsschreiben V

lettuce ['letɪs] (Kopf-)Salat II

level ['levl] (Lern-)Stand, Niveau, Grad V

liberty ['lɪbəti] Freiheit IV

library ['laɪbrəri] Bibliothek, Bücherei I

license plate ['laɪsns pleɪt] (AE) Nummernschild IV

lie (-ing form: **lying**) [laɪ], **lay, lain** liegen IV

lie (to sb.) (-ing form: **lying**) [laɪ] jn. (an)lügen IV

life [laɪf], pl **lives** [laɪvz] Leben I **life coach** Lebensberater/in V **life expectancy** Lebenserwartung V • **life sciences** (pl) Biowissenschaften VI 3 (52) • **life sentence** lebenslängliche Haftstrafe IV **way of life** Lebensart III • **real-life** aus dem echten Leben VI 4 (105)

lifeline ['laɪflaɪn] Rettungsleine VI 4 (90)

lifestyle ['laɪfˌstaɪl] Lebensstil VI 3 (60)

lift [lɪft] (an-, hoch)heben IV

lift [lɪft] Fahrstuhl, Aufzug II

light [laɪt] Licht III • **light bulb** Glühlampe VI 3 (53) • °**light energy** Lichtmenge

°**lighting** ['laɪtɪŋ] Beleuchtung

lights (pl) [laɪts] Beleuchtung VI 2 (32)

like [laɪk]
1. wie I • **just like you** genau wie du II • **language like that** solche Sprache IV • **like what?** wie zum Beispiel? IV • **What was the weather like?** Wie war das Wetter? II
2. (infml) als ob III

like [laɪk] mögen, gernhaben I **like sth. better** etwas lieber mögen II • **like sth. very much** etwas sehr mögen II • **I like dancing/swimming...** Ich tanze/ schwimme... gern. I • **I'd like ... (= I would like ...)** Ich hätte gern ... / Ich möchte gern ... I • **I'd like to go (= I would like to go)** Ich würde gern gehen / Ich möchte gehen I **I wouldn't like to go** Ich würde nicht gern gehen / Ich möchte nicht gehen I • **Would you like ...?** Möchtest du ...? / Möchten Sie ...? I

likely ['laɪkli]: **be likely to do/be sth.** etwas wahrscheinlich tun/ sein VI 2 (39)

likes and dislikes (pl) [laɪks, 'dɪslaɪks] Vorlieben und Abneigungen V

limit ['lɪmɪt] Begrenzung, Beschränkung III • **speed limit** Geschwindigkeitsbegrenzung, -beschränkung III

limit sth./sb. ['lɪmɪt] etwas einschränken; etwas beschränken/ begrenzen (auf) VI 2 (42)

line [laɪn]
1. Zeile II • °**learn your lines** seinen Text lernen
2. (U-Bahn-)Linie III
3. Schlange, Reihe (wartender Menschen) IV • **Line starts here.** Hier anstellen. IV • **line of work** Beruf, berufliche Richtung IV • **be in a line of work** einen Beruf ausüben IV

link [lɪŋk] verbinden, verknüpfen I

link [lɪŋk] Verbindung III

linking word ['lɪŋkɪŋ wɜːd] Bindewort II

lion ['laɪən] Löwe II

lip [lɪp] Lippe IV

list [lɪst] auflisten, aufzählen II

list [lɪst] Liste I • **put one's name on a list** sich eintragen IV

listen (to) ['lɪsn] zuhören; sich etwas anhören I • **listen for sth.** auf etwas horchen, achten III

listener ['lɪsnə] Zuhörer/in II

literature ['lɪtrətʃə] Literatur V

litter ['lɪtə] Abfälle zurücklassen IV

litter ['lɪtə] Abfall IV

little ['lɪtl]
1. klein I
2. wenig IV • **a little** ein bisschen, ein wenig IV

live [lɪv] leben, wohnen I **standard of living** Lebensstandard V

live [laɪv]: **live concert** Livekonzert III • **live music** Livemusik II

lives [laɪvz] Plural von „life" I

living-history museum Freilichtmuseum IV

living room ['lɪvɪŋ ruːm; rʊm] Wohnzimmer I

lizard ['lɪzəd] Eidechse V

load [ləʊd] beladen III

loads of [ləʊdz] viel, viele VI 3 (61)

lobby ['lɒbi] Eingangshalle IV

local ['ləʊkl] örtlich, Lokal-; am/vom Ort III

location [ləʊ'keɪʃn] (Einsatz-)Ort, Platz III

loch [lɒx] (Binnen-)See in Schottland III

lock [lɒk] Schleuse III

lock [lɒk] abschließen, zuschließen I • **lock up** abschließen II

°**log** [lɒg]: **keep a log** Buch führen

°**logic** ['lɒdʒɪk] Logik

logical ['lɒdʒɪkl] logisch (denkend) V

logo ['ləʊgəʊ] Logo, Markenzeichen III

lonely ['ləʊnli] einsam V

long [lɒŋ] lang I • **a long way (from)** weit entfernt (von) I • **a long time** lange III

°**long for sb./sth.** [lɒŋ] sich nach jm./ etwas sehnen

longer ['lɒŋgə]: **no longer** nicht mehr, nicht länger VI 3 (56)

look [lʊk]
1. schauen, gucken I
2. look different/great/old anders/toll/alt aussehen I • **look after sth./sb.** sich um etwas/jn. kümmern; auf etwas/jn. aufpassen II • **look at** ansehen, anschauen I **look at sth. closely** etwas genau anschauen III • **look down on sb.** auf jn. herabsehen VI 1 (12) • **look for** suchen II • **look forward to sb./sth.** sich auf jn./etwas freuen IV • **look left and right** nach links und rechts schauen I • **look around/round** sich umsehen I **look up (from)** hochsehen, aufschauen (von) II • **look up to sb.** zu jm. aufsehen IV • **look up words** Wörter nachschlagen III

°**look** [lʊk]: **the look of sb.'s face** wie jemand aussieht

Lord [lɔːd] Herr(gott) IV
lose [luːz], **lost, lost** verlieren II
loss [lɒs] Verlust VI 4 (93)
lost [lɒst]
  1. *siehe* **lose**
  2. get lost sich verlaufen III
lot [lɒt]: **a lot (of), lots of** eine Menge, viel, viele I / II • **He likes her a lot.** Er mag sie sehr. I • **lots more** viel mehr I • **Thanks a lot!** Vielen Dank! I
loud [laʊd] laut I
love [lʌv] lieben, sehr mögen I
  love sth. very much etwas sehr lieben II
love [lʌv]
  1. Liebe II • **be in love** verliebt sein V • **fall in love (with sb.)** sich verlieben (in jn.) IV • **Love ...** Liebe Grüße, ... *(Grußformel am Ende eines Briefes)* • **love story** Liebesgeschichte VI 4 (76) • **make love** miteinander schlafen, sich lieben V
  2. „Liebes", „Liebling" III
lovely ['lʌvli] schön, hübsch, wunderbar II
low [ləʊ] niedrig VI 2 (30)
lower sth. [ləʊə] etwas hinunterlassen, senken VI 1 (21)
luck [lʌk]: **Good luck (with ...)!** Viel Glück (bei/mit ...)! I
luckily ['lʌkɪli] zum Glück, glücklicherweise II
lucky ['lʌki]: **be lucky** Glück haben III
°lunar rover [ˌluːnə 'rəʊvə] Mondfahrzeug
lunch [lʌntʃ] Mittagessen I • **for lunch** zum Mittagessen III
  lunch break Mittagspause I
  lunchtime ['lʌntʃtaɪm] Mittagszeit III
lyrics *(pl)* ['lɪrɪks] Liedtext(e) III

M

°Ma'am [mæm] Majestät
machine [məˈʃiːn] Maschine, Gerät II
mad [mæd]
  1. verrückt I • **mad about** verrückt nach III
  2. mad (at sb.) *(bes AE, infml)* wütend (auf jn.) VI 1 (10)
madam ['mædəm]: **Dear Sir or Madam ...** Sehr geehrte Damen und Herren IV
made [meɪd]
  1. *siehe* **make**
  2. be made of sth. aus etwas (ge-

macht) sein III • **be made up of sth.** aus etwas bestehen V
magazine [ˌmæɡəˈziːn] Zeitschrift, Magazin I
magical ['mædʒɪkl] zauberhaft, wundervoll V
magnet ['mæɡnət] Magnet V
magnificent [mæɡˈnɪfɪsənt] großartig, herrlich VI 4 (96)
mail sb. [meɪl] jn. anmailen II
  mail sb. sth. jm. etwas schicken, senden *(vor allem per E-Mail)* III
main [meɪn] Haupt- III
mainly ['meɪnli] hauptsächlich, vorwiegend V
maize *(no pl)* [meɪz] *(BE)* Mais IV
°majesty ['mædʒəsti]: **Your Majesty** Eure Majestät
major ['meɪdʒə] groß, bedeutend VI 4 (77)
majority [məˈdʒɒrəti] Mehrheit IV
make [meɪk], **made, made** machen; bauen I • **make a call** ein Telefongespräch führen, telefonieren II
  make a deal ein Abkommen/eine Abmachung treffen III • **make a decision** eine Entscheidung treffen/fällen VI 2 (32/209) • **make an impression** einen Eindruck machen VI 4 (80/226) • **make a mess** alles durcheinanderbringen, alles in Unordnung bringen I • **make a speech** eine Rede halten IV
  make friends (with) Freunde finden; sich anfreunden (mit) II
  make love miteinander schlafen, sich lieben V • **make sense** Sinn ergeben VI 3 (64/221) • **make sb. do sth.** jn. zwingen, etwas zu tun; jn. dazu bringen, etwas zu tun V
  make sb. sth. jn. zu etwas machen III • **make sth. up** etwas bilden V
  make sure sich vergewissern IV
make-up ['meɪkʌp] Make-up II
  make-up artist Maskenbildner/in
male [meɪl] männlich VI 2 (31)
male [meɪl]
  1. männliche Person VI 2 (31)
  2. Männchen II
mall [mɔːl, *BE auch* mæl] *(großes)* Einkaufszentrum III
man [mæn], *pl* **men** [men] Mann I
°manage ['mænɪdʒ] zurechtkommen
manage a problem ['mænɪdʒ] mit einem Problem umgehen, ein Problem lösen V
manager ['mænədʒə] Manager/in III
many ['meni] viele I • **how many?** wie viele? I • **Many thanks.** Vielen Dank. VI 2 (40)
map [mæp] Landkarte, Stadtplan II

March [mɑːtʃ] März I
march [mɑːtʃ] Marsch, Demonstration IV
march [mɑːtʃ] marschieren, demonstrieren VI 2 (42)
marcher ['mɑːtʃə] Demonstrant/in VI 2 (42)
mark [mɑːk] (Schul-)Note, Zensur IV
mark [mɑːk]: **quotation marks** Anführungszeichen, -striche III
mark sth. (up) [ˌmɑːk_ˈʌp] etwas markieren, kennzeichnen II
market ['mɑːkɪt] Markt II
  market forces Marktkräfte VI 2 (28/207)
marmalade ['mɑːməleɪd] Orangenmarmelade I
marriage ['mærɪdʒ] Ehe VI 1 (24)
married (to) ['mærɪd] verheiratet (mit) I • **get married** heiraten V
marry ['mæri] heiraten III
mass [mæs] Messe *(Gottesdienst)* IV
massage ['mæsɑːʒ] Massage II
  have a massage sich massieren lassen II
massive ['mæsɪv] riesig VI 4 (104)
match [mætʃ] Spiel, Wettkampf I
°match sth. (to sth.) [mætʃ] etwas (zu etwas) zuordnen
match [mætʃ] zusammenpassen VI 4 (91)
mate [meɪt] *(infml)* Freund/in, Kumpel V
material [məˈtɪəriəl] Material, Stoff II
maths [mæθs] Mathematik I
matter ['mætə]
  1. Angelegenheit, Sache VI 1 (20)
  no matter what ganz gleich, was VI 2 (28) • **What's the matter?** Was ist los? / Was ist denn? II
  °2. Materie
matter ['mætə] wichtig sein V
mattress ['mætrəs] Matratze V
mature [məˈtʃʊə] reif, vernünftig VI 2 (34)
maximum ['mæksɪməm] Maximum V
may [meɪ] dürfen I • **°May he/she rest in peace.** Ruhe in Frieden.
May [meɪ] Mai I
maybe ['meɪbi] vielleicht I
mayor ['meə] Bürgermeister/in IV
me [miː] mir; mich I • **°me and mine** ich und das meinige • **Me too.** Ich auch. I • **more than me** mehr als ich II • **That's me.** Das bin ich. I • **Why me?** Warum ich? I

Dictionary

meal [miːl] Mahlzeit, Essen III
set meal Menü III
mean [miːn], **meant, meant**
  1. bedeuten II
  2. meinen, sagen wollen I • **mean no harm** es nicht böse meinen VI 1 (14/200)
mean [miːn] gemein IV
meaning ['miːnɪŋ] Bedeutung I
means [miːnz]: **by no means** keineswegs VI 3 (55)
meant [ment] siehe **mean**
meat [miːt] Fleisch I
medal ['medl] Medaille III
media (pl) ['miːdiə] Medien III
mediate ['miːdieɪt] vermitteln IV
mediation [ˌmiːdi'eɪʃn] Vermittlung, Sprachmittlung, Mediation II
medium ['miːdiəm] mittel-, mittlere(r, s); mittelgroß II
medium ['miːdiəm], pl **media** Medium VI 1 (19)
meet [miːt], **met, met**
  1. treffen; kennenlernen I
  2. sich treffen I
meeting ['miːtɪŋ] Versammlung, Besprechung IV
melt [melt] schmelzen VI 3 (62)
member ['membə]: **member of staff** (BE), **staff member** (AE) Mitarbeiter/in IV
membership (of sth.) ['membəʃɪp] Mitgliedschaft (in etwas) V
memorable ['memərəbl] unvergesslich VI 4 (87)
memorial (to sb./sth.) [mə'mɔːriəl] Denkmal (für jn./etwas) V
memory ['meməri]
  1. Gedächtnis VI 1 (16)
  2. Erinnerung VI 1 (16)
  3. Speicher (Computer) VI 1 (16)
men [men] Plural von „man" I
mend [mend] reparieren VI 4 (103)
mention ['menʃn] erwähnen, nennen VI 4 (90)
menu ['menjuː] Speisekarte; Menü (Computer) III
merciless ['mɜːsɪləs] gnadenlos VI 2 (38)
merry-go-round ['merɪɡəʊˌraʊnd] Karussel IV
mess [mes]: **make a mess** alles durcheinanderbringen, alles in Unordnung bringen I
°**mess (it) up** [mes] (infml) etwas vermasseln
message ['mesɪdʒ]
  1. instant message Nachricht, die man im Internet austauscht (in Echtzeit) III
  2. Botschaft, Aussage VI 3 (64)
met [met] siehe **meet**

°**metal** ['metl] Metall
metaphor ['metəfə, 'metəfɔː] Metapher V
meter ['miːtə] (Gas-, Strom-)Zähler VI 3 (62)
method ['meθəd] Methode IV
metre ['miːtə]
  1. Meter II
  2. Metrum VI 4 (91/G)
mice [maɪs] Plural von „mouse" I
microphone ['maɪkrəfəʊn] Mikrofon III
mid [mɪd]: **in the mid-1800s** Mitte des 19. Jahrhunderts V
middle (of) ['mɪdl] Mitte; Mittelteil I • **the middle of nowhere** (infml) etwa: das Ende der Welt V
°**middle-class** [ˌmɪdl 'klɑːs] Mittelstand, -schicht
middle school [ˌmɪdl ˌskuːl] (USA) Schule für 11- bis 14-Jährige IV
might [maɪt]: **you might need help** du könntest (vielleicht) Hilfe brauchen III
migrant worker [ˌmaɪɡrənt 'wɜːkə] Wanderarbeiter/in IV
mild [maɪld] mild III
mile [maɪl] Meile (= ca. 1,6 km) II
  for miles meilenweit II
°**milestone** ['maɪlstəʊn] Meilenstein
military ['mɪlətri] militärisch, Militär- V • **military-style fashion** Mode im Militärstil V
milk [mɪlk] melken IV
milk [mɪlk] Milch I
milkshake ['mɪlkʃeɪk] Milchshake I
Milky Way [ˌmɪlki 'weɪ] Milchstraße VI 1 (16/201)
million ['mɪljən] Million III
millionaire [ˌmɪljə'neə] Millionär/in IV
mime [maɪm] vorspielen, pantomimisch darstellen II
mind (doing) sth. [maɪnd]
  1. etwas dagegen haben (etwas zu tun) V • **Do you mind?** Stört es dich/Sie? V • **I don't mind.** Es macht mir nichts aus. V • **if you don't mind** wenn Sie nichts dagegen haben V • **Would you mind ...?** Würden Sie bitte ...? V
  2. (sich kümmern) **Mind your own business.** Das geht dich nichts an! / Kümmere dich um deine eigenen Angelegenheiten! II **Never mind.** Kümmere dich nicht drum. / Macht nichts. II
mind [maɪnd] Verstand, Kopf V
°**state of mind** Geisteszustand
°**your mind is on sth.** du denkst an etwas

mind map ['maɪnd mæp] Mindmap („Gedankenkarte", „Wissensnetz") I
mine [maɪn] meiner, meine, meins II • °**me and mine** ich und das meinige
miner ['maɪnə] Bergarbeiter/in VI 3 (64)
°**mineral** ['mɪnərəl] Mineral
minimum ['mɪnɪməm] Minimum V
minister ['mɪnɪstə]
  1. Minister/in IV • **prime minister** Premierminister/in IV
  2. Pfarrer/in, Pastor/in IV
minor ['maɪnə] klein, unbedeutend VI 4 (77)
minority [maɪ'nɒrəti] Minderheit IV
mints (pl) [mɪnts] Pfefferminzbonbons I
minus ['maɪnəs] minus VI 1 (21/203)
minute ['mɪnɪt] Minute I • **Wait a minute.** Warte mal! / Moment mal! II • **a 30-minute ride** eine 30-minütige Fahrt III
Minuteman ['mɪnɪtˌmæn] Angehöriger der amerikanischen Miliz IV
mirror ['mɪrə] Spiegel II
Miss White [mɪs] Frau White (unverheiratet) I
miss [mɪs]
  1. vermissen II
  2. verpassen II
  Miss a turn. Einmal aussetzen. II
missing ['mɪsɪŋ]: **be missing** fehlen II
mistake [mɪ'steɪk] Fehler I • **by mistake** aus Versehen IV
misunderstanding [ˌmɪsʌndə'stændɪŋ] Missverständnis VI 2 (41)
mix [mɪks] mischen, mixen III
mix [mɪks] sich vermischen VI 1 (24)
mixed-race [ˌmɪkst 'reɪs] gemischtrassig V
mixture ['mɪkstʃə] Mischung III
mobile (phone) ['məʊbaɪl] Mobiltelefon, Handy I
model ['mɒdl] Modell(-flugzeug, -schiff usw.) I; (Foto-)Modell II
modern ['mɒdən] modern V
mole [məʊl] Maulwurf II
mom [mɑːm] (AE) Mutti, Mama; Mutter III
moment ['məʊmənt] Augenblick, Moment I • **at the moment** im Moment, gerade, zurzeit I • **for a moment** einen Moment lang II
°**momentum** [mə'mentəm]: **gain momentum** in Schwung/Fahrt kommen
monarch ['mɒnək] Monarch/in V
monarchy ['mɒnəki] Monarchie V

Monday ['mʌndeɪ, 'mʌndi] Montag I • **Monday morning** Montagmorgen I

money ['mʌni] Geld I • **Money doesn't grow on trees.** *Redensart:* Geld wächst nicht auf Bäumen; Geld liegt nicht auf der Straße. III **raise money (for)** Geld sammeln (für) IV

monitor ['mɒnɪtə] Bildschirm, Monitor III

monk [mʌŋk] Mönch V

monkey ['mʌŋki] Affe II

°**monologue** ['mɒnəlɒg] Monolog

monster ['mɒnstə] Monster, Ungeheuer III

month [mʌnθ] Monat I

mood [muːd] Laune V • **be in a good/bad mood** gute/schlechte Laune haben V

moon [muːn] Mond II

moped ['məʊped] Moped V

more [mɔː] mehr I • **lots more** viel mehr I • **more boring (than)** langweiliger (als) II • **more or less** mehr oder weniger IV • **more quickly (than)** schneller (als) II • **more than ever** mehr als je (zuvor), mehr denn je V • **more than me** mehr als ich II • **no more music** keine Musik mehr I • **not (...) any more** nicht mehr II • **one more** noch ein(e), ein(e) weitere(r, s) I • **the more ... the more ...** je mehr ... desto mehr ... VI 1 (10)

morning ['mɔːnɪŋ] Morgen, Vormittag I • **in the morning** morgens, am Morgen I • **Monday morning** Montagmorgen I • **on Friday morning** freitagmorgens, am Freitagmorgen I

mosque [mɒsk] Moschee III

mosquito [mɒsˈkiːtəʊ] Stechmücke, Moskito V

most [məʊst] (der/die/das) meiste ...; am meisten II • **most people** die meisten Leute I • **(the) most boring ...** der/die/das langweiligste ...; am langweiligsten II

mostly ['məʊstli] hauptsächlich, meistens VI 1 (10)

motel [məʊˈtel] Motel III

mother ['mʌðə] Mutter I

motorist ['məʊtərɪst] Autofahrer/in VI 3 (54)

motorway ['məʊtəweɪ] *(BE)* Autobahn IV

mountain ['maʊntən] Berg II

mouse [maʊs]**,** *pl* **mice** [maɪs] Maus I

mouth [maʊθ] Mund I

move [muːv]
1. bewegen; sich bewegen II **Move back one space.** Geh ein Feld zurück. II • **Move on one space.** Geh ein Feld vor. II
2. **move (to)** umziehen (nach, in) II • **move in** einziehen II • **move out** ausziehen II

move [muːv] Umzug IV

movement ['muːvmənt] Bewegung II

movie ['muːvi] Film IV

moving ['muːvɪŋ] bewegend VI 4 (87)

MP3 player [ˌempiːˈθriː ˌpleɪə] MP3-Spieler I

Mr, Mr. ... ['mɪstə] Herr ... I

Mrs, Mrs. ... ['mɪsɪz] Frau ... I

Ms, Ms. ... [mɪz, məz] Frau ... II

much [mʌtʃ] viel I • **how much?** wie viel? I • **How much is/are ...?** Was kostet/kosten ...? / Wie viel kostet/kosten ...? I • **like/love sth. very much** etwas sehr mögen / sehr lieben II • **Thanks very much!** Danke sehr! / Vielen Dank! II

mud [mʌd] Schlamm, Matsch V

muddy ['mʌdi] schlammig, matschig V

muesli ['mjuːzli] Müsli I

mug (-gg-) [mʌg] überfallen V

mule [mjuːl] Maultier IV • **mule train** Maultierkarawane IV

multi- ['mʌlti] viel-, mehr-; multi-, Multi- IV • **multi-coloured** mehrfarbig IV • **multi-millionaire** Multimillionär(in) IV • **multitasking** die Fähigkeit, mehrere Sachen gleichzeitig zu machen VI 1 (14)

multiply ['mʌltɪplaɪ] multiplizieren VI 1 (21/203)

mum [mʌm]**, mummy** ['mʌmi], Mama, Mutti; Mutter I

murder ['mɜːdə] (er)morden III

murder ['mɜːdə] Mord III

murderer ['mɜːdərə] Mörder/in III

museum [mjuːˈziːəm] Museum I

music ['mjuːzɪk]
1. Musik I • **Music is for dancing.** *etwa:* Musik ist zum Tanzen da. III
2. Noten III • **I can read music.** Ich kann Noten lesen. III

musical ['mjuːzɪkl] Musical I

musician [mjuːˈzɪʃn] Musiker/in III

Muslim ['mʊzlɪm] Muslim/Muslima, Muslimin; muslimisch V

must [mʌst] müssen I

mustard ['mʌstəd] Senf IV

mustn't do ['mʌsnt] nicht tun dürfen I

my [maɪ] mein/e I • **My name is ...** Ich heiße ... / Mein Name ist ... I

It's my turn. Ich bin dran / an der Reihe. I

myself [maɪˈself]
1. mir/mich III
2. selbst IV

mystery ['mɪstri] Rätsel, Geheimnis II

N

°**nah** [nɑː] *(infml)* nein

naked ['neɪkɪd] nackt V • **with the naked eye** mit dem bloßen Auge V

name [neɪm] Name I • **My name is ...** Ich heiße ... / Mein Name ist ... I • **What's your name?** Wie heißt du? I • **call sb. names** jn. mit Schimpfwörtern hänseln, jm. Schimpfwörter nachrufen III **put one's name on a list** sich eintragen IV

name [neɪm] nennen; benennen II

narrator [nəˈreɪtə] Erzähler/in IV

nation ['neɪʃn] Nation, Volk III **the First Nations** die Ersten Nationen *(indianische Ureinwohner/innen Kanadas)* III

national ['næʃnəl] national III **national park** Nationalpark IV

nationality [ˌnæʃəˈnæləti] Staatsangehörigkeit, Nationalität V

nationwide [ˌneɪʃnˈwaɪd] landesweit, im ganzen Land VI 1 (14)

Native American [ˌneɪtɪv_əˈmerɪkən] amerikanische(r) Ureinwohner/in, Indianer/in IV

natural ['nætʃrəl] natürlich, Natur- II • **natural forces** Naturgewalten VI 2 (28/207) • **natural selection** natürliche Selektion VI 3 (55)

nature ['neɪtʃə] Natur II

near [nɪə] in der Nähe von, nahe (bei) I

nearby [ˌnɪəˈbaɪ] *(adj)* nahegelegen; *(adv)* in der Nähe V

nearly ['nɪəli] fast, beinahe IV

neat [niːt]
1. gepflegt II • **neat and tidy** schön ordentlich II
2. *(AE, infml)* großartig, toll, klasse III

necessary ['nesəsri] notwendig, nötig V

neck [nek] Hals IV

need [niːd] brauchen, benötigen I

need [niːd]**: someone in need** ein/e Notleidende(r) VI 2 (39)

needle ['niːdl] Nadel VI 3 (56)

needn't do ['niːdnt] nicht tun müssen, nicht zu tun brauchen II

Dictionary

negative ['negətɪv] negativ v

neglect [nɪ'glekt] vernachlässigen; versäumen (zu tun) VI 4 (83)

neighbour ['neɪbə] Nachbar/in I

neighbourhood ['neɪbəhʊd] Gegend, Stadtbereich; Nachbarschaft v

°**neighbouring** ['neɪbərɪŋ] benachbart

Neither. ['naɪðə, 'niːðə] Weder noch.; Keiner der beiden. v

nerve [nɜːv] Nerv VI 1 (12) • **get on sb.'s nerves** jm. auf die Nerven gehen VI 1 (12) • **have the nerve to do sth.** die Frechheit besitzen, etwas zu tun VI 1 (12/199)

nervous ['nɜːvəs] nervös, aufgeregt I

network ['netwɜːk] (Fernseh-/ Radio-) Sendernetz IV • **social networking** soziales Netzwerk (vor allem im Internet) VI 1 (8) **social networking site** eine Website zur Bildung und Unterhaltung sozialer Netzwerke VI 1 (8)

neutral ['njuːtrəl] neutral VI 2 (31)

never ['nevə] nie, niemals I **Never mind.** Kümmere dich nicht drum. / Macht nichts. II

nevertheless [ˌnevəðə'les] trotzdem VI 1 (20)

new [njuː] neu I

news (no pl) [njuːz] Nachrichten I

news agency ['njuːz_ˌeɪdʒənsi] Nachrichtenagentur IV

newspaper ['njuːspeɪpə] Zeitung I **do a (news)paper round** Zeitungen austragen v

next [nekst]: **be next** der/die Nächste sein I • **the next day** am nächsten Tag I • **the next photo** das nächste Foto I • **What have we got next?** Was haben wir als Nächstes? I

next to [nekst] neben I

nice [naɪs] schön, nett I; sympathisch VI 2 (28/206) • **nice and cool/ clean/...** schön kühl/sauber/... I **Nice to meet you.** Nett, dich/ euch/Sie kennenzulernen. III

°**nickname** ['nɪkneɪm] Spitzname I

night [naɪt] Nacht, später Abend I **at night** nachts, in der Nacht I **by day and by night** bei Tag und bei Nacht v • **late at night** spät abends v • **on Friday night** freitagnachts, Freitagnacht I

nightclub ['naɪtklʌb] Nachtklub III

nightmare ['naɪtmeə] Albtraum VI 1 (16)

nil [nɪl] null III

no [nəʊ] nein I

no [nəʊ] kein, keine I • **by no means** keineswegs VI 3 (55) • **no longer** nicht mehr, nicht länger VI 3 (56) • **no matter what** ganz gleich, was VI 2 (28) • **no more music** keine Musik mehr I • **no people at all** überhaupt keine Menschen IV • **No way!** [ˌnəʊ 'weɪ] Auf keinen Fall! / Kommt nicht in Frage! II; Was du nicht sagst! / Das kann nicht dein Ernst sein! III

no., pl nos. ['nʌmbə] Nr. III

noble ['nəʊbl] ehrenhaft; adlig IV

nobody ['nəʊbədi] niemand II

nod (-dd-) [nɒd] nicken (mit) II **nod (one's head)** (mit dem Kopf) nicken III

noise [nɔɪz] Geräusch; Lärm I

noisy ['nɔɪzi] laut, lärmend II

°**none** [nʌn] keine(r, s)

non-fiction ['nɒnˌfɪkʃn] Sachliteratur IV

non-living [ˌnɒn'lɪvɪŋ] nichtlebend, tot VI 3 (55)

non-violence [ˌnɒn'vaɪələns] Gewaltlosigkeit, Gewaltfreiheit VI 2 (41)

non-violent [ˌnɒn 'vaɪələnt] gewaltlos, gewaltfrei IV

no one ['nəʊ wʌn] niemand III

north [nɔːθ] Norden; nach Norden; nördlich II • **northbound** ['nɔːθbaʊnd] Richtung Norden III **north-east** [ˌnɔːθ'iːst] Nordosten; nach Nordosten; nordöstlich II **northern** ['nɔːðən] nördlich, Nord- III • **north-west** [ˌnɔːθ'west] Nordwesten; nach Nordwesten; nordwestlich II

nose [nəʊz] Nase I

not [nɒt] nicht I • **not (...) any** kein, keine I • **not (...) any more** nicht mehr II • **not (...) anybody** niemand II • **not (...) anything** nichts II • **not (...) anywhere** nirgendwo(hin) II • **not at all** gar nicht, überhaupt nicht, überhaupt kein(e) IV • **not (...) either** auch nicht II • **not only ... but also ...** nicht nur ... sondern auch ... IV **not (...) yet** noch nicht II

note [nəʊt]
1. Mitteilung, Notiz I • **take notes (on)** sich Notizen machen (über, zu) I
2. Ton III
3. (BE) (Geld-)Schein, Banknote v

note [nəʊt]
1. (be)merken VI 4 (91)
°2. notieren

note sth. down [ˌnəʊt 'daʊn] (sich) etwas notieren VI 1 (11)

nothing ['nʌθɪŋ] nichts II **nothing at all** gar nichts, überhaupt nichts IV

notice ['nəʊtɪs] (be)merken IV

notice board ['nəʊtɪs bɔːd] schwarzes Brett, Anschlagtafel IV

notion ['nəʊʃn] Vorstellung, Idee VI 3 (55)

novel ['nɒvl] Roman IV

November [nəʊ'vembə] November I

now [naʊ] nun, jetzt I • **(and) now for ...** und jetzt ... (kündigt ein neues Thema an) III • **now and again** ab und zu, von Zeit zu Zeit III

nowadays ['naʊədeɪz] heutzutage IV

nowhere ['nəʊweə] nirgendwo(hin) v • **the middle of nowhere** (infml) etwa: das Ende der Welt v

nuclear ['njuːklɪə] Kern-, Atom- VI 3 (53) • **nuclear fusion** Kernfusion VI 3 (53)

number ['nʌmbə] Zahl, Ziffer, Nummer I

number plate ['nʌmbə ˌpleɪt] Nummernschild IV

nun [nʌn] Nonne v

nut [nʌt] Nuss III

O

o [əʊ] null I

obey [ə'beɪ] gehorchen; sich halten an IV

object ['ɒbdʒɪkt] Gegenstand VI 3 (55)

objective [əb'dʒektɪv] objektiv v

observatory [əb'zɜːvətri] Aussichtsplattform v

obtain [əb'teɪn] (fml) erhalten, erwerben VI 3 (55)

obviously ['ɒbvɪəsli] offensichtlich VI 1 (20)

occupy ['ɒkjuːpaɪ] besetzen v

occur (to sb.) [ə'kɜː] jm. einfallen VI 3 (54)

ocean ['əʊʃn] Ozean IV

o'clock [ə'klɒk]: **eleven o'clock** elf Uhr I

October [ɒk'təʊbə] Oktober I

of [əv, ɒv] von I • **of the summer holidays** der Sommerferien I **a kilogram of oranges** ein Kilogramm Orangen III

of course [əv 'kɔːs] natürlich, selbstverständlich I

°**off** [ɒf]: **off a bridge** von einer Brücke (herunter)

offensive [əˈfensɪv] beleidigend, Anstoß erregend VI 2 (31)

offer [ˈɒfə] (an)bieten IV

office [ˈɒfɪs] Büro V

office worker [ˈɒfɪs ˌwɜːkə] Büroangestellte(r) V

official [əˈfɪʃl] amtlich, Amts- V

often [ˈɒfn] oft, häufig I

Oh dear! Oje! II

OHP [ˌəʊˌeɪtʃ ˈpiː] Tageslichtprojektor, Polylux V

Oh well ... [əʊ ˈwel] Na ja ... / Na gut ... I

oil [ɔɪl] Öl VI 3 (56)

OK [əʊˈkeɪ] okay, gut, in Ordnung I

old [əʊld] alt I • **How old are you?** Wie alt bist du? I • **I'm ... years old.** Ich bin ... Jahre alt. I • **old people's home** Altenheim, Seniorenresidenz V

old-fashioned [ˌəʊldˈfæʃənd] altmodisch IV

oldie [ˈəʊldi] (infml) Oldie III

oligarchy [ˈɒlɪɡɑːki] Oligarchie V

Olympic Games [əˌlɪmpɪk ˈɡeɪmz] Olympische Spiele IV

omniscient [ɒmˈnɪsɪənt] (fml) allwissend VI 4 (84/G)

on [ɒn]
  1. auf I
  2. weiter III
  3. (Radio, Licht usw.) an, eingeschaltet II
  be on (in the cinema, theatre, etc.) laufen (im Kino, Theater, usw.) V
  go on angehen III • **on a/my shift** in einer/meiner Schicht IV • **on 13th June** am 13. Juni I • **on foot** zu Fuß III • **on Friday** am Freitag I • **on Friday afternoon** freitagnachmittags, am Freitagnachmittag I • **on Friday evening** freitagabends, am Freitagabend I • **on Friday morning** freitagmorgens, am Freitagmorgen I • **on Friday night** freitagnachts, Freitagnacht I • **on his street** in seiner Straße III • **on the beach** am Strand II • **on the board** an die Tafel I • **on the left** links, auf der linken Seite I • **on the Missouri River** am Missourifluss IV • **on the phone** am Telefon I • **on the plane** im Flugzeug II • **on the radio** im Radio I • **on the right** rechts, auf der rechten Seite I • **on the scene** vor Ort, zur Stelle IV • **on the second floor** im zweiten Stock (BE) / im ersten Stock (AE) IV • **on the train** im Zug I • **on their/your/the way (to)** unterwegs (nach) IV • **on the weekend** (AE) am Wochenende IV

on top of oben auf IV • **on TV** im Fernsehen I • **What page are we on?** Auf welcher Seite sind wir? I • **be on holiday** in Urlaub sein II • **go on holiday** in Urlaub fahren II • **straight on** geradeaus weiter II

once [wʌns] einmal III • **once/twice a week** (einmal/zweimal) pro Woche III • **at once 1.** gleichzeitig, zugleich, auf einmal V **2.** sofort V

one [wʌn] eins, ein, eine I • **one day** eines Tages I • **one more** noch ein/e, ein/e weitere(r, s) I • **a new one** ein neuer / eine neue / ein neues II • **my old ones** meine alten II • **one by one** eins nach dem anderen V • **one tough girl** (AE, infml) etwa: ein wirklich toughes Mädchen III • **our one world** unsere einzige Welt VI 3 (52)

°**oniomania** [ˌɒnɪəʊˈmeɪnɪə] Kaufsucht

onion [ˈʌnjən] Zwiebel III

online [ˌɒnˈlaɪn] online, Online- III

only [ˈəʊnli]
  1. nur, bloß I • **not only ... but also ...** nicht nur ... sondern auch ... IV
  2. erst II
  3. the only guest der einzige Gast I

onto [ˈɒntə, ˈɒntʊ] auf (... hinauf) III

open [ˈəʊpən]
  1. öffnen, aufmachen I
  2. sich öffnen I

open [ˈəʊpən] geöffnet, offen I **open-air concert** [ˌəʊpən ˈeə ˌkɒnsət] Open-Air-Konzert, Konzert im Freien II • **opening times** Öffnungszeiten IV • **open-ended** VI 4 (89/G) offen, nicht entschieden

opera [ˈɒprə] Oper III

opera house [ˈɒprə haʊs] Oper, Opernhaus III

operation (on) [ˌɒpəˈreɪʃn] Operation (an) III

opinion (on/of) [əˈpɪnjən] Meinung (zu/von) IV • **in my opinion** meiner Meinung nach IV

opponent [əˈpəʊnənt] Gegner/in IV

opportunity [ˌɒpəˈtjuːnəti] Gelegenheit, Chance, Möglichkeit V

opposite [ˈɒpəzɪt] gegenüber (von) II

opposite [ˈɒpəzɪt] entgegengesetzt; gegenüberliegende(r, s) V • **the opposite sex** das andere Geschlecht VI 3 (63/221)

opposite [ˈɒpəzɪt] Gegenteil IV

oppressive [əˈpresɪv] repressiv, unterdrückerisch V

or [ɔː] oder I

oral [ˈɔːrəl] mündlich VI 1 (25)

orange [ˈɒrɪndʒ] orange(farben) I

orange [ˈɒrɪndʒ] Orange, Apfelsine I • **orange juice** [ˈɒrɪndʒ dʒuːs] Orangensaft I

orbit sth. [ˈɔːbɪt] etwas umkreisen VI 3 (55)

orchestra [ˈɔːkɪstrə] Orchester V

order [ˈɔːdə]
  1. Befehl, Anweisung, Anordnung V • **break an order** gegen eine Anordnung verstoßen V
  °**2.** Reihenfolge

order [ˈɔːdə]
  1. bestellen II
  2. befehlen V
  °**3.** ordnen

organization [ˌɔːɡənaɪˈzeɪʃn] Organisation IV

organize [ˈɔːɡənaɪz] organisieren, veranstalten III

organized [ˈɔːɡənaɪzd] (gut) organisiert V

origin [ˈɒrɪdʒɪn] Herkunft, Abstammung V; Entstehung, Ursprung VI 3 (52)

original (n; adj) [əˈrɪdʒənl] Original; Original-, ursprünglich IV **original version** Originalfassung IV

orphan [ˈɔːfən] Waise, Waisenkind V

other [ˈʌðə] andere(r, s) I • **the others** die anderen I • **the other way round** anders herum II

otherwise [ˈʌðəwaɪz] sonst IV

Ouch! [aʊtʃ] Autsch! I

ought [ɔːt]: **they ought to do more sport** sie sollten mehr Sport treiben VI 1 (18)

our [ˈaʊə] unser, unsere I

ours [ˈaʊəz] unsere(r, s) II

ourselves [aʊəˈselvz]
  1. uns III
  2. selbst IV

out [aʊt] heraus, hinaus; draußen II **be out** weg sein, nicht da sein I **out of ...** aus ... (heraus/hinaus) I

outback [ˈaʊtbæk]: **the outback** (Australien) das Hinterland V

outdoor [ˈaʊtdɔː] im Freien, Außen- III

outfit [ˈaʊtfɪt] Outfit (Kleidung; Ausrüstung) II

outline [ˈaʊtlaɪn] Gliederung IV

outside [ˌaʊtˈsaɪd]
  1. draußen I; Außen- IV; in der Natur V
  2. nach draußen II
  3. outside the room vor dem Zimmer; außerhalb des Zimmers I

Dictionary

261

oven [ˈʌvn] Ofen, Backofen IV
over [ˈəʊvə]
1. über, oberhalb von I • **all over the world** auf der ganzen Welt III • **from all over the world** aus der ganzen Welt II • **over here** herüber v • **over there** da drüben, dort drüben I • **over to ...** hinüber zu/nach ... II • **over time** im Laufe der Zeit IV
2. be over vorbei sein, zu Ende sein I
overall [ˌəʊvəˈrɔːl] Gesamt-, allgemein VI 3 (64)
overhead projector [ˌəʊvəhed prəˈdʒektə] Tageslichtprojektor, Polylux v
overseas [ˌəʊvəˈsiːz] ausländisch; im Ausland v
own [əʊn] besitzen IV
own [əʊn]: **our own pool** unser eigenes Schwimmbecken II • **on our/my/... own** allein, selbstständig (ohne Hilfe) IV
owner [ˈəʊnə] Besitzer/in, Eigentümer/in IV
°**oxygen** [ˈɒksɪdʒən] Sauerstoff
ozone hole [ˈəʊzəʊn həʊl] Ozonloch v

P

pace [peɪs] Tempo VI 4 (87)
pack [pæk] packen, einpacken II
packet [ˈpækɪt] Päckchen, Packung, Schachtel I • **a packet of mints** ein Päckchen/eine Packung Pfefferminzbonbons I
paddle [ˈpædl] paddeln III
paddle [ˈpædl] Paddel III
pads [pædz] Knieschützer; Schulterpolster III
page [peɪdʒ] (Buch-, Heft-)Seite I • **What page are we on?** Auf welcher Seite sind wir? I • °**page-turner** spannendes Buch
paid [peɪd] siehe **pay**
pain [peɪn] Schmerz(en) I • **cry in pain** vor Schmerzen schreien I
paint [peɪnt] (an)malen I; anstreichen II
paint [peɪnt] Farbe, Lack IV
painter [ˈpeɪntə] Maler/in II
painting [ˈpeɪntɪŋ] Gemälde, Bild; Malerei III
pair [peə]: **a pair (of)** ein Paar II
palace [ˈpæləs] Palast, Schloss III
palm tree [pɑːm] Palme v
panic (-ing form: **panicking**) [ˈpænɪk] in Panik geraten III

panicky [ˈpænɪki] (infml) in Panik, panisch VI 4 (105)
pants (pl) [pænts] (AE) Hose IV
paper [ˈpeɪpə]
1. Papier I
2. Zeitung v
do a paper round Zeitungen austragen v
parade [pəˈreɪd] Parade, Umzug IV
paradise [ˈpærədaɪs] Paradies III
paragraph [ˈpærəɡrɑːf] Absatz (in einem Text) II
Paralympics [ˌpærəˈlɪmpɪks] Paralympische Spiele (Olympische Spiele für Sportler/innen mit körperlicher Behinderung) III
paramedic [ˌpærəˈmedɪk] Sanitäter/in II
paraphrase [ˈpærəfreɪz] umschreiben, anders ausdrücken III
parcel [ˈpɑːsl] Paket I
pardon [ˈpɑːdn] begnadigen IV
parent [ˈpeərənt]: **a single parent** ein(e) Alleinerziehende(r) II
parents [ˈpeərənts] Eltern I
park [pɑːk] Park I • **car park** Parkplatz III • **national park** Nationalpark IV
park [pɑːk] parken v
parking lot [ˈpɑːkɪŋ lɒt] (AE) Parkplatz IV
parliament [ˈpɑːləmənt] Parlament III
parrot [ˈpærət] Papagei I
part [pɑːt] Teil I • **take part in sth.** teilnehmen an etwas III
participate (in) [pɑːˈtɪsɪpeɪt] teilnehmen (an) IV
particular [pəˈtɪkjələ] bestimmte(r, s), spezielle(r, s) v
partly [ˈpɑːtli] zum Teil, teilweise VI 1 (10)
partner [ˈpɑːtnə] Partner/in I
party [ˈpɑːti]
1. Party I
2. Partei VI 2 (34)
party [ˈpɑːti] (infml) feiern v
pass [pɑːs]
1. (herüber)reichen, weitergeben I • **pass sth. on** etwas weiterleiten, -geben IV • **pass round** herumgeben I
2. bestehen (Test, Prüfung usw.) v
3. genehmigen, verabschieden (Gesetz usw.) v
4. an etwas/jn. vorbeigehen/-fahren VI 2 (38)
passenger [ˈpæsɪndʒə] Passagier/in, Fahrgast III
passive [ˈpæsɪv] Passiv III
past [pɑːst] Vergangenheit II

past [pɑːst] vorbei (an), vorüber (an) II • **half past 11** halb zwölf (11.30 / 23.30) I • **quarter past 11** Viertel nach 11 (11.15 / 23.15) I
path [pɑːθ] Pfad, Weg II • **bridle path** [ˈbraɪdl ˌpɑːθ] Reitweg III
pathetic [pəˈθetɪk] jämmerlich; lächerlich VI 3 (61)
°**pathological** [ˌpæθəˈlɒdʒɪkl] pathologisch, krankhaft
patient [ˈpeɪʃnt] geduldig v
patrol [pəˈtrəʊl] Streife, Patrouille IV
pattern [ˈpætn] Muster VI 4 (90)
pause [pɔːz] eine Pause machen VI 4 (94)
pause [pɔːz] Pause VI 4 (94)
pavement [ˈpeɪvmənt] Gehweg, Bürgersteig IV
°**paw** [pɔː] Tatze
pay (for) [peɪ], **paid, paid** bezahlen II • **pay attention (to sth./sb.)** jm. zuhören, auf jn. hören/aufpassen VI 2 (30/208)
PE [ˌpiːˈiː], **Physical Education** [ˌfɪzɪkəl ˌedʒuˈkeɪʃn] Sportunterricht, Turnen I
peace [piːs] Frieden VI 2 (35) • °**May he/she rest in peace.** Ruhe in Frieden.
peaceful [ˈpiːsfl] friedlich; ruhig VI 2 (35)
pedestrian [pəˈdestriən] Fußgänger/in IV
pedestrian crossing [pəˌdestriən ˈkrɒsɪŋ] Fußgängerüberweg IV
°**peer** [pɪə] Ebenbürtige(r), Gleichaltrige(r) • **peer evaluation** Partnerbeurteilung
pen [pen] Kugelschreiber, Füller I
penalty [ˈpenəlti] Strafstoß; Elfmeter (Fußball) III
pence (p) (pl) [pens] Pence (Plural von „penny") I
pencil [ˈpensl] Bleistift I • **pencil case** [ˈpensl keɪs] Federmäppchen I • **pencil sharpener** [ˈpensl ʃɑːpnə] Bleistiftanspitzer I
penny [ˈpeni] kleinste britische Münze I
people [ˈpiːpl] Menschen, Leute I • **old people's home** Altenheim, Seniorenresidenz v
pepper [ˈpepə] Pfeffer v
per [pɜː, pə] pro III
per cent (%) [pəˈsent] Prozent III
percentage [pəˈsentɪdʒ] Prozentsatz, prozentualer Anteil v
perfect [ˈpɜːfɪkt] perfekt; ideal; vollkommen IV
perform [pəˈfɔːm] eine Vorstellung haben, auftreten; vorführen VI 2 (32/G)

performance [pə'fɔːməns] Vorstellung, Auftritt VI 2 (32/G)

performer: **(street) performer** [pə'fɔːmə] Straßenkünstler/in III

perhaps [pə'hæps] vielleicht V

period ['pɪəriəd]
1. (Unterrichts-/Schul-)Stunde IV
2. Zeit(-raum, -spanne) VI 4 (87)

person ['pɜːsn] Person I

personal ['pɜːsənl] persönlich III

personality [ˌpɜːsə'næləti] Persönlichkeit V

perspective [pə'spektɪv] Perspektive, Blickwinkel VI 4 (84/G)

persuade [pə'sweɪd] überreden V

pet [pet] Haustier I • **pet shop** Tierhandlung I

petrol ['petrəl] Benzin IV

petrol station ['petrəl ˌsteɪʃn] Tankstelle IV

phone [fəʊn] anrufen I

phone [fəʊn] Telefon I • **on the phone** am Telefon I • **phone number** Telefonnummer I • **pick up the phone** den Hörer abnehmen II

photo ['fəʊtəʊ] Foto I • **in the photo** auf dem Foto I • **take photos** Fotos machen, fotografieren I

°**photocopy** [ˌfəʊtəʊkɒpi] Fotokopie I

photograph ['fəʊtəɡrɑːf] Fotografie VI 4 (101)

photographer [fə'tɒɡrəfə] Fotograf/in II

photosynthesis [ˌfəʊtəʊ'sɪnθəsɪs] Photosynthese VI 3 (58)

phrase [freɪz] Ausdruck, (Rede-)Wendung II

piano [pi'ænəʊ] Klavier, Piano I
play the piano Klavier spielen I

pick [pɪk]: **pick fruit/flowers** Obst/Blumen pflücken IV • **pick sb. up** jn. abholen III • **pick sth. up** etwas hochheben, aufheben III
pick up the phone den Hörer abnehmen II

picnic ['pɪknɪk] Picknick II

picture ['pɪktʃə] Bild I • **in the picture** auf dem Bild I

pie [paɪ] Obstkuchen; Pastete II

pie chart ['paɪ tʃɑːt] Tortendiagramm V

piece [piːs]: **a piece of** ein Stück I
a piece of paper ein Stück Papier I
a piece of clothing Kleidungsstück IV • **piece of evidence** Beweis, Hinweis VI 3 (55)

°**pile** [paɪl] Haufen

pilgrim ['pɪlɡrɪm] Pilger/in IV

pilot ['paɪlət] Pilot/in IV

pink [pɪŋk] pink(farben), rosa I

pipe [paɪp] Pfeife III

pirate ['paɪrət] Pirat, Piratin I

pitch [pɪtʃ]: **football/hockey pitch** Fußball-/Hockeyplatz, -feld II

pity (for sb.) ['pɪti] Mitleid (mit jm.) VI 4 (78) • **It's a pity (that ...)** Es ist schade, dass ... II

pizza ['piːtsə] Pizza I

place [pleɪs] Ort, Platz I • **place of birth** Geburtsort IV • **take place** stattfinden II • **in other places** an anderen Orten, anderswo III

placement ['pleɪsmənt] Praktikum V

plain [pleɪn] einfach, schlicht IV

plan [plæn] Plan I

plan (-nn-) [plæn] planen II

plane [pleɪn] Flugzeug II • **on the plane** im Flugzeug II

planet ['plænɪt] Planet II

plant [plɑːnt] (ein-, aus-, be-)pflanzen IV

plant [plɑːnt] Pflanze IV

plastic ['plæstɪk] Plastik, Kunststoff IV

plate [pleɪt] Teller I • **a plate of chips** ein Teller Pommes frites I
license plate (AE) Nummernschild IV • **number plate** Nummernschild IV

platform ['plætfɔːm] Bahnsteig, Gleis III

play [pleɪ] spielen I • **play a trick on sb.** jm. einen Streich spielen II
°**play dead** sich totstellen • **play football** Fußball spielen I • **play the drums** Schlagzeug spielen III
play the fiddle Geige spielen III
play the guitar Gitarre spielen I
play the piano Klavier spielen I
play the violin Geige spielen III

play [pleɪ] Theaterstück I

player ['pleɪə] Spieler/in I

playwright ['pleɪraɪt] Dramatiker/in VI 4 (82/G)

pleasant ['pleznt] angenehm VI 1 (20/203)

please [pliːz] bitte (in Fragen und Aufforderungen) I

pleased [pliːzd]: **be pleased** sich freuen IV

pleasure ['pleʒə] Vergnügen VI 4 (93)
for pleasure (zum) Vergnügen VI 4 (93)

plenty of ['plenti_əv] reichlich, viel(e) IV

plot [plɒt] Handlung V

plug [plʌɡ] Stecker III

plus [plʌs] plus VI 1 (21/203)

plutocracy [pluː'tɒkrəsi] Plutokratie V

pm [ˌpiː_'em]: **7 pm** 7 Uhr abends/19 Uhr I

pocket ['pɒkɪt] Tasche (an Kleidungsstück) II • **pocket money** ['pɒkɪt mʌni] Taschengeld II

poem ['pəʊɪm] Gedicht I

poet ['pəʊɪt] Dichter/in VI 4 (78/G)

poetic [pəʊ'etɪk] dichterisch, poetisch VI 4 (87/G) • **poetic device** poetisches (Stil-)Mittel VI 4 (91/G)

poetry ['pəʊətri] Lyrik, Dichtung, Poesie VI 2 (27/G)

point [pɔɪnt] Punkt II • **11.4 (eleven point four)** 11,4 (elf Komma vier) II • **point of view** Standpunkt II • **from my point of view** aus meiner Sicht; von meinem Standpunkt aus gesehen II • **That's a good point.** Das ist ein gutes Argument. V • **There was no point.** Es hatte keinen Sinn. III • **What's the point?** Was soll das? III

point (at/to sth.) [pɔɪnt] zeigen, deuten (auf etwas) II

poison ['pɔɪzn] Gift V

poisonous ['pɔɪzənəs] giftig V

°**polar** ['pəʊlə] Polar-

police (pl) [pə'liːs] Polizei I • **police station** Polizeiwache, Polizeirevier II • **police officer** Polizist/in VI 2 (42)

policy (on sth.) ['pɒləsi] Politik (in Bezug auf etwas) VI 2 (34)

polish ['pɒlɪʃ] polieren VI 4 (103)

polite [pə'laɪt] höflich IV

political [pə'lɪtɪkl] politisch VI 2 (34)

politician [ˌpɒlə'tɪʃn] Politiker/in IV

politics ['pɒlətɪks] (die) Politik IV

°**pollute** [pə'luːt] verschmutzen

polluted [pə'luːtɪd] verseucht, verunreinigt V

pollution [pə'luːʃn] Verschmutzung IV

poltergeist ['pəʊltəɡaɪst] Poltergeist I

pond [pɒnd] Teich V

ponytail ['pəʊniteɪl] Pferdeschwanz (Frisur) III

pool [puːl] Schwimmbad, Schwimmbecken II

poor [pɔː, pʊə]
1. arm I • **poor Sophie** (die) arme Sophie I
2. schlecht VI 1 (14)
▶ S.217 the rich, the poor, etc.

pop (-pp-) [pɒp] (BE, infml) (schnell) irgendwo hingehen VI 3 (62)

pop siehe **population**

pop (music) [pɒp] Pop(musik) III

popcorn ['pɒpkɔːn] Popcorn II

popular ['pɒpjələ] populär, beliebt III

population [ˌpɒpju'leɪʃn] Bevölkerung, Einwohner(zahl) III

Dictionary

port [pɔːt] Hafen(stadt) V

posh [pɒʃ] vornehm, edel *(etwas abwertend)* V

°**position** [pəˈzɪʃn] Platz, Stelle, Standort

positive [ˈpɒzətɪv] positiv V

possession [pəˈzeʃən] Besitz, Besitzung; Eigentum V

possessive [pəˈzesɪv] besitzergreifend, vereinnahmend VI 1 (7)

possibility [ˌpɒsəˈbɪlɪti] Möglichkeit IV

possible [ˈpɒsəbl] möglich II

post [pəʊst] Post *(Briefe, Päckchen, ...)* III

post office [ˈpəʊst ˌɒfɪs] Postamt II

postcard [ˈpəʊstkɑːd] Postkarte II

poster [ˈpəʊstə] Poster I

postscript [ˈpəʊstskrɪpt] Postskript III

potato [pəˈteɪtəʊ], *pl* **potatoes** Kartoffel I • **potato chips** *(AE)* Kartoffelchips IV

pound (£) [paʊnd] Pfund *(britische Währung)* I

pound [paʊnd] Pfund *(Gewichtseinheit)*: **a three-pound ball** ein drei Pfund schwerer Ball III

pour [pɔː] eingießen VI 4 (99)

poverty [ˈpɒvəti] Armut V

power [ˈpaʊə]
1. Macht; Stärke V
2. Kraft, Energie, Strom VI 3 (53)
°**power cut** *(also* **powercut***)* Stromabschaltung, Stromausfall

power sth. [ˈpaʊə] etwas antreiben, etwas mit Energie versorgen VI 3 (53)

powerful [ˈpaʊəfl] mächtig, einflussreich V

practical [ˈpræktɪkl] praktisch; praxisnah, praxisbezogen V

practice [ˈpræktɪs] *im Lehrwerk:* Übungsteil I

practice [ˈpræktɪs] *(AE)* üben; trainieren IV

practise [ˈpræktɪs] üben; trainieren I

praise [preɪz] loben, preisen VI 4 (94)

pray [preɪ] beten IV

prayer [preə] Gebet IV

precinct [ˈpriːsɪŋkt]: **shopping precinct** Einkaufsviertel, Einkaufsstraße III

precise [prɪˈsaɪs] präzise, genau VI 2 (31)

predecessor [ˈpriːdɪsesə] Vorgänger/in, Vorläufer/in VI 3 (55)

predict [prɪˈdɪkt] voraussagen, vorhersagen VI 3 (54)

prefer sth. (to sth.) (-rr-) [prɪˈfɜː] etwas (einer anderen Sache) vorziehen; etwas lieber tun (als etwas) IV

°**preference** [ˈprefrəns] Vorliebe

prefix [ˈpriːfɪks] Präfix III

prejudice (against) [ˈpredʒʊdɪs] Voreingenommenheit (gegen), Vorurteil (gegenüber) IV

prejudiced: [ˈpredʒʊdɪst]: **be prejudiced (against)** voreingenommen sein (gegen), Vorurteile haben (gegenüber) IV

prepare [prɪˈpeə] vorbereiten; sich vorbereiten II • **prepare for** sich vorbereiten auf II

present [ˈpreznt]
1. Gegenwart I
2. Geschenk I

present sth. (to sb.) [prɪˈzent] (jm.) etwas präsentieren, vorstellen I; überreichen III

presentation [ˌpreznˈteɪʃn] Präsentation, Vorstellung I

present-day [ˌpreznt ˈdeɪ] heutige(r, s) IV

presenter [prɪˈzentə] Moderator/in II

preserve [prɪˈzɜːv] konservieren; erhalten, bewahren VI 1 (21)

president [ˈprezɪdənt] Präsident/in IV

°**presidential** [ˌprezɪˈdenʃl]
1. Präsidenten-
2. Präsidentschafts-

press [pres]: **the press** die Presse, Zeitungen VI 2 (29)

pressure [ˈpreʃə] Druck, Belastung VI 2 (28)

pretend [prɪˈtend] so tun, als ob V

°**pretend** [prɪˈtend] Spiel-, rhetorische(r, s)

pretty [ˈprɪti]
1. hübsch I
2. **pretty cool/good/...** ziemlich cool/gut/... II

prevent sth. [prɪˈvent] etwas verhindern IV • **prevent sb./sth. from doing sth.** jn./etwas daran hindern, etwas zu tun IV

previous [ˈpriːvəs] frühere(r, s), vorherige(r, s) VI 1 (16)

prewriting exercise [ˌpriːˈraɪtɪŋ] Übung vor dem Schreiben III

price [praɪs] (Kauf-)Preis I

primary school [ˈpraɪməri] *Grundschule in GB, von 4–5 bis 11 Jahren* V

prime minister [ˌpraɪm ˈmɪnɪstə] Premierminister/in IV

principal [ˈprɪnsəpl] *(bes. AE)* Schulleiter/in IV

print [prɪnt] Druck-, Print- VI 2 (34)

print sth. out [ˌprɪnt ˈaʊt] etwas ausdrucken II

prison [ˈprɪzn] Gefängnis IV • **in prison for murder** im Gefängnis wegen Mordes IV

prisoner [ˈprɪznə] Gefangene(r) IV

privacy [ˈprɪvəsi] Privatsphäre VI 2 (26)

private [ˈpraɪvət] privat V

privilege [ˈprɪvəlɪdʒ] Privileg V

prize [praɪz] Preis, Gewinn I

°**pro** [prəʊ]: **pros and cons** *(pl)* Vor- und Nachteile

probably [ˈprɒbəbli] wahrscheinlich II

problem [ˈprɒbləm] Problem II
manage a problem mit einem Problem umgehen, ein Problem lösen V

produce [prəˈdjuːs] produzieren, erzeugen, herstellen II

°**product** [ˈprɒdʌkt] Produkt, Erzeugnis

°**production** [prəˈdʌkʃn] Inszenierung

professional [prəˈfeʃənl] professionell IV

professor [prəˈfesə] Professor/in V

profile [ˈprəʊfaɪl] Profil; Beschreibung, Porträt V

program [ˈprəʊɡræm] *(AE)* Programm IV

programme [ˈprəʊɡræm] programmieren; planen IV

programme [ˈprəʊɡræm]
1. Programm I
2. (Fernseh-/Radio-)Sendung IV

progress [ˈprəʊɡres] Fortschritt V
°**in progress** im Gange

project (about, on) [ˈprɒdʒekt] Projekt (über, zu) I • **do a project** ein Projekt machen, durchführen II

projector [prəˈdʒektə]: **video projector** Videoprojektor, Beamer V

promise [ˈprɒmɪs] versprechen II

promise [ˈprɒmɪs] Versprechen VI 4 (92)

pronunciation [prəˌnʌnsiˈeɪʃn] Aussprache I

proof *(no pl)* [pruːf] Beweis(e) II

°**proof-read** [ˈpruːfriːd] Korrektur lesen; korrigieren

proper [ˈprɒpə] richtige(r, s), ordentliche(r, s) VI 1 (20)

prospect [ˈprɒspekt] Aussicht, Vorstellung VI 2 (35)

prostitute [ˈprɒstɪtjuːt] Prostituierte(r) V

protagonist [prəˈtæɡənɪst] Protagonist/in VI 4 (76/G)

protect sb./sth. (from sb./sth.) [prə'tekt] jn./etwas (be)schützen (vor jm./etwas) IV

protective [prə'tektɪv] Schutz-, schützend V

protest (against/about) [prə'test] protestieren (gegen) IV

protest ['prəʊtest] Protest IV

protester [prə'testə] Demonstrant/in VI 2 (42)

proud (of sb./sth.) [praʊd] stolz (auf jn./etwas) II

prove [pruːv] (jm.) etwas beweisen, nachweisen VI 1 (10)

provide sb. with sth. [prə'vaɪd] jm. etwas zur Verfügung stellen, jn. mit etwas ausstatten VI 3 (56)

PS [ˌpiː'es] (**postscript** ['pəʊstskrɪpt]) PS, Postskript *(Nachschrift unter Briefen)* III

psychological [ˌsaɪkə'lɒdʒɪkl] psychisch, psychologisch VI 2 (32)

psychologist [ˌsaɪ'kɒlədʒɪst] Psychologe, Psychologin VI 2 (32)

psychology [ˌsaɪ'kɒlədʒi] Psychologie VI 2 (32)

pub [pʌb] Kneipe, Lokal II

public ['pʌblɪk] öffentlich IV
public transport öffentlicher Verkehr IV

public ['pʌblɪk]: **the public** die Öffentlichkeit IV

publish ['pʌblɪʃ] veröffentlichen III

°**publisher** ['pʌblɪʃə] Verleger/in, Verlag V

pull [pʊl] ziehen I

pullover ['pʊləʊvə] Pullover II

punchline ['pʌntʃlaɪn] Pointe VI 4 (93/G)

punctual ['pʌŋktʃuəl] pünktlich V

punish ['pʌnɪʃ] bestrafen V

punishment ['pʌnɪʃmənt] Bestrafung, Strafe V

punk [pʌŋk] Punker/in II

purple ['pɜːpl] violett; lila I

purse [pɜːs] Geldbörse II

push [pʊʃ] drücken, schieben, stoßen I

put (-tt-) [pʊt], **put, put** legen, stellen, (etwas wohin) tun I • **put sth. away** wegräumen IV • °**put sth. down** etwas aus der Hand legen **put sth. in order** etwas in Ordnung bringen IV • **put sb. to bed** jn. ins Bett bringen III • **put sth. on** etwas anziehen *(Kleidung)*; etwas aufsetzen *(Hut, Helm)* II • °**put a play on** ein Theaterstück aufführen • **put out a fire** ein Feuer löschen IV • **put one's name on a list** sich eintragen IV • **You know how to put it.** Sie wissen, wie man es formuliert/ausdrückt. IV

puzzled ['pʌzld] verwirrt II

pyjamas *(pl)* [pə'dʒɑːməz] Schlafanzug II

Q

qualification [ˌkwɒlɪfɪ'keɪʃn] Abschluss, Qualifikation V

quality ['kwɒləti] Eigenschaft; Qualität IV

quarter ['kwɔːtə]: **quarter past 11** Viertel nach 11 (11.15 / 23.15) I **quarter to 12** Viertel vor 12 (11.45 / 23.45) I

quay [kiː] Kai III

queen [kwiːn] Königin III

question ['kwestʃn] Frage I • **ask questions** Fragen stellen I

questionnaire (on sth.) [ˌkwestʃə'neə] Fragebogen (zu etwas) V

queue [kjuː] Schlange, Reihe *(wartender Menschen)* IV

quick [kwɪk] schnell I

quiet ['kwaɪət] leise, still, ruhig I **keep quiet** still sein, leise sein IV

quilt [kwɪlt] Bettdecke, Federbett V

quite [kwaɪt] ziemlich; ganz III

quiz [kwɪz], *pl* **quizzes** ['kwɪzɪz] Quiz, Ratespiel I

quotation [kwəʊ'teɪʃn] Zitat V

quotation marks [kwəʊ'teɪʃn ˌmɑːks] Anführungszeichen, -striche III

°**quote** [kwəʊt] zitieren

R

rabbit ['ræbɪt] Kaninchen I

rabbitproof ['ræbɪtpruːf] kaninchensicher, kaninchen-fest V

race (sb./sth.) [reɪs] (mit jm./etwas) um die Wette laufen/schwimmen/fahren/... V

race [reɪs] Rennen, (Wett-)Lauf V

race [reɪs] Rasse V • **mixed-race** gemischtrassig V

racing ['reɪsɪŋ] (Pferde-)Rennsport V

racist ['reɪsɪst] Rassist/in; rassistisch V

racket ['rækɪt] Schläger *(Badminton, Tennis, Squash)* III

radiate ['reɪdieɪt] ausstrahlen, abstrahlen VI 3 (62)

radio ['reɪdiəʊ] Radio I • **on the radio** im Radio I

raft [rɑːft] Schlauchboot, Floß IV

raft [rɑːft] mit einem Schlauchboot/Floß fahren IV

railway ['reɪlweɪ] Eisenbahn II

rain [reɪn] Regen II

rainfall ['reɪnfɔːl] Niederschlag *(Regen)*; Regenfälle V

°**rainforest** ['reɪnfɒrɪst] Regenwald V

rainproof ['reɪnpruːf] regendicht V

rain [reɪn] regnen II

rainy ['reɪni] regnerisch II • **rainy season** Regenzeit II

raise sth. [reɪz] etwas (er)heben VI 1 (21)

raise [reɪz]: **raise money (for)** Geld sammeln (für) IV

ran [ræn] *siehe* **run**

rang [ræŋ] *siehe* **ring**

ranger ['reɪndʒə] Ranger/in, Aufseher/in III

°**rank** [ræŋk] (an)ordnen

°**ranking** ['ræŋkɪŋ] Rangliste

rap [ræp] Rap(musik) *(rhythmischer Sprechgesang)* I

rapid ['ræpɪd] rapide, schnell V

rapids *(pl)* ['ræpɪdz] Stromschnellen III

rapper ['ræpə] Rapper/in IV

rare [reə] selten VI 1 (21)

rat [ræt] Ratte III

rate [reɪt] Rate V • **birth rate** Geburtsrate V • **death rate** Sterberate V

rate [reɪt] bewerten, einschätzen V

rather ['rɑːðə] ziemlich VI 3 (55)

°**rating** ['reɪtɪŋ] Einschätzung

ration ['ræʃn] rationieren VI 3 (61)

ray [reɪ] (Licht-)Strahl V • **ultraviolet rays** *(pl)* ultraviolette Strahlen V

RE [ˌɑːr'iː], **Religious Education** [rɪˌlɪdʒəs_edʒu'keɪʃn] Religion, Religionsunterricht I

reach [riːtʃ] erreichen III • **reach (an) agreement** sich einigen VI 2 (28)

react (to sth.) [ri'ækt] reagieren (auf/gegen etwas) V

reaction (to) [ri'ækʃn] Reaktion (auf) IV

read [riːd], **read, read** lesen I **easy-to-read** leicht zu lesende(r, s) V

°**read** [riːd] Lesen, Lektüre

reader ['riːdə] Leser/in II

ready ['redi] bereit, fertig I • **get ready (for)** sich fertig machen (für), sich vorbereiten (auf) I • **get things ready** Dinge fertig machen, vorbereiten I

real [rɪəl] echt, wirklich I • **real late** *(AE, infml)* wirklich spät, echt

Dictionary

spät III • **real-life** aus dem echten Leben VI 4 (105)

realistic [ˌrɪəˈlɪstɪk] realistisch, wirklichkeitsnah III

reality [riˈæliti] Wirklichkeit, Realität IV • **reality show** Reality-Show IV

realization [ˌriːəlaɪˈzeɪʃn] Erkenntnis VI 3 (54)

realize [ˈrɪəlaɪz] erkennen, merken I

°**real-life** [ˌrɪəl ˈlaɪf] im/aus dem wirklichen Leben

really [ˈrɪəli] wirklich I

reason [ˈriːzn] Grund, Begründung I • **the reason why** der Grund, warum IV • **for lots of reasons** aus vielen Gründen I

receive [rɪˈsiːv] erhalten III

recent [ˈriːsnt] jüngst, aktuell V

recently [ˈriːsntli] vor kurzem, kürzlich, neulich; in letzter Zeit V

recess [ˈriːses] (AE) Pause (zwischen Schulstunden) IV • **during recess** in der Pause I

recipe [ˈresəpi] Kochrezept VI 3 (59)

recite [rɪˈsaɪt] vortragen, rezitieren, aufsagen VI 4 (90/227)

recognize [ˈrekəgnaɪz] erkennen IV; anerkennen VI 2 (28)

recommend sth. (to sb.) [ˌrekəˈmend] (jm.) etwas empfehlen VI 3 (64)

recommendation [ˌrekəmenˈdeɪʃn] Empfehlung VI 3 (64)

record [rɪˈkɔːd] aufnehmen, aufzeichnen III

°**record** [ˈrekɔːd]: **attendance record** Anwesenheitsliste

recorder [rɪˈkɔːdə] Blockflöte III

recording [rɪˈkɔːdɪŋ] Aufnahme, Aufzeichnung III

recover (from) [rɪˈkʌvə] sich erholen (von) II

recycled [ˌriːˈsaɪkld] wiederverwertet, wiederverwendet, recycelt II

recycling [ˌriːˈsaɪklɪŋ] Wiederverwertung, Recycling II

red [red] rot I

reddish [ˈredɪʃ] rötlich IV

reduce sth. (by) [rɪˈdʒuːs] etwas reduzieren (um) IV

reef [riːf] Riff V

°**refer to sth.** [rɪˈfɜː] sich auf etwas beziehen

referee [ˌrefəˈriː] Schiedsrichter/in III

reference [ˈrefrəns] Referenz, Empfehlung V

reflect [rɪˈflekt] zurückwerfen, reflektieren, spiegeln VI 3 (57) • °**be reflected (in sth.)** sich (in etwas) spiegeln

reflex [ˈriːfleks] Reflex IV

°**reform** [rɪˈfɔːm] Reform

refuse (to do sth.) [rɪˈfjuːz] sich weigern (etwas zu tun); verweigern, ablehnen VI 1 (15)

register [ˈredʒɪstə] Stilebene, Register VI 2 (31/G)

regular [ˈregjələ] regelmäßig III

rehearsal [rɪˈhɜːsl] Probe (am Theater) I

rehearse [rɪˈhɜːs] proben (am Theater) I

°**related** [rɪˈleɪtɪd] verwandt

relations (pl) [rɪˈleɪʃnz] Beziehungen IV

relationship [rɪˈleɪʃnʃɪp] Verhältnis, Beziehung V • **end a relationship** mit jm. Schluss machen V

relative [ˈrelətɪv] Verwandte(r) II

relax [rɪˈlæks] (sich) entspannen, sich ausruhen II

relaxed [rɪˈlækst] entspannt V

release [rɪˈliːs]
1. (CD, Film usw.) herausbringen, auf den Markt bringen III
2. (Gefangene) freilassen VI 3 (60)
3. (Gas) freisetzen, ablassen VI 3 (60)

°**relevance** [ˈreləvəns] Relevanz

relevant (to sth.) [ˈreləvənt] relevant (für etwas) VI 2 (36)

reliable [rɪˈlaɪəbl] zuverlässig IV

religion [rɪˈlɪdʒən] Religion IV

religious [rɪˈlɪdʒəs] gläubig, religiös IV

remain [rɪˈmeɪn] (fml) bleiben VI 2 (38)

remarkable [rɪˈmɑːkəbl] beachtlich, außergewöhnlich VI 3 (55)

remember sth. [rɪˈmembə]
1. sich an etwas erinnern I
2. sich etwas merken I

remove [rɪˈmuːv] (fml) entfernen VI 3 (56)

renewable [rɪˈnjuːəbl] erneuerbar VI 3 (53)

repair [rɪˈpeə] reparieren, ausbessern III

repeat [rɪˈpiːt] wiederholen II

repetition [ˌrepəˈtɪʃn] Wiederholung V

replace sth. (with) [rɪˈpleɪs] etwas ersetzen (durch) III

reply (to) [rɪˈplaɪ] antworten (auf), beantworten; erwidern III

°**reply** [rɪˈplaɪ] Antwort

report (on) [rɪˈpɔːt] Bericht, Reportage (über) I

report (to sb.) [rɪˈpɔːt] jm. berichten, sich bei jm. melden II

reporter [rɪˈpɔːtə] Reporter/in II

represent [ˌreprɪˈzent] repräsentieren, vertreten III

request [rɪˈkwest] Bitte, Wunsch V • **on request** auf Wunsch V

request sth. (from sb.) (fml) [rɪˈkwest] (fml) (jn.) um etwas bitten VI 4 (80)

require sb. to do sth [rɪˈkwaɪə] von jm. verlangen, etwas zu tun V

rescue [ˈreskjuː] Rettung, Rettungsdienst IV

research (no pl) [rɪˈsɜːtʃ, ˈriːsɜːtʃ] Recherche, Forschung(en) III

researcher [rɪˈsɜːtʃə, ˈriːsɜːtʃə] Rechercheur/in III; Forscher/in VI 1 (14)

reservation [ˌrezəˈveɪʃn] Reservat IV

resistance (no pl) [rɪˈzɪstəns] Widerstand VI 3 (56)

resolution [ˌrezəˈluːʃn] Auflösung, Lösung VI 4 (89/G)

resources (pl) [rɪˈzɔːsɪs, rɪˈsɔːsɪz] Mittel, Ressourcen IV

respect (for) [rɪˈspekt] Achtung, Respekt (vor) V • **With respect, …** Bei allem Respekt, … V

respect sb./sth. (for sth.) [rɪˈspekt] jn./etwas (wegen einer Sache) achten, respektieren V

respond (to sth.) [rɪˈspɒnd] (fml) reagieren (auf etwas); antworten (auf etwas) VI 2 (38)

responsibility (for) [rɪˌspɒnsəˈbɪləti]
1. Verantwortung (für) V • **take responsibility (for)** Verantwortung (für) übernehmen
2. Pflicht VI 2 (35)

responsible (for) [rɪˈspɒnsəbl] verantwortlich (für) V

rest [rest] Rest II

rest [rest] ruhen, sich ausruhen VI 2 (35) • °**May he/she rest in peace.** Ruhe in Frieden.

restart [ˌriːˈstɑːt] neu starten (Computer) II

restaurant [ˈrestrɒnt] Restaurant II

restroom [ˈrestˌruːm] (AE) (öffentliche) Toilette IV

result [rɪˈzʌlt] Ergebnis, Resultat I

result in sth. [rɪˈzʌlt] zu etwas führen V

résumé [ˈrezəmeɪ] (AE) Lebenslauf V

retire [rɪˈtaɪə] in den Ruhestand gehen; sich zurückziehen V

return [rɪˈtɜːn] zurückkehren VI 2 (27)

reveal [rɪˈviːl] offenbaren, preisgeben, verraten VI 4 (84)

°**reverse** [rɪˈvɜːs] umgekehrte(r, s)

review [rɪ'vjuː] Rezension, Kritik VI 3 (64)

revise [rɪ'vaɪz] überarbeiten IV

revision [rɪ'vɪʒn] Wiederholung (des Lernstoffs) I

revolution [ˌrevə'luːʃn] Revolution IV

rhino ['raɪnəʊ] Nashorn II

°**rhyme** [raɪm] sich reimen

rhyme [raɪm] Reim VI 4 (91/G)
  end-rhyme Endreim VI 4 (91/G)
  internal rhyme Binnenreim VI 4 (91/G) • **rhyme scheme** Reimschema VI 4 (91/G)

rhythm ['rɪðəm] Rhythmus III

rich [rɪtʃ] reich II
  ▶ S.217 the rich, the poor, etc.

ridden ['rɪdn] siehe ride

riddle ['rɪdl] Rätsel, Scherzfrage III

ride [raɪd], **rode, ridden** reiten I
  ride a (motor)bike (Motor-)Rad fahren I

ride [raɪd]: **(bike) ride** (Rad-)Fahrt, (Rad-)Tour II • **(bus) ride** (Bus-)Fahrt II • **take a ride** eine Spritztour/Fahrt machen III

riding ['raɪdɪŋ] Reiten, Reitsport I
  go riding ['raɪdɪŋ] reiten gehen I
  riding boots (pl) Reitstiefel III **riding hat** Reitkappe, Reiterhelm III

right [raɪt] richtig I • **all right** [ɔːl 'raɪt] gut, in Ordnung II • **be right** Recht haben I • **get sth. right** etwas richtig machen III • **That's right.** Das ist richtig. / Das stimmt. I • **You need a school bag, right?** Du brauchst eine Schultasche, stimmt's? / nicht wahr? I

right (to sth.) [raɪt] Recht (auf etwas) IV • **civil rights** (pl) Bürgerrechte IV

right [raɪt] rechte(r, s) I • **look right** nach rechts schauen I • **on the right** rechts, auf der rechten Seite I • **to the right** nach rechts III • **turn right** (nach) rechts abbiegen II • **take a right** (AE) nach links/rechts abbiegen IV

right [raɪt]: **right behind you** direkt/genau hinter dir II • **right now** jetzt sofort; jetzt gerade I

°**rigor mortis** [ˌrɪgə 'mɔːtɪs] Totenstarre

rim [rɪm] Rand, Kante IV

ring [rɪŋ] Ring II

ring [rɪŋ], **rang, rung** klingeln, läuten II

ringtone ['rɪŋtəʊn] Klingelton III

riot ['raɪət] Aufruhr, Krawall IV

rip sb. off (-pp-) [ˌrɪp_'ɒf] jn. übers Ohr hauen, jn. abzocken VI 3 (62)

ripe [raɪp] reif IV

rise [raɪz], **rose, risen** (auf)steigen IV

risen ['rɪzn] siehe rise

ritual ['rɪtʃuəl] Ritual VI 1 (24)

river ['rɪvə] Fluss II

road [rəʊd] Straße I • **Park Road** [ˌpɑːk 'rəʊd] Parkstraße I

robot ['rəʊbɒt] Roboter VI 3 (64)

rock [rɒk] Fels, Felsen III • **rock art** (no pl) Felsmalerei(en) V

rock (music) [rɒk] Rock(musik) III

rode [rəʊd] siehe ride

role [rəʊl] Rolle III

role model ['rəʊl ˌmɒdl] Vorbild V

role play ['rəʊl pleɪ] Rollenspiel VI 1 (15)

roll [rəʊl] Brötchen II

roll [rəʊl] rollen VI 4 (94)

Roman ['rəʊmən] römisch; Römer, Römerin II

romantic [rəʊ'mæntɪk] romantisch VI 4 (87)

roof [ruːf] Dach II

room [ruːm, rʊm] Raum, Zimmer I

root [ruːt] Wurzel VI 3 (58)

rope [rəʊp] Seil IV

rose [rəʊz] siehe rise

°**rough** [rʌf]
  1. rau
  2. roh, grob

round [raʊnd] rund II • **round brackets** runde Klammern IV

round [raʊnd] um ... (herum); in ... umher II • **round here** hier (in der Gegend) IV • **the other way round** anders herum II

round [raʊnd]: **do a paper round** Zeitungen austragen V

route [ruːt] Strecke, Route IV

routine [ruː'tiːn] Routine IV

°**rover** ['rəʊvə]: **lunar rover** Mondfahrzeug

row [rəʊ] Reihe IV

royal ['rɔɪəl] königlich, Königs II

rubber ['rʌbə] Radiergummi I

rubbish ['rʌbɪʃ] (Haus-)Müll, Abfall II • **rubbish collection** Müllabfuhr II

rucksack ['rʌksæk] Rucksack III

rude [ruːd] unhöflich, unverschämt II

rugby ['rʌgbi] Rugby III

ruin ['ruːɪn] Ruine IV

ruin ['ruːɪn] verderben; ruinieren V

rule [ruːl] Regel, Vorschrift III
  break a rule gegen eine Regel verstoßen IV • **set of rules** Regelwerk V

ruler ['ruːlə] Lineal I

run [rʌn] (Wett-)Lauf I • **go for a run** laufen gehen IV

run (-nn-) [rʌn], **ran, run**
  1. laufen, rennen I • **run away** weglaufen V
  2. verlaufen (Straße; Grenze) IV
  3. etwas leiten (Hotel, Firma usw.) V

rung [rʌŋ] siehe ring

runner ['rʌnə] Läufer/in II

running shoes ['rʌnɪŋ ʃuːz] Laufschuhe III

running track ['rʌnɪŋ træk] Laufbahn (Sport) III

rural ['rʊərəl] ländlich, Land- V

rush [rʌʃ] Ansturm V

S

sad [sæd] traurig II

saddle ['sædl] Sattel III

sadly ['sædli] leider; traurig V

sadness ['sædnəs] Traurigkeit IV

safe [seɪf] Tresor, Safe IV

safe (from) [seɪf] sicher, in Sicherheit (vor) II

safety ['seɪfti] Sicherheit IV

said [sed]
  1. siehe say
  2. be said to do sth. etwas (angeblich) tun sollen VI 1 (14/180)
  °**3.** besagte(r, s)

sail [seɪl] (mit dem Schiff) fahren; segeln IV

saint [seɪnt] Heilige(r) IV

salad ['sæləd] Salat (als Gericht oder Beilage) I

sale [seɪl] (Aus-, Schluss-)Verkauf IV

salmon ['sæmən], pl **salmon** Lachs III

salt [sɔːlt] Salz V

same [seɪm]: **the same ...** der-/die-/dasselbe ...; dieselben ... I • **be/look the same** gleich sein/aussehen I

sandwich ['sænwɪtʃ, 'sænwɪdʒ] Sandwich, (zusammengeklapptes) belegtes Brot I

sandy ['sændi] sandig IV

sang [sæŋ] siehe sing

sank [sæŋk] siehe sink

sarcastic [sɑː'kæstɪk] sarkastisch VI 2 (30)

sat [sæt] siehe sit

Saturday ['sætədeɪ, 'sætədi] Samstag, Sonnabend I

sauce [sɔːs] Soße III

sauna ['sɔːnə] Sauna II • **have a sauna** in die Sauna gehen II

sausage ['sɒsɪdʒ] (Brat-, Bock-)Würstchen, Wurst I

save [seɪv]
  1. retten II
  2. sparen II

Dictionary

saw [sɔː] *siehe* **see**

saxophone ['sæksəfəʊn] Saxophon III

say [seɪ], **said, said** sagen I • **It says here: ...** Hier steht: ... / Es heißt hier: ... II • **say goodbye** sich verabschieden I • **Say hi to your parents for me.** Grüß deine Eltern von mir. I • **say sorry** sich entschuldigen II • **They say ...** Man sagt, ... III

°**scale** [skeɪl] Skala

scan (-nn-) [skæn]: **scan a text** einen Text schnell nach bestimmten Wörtern/Informationen absuchen II

scare sb. [skeə] jn. erschrecken, jm. Angst machen VI 4 (104)

scared [skeəd] verängstigt I • **be scared (of)** Angst haben (vor) I

scary ['skeəri] unheimlich; gruselig I • **kind of scary** (*infml*) irgendwie unheimlich III

scene [siːn] Szene I • **on the scene** vor Ort, zur Stelle IV

scenery ['siːnəri] Landschaft III

scent [sent] Duft V

schedule [*AE:* 'skedʒuːl, *BE:* 'ʃedjuːl] (*bes. AE*) Stundenplan IV

scheme [skiːm]: **rhyme scheme** Reimschema VI 4 (91/G)

school [skuːl] Schule I • **at school** in der Schule I • **from school** aus der Schule III • **in school** (*AE*) in der Schule IV • **school bag** Schultasche I • **school office** Sekretariat IV • **school subject** Schulfach I

science ['saɪəns] Naturwissenschaft I • **life sciences** (*pl*) Biowissenschaften VI 3 (52)

science fiction [ˌsaɪəns 'fɪkʃn] Sciencefiction V

scientific [ˌsaɪən'tɪfɪk] (natur)wissenschaftlich VI 3 (54)

scientist ['saɪəntɪst] Naturwissenschaftler/in V

score [skɔː] Spielstand; Punktestand III • **final score** Endstand (*beim Sport*) III • **What's the score?** Wie steht es? (*beim Sport*) III

score (a goal) [skɔː], [gəʊl] ein Tor schießen, einen Treffer erzielen III

Scottish ['skɒtɪʃ] schottisch III

scrapbook ['skræpbʊk] Sammelalbum IV

scream [skriːm] schreien IV

scream [skriːm] Schrei IV

sea [siː] Meer, (die) See I • **at sea** auf See II

search sth./sb. (for sth./sb.) [sɜːtʃ] etwas/jn. (nach etwas/jm.) durchsuchen V

search [sɜːtʃ] Suche VI 1 (16) • **in search of** auf der Suche nach VI 1 (16)

season ['siːzn] Jahreszeit II • **rainy season** Regenzeit II

seat [siːt] Sitz, Platz IV

second ['sekənd] Sekunde I

second ['sekənd] zweite(r, s) I **second-hand** [ˌsekənd 'hænd] gebraucht; aus zweiter Hand III **a second-half goal** ein Tor in der zweiten Hälfte/Halbzeit III

secondary school ['sekəndri] *weiterführende Schule* V

secret ['siːkrət] Geheimnis IV

secret ['siːkrət] geheim IV

secretly ['siːkrətli] heimlich, insgeheim V

section ['sekʃn] Abschnitt, Teil II; (Themen-)Bereich III

secure [sɪ'kjʊə] sicher; selbstsicher VI 1 (8)

security [sɪ'kjʊərəti] Sicherheit(svorkehrungen) V • **security forces** Sicherheitskräfte VI 2 (28/207)

see [siː], **saw, seen**
1. sehen I
2. see sb. jn. besuchen, jn. aufsuchen II
See? Siehst du? I • **See you.** Bis bald. / Tschüs. I

seek [siːk], **sought, sought,** suchen V

seem (to be / to do) [siːm] (zu sein/ tun) scheinen III

seen [siːn] *siehe* **see**

see-through ['siː'θruː] durchsichtig IV

segregate ['segrɪgeɪt] trennen (*nach Rasse, Religion, Geschlecht*) IV

segregation [ˌsegrɪ'geɪʃn] Trennung (*nach Rasse, Religion, Geschlecht*) IV

selection (of) [sɪ'lekʃn] Auswahl (an) II • **natural selection** natürliche Selektion VI 3 (55)

self [self]: **self-adjusting** sich selbst regulierend VI 3 (56)

selfish ['selfɪʃ] egoistisch VI 4 (88)

sell [sel], **sold, sold** verkaufen I °**hard sell** aggressive Verkaufstechnik

semester [sɪ'mestə] Semester (*Schulhalbjahr in den USA*) IV

semi-final [ˌsemi'faɪnl] Halbfinale III

send [send], **sent, sent** senden, schicken II

senior ['siːniə]
1. senior (to sb.) (rang)höher (als jd.) IV
2. leitende(r, s) IV

senior ['siːniə] Rentner/in, Senior/in IV

sense [sens] Sinn VI 3 (64) • **make sense** Sinn ergeben VI 3 (64/221)

sensible ['sensəbl] vernünftig VI 3 (65)

sensitive ['sensətɪv] einfühlsam, empfindsam; empfindlich, sensibel VI 1 (10)

sent [sent] *siehe* **send**

sentence sb. (to sth.) ['sentəns] jn. verurteilen (zu etwas) IV

sentence ['sentəns]
1. Satz I • **sentence for sentence** Satz um Satz III
2. Urteil, Strafe IV • **death sentence** Todesstrafe IV • **life sentence** lebenslängliche Haftstrafe IV

separate ['seprət] getrennt, separat, extra IV

separate ['sepəreɪt] trennen V

separation [ˌsepə'reɪʃn] Trennung VI 4 (80) • **trial separation** (Ehe-) Trennung auf Probe VI 4 (80)

September [sep'tembə] September I

sequence ['siːkwəns] Abfolge, Reihenfolge VI 4 (91)

series, *pl* **series** ['sɪəriːz] (Sende-) Reihe, Serie II

serious ['sɪəriəs] ernst(haft) V

seriously ['sɪəriəsli] ernsthaft; (*infml*) sehr V

service ['sɜːvɪs]
1. Dienst (am Kunden), Service II **social services** Sozialeinrichtungen V
2. Gottesdienst IV

session ['seʃn]: **training session** Trainingsstunde, -einheit III

set (-tt-) [set], **set, set**
1. set a goal ein Ziel setzen VI 2 (35) • **set a trap (for sb.)** (jm.) eine Falle stellen II • **set sth. up** etwas aufstellen, aufbauen III
2. be set in spielen in V

set [set] Reihe, Set, Satz V • **set of rules** Regelwerk V

set meal [ˌset 'miːl] Menü III

°**Setswana** [set'swɑːnə] Setswana (*neben Englisch die Amtssprache in Botswana*)

setting ['setɪŋ] Schauplatz V

settle down [ˌsetl 'daʊn] zur Ruhe kommen, sesshaft werden V

settler ['setlə] Siedler/in IV

several ['sevrəl] mehrere, verschiedene IV

sew (on) [səʊ]**, sewed, sewn** (an)nähen IV

sewn [səʊn] *siehe* **sew**

sex [seks] Sex, Geschlechtsverkehr VI 1 (24) • **have sex** miteinander schlafen, sich lieben V • °**sex education** Sexualkunde • **the opposite sex** das andere Geschlecht VI 3 (63/221)

°**sexy** ['seksi] sexy

shade [ʃeɪd] Schatten *(von der Sonne geschützt)* V

shadow ['ʃædəʊ] Schatten *(Umriss)* III

shake [ʃeɪk]**, shook, shaken** zittern; schütteln IV • **shake one's head** den Kopf schütteln III

Shall we ...? [ʃæl] Wollen wir ...? / Sollen wir ...? III

°**shall** [ʃæl]
1. sollen; **2.** dürfen; **3.** werden

shape [ʃeɪp] Form, Gestalt II

share sth. (with sb.) [ʃeə]
1. sich etwas teilen (mit jm.) I; etwas gemeinsam (mit jm.) haben/nutzen IV
2. jm. etwas mitteilen IV

sharp [ʃɑ:p] scharf VI 4 (91)

she [ʃi:] sie I

sheep, *pl* **sheep** [ʃi:p] Schaf II

sheet [ʃi:t]
1. Blatt, Bogen *(Papier)* V
2. Laken V

shelf [ʃelf], *pl* **shelves** [ʃelvz] Regal(brett) I

shell [ʃel] Muschel(schale) V

shift [ʃɪft] Schicht *(bei der Arbeit)* IV

shine [ʃaɪn]**, shone, shone**
1. scheinen *(Sonne)* II
2. glänzen IV

ship [ʃɪp] Schiff I

shirt [ʃɜ:t] Hemd I • **football shirt** (Fußball-)Trikot III

°**shit** [ʃɪt] Mist

shiver ['ʃɪvə] zittern II

shock [ʃɒk] Schock, Schreck V

shocked [ʃɒkt] schockiert III

shocking ['ʃɒkɪŋ] schockierend V

shoe [ʃu:] Schuh I

shone [ʃɒn, *AE* ʃəʊn] *siehe* **shine**

shoot [ʃu:t] **shot, shot**
1. (er)schießen IV • **shoot at sth./ sb.** auf jn./etwas schießen IV
2. *(Film)* drehen; fotografieren IV

shop [ʃɒp] Laden, Geschäft I
shop assistant ['ʃɒp‿ə,sɪstənt] Verkäufer/in I

shop (-pp-) [ʃɒp] einkaufen (gehen) I

shopping ['ʃɒpɪŋ] (das) Einkaufen I
go shopping einkaufen gehen I
shopping list Einkaufsliste I
shopping mall (großes) Einkaufszentrum III • **shopping precinct** Einkaufsviertel, -straße *(autofrei)* III

short [ʃɔ:t] kurz I • **a short time** kurz IV

shorts *(pl)* [ʃɔ:ts] Shorts, kurze Hose I

shot [ʃɒt] *siehe* **shoot**

shot [ʃɒt]
1. Schuss III
2. (Film-)Aufnahme, Dreh VI 2 (30)

should [ʃəd, ʃʊd]**: you should ...** du solltest ... / ihr solltet ... I • **you should have asked** du hättest fragen sollen IV

shoulder ['ʃəʊldə] Schulter I

shout [ʃaʊt] schreien, rufen I
shout at sb. jn. anschreien I

show [ʃəʊ] Show, Vorstellung I

show [ʃəʊ]**, showed, shown** zeigen I • **show sb. around** jn. (in der Stadt/im Museum/... herumführen) III

show off [ˌʃəʊ‿'ɒf]**, showed off, shown off** angeben, prahlen IV

shower ['ʃaʊə] Dusche I • **have a shower** (sich) duschen I

shown [ʃəʊn] *siehe* **show**

shut up [ˌʃʌt‿'ʌp]**, shut, shut** den Mund halten II

shy [ʃaɪ] schüchtern, scheu II

sick [sɪk] krank IV • **I feel sick.** Mir ist schlecht. IV

side [saɪd] Seite II • **side door** Seitentür IV

sidetrack ['saɪdtræk]**: get sidetracked** abgelenkt werden V

sidewalk ['saɪdwɔ:k] *(AE)* Gehweg, Bürgersteig IV

sight [saɪt]**: Get out of my sight.** Geh mir aus den Augen. IV

sight [saɪt] Sehen, visuelle Wahrnehmung VI 3 (64/221)

sights *(pl)* [saɪts] Sehenswürdigkeiten II

sightseeing ['saɪt,si:ɪŋ] Sightseeing; das Anschauen von Sehenswürdigkeiten IV

sign [saɪn] unterschreiben III

sign [saɪn] Schild; Zeichen III

significant [sɪg'nɪfɪkənt] bedeutend; wichtig VI 2 (31)

silence ['saɪləns] Stille, Schweigen VI 2 (29)

silent ['saɪlənt] still, schweigend VI 2 (29) • **silent letter** „stummer" Buchstabe *(nicht gesprochener Buchstabe)* II

silly ['sɪli] albern, dumm II

similar (to sth./sb.) ['sɪmələ] (etwas/jm.) ähnlich VI 2 (38)

similarity (to, between) [ˌsɪmə'lærəti] Ähnlichkeit (mit, zwischen) VI 4 (77)

simile ['sɪməli] Vergleich VI 4 (93/G)

°**sin (-nn-)** [sɪn] sündigen

since September [sɪns] seit September III • **ever since** (ununterbrochen) seit VI 1 (9)

since [sɪns] weil, da VI 3 (55)

Sincerely (yours) [sɪn'sɪəli] *(AE)* mit freundlichen Grüßen IV

sing [sɪŋ]**, sang, sung** singen I

singer ['sɪŋə] Sänger/in II

single ['sɪŋgl]
1. ledig, alleinstehend I • **single bed** Einzelbett V • **a single parent** ein(e) Alleinerziehende(r) II
2. einzige(r, s), nur ein(e/n) VI 1 (8) **not a single friend** kein einziger Freund VI 1 (8/198)

sink [sɪŋk] Spüle, Spülbecken I

sink [sɪŋk]**, sank, sunk** sinken V

sir [sɜ:] Sir *(höfliche Anrede, z. B. für Kunden, Vorgesetzte oder Lehrer)* IV • **Dear Sir or Madam ...** Sehr geehrte Damen und Herren IV

sister ['sɪstə] Schwester I

sister city ['sɪstə ˌsɪti] *(AE)* Partnerstadt IV

sit (-tt-) [sɪt]**, sat, sat** sitzen; sich setzen I • **sit down** sich hinsetzen II • **sit up** sich aufsetzen II **Sit with me.** Setz dich zu mir. / Setzt euch zu mir. I

site [saɪt] *siehe* **website** • **social networking (web)site** *eine Website zur Bildung und Unterhaltung sozialer Netzwerke* VI 1 (8)

situation [ˌsɪtju'eɪʃn] Situation IV

sixth [sɪksθ] Sechstel V

size [saɪz] Größe I

skate [skeɪt] Inliner/Skateboard fahren I

skateboard ['skeɪtbɔ:d] Skateboard I

skates *(pl)* [skeɪts] Inliner I

sketch [sketʃ] Sketch I

ski [ski:] Ski III • **ski slope** Skipiste III

ski [ski:] Ski laufen/fahren III • **go skiing** [ski:ɪŋ] Ski laufen/fahren III • **skiing instructor** Skilehrer/in V

skiing: go skiing [ski:ɪŋ] Ski laufen/fahren III

skill [skɪl] Fähigkeit, Fertigkeit IV

skills file ['skɪlz faɪl] Anhang mit Lern- und Arbeitstechniken I

Dictionary

skim a text (-mm-) [skɪm] einen Text überfliegen *(um den Inhalt grob zu erfassen)* III
skin [skɪn] Haut IV
skirt [skɜːt] Rock II
sky [skaɪ] Himmel II • **in the sky** am Himmel II
skyline ['skaɪˌlaɪn] Horizont, Skyline IV
skyscraper ['skaɪskreɪpə] Wolkenkratzer IV
°**skyward(s)** ['skaɪwəd] himmelwärts, nach oben
slang [slæŋ] Slang VI 2 (31)
slave [sleɪv] Sklave, Sklavin II
slavery ['sleɪvəri] Sklaverei IV
sledge [sledʒ] Schlitten III
°**sleek** [sliːk] elegant
sleep [sliːp]**, slept, slept** schlafen I
sleep in ausschlafen VI 2 (36)
sleep [sliːp] Schlaf III
sleepover ['sliːpəʊvə] Schlafparty III
slept [slept] *siehe* **sleep**
°**slid** [slɪd] *siehe* **slide**
slide [slaɪd] Folie *(bei Präsentationsprogrammen)* V
°**slide** [slaɪd]**, slid, slid** rutschen
slight [slaɪt] klein, leicht, unwichtig VI 4 (98)
slogan ['sləʊgən] Slogan, Losung IV
slope: ski slope Skipiste III
slow [sləʊ] langsam II
slow down [ˌsləʊ 'daʊn] langsamer werden VI 1 (25)
slum [slʌm] Slum, Elendsviertel V
small [smɔːl] klein II • **small letters** Kleinbuchstaben III
smart [smɑːt] schlau IV
smell [smel] riechen I
smell [smel] Geruch II; Riechen, olfaktorische Wahrnehmung VI 3 (64/221)
smile [smaɪl] lächeln I • **smile at sb.** jn. anlächeln II
smile [smaɪl] Lächeln II • **give (sb.) a smile** lächeln, jn. anlächeln IV
smoke [sməʊk] rauchen IV
smoke [sməʊk] Rauch IV • **There's no smoke without fire.** Wo Rauch ist, ist auch Feuer. IV
smoker ['sməʊkə] Raucher/in VI 2 (37)
°**smooth** [smuːð] glatt
smoothie ['smuːði] *dickflüssiger Fruchtshake mit Milch, Joghurt oder Eiscreme* II
smuggle ['smʌgl] schmuggeln IV
snack [snæk] Snack, Imbiss II
snake [sneɪk] Schlange I
°**snippet** ['snɪpɪt] Ausschnitt
snow [snəʊ] Schnee II

snowball ['snəʊbɔːl] Schneeball IV
so [səʊ]
1. also; deshalb, daher I • **So?** Und? / Na und? II • **So what?** [səʊ 'wɒt] Und? / Na und? II
2. so sweet so süß I • **so far** bis jetzt, bis hierher III • **so (that)** sodass, damit III
3. I hope so. Ich hoffe es. II **I think so.** Ich glaube (ja). I **I don't think so.** Das finde/glaube ich nicht. I • **Do you really think so?** Meinst du wirklich? / Glaubst du das wirklich? II
4. so has crime die Kriminalität auch V
soap [səʊp] Seife I
soap (opera) ['səʊp ˌɒprə] Seifenoper IV
sob (-bb-) [sɒb] schluchzen VI 3 (61)
so-called [ˌsəʊ'kɔːld] so genannt V
social ['səʊʃl] sozial, Sozial-, gesellschaftlich V • **social networking** soziales Netzwerk *(vor allem im Internet)* VI 1 (8) • **social networking site** *eine Website zur Bildung und Unterhaltung sozialer Netzwerke* VI 1 (8) • **social services** Sozialeinrichtungen V
Social Studies [ˌsəʊʃl 'stʌdiz] Gemeinschaftskunde, Politische Bildung, Sozialkunde IV
society [sə'saɪəti] (die) Gesellschaft VI 1 (18)
sock [sɒk] Socke, Strumpf I
soda ['səʊdə] *(AE)* Limonade IV
sofa ['səʊfə] Sofa I
soft [sɒft] weich, sanft III • **soft drink** alkoholfreies Getränk IV
software ['sɒftweə] Software II
soil [sɔɪl] *(Erdreich)* Erde IV
solar ['səʊlə] Solar-, Sonnen- VI 3 (53)
sold [səʊld]
1. *siehe* **sell**
2. sold out [ˌsəʊld_'aʊt]: **be sold out** ausverkauft/vergriffen sein III
soldier ['səʊldʒə] Soldat/in IV
°**child soldier** Kindersoldat/in
solution (to) [sə'luːʃn] (Auf-)Lösung (für) VI 3 (55)
solve [sɒlv] lösen IV
some [səm, sʌm] einige, ein paar I **some cheese/juice/money/English** etwas Käse/Saft/Geld/Englisch I
somebody ['sʌmbədi] jemand I **Find/Ask somebody who ...** Finde/Frage jemanden, der ... I
somehow ['sʌmhaʊ] irgendwie IV
someone ['sʌmwʌn] jemand III
something ['sʌmθɪŋ] etwas I
sometimes ['sʌmtaɪmz] manchmal I

somewhere ['sʌmweə] irgendwo(hin) II
son [sʌn] Sohn I
song [sɒŋ] Lied, Song I
soon [suːn] bald I • **as soon as** sobald, sowie II
sore [sɔː]: **be sore** wund sein, wehtun II • **have a sore throat** Halsschmerzen haben II
sorry ['sɒri]: **(I'm) sorry.** Entschuldigung. / Tut mir leid. I • **Sorry, I'm late.** Entschuldigung, dass ich zu spät bin/komme. I • **Sorry?** Wie bitte? I • **say sorry** sich entschuldigen I
sort [sɔːt] einteilen; sortieren IV
sort (of) [sɔːt] Art, Sorte II
sought [sɔːt] *siehe* **seek**
soul [səʊl] Soul(musik) III
sound [saʊnd] klingen, sich (gut usw.) anhören I
sound [saʊnd] Laut; Klang I
sound file ['saʊnd faɪl] Tondatei, Soundfile III
soup [suːp] Suppe II
sour ['saʊə] sauer III
source [sɔːs] Quelle *(Informationsquelle, Textquelle)* IV
south [saʊθ] Süden; nach Süden; südlich II • **southbound** ['saʊθbaʊnd] Richtung Süden III **south-east** [ˌsaʊθ'iːst] Südosten; nach Südosten; südöstlich II **southern** ['sʌðən] südlich, Süd- III • **south-west** [ˌsaʊθ'west] Südwesten; nach Südwesten; südwestlich II
souvenir [ˌsuːvə'nɪə] Andenken, Souvenir III
space ['speɪs]
1. Weltraum II
2. Move back one space. Geh ein Feld zurück. II • **Move on one space.** Geh ein Feld vor. II
°**3.** Platz
spaghetti [spə'geti] Spaghetti II
spark [spɑːk] Funke IV
speak (to) [spiːk]**, spoke, spoken** sprechen (mit), reden (mit) II **speak out** seine Meinung (offen) sagen VI 2 (28) • °**speak to sb.** jn. ansprechen
special ['speʃl] besondere(r, s) II **Did you do anything special?** Habt ihr irgendetwas Besonderes gemacht? II • **be special (to sb.)** (jm.) besonders, außergewöhnlich sein; (jm.) viel bedeuten VI 1 (9)
species ['spiːʃiːz] Art *(biologisch)*, Spezies V
specific [spə'sɪfɪk] bestimmte(r, s), spezifische(r, s) IV

spectacular [spek'tækjələ] spektakulär IV

°**speculate (about sth.)** ['spekjuleɪt] (über etwas) Vermutungen anstellen, (über etwas) spekulieren

speech [spiːtʃ]
1. Rede IV • °**hate speech** Hetzrede • **make/give a speech** eine Rede halten IV
2. Sprechpassage, -abschnitt VI 4 (105/G)

speech bubble ['bʌbl] Sprechblase VI 2 (28/207)

speed [spiːd] rasen, schnell fliegen III • **speed up** schneller werden VI 1 (25)

speed [spiːd] Geschwindigkeit III **speed limit** Geschwindigkeitsbegrenzung, -beschränkung III

spell [spel] buchstabieren I

spelling ['spelɪŋ] Rechtschreibung V

spend [spend]**, spent, spent:** **spend money (on)** Geld ausgeben (für) II • **spend time (on)** Zeit verbringen (mit) II

spent [spent] *siehe* **spend**

sphere [sfɪə] Kugel VI 3 (54)

spice [spaɪs] Gewürz III

spicy ['spaɪsi] würzig, scharf gewürzt III

spill [spɪl] verschütten IV

spirit ['spɪrɪt] Geist; Seele VI 2 (26)

spit (at sb.) (-tt-) [spɪt]**, spat, spat** (jn. an)spucken IV

splash [splæʃ] spritzen IV

spoil sth. (for sb.) [spɔɪl] (jm.) etwas verderben VI 3 (65)

spoke [spəʊk] *siehe* **speak**

spoken ['spəʊkən]
1. *siehe* **speak**
2. mündlich V

spoon [spuːn] Löffel III

sport [spɔːt] Sport; Sportart I • **do sport** Sport treiben I

sports gear *(no pl)* ['spɔːts gɪə] Sportausrüstung, Sportsachen II

sports hall ['spɔːts hɔːl] Sporthalle III

spot (-tt-) [spɒt] entdecken III

spray [spreɪ] spritzen, (be)sprühen, sprayen IV

spray can ['spreɪ ˌkæn] Spraydose V

spread [spred]**, spread, spread** (sich) ausbreiten, (sich) verbreiten IV

spring [sprɪŋ]
1. Frühling I
2. Quelle *(Wasser)* IV

spy [spaɪ] Spion/in I

square [skweə]
1. Platz *(in der Stadt)* II
2. Quadrat VI 1 (21/203) • **the square**

of two is four zwei im Quadrat ist vier VI 1 (21/203)

square [skweə] quadrieren VI 1 (21/203) • **two squared is four** zwei im Quadrat ist vier VI 1 (21/203)

°**square** [skweə] quadratisch

square brackets [ˌskweə 'brækɪts] eckige Klammern IV

square km (sq km) [skweə] Quadratkilometer III

square root [ˌskweə 'ruːt] Quadratwurzel VI 1 (21/203)

squash [skwɒʃ]**,** *pl* **squash** Kürbis IV

°**squat (-tt-)** [skwɒt] hocken

squatter ['skwɒtə] Haus-, Landbesetzer/in IV

squeeze [skwiːz] drücken; (aus)pressen II

squirrel ['skwɪrəl] Eichhörnchen II

stadium ['steɪdiəm] Stadion III

staff [stɑːf] Personal, Belegschaft; Lehrerkollegium IV • **member of staff** *(BE)* Mitarbeiter/in IV • **staff member** *(AE)* Mitarbeiter/in IV

stage [steɪdʒ] Bühne I • °**on stage** auf die/der Bühne • **stage directions** Regieanweisungen VI 4 (105/G)

stairs *(pl)* [steəz] Treppe; Treppenstufen I

stamp [stæmp] Briefmarke I

stand [stænd]**, stood, stood**
1. stehen; sich (hin)stellen II
2. ertragen, aushalten, ausstehen II • **I can't stand it.** Ich kann es nicht ertragen/aushalten/ausstehen.
stand out hervorstechen, auffallen VI 4 (76) • **stand up (for sth./sb.)** eintreten/sich einsetzen (für etwas/jn.) VI 2 (26)

standard of living ['stændəd] Lebensstandard V

star [stɑː]
1. Stern II
2. (Film-, Pop-)Star I

°**starch** [stɑːtʃ] Stärke

stare (at sb./sth.) [steə] (jn./etwas an)starren V

start [stɑːt] starten, anfangen, beginnen (mit) I • **start a business** ein Unternehmen gründen V

start [stɑːt] Anfang V

state [steɪt]
1. Staat III; die öffentliche Hand V
2. Zustand VI 2 (33) • °**state of mind** Geisteszustand

static (electricity) ['stætɪk, ˌstætɪk ˌɪ,lek'trɪsəti] elektrische Aufladung IV

station ['steɪʃn]
1. Bahnhof I • **at the station** am Bahnhof I
2. (radio/pop) station (Radio-/Pop-)Sender III

statistics *(pl)* [stə'tɪstɪks] Statistik V

statue ['stætʃuː] Statue II

status ['steɪtəs] Status, Stand V

stay [steɪ] bleiben; wohnen, übernachten II • **stay on** anbleiben VI 3 (58) • **stay out** nicht nach Hause kommen, draußenbleiben III

steady ['stedi] stetig V

steak [steɪk] (Rinder-)Steak IV

steal [stiːl]**, stole, stolen** stehlen II

steam [stiːm] Dampf VI 3 (52) **steam engine** Dampfmaschine VI 3 (52)

steel [stiːl] Stahl III

steel drum [ˌstiːl 'drʌm] Steeldrum III

steer [stɪə] lenken, steuern III

step [step]
1. Schritt I • **take steps** Schritte machen/unternehmen III • **take sth. a step at a time** etwas eins nach dem anderen tun; etwas Schritt für Schritt tun IV
2. Stufe IV

step (-pp-) [step]**: step forward** vortreten, sich melden VI 2 (39)

stereo ['steriəʊ] Stereoanlage III

stereotype ['steriətaɪp] Klischeevorstellung, Stereotyp VI 4 (89/G)

stew [stjuː] Eintopf(gericht) III

stick (on) [ˌstɪk_'ɒn]**, stuck, stuck** (auf)kleben I

°**stick** [stɪk] Stock

stick: (drum-)stick [stɪk] Trommelstock III

stick out of sth. [stɪk]**, stuck, stuck** aus etwas herausragen, herausstehen III

still [stɪl]
1. (immer) noch I
2. trotzdem, dennoch II

still [stɪl] still *(bewegungslos)* IV

°**still** [stɪl] Standfoto

stole [stəʊl] *siehe* **steal**

stolen ['stəʊlən] *siehe* **steal**

stomach ['stʌmək] Magen II **stomach ache** Magenschmerzen, Bauchweh II

stone [stəʊn] Stein II

stood [stʊd] *siehe* **stand**

stop (-pp-) [stɒp]
1. aufhören I
2. anhalten I
stop sb. doing sth. jn. daran hindern, etwas zu tun VI 1 (20) • **Stop that!** Hör auf damit! / Lass das! I

Dictionary

stop [stɒp] Halt, Anhalten IV
store *(AE)* [stɔː] Laden V
store [stɔː] speichern VI 3 (58)
storm [stɔːm] Sturm; Gewitter II
stormy [ˈstɔːmi] stürmisch II
story [ˈstɔːri] Geschichte, Erzählung I • **crime story** Krimi IV
straight [streɪt] direkt IV
straight on [streɪt ˈɒn] geradeaus weiter II
straightaway [ˌstreɪtəˈweɪ] sofort, gleich III
straighten sth. up [ˌstreɪtn ˈʌp] etwas aufräumen, etwas in Ordnung bringen V
°**stranded** [ˈstrændɪd] liegengeblieben
strange [streɪndʒ]
  1. seltsam, sonderbar I
  2. fremd V
stranger [ˈstreɪndʒə] Unbekannte(r), Fremde(r) V
strawberry [ˈstrɔːbəri] Erdbeere II
street [striːt] Straße I • **at 7 Park Street** in der Parkstraße 7 I
street performer [pəˈfɔːmə] Straßenkünstler/in III
strength [streŋθ] Kraft, Stärke V
stress [ˈstres] Betonung III
stress [stres] betonen V
stressful [ˈstresfl] anstrengend, stressig V
stretch [stretʃ] sich (er)strecken IV
strict [strɪkt] streng III
strike [straɪk] Streik III • **be on strike** streiken, sich im Streik befinden III • **go on strike** streiken, in den Streik treten III
striking [ˈstraɪkɪŋ] auffallend VI 4 (87)
string [strɪŋ] Saite III
°**stripe** [straɪp] Streifen III
strong [strɒŋ] stark II
structure [ˈstrʌktʃə] strukturieren, aufbauen II
structure [ˈstrʌktʃə] Struktur; Gliederung III
stuck [stʌk] *siehe* **stick**
student [ˈstjuːdənt] Schüler/in; Student/in I • **exchange student** Austauschschüler/in III
studio [ˈstjuːdiəʊ] Studio I
study [ˈstʌdi] lernen; studieren III
study [ˈstʌdi] Studie VI 1 (14)
study [ˈstʌdi] Arbeitszimmer VI 3 (62)
study hall [ˈstʌdi hɔːl] *Zeit zum selbstständigen Lernen in der Schule* IV
study skills *(pl)* [ˈstʌdi skɪlz] Lern- und Arbeitstechniken I
stuff [stʌf] Zeug, Kram I

stupid [ˈstjuːpɪd] blöd, dämlich V
style [staɪl] Stil III • **military-style fashion** Mode im Militärstil V
sub-heading [ˈsʌbˌhedɪŋ] Zwischenüberschrift IV
subject [ˈsʌbdʒɪkt]
  1. Subjekt I
  2. Schulfach I
  3. Thema IV
  4. Untertan/in; Staatsangehörige(r) *(in einer Monarchie)* IV
subjective [səbˈdʒektɪv] subjektiv V
subscribe (to sth.) [səbˈskraɪb] etwas abonnieren; etwas abonniert haben V
substantial [səbˈstænʃl] erheblich, beträchtlich VI 3 (56)
subtract [səbˈtrækt] subtrahieren VI 1 (21/203)
suburb [ˈsʌbɜːb] Vorort V
subway [ˈsʌbweɪ]: **the subway** *(AE)* die U-Bahn II
succeed (in sth.) [səkˈsiːd] Erfolg haben, erfolgreich sein (mit etwas, bei etwas) IV
success [səkˈses] Erfolg III
successful [səkˈsesfəl] erfolgreich V
such [sʌtʃ]: **such a nice person** so ein netter Mensch III • **such good books** so gute Bücher III • **such as** wie zum Beispiel III
°**suck-up** [ˈsʌk ʌp] Streber/in, Schleimer/in
sudden [ˈsʌdn] plötzlich IV
suddenly [ˈsʌdnli] plötzlich, auf einmal I
suffer (from) [ˈsʌfə] leiden (an) IV
suffix [ˈsʌfɪks] Suffix, Nachsilbe IV
sugar [ˈʃʊgə] Zucker II
suggest sth. [səˈdʒest]
  1. auf etwas hindeuten VI 3 (56)
  °**2.** vorschlagen
°**suggestion** [səˈdʒestʃn] Vorschlag III
suicide [ˈsuːɪsaɪd] Selbstmord VI 3 (64)
suitable [ˈsuːtəbl] geeignet, passend V
suitcase [ˈsuːtkeɪs] Koffer VI 4 (80)
°**suited** [ˈsuːtɪd]: **be suited to sb.** zu jm. passen
°**sulk** [sʌlk] schmollen, eingeschnapptsein, beleidigtsein, maulen
sum (sth.) up (-mm-) [ˌsʌm ˈʌp] (etwas) zusammenfassen V
  To sum up, ... Resümee: ...; Zusammenfassend: ... V
sum [sʌm] Summe VI 1 (21) • **do sums** rechnen VI 1 (21/203)
summarize [ˈsʌməraɪz] zusammenfassen V

summary [ˈsʌməri] Zusammenfassung IV
summer [ˈsʌmə] Sommer I
sun [sʌn] *(also Sun)* Sonne II
Sunday [ˈsʌndeɪ, ˈsʌndi] Sonntag I
sung [sʌŋ] *siehe* **sing**
sunglasses *(pl)* [ˈsʌnglɑːsɪz] (eine) Sonnenbrille I
sunk [sʌŋk] *siehe* **sink**
sunlight [ˈsʌnlaɪt] Sonnenlicht VI 3 (58)
sunny [ˈsʌni] sonnig II
sunrise [ˈsʌnraɪz] Sonnenaufgang IV
sunscreen [ˈsʌnskriːn] Sonnenschutzmittel V
sunset [ˈsʌnset] Sonnenuntergang IV
sunshine [ˈsʌnʃaɪn] Sonnenschein IV
suntan [ˈsʌntæn] Sonnenbräune V • **have a suntan** sonnengebräunt sein III
supermarket [ˈsuːpəmɑːkɪt] Supermarkt I
supper [ˈsʌpə] Abendessen, Abendbrot IV
support [səˈpɔːt] unterstützen, befürworten V • **support a team** eine Mannschaft unterstützen; Fan einer Mannschaft sein III
support [səˈpɔːt] Unterstützung IV
supporter [səˈpɔːtə]
  1. Anhänger/in, Fan III
  2. Befürworter/in, Unterstützer/in VI 2 (34)
suppose [səˈpəʊz] annehmen, vermuten I • **be supposed to do/be sth.** tun sollen / angeblich sein sollen VI 1 (14)
sure [ʃʊə, ʃɔː] sicher I • **make sure** sich vergewissern IV
surely [ˌʃʊəli] sicher VI 2 (34)
  ▶ S.210 certainly – surely
surf [sɜːf] surfen V • **go surfing** wellenreiten gehen, surfen gehen II • **surf the internet** im Internet surfen II • **surf instructor** Surflehrer/in V
surfboard [ˈsɜːfbɔːd] Surfbrett II
surprise (for/to) [səˈpraɪz] Überraschung (für) III
surprise sb. [səˈpraɪz] jn. überraschen III
surprised (at sth.) [səˈpraɪzd] überrascht (über etwas) III
surprising [səˈpraɪzɪŋ] überraschend V
surround [səˈraʊnd]: **be surrounded** umgeben sein IV
survey (on) [ˈsɜːveɪ] Umfrage, Untersuchung (über) II

°**survey sb.** [ˈsɜ:veɪ] jn. befragen
survival [səˈvaɪvl] Überleben II
survive [səˈvaɪv] überleben II
suspect [səˈspekt] vermuten VI 3 (54)
suspense [səˈspens] Spannung V
suspicious [səˈspɪʃəs] misstrauisch (gegenüber); verdächtig VI 4 (105)
swam [swæm] *siehe* **swim**
swap (-pp-) [swɒp] tauschen I
swap sth. (for sth.) etwas (ein)tauschen (für/gegen etwas) IV
sweat [swet] schwitzen IV
sweat [swet] Schweiß IV
sweatshirt [ˈswetʃɜ:t] Sweatshirt I
sweep [swi:p], **swept, swept** fegen, kehren IV
sweet [swi:t] süß I
sweetheart [ˈswi:tha:t] Liebling, Schatz I
sweets *(pl)* Süßigkeiten I
swept [swept] *siehe* sweep
swim (-mm-) [swɪm], **swam, swum** schwimmen I
swimmer [ˈswɪmə] Schwimmer/in II
swimming [ˈswɪmɪŋ] Schwimmen I • **go swimming** schwimmen gehen I • **swimming instructor** Schwimmlehrer/in V
swimming pool [ˈswɪmɪŋ pu:l] Schwimmbad, -becken II
swimming trunks [trʌŋks] Badehose III
swimsuit [ˈswɪmsu:t] Badeanzug III
swipe a card [swaɪp] eine Karte durchziehen VI 3 (61)
switch sth. off [ˌswɪtʃ ˈɒf] etwas ausschalten VI 3 (62/221)
switch sth. on [ˌswɪtʃ ˈɒn] etwas anschalten VI 3 (62)
swum [swʌm] *siehe* swim
syllable [ˈsɪləbl] Silbe I
symbol (of sth.) [ˈsɪmbl] Symbol (für etwas) VI 4 (77)
sympathetic [ˌsɪmpəˈθetɪk] mitfühlend, verständnisvoll, wohlwollend VI 2 (28)
sympathy [ˈsɪmpəθi] Mitgefühl, Verständnis, Anteilnahme (für jn., jm. gegenüber) VI 2 (28)
symptom [ˈsɪmptəm] Symptom, Anzeichen VI 1 (14)
synagogue [ˈsɪnəgɒg] Synagoge III
synonym [ˈsɪnənɪm] Synonym *(Wort mit gleicher oder sehr ähnlicher Bedeutung)* IV
syringe [sɪˈrɪndʒ] Injektionsspritze VI 3 (56)
system [ˈsɪstəm] System IV

T

table [ˈteɪbl]
1. Tisch I • **table tennis** Tischtennis I • **table tennis bat** Tischtennisschläger III
2. Tabelle V • **table of contents** Inhaltsverzeichnis V
tablecloth [ˈteɪblklɒθ] Tischdecke IV
tail [teɪl] Schwanz VI 4 (101)
tailor [ˈteɪlə] Schneider/in VI 3 (56)
take [teɪk], **took, taken**
1. nehmen I
2. (weg-, hin)bringen I
3. dauern, *(Zeit)* brauchen III
I can take it. Ich halt's aus. / Ich kann's aushalten. IV • **take a break** eine Pause machen IV • **take a left/right** *(AE)* nach links/rechts abbiegen IV • **take a trip** *(AE)* einen Ausflug/eine Reise machen IV • **Take another turn.** *(beim Spielen)* Würfel noch einmal. II • **take care of sth./sb.** sich um etwas/jn. kümmern III • **take sth. for granted** etwas für (allzu) selbstverständlich halten VI 4 (76) **take interest in sb./sth.** sich für jn./etwas interessieren VI 1 (12) **take notes** sich Notizen machen I • **take sth. off** etwas ausziehen *(Kleidung)*; etwas absetzen *(Hut, Helm)* II • **take 10 c off** 10 Cent abziehen I • **take sth. out** etwas herausnehmen I • **take sth. over** etwas übernehmen; etwas in seine Macht bringen IV • **take part in sth.** teilnehmen an etwas III **take photos** Fotos machen, fotografieren II • **take place** stattfinden II • **take responsibility (for)** Verantwortung (für) übernehmen V • **take a ride** eine Spritztour/Fahrt machen III • **take sth. a step at a time** etwas eins nach dem anderen tun; etwas Schritt für Schritt tun IV • **take steps** Schritte machen/unternehmen III • **take turns to do sth.** sich abwechseln, etwas zu tun IV • **take sth. up** etwas in Anspruch nehmen, etwas einnehmen (Zeit, Raum) VI 1 (15)
I'll take it. *(beim Einkaufen)* Ich werde es (ihn, sie) nehmen. / Ich nehme es (ihn, sie). I
°**take** [teɪk] *(infml)* Einstellung
takeaway [ˈteɪkəweɪ] *Restaurant, das auch Essen zum Mitnehmen verkauft; Essen zum Mitnehmen* III
taken [ˈteɪkən] *siehe* take
talent [ˈtælənt] Talent, Begabung III

talk [tɔ:k]: **talk (about)** reden (über), sich unterhalten (über) I **talk (to)** reden (mit), sich unterhalten (mit) I
talk [tɔ:k] Rede, Gespräch; Vortrag, Referat IV
talk show [ˈtɔ:k ʃəʊ] Talkshow V
tall [tɔ:l]
1. groß *(Person)* III
2. hoch *(Gebäude, Baum)* IV
Taoism [ˈtaʊɪzm] Taoismus V
Taoist [ˈtaʊɪst] Taoist/in, taoistisch V
tap [tæp] Wasserhahn V
target [ˈtɑ:gɪt] Ziel(scheibe) VI 1 (17)
target group Zielgruppe VI 1 (17)
task [tɑ:sk] Aufgabe VI 1 (11)
taste [teɪst] schmecken; kosten, probieren IV
taste [teɪst]
1. Geschmack IV • **be in good/bad taste** geschmackvoll/geschmacklos sein IV
2. Schmecken, gustatorische Wahrnehmung VI 3 (64/221)
taught [tɔ:t] *siehe* teach
tavern [ˈtævən] Schenke, Gastwirtschaft IV
tax (on) [tæks] Steuer (auf) VI 2 (28)
taxi [ˈtæksi] Taxi III
tea [ti:] Tee; (auch:) leichte Nachmittags- oder Abendmahlzeit I
tea bag Teebeutel IV
teach [ti:tʃ], **taught, taught** unterrichten, lehren I
teacher [ˈti:tʃə] Lehrer/in I • **head teacher** Schulleiter/in III
team [ti:m] Team, Mannschaft I
tear [teə], **tore, torn** (zer)reißen IV
tear [tɪə] Träne II
tease [ti:z] necken, auf den Arm nehmen III
teaspoon [ˈti:spu:n] Teelöffel III
°**technical** [ˈteknɪkəl] technisch
technique [tekˈni:k] (Arbeits-)Verfahren, Technik, Methode IV
technology [tekˈnɒlədʒi] Technologie V
teddy bear [ˈtedi beə] Teddybär III
teen *(bes. AE)* [ti:n]
1. Teenager- III
2. Teenager/in V
teenage [ˈti:neɪdʒ] Teenage- V
teenager [ˈti:neɪdʒə] Teenager, Jugendliche(r) II
teeth [ti:θ] *Plural von „tooth"* I
telephone [ˈtelɪfəʊn] Telefon I
telephone number Telefonnummer I
television [ˈtelɪvɪʒn] Fernsehen I
tell (about) [tel], **told, told** erzählen (von), berichten (über) I • **Tell me**

your names. Sagt mir eure Namen. I • **tell sb. the way** jm. den Weg beschreiben II

°**telly** ['teli] (infml) Fernsehen

temperature ['temprətʃə] Temperatur II • **have a temperature** Fieber haben II

temple ['templ] Tempel V

tempt [tempt] in Versuchung führen VI 4 (99)

tennis ['tenɪs] Tennis I

tense [tens] (grammatische) Zeit, Tempus III

tension ['tenʃn] Spannung VI 4 (94)

tent [tent] Zelt IV

term [tɜːm] Trimester II

terrible ['terəbl] schrecklich, furchtbar I

terrified ['terɪfaɪd]: **be terrified (of)** schreckliche Angst haben (vor) IV

terrifying ['terɪfaɪɪŋ] schrecklich, unheimlich VI 2 (35)

terrorism ['terərɪzm] Terrorismus IV

test [test] Klassenarbeit, Test, Prüfung II

text [tekst] Text I

text (message) ['tekst ˌmesɪdʒ] SMS II

text sb. [tekst] jm. eine SMS schicken II

°**texture** ['tekstʃə] Materialbeschaffenheit

than [ðæn, ðən] als II • **more than me** mehr als ich II

thank [θæŋk]: **Thank God.** Gott sei Dank. IV • **Thank you.** Danke (schön). I • **Thanks.** Danke. I **Thanks a lot!** Vielen Dank! I **Thanks very much!** Danke sehr! / Vielen Dank! II • **give thanks** danken, feierlich danksagen IV **Many thanks.** Vielen Dank. VI 2 (40)

thank sb. [θæŋk] jm. danken; sich bei jm. bedanken VI 1 (21)

that [ðət, ðæt]
1. das (dort) I
2. jene(r, s) I • **that day** an jenem Tag III • **That's me.** Das bin ich. I **That's right.** Das ist richtig. / Das stimmt. I • **That's up to you.** Das liegt bei dir. / Das kannst/musst du (selbst) entscheiden. III • **that's why** deshalb, darum I

that [ðət, ðæt] dass I

that [ðət, ðæt] der, die, das; die (Relativpronomen) III

the [ðə, ði] der, die, das; die I

theatre ['θɪətə] Theater II

their [ðeə]
1. ihr, ihre (Plural) I
2. sein oder ihr (= **his or her**) IV

theirs [ðeəz] ihrer, ihre, ihrs II

them [ðəm, ðem]
1. sie; ihnen I • **the two of them** die beiden; alle beide II
2. ihn oder sie (= **him or her**) IV

theme park ['θiːm pɑːk] Themenpark II

themselves [ðəm'selvz]
1. sich III
2. selbst IV

then [ðen]
1. dann, danach I
2. damals II
Then what? Was dann? II • **just then** genau in dem Moment; gerade dann II

theocracy [θiˈɒkrəsi] Theokratie V

there [ðeə]
1. da, dort I
2. dahin, dorthin I
down there (nach) dort unten II **in there** dort drinnen I • **over there** da drüben, dort drüben I **up there** dort oben III • **there are** es sind (vorhanden); es gibt I **there's** es ist (vorhanden); es gibt I • **there isn't a …** es ist kein/e …; es gibt kein/e … I

thermometer [θəˈmɒmɪtə] Thermometer II

these [ðiːz] diese, die (hier) I

they [ðeɪ]
1. sie (Plural) I • **They say …** Man sagt, … III
2. er oder sie (= **he or she**) IV

thick [θɪk] dick VI 3 (56)

thief [θiːf], pl **thieves** [θiːvz] Dieb/in II

thin [θɪn] dünn VI 3 (56)

thing [θɪŋ] Ding, Sache I • **What was the best thing about …?** Was war das Beste an …? II

think [θɪŋk], **thought, thought** glauben, meinen, denken I • **Do you really think so?** Meinst du wirklich? / Glaubst du das wirklich? II • **I think so.** Ich glaube (ja). I • **I don't think so.** Das finde/glaube ich nicht. I • **think about 1.** nachdenken über II; **2.** denken über, halten von II **think of 1.** denken über, halten von II **2.** denken an; sich ausdenken II

third [θɜːd] dritte(r, s) I • **the Third World** die Dritte Welt VI 3 (56)

thirsty ['θɜːsti] durstig I • **be thirsty** Durst haben, durstig sein I

this [ðɪs]
1. dies (hier) I
2. diese(r, s) I

This is Isabel. Hier spricht Isabel. / Hier ist Isabel. (am Telefon) II **this morning/afternoon/evening** heute Morgen/Nachmittag/Abend I • **this way** hier entlang, in diese Richtung II

those [ðəʊz] die (da), jene (dort) I

thought [θɔːt]
1. siehe **think**
2. Gedanke IV

thought bubble ['bʌbl] Denkblase VI 2 (28/207)

thousand ['θaʊznd] tausend, Tausend I

°**thread** [θred] Folge von Diskussionsbeiträgen in einem Blog oder Forum

°**thread** [θred] einfädeln

threaten ['θretn] jn. bedrohen, jm. drohen VI 2 (38)

threatening ['θretnɪŋ] drohend, bedrohlich VI 2 (38)

threw [θruː] siehe **throw**

thriller ['θrɪlə] Thriller VI 4 (76)

thrilling ['θrɪlɪŋ] aufregend, spannend VI 4 (87)

throat Hals, Kehle II • **have a sore throat** [sɔː 'θrəʊt] Halsschmerzen haben II

through [θruː] durch II

throughout October [θruːˈaʊt] den ganzen Oktober hindurch IV

throw [θrəʊ], **threw, thrown** werfen I • **throw the dice** würfeln II **throw up** sich übergeben IV

thrown [θrəʊn] siehe **throw**

thunderstorm ['θʌndəstɔːm] Gewitter V

Thursday ['θɜːzdeɪ, 'θɜːzdi] Donnerstag I

thus (fml) [ðʌs] daher, folglich VI 4 (88)

ticket ['tɪkɪt]
1. Eintrittskarte I
2. Fahrkarte III

ticket machine ['tɪkɪt məˌʃiːn] Fahrkartenautomat III

ticket office ['tɪkɪt ˌɒfɪs] Kasse (für den Verkauf von Eintrittskarten); Fahrkartenschalter IV

tide [taɪd] Gezeiten, Ebbe und Flut II • **the tide is in** es ist Flut II **the tide is out** es ist Ebbe II

tidy ['taɪdi] aufräumen I

tidy ['taɪdi] ordentlich, aufgeräumt II

tie (-ing form: **tying**) [taɪ] (fest)binden IV

tiger ['taɪgə] Tiger II

tight [taɪt] eng; fest IV

tights (pl) [taɪts] Strumpfhose III

till [tɪl] bis (zeitlich) I

time [taɪm] Zeit; Uhrzeit I • **in time** rechtzeitig II • **What's the time?** Wie spät ist es? I • **a long time** lange III • **a short time** kurz IV • **time zone** Zeitzone IV

time(s) [taɪmz] Mal(e); -mal II **for the first time** zum ersten Mal II

timeline ['taɪmlaɪn] Zeitstrahl, Zeitleiste IV

timetable ['taɪmteɪbl] Stundenplan I

timing ['taɪmɪŋ]: **bad timing** schlechtes Timing, schlechte Wahl des Zeitpunkts III

tin [tɪn] Dose V

tip [tɪp]
1. Tipp III
2. Spitze IV

tired ['taɪəd] müde I • **be tired of sth.** genug von etwas haben, etwas satt haben IV • **get tired of sth.** einer Sache überdrüssig werden, die Lust an etwas verlieren IV

title ['taɪtl] Titel, Überschrift I

to [tə, tu]
1. zu, nach I • **an e-mail to** eine E-Mail an I • **to Jenny's** zu Jenny I • **to the doctor's** zum Arzt III **to the front** nach vorn I • **I've never been to Bath.** Ich bin noch nie in Bath gewesen. II • **write to** schreiben an I
2. **quarter to 12** Viertel vor 12 (11.45 / 23.45) I • **from Monday to Friday** von Montag bis Freitag III
3. **try to do** versuchen, zu tun I
4. um zu I

toast [təʊst] Toast(brot) I

today [tə'deɪ] heute I

toe [təʊ] Zeh I

together [tə'geðə] zusammen I

toilet ['tɔɪlət] Toilette I • **toilet paper** Toilettenpapier V

told [təʊld] siehe **tell**

tolerant (of sth./sb.) ['tɒlərənt] tolerant, verständnisvoll (etwas/jm. gegenüber) VI 2 (29/207)

tomato [tə'mɑːtəʊ], pl **tomatoes** Tomate II

tomorrow [tə'mɒrəʊ] morgen I

tone of voice [təʊn] Ton(fall) V

°**tone** [təʊn] Klang, Ton

tonight [tə'naɪt] heute Nacht, heute Abend I

tonne [tʌn] Tonne (Gewichtseinheit) VI 3 (58)

too [tuː]: **from Bristol too** auch aus Bristol I • **Me too.** Ich auch. I

too much/big/... [tuː] zu viel/groß/... I

took [tʊk] siehe **take**

---

tool [tuːl] Werkzeug IV

tooth [tuːθ], pl **teeth** [tiːθ] Zahn I

toothache ['tuːθeɪk] Zahnschmerzen II

top [tɒp]
1. Spitze, oberes Ende I • **at the top (of)** oben, am oberen Ende, an der Spitze (von) I • °**at the top of your voice** aus vollem Hals
2. Top, Oberteil I

top [tɒp] (adj) Spitzen-, oberste(r, s) III

topic ['tɒpɪk] Thema, Themenbereich I • **topic sentence** Satz, der in das Thema eines Absatzes einführt II

torch [tɔːtʃ] Taschenlampe VI 4 (98)

tore [tɔː] siehe **tear**

°**tormentor** [tɔː'mentə] (fml) Peiniger/in

torn [tɔːn] siehe **tear**

tortoise ['tɔːtəs] Schildkröte I

torture ['tɔːtʃə] Folter VI 2 (26)

total ['təʊtl] Gesamt-, gesamt, völlig, total VI 1 (10)

touch [tʌtʃ] berühren, anfassen I

touch [tʌtʃ]: **keep in touch** in Verbindung bleiben, Kontakt halten III

touch [tʌtʃ] Tasten, haptische Wahrnehmung VI 3 (64/221)

°**touchline** ['tʌtʃlaɪn] Seitenlinie

tough [tʌf] tough, selbstsicher, zäh III; schwierig, hart IV

tour [tʊə]
1. (of the house) Rundgang, Tour (durch das Haus) I
2. Tournee • **go on tour** auf Tournee gehen VI 2 (39)

tourist ['tʊərɪst] Tourist/in II **tourist information** Fremdenverkehrsamt II

toward [tə'wɔːd] (AE) siehe **towards**

towards [tə'wɔːdz]
1. **towards Mr Green** auf Mr Green zu, in Mr Greens Richtung I
2. **towards sb.** jm. gegenüber VI 2 (26)

towel ['taʊəl] Handtuch II

tower ['taʊə] Turm I

town [taʊn] Stadt I • **the centre of town** die Mitte der Stadt III • **in town** in der Stadt III • **into town** in die Stadt III

track [træk]
1. Stück, Titel, Track (auf einer CD) III
2. Spur, Fährte; Pfad, Weg V

trade [treɪd] Handel II

trade [treɪd] Handel treiben V

tradition [trə'dɪʃn] Tradition IV

traditional [trə'dɪʃənl] traditionell III

---

traffic ['træfɪk] Verkehr II

trail [treɪl] (Lehr-)Pfad IV

train [treɪn] Zug I • **on the train** im Zug I • **mule train** Maultierkarawane IV

train [treɪn]
1. trainieren III
2. **train as ...** eine Ausbildung machen zu ... V

trained [treɪnd] ausgebildet V

trainers (pl) ['treɪnəz] Turnschuhe II

training session ['seʃn] Trainingsstunde, -einheit III

tram [træm] Straßenbahn III

transfer [træns'fɜː] übertragen VI 3 (57)

translate (from ... into) [træns'leɪt] übersetzen (aus ... in) III

translation [træns'leɪʃn] Übersetzung III

translator [ˌtræns'leɪtə] Übersetzer/in VI 3 (59)

transparency [træns'pærənsi] Folie V

transport (no pl) ['trænspɔːt] Transport(wesen) III • **public transport** öffentlicher Verkehr IV

trap [træp] Falle II

trap (-pp-) [træp] (mit einer Falle) fangen III

trash [træʃ] (AE) Abfall, Müll V

travel (-ll-) ['trævl] reisen II

Travelcard ['trævlkɑːd] Tages-/Wochen-/Monatsfahrkarte (der Londoner Verkehrsbetriebe) III

travel guide ['trævl ˌgaɪd] Reiseführer (Buch) V

treason ['triːzn] Hochverrat IV

treat [triːt] behandeln V

treatment ['triːtmənt] Behandlung (auch medizinisch) VI 2 (26)

tree [triː] Baum I • **Christmas tree** Christ-, Weihnachtsbaum V **palm tree** Palme V

trend [trend] Trend V

trendy ['trendi] modisch, schick III

trial ['traɪəl] Test, Probe, Versuch VI 4 (80) • **trial separation** (Ehe-)Trennung auf Probe VI 4 (80)

tribal ['traɪbl] Stammes- IV

tribe [traɪb] (Volks-)Stamm IV

trick [trɪk]
1. (Zauber-)Kunststück, Trick I **do tricks** (Zauber-)Kunststücke machen I
2. Streich II • **play a trick on sb.** jm. einen Streich spielen II

trick sb. [trɪk] jn. austricksen, reinlegen V

trick sb. into doing sth. [trɪk] jn. mit einer List / einem Trick dazu bringen, etwas zu tun V

tricky ['trɪki] verzwickt, heikel V

trillion ['trɪlɪən] Billion v

trip [trɪp] Reise; Ausflug I • **go on a trip** einen Ausflug/eine Reise machen II • **take a trip** (AE) einen Ausflug/eine Reise machen IV

trombone [trɒm'bəʊn] Posaune III

trouble ['trʌbl] Schwierigkeiten, Ärger II • **be in trouble** in Schwierigkeiten sein; Ärger kriegen II

troublemaker ['trʌbl,meɪkə] Unruhestifter/in v

trousers (pl) ['traʊzəz] Hose II

truck [trʌk] Lastwagen, LKW v

true [truː] wahr II • **come true** wahr werden II

truly ['truːli]: **Yours truly** (AE) mit freundlichen Grüßen IV

trumpet ['trʌmpɪt] Trompete III

°**trunk** [trʌŋk] Baumstamm

trust [trʌst] trauen, vertrauen v

trust [trʌst] Vertrauen; vertrauliche Mitteilung VI 1 (9)

try [traɪ]
1. versuchen I
2. probieren, kosten I
try and do sth. / try to do sth. versuchen, etwas zu tun I • **try sth. on** etwas anprobieren (Kleidung) I

T-shirt ['tiː,ʃɜːt] T-Shirt I

tsunami [tsuː'nɑːmi] Tsunami III

tube [tjuːb]: **the Tube** (no pl) (BE) die Londoner U-Bahn III

Tuesday ['tjuːzdeɪ, -di] Dienstag I

tuition [tjuː'ɪʃn] (Nachhilfe-)Unterricht v

tune [tjuːn]: **tune a radio to a station** ein Radio auf einen Sender einstellen IV • **You're tuned to Radio Bristol.** Sie hören gerade Radio Bristol. IV

tune [tjuːn] Melodie III

tunnel ['tʌnl] Tunnel II

turkey ['tɜːki] Pute, Truthahn IV

turn [tɜːn]
1. sich umdrehen II • **turn around** sich umdrehen IV • **turn left/right** (nach) links/rechts abbiegen II **turn to sb.** sich jm. zuwenden; sich an jn. wenden II
2. **turn sth. off/on** etwas aus-/einschalten I • **turn sth. down/up** etwas leiser/lauter stellen III
3. **turn out to be sth.** sich (als etwas) herausstellen VI 3 (55)
4. **turn sth. into sth.** jn./etwas in etwas verwandeln VI 2 (29)

turn [tɜːn]: **(It's) my turn.** Ich bin dran / an der Reihe. I • **Miss a turn.** Einmal aussetzen. II • **Take another turn.** (beim Spielen) Würfel noch einmal. II • **take turns to do sth.** sich abwechseln IV

turtle ['tɜːtl] Wasserschildkröte v

TV [tiː'viː] Fernsehen I • **on TV** im Fernsehen I • **watch TV** fernsehen I

twice [twaɪs] zweimal III

twin [twɪn]: **twin brother** Zwillingsbruder I • **twins** (pl) Zwillinge I **twin town** Partnerstadt I

twist [twɪst] (überraschende) Wendung VI 4 (96)

typical (of) ['tɪpɪkl] typisch (für) v

U

ugly ['ʌgli] hässlich v

ultimate ['ʌltɪmət] ultimativ, perfekt IV

ultraviolet rays (UV rays) (pl) [,ʌltrə,vaɪələt 'reɪz] ultraviolette Strahlen v

umbrella [ʌm'brelə] Regenschirm VI 3 (54)

unable [ʌn'eɪbl]: **be unable to do sth.** etwas nicht können v

unafraid [,ʌnə'freɪd]: **be unafraid** keine Angst haben v

unanswered [,ʌn'ɑːnsəd] unbeantwortet IV

unavailable [,ʌnə'veɪləbl] nicht erhältlich, nicht vorrätig v

uncle ['ʌŋkl] Onkel I

unclear [,ʌn'klɪə] unklar, undeutlich II

uncomfortable [ʌn'kʌmftəbl] unbequem II

unconscious [ʌn'kɒnʃəs] bewusstlos II

uncool [,ʌn'kuːl] (infml) uncool III

under ['ʌndə] unter I

under age [,ʌndər_'eɪdʒ] minderjährig v

under control [kən'trəʊl] unter Kontrolle IV

underground ['ʌndəgraʊnd]: **the underground** die U-Bahn II

underground [,ʌndə'graʊnd] unterirdisch IV

°**underline** ['ʌndə'laɪn]
1. unterstreichen
2. betonen

understand [,ʌndə'stænd], **understood, understood** verstehen, begreifen I

understanding [,ʌndə'stændɪŋ] verständnisvoll IV

°**understanding** [,ʌndə'stændɪŋ] Kenntnis(se)

understood [,ʌndə'stʊd] siehe **understand**

underwear (no pl) ['ʌndəweə] Unterwäsche v

unequal [ʌn'iːkwəl] ungleich v

unexpected [,ʌnɪk'spektɪd] unerwartet, überraschend v

unfair [,ʌn'feə] unfair, ungerecht II

unfortunately [ʌn'fɔːtʃənətli] leider, unglücklicherweise VI 1 (14)

unfriendliness [,ʌn'frendlɪnəs] Unfreundlichkeit VI 2 (41)

unfriendly [ʌn'frendli] unfreundlich II

unhappy [ʌn'hæpi] unglücklich II

unhealthy [ʌn'helθi] ungesund III

uniform ['juːnɪfɔːm] Uniform I

unimportant [,ʌnɪm'pɔːtnt] unwichtig III

uninteresting [ʌn'ɪntrəstɪŋ] uninteressant II

°**Union Jack** [,juːnɪən 'dʒæk] britische Nationalflagge

unique [juː'niːk] einzigartig, einmalig v

unit ['juːnɪt] Kapitel, Lektion I

unite (with sb./sth.) [juː'naɪt] sich (mit jm./etwas) vereinigen, vereinen v • **the United Kingdom (UK)** [juː,naɪtɪd 'kɪŋdəm], [,juː' keɪ] das Vereinigte Königreich (Großbritannien und Nordirland) III • **the United States (US)** [juː,naɪtɪd 'steɪts], [,juː_'es] die Vereinigten Staaten (von Amerika) III

°**universal declaration** [juːnɪ,vɜːsl ,deklə'reɪʃn] Allgemeine Erklärung v

universe ['juːnɪvɜːs] (also **Universe**) Universum VI 3 (54)

university [,juːnɪ'vɜːsəti] Universität, Hochschule v • **go to university** mit dem Studium anfangen v

unkind [,ʌn'kaɪnd] unfreundlich VI 1 (20)

unknown [,ʌn'nəʊn] unbekannt IV

unless [ən'les] es sei denn, außer (wenn) v

unlike [,ʌn'laɪk] im Gegensatz zu III

unlimited [ʌn'lɪmɪtɪd] unbegrenzt VI 4 (84)

unload [ʌn'ləʊd] entladen III

unlucky [ʌn'lʌki]: **be unlucky** Pech haben v

unnecessary [ʌn'nesəsəri] unnötig VI 4 (105)

unpleasant [ʌn'pleznt] unangenehm VI 1 (20)

unpopular [ʌn'pɒpjələ] unpopulär, unbeliebt v

°**unpredictable** [prɪ'dɪktəbl] unvorhersagbar, unvorhersehbar v

unreal [,ʌn'rɪəl] unwirklich v

unrealistic [,ʌnrɪə'lɪstɪk] unrealistisch v

unreliable [,ʌnrɪ'laɪəbl] unzuverlässig v

unsafe [ʌn'seɪf] nicht sicher, gefähr-lich III

°**unspoken** [ˌʌn'spəʊkən] unausge-sprochen

unsure [ʌn'ʃʊə, ʌn'ʃɔː] unsicher II
untidy [ʌn'taɪdi] unordentlich III
until [ən'tɪl] bis III
unusual [ʌn'juːʒʊəl] ungewöhnlich VI 2 (31)

unwanted [ˌʌn'wɒntɪd] uner-wünscht, ungewollt v

unwrap (-pp-) [ʌn'ræp] auspacken, auswickeln VI 3 (61)

up [ʌp] hinauf, herauf, nach oben I
up the hill den Hügel hinauf II
up there dort oben III • **That's up to you.** Das liegt bei dir. / Das kannst/musst du (selbst) entschei-den. III • **What's up?** Was ist los? IV • °**be up to sth.** (infml) etwas vorhaben, etwas anstellen

upper-class [ˌʌpə 'klɑːs] der Ober-schicht zugehörig, vornehm, edel v

uprising ['ʌpraɪzɪŋ] Aufstand v

upset (about) [ʌp'set] aufgebracht, gekränkt, mitgenommen (wegen) III

upset sb. **(-tt-)** [ʌp'set]**,** upset, upset jn. ärgern, kränken, aus der Fas-sung bringen III

upstairs [ʌp'steəz] oben; nach oben I

urban ['ɜːbən] städtisch, Stadt- v

urge [ɜːdʒ] Bedürfnis, Verlangen VI 3 (54)

us [əs, ʌs] uns I

US [juː'es] US-amerikanische(r, s) IV

use [juːz] benutzen, verwenden I
use force Gewalt anwenden v
use sth. up etwas aufbrauchen VI 3 (61)

use [juːs] Gebrauch III

used [juːst]**: get used to sth./sb.** sich gewöhnen an jn./etwas IV
I used to be Früher war ich (immer) ... v

useful ['juːsfl] nützlich v
useless ['juːsləs] nutzlos, unfähig IV
usual ['juːʒʊəl] gewöhnlich, üblich IV

usually ['juːʒʊəli] meistens, ge-wöhnlich, normalerweise I

°**utopia** [juː'təʊpiə] Utopie

V

vacation [və'keɪʃn, AE: veɪ'keɪʃn] (AE) Urlaub, Ferien III

valley ['væli] Tal II • **valley floor** Talboden II

valuable ['væljuəbl] wertvoll, nütz-lich v

value ['væljuː] Wert IV

vandalism ['vændəlɪzəm] Vandalis-mus, Zerstörungswut v

vandalize ['vændəlaɪz] mutwillig beschädigen, mutwillig zerstören v

various ['veəriəs] verschieden VI 4 (98)

vast [vɑːst] riesig VI 4 (78)

vastly ['vɑːstli] äußerst, völlig VI 4 (78)

vegetable ['vedʒtəbl] (ein) Gemüse III

verse [vɜːs] Vers (von der Bibel); Strophe IV

version ['vɜːʃn] Fassung IV
original version Originalfassung IV

very ['veri]
1. sehr I • **like/love sth. very much** etwas sehr mögen/lieben II
Thanks very much! Danke sehr! / Vielen Dank! II
2. very best/most/... allerbes-te(r, s), allermeiste(r, s), ... VI 1 (10)

victim ['vɪktɪm] Opfer III

victory ['vɪktəri] Sieg IV

video ['vɪdiəʊ] Video III • **video projector** Videoprojektor, Beamer v

view (of) [vjuː]
1. Aussicht, Blick (auf) II
2. Ansicht, Meinung III
in my view meiner Ansicht nach III • **point of view** [ˌpɔɪnt_əv 'vjuː] Standpunkt II • **from my point of view** aus meiner Sicht; von mei-nem Standpunkt aus gesehen II

view [vjuː] betrachten, sehen; fern-sehen VI 1 (23)

villa ['vɪlə] Ferienhaus; Villa II
village ['vɪlɪdʒ] Dorf II
vineyard ['vɪnjəd] Weinberg IV

°**violation** [ˌvaɪə'leɪʃn] Verletzung

violence ['vaɪələns] Gewalt, Gewalt-tätigkeit IV

violent ['vaɪələnt] gewalttätig, ge-waltsam IV

violin [ˌvaɪə'lɪn] Violine, Geige III
play the violin Geige spielen III

visibility [ˌvɪzə'bɪləti] Sicht(weite) IV

vision ['vɪʒn]
1. Sehvermögen VI 3 (56)
°**2.** Vision, Vorstellung

visit ['vɪzɪt] besuchen, aufsuchen II
visit ['vɪzɪt] Besuch II
visitor ['vɪzɪtə] Besucher/in, Gast I
visual ['vɪʒʊəl] optisch, visuell VI 4 (86) • **visual aids** (pl) An-schauungsmaterialien v

°**vivid** ['vɪvɪd] lebendig

vocabulary [və'kæbjələri] Vokabel-verzeichnis, Wörterverzeichnis I

voice [vɔɪs] Stimme I • **tone of voice** Ton(fall) v • °**at the top of your voice** aus vollem Hals

voiceover ['vɔɪsəʊvə] Voiceover (Kommentar einer Figur oder eines Erzählers, der nicht „in der Szene" gesprochen wird, sondern sozusa-gen „über der Szene") VI 2 (30)

volleyball ['vɒlibɔːl] Volleyball I

volume ['vɒljuːm] Lautstärke VI 3 (66)

volunteer [ˌvɒlən'tɪə] sich freiwillig melden, sich bereit erklären IV; ehrenamtliche Arbeit leisten für/ bei v

volunteer work [ˌvɒlən'tɪə] Arbeit als Freiwillige(r) III

vote [vəʊt]
1. (for/against sb./sth.) für/gegen jn./etwas stimmen IV
2. zur Wahl gehen, wählen v
voting age Wahlalter VI 2 (34)

vote [vəʊt] (die) Stimme(n); Stimm-recht II

vowel sound ['vaʊəl saʊnd] Vokal-laut II

W

wages (pl) ['weɪdʒɪz] Lohn VI 3 (56)
waist [weɪst] Taille VI 4 (81)
wait (for) ['weɪt fɔː] warten (auf) I
I can't wait to see ... ich kann es kaum erwarten, ... zu sehen I
Wait a minute. Warte mal! / Mo-ment mal! II • **Wait and see!** Wart's ab! III

wake [weɪk]**, woke, woken**
1. wake sb. (up) jn. (auf)wecken III
2. wake up aufwachen III

walk [wɔːk] (zu Fuß) gehen, laufen I; spazieren gehen III • **walk on** weiterlaufen III • **walk around** herumlaufen III • °**walk away from sb./sth** von jm./etwas weg-laufen • **walk the dog** den Hund ausführen v

walk [wɔːk] Spaziergang II • **go for a walk** spazieren gehen, einen Spaziergang machen II

wall [wɔːl] Wand; Mauer II

wander ['wɒndə] schlendern, her-umirren IV

want [wɒnt] (haben) wollen I
want to do tun wollen I • **They want me to say something.** Sie möchten, dass ich etwas sage IV
want sth. (to be) done wollen,

Dictionary

dass etwas geschieht; wollen, dass etwas getan wird VI 2 (34)

war [wɔː] Krieg III

wardrobe ['wɔːdrəʊb] Kleiderschrank I

warm [wɔːm] warm II

warming ['gləʊbl]: **global warming** Erwärmung der Erdatmosphäre V

warn sb. (about/of sth.) [wɔːn] jn. vor etwas warnen IV

warning ['wɔːnɪŋ] Warnung IV

was [wəz, wɒz] *siehe* **be**

wash [wɒʃ] waschen I • **I wash my hands.** Ich wasche mir die Hände. I

washing machine ['wɒʃɪŋ məˌʃiːn] Waschmaschine II

waste sth. (on) [weɪst] etwas verschwenden, vergeuden (für) III

waste [weɪst]
  1. Verschwendung IV
  2. Abfall V

watch [wɒtʃ] beobachten, sich etwas ansehen; zusehen I
  watch TV fernsehen I

°**watch** [wɒtʃ] aufpassen

watch [wɒtʃ] Armbanduhr I

water ['wɔːtə] Wasser I

waterfall ['wɔːtəfɔːl] Wasserfall III

waterproof ['wɔːtəpruːf] wasserdicht, -fest V

wave [weɪv] winken II • **wave at sb.** jm. zuwinken V

wave [weɪv] Welle IV

way [weɪ]
  1. Weg; Strecke II • **a long way (from)** weit entfernt (von) I **ask sb. the way** jn. nach dem Weg fragen II • **on the way (to)** auf dem Weg (zu/nach) II • **tell sb. the way** jm. den Weg beschreiben II • **What's the best way to get there?** Wie komme ich am besten dahin? III • **I'm on my way.** Ich bin (schon) unterwegs. IV
  2. Richtung II • **the other way round** anders herum II • **the wrong way** in die falsche Richtung II • **this way** hier entlang, in diese Richtung II • **which way?** in welche Richtung? / wohin? II
  3. No way! [ˌnəʊ 'weɪ] Auf keinen Fall! / Kommt nicht in Frage! II; Was du nicht sagst! / Das kann nicht dein Ernst sein! III
  4. by the way übrigens, nebenbei (bemerkt) III
  5. Art und Weise • **way of life** Lebensart III • **the way you ...** so wie du ..., auf dieselbe Weise wie du ... IV

we [wiː] wir I

weak [wiːk] schwach II

weakness ['wiːknəs] Schwäche, Schwachpunkt V

wealth [welθ] Reichtum IV

wealthy ['welθi] reich IV

wear [weə], **wore, worn** tragen, anhaben (Kleidung) I

wearer ['weərə] Träger/in VI 3 (56)

weather ['weðə] Wetter II

weatherproof ['weðəpruːf] wetterbeständig, -fest V

web address [web ə'dres] Webadresse VI 2 (34)

webcam ['webkæm] Webcam, Internetkamera II

web design ['webdɪˌzaɪn] Webgestaltung V

website ['websaɪt] Website II

Wednesday ['wenzdeɪ, 'wenzdi] Mittwoch I

week [wiːk] Woche I • **days of the week** Wochentage I • **a three-week holiday** ein dreiwöchiger Urlaub III • **once a week** einmal pro Woche III

weekend [ˌwiːk'end] Wochenende I • **at the weekend** am Wochenende I • **on the weekend** (AE) am Wochenende IV

weigh [weɪ] wiegen III

weight [weɪt] Gewicht IV

weird [wɪəd] seltsam III

welcome ['welkəm]
  1. Welcome (to Bristol). Willkommen (in Bristol). I
  2. You're welcome. Gern geschehen. / Nichts zu danken. I

welcome sb. (to) ['welkəm] jn. begrüßen, willkommen heißen (in) I **They welcome you to ...** Sie heißen dich in ... willkommen I

welcoming ['welkəmɪŋ] gastfreundlich, einladend (place) V

well [wel] (*gesundheitlich*) gut; gesund, wohlauf II

well [wel] gut II • **go well** gut (ver)laufen, gutgehen II • **You looked after them well.** Du hast dich gut um sie gekümmert. II **Oh well ...** Na ja ... / Na gut ... I **Well, ...** Nun, ... / Also, ... I • **well-structured** gut aufgebaut, gut strukturiert V • °**well-worn** abgenutzt

Welsh [welʃ] walisisch; Walisisch II

went [went] *siehe* **go**

were [wə, wɜː]: **(we/you/they) were** *siehe* **be**

west [west] Westen; nach Westen; westlich II • **westbound** ['westbaʊnd] Richtung Westen III

western ['westən] westlich, West-III

wet [wet] feucht, nass II

wetsuit ['wetsuːt] Nassanzug *(Tauch- oder Surfanzug)* V

whale [weɪl] Wal V

what [wɒt]
  1. was I
  2. welche(r, s) I
  like what? wie zum Beispiel? IV **So what?** [səʊ 'wɒt] Und? / Na und? II • **Then what?** Was dann? II • **they didn't know what to do** sie wussten nicht, was sie tun sollten; sie wussten nicht, was zu tun war III • **What a bummer!** *(infml)* So ein Mist! / Wie schade! III **What about ...? 1.** Was ist mit ...? / Und ...? I; **2.** Wie wär's mit ...? I **What are you talking about?** Wovon redest du? I • **What can I get you?** Was kann/darf ich euch/ Ihnen bringen? II • **What colour is ...?** Welche Farbe hat ...? I **What for?** [ˌwɒt 'fɔː] Wofür? II **What have we got next?** Was haben wir als Nächstes? I • **What kind of car ...?** Was für ein Auto ...? III • **What page are we on?** Auf welcher Seite sind wir? I • **What's for homework?** Was haben wir als Hausaufgabe auf? I • **What's the best way to get there?** Wie komme ich am besten dahin? III **What's the point?** Was soll das? III **What's the time?** Wie spät ist es? I • **What's the matter?** Was ist los? / Was ist denn? II • **What's up?** Was ist los? IV • **What's wrong with you?** Was fehlt dir? II **What's your name?** Wie heißt du? I • **What was the weather like?** Wie war das Wetter? II

whatever [ˌwɒt'evə] egal; wie dem auch sei; was (auch) immer IV **whatever the movie** egal, in welchem Film IV

wheel [wiːl] Rad III • **big wheel** Riesenrad III

wheelchair ['wiːltʃeə] Rollstuhl I

when [wen] wann I • **When's your birthday?** Wann hast du Geburtstag? I

when [wen]
  1. wenn I
  2. als I

whenever [ˌwen'evə] wann (auch) immer; egal, wann IV

where [weə]
  1. wo I
  2. wohin I
  Where are you from? Wo kommst

du her? I • **He had no idea where to go.** Er hatte keine Ahnung, wo er gehen sollte. IV

wherever [ˌwerˈevə] wo(hin) (auch) immer; egal, wo(hin) IV

whether [ˈweðə] ob IV

which [wɪtʃ] welche(r, s) I • **Which picture …?** Welches Bild …? I **which way?** in welche Richtung? / wohin? II

which [wɪtʃ] der, die, das; die *(Relativpronomen)* III

while [waɪl]
1. *(conj)* während III
2. *(n)* **(for) a while** eine Weile, einige Zeit IV

whisper [ˈwɪspə] flüstern I

whistle [ˈwɪsl] pfeifen II

whistle [ˈwɪsl] Pfiff; (Triller-)Pfeife II

white [waɪt] weiß I

who [huː]
1. wer I
2. wen / wem II
Who did she talk to? Mit wem hat sie geredet? II • **He had no idea who to ask.** Er hatte keine Ahnung, wen er fragen sollte. IV

who [huː] der, die, das; die *(Relativpronomen)* III

whoever [ˌhuːˈevə] wer/wen/wem (auch) immer; egal, wer/wen/wem IV

whole [həʊl] ganze(r, s), gesamte(r, s) II • **the whole of 2006** das ganze Jahr 2006 II

whom [huːm]: **To whom it may concern** *(bes. AE)* Sehr geehrte Damen und Herren IV

whose [huːz] wessen II • **Whose are these?** Wem gehören diese? II

whose [huːz]: **the man whose statue …** der Mann, dessen Statue … II

why [waɪ] warum I • **Why me?** Warum ich? I • **that's why** deshalb, darum I

wicked [ˈwɪkɪd] böse, schlecht VI 3 (62)

wide [waɪd] weit, breit III • **far and wide** weit und breit IV

wife [waɪf], *pl* **wives** [waɪvz] Ehefrau II

wild [waɪld] wild II

wildfire [ˈwaɪldfaɪə] Waldbrand, Buschbrand III

wildlife [ˈwaɪldlaɪf] Tierwelt, frei lebende Tiere IV

will [wɪl]: **you'll be cold (= you will be cold)** du wirst frieren; ihr werdet frieren II • **you'll have travelled** du wirst gereist sein III

willing [ˈwɪlɪŋ]: **be willing to do sth.** bereit/gewillt sein, etwas zu tun VI 2 (39)

win (-nn-) [wɪn], **won, won** gewinnen I

win [wɪn] Sieg III

wind [wɪnd] Wind I

window [ˈwɪndəʊ] Fenster I

windproof [ˈwɪndpruːf] winddicht V

windy [ˈwɪndi] windig I

wine [waɪn] Wein IV

winemaker [ˈwaɪnmeɪkə] Winzer/in IV

winemaking [ˈwaɪnmeɪkɪŋ] Weinherstellung IV

wing [wɪŋ] Flügel IV

winner [ˈwɪnə] Gewinner/in, Sieger/in II

winter [ˈwɪntə] Winter I

wipe [waɪp] (ab)wischen IV

wish [wɪʃ] sich etwas wünschen III • **You wish!** *etwa:* Das hättest du wohl gerne! III

wish [wɪʃ]: **Best wishes** Viele Grüße IV

witch [wɪtʃ] Hexe VI 4 (76)

with [wɪð]
1. mit I
2. bei I
Sit with me. Setz dich zu mir. / Setzt euch zu mir. I • **be with sb.** mit jm. zusammen sein IV

within [wɪˈðɪn] innerhalb (von) V

without [wɪˈðaʊt] ohne I

witness (to sth.) [ˈwɪtnəs] Zeuge, Zeugin (für/von etwas) V

witness sth. [ˈwɪtnəs] bei/von etwas Zeuge sein VI 2 (38)

wives [waɪvz] *pl von „wife"* II

woke [wəʊk] *siehe* **wake**

woken [ˈwəʊkn] *siehe* **wake**

wolf [wʊlf], *pl* **wolves** [wʊlvz] Wolf II

woman [ˈwʊmən], *pl* **women** [ˈwɪmɪn] Frau I

won [wʌn] *siehe* **win**

wonder [ˈwʌndə] sich fragen, gern wissen wollen II

°**wonder** [ˈwʌndə] Staunen V

wonderful [ˈwʌndəfəl] wunderbar II

won't [wəʊnt]: **you won't be cold (= you will not be cold)** du wirst nicht frieren; ihr werdet nicht frieren II

wood [wʊd]
1. Holz II
2. *(also* **woods** *(pl))* Wald, Wälder II

woodpecker [ˈwʊdpekə] Specht II

word [wɜːd] Wort I • **word building** Wortbildung II • **word field**

Wortfeld III • **word for word** Wort für Wort, wortwörtlich VI 1 (25) • °**word order** Wortstellung II

wore [wɔː] *siehe* **wear**

work [wɜːk]
1. arbeiten I • **work hard** hart arbeiten II • **work on sb./sth.** an jn./etwas arbeiten I • **work out** klappen, gutgehen IV • **work sth. out** etwas herausfinden, etwas herausarbeiten IV
2. funktionieren III

work [wɜːk] Arbeit I • **at work** bei der Arbeit / am Arbeitsplatz I **be in a line of work** einen Beruf ausüben IV • **volunteer work** Arbeit als Freiwillige(r) III • **work experience** *(no pl)* Arbeits-, Praxiserfahrung(en) V

worker [ˈwɜːkə] Arbeiter/in II

work(place) [ˈwɜːkpleɪs] Arbeitsplatz *(Ort)* IV

worksheet [ˈwɜːkʃiːt] Arbeitsblatt I

workshop [ˈwɜːkʃɒp] Workshop, Lehrgang III

world [wɜːld] Welt I • **all over the world** auf der ganzen Welt III **developing world** Entwicklungsländer VI 3 (56) • **from all over the world** aus der ganzen Welt II **in the world** auf der Welt II **the Third World** die Dritte Welt VI 3 (56) • **world music** Weltmusik III

world-famous [ˌwɜːld ˈfeɪməs] weltberühmt IV

worldwide [ˌwɜːldˈwaɪd] weltweit IV

worn [wɔːn] *siehe* **wear**

worried [ˈwʌrid]: **be worried (about)** beunruhigt sein, besorgt sein (wegen) I

worry [ˈwʌri] Sorge, Kummer II **No worries!** *(bes. Australisches E)* Kein Problem! V

worry (about) [ˈwʌri] sich Sorgen machen (wegen, um) I • **Don't worry.** Mach dir keine Sorgen. I **worry sb.** jm. Sorgen machen, jn. beunruhigen VI 2 (38)

worse (than) [wɜːs] schlechter, schlimmer (als) II

worst [wɜːst]: **(the) worst** am schlechtesten, schlimmsten; der/die/das schlechteste, schlimmste … II

worth [wɜːθ]: **it is worth doing sth.** es lohnt sich, etwas zu tun IV **It's worth it.** Es lohnt sich. IV **It isn't worth it.** Es lohnt sich nicht. IV

Dictionary

would [wəd, wʊd]
1. würde, würdest, würden II • **I'd like ... (= I would like ...)** Ich hätte gern ... / Ich möchte gern ... I **Would you like ...?** Möchtest du ...? / Möchten Sie ...? I • **I'd like to go (= I would like to go)** Ich würde gern gehen / Ich möchte gehen I • **I wouldn't like to go** ich würde nicht gern gehen / ich möchte nicht gehen I
2. I'd (= I would) go ich pflegte zu gehen; ich ging oft VI 1 (10)
wrap (-pp-) [ræp] einwickeln VI 3 (61)
wrist [rɪst] Handgelenk IV
write [raɪt]**, wrote, written** schreiben I • **write down** aufschreiben I • **write to** schreiben an I
writer ['raɪtə] Schreiber/in; Schriftsteller/in II
written ['rɪtn]
1. siehe **write**
2. schriftlich V
wrong [rɒŋ] falsch, verkehrt I **get sth. wrong** etwas falsch machen III • **the wrong way** in die falsche Richtung II • **What's wrong with you?** Was fehlt dir? II
wrote [rəʊt] siehe **write**

X

xenophobic [ˌzenəˈfəʊbɪk] fremdenfeindlich, xenophob VI 2 (29)

Y

yard [jɑːd]
1. Hof II • **in the yard** auf dem Hof II
2. Yard (Längenmaß, 0,91m) IV
yawn [jɔːn] gähnen II
year [jɪə]
1. Jahr I • **a 70-year-old teacher** ein 70-jähriger Lehrer III
2. Jahrgangsstufe I
yellow ['jeləʊ] gelb I
yes [jes] ja I
yesterday ['jestədeɪ, 'jestədi] gestern I • **the day before yesterday** vorgestern II • **yesterday morning/afternoon/evening** gestern Morgen/Nachmittag/Abend I
yet [jet]: **not (...) yet** noch nicht II **yet?** schon? II
yoga ['jəʊgə] Yoga I
yogurt ['jɒgət] Jogurt III
you [juː]
1. du; Sie I
2. ihr I
3. dir; dich; euch I
4. man III
How are you? Wie geht es dir/Ihnen/euch? II • **You're welcome.** Gern geschehen. / Nichts zu danken. I • **you two** ihr zwei I • **You wish!** etwa: Das hättest du wohl gerne! III • °**you and yours** du und das Deinige
young [jʌŋ] jung I

your [jɔː]
1. dein/e I
2. Ihr I
3. euer/eure I
°**Your Majesty** Eure Majestät
yours [jɔːz]
1. deiner, deine, deins II
2. eurer, eure, eures II
Yours faithfully mit freundlichen Grüßen IV • **Yours sincerely** (BE) mit freundlichen Grüßen IV **Yours truly** (AE) mit freundlichen Grüßen IV
yourself [jəˈself, jɔːˈself]
1. dir/dich III • **about yourself** über dich selbst III
2. selbst III
yourselves [jəˈselvz, jɔːˈselvz]
1. euch/sich III
2. selbst IV
youth [juːθ] Jugend III
youth group ['juːθ ˌgruːp] Jugendgruppe IV
youth hostel ['juːθ ˌhɒstəl] Jugendherberge III
yummy ['jʌmi] (infml) lecker III

Z

zebra ['zebrə] Zebra II
zero ['zɪərəʊ] null I
zone [zəʊn] Zone, Bereich III **time zone** Zeitzone IV
zoo [zuː] Zoo, Tierpark I

Irregular verbs

Infinitive	Simple past form	Past participle	
(to) **be**	**was/were**	**been**	sein
(to) **beat**	**beat**	**beaten**	schlagen; besiegen
(to) **become**	**became**	**become**	werden
(to) **begin**	**began**	**begun**	beginnen, anfangen (mit)
(to) **bend**	**bent**	**bent**	sich beugen
(to) **bleed** [iː]	**bled** [e]	**bled** [e]	bluten
(to) **blow**	**blew**	**blown**	wehen, blasen, pusten
(to) **break**	**broke**	**broken**	zerbrechen, kaputt machen
(to) **bring**	**brought**	**brought**	(mit-, her)bringen
(to) **broadcast**	**broadcast**	**broadcast**	ausstrahlen; senden
(to) **build**	**built**	**built**	bauen
(to) **buy**	**bought**	**bought**	kaufen
(to) **catch**	**caught**	**caught**	fangen; erwischen
(to) **choose** [uː]	**chose** [əʊ]	**chosen** [əʊ]	(aus)wählen; (sich) aussuchen
(to) **come**	**came**	**come**	kommen
(to) **creep** [iː]	**crept** [e]	**crept**	kriechen
(to) **cut**	**cut**	**cut**	schneiden
(to) **deal** with [iː]	**dealt** [e]	**dealt** [e]	sich beschäftigen mit
(to) **do**	**did**	**done** [ʌ]	tun, machen
(to) **draw**	**drew**	**drawn**	zeichnen
(to) **drink**	**drank**	**drunk**	trinken
(to) **drive** [aɪ]	**drove**	**driven** [ɪ]	(ein Auto) fahren
(to) **eat**	**ate** [et, eɪt]	**eaten**	essen
(to) **fall**	**fell**	**fallen**	(hin)fallen, stürzen
(to) **feed**	**fed**	**fed**	füttern
(to) **feel**	**felt**	**felt**	(sich) fühlen; sich anfühlen
(to) **fight**	**fought**	**fought**	kämpfen
(to) **find**	**found**	**found**	finden
(to) **fly**	**flew**	**flown**	fliegen
(to) **forget**	**forgot**	**forgotten**	vergessen
(to) **forgive**	**forgave**	**forgiven**	vergeben, verzeihen
(to) **get**	**got**	**got** (AE also: **gotten**)	bekommen; holen; werden; (hin)kommen
(to) **give**	**gave**	**given**	geben
(to) **go**	**went**	**gone** [ɒ]	gehen, fahren
(to) **grow**	**grew**	**grown**	wachsen; anbauen, anpflanzen
(to) **hang**	**hung**	**hung**	(etwas) aufhängen
(to) **have (have got)**	**had**	**had**	haben, besitzen
(to) **hear** [ɪə]	**heard** [ɜː]	**heard** [ɜː]	hören
(to) **hide** [aɪ]	**hid** [ɪ]	**hidden** [ɪ]	(sich) verstecken
(to) **hit**	**hit**	**hit**	treffen; schlagen
(to) **hold**	**held**	**held**	halten
(to) **hurt**	**hurt**	**hurt**	wehtun; verletzen
(to) **keep**	**kept**	**kept**	(be)halten; aufbewahren
(to) **kneel** [niːl]	**knelt** [nelt]	**knelt**	sich hinknien
(to) **know** [nəʊ]	**knew** [njuː]	**known** [nəʊn]	wissen; kennen
(to) **lay** the table	**laid**	**laid**	den Tisch decken
(to) **lead** [iː]	**led** [e]	**led** [e]	führen
(to) **leave**	**left**	**left**	(weg)gehen; abfahren; verlassen; zurücklassen
(to) **lend**	**lent**	**lent**	leihen
(to) **let**	**let**	**let**	lassen

Irregular verbs

Infinitive	Simple past form	Past participle	
(to) lie	lay	lain	liegen
(to) lose [uː]	lost [ɒ]	lost [ɒ]	verlieren
(to) make	made	made	machen; bauen; bilden
(to) mean [iː]	meant [e]	meant [e]	bedeuten; meinen
(to) meet	met	met	(sich) treffen
(to) pay	paid	paid	bezahlen
(to) put	put	put	legen, stellen, *(wohin)* tun
(to) read [iː]	read [e]	read [e]	lesen
(to) ride [aɪ]	rode	ridden [ɪ]	reiten; *(Rad)* fahren
(to) ring	rang	rung	klingeln, läuten
(to) rise [aɪ]	rose	risen [ɪ]	(auf)steigen
(to) run	ran	run	rennen, (ver)laufen
(to) say [eɪ]	said [e]	said [e]	sagen
(to) see	saw	seen	sehen; besuchen, aufsuchen
(to) seek [iː]	sought [ɔː]	sought	suchen
(to) sell	sold	sold	verkaufen
(to) send	sent	sent	schicken, senden
(to) set a trap	set	set	eine Falle stellen
(to) sew	sewed	sewn	(an)nähen
(to) shake	shook	shaken	schütteln
(to) shine	shone [ɒ, *AE* əʊ]	shone [ɒ]	scheinen *(Sonne)*
(to) shoot [uː]	shot [ɒ]	shot [ɒ]	(er)schießen
(to) show	showed	shown	zeigen
(to) shut up	shut	shut	den Mund halten
(to) sing	sang	sung	singen
(to) sink	sank	sunk	sinken
(to) sit	sat	sat	sitzen; sich setzen
(to) sleep	slept	slept	schlafen
(to) speak	spoke	spoken	sprechen
(to) spend	spent	spent	*(Zeit)* verbringen; *(Geld)* ausgeben
(to) spit	spat	spat	spucken
(to) spread [e]	spread [e]	spread [e]	(sich) ausbreiten, (sich) verbreiten
(to) stand	stood	stood	stehen; sich (hin)stellen
(to) steal	stole	stolen	stehlen
(to) stick	stuck	stuck	herausragen, herausstehen; (auf)kleben
(to) sweep [iː]	swept [e]	swept [e]	fegen, kehren
(to) swim	swam	swum	schwimmen
(to) take	took	taken	nehmen; (weg-, hin)bringen; dauern, *(Zeit)* brauchen
(to) teach	taught	taught	unterrichten, lehren
(to) tear [eə]	tore [ɔː]	torn [ɔː]	(zer)reißen
(to) tell	told	told	erzählen, berichten
(to) think	thought	thought	denken, glauben, meinen
(to) throw	threw	thrown	werfen
(to) understand	understood	understood	verstehen
(to) upset	upset	upset	ärgern, kränken, aus der Fassung bringen
(to) wake up	woke	woken	aufwachen; wecken
(to) wear [eə]	wore [ɔː]	worn [ɔː]	tragen *(Kleidung)*
(to) win	won [ʌ]	won [ʌ]	gewinnen
(to) write	wrote	written	schreiben

List of names

First names

Adam ['ædəm]
Adisa [ə'di:sə]
Afra ['æfrə]
Alaska [ə'læskə]
Albert ['ælbət]
Alex ['æliks]
Alfred ['ælfrid]
Alfredo [al'fri:dəu]
Amal [ə'mæl, ə'mɑ:l]
Andreas [æn'dreɪəs]
Archimedes [ˌɑ:kɪ'mɪːdiːz]
Bernard ['bɜ:nəd]
Betsy ['betsi]
Bianca [bi'æŋkə]
Bridget ['brɪdʒɪt]
Bryan ['braɪən]
Carol ['kærəl]
Charles [tʃɑ:lz]
Christopher ['krɪstəfə]
David ['deɪvɪd]
Douglas ['dʌgləs]
Duncan ['dʌŋkən]
Edith ['iːdɪθ]
Eileen ['aɪliːn]
Emmanuel [i'mænjuːəl]
Emmeline ['eməliːn]
Ernest ['ɜ:nɪst]
Francis ['frɑːnsɪz]
Galileo [gælɪ'leɪəu]
Geoffrey ['dʒefri]
George [dʒɔ:dʒ]
Gerty ['gɜ:ti]
Gideon ['gɪdiən]
Gilbert ['gɪlbət]
Godric ['gɒdrɪk]
Grace [greɪs]
Haylie ['heɪli]
Henry ['henri]
Howard ['haʊəd]
Humphrey ['hʌmfri]
Jaz [dʒæz]
Jeanette [dʒə'net]
Jesus ['dʒiːzəz]
Jill [dʒɪl]
Jimmy ['dʒɪmi]
Joshua ['dʒɒʃjuə]
Junior ['dʒuːniə]
Kalino [kə'liːnəu]
Kevin ['kevɪn]
Kirsty ['kɜ:sti]
Laura [lɔ:rə]
Laurie ['lɒri]
Lawrence ['lɒrəns]
Lucy [luːsi]
Lyra ['laɪrə]
Margaret ['mɑːgrət]
Marie [mə'riː]
Mary ['meəri]
Matthew ['mæθjuː]
Maurice ['mɒrɪs]
Maya [meɪə, maɪə]
Melinda [mə'lɪndə]
Michael ['maɪkl]
Mike [maɪk]

Miles [maɪlz]
Nicolaus ['nɪkələus]
Oscar ['ɒskə]
Peter ['piːtə]
Prudence ['pruːdəns]
Puma ['pjuːmə]
Roald ['rəuəld]
Robert ['rɒbəts]
Roger ['rɒdʒə]
Rosalind ['rɒsəlɪnd]
Rowena [rəu'iːnə]
Saci ['sæʃi]
Salazar ['sæləzɑː]
Samantha [sə'mænθə]
Sean [ʃɔːn]
Sharon ['ʃærən]
Sherman ['ʃɜːmən]
Simone [sɪməun]
Stephen ['stiːvn]
Stewart [stjuːət]
Susan ['suːzən]
Tau [tau]
Thomas ['tɒməs]
Tony ['təuni]
Troy [trɔɪ]
Victoria [vɪk'tɔːriə]
William ['wɪliəm]
Yamila [jə'mɪlə]

Family names

Adjei-Mensah [əˌdʒeɪ 'mensə]
Alexie [ə'leksi]
Anderson ['ændəsən]
Angelou ['ændʒəluː]
Atwood ['ætwʊd]
Baldwin [bɔːldwɪn]
Belacqua [bel'ækwə]
Blunt [blʌnt]
Bogart ['bəugɑːt]
Bowie ['bəuɪ]
Bryson ['braɪsən]
Calvin ['kælvɪn]
Copernicus [kə'pɜːnɪkəs]
Cowling ['kaulɪŋ]
Cromwell ['krɒmwel]
Darwin ['dɑːwɪn]
Edison ['edɪsən]
Eggers ['egəz]
Einstein ['aɪnstaɪn]
Ferlinghetti [ˌfɜːlɪŋ'geti]
Franklin ['fræŋklɪn]
Gabriel ['geɪbriəl]
Gentile ['dʒentaɪl]
Gribbin ['grɪbɪn]
Gryffindor ['grɪfɪndɔː]
Gunn [gʌn]
Haddon ['hædn]
Halse [hæls]
Halter ['hɔːltə]
Hemingway ['hemɪŋweɪ]
Herrick ['herɪk]
Hufflepuff ['hʌflpʌf]
Jagger ['dʒægə]
Jal [dʒɑːl]
Johnson ['dʒɒnsən]

Jones [dʒəunz]
Jordan ['dʒɔːdən]
Joyce [dʒɔɪs]
Kamkwamba [kæm'kwæmbə]
Kelso ['kelsəu]
Kennedy ['kenədi]
Lanning ['lænɪŋ]
Lawson ['lɔːsən]
Lewis ['luːɪs]
Lloyd [lɔɪd]
Logue [ləug]
Marsden ['mɑːzdən]
Martin ['mɑːtɪn]
Mealer ['miːlə]
Miles [maɪlz]
Mitton ['mɪtn]
Moynahan ['mɔɪnəhən]
Pankhurst [ˌpæŋkhɜːst]
Petrakis [pə'trɑːkɪs]
Phiri ['fɪri]
Preston ['prestən]
Proyas ['prɔɪəs]
Pullman ['pulmən]
Ravenclaw ['reɪvnklɔː]
Ridley ['rɪdli]
Roberts ['rɒbəts]
Rockwell ['rɒkwel]
Sagan ['seɪgən]
Sikelo [sɪ'keɪləu]
Slytherin ['slɪðərɪn]
Smith [smɪθ]
Spacey ['speɪsi]
Spooner ['spuːnə]
Stevens ['stiːvəns]
Tembo ['tembəu]
Tennyson ['tenɪsən]
Ustinov ['juːstɪnɒf]
Vesalius [və'seɪliəs]
Waldrop ['wɔːldrɒp]
Wallace ['wɒlɪs]
Washington ['wɒʃɪŋtən]
Watson ['wɒtsən]
Watt [wɒt]
Wilde [waɪld]
Wilkins ['wɪlkɪnz]
Wordsworth ['wɜːdzwəθ]

Place names

Alabama [ˌælə'bæmə]
Belfast [ˌbel'fɑːst]
Birmingham (US) ['bɜːmɪŋhæm]
Broughton ['brɔːtn]
Brussels ['brʌsəlz]
Budapest [ˌbjuːdə'pest]
California [ˌkælə'fɔːniə]
Chandigarh ['tʃændɪgɑː]
Cicero ['sɪsərəu]
Connecticut [kə'netɪkət]
Culver Creek [ˌkʌlvə 'kriːk]
Darfur [dɑː'fuə]
Florida ['flɒrɪdə]
the Great Lakes [ˌgreɪt 'leɪks]
Hades ['heɪdiːz]
Hamburg ['hæmbɜːg]

Haybrook ['heɪbruk]
Illinois [ˌɪlə'nɔɪ]
Irbid ['ɪəbɪd]
London ['lʌndən]
Majorca [mə'jɔːkə]
Milan [mɪ'læn]
Molepolole [ˌməuləpə'ləuleɪ]
Mostyn ['mɒstɪn]
New Hope [ˌnjuː 'həup]
New York City [ˌnjuː jɔːk 'sɪti]
the North Pole [ˌnɔːθ 'pəul]
Orange ['ɒrɪndʒ] Oranien
Oxford ['ɒksfəd]
the Pacific [pə'sɪfɪk]
Paris ['pærɪs]
Rome [rəum]
Spokane [spəu'kæn]
Tallinn ['tælɪn]
Tianjin [tiˌæn'dʒɪn]
Toledo [tə'liːdəu]
Toulouse [tuː'luːz]
the Vatican (City) ['vætɪkən]
Washington ['wɒʃɪŋtən]
Wimbe ['wɪmbeɪ]
Woodstock ['wudstɒk]

Other names

Adonis [ə'dəunɪs]
Beluga [bə'luːgə]
Boeing ['bəuɪŋ]
Buckingham Palace [ˌbʌkɪŋəm 'pæləs]
the Colonel ['kɜːnəl]
the Conservative party [kən'sɜːvətɪv] „Konservative Partei"
the (River) Dove [dʌv]
Durex [djuəreks]
Jupiter ['dʒuːpɪtə]
the Labour party ['leɪbə] „Partei der Arbeit"
the Liberal Democrats [ˌlɪbrəl 'deməkræts] „Liberaldemokraten"
Little Red Riding Hood [ˌ--ˌ-'---] Rotkäppchen
McCleans [mə'kliːnz]
NASA ['næsə]
Neptune ['neptjuːn]
the Nile [naɪl] Nil
Plaid Cymru [ˌplaɪd 'kʌmrɪ] (walisisch) „Partei von Wales"
Pudge [pʌdʒ]
the Scottish National Party [ˌskɒtɪʃ 'næʃnəl ˌpɑːti]
Saturn ['sætɜːn]
St Joseph's [ˌseɪnt 'dʒəusefs]
United Nations [juˌnaɪtɪd 'neɪʃənz]
Uranus ['juərənəs]
Vigo ['vaɪgəu]
Voyager ['vɔɪɪdʒə]
Zorba ['zɔːbə]

Countries and continents

Country/Continent	Adjective	Person	People
Afghanistan [æfˈgænɪstɑːn] *Afghanistan*	Afghan [ˈæfgæn]	an Afghan	the Afghans
Africa [ˈæfrɪkə] *Afrika*	African [ˈæfrɪkən]	an African	the Africans
Albania [ælˈbeɪniə] *Albanien*	Albanian [ælˈbeɪniən]	an Albanian	the Albanians
Algeria [ælˈdʒɪəriə] *Algerien*	Algerian [ælˈdʒɪəriən]	an Algerian	the Algerians
America [əˈmerɪkə] *Amerika*	American [əˈmerɪkən]	an American	the Americans
American Samoa [əˌmerɪkən səˈməʊə] *Amerikanisch-Samoa*	American Samoan [səˈməʊən]	an American Samoan	the American Samoans
Andorra [ænˈdɔːrə] *Andorra*	Andorran [ænˈdɔːrən]	an Andorran	the Andorrans
Asia [ˈeɪʃə, ˈeɪʒə] *Asien*	Asian [ˈeɪʃn, ˈeɪʒn]	an Asian	the Asians
Australia [ɒˈstreɪliə] *Australien*	Australian [ɒˈstreɪliən]	an Australian	the Australians
Austria [ˈɒstriə] *Österreich*	Austrian [ˈɒstriən]	an Austrian	the Austrians
Belgium [ˈbeldʒəm] *Belgien*	Belgian [ˈbeldʒən]	a Belgian	the Belgians
Bosnia [ˈbɒzniə] *Bosnien*	Bosnian [ˈbɒzniən]	a Bosnian	the Bosnians
Botswana [bɒtˈswɑːnə] *Botsuana*	Botswanan [bɒtˈswɑːnən]	a Motswana [mɒtˈswɑːnə]	the Batswana [bætˈswɑːnə]
Canada [ˈkænədə] *Kanada*	Canadian [kəˈneɪdiən]	a Canadian	the Canadians
China [ˈtʃaɪnə] *China*	Chinese [ˌtʃaɪˈniːz]	a Chinese	the Chinese
Croatia [krəʊˈeɪʃə] *Kroatien*	Croatian [krəʊˈeɪʃn]	a Croatian	the Croatians
the Czech Republic [ˌtʃek rɪˈpʌblɪk] *Tschechien, die Tschechische Republik*	Czech [tʃek]	a Czech	the Czechs
Denmark [ˈdenmɑːk] *Dänemark*	Danish [ˈdeɪnɪʃ]	a Dane [deɪn]	the Danes
England [ˈɪŋglənd] *England*	English [ˈɪŋglɪʃ]	an Englishman/-woman	the English
Europe [ˈjʊərəp] *Europa*	European [ˌjʊərəˈpiːən]	a European	the Europeans
Finland [ˈfɪnlənd] *Finnland*	Finnish [ˈfɪnɪʃ]	a Finn [fɪn]	the Finns
France [frɑːns] *Frankreich*	French [frentʃ]	a Frenchman/-woman	the French
Germany [ˈdʒɜːməni] *Deutschland*	German [ˈdʒɜːmən]	a German	the Germans
Ghana [ˈgɑːnə] *Ghana*	Ghanaian [gɑːˈneɪən]	a Ghanaian	the Ghanaians
(Great) Britain [ˈbrɪtn] *Großbritannien*	British [ˈbrɪtɪʃ]	a Briton [ˈbrɪtn]	the British
Greece [griːs] *Griechenland*	Greek [griːk]	a Greek	the Greeks
Holland [ˈhɒlənd] *Holland, die Niederlande*	Dutch [dʌtʃ]	a Dutchman/-woman	the Dutch
Hungary [ˈhʌŋgəri] *Ungarn*	Hungarian [hʌŋˈgeəriən]	a Hungarian	the Hungarians
India [ˈɪndiə] *Indien*	Indian [ˈɪndiən]	an Indian	the Indians
Ireland [ˈaɪələnd] *Irland*	Irish [ˈaɪrɪʃ]	an Irishman/-woman	the Irish
Italy [ˈɪtəli] *Italien*	Italian [ɪˈtæliən]	an Italian	the Italians
Japan [dʒəˈpæn] *Japan*	Japanese [ˌdʒæpəˈniːz]	a Japanese	the Japanese
Jordan [ˈdʒɔːdən] *Jordanien*	Jordanian [dʒɔːˈdeɪniən]	a Jordanian	the Jordanians
Malawi [məˈlɑːwi] *Malawi*	Malawian [məˈlɑːwiən]	a Malawian	the Malawians
the Maldives [ˈmɔːldaɪvz, ˈmɔːldiːvz] *die Malediven*	Maldivian [mɔːlˈdɪviən]	a Maldivian	the Maldivians
Mexico [ˈmeksɪkəʊ] *Mexiko*	Mexican [kəˈriən]	a Mexican	the Mexicans
the Netherlands [ˈneðələndz] *die Niederlande, Holland*	Dutch [dʌtʃ]	a Dutchman/-woman	the Dutch
New Zealand [ˌnjuː ˈziːlənd] *Neuseeland*	New Zealand [ˌnjuː ˈziːlənd]	a New Zealander	the New Zealanders
Nicaragua [ˌnɪkəˈrægjuə] *Nicaragua*	Nicaraguan [ˌnɪkəˈrægjuən]	a Nicaraguan	the Nicaraguans
Norway [ˈnɔːweɪ] *Norwegen*	Norwegian [nɔːˈwiːdʒən]	a Norwegian	the Norwegians
Pakistan [ˌpækɪˈstæn, ˌpɑːkɪˈstɑːn] *Pakistan*	Pakistani [ˌpækɪˈstæni, ˌpɑːkɪˈstɑːni]	a Pakistani	the Pakistanis
Poland [ˈpəʊlənd] *Polen*	Polish [ˈpəʊlɪʃ]	a Pole [pəʊl]	the Poles
Portugal [ˈpɔːtʃʊgl] *Portugal*	Portuguese [ˌpɔːtʃuˈgiːz]	a Portuguese	the Portuguese
Russia [ˈrʌʃə] *Russland*	Russian [ˈrʌʃn]	a Russian	the Russians
Scotland [ˈskɒtlənd] *Schottland*	Scottish [ˈskɒtɪʃ]	a Scotsman/-woman, a Scot [skɒt]	the Scots, the Scottish
Slovakia [sləʊˈvɑːkiə, sləʊˈvækiə] *die Slowakei*	Slovak [ˈsləʊvæk]	a Slovak	the Slovaks
Slovenia [sləʊˈviːniə] *Slowenien*	Slovenian [sləʊˈviːniən], Slovene [ˈsləʊviːn]	a Slovene, a Slovenian	the Slovenes, the Slovenians

Countries and continents

Country/Continent	Adjective	Person	People
Spain [speɪn] *Spanien*	Spanish [ˈspænɪʃ]	a Spaniard [ˈspænɪəd]	the Spaniards
Sudan [suˈdɑːn] *Sudan*	Sudanese [ˌsuːdəˈniːz]	a Sudanese	the Sudanese
Sweden [ˈswiːdn] *Schweden*	Swedish [ˈswiːdɪʃ]	a Swede [swiːd]	the Swedes
Switzerland [ˈswɪtsələnd] *die Schweiz*	Swiss [swɪs]	a Swiss	the Swiss
Tanzania [ˌtænzəˈniːə] *Tansania*	Tanzania [ˌtænzəˈniːən]	a Tanzanian	the Tanzanians
Turkey [ˈtɜːki] *die Türkei*	Turkish [ˈtɜːkɪʃ]	a Turk [tɜːk]	the Turks
the United Kingdom (the UK) [juˌnaɪtɪd ˈkɪŋdəm, juːˈkeɪ] *das Vereinigte Königreich (Großbritannien und Nordirland)*	British [ˈbrɪtɪʃ]	a Briton [ˈbrɪtn]	the British
the United States of America (the USA) [juˌnaɪtɪd ˌsteɪts_əv_əˈmerɪkə, juːˌes_ˈeɪ] *die Vereinigten Staaten von Amerika*	American [əˈmerɪkən]	an American	the Americans
Wales [weɪlz] *Wales*	Welsh [welʃ]	a Welshman/-woman	the Welsh

English sounds (Englische Laute)

Die Lautschrift in den eckigen Klammern zeigt dir, wie ein Wort ausgesprochen wird.
In der folgenden Übersicht findest du alle Lautzeichen.

Vokale (Selbstlaute)

[iː]	gr**ee**n	[ʊ]	b**oo**k	[ɪə]	h**ere**
[i]	happ**y**	[ʌ]	m**u**m	[eə]	wh**ere**
[ɪ]	**i**n	[ɜː]	T-sh**ir**t	[ʊə]	t**our**
[e]	y**e**s	[ə]	**a** partn**er**		
[æ]	bl**a**ck	[eɪ]	sk**a**te		
[ɑː]	p**ar**k	[aɪ]	t**i**me		
[ɒ]	s**o**ng	[ɔɪ]	b**oy**		
[ɔː]	m**or**ning	[əʊ]	**o**ld		
[uː]	bl**ue**	[aʊ]	n**ow**		

Konsonanten (Mitlaute)

[b]	**b**ox	[l]	he**ll**o	[ʒ]	televi**si**on
[p]	**p**lay	[r]	**r**ed	[tʃ]	tea**ch**er
[d]	**d**ad	[w]	**w**e	[dʒ]	**G**ermany
[t]	**t**en	[j]	**y**ou	[θ]	**th**anks
[g]	**g**ood	[f]	**f**ull	[ð]	**th**is
[k]	**c**at	[v]	**v**ery	[h]	**h**e
[m]	**m**um	[s]	**s**ister	[x]	lo**ch**
[n]	**n**o	[z]	plea**s**e		
[ŋ]	si**ng**	[ʃ]	**sh**op		

The English alphabet (Das englische Alphabet)

a [eɪ]	**h** [eɪtʃ]	**o** [əʊ]	**v** [viː]	
b [biː]	**i** [aɪ]	**p** [piː]	**w** [ˈdʌbljuː]	
c [siː]	**j** [dʒeɪ]	**q** [kjuː]	**x** [eks]	
d [diː]	**k** [keɪ]	**r** [ɑː]	**y** [waɪ]	
e [iː]	**l** [el]	**s** [es]	**z** [zed]	
f [ef]	**m** [em]	**t** [tiː]		
g [dʒiː]	**n** [en]	**u** [juː]		

Acknowledgments

Illustrationen

Roland Beier, Berlin (S. 125–126; 131; 133 Mitte, unten; 134–139; 141; 145–155; 158; 168–230); **Dr. Volkhard Binder**, Berlin (S. 133 oben); **Carlos Borrell**, Berlin (Umschlaginnenseite 2); **Christian Görke**, Berlin (S. 129); **Karin Mall**, Berlin (S. 53 unten re.; 124)

Bildquellen

action press, Hamburg (Inhaltsverz. (u. 35 unten): ZUMA PRESS, INC., Inhaltsverz. (u. 39 unten): ISOPIX SPRL; S. 116 unten re.: REX FEATURES LTD.); **Agentur Focus**, Hamburg (Inhaltsverz. (u. 53 unten li.)); **Alamy**, Abingdon (Inhaltsverz. (u. 77) Alaska cover girl (M): Itani Images; S. 16 oben (M): Carol and Mike Werner; S. 24 oben re.: dbimages, unten li.: Jaggat Images; S. 31 girl (M): PhotoAlto (RF); S. 42 unten: UpperCut Images (RF); S. 50 oben re.: Ian Francis; S. 52 unten li.: Angelo Hornak; S. 53 oben li.: The Art Gallery Collection; S. 85: Corbis RF (RF); S. 93 li.: Mary Evans Picture Library; S. 94 li.: Geraint Lewis; S. 144 unten: Mode Images Limited; S. 156: Beyond Fotomedia GmbH (RF); S. 157 oben: Jeff Morgan 15, unten: Photos 12); **Appian way** (S. 35 oben: Taken from "Five more friends". Courtesy of Appian way); **HL Böhme** (S. 97 Bild 3); **Bridgeman Art**, Berlin / www.bridgemanart.com (S. 90); **www.carbonfootprint.com** (S. 60 oben u. Mitte); **The Cartoon Bank** / www.cartoonbank.com, New York (S. 18 oben: Mick Stevens/Condé Nast Publications; S. 87: the New Yorker Collection/David Sipress); **CartoonStock**, Bath (S. 15: Phil Judd); **Alessio del Cave**, Trentino (S. 96 unten li.); **Centre for Vision in the Developing World** / www.vdw.ox.ac.uk (S. 56); Courtesy of **Alice M. Chalk**, United Kingdom (S. 86 unten); **Cinetext**, Frankfurt/Main (S. 64 re.: 20th Century Fox; S. 157 Mitte: Concorde); **Corbis**, Düsseldorf (S. 9 (u. 10 Hintergrund) sad girl (M): Emely; S. 50 unten Mitte: moodboard (RF); S. 143 unten re.: Rick Gomez); **Cornelsen Verlag GmbH** (S. 22; S. 116 unten li.); **ddp images**, Hamburg (S. 46: AP Photo/Compound Security Systems; S. 67: AP Photo/Axel Heimken); Courtesy of **ECHO BRIDGE ENTERTAINMENT LLC**, Needham, USA (S. 30 Bild 1–4); **Europäisches Parlament**, 2009 (S. 115); **Gareth Evans**, Berlin (S. 25 oben; S. 160); **5W Infographics**, New York / www.5wgraphics.com (S. 57); **Agentur Focus**, Hamburg (Inhaltsverz. (u. 53 unten li.); **Sammlung Gesellschaft für ökologische Forschung**, München (S. 123 oben); **Getty Images**, München (S. 14: Digital Vision/James Woodson (RF); S. 23: Archive Films; S. 27 unten; S. 50 oben li.: Andersen Ross (RF); S. 53 oben re.: Harald Sund; S. 94 re.; S. 96 oben: Comstock Images (RF), unten re.: Tim Hawley; S. 112 oben: AFP/ARTHUR EDWARDS; S. 120: ABC/Ida Mae Astute); **Allan E. Goldstein, Gold Seal Photography and Aerial Images Photography**, Elk Grove Village (S. 19); **Orélie Grimaldi Photographe Auteur**, Paris (S. 97 Bild 2); **Dieter Grote** / glteam.de (S. 58 oben); **Hachette**, London (S. 61: From "The Carbon Diaries" by Saci Lloyd, first published in the UK by Hodder Children's, an imprint of Hachette Children's Books, 338 Euston Road, London NW1 3BH); Courtesy of **Independent Film Company** (S. 65: film still taken from "Moon"); **iStockphoto**, Calgary (S. 18 unten: quavondo; S. 24 oben li.: Kevin Russ; S. 25 funnel: Paul Erickson, sails: Connie Alexander, anchor: Geoffrey Holman; S. 26 Bild D: mandygodbehear; S. 32: Chris Hepburn; S. 42 oben: Christine Glade, Mitte: Johnny Greig; S. 44: Leigh Schindler; S. 68 oben: Robert Byron; S. 106 Mitte: Claudio Arnese, re.: steve weber; S. 107 TF 3 (u. 113 oben li.): Jolande Gerritsen; S. 117: Shelly Perry; S. 140 unten: james steidl; S. 143 li.: AVAVA); © **I Theatre Ltd.**, Singapore (S. 97 Bild 1 u. 4: Photography by Ung Ruey Loon); **Library of Congress**, Washington, D. C. (S. 36: Painting by G. Liebscher, © F. A. Schneider); **Jay Matternes**, Fairfax (S. 52 oben li.); **NASA** (S. 107 TF 5; S. 118); **The New York Times Syndicate**, New York (S. 26 Bild A, Bild C (u. 128): CartoonArts International); © **Pancho**, Paris (S. 26 Bild E); Courtesy of **Pan Macmillan Australia Pty Ltd** (Inhaltsverz. (u. 76 unten re.) Australian cover "Tomorrow when the war began"); **Photolibrary**, London (Inhaltsverz. (u. 77) cover candle (M); S. 24 unten re.: Imagesource (RF); S. 50 unten li.: Comstock (RF)); **Picture-Alliance**, Frankfurt/Main (Inhaltsverz. (u. 52/53 Hintergrund): dieKLEINERT.de / Enno Kleinert; S. 34: Anthony Devlin; S. 38: KEYSTONE; S. 52 oben re.: united archives; S. 107 TF 4 re. (u. 116 oben): dpa; S. 112 unten: dpa_Bildarchiv; S. 113 re.: empics); **Picture-Desk**, London (S. 64 li.: THE KOBAL COLLECTION/LIBERTY FILMS UK); **The Random House Group Ltd.** (S. 54: From "A Short History of Nearly Everything" by Bill Bryson. Published by Doubleday. Reprinted by permission of The Random House Group Ltd.); **Reuters**, Berlin (S. 26 Bild B (u. Hintergrund 26/27): Brian Snyder); **Rex Features Ltd**, London (S. 39 oben); © **ROLAND Corporation**. Mit freundlicher Genehmigung (S. 59); Courtesy of **Jason Sattler**, USA (S. 86 oben); **Schapowalow**, Hamburg (Inhaltsverz. (u. 77) cover tulips (M): Zoellner); **Marion Schönenberger**, Berlin (Inhaltsverz. (u. 6/7)); **Scholastic Ltd**, London (Inhaltsverz. (u. 76 oben re.) cover "Northern Lights". Cover artwork by David Scutt;

S. 107 TF 1 (u. 108): "Does My Head Look Big in This?", Cover artwork by Scholastic Ltd, Copyright © Scholastic Ltd. Reproduced with kind permission of Scholastic Ltd. All Rights Reserved); **Shooting Jozi**, a project of Global Studio 2007 and the individuals who participated (S. 130); **Shutterstock**, New York (Inhaltsverz. unten re.: Yuri Arcurs; S. 8 Hintergrund: Rafa Irusta; S. 9 (u. 11) mobile (M): Jaroslaw Grudzinski; S. 16 unten (M): Rannev; S. 26 oben: keellla; S. 50 oben Mitte: Monkey Business Images, unten re.: Stuart Whitmore; S. 54/55 Hintergrund: Roman Sigaev; S. 58 unten: Andrea Danti; S. 68 unten: Inc; S. 69 oben: Rob Wilson, unten: Gravicapa; S. 71 li.: blueking, re.: PSD photography; S. 72 li.: NatUlrich, Mitte: Vereshchagin Dmitry; S. 106 li.: electra; S. 107 TF 2 (u. 111 re.): Gary Blakeley, TF 4 li.: tatniz, TF 7: Jan Martin Will; S. 111 oben: Condor 36, unten li.: Jonathan Larsen; S. 138: Holger Mette; S. 140 oben: Tatiana Popova; S. 143 oben re.: Monkey Business Images); **Jill Stevens**, Hove, UK (S. 93 re.); © **Tate**, London 2010 (S. 74/75: Painting by Paul Nash "Landscape from a Dream"); **Thomas Thesen**, Seoul (Inhaltsverz. (u. 76 unten li.) cover "The Absolutely True Diary" (M), Inhaltsverz. (u. S. 76 oben li.) cover "The Curious Incident" (M)); **ullsteinbild**, Berlin (S. 52 unten re.; S. 116 Mitte re.: Rauhe); **Umweltbundesamt**, Dessau-Roßlau (S. 72 re.); **U.S. Global Change Research Program** / www.globalchange.gov (S. 123 diagrams); **whiteafrican/ Erik (HASH) Hersman** (S. 107 TF 6 (u. 122))

Titelbild

Corbis, Düsseldorf (cyclist (M): Motofish Images); **iStockphoto**, Calgary (Capitol (M): Cheng Chang)

Textquellen

S. 9–10: *My Best Friend Dumped Me*. Abridged from Discovery Girls magazine, June/July 2009, Vol. 9, No. 4, pp 30–31. © 2009 Discovery Girls, Inc. Reprinted with permission; **S. 14:** *1 in 12 Teens Addicted to Video Games* by PSYCH CENTRAL NEWS EDITOR. Reviewed by John M. Grohol, Psy.D. on April 20, 2009. Source: Association for Psychological Science. Adapted from http://psychcentral.com/news/2009/04/20/1-in-12-teens-addicted-to-video-games/5438.html. (Stand: 3.11.2009); **S. 20–21:** *I hate my dad*. Abridged from „LOVE LESSONS" by Jacqueline Wilson. © Jacqueline Wilson 2005. Published by Corgi Books / Random House Children's Books, London; **S. 27:** *Forced to sin*. Excerpts from the poem "Forced to sin" by Emmanuel Jal. © Emmanuel Jal/www.emmanueljal.com. Reprinted

by permission of Mark Lea, Co-Manager of Emmanuel Jal./Jal Music, London; **S. 28–29:** *First Amendment*. Excerpt from "Job Day" from SPEAK by Laurie Halse Anderson. Copyright © 1999 by Laurie Halse Anderson. Reprinted by permission of Farrar, Straus and Giroux, LLC; **S. 34:** *Should the voting age be 16?* Copyright Guardian News & Media Ltd 2009; **S. 38:** *We are all bystanders*. Abridged and adapted from Greater Good magazine, Volume III, Issue 2 (Fall/Winter 2006–07). www.greatergoodmag.org; **S. 39:** *The bystander effect*. Abridged and adapted from „Act now to defy ‚bystander effect'" by Craig and Marc Kielbruger, March 29, 2007; **S. 40:** *ZivilCOURAGE zeigen*. SOS-Rassismus-NRW; **S. 54:** *Science – what is it good for? Text A*. Abridged from "A Short History of Nearly Everything" by Bill Bryson. Published by Doubleday. Reprinted by permission of The Random House Group Ltd; **S. 55:** *Text B*. Abridged from „SCIENCE, A HISTORY" by John Gribbin. Published by Penguin; **S. 56:** *Self-Adjusting Lenses for the Poor*. Abridged and adapted from "From a Visionary English Physicist, Self-Adjusting Lenses for the Poor" by Mary Jordan. The Washington Post, January, 10, 2009; **S. 61–62:** *Welcome to the future*. Abridged from "The Carbon Diaries" by Saci Lloyd, first published in the UK by Hodder Children's, an imprint of Hachette Children's Books, 338 Euston Road, London NW1 3BH; **S. 77–83:** *Reading a novel*. Abridged from "Looking for Alaska" by John Green. All rights reserved including the right of reproduction in whole or in part in any form. This extract published by arrangement with Dutton Children's Books, a division of Penguin Young Readers Group, a member of Penguin Group (USA) Inc.; **S. 88:** *How to do it*. From "HOW THE WATER FEELS TO THE FISHES" by Dave Eggers. © 2007, Dave Eggers. Reprinted by permission. All rights reserved. No cuts or changes shall be made to the text of the Story without the written consent of the Author or his agent. No further use of this material in extended distribution, other media, or future editions shall be made without the express written consent of the Wylie Agency (UK) Ltd; **S. 90:** *London Airport* by Christopher Logue, copyright © Christopher Logue, 1996, *Willow Pattern*. Taken from "PLUM" by Tony Mitton. © Toni Mitton. Re-published by Barn Owl Books, London, 2010; **S. 91:** *Little Red Riding Hood and the Wolf*. Copyright © 1982 by Roald Dahl. Taken from "REVOLTING RHYMES" by Roald Dahl. Published by Jonathan Cape Ltd & Penguin Books Ltd; **S. 92:** *Haiku* by Sue Cowling. © Sue Cowling. Reproduced by permission of the author, *Amsterdam Avenue* from JAZMIN'S NOTEBOOK by Nikki Grimes,

Acknowledgments

copyright © 1998 by Nikki Grimes. Used by permission of Dial Books for Young Readers, A Division of Penguin Young Readers Group, A Member of Penguin Group (USA) Inc., 345 Hudson Street, New York, NY 10014. All rights reserved, (u. 142) *Castaway*. Copyright © 2010 by Stephen Brock, Reproduced by permission of the author, *Stopping by Woods on a Snowy Evening* by Robert Frost. Taken from the book, "THE POETRY OF ROBERT FROST" edited by Edward Connery Lathem. Copyright 1923, 1969 by Henry Holt and Company. Copyright 1951 by Robert Frost. Reprinted by arrangement with Henry Holt and Company, LLC; **S. 93:** *Sonnet number one*. Taken from "The Monster That Ate the Universe." published by Macmillan, UK. © Roger Stevens/poetryzone@googlemail.com. Reprinted by kind permission of the author; **S. 94:** *Come. And Be My Baby*, copyright © 1975 by Maya Angelou, from "OH PRAY MY WINGS ARE GONNA FIT ME WELL" by Maya Angelou. Used by permission of Random House, Inc., *Meeting Midnight* by Carol Ann Duffy. Copyright © Carol Ann Duffy by kind permission of the author c/o Rogers, Coleridge & White Ltd., 20 Powis Mews, London W11 1JN; **S. 95:** *Absent*. Copyright © by Bernard Young. Reprinted by kind permission of the author, *The world is a beautiful place*. From "The world is a beautiful place to be born into" by Lawrence Ferlinghetti, from "A CONEY ISLAND OF THE MIND", copyright © 1955 by Lawrence Ferlinghetti. Reprinted by permission of New Directions Publishing Corp., *Natural numbers*. Copyright © by Mike Johnson. Reprinted by kind permission of the author; **S. 98–104:** *Kirsty and Gideon*. Abridged from "Fairytaleheart", published in "Two Plays for Young People: Fairytaleheart and Sparkleshark", by Philip Ridley. Published by Faber and Faber Ltd. © 1998; **S. 108–110:** *Amal's decision*. Abridged from "Does My Head Look Big in This?" Text Copyright © Randa Abdel-Fattah, 2006. Reproduced with the permission of Scholastic Ltd. All Rights Reserved; **S. 115:** *Young people in Europe*. Abridged speech by Jerzy Buzek, President of the European Parliament, 11. 11. 2009. http://www.europarl.europa.eu/president/view/en-de/press/speeches/sp-2009/sp-2009-November/speeches-2009-November-3.html (Stand: 30. 09. 2010). Used with permission; **S. 120–122:** *Electric Wind*. Abridged text totaling 1608 words from "THE BOY WHO HARNESSED THE WIND" by WILLIAM KAMKWAMBA and BRYAN MEALER. Copyright © 2009 BY WILLIAM KAMKWAMBA AND BRYAN MEALER. Reprinted by permission of HarperCollins Publishers; **S. 126:** Auszug v. S. 516 des „English G 2000 Wörterbuch – Das Wörterbuch zum Lehrwerk". Herausgegeben von der Langenscheidt-Redaktion Wörterbücher und der Cornelsen-Redaktion Englisch. © 2002 Cornelsen Verlag GmbH & Co. OHG, Berlin und Langenscheidt KG, Berlin und München.